W9-ATE-881

THE KARL MARX LIBRARY

EDITED AND TRANSLATED BY

SAUL K. PADOVER

Distinguished Service Professor of Political Science,
Graduate Faculty, New School for Social Research

ALREADY PUBLISHED

On Revolution

TITLES IN PREPARATION

On America and the Civil War

On the First International

On Freedom of the Press and Censorship

On Revolution

KARL MARX (1818–1883)

THE KARL MARX LIBRARY
VOLUME I

On Revolution

KARL MARX

ARRANGED AND EDITED, WITH AN
INTRODUCTION AND NEW TRANSLATIONS
by Saul K. Padover

McGraw-Hill Book Company

NEW YORK   ST. LOUIS   SAN FRANCISCO
DÜSSELDORF   LONDON   MEXICO   PANAMA
SYDNEY   TORONTO

Design: *Herb Johnson*
Art Direction: *Harris Lewine*

Library of Congress Catalog Card Number: 78-172260

FIRST EDITION

07-048079-6

Contents

France

Germany

viii

viii
CONTENTS

Spain

Photographs following pages 232 and 448

Introduction:
Karl Marx As Revolutionist

KARL MARX, the German exile who died in relative obscurity in Victorian London in 1883, two months before his sixty-fifth birthday, has become the world-wide personification of revolution in the twentieth century. The very words "Marxism" and "Marxist" have acquired the connotation—indeed, the equivalence—of revolution, however the latter is interpreted. His physical appearance, too, conveys this idea. To millions of people everywhere, Marx's leonine head, with its wild hair, bushy beard, flashing eyes, is in itself the symbol of a revolutionist.

Marx was of medium height, thickset; wide-shouldered, strongly built. He had a finely shaped forehead, a somewhat blunt nose, and, in his youth, thick black hair. To some, including his friend Dr. Ludwig Kugelmann, Marx's head was so powerful that he looked like Zeus ready to flash thunder. Marx had the energy and stance of a fighter; he impressed Albert Brisbane, an American newspaperman who saw him in Cologne in 1848, as possessing the "passionate fire of an intrepid spirit."

This physical appearance was not misleading. Marx *was* a revolutionist in his "life style" as well as in his writings. A highly educated middle-class intellectual—a German *Herr Doktor* at a time when the Ph.D. was the achievement of a select few—Marx diverged from "bourgeois" norms in the whole pattern of his life.

In his youth he was noted for his exuberance and extremism. Pampered in his own family as the oldest (and brightest) son, he alternately bullied his siblings and then charmed them with imaginative stories, for Marx was a gifted raconteur and wit. At school in Trier he exasperated his classmates, among whom he made no lasting friends. His daughter Eleanor wrote in later years that her father was "loved and feared by his schoolmates—loved, because he was always ready for boyish pranks, and feared because he wrote biting, satiric verse, in which he exposed his enemies to ridicule."

Karl's doting parents were concerned because his basic habits were not those of their other children, of whom there were seven,[1] or those of their middle-class neighbors. His father, Heinrich Marx, a cautious and moderate provincial lawyer, saw an unbridled "daemon" in the son: he was convinced that this quality would lead either to great creative achievement or to great personal tragedy. In truth, it led to both. His mother, Henriette Presburg Marx, a sturdy and solidly practical Dutchwoman, fussed over Karl, whom she called her *"Glückskind"*—child of fortune—and worried about his personal habits. Both parents feared that his lack of restraint would end sooner or later in a breakdown of his health, which, despite spurts of energy, was always fragile. Their fears were to be justified.

Karl's teachers found him undisciplined and given to exaggeration. His exuberance and intelligence were not easily subjugated to the Germanic order. With the possible exception of Johann Abraham Küpper, the Evangelical pastor who baptized Karl and his siblings, his teachers do not seem to have liked or admired him. In the Trier Gymnasium, which he attended for five years, his grades were middling; he graduated with the equivalent of an American "B" average. The director of the Gymnasium, Johann Hugo Wyttenbach, a pro-French liberal-minded scholar who taught history, noted in the record that Karl, who then had a passion for poetry instead of politics, lacked scholarly discipline and was prone to hyperbole.

His mother's first known letter to him, written on November 29, 1835, when the seventeen-year-old Karl was at Bonn University, casts an illuminating light on the early character of the modern world's foremost revolutionist. The letter of Henriette Marx, who never fully mastered the German language, given here in English translation for the first time, includes her own syntax and punctuation: "Greatly beloved dear Carl![2] with much pleasure I take the pen to write to you . . . for you can believe me that I really very much long for you thank Heaven we are all quite healthy everything is active and diligent . . . now you cannot ascribe it to the weakness of my sex if I am curious to know how you have arranged your small household, if frugality plays the main role in big as well as in little

---

1. Sophie (1816–83), Hermann (1819–42), Henriette (1820–56), Luise (1821–65), Emilie (1822–88), Karoline (1824–47), and Eduard (1826–37).
2. Carl—with a "C"—is used on Marx's birth certificate, school diplomas, and other official documents.

household expenses which is an indispensable necessity, in addition I permit myself to remark dear Carl that you must never regard cleanliness and orderliness as unimportant because health and cheerfulness depend upon them see to it punctually that your rooms are scrubbed often set a regular time for it—and scrub my beloved Carl weekly with sponge and soap—how goes it with the coffee? Do you cook it yourself or what? . . . keep well my beloved Carl be worthy and good always keep God and your parents before your eyes adieu your loving mother Henriette Marx."

A few months later, after hearing that Karl was sick, his mother wrote him a maternal warning against overindulgence: "Beloved dear Carl! . . . I am convinced that you darling Carl can reach a high old age if you behave sensibly, you should not get heated up or drink much wine or coffee and not consume sharp stuff like pepper or other sorts of spices, you ought not to smoke tobacco or stay up too late at night and rise early. Beware also of catching cold and don't dance dear Carl until you are fully recovered. . . ."

Karl paid little, if any, attention. At Bonn University he joined a student *Landsmannschaft* [regional fraternity] and became its leader. He did attend lectures—on jurisprudence, art history, and Greek mythology—but he spent much time carousing and drinking with his fellow students. He fought at least one duel, and suffered a cut near his right eye. He spent money riotously. In Cologne, where he was on a revel with some students, he was arrested for carrying a "forbidden weapon." In Bonn, according to the university record,[3] "because of nightly uproarious disturbances of the peace and drunkenness, he incurred the penalty of one day's imprisonment." For a German university student of those days, such activities were relatively normal and popular, but they horrified Karl's conservative father, who took him out of Bonn after the second semester and sent him to the University of Berlin. Unlike Germany's older universities, the one in Berlin was not a colorful place for student revelry but an institution designed for hard and sober study. Ludwig Feuerbach, the Bavarian philosopher, who studied there under Hegel about a decade earlier, said of it: "Other universities are actual pubs compared to this workhouse."

In Berlin Marx registered in the Faculty of Jurisprudence, to prepare himself, at his father's urgent wish, to become a lawyer. He plunged into his studies with an immoderateness that appalled his father when he heard about it. Young Marx devoured and excerpted from vast tomes of Germanic law and Latin Pandects. He made

---

3. University Leaving-Certificate, August 22, 1836.

frantic attempts to master the world of Roman law and to organize it into a coherent system that would yield some philosophic meaning. Soon, however, he abandoned the whole effort as crude and meaningless, deciding that it was "written with tiresome prolixity and it abused the Roman concepts most barbarously in order to force them into my system." Nevertheless, he thought the exercise, his first attempt at system building, was not altogether wasted. "I acquired thereby," he wrote later, "a love for a general view of the material."

He was studying jurisprudence only to please his father. His own love was not for law, but for literature and art. He nursed a passionate ambition to become a poet, a playwright, and a dramatic critic. While racing through the immense Sahara of jurisprudence, he found oases in writing his own literature, or what he thought literature. He wrote poetry—love poems (to Jenny von Westphalen), romantic poems (dedicated to his father), epigrammatic poems. He also concocted a "humorous romance" (*Scorpion and Felix*), a "fantastic drama" (*Oulanem*), and a philosophic playlet (*Cleanthes*). The latter, he said, was designed to demonstrate the "philosophical-dialectical development of the godhead as it manifests itself as the concept itself, as religion, as nature, as history." In all this literary outpouring he sought, as he said, "the dances of the Muses and the music of Satyrs."

At the same time he was driven by "an urge to grapple with philosophy." Among other things, he began to read the *Phänomenologie des Geistes* by Hegel, who had died five years before Marx entered the university but whose spirit and philosophy still permeated it. Two of Marx's professors, Friedrich Karl von Savigny and Eduard Gans, had been students of the philosopher. Marx's first dip into Hegel was unsatisfying. "The grotesque, rocklike melody" of Hegel's philosophy, he wrote, "did not appeal to me." It took another year or two, under the stimulus of the Young Hegelians Club in Berlin, which he joined, to return to Hegel and study him thoroughly. Hegel, particularly his dialectics, was to have a profound influence on Marx, providing him with indispensable tools for his revolutionary thought and action.

Young Marx was then in frantic search of the Absolute. He was in a hurry to combine art, aesthetics, literature, and philosophy into a single system that would embrace the totality of human experience. He tried, as he said, to establish a "new system of logic," and filled three hundred notebook pages with "metaphysical propositions," until he was unable to read his own scribblings. The Absolute continued to elude him. Finally, in a rage of bafflement and frustration, he destroyed his notes and his writings; the hunger for System and for

Universals remained unappeased. It was to characterize his whole life.

Such pursuits involved staying up night after night, eating irregularly, and smoking heavily. The smoke-filled room and the sleepless nights were too much for Marx's delicate lungs. Moreover, his "fruitless intellectual labors," as he phrased it, filled him with a "consuming anger." As his parents had always feared and warned against, his immoderation led to a physical and nervous breakdown. He began to spit blood. A doctor recommended fresh country air, and Marx went to Stralow (Strelau), a village near Berlin, on the Spree River. For the first two days he ran around the garden "like a madman." Then he calmed down and began to enjoy the fresh air and country life. He recovered his health, returned to Berlin—and soon resumed his hectic intellectual pace.

From Trier, Karl's worried father, in poor health himself and with a declining law practice, kept writing his son letters of admonition and urgent advice. It was time, he reminded Karl, that a young man of nineteen or twenty should begin to devote serious thought to the practical things of life. He could not give financial support to his son forever; there were the other children to think about. Poetry and drama were praiseworthy enough as avocations, but even a genius like Gotthold Ephraim Lessing, whom Heinrich Marx greatly admired, could hardly make a living and had to depend upon the whim of patrons. Karl's father pleaded with him to take himself in hand, to lead a normal and disciplined life, and above all, to begin preparing himself for a career in law or government if he were to support a wife (young Marx was then secretly engaged to Jenny von Westphalen, in Trier) and family.

These exhortations had no effect whatever on the strong-willed Karl, whose ear was not attuned to the voice of his cautious, practical father. As Henry David Thoreau once wrote: "If a man does not keep pace with his companions, perhaps it is because he hears a different drummer." And the rhythms Karl Marx heard were neither those of his "bourgeois" parents nor of "bourgeois" civilization. He followed his own drummer, moved only by personal passions and visions, regardless of consequence.

From the very first, Marx's life differed sharply from middle-class expectations. Boy and man, he had no sense of the practical. He despised money, of which he had a deep philosophical understanding but neither desire for its acquisition nor appreciation of its utility— which helps explain why he was desperately poor and generally in debt most of his life. When he had money—he inherited fairly substantial sums two or three times—he mismanaged and quickly squandered it. He loathed "capitalists," whose historic and economic functions he came to understand profoundly but whose values he could judge only with disdain. His disinclination to accumulate any kind of property (except for personal things, such as books) amounted to a moral repugnance. Even when he had a wife and children to support, he would not take a regular, paying job—as did his closest friend and associate, Frederick Engels—or engage in any pecuniarily rewarding business, although this meant exposing his family, whom he deeply loved, to virtually lifelong economic insecurity, penury, and dependence. He rejected "bourgeois" and "capitalist" values and behavior—frugality, acquisitions, savings, orderliness—as "philistinism," but accepted constant financial help from Engels, who made his money in the market place: manufacturing, buying, selling, and investing.

Five days before Marx's twentieth birthday, in May, 1838, his father died, wracked with misgivings about his son's future. Toward the end of his life Heinrich Marx realized in despair that the "daemon" he had detected in his gifted son was now beyond his (or anybody else's) control.

After his father's death Marx gave up all pretense of preparing for a lawyer's career. He stopped attending lectures regularly and pursued his own course of immense reading, poetizing, and philosophizing, the latter including endless conversations and argumentations in the perfervid circle of Young Hegelians. In his last two years in Berlin, Marx studied the Greek classical philosophers—in Greek—in preparation for his doctorate. In 1841 he was awarded his Ph.D. degree by Jena University, to which he sent his dissertation, which included lengthy Greek excerpts, entitled: *Differenz der demokritischen und epikureischen Naturphilosophie* [*Difference between the Democritean and Epicurean Philosophy of Nature*].

Dr. Marx, aged twenty-three, joined his friend Bruno Bauer in Bonn, expecting to get a professorship there, but the Prussian Government opposed the appointment of radicals. In the Germany of that day there was no academic future for men like Marx. Careers in established institutions—universities as well as government—were closed even to the most gifted individuals if they had the temerity to question the mystical foundations of Christianity, as Bruno Bauer and Ludwig Feuerbach did, or the social system, as Marx and other Young Hegelians did. Germany, and for that matter the rest of Europe, provided no institutionalized outlet for the energies and imaginations of the most talented and idealistic young men.

Marx, like many other *déraciné* intellectuals of the time, entered one of the few fields open to him—journalism. Given the conditions of the time, with Germany and Europe in general in a ferment of both nationalism and social revolution, and with governments monarchistic and oppressive, journalism could not be a neutral occupation. The writer or editor had the choice of either defending the status quo, in which case he was likely to be rewarded with money and other favors, or attacking it, which was certain to expose him to censorship, legal prosecution, and, in the end, exile. Marx, by instinct a nonconformist and by philosophical conviction a rebel determined to rearrange the universe around him, chose the latter alternative. As he stated in his "Theses on Feuerbach": "The philosophers have only *interpreted* the world in various ways; the point, however, is to change it." Marx thus became a radical journalist. Journalism was the only profession he ever had and the only career he ever pursued.

He made contact with other radical intellectuals in Cologne, which was then one of Germany's most economically advanced and progressive cities. He impressed like-minded persons with his flash and fire. Moses Hess, a philosophical socialist six years older than Marx, wrote to his friend, the German novelist Berthold Auerbach, in September, 1841: "Dr. Marx, the name of my idol, is still a very young man (hardly twenty-four years old, at most) who will administer the last *coup* to our medieval religion and politics; he combines the profoundest philosophic seriousness with the most cutting wit. Imagine Rousseau, Voltaire, d'Holbach, Lessing, Heine, and Hegel united in one person—I say *united*, and not tossed together—and you have Dr. Marx."

Marx became a contributor to the Cologne *Rheinische Zeitung* and half a year later, in May, 1842, its editor. He attacked sacrosanct Prussian institutions, including the divorce laws and censorship. On April 1, 1843, the censors closed the newspaper and Marx, disgusted with what he regarded as German philistinism and general backwardness, decided to leave the country. He wrote to Arnold Ruge, with whom he was planning to publish a journal, the *Deutsch-Französische Jahrbücher*, in Paris, "Not even a dog can live without a police permit" in Prussia. He could no longer breathe the oppressive air of his native land, where "everything is suppressed violently" by a "regime of stupidity itself." In Paris, where a freer intellectual atmosphere prevailed, a rallying point could be established for the formulation of critical and philosophical ideas that would lead to the social transformation of Europe, including Germany and France.

In planning the *Deutsch-Französische Jahrbücher*, in the fall of 1843, Marx made it clear that he was not a communist, at least not the kind fashionable in radical circles in those days, especially in Paris. He was not, he wrote to Ruge, "in favor of raising a dogmatic flag; quite the contrary." He considered the communist ideas of Étienne Cabet and Wilhelm Weitling "dogmatic abstractions," and those of Charles Fourier and Pierre Joseph Proudhon a "one-sided consummation of socialist principles." He himself, he wrote to Ruge, was opposed to any "ready-made system."

Only two issues of the *Deutsch-Französische Jahrbücher* came out. They contained articles by Marx sharply attacking religion, including Judaism, and the philosophical-theological foundations of Germany, a land, he wrote, ruled by "ignorant bumpkins and philistines." After the March, 1844, issue of the journal reached Berlin, the Prussian Government put Marx, a Prussian citizen, on a proscription list, to be arrested the moment he reentered the country. On April 16, 1844, the Prussian Minister of Interior, Heinrich von Arnim-Boitzenburg, issued the following order to all provincial governors, who were in turn to inform their police chiefs: "The first and second issues of the *Deutsche-Französische Jahrbücher*, as well as the whole tone of that journal, published in Paris by Arnold Ruge and Carl Marx, contains numerous passages, in effect constituting attempted high treason and *lèse majesté*. The publisher and the authors of the individual articles are to be held responsible. I . . . hereby enjoin the respective police authorities to arrest, and seize the papers of, Dr. Arnold Ruge, Carl Marx, Heinrich Heine, and . . . Bernays as soon as they cross our frontier. . . ."

Marx, however, did not oblige the Prussian police by crossing the frontier. He remained in Paris, the febrile center of European radicalism, where he made contact with radical intellectuals, such as Pierre Joseph Proudhon, and radical workingmen's circles, including those of German refugee artisans, and began seriously to study economics, a subject of which he, a philosopher and littérateur, had been hitherto largely ignorant. For the next quarter of a century and more, in Paris, in Brussels, and finally in London's immense British Museum library, Marx was to pursue this subject in all available languages. Unlike his fellow radical journalists and agitators, who spouted economic and social theories derived from imagination, Marx was to become a master of economic facts, as can be seen in his great work, *Capital*, with its voluminous and erudite notes.[4]

An equally fateful event was Marx's meeting with Frederick Engels in the summer of 1844. The two men had once met briefly in Cologne,

4. Only Volume I (1867) of *Capital* appeared in Marx's lifetime. Volumes II and III were brought out by Engels in 1893 and 1894, respectively, on the basis of Marx's drafts and notes. So-called Volume IV, entitled *Theories of Surplus Value*, was published, in two parts, by Dietz Verlag, Berlin, 1959; and in English translation by Progress Publishers, Moscow, 1963 and 1968. Strictly speaking, Volume IV is more a collection of notes than an integrated work on economics.

but this time they struck up a permanent friendship that was profoundly to affect both their lives and, for that matter, the course of modern history. Engels, on his way back to Germany from Manchester, where he had spent almost two years in business and had, among other things, collected materials for his notable book, *The Condition of the Working Class in England in 1844* (published in German in 1845 and in English translation in 1892), stopped over in Paris. He was tall, blond, and athletic-looking, in the words of Pavel Annenkov, a Russian writer, "like a distinguished Englishman." His rapport with the stocky, swarthy, and nonathletic Marx was immediate. The two young Germans—Marx, then twenty-six, was two years older than Engels—found that they were of the same opinion about virtually everything, and they decided to collaborate in their future writings. They did, in fact, have so much to say to each other that their conversation lasted ten days, and, given the compulsive talkativeness of young intellectuals, probably as many nights as well.

Henceforth the lives and destinies of the two men were to be so intertwined as to be practically inseparable. The personal and intellectual influence of one upon the other was to be of such a nature as to justify the use of the term "Marx-Engels" in discussing Marx and Marxism, particularly in connection with revolution.

A brief look at Engels, as well as his career, is therefore in order.

Engels was born in 1820, in Barmen, an industrial town near Elberfeld in the Ruhr area. He was the son of a Protestant Pietist and religious fanatic who owned textile factories in Barmen and in Manchester. Even as a boy he could hardly bear his joyless home—a "Zion of obscurantism," as he called it—and in his teens he was already in full rebellion not only against his dour, tyrannical father but also against the whole world of commerce, which he termed *"Schacher,"* haggling or huckstering. He also developed, as did Marx, a lifelong aversion for organized religion and churches, an antipathy no less deep than that which he felt for capitalism and the whole social-political system with which it was interconnected.

Despite his father's continuous pressure to pursue a business career, Engels chose writing and radical journalism. For five years after his meeting with Marx in Paris he pursued a writing and revolutionary career. In the circle of young German refugees, including Marx, who gathered in Brussels between 1845 and 1848, planning and plotting revolution, Engels reminded one fellow communist—the so-called "proletarian poet" Georg Weerth—of Ulrich von Hutten (1488-1523), the humanist poet laureate who had given staunch support to a great German rebel of another age—Martin Luther.

Engels fought in the revolutionary uprisings in Baden, participating in four military engagements; he was to be proud of that all his life. Military affairs, in fact, became a lifelong interest and hobby, so that his friends, including Marx's children, came to call him affectionately "the General," a title he enjoyed, and perhaps even deserved.

After the collapse of the Baden revolution Engels escaped to London, where he joined Marx, but he soon found that he could not support himself (or help the indigent Marx family) by journalism. Reluctantly he returned to his father's business in Manchester, where he remained for nineteen years, sending the desperately poor Marx family money almost weekly. When Engels decided he had accumulated enough capital for himself and for an annuity (£350) for Marx, he sold his share of the business and moved to London, where he spent the last twenty-five years of his life writing his own books and articles, editing Marx's works, and keeping close contact with European socialists. He died, of cancer of the larynx, on August 5, 1895, and his ashes were scattered over the ocean at Eastbourne, one of his favorite resorts.

Engels was a brilliant man with great intellectual powers. Although he never attended a university, by dint of voracious reading he became a person of immense erudition, with an easy mastery of the natural sciences, history, philosophy, economics, and literature. He knew Germanic, Latin, Slavic, and Semitic tongues. It took him only a few weeks to learn Arabic and Persian. Because he was given to stuttering when excited, it was said of him that he could "stutter in twenty languages."

Even as a hard-working businessman, often laboring past midnight to catch up with his reading and writing,[5] he indulged in aristocratic tastes and habits, including fox hunting and riding. Tough-minded and sentimental, generous and cynical, cocky and modest, gentlemanly and bawdy, grave and witty, practical and utopian, Engels was a worldly and complicated personality. He was also a totally dedicated revolutionist. He became one of the major theorists of revolution through radical ("Marxist") socialism or communism—two words which he and

---

5. Engels collaborated with Marx on a number of books and articles. Among his collaborations are *The Holy Family* (1845), *The German Ideology* (written in 1845–46 but not published until 1932), and, of course, *The Communist Manifesto* (1848). He also wrote a number of prefaces to Marx's works. Engels' own writings include: *The Peasant War in Germany* (1870); *Herr Eugen Dühring's Revolution in Science* (known in English translation as *Anti-Dühring*) (1878); *Development of Socialism from Utopia to Science* (1882), known in English translation (1892) as *Socialism, Utopian and Scientific; The Origins of the Family, Private Property, and the State* (1884); and *Ludwig Feuerbach and the End of Classical German Philosophy* (1888). Two of his books were published posthumously: *Germany, Revolution and Counter-Revolution* (German, 1896; English, 1933), and *Dialectics of Nature*, begun in 1895 but never completed (English translation, 1964).

Marx used interchangeably. After he and Marx joined forces in 1844, Engels never swerved from his devotion to revolution.

Throughout that year, in Paris, Marx continued to be busy with radical activities and studies. He contributed to *Vorwärts*, a German-language semiweekly published by radical émigrés. The Prussian authorities, in contact with the Paris police, continued their surveillance of him, as well as of other German radicals. On December 21, 1844, Minister von Arnim-Boitzenburg issued a supplementary order to the Prussian police: "The descriptions of Dr. Ruge, Bernays, and Marx are so far not yet available. In any case, these individuals, should they be apprehended, are to be transported and delivered, under secure guard, to the Royal Police Headquarters here [in Berlin]...."

Thus at the age of twenty-six Marx was declared an outlaw by his government. He was never thereafter to be free of some form of police attention.

Marx soon discovered that the Prussian Government had a long reach. In January, 1845, the Paris police ordered him expelled within twenty-four hours. Penniless, he departed for Brussels.

His appeal to King Leopold I for the right to settle in Belgium was ignored, but he was permitted to remain in Brussels on condition that he keep out of Belgian politics. He signed a statement to that effect in the office of the *Sûreté Publique*. The records show that every time he changed his address in Brussels the police promptly reported it to the *Sûreté*. The Marx family, with their three young children (Jenny, Laura, and Edgar), moved at least three times, from one "pauper colony" in the workers' quarter to another.

The police in Brussels, as in the rest of Europe, were ubiquitous, if not always efficient. In response to the seething social discontent and nationalistic ferment which exploded in revolutionary violence throughout Europe in 1848 and 1849, the Continent's rulers used what seems to have been a loose network of spies. Police agents, open and secret, operated in European capitals: Berlin, Brussels, Madrid, Paris, Vienna, and wherever radicals and revolutionists congregated.

Not all the revolutionists who were spied upon were radicals in the social-economic sense. Many of the leading ones—men like Italy's Giuseppe Mazzini and Hungary's Louis Kossuth—were simply patriotic nationalists fighting for the independence of their respective countries. But others were actual revolutionists, determined to destroy Europe's political, economic, and religious institutions. All were kept under surveillance. Police agents successfully infiltrated radical circles and secret communist organizations such as the League of the Just in Paris and the Communist League in Brussels.

To escape Prussian police harassment Marx took a rash step. He let

XX INTRODUCTION: MARX AS REVOLUTIONIST

it be known that he was planning to emigrate to America—to Texas—
and on November 10, 1845, he wrote to Franz Damian Görtz, the Ober-
bürgermeister of his native Trier, that to avoid being prevented by his
native country from emigrating, he was requesting an *"Entlassung"*
[release] from the "Royal Prussian citizens' union," as he put it. Marx's
request was forwarded to Berlin, which on November 23, 1845, officially denaturalized him. He lived to regret it, for henceforth he was to
be a man without a country.

Watched by the police, Marx remained in Brussels for three years.
In some ways this may have been the most crucial time in his life, for it
was in this period that he seems to have made the definite transition
from Hegelianism to materialism and from idealism to communism. It
was in Brussels that his ideas—known to the world as "Marxism"—
began to crystallize and to take written form. It was in Brussels that he
wrote much of his important noneconomic work, crossing the bridge
from the still-Hegelian *Economic and Philosophic Manuscripts of
1844*, which he wrote in Paris that year, to the materialist-oriented and
action-directed "Theses on Feuerbach," written in 1845. Engels, who
published the "Theses," consisting of eleven terse paragraphs totaling
about 500 words, in 1888, called it "the first document in which the
brilliant germ of the new philosophy is laid down." In Brussels, Marx
collaborated with Engels in writing *The Holy Family*, a criticism of the
Young Hegelians, and *The German Ideology*, a critique of idealism. He
also attacked Proudhonism in the *Poverty of Philosophy*, the first book
written solely by himself (in French). Finally, it was in Brussels that
Marx, in collaboration with Engels, wrote the *Manifesto of the Communist Party.*

In Brussels, Marx helped to organize a Communist Correspondence
Committee. He also became a member of the secret Communist League,
which had for its aim, according to Article One of its statutes (June,
1847), "the overthrow of the bourgeoisie, the rule of the proletariat, the
breaking-up of the old society based on class laws, and the founding of
a new society without classes and without private property." At its
second congress, held in London at the end of November, 1847, the
League commissioned Marx and Engels, who were delegates, to write
the *Communist Manifesto.*

The German radicals with whom Marx associated consisted of some
talented individuals, among them the poets Ferdinand Freiligrath and
Georg Weerth and the Westphalian artillery lieutenant Joseph Weydemeyer (later a colonel in the Union Army during the Civil War);
others were the usual lot of argumentative loudmouths. To the blunt-
speaking Russian refugee revolutionist Michael Bakunin, who encountered German radicals in Paris and Brussels, they were a pack of vain,

arrogant malicious petty bourgeois, full of "stupidities and lies." But it must be said that Bakunin had a Slav's deep-rooted suspicion and antipathy for anything Teutonic, including Marx, whom he admired for his "passionate devotion to the cause of the proletariat," but considered a vain doctrinaire extremist and, in later years, a secret German agent in the pay of Bismarck.

Pavel Annenkov furnishes an illuminating glimpse of Marx, whom he knew in Brussels in 1845. One evening Marx invited Annenkov to his house to attend a meeting with radicals to decide the course of action the communists were to take. Among those present were Engels and Weitling, a self-taught tailor, "in a coat of elegant cut, a coquettishly trimmed small beard, more like a traveling salesman than the stern, embittered worker that I had expected to meet." And there was the host, Marx himself, "most remarkable in his appearance. He had a shock of deep black hair and hairy hands and his coat was buttoned wrong; but he looked like a man with the right and power to demand respect. . . . His movements were clumsy but confident and self-reliant, his manners defied the usual conventions in human relationships, but they were dignified and somewhat disdainful; his sharp metallic voice was wonderfully adapted to the radical judgments that he passed on persons and things."

At the meeting, Marx sat at one end of a small green table, pencil in hand, his great head bent over a sheet of paper. Engels made an opening speech to the effect that the time had come for the revolutionists to unite on a common theory to be used as propaganda among the German workers. Emotion-appealing revolutionary clichés such as Weitling was accustomed to hurl at German workers only misled them. The proletariat must be provided with a systematic theory.

Before Engels finished speaking, Marx raised his head and rasped: "Tell us, Weitling, you who have made such a noise in Germany with your preaching: on what grounds do you justify your activity and what do you intend to base it on in the future?" Weitling, a simple agitator untrained in philosophical theory, launched into his usual commonplace harangue that workingmen should not trust their rulers, etc., until a seethingly impatient Marx cut in. "Your speech," he said sarcastically, "amounts to this: You don't realize that if you stir up the people without providing them with a firm, carefully thought out theory you simply deceive them." Weitling, his face suffused with anger, his voice trembling with outrage, cried out that hundreds of letters proved that his activities among workers were worth more than all the talk here about theories.[6] Marx, in a great fury, jumped

---

6. See Weitling's letter to Hess, pp. 130–132.

up, pounded his fist on the table so that the lamp rattled, and shouted: "Ignorance never yet helped anybody!" The meeting broke up, with Marx pacing up and down the room in a violent rage.

In February, 1848, revolutions broke out in Europe. At the news of the uprising in Paris, demonstrations started in Brussels. Red flags appeared in the streets; there were shouts of *"Vive la République!"* Workers began to arm. Sure that the moment of revolutionary triumph had arrived, Marx urged the German refugees to join the Belgian rebels. He had just received 6,000 francs in settlement of his father's estate, and he contributed 5,000 francs to buy weapons. This was reported to the police. The government of King Leopold I acted swiftly. It brought in troops, declared martial law, smashed workers' meetings, and savaged German radicals. Marx and his wife were arrested in the middle of the night. The following morning they were expelled from Brussels.

The Marx family went to Paris, then in revolutionary ferment. German refugees were forming volunteer battalions in preparation for action in Germany. Berlin and Cologne were in revolt.

Early in April Marx left for Cologne. Within a few weeks, on June 1, he brought out the first issue of the *Neue Rheinische Zeitung*, a revival of his old newspaper, with the word *Neue* added to its title. The subtitle of the paper was *Organ der Demokratie*. All the editors, including Engels, were members of the Communist League. The *Neue Rheinische Zeitung*, according to Engels, was under "Marx's dictatorship," one that was gladly accepted.

The subtitle of the *Neue Rheinische Zeitung* was misleading. The paper was not an "Organ of Democracy," but of communism. Its aim was to goad and stimulate proletarian revolution and to report uprisings everywhere, including Austria, France, and Hungary. In that sense it was not a local, conventional newspaper. Nor was Marx a democrat, then or ever, in any meaningful sense of the term. He used the word "democracy," not to mislead anybody—he was much too doctrinaire and blunt for deception—but in the honest conviction that it meant the power of the common people, and more specifically of the lowest and most exploited stratum of the population: the proletariat. To Marx, the "people" connoted a particular class of people, with the emphasis on class rather than on people. The proletariat was an abstraction, a faceless and unindividuated force. It was, in Marx's view, destined to do the impersonal work of history. The individual proletarian had nothing to say about his assigned historic role.

The classic conception of democracy as being government of, for, and by all the people was alien to Marx's thinking. Government as he knew it on the European continent was rule by an old upper class, and it was only historically right and morally just that it should be overthrown by a new lower class, and that a dictatorship of monarchs and aristocrats should be replaced by a dictatorship of proletarians. Since the proletarians were the "people," their rule would thus be "democratic."

This view left no room for individual human beings and their "inalienable rights" to life, liberty, and the pursuit of happiness. Nor was there a role for other classes—high or low—of the human family, except submission to the proletariat. For peasants, then the majority of Europe's population, Marx had scant sympathy and less understanding; if landless, they were simply subsumed under the general concept of "proletariat." For the influential middle classes, a large and growing element in Western Europe, Marx had no political use at all. The Marxist philosophy assigned no role to them except as doomed (although not necessarily passive) occupiers of the final stage of history, to be liquidated by its inexorable march. They were contemptuously dismissed as "bourgeois," a term of opprobrium in Marx's universe of discourse.

Since, therefore, democracy means the free participation of all the members of the community in the processes of government, on a level of political equality, then Marx was not and—given his conception of the select role of the proletariat and the class struggle—could not be a democrat. To call him a democrat is to misuse the term.

In Cologne, Marx was in his element as a fighting revolutionist, convinced that he was spearheading the political and social transformation of Germany and of Europe. He joined a number of radical workers' groups and became an active organizer and agitator in Cologne and throughout the Rhineland. His newspaper, an instrument and sounding board of revolution, boldly challenged the foundations of existing government and exposed its evil doings. The *Neue Rheinische Zeitung*, which opened with 6,000 subscribers, spoke for a relatively small minority, but to Marx it was the clarion call of history.

His intrepid and uncompromising stand made him something of a hero to the radicals. But he was less than that to moderates, among them nondoctrinaire believers in freedom who soon withdrew financial support from his newspaper. Dogmatic in his opinions and contemptuous of those of others, harsh in his judgments and arrogant in his manner, he antagonized those who might normally have been sympathetic to his fight against royal absolutism, censorship, and militarism. In haste to remake history, he did not seem to care that he made enemies in the process.

Throughout Germany and Austria the uprisings were being systematically suppressed, in some cases, as in Vienna, with great ferocity. Poorly organized revolutionists, not infrequently romantic nationalists heavily armed with slogans, proved no match for disciplined troops led by professional officers. The rulers, moreover, had an identity of interests (Czarist Russian troops effectively aided the Austrian monarchy in suppressing the Hungarian revolution) and unrelenting determination. The revolutionary activists, a small minority everywhere, had neither unity nor common objectives. Some strove for national independence, others fought for jobs for themselves and bread for their families. At cross-purposes, they failed to get mass support at critical junctures, as the frustrated Marx bitterly observed.

In Prussia, the middle classes, desiring primarily to curb the absolute power of the government through the establishment of a British type of constitutional system, recoiled at the idea of joining active forces with revolutionaries for the overthrow of existing institutions. In the showdown they made compromises with the hereditary government, leaving it in power but curtailing it to a considerable extent through a freely elected Reichstag. They did not act according to the role that Marx's theory assigned to them. This was also true in the rest of Germany and in Austria. The all-German *Nationalversammlung* (National Assembly), which met in Frankfurt in May, 1848, to draft a democratic constitution for a united Germany, accurately reflected the country's lack of revolutionary purpose, as well as its lack of unity. The Frankfurt Assembly was dissolved in futility in April, 1849. In the final analysis, the uprisings in Germany, as in the rest of Europe, failed because the revolutionaries had no widespread support among the people at large.

At the end of 1848 Marx was indicted in Cologne for *lèse majesté* and for incitement to rebellion. He underwent intensive police-magistrate interrogations. Censorship continued to harass his paper and hound his person. In February, 1849, he was tried in court and acquitted by a friendly (anti-Prussian) jury. It proved, however, an uneven battle. Marx had the voice of the newspaper, but the Prussian Government had the power—sanctions backed by force. Power won. In May, 1849, the *Neue Rheinische Zeitung* was suspended and Marx was expelled from Prussia.

He moved back to Paris with his wife and children, but within a few weeks received an order of expulsion. Everywhere Europe's routed revolutionists were either in flight or in hiding. Thousands, including a number of Marx's friends and acquaintances, emigrated to the United States; many others moved to London, where they remained either permanently or temporarily, moving to other countries later. Marx chose London. He arrived there, a penniless and stateless refugee of thirty-one, on August 24. London was to be his home for the rest of his life.

The British capital offered three major advantages. In the first place, after the 1848–49 revolutions, London replaced Paris as the center of European radical émigrés. There Frenchmen, Germans, Hungarians, Italians, Poles, and other refugees freely commingled, squabbled, and intrigued among themselves. They met in particular coffee houses, brought out their own little publications, organized and reorganized their specialized groupings, made and unmade friendships, and when in desperate need sought one another's advice and assistance. Marx joined the refugee circles, where he made friends and enemies, but within a few years he withdrew from them, disgusted with what he considered the endless bickerings and hollow rhetoric of self-centered and ignorant egoists, many of whom possessed his dogmatism but not his genius.

The second advantage of London was the relative mildness of the British Government. Compared to the Continent, England was a haven of freedom. Parliament was in power and enjoyed the respect of the citizenry. Public life was orderly and decent. There was no police brutality and no crippling censorship. The British did not hound radicals, their own or those who were foreign. It is noteworthy that Marx remained generally unmolested by the British authorities, although he did occasionally complain that the post office sometimes opened or delayed his mail, a charge that may or may not have been true in fact.

Finally, London had the advantage of being close to the Continent. For Marx this was especially important, since he was committed to the idea of revolution in Europe, to be followed by revolution in the rest of the world, and was convinced that the 1848–49 defeats were not final but only temporary setbacks in the inexorable march of history. London, where contact with continental radicals and their sympathizers could be easily maintained, was, he felt, the best place to prepare for the next revolutionary round.

London also provided Marx with the opportunity for his study of economics, a subject which came to absorb him increasingly and to which he was to devote most of his energies. Besides being the center of world capitalism, the city possessed the British Museum, then probably the world's greatest library, where Marx spent his working years, utilizing its rich collection of books, newspapers, pamphlets, and government reports. The British Museum provided him with materials not only for his economic writings, notably *Capital*, but also for his journalistic articles, which were largely political, including those he contributed to the *New-York Daily Tribune*.

In the preface to his first book on economics, *Critique of Political Economy*, which he published a decade after he arrived in London, Marx gave this autobiographical account: "The editing of the *Neue Rheinische Zeitung* in 1848 and 1849, and subsequent events, interrupted my economic studies, which I could not resume until 1850 in London. The enormous amount of material on the history of political economy which is accumulated in the British Museum, the favorable vantage point which London offers for the observation of bourgeois society . . . determined me to resume my studies from the very beginning and to work through the new materials critically . . . The time at my disposal was curtailed by the imperative necessity of earning a living. My work as contributor to the foremost English-language American newspaper, the *New-York Tribune* . . . compelled an extraordinary scattering of my researches, since I occupy myself with newspaper correspondence proper only in exceptional cases. Nevertheless, articles on important economic events in England and on the Continent have constituted so considerable a part of my contributions that I was obliged to familiarize myself with practical details which lie outside the science of political economy proper."

Marx's economic studies and observations in London led to modifications in his theories of revolution. Greater economic knowledge and insight deepened his conception of the real nature of modern revolution, and the experience of living in a well-functioning parliamentary democracy, which offered obvious possibilities of social-economic reform through legislation, made him moderate his views about the universal inevitability of violent political change.

Marx did not relinquish his concept of the class struggle, which, he said, he did not invent, because classes did actually exist in human society.[7] Nor did he give up his belief in ultimate revolution, but he now took a longer view, which in fact amounted to a considerable shift in position. The new view attenuated the sweeping doctrinairism found in the *Communist Manifesto*.

In a little speech which he delivered (in English) on April 16, 1856, at a banquet celebrating the anniversary of the Chartist weekly, the *People's Paper*, Marx revealed the change in his thinking. "The so-called revolutions of 1848," he said, were but pathetic episodes that merely exposed the fissures and fractures of the hard crust of European society. Those uprisings proclaimed the emancipation of the proletariat "noisily and confusedly." The real revolution, he stated,

7. Classes existed not only in life but also in death. They were to be found in cemeteries too. In 1640, for example, when Hartford, Conn., appointed a sexton and gravedigger (Thomas Woodford), it provided that he be paid according to whether the grave was "the lesser sort," "the middle sort," or "the highest sort."

lay elsewhere. It was to be found in the products of science, which were causing fundamental transformations, first in the economic structure and then unavoidably in the social superstructure. Steam, electricity, powered machinery, Marx said sardonically, with an eye to his former Paris colleagues-in-revolution, were "revolutions of a more dangerous character than even Citizens Barbès, Raspail, and Blanqui."

The revolutionary force of science was creating new conditions and a new world in which industrialization must spread and the workers must inevitably increase in numbers. At some point in history the working class would unavoidably be numerous and strong enough to make a successful bid for power. Meanwhile it must be made aware that it needed to buy time to train itself for its historic role. With this in mind, in September, 1864, Marx helped to organize the International Working Men's Association—the so-called First International —of which he was the leading spirit until its dissolution in 1872.

The objective of the Association was to unite the workers on an international scale, to instill in them the idea of and need for international cooperation, to provide them with a program and give them direction. The tone of the International was set in the "Inaugural Address," which Marx wrote, and which differed from the *Communist Manifesto* in its appreciation of realities. "To conquer political power," Marx stated in the "Address," "has, therefore, become the great duty of the working classes. . . . One element of success they possess—numbers; but numbers weigh in the balance only if united by combination and led by knowledge."

In shaping the policy of the International Marx vehemently opposed secret conspiracies and individualistic activisms, such as were advocated by the wilder kind of radicals, particularly the anarchist followers of Bakunin and Proudhon. Their fantasies about power exceeded their grasp of its realities. Secret conspiracies and individual violence, Marx believed, were not merely nugatory but also self-defeating in that they played directly into the hands of the repressive authorities. He insisted on open organization, open agitation, and open political action, based on a systematic theory of revolution, which held that the workers were bound to win in the long run because they were going to be in the majority. Speaking in the General Council of the International on May 3, 1870, he said: "[Our] statutes bind all the sections of our Association to act in open daylight. If our statutes were not formal on that point, the very nature of an Association which identifies itself with the working classes would exclude from it every form of secret society. If the working classes, who form the great bulk of all nations, who produce all their wealth, and in the name of whom even the usurping powers always pretend to rule, conspire, they conspire publicly, as the sun conspires against darkness, in the full consciousness that without their pale there exists no legitimate power."

His views did not meet with immediate success. The Paris Commune of 1871, which was a brief proletarian dictatorship animated by an assortment of Bakuninists, Blanquists, Proudhonists, and other zealots, ended in a frightful slaughter of the innocent. In one "Bloody May Week" about 20,000 civilians were butchered in Paris by the troops of Adolphe Thiers's conservative French government. Tens of thousands of people were thrown in jail and tortured. In a continuing reign of terror, 20,000 workers, craftsmen, and artisans—mechanics, silversmiths, masons, carpenters, shoemakers, watchmakers, tailors, printers, binders—as well as teachers, journalists, and salesmen, were court-martialed; thousands were condemned to penal colonies. The Twentieth Arrondissement, a workingmen's district, was laid waste. Altogether, the anti-Commune forces claimed around 100,000 victims.[8]

The European press blamed Marx for the horrors of the Commune because a number of the Communards were members of the International. In truth, he had no control over them; they neither consulted him nor heeded what advice he offered. He was horrified by the Paris saturnalia and dreaded a repetition of it so long as Bakuninists and other fanatical nihilists were at large and at liberty to continue stirring up the smoldering resentments of radical workers.

The undisciplined anarchists had not learned the lesson of the blood-drenched Commune—that a handful of fanatics, even heroic ones, as some of the Communards were, could not make a successful revolution if they did not have the support of the majority, and if they were unable or unwilling to utilize the existing machinery for their own purposes. Marx read the lesson clearly. In the year following the Commune disaster he attended the last congress of the International, held in The Hague early in September, determined to prevent the organization from falling into the hands of the Bakuninists. In this he succeeded.

It was in The Hague that Marx delivered a speech in which he made what was for him a remarkable admission. For the first time he seemed to edge close to an evolutionary idea of revolution. While revolutionary transformation was still unavoidably the world-wide goal, he remarked, the method of achieving it could vary in different countries. Where democracy really existed, and the workers had political rights and knew how to use them legally, violence might not be necessary. He said: "You know that the institutions, mores, and

---

8. See also Volume II in this series.

traditions of various countries must be taken into consideration, and we do not deny that there are countries—such as America, England, and if I were more familiar with your institutions, I would perhaps also add Holland—where the workers can attain their goal by peaceful means."

Marx repeated this relatively evolutionary idea of revolution, with emphasis on the ripeness of social-economic conditions as a necessary prerequisite, in subsequent press interviews and statements.

In the long run, Marx's later insistence on disciplined labor organization, fueled by systematic revolutionary theory, to achieve the aims of the working class has proved to be far-sighted. In Germany and France Social-Democratic parties were organized by Marx's followers and served as models for other countries, in many of which, notably Scandinavia, they attained power and carried through far-reaching social and economic reforms democratically, without bloodshed or tyranny. Elsewhere, most strikingly in Russia and China, Marx-inspired parties have seized power by force. Both the democratic socialists (who nowadays no longer call themselves "Marxist") and the totalitarian communists have interpreted Marx to suit their own purposes.

Such varied interpretations have been made possible by Marx's own ambiguities, exaggerations, imprecisions, and lacunae. He never, for example, defined his key terms, or developed a theory of the state in practice, or offered concrete solutions for society's ailments. As his frank wife said in a private letter to a friend, written a few months after publication of *Capital* in 1867: "Of course, Marx has no specific ready-made panaceas—for which the bourgeois world that now calls itself socialist cries out so loudly: no pills, no salves, no bandages, with which to heal the gaping and bloody wounds of our society."

But the ambiguities and "terminological inexactitudes," in Winston Churchill's phrase, have also been the main source of Marx's strength, universality, and enduring appeal. His writings have become a sort of secular Bible, in which men in search of a better world find hope, rationalization, and inspiration. Marx's language, imbued with moral passion and historic sweep, lends itself, like the Bible, to a great variety of interpretations. And, again like the Bible, it has enormous vision and universality.

This volume, the first of its kind, contains Marx's basic writings on every aspect of revolution. It will enable the reader to see Marx's ideas, presented here developmentally and in context, in their total perspective.

No major editorial changes have been made in the texts. Among the few minor alterations are the elimination of italics for some words and phrases, primarily those that Marx was in the habit of underlining in nineteenth-century polemical fashion. Otherwise his writings are given here as in the original.

Translations and brief explanations by the editor are given in brackets. Footnotes are the editor's except for those keyed "K.M.," "NOTE BY ENGELS," etc. All the translations, except when otherwise indicated, are by the editor.

Chronology:
The Life of Karl Marx

1814

FEBRUARY 12   *Birth of Jenny von Westphalen, Marx's future wife, in Salzwedel, Prussia.*

1818

MAY 5   *Birth of Karl Marx, son of lawyer Heinrich Marx and Dutch-born Henriette Marx (née Presborg or Presburg or Presborck), in Trier, No. 664 Brückengasse (now No. 10 Brückenstrasse).*

1824

AUGUST 26   *Baptized, together with seven siblings (Sophie, Hermann, Henriette, Luise, Emilie, Karoline, and Eduard), in Lutheran church. The Marx family had been Jewish.*

1830

OCTOBER   *Enters Friedrich Wilhelm Gymnasium in Trier.*

1835

SEPTEMBER 24   *Graduates from Gymnasium.*
OCTOBER 15   *Matriculates at Bonn University as "Studiosus juris et cameralium," attending lectures in law, Roman history, and Greek mythology. Address: 1 Stocken Strasse, then 764 Joseph Strasse.*

1836

AUGUST   *Fights a student duel, is wounded in right eye.*

AUGUST 22   *Leaves Bonn for Trier, where he becomes secretly engaged to Jenny von Westphalen.*

MID OCTOBER   *By post coach to Berlin, taking up quarters first at 61 Mittelstrasse, then 50 Alte Jacobstrasse.*

OCTOBER 22   *Matriculates at Berlin University, Faculty of Law, attending lectures in philosophy, law, art history. He remains in Berlin four and a half years.*

1837

Reads Hegel, other philosophers and jurists; writes plays, fifty-six poems ("Book of Love" and "Book of Poems," dedicated to Jenny von Westphalen; and "Wild Songs," dedicated to his father); meets Young Hegelians, the so-called Freien; *has a nervous breakdown.*

NOVEMBER 10   *Writes 4,000-word letter to father, explaining his readings, writings, search for truth, and his undisciplined behavior.*

1838

MAY 10   *Death of his father, Heinrich Marx, in Trier.*

1839–40

Studies Greek philosophers and works on his doctoral dissertation, Differenz der demokritischen und epikureischen Naturphilosophie (Difference Between the Democritean and Epicurean Philosophy of Nature).

1841

JANUARY 23   *Publication of two poems, "Der Spielmann" and "Nachtliebe," in* Athenaeum; *the only poems Marx ever published.*

MARCH 30   *Completes studies at Berlin University.*

APRIL 15   *Receives Ph.D. degree from Jena University, in absentia.*

MID APRIL   *Leaves Berlin for Trier, where he remains until early July.*

MAY 4   *Declared unfit for military service because of affected lungs.*

EARLY JULY–   *Moves to Bonn in vain expectation of a university*
MID-OCTOBER   *professorship.*

1842

JANUARY 15–   *Writes on Prussian censorship for Ruge's* Deutsch-
FEBRUARY 10   Französische Jahrbücher; *because of censorship diffi-
               culties the article is not published until February,
               1843, in Swiss-based* Anekdota zur neuesten deutschen
               Philosophie und Publicistik, *Vol. I.*

LATE JANUARY   *Writes article, "Luther As Arbiter Between Strauss
               and Feuerbach," published in* Anekdota, *Vol. II,
               1843.*

MAY 5   *Begins a series of six articles on debates over freedom
               of the press in the Rhenish Landtag, in* Rheinische
               Zeitung *(May 5, 8, 10, 12, 15, 19).*

AUGUST 9   *Publishes "The Philosophical Manifesto of the His-
               torical School of Law," in* Rheinische Zeitung *(the
               censor cut out the section on marriage).*

MID-OCTOBER   *Becomes editor in chief of* Rheinische Zeitung *and
               moves to Cologne from Bonn.*

OCTOBER 16   *Publishes article on communism in* Rheinische Zei-
               tung.

OCTOBER–   *Begins study of French utopians: Fourier, Cabet,*
EARLY 1843   *Proudhon, etc.*

NOVEMBER   *Marx and Engels meet for the first time, in office of*
               Rheinische Zeitung.

NOVEMBER 15   *Publishes critical article on religious aspects of di-
               vorce law in* Rheinische Zeitung.

LATE   *Breaks with Young Hegelians over* Rheinische Zei-
NOVEMBER   tung *policy.*

DECEMBER 19   *Publishes critical article on divorce law in* Rheinische
               Zeitung.

1843

JANUARY 1–16   *Publishes a series of seven articles on the suppression
               of the* Leipziger Allgemeine Zeitung *in* Rheinische
               Zeitung *(January 1, 4, 6, 8, 10, 13, 16).*

MARCH 17   *Resigns from* Rheinische Zeitung (*closed by censorship on April 1*).

LATE MARCH   *Travels in Holland.*

JUNE 19   *Marries Jenny von Westphalen at Kreuznach.*

SUMMER   *Writes "Critique of Hegel's Philosophy of Law" and "On the Jewish Question."*

LATE OCTOBER   *Moves to Paris: 41 Rue Vaneau, Fbg. St. Germain;* and becomes coeditor (*with Ruge*) of Deutsch-Französische Jahrbücher.

1844

LATE FEBRUARY   *Publishes first double issue of* Deutsch-Französische Jahrbücher, *containing his two articles "Critique of Hegel's Philosophy of Law" and "On the Jewish Question."*

MARCH 23   *Meets Mikhail Bakunin in Paris.*

MARCH 26   *Break with Arnold Ruge and suspension of* Deutsch-Französische Jahrbücher.

APRIL–AUGUST   *Works on the* Economic and Philosophic Manuscripts *of 1844 (first published in Berlin, 1932).*

APRIL 16   *Prussian Government issues order for Marx's arrest for "high treason and* lèse majesté" *if he enters Prussia.*

MAY 1   *Birth of daughter Jenny in Paris.*

JULY   *Meets Pierre Joseph Proudhon.*

AUGUST 7, 10   *Publishes anti-Ruge articles, "The King of Prussia," etc., in* Vorwärts, *a twice-weekly German-language publication in Paris.*

AUGUST 28   *Meets Engels for the second time, and strikes up a permanent friendship.*

SEPTEMBER   *Begins to meet with French workingmen's groups and to study economic and socialist theorists.*

1845

MID JANUARY   *Receives order of expulsion from Paris.*

FEBRUARY 1   *Signs contract with Darmstadt publisher, Karl Leske, for a two-volume work,* Critique of Political and National Economy.

FEBRUARY 2   *Meets utopian communist Étienne Cabet.*

FEBRUARY 3	*Moves to Brussels: 4 Rue d'Alliance, outside Porte de Louvain.*
FEBRUARY 24	*Publication of* Die Heilige Familie (*The Holy Family*)*, a polemic against Bruno Bauer and colleagues, written in collaboration with Engels.*
SPRING	*Writes "Thesis on Feuerbach" (first published by Engels in his* Ludwig Feuerbach, *in 1888).*
JULY 12	*In company of Engels visits London and Manchester for first time.*
AUGUST 20	*Participates in Chartist conference in London.*
AUGUST 24	*Returns to Brussels.*
SEPTEMBER	*Begins work on the* Deutsche Ideologie (*The German Ideology*)*.*
SEPTEMBER 6	*Birth of daughter Laura.*
NOVEMBER 10	*Requests release from Prussian citizenship.*
DECEMBER 1	*Gives up Prussian citizenship.*

1846

EARLY IN YEAR	*Founds, with Engels, a Communist Correspondence Committee in Brussels.*
MARCH 30	*Vehement confrontation with German radical Wilhelm Weitling.*
LATE APRIL	*Meets German radical Wilhelm Wolff, who becomes a lifelong friend.*
MAY	*Moves to hotel Au Bois Sauvage: 19/21 Plaine Ste. Gudule.*
SUMMER	*Completes, with Engels,* The Germany Ideology*, but can find no publisher in Germany.*

1847

JANUARY 3–FEBRUARY, 1848	*Writes for* Deutsche Brüsseler Zeitung, *a radical paper in Brussels.*
MID JANUARY	*Moves to new address: 42 Rue d'Orléans, Fbg. de Namour, Brussels.*
JANUARY–APRIL	*Works on* Misère de la Philosophie (*Poverty of Philosophy*)*.*
EARLY JUNE	*Organizes, with Engels, German Communist League, in Brussels.*

EARLY JULY   *Publication, in French, of* Misère de la Philosophie. Réponse à la Philosophie de la Misère de M. Proudhon, *in Paris and Brussels (a German edition came out in 1885).*

LATE AUGUST   *Founds, with Engels, German Workers' Association, for propagation of communist ideas.*

NOVEMBER 15   *Elected vice-president of the Brussels* Association Démocratique.

NOVEMBER 29   *Participates, with Engels, in international meeting of Fraternal Democrats in London.*

NOVEMBER 29– DECEMBER 8   *Participates, with Engels, in London congress of Communist League, which commissions them to draw up the* Manifesto.

DECEMBER 13   *Returns to Brussels from London.*

DECEMBER 17   *Birth of son Edgar.*

LATE DECEMBER   *Lectures before German Workers' Association on* Wage Labor and Capital, *published later as a pamphlet in 1884, 1891, and 1925.*

1848

LATE JANUARY   *Completes, with Engels,* Manifesto of the Communist Party *and sends it to London to be printed.*

FEBRUARY 24   *Publication, in German, of* Manifesto.

FEBRUARY 25   *Resigns as vice-president of the Brussels* Association Démocratique.

MARCH 1   *Receives invitation from French Provisional Government to return to Paris.*

MARCH 3   *Receives order of expulsion from Brussels.*

MARCH 5   *Arrives in Paris; address: 10 Rue Neuve Ménilmontant (Bld. Beaumarchais).*

MARCH 8–9   *Helps found Club of German Workers in Paris.*

MARCH 12   *Elected president of Communist League.*

MARCH 21, 29   *Writes, with Engels, "Demands of the Communist Party in Germany."*

APRIL 6   *Leaves Paris, with Engels, to participate in German revolution.*

APRIL 11   *Arrives in Cologne; address: No. 7 Apostelstrasse.*

MID APRIL– JUNE   *Works on plans to establish the daily,* Neue Rheinische Zeitung.

JUNE 1 — *Publishes first issue of* Neue Rheinische Zeitung, *subtitled* Organ der Demokratie (*Organ of Democracy*). *It started with 6,000 subscribers, and appeared until May 19, 1849.*

EARLY JULY — Neue Rheinische Zeitung *investigated by police.*

JULY 20 — *Attacks Prussian censorship in an article in* Neue Rheinische Zeitung.

JULY 21 — *Elected member of Cologne Democratic Society.* •

AUGUST 3 — *Denial of his citizenship by Prussian Government.*

AUGUST 23– SEPTEMBER 11 — *Trip to Berlin and Vienna to raise money for* Neue Rheinische Zeitung.

SEPTEMBER 11 — *Returns to Cologne.*

SEPTEMBER 25 — *Outbreak of revolution in Cologne.*

SEPTEMBER 26 — Neue Rheinische Zeitung *suspended under martial law.*

OCTOBER 5 — *Reappearance of* Neue Rheinische Zeitung.

NOVEMBER — *Meets Charles A. Dana, who is later (1852) to appoint him London correspondent of* New-York Daily Tribune.

NOVEMBER 14, 20, 23, 26 — *Appears in court on charges of* lèse majesté *and incitement to rebellion.*

DECEMBER 2 — *Summoned to court again.*

DECEMBER 6 — *Indicted.*

DECEMBER 20–21 — *Court trial. Decision postponed.*

1849

FEBRUARY 7–8 — *Tried in Cologne court and acquitted by jury.*

MAY 16 — *Receives order of expulsion from Prussia.*

MAY 19 — *Publication of last issue of* Neue Rheinische Zeitung.

JUNE 3 — *Arrives in Paris.*

JULY — *Joined by wife and children; address: 45 Rue de Lille.*

JULY 19 — *Receives order of expulsion from Paris.*

AUGUST 24 — *Leaves Paris for London.*

LATE AUGUST — *Helps to reconstitute Communist League in London.*

EARLY SEPTEMBER — *Joins German Workers' Educational Society.*

SEPTEMBER 17   *Joined by pregnant wife and their children; lives in rooming house on Leicester Square.*

NOVEMBER 5   *Birth of son, Heinrich Guido, called "Föxchen," because he was born on Guy Fawkes Day.*

NOVEMBER 10   *Engels arrives in London.*

DECEMBER   *Works, with Engels, on publication of* Neue Rheinische Zeitung Politisch-Ökonomische Revue.

1850

JANUARY   *Illness.*

MARCH 6   *First issue of* Neue Rheinische Zeitung Politisch-Ökonomische Revue, *printed in Hamburg in an edition of 2,500 copies, and dated January, 1850.*

LATE MARCH   *Second issue of the* Revue, *dated February, 1850, 2,000 copies.*

APRIL 17   *Third issue of the* Revue, *dated March, 1850.*

MAY 19   *Fourth issue of the Revue, dated March–April, 1850.*

NOVEMBER 29   *Fifth-sixth, and last, double issue of the* Revue, *dated May–October, 1850.*

MARCH–NOVEMBER   *Publication of* The Class Struggles in France, 1848 *to 1850, as a series in the* Revue. *In 1895 Engels published the whole in book form under this title.*

SPRING   *Evicted from German hotel in Leicester Square and moves to squalid quarters: 64 Dean Street, Soho.*

MID APRIL   *Meets Wilhelm Liebknecht on excursion of German Workers' Educational Society.*

JULY   *Begins study of political economy in British Museum.*

SEPTEMBER 17   *Quits Workers' Educational Society over doctrinal dispute.*

LATE NOVEMBER   *Engels moves to Manchester, to enter business and help support Marx financially, which he will do for the rest of the latter's life.*

NOVEMBER 19   *Death of one-year-old son Heinrich Guido.*

NOVEMBER 30   *First publication of* Manifesto of the Communist Party *in English (translation by Helen Macfarlane), in George Julian Harney's* Red Republican, *a Chartist weekly.*

DECEMBER   *Moves to small three-room furnished apartment: 28 Dean Street, Soho, where the Marx family lives until September 1856.*

1851

MARCH 28	*Birth of daughter Franziska.*
APRIL 17	*Visits Engels in Manchester.*
LATE APRIL	*Publication of first part of* Gesammelte Aufsätze von Karl Marx (Collected Essays by Karl Marx), *by Hermann Becker in Cologne.*
MAY– DECEMBER	*Works in British Museum daily "from 10* A.M. *to 7* P.M.*"*
JUNE 23	*Birth of Frederick Demuth, Marx's illegitimate son by his housekeeper, Helene Demuth.*
AUGUST 7	*Receives invitation from Dana to write for* New-York Daily Tribune.
NOVEMBER 5–15	*Visits Engels in Manchester.*
DECEMBER 19–MARCH 25, 1852	*Works on* Der achtzehnte Brumaire des Louis Bonaparte (*The Eighteenth Brumaire of Louis Bonaparte*).

1852

JANUARY	*Ill with hemorrhoids and barely able to work.*
JANUARY– MAY	*Publication of* Der achtzehnte Brumaire des Louis Bonaparte, *in two installments, in Joseph Weydemeyer's New York German-language weekly,* Die Revolution. *A revised edition came out in book form in Hamburg, 1869.*
APRIL 14	*Death of daughter Franziska.*
LATE MAY– MID JUNE	*Visits Engels in Manchester, where they work on booklet,* Die grossen Männer des Exils (The Great Men of the Exile).
JULY–AUGUST	*Resumes research in British Museum.*
AUGUST 21	*Publication of Marx's own article (translated by Engels), "The Elections in England: Tories and Whigs," in* New-York Daily Tribune. (*His last Tribune article was published March 10, 1862.*)
OCTOBER 2–23	*Reprint of the* Tribune *article in the Chartist weekly, the* People's Paper (*October 2, 9, 16, 23*).
NOVEMBER 17	*Dissolution, at Marx's suggestion, of Communist League.*
DECEMBER 14	*Ill with hemorrhoids.*

1853

LATE JANUARY — *Publication of* Enthüllungen über den Kölner Kommunisten Prozess *(Revelations About the Cologne Communist Trial), in Basel.*

MARCH — *Grave liver inflammation ("I came near to croaking this week," Marx to Engels, March 10).*

APRIL 24 — *Publication of* Enthüllungen *as a pamphlet in Boston.*

APRIL 30–
MAY 19 — *Visit to Engels in Manchester.*

OCTOBER 19–
JANUARY 11,
1854 — *Publishes six articles, "Lord Palmerston," in* New-York Daily Tribune; *the series also appeared, in eight articles, in the Chartist weekly, the* People's Paper *(October 22, 29, November 5, 12, 19, December 10, 17, 24, 1853).*

NOVEMBER
21–28 — *Writes* Der Ritter vom edelmütigen Bewusstsein *(The Knight of Magnanimous Consciousness), a satire against August Willich.*

1854

MID JANUARY — *Publication of* Der Ritter *as a brochure in New York.*

MARCH 6 — *Publishes article, "The Oriental War," in the* Capetown Zuid Afrikaan.

MAY — *Illness—tumors, toothaches, etc.—and inability to work.*

SEPTEMBER 9–
DECEMBER 2 — *Publishes a series of eight articles, "Revolutionary Spain," in* New-York Daily Tribune *(September 9, 25, October 20, 27, 30, November 24, December 1, 2).*

1855

JANUARY 2–
OCTOBER 8 — *Publication of first article, "Rückblicke" ("Retrospects"), in the Breslau daily,* Neue Oder-Zeitung. *Altogether, Marx contributed 112 articles (a few of them in collaboration with Engels), many of which also appeared in the* New-York Daily Tribune, *to the* Neue Oder-Zeitung. *The last article, "The French Bank—Reinforcements for the Crimea—The New Field Marshals," came out October 8, 1855.*

JANUARY 16   *Birth of daughter Eleanor (Tussy).*

FEBRUARY 9–
MARCH   *Illness and eye inflammation.*

APRIL 6   *Death of eight-year-old son Edgar (Musch).*

APRIL 18–
MAY 6   *Marx and wife visit Engels in Manchester.*

MAY 16   *Publication of Palmerston articles as a pamphlet in Tucker's* Political Fly-Sheets.

JUNE   *Illness and "atrocious toothache."*

JULY 28–
AUGUST 15   *Publication of a series of six articles, "Lord John Russell," in* Neue Oder-Zeitung *(July 28, August 4, 7, 8, 10, 15).*

JULY–
SEPTEMBER 12   *Lives with family in Peter Imandt's cottage: 3 York Place, Denmark Street, Camberwell.*

SEPTEMBER
12–EARLY
DECEMBER   *Marx family lives with Engels in Manchester: 34 Butler Street, Green Keys.*

DECEMBER
29–FEBRUARY
16, 1856   *Republication of Palmerston articles from the* People's Paper *in Urquhart's* Free Press; *they were also published as a separate brochure, No. 5 of "Free Press Serials."*

1856

JANUARY–
FEBRUARY   *Ill with hemorrhoids.*

FEBRUARY–
APRIL   *Research in British Museum (though "plagued by hemorrhoids") on Russo-British diplomatic relations in seventeenth and eighteenth centuries.*

APRIL 5–26   *Publishes a series of four articles, "The Fall of Kars," in the* People's Paper *(April 5, 12, 19, 26).*

APRIL 14   *Speech at anniversary banquet of the* People's Paper *on revolution and the proletariat.*

MAY 18–
JUNE 5   *Illness and inability to work.*

JUNE 7–
MID JUNE   *Visits Engels in Manchester.*

JUNE 21–
JULY 11   *Publication of a series of three articles, "The French Crédit Mobilier," in* New-York Daily Tribune *(June 21, 24, July 11).*

JUNE 21   *Begins writing* Diplomatic History of the Seventeenth Century. (*This work was not completed.*)

EARLY   *Moves from Soho to new house in undeveloped*
OCTOBER   *suburb: 9 Grafton Terrace, Maitland Park, Haverstock Hill. The Marx family lived here until 1864.*

1857

JANUARY–   *Illness and inability to work* (*Mrs. Marx to Engels,
JULY   April 12:* "*Der Chaley has a headache, terrible toothaches, pains in the ears, head, eyes, throat, and God
knows what else. Neither opium pills nor creosote
helps*").

MAY   *Studies Danish and Swedish.*

LATE AUGUST– *Works on introduction to a book on political econ-
MID SEPTEM-   omy. The introduction was first published in* Die
BER   Neue Zeit *in 1903.*

SEPTEMBER–   *Writes sixteen articles—eight in collaboration with
APRIL, 1858   Engels—for the* New American Cyclopaedia, *published in New York:*

Title	Written	Published
"Armada"*	September–October	Vol. II, 1858
"Ayacucho"*	September 20–October 23	Vol. II, 1858
"Barclay de Tolly"*	September 10–15	Vol. II, 1858
"Bem"*	late September	Vol. III, 1858
"Bennigsen"*	September 10–22	Vol. III, 1858
"Beresford"*	March–April 9	Vol. III, 1858
"Bernadotte"	September 17–October 15	Vol. III, 1858
"Berthier"	September 15	Vol. III, 1858
"Bessières"	September 29	Vol. III, 1858
"Blücher"*	September 22–October 30	Vol. III, 1858
"Blum"	September 22	Vol. III, 1858
"Bolivar y Ponte"	January 8, 1858	Vol. III, 1858
"Bosquet"*	September 22–29	Vol. III, 1858
"Bourrienne"	September 22	Vol. III, 1858
"Brune"	September 23–29	Vol. IV, 1859
"Bugeaud"	November 27	Vol. IV, 1859
* In collaboration with Engels.		

1858

FEBRUARY–
LATE MAY   *Illness—liver, toothaches, etc.—and inability to work.*

MAY 6–24   *Visits Engels in Manchester.*

AUGUST   *Begins writing* Zur Kritik der Politischen Ökonomie (Critique of Political Economy).

EARLY
NOVEMBER   *Toothaches and inability to work.*

1859

JANUARY 26   *Manuscript of* Critique of Political Economy *sent to publisher Franz Duncker in Berlin.*

JUNE 4   *Introduction to* Zur Kritik *published in* Das Volk, *a radical German-language London weekly.*

JUNE 11   *Publication of* Zur Kritik, First Part, *in an edition of 1,000 copies. (An English translation did not appear until 1909.)*

JUNE 12–
JULY 2   *Visits Engels in Manchester.*

JULY 3   *Becomes editor of* Das Volk.

JULY 30   *Publishes article, "Invasion!" in* Das Volk.

JULY 30–
AUGUST 20   *Series of four articles, "Quid pro Quo," published in* Das Volk *(July 30, August 6, 13, 20).*

AUGUST 20   Das Volk *ceases publication.*

1860

JANUARY–
EARLY
FEBRUARY   *Works on Second Part of* Zur Kritik der Politischen Ökonomie *(never completed).*

MAY–
NOVEMBER 17   *Works on* Herr Vogt, *a bitter, violent, and financially ruinous pamphlet against Karl Vogt, whom Marx accused of being a Bonapartist agent.*

LATE
NOVEMBER   *Illness and toothaches.*

DECEMBER 1   *Publication of* Herr Vogt, *by A. Petsch & Co., "German Bookseller," 78 Fenchurch Street, London, E.C.*

DECEMBER   *Illness; reading Darwin's* Natural Selection *(Marx to Engels, December 19: ". . . it is the book that contains the natural-history basis of our philosophy").*

1861

JANUARY	*Suffers from inflammation of the liver.*
JANUARY–OCTOBER 11	New-York Daily Tribune *suspend's Marx's correspondenceship, printing none of his articles.*
FEBRUARY 28–MARCH 16	*Visits uncle, Lion Philips, in Zaltbommel, Holland.*
MARCH 17–APRIL 12	*Visit with Ferdinand Lassalle in Berlin.*
APRIL 10	*Applies for restoration of Prussian citizenship.*
APRIL 12–29	*Travels from Berlin to the Rhineland, visiting his mother in Trier and returning to London via Holland.*
EARLY JUNE	*Begins work on* Capital.
JUNE	*Research on U.S. Civil War.*
EARLY JULY	*Eye inflammation (Marx to Engels, July 5: "For three days now I have had a disgusting eye inflammation, which prevents all writing and reading").*
LATE AUGUST–MID SEPTEMBER	*Visits Engels in Manchester.*
SEPTEMBER 18	*Writes "The American Question in England," the first article of his to be published in* New-York Daily Tribune *in the year 1861 (October 11). For the rest of the year the* Tribune *publishes only seven more of his articles.*
OCTOBER 25	*First publication ("The North American Civil War") in* Die Presse, *a Vienna daily.*
NOVEMBER	*Prussian Government denies Marx's application for restoration of citizenship.*

1862

JANUARY–FEBRUARY	*Work on "Theories of Surplus Value."*
MARCH 10	*Publishes last article, "The Mexican Imbroglio," in* New-York Herald Tribune.
MARCH 30–APRIL 25	*Visits Engels in Manchester.*
AUGUST 28–SEPTEMBER 27	*Visits mother in Trier and uncle Lion Philips in Zaltbommel in connection with money matters.*

DECEMBER 5–
13   *Visits Engels in Manchester.*

1863

FEBRUARY–   *Illness—inflammation of eyes and liver, coughing—*
LATE MAY   *and inability to work.*

MAY–AUGUST   *Intermittent research in British Museum.*

SEPTEMBER–   *Ill with carbuncles and furuncles; carbuncle opera-*
DECEMBER   *tion in November.*

DECEMBER 2   *Death of mother, Henriette Marx, in Trier.*

DECEMBER 7   *Leaves London for Germany and Holland; in Trier, stays in inn, Gasthof von Venedig.*

DECEMBER 21–
FEBRUARY 19,   *Stays with Philips family in Zaltbommel, where he*
1864   *is ill.*

1864

FEBRUARY 19   *Returns to London.*

MARCH   *Moves to new house: 1 Modena Villas, Maitland Park, Haverstock Hill, N.W. The Marx family lived here until 1873.*

MARCH 12   *Visits Engels in Manchester, to report on his trip to Germany and Holland.*

MAY 3–13   *In Manchester during final illness and death (May 9) of friend, Wilhelm Wolff, who left the Marx family the bulk of his estate, valued at £320.*

LATE MAY   *Ill with carbuncles.*

JULY 1–
AUGUST 31   *Ill with influenza and carbuncles.*

JULY 20–
AUGUST 10   *On cure in Ramsgate, 46 Hardres Street.*

SEPTEMBER 28   *Attends meeting which founds International Working Men's Association (First International), at St. Martin's Hall, London; chosen member of Provisional Committee.*

OCTOBER 6–17   *Illness and inability to work.*

OCTOBER 21–
27   *Drafts Provisional Rules and Inaugural Address of the International, adopted by the Provisional Committee November 1.*

NOVEMBER 3   *Meets Michael Bakunin for first time in sixteen years.*

EARLY No-
VEMBER–MID
DECEMBER   *Ill with new carbuncles.*

NOVEMBER 29   *Completes "Address of the International Working Men's Association to Abraham Lincoln," congratulating him on his reelection to Presidency.*

DECEMBER 21,
30   *Publication of "Address and Provisional Rules of the Working Men's Association," in* Der Social-Demokrat; *also published as pamphlet by* Bee-Hive Newspaper Office, *10 Bolt Court, Fleet Street.*

1865

JANUARY 7–14   *Visits Engels in Manchester.*

FEBRUARY–
MID MARCH   *Ill with carbuncles.*

MARCH 19–
APRIL 8   *Visits relatives in Zaltbommel.*

APRIL 11   *Becomes the International's corresponding secretary for Belgium (Marx held this office until January, 1866).*

MAY 2–9   *Drafts International's Address to President Andrew Johnson.*

LATE MAY–
JUNE 17   *Writes "Wages, Price and Profit."*

JUNE 20   *Delivers "Wages, Price and Profit" as a lecture before the General Council of the International.*

MAY–
AUGUST   *Ill with influenza, carbuncles, etc., but working intermittently on* Capital.

LATE AUGUST   *Chosen for editorial board of* Workmen's Advocate, *organ of the International.*

SEPTEMBER
25–29   *Attends sessions of London conference of the International.*

SEPTEMBER
29–MID
OCTOBER   *Illness and inability to work.*

OCTOBER 20–
NOVEMBER 2   *Visits Engels in Manchester.*

LATE
DECEMBER   *Completes first draft of* Capital.

1866

JANUARY	*Begins preparing manuscript of* Capital *for publisher.*
MID JANUARY– MID MARCH	*Desperately ill with carbuncles and boils, interrupting work on* Capital.
MARCH 15– APRIL 10	*On cure in Margate, 5 Lansell's Place.*
MID APRIL– LATE DECEMBER	*Continuing illnesses—toothaches, carbuncles, rheumatism, liver inflammation, etc.; working intermittently.*
SEPTEMBER 2	*Elected International's corresponding secretary for Germany.*
MID NOVEMBER	*Sends first part of* Capital *to Meissner, Hamburg publisher.*

1867

LATE MARCH	*Completes* Capital.
APRIL 10	*Leaves for Hamburg to see Meissner, his publisher.*
APRIL 12–16	*Discusses publication of* Capital *with Meissner.*
APRIL 17– MAY 15	*Visits Dr. Ludwig Kugelmann, a friend and admirer, in Hanover.*
MAY 16–17	*On way back to London, again visits Meissner in Hamburg.*
MAY 19	*Arrives in London.*
MAY 21– JUNE 2	*Visits Engels in Manchester.*
AUGUST 15– 16	*Finishes correcting proofs of* Capital.
SEPTEMBER 14	*Publication of* Capital (*Vol. I*).
LATE NOVEMBER	*New outbreak of carbuncles.*

1868

JANUARY– MID MAY	*Festering carbuncles all over his body; taking prescribed arsenic treatment.*
APRIL 2	*Marriage of Laura Marx to Paul Lafargue.*
APRIL 22	*Begins intermittent work, for brief periods, on Vol. II of* Capital.
MAY 29– JUNE 15	*Visits Engels in Manchester with daughter Eleanor.*

AUGUST 21–
24   *On cure in Ramsgate.*

SEPTEMBER 24   *Reelected International's corresponding secretary for Germany.*

EARLY
OCTOBER   *Bakunin begins translation of* Capital *into Russian.*

MID
NOVEMBER   *Reappearance of carbuncles.*

NOVEMBER 29 *Engels offers Marx annuity of £350 to relieve him permanently of financial distress.*

DECEMBER 1   *Appointed archivist of the International.*

1869

LATE JANUARY   *Ill with cold and fever; prepares second edition of* The Eighteenth Brumaire of Louis Bonaparte *and sends it to Meissner in Hamburg.*

MID FEBRUARY–
LATE MAY   *Liver illness and carbuncles.*

MAY 25–
JUNE 14   *Visits Engels in Manchester, with daughter Eleanor.*

JULY 1   *Engels gives up his business in Manchester (Engels to Marx, July 1: "Hurrah! Today . . . I am a free man").*

JULY 6–12   *Incognito visit to daughter Laura Lafargue in Paris, under pseudonym of "J. Williams."*

LATE JULY   *Ill with carbuncles. Publication of second edition of* Eighteenth Brumaire *in Hamburg.*

LATE AUGUST–
EARLY SEP-
TEMBER   *Writes "Report . . . of the International . . . to the Fourth Congress in Basel."*

SEPTEMBER 7–
11   *At Basel Congress, the absent Marx is unanimously reelected member of International's General Council.*

SEPTEMBER 10 *Leaves, with daughter Eleanor, for Germany, traveling through Belgium.*

SEPTEMBER 18–
OCTOBER 7   *Visits Dr. Kugelmann in Hanover.*

OCTOBER 8–9 *Visits publisher, Meissner, in Hamburg.*

OCTOBER 11   *Returns to London.*

LATE OCTOBER *Begins to study Russian.*

NOVEMBER 30   *Becomes member of Land and Labour League, a radical organization founded October, 1869.*

1870

MID JANUARY–
APRIL   *Ill with liver inflammation, carbuncles and abscesses; undergoes two operations.*

APRIL 29   *Receives Russian translation of the* Manifesto, *to be published in Geneva.*

MAY 23–
JUNE 23   *Visits Engels in Manchester with daughter Eleanor. Review of* Capital, *by Hermann Karl Friedrich Rösler, in* Jahrbücher für Nationalökonomie und Statistik, *which Marx considered so ridiculous that he laughed until he had tears in his eyes.*

JULY 19–23   *Writes First Address of the International on the Franco-Prussian War, published, in German and French, in an edition of 30,000 copies.*

AUGUST 9–31   *On cure (for sciatica) at Ramsgate, 36 Hardres Street.*

SEPTEMBER 6–
9   *Writes Second Address of the International on the Franco-Prussian War, protesting annexation of Alsace-Lorraine.*

SEPTEMBER 16   *Writes last letter to Engels in Manchester.*

SEPTEMBER 22   *Engels moves to London, 122 Regents Park Road, N.W., to be near Marx.*

1871

JANUARY ON   *Continued illness—bronchitis, coughing, sleeplessness.*

APRIL 18–
MAY 29   *Writes* The Civil War in France, *a pamphlet defending the Paris Commune, published in English in London, in German in Leipzig (July), and in a later edition by Engels in 1891.*

MAY 2–22   *Inability to work, due to continued illness.*

JUNE–
DECEMBER   *Organizes financial assistance for Paris Commune refugees in London.*

JULY 3   *Gives interview to R. Landor, correspondent of* New York World *(published in the* World, *July 18, and in* Woodhull & Claflin's Weekly, *August 12).*

AUGUST 16–29   *On cure in Brighton, Globe Hotel, Manchester Street.*

SEPTEMBER 17–23   *Participates in London conference of the International.*

SEPTEMBER 28–OCTOBER 3   *On cure in Ramsgate with Mrs. Marx and Engels.*

OCTOBER 3   *Elected International's corresponding secretary for Russia.*

OCTOBER– LATE NOVEM- BER   *Inability to work, due to illness.*

1872

JANUARY– EARLY MARCH   *Prepares, with Engels, the anti-Bakunin circular, "Fictitious Splits in the International."*

JANUARY 15– FEBRUARY 15   *Negotiates with Joseph Roy for the translation, and with Paris publisher Maurice Lachatre for the publication, of a French edition of* Capital.

MARCH 27   *Publication of first foreign translation—in Russian— of* Capital *(translation begun by Bakunin, completed by Nicolai F. Danielson). Of an edition of 3,000 copies, 900 were sold in first six weeks.*

APRIL–MAY   *Edits French translation of* The Civil War in France, *published in June in Brussels in an edition of 2,000 copies.*

JULY 9–15   *On cure in Ramsgate with Engels.*

JULY   *Publication in Leipzig of new German edition of the* Manifesto, *with introduction by Marx and Engels.*

MID JULY   *Publication of first part of second German edition of* Capital.

LATE AUGUST   *Chosen delegate to Hague Congress of the International.*

SEPTEMBER 1   *Arrives, with wife and daughter Eleanor, in The Hague.*

SEPTEMBER 2–7   *Participates actively in the Congress and in the struggle with the Bakuninists which led to dissolution of the International.*

SEPTEMBER 17   *Returns to London. Publication of first installments of French edition of* Capital.

OCTOBER   *Marriage of Jenny Marx to French socialist Charles Longuet.*

1873

JANUARY 24   *Writes Epilogue for second German edition of Capital.*

MAY–JUNE   *Corrects and retranslates French edition of Capital.*

MAY 22–
JUNE 3   *Visits Dr. Eduard Gumpert (for medical consultation) and friends, including Carl Schorlemmer and Samuel Moore, the English translator of Capital, in Manchester.*

EARLY JUNE   *Publication of second German edition of Capital.*

JULY–
OCTOBER   *Works in British Museum, despite ill health.*

NOVEMBER 24–
DECEMBER 15   *On cure in Harrogate with daughter Eleanor.*

1874

FEBRUARY–
MID APRIL   *Continued illness.*

MID APRIL–
MAY 5   *On cure in Ramsgate, 16 Abbott's Hill.*

MID JULY–
LATE JULY   *On cure in Ryde, Isle of Wight, 11 Nelson Street.*

AUGUST 1   *Applies for British citizenship, to obtain passport for European travel.*

AUGUST 4–9   *In Ramsgate with sick daughter, Jenny Longuet.*

AUGUST 17   *Application for citizenship rejected by Scotland Yard.*

AUGUST 19–
SEPTEMBER 21   *On cure in Karlsbad, Hotel Germania, am Schlossberg.*

OCTOBER 3   *Returns to London.*

OCTOBER 28–
DECEMBER 18   *First publication in Germany—in* Der Volksstaat, *a social-democratic journal appearing twice weekly in Leipzig—of* Revelations About the Cologne Communist Trial; *it was published as a brochure in 1875.*

1875

MARCH   *Moves to 41 Maitland Park Road (or Crescent), N.W., where he is to live until his death in 1883.*

MAY 5   *Sends* Critique of the Gotha Program *to Wilhelm Bracke for the social-democratic congress in Eisenach, Germany.*

AUGUST 15–
SEPTEMBER 11   *On cure in Karlsbad, Hotel Germania.*

SEPTEMBER 20   *Returns to London after visiting several European cities.*

LATE
NOVEMBER   *Publication of French edition of* Capital *(translation begun by Joseph Roy, corrected by Marx, completed by Charles Keller and others).*

1876

JULY 15   *The General Council of the International, which Marx had moved to America in 1872 (to keep it out of the hands of the Bakuninists), dissolves itself at a conference in Philadelphia.*

AUGUST 16–
SEPTEMBER 15   *On cure for third time in Karlsbad, Hotel Germania, with daughter Eleanor.*

1877

MARCH 5   *Completes first part of Chapter 10 for Engels' Anti-Dühring.*

LATE MARCH   *Resumes intermittent work on second volume of* Capital.

AUGUST 8   *Completes second part of Chapter 10 for Anti-Dühring.*

AUGUST 8–
SEPTEMBER 27   *On cure, with sick wife, in Bad Neuenahr, Germany, Hotel Flora.*

NOVEMBER–
JULY, 1878   *Works on first chapter of second volume of* Capital.

1878

SEPTEMBER 4–
14   *On cure, with wife and daughter Jenny Longuet, in Malvern.*

1879

AUGUST 8-20   *On cure in St. Aubin's, Isle of Jersey; Trafalgar Hotel.*

AUGUST 21– *On cure with wife in Ramsgate, 62 Plains of Water-*
SEPTEMBER 17 *loo.*

1880

JANUARY– *While ill, works intermittently on second and third*
DECEMBER *volumes of* Capital.
EARLY AUGUST–
SEPTEMBER 13 *On cure, with wife and children, in Ramsgate.*

1881

LATE JUNE– *On cure with wife in Eastbourne, 43 Terminus*
JULY 20 *Road.*
JULY 26– *With sick wife, visits daughter Jenny Longuet in*
AUGUST 16 *Argenteuil, 11 Boulevard Thiers.*
OCTOBER 13–
MID
DECEMBER *Gravely ill.*
DECEMBER 1 *Publication of "Karl Marx," by Ernest Belfort Bax,*
in Modern Thought, *a London monthly—the first*
serious pro-Marx article in the English language.
DECEMBER 2 *Death of wife, Jenny Marx, of cancer; Marx too ill*
to attend funeral.
DECEMBER
29–JANUARY *On cure in Ventnor, Isle of Wight, 1 St. Boniface*
16, 1882 *Gardens.*

1882

JANUARY 16 *Returns to London from Ventnor.*
JANUARY 21 *Writes (with Engels) preface to Russian translation*
(by G. Plekhanov) of the Manifesto; *preface pub-*
lished in Russian weekly, Narodnaya Volya, *Feb-*
ruary 5.
FEBRUARY 9– *Visits daughter Jenny Longuet in Argenteuil, on way*
16 *to cure for pleurisy and bronchitis in Algiers.*
FEBRUARY 20–
MAY 2 *On cure in Algiers, Hotel Victoria.*
EARLY MAY– *In Nice and Monte Carlo, Hotel de Russie, in search*
JUNE 3 *of sun.*
JUNE 3–5 *In Cannes.*

JUNE 6–
   AUGUST 22   *Visits daughter Jenny Longuet in Argenteuil, taking sulphur baths at Enghien.*

AUGUST 23–27   *Visits Lausanne with daughter Laura Lafargue.*

AUGUST 27–
SEPTEMBER 25   *Visits Vevey, Switzerland, with Laura.*

OCTOBER 30–
JANUARY 12,
      1883   *On cure in Ventnor, 1 St. Boniface Gardens.*

1883

JANUARY 11   *Death of Jenny Longuet, in Argenteuil, of cancer, causing the shocked Marx to return to London.*

JANUARY–
   MARCH 14   *Gravely ill with laryngitis, bronchitis, lung tumor, etc.*

MARCH 14,
  2:45 P.M.   *Dies at home in London, sitting in easy chair.*

MARCH 17   *Buried in Highgate Cemetery, London, in presence of about a dozen people—sons-in-law Paul Lafargue and Charles Longuet, fellow Communists Friedrich Lessner and Georg Lochner, German socialist leader Wilhelm Liebknecht, scientists Sir Edwin Ray Lankester and Carl Schorlemmer. Liebknecht and Engels speak at the grave, the latter saying: "His name and his works will live on through the centuries."*

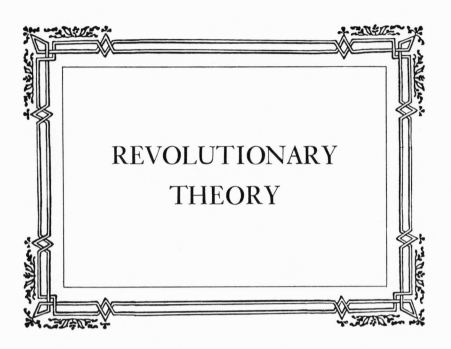

REVOLUTIONARY
THEORY

Communism and the Augsburg
*Allgemeine Zeitung**

Cologne, October 15

ISSUE NO. 284 of the Augsburg paper is so inept as to find the *Rheinische Zeitung* to be a Prussian *communist*—not a real communist, to be sure, but still one that fantastically flirts with and platonically ogles communism.

Whether this ill-mannered fantasy of the Augsburger is unselfish or whether this idle trick of its excited imagination is connected with speculation and diplomatic affairs, the reader may decide—after we have presented the alleged corpus delicti.

The *Rheinische Zeitung*, they say, has printed a communistic essay on Berlin family dwellings,[1] accompanied by the following comment: This report "might not be without interest for the history of this important issue." From this it follows, according to the Augsburger's logic, that the *Rheinische Zeitung* "served up such dirty linen with approval." Thus, for example, if I say: "The following report from *Mefistofeles*[2] about the household affairs of the Augsburg paper might *not be without interest* for the history of this pretentious lady," do I thereby recommend dirty "material" from which the Augsburg lady could tailor a colorful wardrobe? Or should we not consider communism an important current issue because it's not a current issue privileged to appear at court, since it wears dirty linen and does not smell of rosewater?

---

* *Rheinische Zeitung*, October 16, 1842. This article was written the day Marx was appointed editor of the paper. It was his first published essay on communism.

1. On September 30, 1842, the *Rheinische Zeitung* reprinted an article from the communist Wilhelm Weitling's weekly magazine, *Die Junge Generation* (*The Young Generation*).

2. A journal published in Leipzig between 1842 and 1844.

But the Augsburg paper has reason to be angry at our misunderstanding. The importance of communism does not lie in its being a current issue of highest moment for France and England. Communism has "European significance," to repeat the phrase used by the Augsburg paper. One of its Paris correspondents, a convert who treats history the way a pastry cook treats botony, has recently had the notion that monarchy, in its own fashion, must seek to appropriate socialist-communist ideas. Now you understand the displeasure of the Augsburg paper, which will never forgive us for revealing communism to the public in its *unwashed* nakedness; now you understand the sullen irony that tells us: So you recommend communism, which once had the fortunate elegance of being a phrase in the Augsburg paper!

The second reproach to the *Rheinische Zeitung* deals with the conclusion of a report on the communist speeches given at the congress in Strasbourg, because the two stepsister papers had so divided the booty that the Rhineland sister took the proceedings and the Bavarian one the fruits of the Strasbourg scholars. The exact wording of the incriminating passage is: "It is with the middle class today as it was with the nobility in 1789. At that time the middle class claimed the privileges of the nobility and got them; *today the class which possesses nothing demands to share in the wealth of the middle classes that are now in control.* Today, however, the middle class is better prepared for a surprise attack than the nobility was in 1789, and it is to be expected that the problem will be solved peacefully."

That Sieyès' prophecy has come true and that the *tiers état* [Third Estate] has become everything and wants to be everything—all this is recognized with the most sorrowful indignation by Bülow-Cummerow, by the former *Berliner Politische Wochenblatt* [*Berlin Political Weekly*], by Dr. Kosegarten, and by all the feudalistic writers. That the class that today possesses nothing demands to share in the wealth of the middle classes is a fact that, without the Strasbourg speeches and the silence of the Augsburg paper, is clearly recognized in the streets of Manchester, Paris, and Lyon. Does the Augsburger really believe that indignation and silence refute the facts of the time? The Augsburger is impertinent in fleeing. The Augsburg paper runs away from captious issues and believes that the dust it stirs up, and the nervous invectives it mutters in its flight, will blind and confuse the uncomfortable issue as well as the comfortable reader.

Or is the Augsburger angry at our correspondent's expectation that the undeniable collision will be solved in a "peaceful way"? Or does the Augsburger reproach us for not having given immediately a good prescription and not having put into the surprised reader's pocket a report as clear as daylight on the solution of the enormous problem?

We do not possess the art of mastering problems which two nations are working on with one phrase.

But my dear, best Augsburger! In connection with communism, you give us to understand that Germany is now poor in independent people, that nine-tenths of the better educated youth are begging the state for their future bread, that our rivers are neglected, that shipping has declined, that our once-flourishing commercial cities have faded, that in Prussia very slow progress is made toward free institutions, that the surplus of our population helplessly wanders away and ceases to be German among foreign nations—and for all these problems there is not a single prescription, no attempt to become "clearer about the means of achieving" the great act that is to redeem us from all these sins! Or don't you expect a peaceful solution? It almost seems that another article in the same issue, date-lined from Karlsruhe, points in that direction when you pose for Prussia the insidious question of the Customs Union: "Does anyone believe that such a crisis would pass like a brawl over smoking in the Tiergarten?" The reason you offer for your disbelief is *communistic:* "Let a crisis break out in industry; let millions in capital be lost; let thousands of workers go hungry." How inopportune our "peaceful expectation," after you had decided to let a bloody revolution break out! Perhaps for this reason, your article on Great Britain by your own logic points approvingly to the demagogic physician, Dr. M'Douall, who emigrated to America because "nothing can be done with this royal family after all."

Before we part from you, we would, in passing, like to call your attention to your own wisdom—your method which, with no shortage of phrases but without even a harmless idea here and there, makes you nevertheless *speak up.* You find that the polemic of Mr. Hennequin in Paris against parceling out the land puts him in surprising harmony with the *Autonomes* [aristocratic landowners]! Surprise, says Aristotle, is the beginning of philosophizing. You have ended at the beginning. Otherwise, would the surprising fact have escaped you that in Germany communistic principles are spread, not by the liberals, but by your reactionary friends?

Who speaks of handicraft corporations? The reactionaries. The artisan class is to form a state within a state. Do you find it extraordinary that such ideas, couched in modern terms, thus read: "The state should transform itself into an artisan class"? If the state is to be a state for the artisan, but if the modern artisan, like any modern man, understands and can understand the state only as a sphere shared by all his fellow citizens—how can you synthesize both of these ideas in any other way except in an *artisan state?*

Who polemicizes about parceling out the land? The reactionaries.

A recently published feudalistic writing (Kosegarten on land parceling) went so far as to call private property a privilege. This is Fourier's principle. Once there is agreement on principles, may not there then be disagreement over consequences and implications?

The *Rheinische Zeitung*, which cannot concede the theoretical reality of communist ideas even in their present form, and can even less wish or consider possible their practical realization, will submit these ideas to a thorough criticism. If the Augsburg paper demanded and wanted more than slick phrases, it would see that writings such as those of Leroux, Considérant, and above all Proudhon's penetrating work can be criticized, not through superficial notions of the moment, but only after long and deep study. We consider such "theoretical" works the more seriously as we do not agree with the Augsburg paper, which finds the "reality" of communist ideas not in Plato but in some obscure acquaintance who, not without some merit in some branches of scientific research, gave up the entire fortune that was at his disposal at the time and polished his confederates' dishes and boots, according to the will of Father Enfantin. We are firmly convinced that it is not the *practical attempt*, but rather the *theoretical application* of communist ideas, that constitutes the real *danger;* for practical attempts, even those on a large scale, can be answered with cannon as soon as they become dangerous, but ideas, which conquer our intelligence, which overcome the outlook that reason has riveted to our conscience, are chains from which we cannot tear ourselves away without tearing our hearts; they are demons that man can overcome only by submitting to them. But the Augsburg paper has never come to know the troubled conscience that is evoked by a rebellion of man's subjective wishes against the objective insights of his own reason, *because it possesses neither reason nor insight nor conscience.*

Socialism, Democracy, and
Revolution*

August 7

NUMBER 60 of the *Vorwärts* contains an article titled "The King of Prussia and Social Reform," signed by: "A Prussian."

The so-called Prussian sums up the contents of the Royal Prussian Cabinet Order on the revolt of the Silesian workers[1] and the view of the French journal *La Réforme*[2] on that Cabinet Order. *La Réforme* ascribes the Cabinet Order to the King's "fears and religious feeling." It even finds in that document the anticipation of great reforms which are in prospect for bourgeois society. . . .

The so-called Prussian denies the existence of the King's "fears" on the ground, among others, that a few soldiers sufficed to deal with the weak weavers.

In a country, then, where banquets with liberal toasts and foaming champagne—one recalls the Düsseldorf celebration [of June 18, 1843]—provoke a Royal Cabinet Order, where *not a single soldier* is required to crush the aspiration of the entire liberal bourgeoisie for freedom of the press and a constitution; in a country where passive obedience is the order of the day; in such a country, would the compulsory application of armed force against weak weavers not be an

---

* From "Critical Marginal Notes on the Article 'The King of Prussia and Social Reform. By a Prussian,'" in *Vorwärts*, August 7 and 10, 1844. Written in Paris, July 31, 1844. The "Prussian" was Arnold Ruge, with whom Marx had recently broken over the *Deutsch-Französische Jahrbücher*, for which Ruge refused further financial support. Marx wrote in a footnote: "Special reasons lead me to explain that this article is the first which I have contributed to the *Vorwärts.*"

1. June 4-6, 1844, the Silesian weavers revolted against their miserable conditions.

2. A democratic-republican daily published in Paris.

event, and a fearful event? And the weak weavers were victorious at
the first encounter. They were suppressed by a later reinforcement of
troops. Is the revolt of a crowd of workers the less dangerous because
it requires no army to suppress it? If the clever Prussian compares the
Silesian weavers' revolt with the English labor revolts, the Silesian
weavers will appear to him to be strong weavers.

On the basis of the general relation of politics to social need, we
shall explain why the weavers' revolt could inspire no special "fear"
in the King. Provisionally, we say only this much: The revolt was not
directed immediately against the King of Prussia but against the bourgeoisie. As an aristocrat and an absolute monarch, the King of Prussia
cannot love the bourgeoisie; he can have even less cause for fear when
their submission and their impotence are heightened by a strained and
difficult relation to the proletariat. Furthermore, an orthodox Catholic
is more hostile to an orthodox Protestant than he is to an atheist, just
as a legitimist is more inimical to a liberal than he is to a communist.
Not that an atheist and a communist are closer to a Catholic than a
legitimist, but that they are more alien to him than the Protestant and
the liberal, since they stand outside his circle. As a politician, the King
of Prussia has his immediate opposition in politics itself, in liberalism.
For the King, the opposition of the proletariat exists as little as the
King exists for the proletariat. The proletariat would have to achieve
decisive power to stifle antipathies, political oppositions, and turn
against itself the whole enmity of politics. Finally, in view of the
King's well-known character of yearning for what is "interesting" and
"significant," he must even be pleasantly surprised to find "interesting"
and "much discussed" pauperism on his own soil, and thus have a new
opportunity to make himself talked about. How pleased he must have
been at the news that now he possessed his "own" Royal Prussian
pauperism!

Our "Prussian" is even more unfortunate when he denies that
"religious feeling" is the source of the Royal Cabinet Order.

Why is religious feeling not the source of this Cabinet Order?
Because it is a "very sober expression of Christian statecraft," a "sober"
expression of the doctrine that "lets no obstacle stand in the way of its
own medicine, the good intentions of Christian hearts."

Is not religious feeling the source of Christian statecraft? Is not a
doctrine whose universal panacea lies in the good intentions of Christian hearts based on religious feeling? Does a sober expression of religious feeling cease to be an expression of religious feeling? More than
that! I maintain that it must be a religious feeling greatly infatuated,
even intoxicated, with itself which seeks in the "union of Christian
hearts" the "remedy for great evils" that it denies to the "state and

the authorities." It is a very intoxicated religious feeling that—according to the "Prussian's" admission—finds the whole evil in the lack of Christian sentiment and hence refers the authorities to "exhortation" as the only means of strengthening this sentiment. According to the "Prussian," the purpose of the Cabinet Order is Christian conviction. Obviously, when religious feeling is intoxicated, when it is not sober, it considers itself the sole good. Where it sees evil, it ascribes evil to its own absence, for as it is the only good, it alone can produce the good. The Cabinet Order dictated by religious feeling consequently dictates the religious feeling. A politician of "sober" religious feeling would not, in his "perplexity," seek "help" in the "exhortation of pious preachers to Christian sentiment."

How, then, does the so-called Prussian of *La Réforme* prove that the Cabinet Order is not an emanation of religious feeling? By everywhere depicting the Cabinet Order as an emanation of religious feeling. Is insight into social movements to be expected from such an illogical mind? Let us listen to his chatter about the relation of German society to the labor movement and to social reform in general.

Let us distinguish, which the "Prussian" neglects to do, among the various categories comprised in the expression "German society": government, the bourgeoisie, the press, and finally the workers themselves. These are the various groups we are concerned with here. The "Prussian" lumps them together and judges them en masse from his superior standpoint. German society, according to him, has "not yet even reached the stage of *anticipating* its 'reform.'"

Why does it lack this instinct? "In an *unpolitical* country like Germany," answers the "Prussian," "it is impossible to regard the partial misery of the factory districts as a general concern, let alone as a a blot before the whole civilized world. For the Germans, this event has the same character as any local drought or famine. Hence the King regards it as an administrative and charity defect."

The "Prussian" thus ascribes this inverted view of the misery of labor to the peculiarity of an unpolitical country.

One will admit: England is a political country. One will further admit: England is the country of pauperism, for even the word is of English origin. An inquiry into England is thus the surest experiment for getting to know the *relation* of a political country to pauperism. In England the misery of labor is not partial but universal; it is not confined to factory districts but extends to rural districts. The movements there are not at the beginning; they have recurred periodically for nearly a century.

Now how do the English bourgeoisie and the government and press associated with it view pauperism?

Insofar as the English bourgeoisie admits pauperism to be the fault of politics, the Whig considers the Tory, and the Tory the Whig, the cause of pauperism. According to the Whig, the monopoly of large estates and the prohibition against the import of grain are the main source of pauperism. According to the Tory, the entire evil lies with liberalism, competition, and the factory system which is carried too far. Neither party finds the cause in politics in general, but only in the politics of its opponent; neither party permits itself to dream of a reform of society.

The most decisive expression of English insight into pauperism—we are referring always to the insight of the English bourgeoisie and government—is the English national economy, that is, the scientific reflection of English economic conditions.

MacCulloch, one of the best and most famous of English economists, a pupil of the cynical Ricardo, and one who knows existing conditions and should have a thorough overall view of the movement of civil society, ventured at a public lecture, amidst applause, to apply to economics what Bacon said of philosophy: "The man who suspends his judgment with true and untiring wisdom, who progresses gradually, and who successively surmounts obstacles which impede the course of study like mountains, will in time reach the summit of knowledge where rest and pure air may be enjoyed, where Nature may be viewed in all her beauty, and whence one may descend by an easy path to the final details of practice."

Good and pure air—the pestilential atmosphere of English basement dwellings! Great natural beauty—the fantastic beggars' rags of the English poor, and the withered flesh of the women who are consumed by work and misery; children lying in filth; the monsters produced by overwork in the monotonous mechanization of the factories! And the most delightful final detail of the whole thing: prostitution, murder, and the gallows!

Even the part of the English bourgeoisie that is sensitive to the dangers of pauperism views this peril and the means of curing it not only in special ways but, to speak bluntly, in childish and silly ways.

Thus Dr. Kay in his brochure, "Recent Measures for the Promotion of Education in England," for example, reduces everything to *neglected education*. Guess on what grounds! From lack of education the worker fails to comprehend the "natural laws of commerce," laws which *necessarily* reduce him to pauperism. Hence he resists. This can only "embarrass the prosperity of English manufacturers and English commerce, shake the mutual confidence of businessmen, diminish the stability of political and social institutions."

So great is the brainlessness of the English bourgeoisie and its press concerning pauperism, this national epidemic of England!

Granted, then, that the reproaches directed by our "Prussian" against German society are justified. Does the cause lie in the unpolitical condition of Germany? But if the bourgeoisie of unpolitical Germany cannot grasp the general significance of a partial misery, the bourgeoisie of political England, on the other hand, has failed to appreciate the significance of a universal misery which has brought its universal significance to attention partly by periodic recurrence in time, partly by extension in space, and partly by the frustration of all attempts to remedy it.

The "Prussian," furthermore, blames the unpolitical condition of Germany when the King of Prussia finds the cause of pauperism in an administrative and charity defect, and hence seeks the remedy for pauperism in administrative and charitable measures.

Is this point of view peculiar to the King of Prussia? Let us take a quick look at England, the only country in which one can refer to major political action on pauperism.

The present English Poor Law dates from the Forty-third Act in the reign of Elizabeth.[3] What were the provisions of that legislation? The obligation laid on parishes to support their poor laborers, the Poor Tax, legal benevolence. This law—benevolence by way of administration—has lasted two hundred years. After long and painful experiences, what is the viewpoint of Parliament in its Amendment Bill of 1834?

First it ascribes the frightful increase of pauperism to an "administrative defect."

The Poor Tax administration, which consisted of officials from the respective parties, is hence reformed. Some twenty parishes are united into a single administration. A bureau of officials—Board of Guardians —elected by taxpayers meets on a specified day in the headquarters of the unions and decides on the granting of relief. These boards are guided and supervised by deputies of the government, the Central Commission of Somerset House—the Ministry of Pauperism, as it has been aptly described by a Frenchman. The capital supervised by this administration almost equals the amount the French War Department costs. The number of local administrations it employs comes to five hundred, and each of these local administrations in turn keeps at least twelve officials busy.

The English Parliament did not stop with the *formal* reform of administration.

It found the main source of the acute condition of English pauperism in the Poor Law itself: The legal remedy for social misery—

---

3. For our purpose it is not necessary to go back to the Statute of Labor under Edward III.—K.M.

charity—encourages social misery. So far as pauperism in general is concerned, it is, according to Malthus' theory, an eternal law of nature: "Since population continually tends to exceed the means of subsistence, charity is folly, an open encouragement to poverty. The state can therefore do nothing more than leave poverty to its fate and at most ease death for the poor."

With this philanthropic theory the English Parliament combines the view that pauperism is *distress caused by the workers themselves* and should not be regarded as a misfortune but rather be suppressed and punished as a crime.

Thus arose the regime of workhouses—that is, poorhouses—whose internal arrangement frightens the poverty-stricken from seeking in them any refuge from death by starvation. In the workhouses charity is ingeniously enlaced with the revenge of the bourgeoisie on the poor who appeal to its charity.

Thus England first attempted to abolish pauperism through charity and through administrative regulations. Then it saw the progressive increase of pauperism not as the necessary consequence of modern industry, but rather as the consequence of the English Poor Tax. It regarded the universal misery as merely a peculiarity of English legislation. What had been previously attributed to a lack of charity was now ascribed to a surplus of charity. Finally, poverty was regarded as the fault of the poor and they were punished accordingly.

The general importance that pauperism has achieved in political England is confined to the fact that in the course of development, and despite administrative measures, pauperism has risen to a national institution and hence has inevitably become an object of ramified and extensive administration—an administration, however, whose aim is no longer to suppress it but to *discipline* and perpetuate it. This administration has abandoned all efforts to stop pauperism at its source by positive means; it is satisfied with digging its grave with a policeman's tenderness whenever it boils up to the surface of the official's territory. The English state, far from going beyond administrative and charitable measures, has in fact lessened them. It administers only those paupers who are desperate enough to permit themselves to be apprehended and jailed.

Thus far the "Prussian" has not proved anything peculiar in the procedure of the King of Prussia. But *why*, the great man exclaims with rare naïveté: "Why does not the King of Prussia immediately order the education of all destitute children?" Why does he first turn to the authorities and wait upon their plans and proposals?

The overclever "Prussian" will calm himself when he learns that the King of Prussia is no more original in this respect than he has been in other actions, that in fact he has taken the only course a chief of state *can* take.

Napoleon wanted to destroy beggary at one stroke. He ordered his officials to prepare plans for the eradication of beggary throughout France. The project kept him waiting; he lost patience and wrote to his Minister of the Interior, Crétet, commanding him to destroy beggary within one month, saying; "One should not depart from this world without leaving traces that commend our memory to posterity. Do not make me wait another three or four months for a report. You have young lawyers, clever prefects, well-trained engineers of bridges and roads; put them all to work, and do not fall asleep in the routine office work."

In a few months everything was done. On July 5, 1808, a decree suppressing beggary was issued. How? By means of *dépôts*, which were so quickly transformed into penal establishments that soon the poor could be admitted to them only by way of the police court. And despite that, M. Noailles du Gard, member of the legislative corps, exclaimed, "Eternal gratitude to the hero who secures for the needy a place of refuge and for the poor a means of life. Childhood will no longer be neglected, poor families will no longer be deprived of resources, nor workers of encouragement and employment. Our progress shall no longer be retarded by the disgusting spectacle of infirmities and shameful poverty."

The last cynical passage is the only truth in this eulogy.

If Napoleon seeks the views of his officers of justice, prefects, and engineers, why shouldn't the King of Prussia do the same with his officials?

Why did not Napoleon *immediately* order the abolition of beggary? Of equal value is the "Prussian" question: "Why does not the King of Prussia immediately order the education of destitute children?" Does the "Prussian" know what the King must decree? Nothing less than the *abolition of the proletariat*. To educate children, one must feed them and free them from paid labor. The feeding and educating of destitute children—that is, the feeding and educating of the entire growing proletariat—would be the abolition of the proletariat and of pauperism.

For a short time the [French Revolutionary] Convention had the courage to order the abolition of pauperism—not immediately, to be sure, as the "Prussian" demands of his King, but only after having entrusted the Committee of Public Safety with the preparation of the necessary plans and proposals and only after these had utilized the Constituent Assembly's far-reaching investigations of poverty in France and had proposed, through Barère, the founding of the *Livre*

de la bienfaisance nationale [*Book of National Benevolence*], etc.
What was the consequence of the Convention's ordinance? Only that
there was one more ordinance in the world and that one year later the
Convention was besieged by starving women.

Yet the Convention was the maximum of political energy, political
power, and political intelligence.

No government in the world has issued ordinances on pauperism
without an agreement with its officials. The English Parliament even
sent commissioners to all European countries to get information about
the various administrative remedies for pauperism. Insofar as states
have occupied themselves with pauperism, they have confined themselves to administrative and charitable measures or have done even less.

Can the state act differently?

The state will never find the cause of social want in the "state and
the organization of society," as the "Prussian" requires of his King.
When there are political parties, each finds the cause of every evil in
the fact that its counterpart, instead of itself, is at the helm of the
state. Even radical and revolutionary politicians seek the cause of the
evil not in the *nature* of the state, but in a specific *form of state*,
which they want to replace with another form of state.

The state and the organization of society, from a *political* standpoint, are not two different things. The state is the organization of
society. Insofar as the state admits social evils, it attributes them either
to natural laws, which no human power can change, or to private life,
which is independent of the state, or to the inadequacy of the administration, which is dependent on it. Thus England finds poverty rooted
in the law of nature, according to which the population always ex-
ceeds the means of subsistence. From another side, England explains
pauperism as the consequence of the ill will of the poor, just as the
King of Prussia explains it as caused by the un-Christian spirit of the
rich and the Convention explains it as a result of a suspect, counterrevolutionary attitude of the property owners. Hence England pun-
ishes the poor, the King of Prussia admonishes the rich, and the Convention decapitates property owners.

Finally, *all* states seek the cause of their ills in *accidental* or *inten-
tional* defects of administration, and therefore they seek the remedy
in administrative measures. Why? Precisely because the administration
is the organizing activity of the state.

The state cannot transcend the contradiction between the aim and
good intentions of the administration, on the one hand, and its means
and resources, on the other, without transcending itself, for it is based
on this contradiction. It is based on the contradiction between *public*
and *private* life, on the contradiction between general interests and

particular interests. Hence the administration must confine itself to a formal and negative activity, for where private life and work begin, there its power ceases. Indeed, as against the consequences which spring from the unsocial nature of this civil life, of private property, trade, industry, and the mutual plundering of different civil groups—as against these consequences, impotence is the natural law of administration. This dismemberment, this debasement, this *slavery of civil society* is the natural foundation on which the modern state rests, just as the *civil society of slavery* was the natural foundation on which in antiquity the state rested. The existence of the state and the existence of slavery are indivisible. The state of antiquity and the slavery of antiquity—patent classical antitheses—were no less closely welded than the modern state and the modern world of huckstering—sanctimonious Christian antitheses. If the modern state wanted to do away with the impotence of its administration, it would have to do away with the present form of private life. If it wanted to do away with private life, it would have to do away with itself, because it exists *only* in contrast to that life. No living person, however, believes that the shortcomings of his existence are rooted in the principle, or essence, of his life, but in circumstances *outside* his life. Suicide is unnatural. Hence the state cannot believe in the inner impotence of its administration, that is, of its own self. It can notice only formal, accidental defects and seek to remedy them. If such modifications are fruitless, then the social ill is either a natural imperfection independent of mankind, a *law of God*, or else the will of private individuals is too corrupted to meet the good objectives of the administration. And what perverse private individuals! They grumble against the government whenever it restricts freedom, and they demand that the government prevent the necessary consequences of that freedom!

The more powerful the state, and hence the more political a country is, the less it is inclined to seek the basis and understanding of the general principle of social ills in the principle of the state itself, and hence in the existing organization of society, of which the state is the active, self-conscious, and official expression. Political thought is political precisely because it operates within the confines of politics. The more acute and the more vigorous it is, the more it is incapable of understanding social ills. The classical period of political thought is the French Revolution. Far from perceiving the source of social defects in the principle of the state, the heroes of the French Revolution see the source of social defects in the political abuses. Thus Robespierre sees in great poverty and great wealth only an obstacle to pure democracy. He wants, therefore, to establish a general Spartan frugality. The principle of politics is the *will*. The more one-sided

and hence the more perfected the political thought is, the more he
believes in the omnipotence of the will; the more blind he is to the
natural and intellectual restrictions on the will, the more incapable he
is of discovering the source of social ills. No further proof is needed
against the foolish hope of the "Prussian," whereby "political thought"
is called upon "to discover the root of social misery in Germany."

It was silly to impute to the King of Prussia not only a power
which the Convention and Napoleon combined did not possess, but
also a view exceeding the boundaries of *all* politics, a view that the
clever "Prussian" possesses no more deeply than his King. This entire
declaration was the more silly, as the "Prussian" admits: "Good words
and good intentions are cheap, insight and successful deeds are dear;
in this case they are more than dear, they are as yet not available."

If they are not yet available, one ought to take cognizance of anyone who tries to do what is possible from his position. For the rest,
I leave it to the tact of the reader whether on this occasion the
mercantile-gypsy language of "cheap," "dear," "more than dear," "as
yet not available," belong in the category of "good words" and "good
intentions."

Suppose, then, that the "Prussian's" remarks on the German government and the German bourgeoisie—the latter is surely included in
"German society"—are entirely proved. Is this part of society more
perplexed in Germany than in England and France? Can one be more
perplexed than, for example, in England, where perplexity has been
made into a system? If labor uprisings are now breaking out all over
England, then the bourgeoisie and government there are no better
advised than in the last third of the eighteenth century. Their only
expedient is material force, and as material force diminishes at the
same rate as the spread of pauperism and the insight of the proletariat
increase, English perplexity necessarily grows in geometrical proportion.

Finally, it is untrue, factually untrue, that the German bourgeoisie
has entirely misunderstood the general significance of the Silesian uprising. In several towns the [guild] masters are trying to associate
themselves with the journeymen. All the liberal German newspapers,
the organs of the liberal bourgeoisie, are overflowing with the organization of labor, reform of society, criticism of monopoly and
competition, etc. All this as a consequence of the labor movements.
The newspapers of Trier, Aachen, Cologne, Wesel, Mannheim,
Breslau, and even Berlin often print intelligent articles on social
matters, from which the "Prussian" could always learn something.
Indeed, letters from Germany constantly express astonishment at the
meager opposition of the bourgeoisie to *social* tendencies and ideas.

Had he been better acquainted with the history of the social movement, the "Prussian" would have put his question in reverse. Why does the German bourgeoisie itself interpret this partial misery as a relatively universal one? Whence the animosity and the cynicism of the *political* bourgeoisie, whence the lack of resistance and the sympathy of the *unpolitical* bourgeoisie in connection with the proletariat?

August 10

Now let us turn to the "Prussian's" oracular pronouncements on the German workers.

"The German poor," he puns, "are not more intelligent than the poor Germans; that is, *nowhere* can they see beyond their hearth, their factory, their district: the whole question has hitherto been neglected by the omnipresent political soul."

To be able to compare the situation of the German worker with that of the French and English, the "Prussian" must compare the *first form*, the beginning of the English and French labor movement, with the German movement that is just beginning. He fails to do this. Hence his reasoning amounts to a triviality, such as that industry in Germany is not yet as developed as in England, or that a movement at its beginning looks different from the way it looks during its progress. He wanted to talk about the *specific characteristics* of the German labor movement. He does not say one word on this subject of his.

But if the "Prussian" took the correct position, he would find that not a single French or English labor uprising has possessed such a theoretical and conscious character as the revolt of the Silesian weavers.

First, let us recall the *"Weberlied,"*[4] those bold watchwords of the struggle, wherein hearth, factory, and district are not mentioned at all; but wherein the proletariat cries out its immediate opposition to the society of private property in a striking, sharp, ruthless, and powerful way. The Silesian revolt begins precisely where the French and English labor uprisings end, with the consciousness of the nature of the proletariat. The action itself bears this superior character. Not only the machines, those rivals of the workers, are destroyed, but also the merchants' account books and titles to property. While all other movements were directed first of all against the industrial lords, the visible enemy, this movement is directed at the same time against the

---

4. The title of the song, popular among the Silesian textile workers, was not *"Weberlied"* ("Weavers' Song") but *"Das Blutgericht"* ("Criminal Court").

banker, the hidden enemy. Finally, not a single English labor revolt has been conducted with similar courage, deliberation, and endurance.

As for the state of education among German workers, or their capacity for it in general, I recall Weitling's gifted writings, which frequently surpass Proudhon in theory although they are inferior in execution. Where has the bourgeoisie—its philosophers and academically educated members included—produced a work similar to Weitling's *Garantien der Harmonie und Freiheit* [*Guarantees of Harmony and Freedom*] pertaining to the emancipation of the bourgeoisie—*political* emancipation? If one compares the prosaic, low-spirited mediocrity of German political literature with this tremendous and brilliant literary debut of the German workers; if one compares these gigantic children's shoes of the proletariat with the dwarfishness of the worn-out political shoes of the German bourgeoisie, one must predict an athletic figure for the German Cinderella. It must be admitted that the German proletariat is the theorist of the European proletariat, just as the English proletariat is its economist and the French proletariat its politician. It must be admitted that Germany possesses a classical vocation for social revolution, although it has no capacity for a political one. Just as the impotence of the German bourgeoisie is the political impotence of Germany, so the talent of the German proletariat—even apart from German theory—is the social talent of Germany. The disparity between philosophical and political development in Germany is no abnormality. It is a necessary disparity. Only in socialism can a philosophical people find its adequate practice, and hence only in the proletariat can it find the active element of its emancipation.

Still, at this moment I have neither the time nor the inclination to explain to the "Prussian" the relation of "German society" to social transformation, and from this relation to explain, on the one hand, the weak reaction of the German bourgeoisie to socialism and, on the other hand, the excellent talents of the German proletariat for socialism. He will find the main elements for an understanding of this phenomenon in the introduction to my "Critique of Hegel's Philosophy of Law."[5]

Thus the intelligence of the "German poor" stands in inverse relationship to the intelligence of the "poor Germans." But people who must treat every subject as a public exercise in style, by this formal activity get an inverted content, and such content, in turn, puts a seal of vulgarity on the form. Thus on the occasion of the

5."Zur Kritik der Hegelschen Rechtsphilosophie," in *Deutsch-Französische Jahrbücher*, 1844.

Silesian labor unrest the "Prussian's" attempt to proceed in the form of antithesis led to the greatest antithesis against the truth. The only task of a thoughtful and truth-loving mind in regard to the first outbreak of the Silesian labor revolt consisted of not playing the role of schoolmaster to the event but rather of studying its peculiar character. For the latter, some scientific insight and some love of humanity are required, while for the other operation a glib phraseology, soaked in a hollow egoism, is entirely sufficient.

Why does the "Prussian" criticize the German workers so contemptuously? Because he finds that the "whole question"—namely, the question of labor's misery—"until now" has been abandoned by the "omnipresent political soul." He explains in greater detail his Platonic love for the political soul:

"All revolts that break out in this disastrous isolation of men from the community and of their thoughts from social principles will be smothered in blood and folly; but if misery first produces understanding and the political understanding of the Germans discovers the root of social misery, then these events will also be felt in Germany as symptoms of a great transformation."

First of all, let the "Prussian" permit us to make a stylistic observation. His antithesis is incomplete. The first half of the sentence says: if misery produces *understanding;* and the second half: if political understanding discovers the root of social misery. *Simple* understanding in the first half of the antithesis becomes *political* understanding in the second half, just as the simple misery of the first half becomes *social* misery in the second. Why has the stylistic artist endowed the two halves of the sentences so unequally? I do not believe he thought about that. I want to explain to him his real instinct. If the "Prussian" had written: "if social misery produces political understanding and if political understanding discovers the root of social misery," no unprejudiced reader could have missed the absurdity of this antithesis. In the first place, any such reader would have wondered why the anonymous writer did not join social understanding with social misery and political understanding with political misery, as the simplest logic requires. Now to the point!

It is so false [to say] that social misery creates political understanding, that the reverse is rather the case: social well-being produces political understanding. Political understanding is a spiritual matter and is given to him who already has, who already sits in comfort. On this subject our "Prussian" should listen to a French economist, M. Michel Chevalier:

"In the year 1789, when the bourgeoisie rose in revolt, all it lacked to be free was a share in the government of the country. For it, emancipation consisted in taking the direction of public affairs—the major civil, military, and religious functions—from the hands of the privileged who possessed the monopoly of these functions. Rich and enlightened, capable of self-sufficiency and self-government, it wanted to get rid of the *régime du bon plaisir*."

We have already shown the "Prussian" how incapable political understanding is of discovering the source of social misery. One word more on this view of his: The more developed and general the political intelligence of a people is, the more the proletariat—at least at the beginning of the movement—wastes its energies in irrational and useless uprisings which are smothered in blood. Because it thinks of the forms of politics, it sees the cause of all evils in *will* and all remedies in *force* and the overthrow of a particular form of state. For proof, consider the first outbreaks of the French proletariat.[6] The workers of Lyon believed that they were pursuing only political aims, that they were merely soldiers of the Republic, while in reality they were soldiers of socialism. Thus their political understanding obscured the roots of their social misery and falsified their insight into their actual aims, so that their political understanding deceived their social instinct.

But if the "Prussian" expects the creation of understanding through misery, why does he put smothering in blood and smothering in folly together? If misery is generally a means, bloody misery is a very acute means for the creation of understanding. The "Prussian" must thus say: Smothering in blood will smother irrationality and provide the understanding with proper air to breathe.

The "Prussian" prophesies the smothering of revolts that break out in the "disastrous isolation of men from the community and of their thoughts from social principles."

We have shown that the Silesian uprising in no way came from the separation of thoughts from social principles. We have only to deal with the "disastrous isolation of men from the community." By community is here to be understood the political community, the *state system*. It is the old story of "unpolitical" Germany.

But do not all uprisings without exception break out in the "disastrous isolation of men from the community"? Does not every revolt necessarily presuppose this isolation? Would the Revolution of 1789 have occurred without the disastrous isolation of the French citizens from the community? Its aim was precisely to end this isolation.

But the community from which the worker is isolated is of a very different order and a very different extent from the political com-

6. The revolts of the workers in Lyon in November, 1831, and April, 1834.

munity. This community, from which *his own labor* separates him, is life itself, physical and spiritual life, human morality, human activity, human enjoyment, human existence. *Human existence* is the *real community* of men. Just as the disastrous isolation from this existence is definitely more many-sided, more intolerable, more frightful, and more contradictory than isolation from the political community, so also is the elimination of this isolation; and even a partial reaction, a revolt against it, means all the more, as man is infinitely more than a citizen and human life more than political life. Thus, however partial the *industrial* revolt may be, it contains within itself a universal soul: no matter how universal a *political* revolt may be, it conceals a narrow-minded spirit under the most colossal form.

The "Prussian" worthily concludes his article with the following sentence: "A social revolution without a political soul (that is, without organized insight from the standpoint of the whole) is impossible."

We know this. A social revolution involves the standpoint of the whole—even if it takes place in only one factory district—because it is a protest of man against dehumanized life, because it proceeds from the standpoint of the single actual individual, because the community against whose separation from himself the individual reacts is the true community of men, human existence. The political soul of a revolution, on the other hand, consists of the tendency of politically uninfluential classes to end their isolation from the state system and from power. Its standpoint is that of the state, an abstract whole, which exists only through separation from actual life and which is unthinkable without the organized antithesis between the universal idea and the individual existence of men. Hence a revolution of the political soul also organizes, in accordance with the limited and split nature of this soul, a ruling group in society at the expense of society.

We want to confide to the "Prussian" what a social revolution *with* a political soul is; at the same time, we also confide to him the secret that he does not know how to raise himself above the narrow political standpoint even in phraseology.

A "social" revolution with a political soul is either a compounded absurdity—if the "Prussian" means by "social" a revolution in *contrast* to a political one and, nevertheless, attributes to this social revolution a political, rather than a social, soul—or a "social revolution with a political soul" is merely a paraphrase of what used to be called a "political revolution" or a "revolution pure and simple." Any revolution dissolves the *old society;* to that extent it is *social.* Any revolution overthrows the *old power;* to that extent it is *political.*

The "Prussian" may choose between the paraphrase and the absurdity. But though it is paraphrastic or senseless to speak of a social revolution with a political soul, it is sensible to talk about a political revolution with a social soul. Revolution in general—the overthrow of the existing power and the dissolution of the old conditions —is a political act. But without revolution, socialism cannot come about. It requires this political act, insofar as it needs overthrow and dissolution. But where its organizing activity begins, where its own aim and soul emerge, there socialism casts away the political hull.

All this long-windedness was necessary to tear up the web of errors hidden in a single newspaper column. Not all readers can have the education and the time to settle accounts with such literary charlatanism. For the time being, does not the anonymous "Prussian" have the duty to the reading public to refrain from political and social writings, such as declamations about German conditions, and rather to begin with a conscientious self-analysis of his own condition?

The Role of the Proletariat*

WHEN SOCIALIST WRITERS ascribe this world-historical role to the proletariat, they in no way do it, as the critical survey claims, because they consider proletarians gods. Rather the reverse. They do it because the abstraction of all humanity, even the very semblance of humanity, is in practice consummated in the perfected proletariat; because in the life conditions of the proletariat all the life conditions of modern society are contained in their most inhuman acuteness; because man himself is lost in it, without at the same time having acquired a theoretical awareness of his loss, but through the impossibility of avoiding or prettifying any longer the absolutely imperative *misery* —the practical expression of *necessity*—he is also directly driven to rebellion against all this inhumanity; hence the proletariat can and must emancipate itself. It cannot, however, emancipate itself without removing its own life conditions. It cannot remove its own life conditions without doing the same to *all* the inhuman life conditions of modern society which are comprehended in its situation. It does not go through the hard but steeling school of *work* in vain. It is not a question of what this or that proletarian, or even the whole proletariat itself, imagines the goal to be for the moment. It is a question of what it *is* and what, conformable to the proletariat's essence, it will be compelled to be historically. Its goal and its historical action are perceptibly and irrevocably predetermined in its own life situation, as well as in the whole organization of modern bourgeois society. One does not need to explain here that a large portion of the English and French proletariat is already aware of its own historic task and is constantly engaged in the process of fully clarifying this awareness.

---

* From Marx and Engels, *The Holy Family* (1845).

Class Struggle and a New Society*

AN OPPRESSED CLASS is the vital condition for every society founded on the antagonism of classes. The emancipation of the oppressed class thus necessarily implies the creation of a new society. For the oppressed class to be able to emancipate itself, it is necessary that the productive powers already acquired and the existing social relations should no longer be capable of existing side by side. Of all the instruments of production, the greatest productive power is the revolutionary class itself. The organization of revolutionary elements as a class presupposes the existence of all the productive forces which could be engendered in the bosom of the old society.

Does this mean that after the fall of the old society there will be a new class domination culminating in a new political power? No.

The condition for the emancipation of the working class is the abolition of every class, just as the condition for the liberation of the Third Estate, of the bourgeois order, was the abolition of all estates and all order.

The working class, in the course of its development, will substitute for the old civil society an association which will exclude classes and their antagonism, and there will be no more political power properly so called, since political power is precisely the official expression of antagonism in civil society.

Meanwhile the antagonism between the proletariat and the bourgeoisie is a struggle of class against class, a struggle which carried to its highest expression is a total revolution. Indeed, is it at all sur-

---

* From *The Poverty of Philosophy* (1847), concluding paragraphs. Translation from the edition of Progress Publishers, Moscow, 1955.

[24]

prising that a society founded on the opposition of classes should culminate in brutal *contradiction,* the shock of body against body, as its final denouement?

Do not say that social movement excludes political movement. There is never a political movement which is not at the same time social.

It is only in an order of things in which there are no more classes and class antagonisms that *social evolutions* will cease to be *political revolutions.* Till then, on the eve of every general reshuffling of society, the last word of social science will always be: *"Le combat ou la mort; la lutte sanguinaire ou le néant. C'est ainsi que la question est invinciblement posée."*—George Sand.[1]

---

1. "Combat or death; sanguinary struggle or nothingness. It is thus that the question is invincibly posed"; from George Sand's introduction to her historical novel, *Jean Ziska.*

Heinzen's *Grobianisch* Anticommunism*

October 28

SHORTLY before the Reformation there developed in Germany a kind of literature whose very name was striking—*grobianisch* [coarse]. Nowadays we are confronting a revolutionary period analogous to that of the sixteenth century. No wonder a *grobianisch* literature is again emerging among Germans. Interest in historical development easily overcomes the esthetic disgust that such writing arouses, even among those with poorly educated taste, and that it aroused even in the fifteenth and sixteenth centuries.

Vulgar, bragging, blustering, bold, pretentious, and crude in attack, hysterically sensitive to the uncouthness of others; swinging and flailing the sword with a vast waste of energy, only to let it fall flat; always preaching morality, always violating morality; pathetic and cheap in its comical confusion; grieving over things but rarely analyzing them; contrasting half-baked petty-bourgeois sense with so-called scientific "sane common sense" in the same obscurantist way; gushing forth into limitless horizons with a certain complacent agility; plebeian form for philistinish content; wrestling with the written word in order to give it so to speak a purely corporeal character; in the background, preferably pointing to the body of the writer himself, itching to give examples of his virility, to show his wide shoulders, to stretch his limbs publicly; proclaiming a sound mind in a sound body; unconsciously infected by the most cunning disputes and the physical fever of the sixteenth century; firmly tied to stupid, dogmatic concepts, as well as pretentiously philosophizing

* From "Moralizing Criticism and Criticizing Morality," in *Deutsche-Brüsseler Zeitung*, October 28, November 11, 1847. "A Contribution to German Cultural History. Against Karl Heinzen."

over any petty doings; blustering against reaction, reacting against progress; incapable of portraying the enemy with ridicule, scolding him ridiculously through the whole tone scale; Solomon and Marcolph,[1] Don Quixote and Sancho Panza, fanatic and urbane in the same person; a boorish form of indignation, a form of indignant boorishness; the honest consciousness of the self-satisfied philistine hovering in the atmosphere over the whole—such was the *grobianisch* literature of the sixteenth century. If memory does not deceive us, German folk humor erected a monument to it in the song *"Heinecke, dem starken Knecht."*[2] Herr Heinzen has the merit of being the restorer of the *grobianisch* literature and, as such, one of the German swallows of the approaching people's spring.

Heinzen's Manifesto against the communists in issue No. 84 of the *Deutsche-Brüsseler Zeitung* gives us a reason next time to analyze that degenerate form of literature whose historically interesting aspect for Germany we have already indicated. We will present the literary species which Herr Heinzen represents as much on the basis of his Manifesto as on the historical literary characteristics of the writings and writers remembered from the sixteenth century, for example, the "Goose Preacher" [Thomas Murner].

November 11

"I was a republican, Herr Engels, so long as I occupied myself with politics, and my convictions did not turn inconstantly and rootlessly, like the head of many a communist.

"Indeed, I became a revolutionary at first. It is part of the tactics of communists that in the consciousness of their own incorrigibility they reproach their opponents as soon as the latter improve themselves."[3]

Herr Heinzen never *became* a republican, he *was* one from his political birth. He therefore possesses immutability, immovable completeness, consistency. Herr Heinzen was not always a revolutionary, he *became* one. Currently, indeed, the "turning" is done by Herr Heinzen, but it is done on the basis of his *immoral* character, and it is then called "improving oneself." For the communists, on the other hand, immutability lost its highly moral character. What became of it? "Incorrigibility."

---

1. Solomon and Marcolph (or Marcolf) were the figures of a fourteenth-century gnomic poem, Solomon being a sage and Marcolph a sly peasant.
2. *"Henneke Knecht"* is the title of an old Low German folk song.
3. From Heinzen's Manifesto, in *Deutsche-Brüsseler Zeitung*, No. 84.

Standing or turning—both are moral, both are immoral; moral on the part of the philistine, immoral on the part of his opponent. The art of the criticizing philistine consists precisely of calling out *rouge* and *noir*[4] at the right moment, the right word at the right time.

Ignorance is generally considered a deficiency. One is accustomed to regard it as a negative quantity. We see how the magic wand of philistinish criticism transforms a minus of intelligence into a plus of morality.

Herr Heinzen reports, among other things, that he is still as ig- norant of philosophy as he was in the year 1844. Hegel's "language" "still remains indigestible" to him.

Thus far the facts of the case. Now the moral seasoning.

If Hegel's language has always been "indigestible" to Herr Hein- zen, he did not, like "Engels and others," fall into the presump- tuousness of ever doing himself any good with this Hegelian lan- guage, any more than a Westphalian peasant would do himself much good with Sanskrit. But moral behavior consists of an avoidance of the stimulus to immoral behavior, and how can one better assure oneself against the immoral "effect" of a language than by being careful not to understand it?

Therefore, by his own statement, Herr Heinzen, who knows nothing about philosophy, also never attended the "school" of any philosopher. His school was that of "sound common sense" and the "full life."

"At the same time," he exclaims with the modest pride of the just, "I was spared the danger of having to disavow my school."

Against the moral danger of disavowing a school there is no surer protection than not having gone to school.

Every development, whatever its content, is capable of being pre- sented as one of a series of various stages of development, which are linked in such a way that one is a negation of the other. For example, if a nation develops from absolute monarchy to constitutional mon- archy, it negates a previous political existence. One cannot pass through any development in any field without negating the preceding mode of existence. Negation, translated into the language of morality, means disavowal.

Disavowal! With this slogan the criticizing philistine can stigma- tize any development without understanding it; he can solemnly posit a development-less undevelopment as moral purity. Thus has the religious fantasy of nations stigmatized history at large, placing the Age of Innocence, the Golden Age, in the stage of prehistory, in

---

4. Red and black, as in roulette.

the period when there was as yet no historical development at all, and hence no negation, no disavowal. Thus there appear in the most stirring revolutionary periods, in periods of strong and passionate negations and disavowals, as in the eighteenth century, excellent, well-meaning men, well bred and decent satyrs like Gessner, who put historical corruption in apposition to the development-less condition of the idyllic. In praise of these idyllic poets, who are also a species of criticizing moralists and moralizing critics, it should nevertheless be said that they conscientiously hesitated as to whom they should award the palms of morality, the shepherd or the sheep.

Still, let us allow the philistine to graze undisturbed on his own efficiency! Let us follow him where he fancies himself an expert on the "subject." We will find the same method repeated everywhere.

"I cannot help it if Herr Engels and other communists are too blind to see that power also rules over property and that the injustice in property relationships is maintained only by power. I call anyone a fool and a coward who shows enmity to a bourgeois because of his acquisition of money but leaves a king in peace because of his acquisition of power."

"Power also rules over property"!

Property is in any case a kind of power. Economists call capital, for example, "power over labor that is not one's own."

We thus have two kinds of power, the power of property—that is, of owners—on the one hand, and political power, the power of the state, on the other. "Power also rules over property" means: Property does not have the political power in its own hands, but is rather vexed by it through arbitrary taxes, through confiscations, through privileges, through annoying meddling by the bureaucracy in industry, commerce, and the like.

In other words: The bourgeoisie is not yet constituted as a political class. The power of the state is not yet the bourgeoisie's power. In countries where the bourgeoisie has already taken over political power, and where political rule is nothing but the rule, not of an individual bourgeois over his workers, but of the bourgeois class over the totality of society, Herr Heinzen's sentences lose all sense. The propertyless, of course, are not touched by political power, insofar as the latter relates to property directly.

While Herr Heinzen fancied himself as expressing an eternal and original truth, he expressed only the fact that the German bourgeoisie must achieve political power; that is, he says what Engels says, but does so only unconsciously, only in the fine intention of saying the opposite. Pathetically, he writes about the transitory relationship of the German bourgeoisie to German political power as if it were an eternal verity, and thus shows how one makes a "static kernel" out of a "movement."

"The injustice in property relationships," Herr Heinzen continues, "is maintained only by power."

Either Herr Heinzen understands by "injustice in property relationships" the above-mentioned pressures which the "most sacred" interests of the German bourgeoisie still suffer from the absolute monarchy—in which case he repeats what was just said—or he understands by "injustice in property relationships" the economic relationships of the workers, in which case his disclosure means that the present bourgeois property relationships are "maintained" by the power of the state, which the bourgeoisie has organized for the protection of its property relationships. Hence the proletarians must overthrow the political power, which is already in the hands of the bourgeoisie. They must themselves come to power, and then become the revolutionary power.

Unconsciously Herr Heinzen again says the same thing that Engels says, but again in the naïve conviction of having said the opposite. What he says he does not mean; what he means he does not say.

For the rest, while the bourgeoisie maintains "injustice in property relationships" politically—that is, through the power of the state— it does not *produce* it. The injustice in property relationships is conditioned by the modern division of labor, by the modern form of exchange, by competition, by concentration, etc., and it does not in any way arise from the political rule of the bourgeois class, but the reverse: the political rule of the bourgeois class arises from these modern production relationships, which are proclaimed by bourgeois economists as necessary, eternal laws. Hence if the proletariat overthrew the rule of the bourgeoisie, this would be only a transitory victory, only a moment in the service of the *bourgeois revolution* itself, as in the year 1794, so long as in the course of history, in its "movement," the material conditions were not yet created for the elimination of the bourgeois means of production, which would mean also the definite overthrow of the bourgeois political rule. The French Reign of Terror, with its mighty hammer blows, merely served to conjure away the feudal ruins from French soil. In many decades, the anxiously considerate bourgeoisie has not yet finished this work. The bloody action of the people only prepared the way for it. Similarly, the overthrow of the absolute monarchy would be only momentary, so long as the economic conditions for bourgeois rule were not yet ripe. People build a new world, not out of "material goods," as the *grobianisch* superstition imagines, but out of the historical achievements of their declining world. In the course of their development they must first *produce* the *material conditions* for a new society, and no amount of effort of opinion or will can liberate them from this fate.

It is characteristic of the whole Grobianism of "sound common sense," which draws from the "full life" and is not crippled in its "natural" talents by any philosophical or other studies, that it succeeds in seeing the difference but not the unity, and where it sees the unity, in not seeing the difference. As soon as it posits different conditions, the latter immediately become immovable, and "sound common sense" sees the most reprehensible sophistication when these idea blocks are smashed up ready for burning.

Insofar as Herr Heinzen says, for example, that money and power, property and rule, acquisition of money and acquisition of power, are not the same, he expresses a tautology which lies in the very words themselves, and these very word differences count for him as a heroic deed, which is applied with all the consciousness of a clairvoyant against the communists who are so "blind" as not to stand still with this first childish perception.

"Acquisition of money" turns into "acquisition of power" and "property" turns into "political rule"; that is, instead of the fixed difference which Herr Heinzen sanctions as a dogma, the relationship of the two powers rather tends toward union. Herr Heinzen could convince himself of this very quickly by seeing how serfs *bought* their freedom; how municipalities *bought* their municipal rights; how citizens through commerce and industry enticed the money from the pockets of the feudal lords and dissipated their real property in bills of exchange, on the one hand, and on the other helped the absolute monarchy win victory over the great feudalists who undermined it and *bought* their privileges; how later they themselves exploited the financial crises of the absolute monarchy, etc., etc.; how the absolute monarchies, through the system of debts—a product of modern industry and modern commerce—became dependent on the stock-exchange barons; how industrial monopoly changed the international relations of nations directly into political rule—as, for example, when the princes of the Holy Alliance during the "German War of Liberation" became only the paid mercenaries of England, etc., etc.

While the arrogant Grobianism of "sound common sense" affirms such differences as acquisition of money and acquisition of power, with which it has made such-and-such "arrangements," as eternal verities and unshakable dogmas, it creates the desirable situation of being able to pour out its moral indignation over the "blindness," "folly," or "wickedness" of the adversaries of such articles of faith— a self-indulgence which in its wild spittings must at the same time reveal the rhetorical mush which has only a couple of thin and bony truths swimming in it.

Herr Heinzen will yet experience the day when the power of property will bring about a *mariage forcé* with political power even in Prussia. Let us hear further: "You want to lay the stress of our time on social questions, and you do not see that there is no more important question than that of monarchy or republic."

A while ago Herr Heinzen saw only the *difference* between money power and political power; now he sees only the *unity* between the political question and the social question. At the same time, of course, he sees only "ridiculous blindness" and "cowardly despicableness" in his antipodes.

The *political* relationships of men are, of course, also *social* and *societal* relationships, as are all relationships of men with their fellow men. Hence all questions that have to do with relationships of men to one another are also social questions.

With this insight, which belongs in a catechism for eight-year-old children, the *grobianisch* naïveté not only thinks it has said something, but also that it has laid a weight in the scale of modern conflicts.

One finds fortuitously that the "social questions" which are "being discussed in our time" assume importance to the degree that they leave the sphere of the absolute monarchy. Socialism and communism did not originate in Germany, but in England, France, and North America.

The first appearance of a really active Communist party occurred within the bourgeois revolution, at the moment when the constitutional monarchy was eliminated. The most consistent republicans—in England the Levellers, in France Babeuf, Buonarroti, etc.—were the first to proclaim the "social questions." *Babeuf's Conspiracy*, written by his friend and party comrade Buonarroti, shows how these republicans drew from the historical "movement" the insight that even with the elimination of the social question in a principality or a republic, not a single "social question" in the proletarian sense would be solved.

The property question posed in "our time" cannot, as Heinzen formulates it, be in any way recognized as a real question: "Whether it is right that one man should possess everything and another man nothing, whether any man may possess anything at all," and similar simplistic questions of conscience and righteous phrases.

The property question is a very different one, depending on the different stages of industrial development in general and on the particular stage of such development in various countries.

For the Galician peasant, for example, the property question reduces itself to the transformation of feudal landed property into small bourgeois holdings. For him this has the same meaning it did for the French peasant before 1789, while on the other hand the English farm day laborer has no relationship to the landowner at all. He stands in relationship only to the tenant farmer, that is, the industrial capitalist, who operates agriculture like a factory. For his part, this industrial capitalist, who pays rent to the landowner, stands in direct relationship to the landowner. The abolition of landownership is therefore the most important property question for the English industrial bourgeoisie, and its struggle against the Corn Laws cannot be explained in any other way. The abolition of capital, on the other hand, is a property question for the English farm day laborer as well as the English factory worker.

In the English as well as the French revolutions the property question involved the legitimization of competition and the abolition of all feudal property relationships, such as manorial lordship, guilds, monopolies, etc., etc., which had become fetters on the industry that was developing between the sixteenth and eighteenth centuries.

In "our time," finally, the property question means the abolition of conflict that has emerged from large-scale industry, the development of a world market, and free competition.

The property question, depending on the various stages of industrial development, has always been the life question of every definite class. In the seventeenth and eighteenth centuries, when the abolition of feudal property relationships was involved, the property question was the life question for the bourgeois class. In the nineteenth century, when the abolition of bourgeois property relationships is involved, the property question is a life question for the working class.

The property question, which is a world-historical question in "our time," therefore has meaning only in modern bourgeois society. The more developed a society, and the more the bourgeoisie is developed in a country where the power of the state has a bourgeois aspect, the more glaringly does the *social* question emerge—in France more glaringly than in Germany, in England more glaringly than in France, in a constitutional monarchy more glaringly than in an absolute one, in a republic more glaringly than in a constitutional monarchy. For example, conflicts over the credit system, speculation, etc., are nowhere more acute than in North America. Also, nowhere does social inequality appear more harshly than in the eastern states of North America, because nowhere else is it less whitewashed by political inequality. If pauperism has not yet developed there as extensively as in England, it is due to economic relationships which will not be gone into here. Nevertheless, pauperism is making the most gratifying progress.

"In this country, where there are no privileged classes, where all classes of society have equal rights [the difficulty, however, is the existence of *classes*[5]], and where our population is a long way from pressing on the means of subsistence, it is in fact alarming to see pauperism growing with such rapidity."[6]

"It is proven that in Massachusetts pauperism has increased by 60 percent in twenty-five years."[7]

Thomas Cooper, one of the most famous North American economists, who is a radical to boot, proposes: (1) that the propertyless should not be allowed to marry, and (2) that universal suffrage be abolished. Then he exclaims: "Society is established for the protection of property. What reasonable claim can be made by those who, according to eternal economic laws, will always be propertyless to legislate over the property of others? What common motive and interest exists between these two classes of inhabitants?

"Either the working class is not revolutionary, in which case it represents the interests of the employers, on whom its existence depends—thus in the last elections in New England the factory owners, to assure themselves of votes, had the names of candidates printed on calico, and every one of their workers wore such a piece of calico on his breeches flap—or the working class becomes revolutionary in consequence of its common living together, etc., in which case the political power of the country must sooner or later come into its hands, and property would no longer be safe under such a system."[8]

As in England under the name of Chartists, so in North America under the name of National Reformers, the workers have formed a political party whose battle slogan in no way includes republic or principality, but *rule of the working class* against *rule of the bourgeois class*.

While it was precisely in modern bourgeois society with its corresponding political forms, either the constitutional or the republican-representative state, that the "property question" became the most important "social question," it is definitely the stupid need of the *German* bourgeois that exclaims: The question of the monarchy is the most important social question of our time. Entirely in the same manner does Dr. List, in the preface to his *National Economy*, express his naïve anger at the "mistake" that *pauperism*, and not the protective tariff, is being dealt with as the most important social question of our time.

---

5. The words in brackets are Marx's.
6. Report by William Morris Meredith, in *The Register of Pennsylvania*, August 16, 1828.—K.M.
7. From *Niles' Weekly Register* (no date given).—K.M.
8. Thomas Cooper, *Lectures on the Elements of Political Economy* (Columbia, S.C., 1826).

International Class Conflict*

THE UNIFICATION and fraternization of nations is a phrase used today by all parties, particularly the bourgeois free-trade men. Of course there does exist a certain kind of fraternization among the bourgeois classes of all nations. It is the fraternization of the oppressors against the oppressed, the exploiters against the exploited. Just as the bourgeois class of any one country unites and fraternizes against the proletarians of that country, despite competition and conflict among the members of the bourgeoisie themselves, so also the bourgeoisie of all countries fraternize and unite against the proletarians of all countries, despite their mutual conflict and competition in the world market. For nations really to unite, they must have a mutual interest. For their interest to become mutual, the present property relationships must be abolished, for they condition the exploitation of nations among themselves. To abolish the present property relationships is the interest of the working class. It alone, moreover, possesses the means to do it. The victory of the proletariat over the bourgeoisie is at the same time a victory over the national and industrial conflicts with which the various nations nowadays confront each other inimically. The victory of the proletariat over the bourgeoisie is therefore at the same time the liberation signal of all oppressed nations.

The old Poland is indeed lost, and we would be the last to wish its restoration. But not only is the old Poland lost. The old Germany, the old France, the old England, the whole old social system is lost. The

* A speech on Poland at the international meeting organized by the Fraternal Democrats in London, November 29, 1847, on the occasion of the seventeenth anniversary of the Polish revolution of 1830. Published in *Deutsche-Brüsseler Zeitung*, December 9, 1847.

[35]

loss of the old social system, however, is no loss for those who have nothing to lose by it, and in all contemporary countries this is the case with the great majority. They have, rather, everything to gain through the ruin of the old system, which will lead to the creation of a new one that is no longer based on class conflicts.

Of all countries, England is the one where the conflict between proletariat and bourgeoisie is most developed. Hence the victory of the English proletarians over the English bourgeoisie is decisive for the victory of all the oppressed over their oppressors. Hence Poland is not to be freed in Poland, but in England. You Chartists therefore do not have to express pious wishes for the liberation of nations. Defeat your own internal enemies and you will have the proud awareness of having defeated the entire old social system.

Communism, Revolution, and a Free Poland*

Gentlemen:

There are striking analogies in history. The Jacobin of 1793 has become the communist of our day. When Russia, Austria, and Prussia partitioned Poland among themselves in 1793, the three powers relied on the Constitution of 1791 which they had unanimously condemned for its alleged Jacobin principles.

And what did that Polish Constitution of 1791 proclaim? Nothing but a constitutional monarchy: legislative power in the hands of the representatives of the country; freedom of the press; freedom of conscience; open court proceedings; abolition of serfdom, etc. And all that was then called Jacobinism! Thus, gentlemen, you see that history has moved forward. What was then Jacobinism has today become liberalism, and in its most moderate form at that.

The three powers marched with history. In 1846, when they incorporated Cracow into Austria and robbed the Poles of their last vestige of independence, they designated as communism what had previously been called Jacobinism.

But what did the communism of the Cracow revolution consist of? Was it communist because it wanted to restore the Polish nationality? One could as well say that the war which the European Coalition waged against Napoleon was communistic and that the Congress of Vienna [1815] was made up of crowned communists. Or was the Cracow revolution communistic because it wanted to install a democratic government? Nobody would accuse the millions of citizens of Bern and New York of communistic impulses.

Communism denies the necessity of the existence of classes; it wants

---

* A speech delivered in French at Brussels, February 22, 1848, at the commemoration of the second anniversary of the Cracow uprising of 1846.

to abolish all classes, all class distinctions. The Cracow revolution wanted to extirpate only the political distinctions among classes; it wanted to give equal rights to all classes.

So in what respect, finally, was this Cracow revolution communistic?

Perchance because it wanted to break the chains of feudalism, to liberate property from feudal obligations and to transform it into modern property?

If one asked French property owners, "Do you know what the Polish democrats want? The Polish democrats want to introduce in their country the form of property that exists among you," the French property owners would answer, "That is very good." But if one says to the French property owners, as Guizot did, "The Poles want to abolish the form of property you established by your Revolution of 1789 and which still exists among you," then they exclaim, "What! They are all revolutionists, communists! The scoundrels should be destroyed!" The abolition of corporations and guilds, and the introduction of free competition—this is now called communism in Sweden. The *Journal des Débats*[1] goes even further: the abolition of revenues guaranteed to 200,000 voters by a corrupt law as a source of income, which the *Journal* considers rightfully acquired property, this it calls communism. Undoubtedly the Cracow revolution wanted to abolish a certain kind of property. But what kind of property? The kind that in the rest of Europe can no more be abolished than the Swiss *Sonderbund* [Federation]—because neither one exists any more.

Nobody will deny that in Poland the political question is tied up with the social one. For a long time they have been inseparable from each other.

Just ask the reactionaries about it! Did they fight during the Restoration purely against political liberalism and the Voltaireanism that was necessarily dragged along with it?

A very famous reactionary author has openly admitted that the loftiest metaphysics of a de Maistre and a de Bonald reduces itself in the last analysis to a money question—and is not every money question directly a social question? The men of the Restoration did not conceal the fact that in order to return to the policies of the good old days one must restore the good old property, the feudal property and the moral property. Everybody knows that fealty to the monarch is unthinkable without tithes and socages.

Let us go back further. In 1789 the political question of human rights absorbed in itself the social rights of free competition.

---

1. *Journal des Débats Politiques et Littéraires,* a Paris daily.

And what is it all about in England? Did the political parties there, in all questions, from the Reform Bill [June 7, 1832] to the abolition of the Corn Laws [June, 1846], fight for anything other than changes of property, questions of property, social questions?

Here in Belgium itself, is the struggle between liberalism and Catholicism anything else than a struggle between industrial capital and big landownership?

And the political questions that have been debated for seventeen years, are they not at bottom social questions?

Thus no matter what position one takes—be it liberal or radical or conservative—nobody can reproach the Cracow revolution with having entangled a social question with a political one!

The men at the head of the revolutionary movement in Cracow were most deeply convinced that only a democratic Poland could be independent, and that a Polish democracy was impossible without an abolition of feudal rights, without an agrarian movement that would transform the feudally obligated peasants into modern owners. Put Russian autocrats over Polish aristocrats; thereby you have merely naturalized the despotism. In exactly the same way, in their war against foreign rule, the Germans have exchanged one Napoleon for thirty-six Metternichs.

If the Polish feudal lord no longer has a Russian feudal lord over him, the Polish peasant has not less a feudal lord over him—indeed, a free, in place of an enslaved, lord. This political change has changed nothing in the peasant's social position.

The Cracow revolution has set all of Europe a glorious example, because it identified the question of nationalism with democracy and with the liberation of the oppressed class.

Even though this revolution has been strangled with the bloody hands of paid murderers, it now nevertheless rises gloriously and triumphantly in Switzerland and in Italy. It finds its principles confirmed in Ireland, where O'Connell's party with its narrowly restricted nationalistic aims has sunk into the grave, and the new national party is pledged above all to reform and democracy.[2]

Again it is Poland that has seized the initiative, and no longer a feudal Poland but a democratic Poland; and from this point on its liberation has become a matter of honor for all the democrats of Europe.

---

2. The Irish Confederation, founded in January, 1847.

The Bourgeoisie and the
Counterrevolution*

Croatian[1] *Freedom and Order won*, and celebrated its victory with arson, rape, plundering, and infamous outrages. *Vienna is in the hands of Windischgraetz, Jellachich, and Auersperg.* Hecatombs of human sacrifices are thrown into the grave of the old traitor Latour.

All the gloomy predictions of our Vienna correspondent have been confirmed, and perhaps he himself has already been slain.

For a moment we hoped for Vienna's liberation by the Hungarians, and the movement of the Hungarian army still remains a mystery to us.

Every kind of treason preceded the fall of Vienna. The whole history of the Diet and the City Council since October 6 is nothing but a continuing history of treason. Who was represented in the Diet and the City Council?

The *bourgeoisie.*

A portion of the Vienna National Guard openly took sides with the camarilla from the beginning of the October revolution. And at the end of that revolution we find another portion of the National Guard in battle with the proletariat and the Academic Legion,[2] in secret agreement with the imperial bandits. To whom did these fractions of the National Guard belong?

The *bourgeoisie.*

In France, however, the bourgeoisie took charge of the counter-

---

* "Victory of the Counterrevolution in Vienna," in *Neue Rheinische Zeitung*, November 7, 1848.
1. The Austrian government used half-savage Croatian troops to suppress the Vienna rebellion.
2. Radical university students.

revolution only after that class had eliminated every obstacle that stood in the way of its domination. In Germany the bourgeoisie finds itself suppressed in its adherence to the absolute monarchy and feudalism even before it has secured the first necessary conditions for its own freedom and domination. In France it came out as a despot and made its own counterrevolution. In Germany it appeared as a slave and made the counterrevolution its own despot. In France it won so as to humiliate the people. In Germany it humiliates itself so that the people should not win. History shows no more ignominious pettiness than that of the *German bourgeoisie.*

Who fled in droves from Vienna and left to the magnanimity of the people the watch over its wealth, only to calumniate them for their services during the flight and to see them slaughtered upon its return?

The *bourgeoisie.*

Whose innermost secrets did the thermometer show when it fell with every breath of the Viennese people and rose with every one of their death rattles? Who speaks in the rune language of the stock exchange?

The *bourgeoisie.*

The "German National Assembly" and its "Central Authority" have betrayed Vienna. Whom do they represent?

Above all, the *bourgeoisie.*

The victory of Croatian Freedom and Order in Vienna was made possible by the victory of the "honest" republic in Paris. Who was victorious in the June days there?

The *bourgeoisie.*

With its victory in Paris, the European counterrevolution began its orgies.

In the February and March days [of 1848] armed might was wrecked everywhere. Why? Because it represented nothing but governments themselves. After the June days armed might was victorious everywhere because everywhere the bourgeoisie was in secret understanding with the armed forces, while at the same time it held the revolutionary movement in its hands and set into motion those half-measures whose natural fruit is abortion.

The national fanaticism of the Czechs was the mightiest tool of the Vienna camarilla. *The allies had already fallen out among themselves.* Our readers will find in this issue of our paper the story of the Prague deputation's protest against the despicable insolence with which it was greeted at Olmütz.

Here was the first symptom of the war between the Slavic party and its hero Jellachich and the party of the simple, supranational camarilla and its hero Windischgraetz. For their part, the German countryfolk of Austria are not yet pacified. Their voices are drowned out by the shrill Austrian multinational caterwauling. On the third side, one can hear all the way to Pest the voice of the people-loving Czar; his executioners await the decisive order in the Danube principalities.

Finally, the latest decision of the German National Assembly at Frankfurt, which incorporates German Austria in the German Reich, must by itself lead to a gigantic conflict, if the German Central Authority and the German National Assembly are not to find themselves entering the stage only to be hissed off it by the European public. Despite the Assembly's fatalistic resignation, the struggle in Austria will unfold in gigantic dimensions such as world history has never yet witnessed.

In Vienna, then, the second act of the drama has been performed, the first act having been played in Paris under the title "The June Days." In Paris the Guard Mobile; in Vienna the "Croats"—in both *lazzaroni* [beggars], armed and bought lumpen proletariat against the working and thinking proletariat. We will soon see the third act *in Berlin*.

Supposing it to be true that the counterrevolution lives in all of Europe through *arms*, it will die in all of Europe through *money*. The fate that will clinch the victory will be European bankruptcy, the bankruptcy of the state. On the "economic" points, the tips of the bayonets will shatter like tinder.

But development does not wait for the due date of the promissory note which the European states have drawn on European society. In Paris the devastating counter stroke of the June revolution will be defeated. With the victory of the "red republic" in Paris, armies from the countryside will pour over the frontiers, and the real power of the contending parties will emerge clearly. Then we will remember June and October, and we too will cry out: *Vae victis!*[3]

The fruitless butcheries since the days of June and October, the tedious invocations of the martyrs since February and March, the cannibalism of the counterrevolution itself, will convince the nations that there is only one way to shorten, to simplify, to concentrate, the murderous death pains of the old society and the bloody birth pains of the new society: only one way—*revolutionary terrorism*.

---

3. Woe to the victim! An exclamation made by Brennus at the capture and destruction of Rome by the Gauls in 390 A.D.

The 1848 Revolution and the Overthrow of England*

THE DEFEAT of the working class in France [in June, 1848] and the victory of the French bourgeoisie have meant at the same time the clubbing down of the nationalities that responded to the crowing of the Gallic cock with heroic attempts at emancipation. Poland, Italy, and Ireland are once again ravaged, ravished, assassinated by Prussian, Austrian, and English hordes. The defeat of the French working class and the victory of the French bourgeoisie have been at the same time the defeat of the middle classes in all the European countries where, united for a moment with the people, they responded to the crowing of the Gallic cock by attempting a bloody revolt against feudalism. Naples, Vienna, Berlin! The defeat of the French working class and the victory of the French bourgeoisie have been at the same time the victory of the East over the West, the defeat of civilization by barbarism. In Wallachia the oppression of the Romance people was initiated by the tools of the Russians, the Turks; in Vienna, Croats, Pandurs, Czechs, Seressaner and such lumpen rabble strangled German freedom; and at this moment the Czar is all over Europe. Hence the downfall of the bourgeoisie in France, the triumph of the French working class, and the emancipation of the working class in general must become the watchword for Europe's liberation.

But the country which has transformed whole nations into its proletarians, which has clasped the whole world in its giant arms, which has defrayed the costs of the European Restoration with its own money; the country where internal class contradictions exist in their

* "The Revolutionary Movement," in *Neue Rheinische Zeitung*, January 1, 1849.

most pronounced and shameless form—*England*—seems to be the rock on which revolutionary waves are shattered, where the new society perishes in its mother's lap. England dominates the world market. A transformation of national economic relations in every country of the European continent, on the entire European continent, without England, would be a storm in a teacup. Industrial and commercial relations in every country are dominated by its commerce with other nations and conditioned by its relations to the world market. But England dominates the world market, and the bourgeoisie dominates England.

The liberation of Europe, whether it is the revolt of oppressed nationalities for freedom or the overthrow of feudal absolutism, must therefore depend on the victorious uprising of the French working class. But every French social revolution necessarily shatters on the English bourgeoisie, on the industrial and commercial world domination of Great Britain. Every partial social reform in France, and on the European continent in general, is and remains, insofar as it is definitive at all, a hollow and pious wish. And old England can be overthrown only by a *world war*, which is the only possible opportunity for the Chartists, the organized English labor party, to make a successful revolt against their gigantic oppressors. From the moment the Chartists are at the helm in the English government, social revolution moves from the realm of utopia into the realm of reality. But every European war in which England is involved is a world war. It is waged in Canada as well as in Italy, in the East Indies as well as in Prussia, in Africa as well as on the Danube. And a European war is the first consequence of a successful workers' revolution in France. As it was in Napoleon's time, England will be at the head of the counter-revolutionary armies, but in war it will be defeated by the spearhead of the revolutionary movement and will pay for its sins against the revolution of the eighteenth century.

REVOLUTIONARY UPRISING OF THE FRENCH WORKING CLASS, AND WORLD WAR—these are the auguries of the year 1849.

England's Seventeenth-Century Revolution[*]

IN THIS PAMPHLET M. Guizot intends to prove that Louis Philippe and the politics pursued by M. Guizot should not really have been overthrown on February 24, 1848, and that only the wicked character of the French is to be blamed for the fact that the July Monarchy of 1830, after an existence of eighteen troublesome years, collapsed so ignominiously and did not acquire the endurance that the English monarchy has enjoyed since 1688.

Reading this pamphlet, one realizes that even the ablest men of the *ancien régime*, as well as men who cannot be denied certain historical talents, have become so confused by the fateful events of that February that they have lost all sense of history and, indeed, no longer understand their previous actions. Instead of gaining, from the experience of the February Revolution, some insight into the totally different historical situation and into the entirely different position that the classes occupied in society under the French Monarchy of 1830 and under the English Monarchy of 1688, M. Guizot dissolves these differences with a few moralistic phrases and asserts in conclusion that the policy overthrown on February 24 was the "only one that could master the revolution, in the same way that it had controlled the state."

Specifically formulated, the question Mr. Guizot sets out to answer is: Why did bourgeois society in England develop as a constitutional monarchy longer than it did in France?

Characteristic of M. Guizot's knowledge of the course of bour-

---

* Marx and Engels, review of Guizot's *Pourquoi la révolution d'Angleterre a-t-elle réussi?* (Paris, 1850), in *Neue Rheinische Zeitung. Politisch-Ökonomische Revue*, Second Issue, February, 1850. This journal was founded by Marx and Engels in December, 1849. Translated by the editor and Ann Dreyer.

geois development in England is the following passage: "Under
George I and George II the public spirit took a different direction:
Foreign policy ceased to be the major interest; internal administration,
the maintenance of peace, financial, colonial, and commercial questions, and the development and struggle for parliamentary government became the major issues occupying the government and the
public."

M. Guizot finds in the reign of William III only two points worth
mentioning: the preservation of the balance of power between Parliament and crown, and the preservation of the European balance of
power through the wars against Louis XIV. Under the Hanoverian
dynasty "public opinion" suddenly takes a "different direction," nobody knows how or why. Here one sees how M. Guizot super-
imposes the most commonplace phrases of French parliamentary
debates on English history, believing he has thereby explained it. In
the same way, Guizot also imagines that, as French Prime Minister, he
carried on his shoulders the responsibility of preserving the proper
equilibrium between Parliament and crown, as well as the European
balance of power, while in reality he did nothing but huckster French
society away piecemeal to the moneyed Jews of the Paris Bourse.

M. Guizot does not think it worth mentioning that the struggle
against Louis XIV was simply a war of competition aimed at the
destruction of French naval power and commerce; nor does he mention the rule of the finance bourgeoisie through the establishment of
the Bank of England under William III, nor the introduction of the
public debt which then received its first sanction, nor that the manufacturing bourgeoisie received a new impetus by the consistent application of a system of protective tariffs. For Guizot, only political
phrases are meaningful. He does not even mention that under Queen
Anne the ruling parties could preserve themselves, as well as the constitutional monarchy, only by forcibly extending the term of Parliament to seven years, thus all but destroying any influence the people
might have had on the government.

Under the Hanoverian dynasty England had already reached a
stage of development where it could fight its wars of competition
against France with modern means. England herself challenged France
directly only in America and the East Indies, whereas on the Continent she contented herself with paying foreign sovereigns, such as
Frederick II, to wage war against France. And while foreign policy
assumed such a new form, M. Guizot has this to say: "Foreign policy
ceased to be the major interest," being replaced by "the maintenance
of peace." Regarding the statement that the "development and struggle for parliamentary government" became a major concern, one may

recall the incidents of corruption under the Walpole Ministry, which, indeed, resemble very closely the scandals that became daily events under M. Guizot.

The fact that the English Revolution developed more successfully than the French can be attributed, according to M. Guizot, to two factors: first, that the English Revolution had a thoroughly religious character, and hence in no way broke with all past traditions; and second, that from the very beginning it was not destructive but conservative, Parliament defending the old existing laws against encroachments by the crown.

In regard to the first point, M. Guizot seems to have forgotten that the free-thinking philosophy which makes him shudder so terribly when he sees it in the French Revolution was imported to France from no other country than England. Its father was Locke, and in Shaftesbury and Bolingbroke it had already achieved that ingenious form which later found such a brilliant development in France. We thus arrive at the strange conclusion that the same free-thinking philosophy which, according to M. Guizot, wrecked the French Revolution, was one of the most essential products of the religious English Revolution.

In regard to the second point, Guizot completely forgets that the French Revolution, equally conservative, began even more conservatively than the English. Absolutism, particularly as it finally appeared in France, was an innovation there too, and it was against this innovation that the *parlements* [French Diets] revolted to defend the old laws, the *us et coutumes* [usages and customs] of the old monarchy with its Estates General. And whereas the French Revolution was to revive the old Estates General that had quietly died since Henry IV and Louis XIV, the English Revolution, on the contrary, could show no comparable classical-conservative element.

According to M. Guizot, the main result of the English Revolution was that it made it impossible for the king to rule against the will of Parliament and the House of Commons. Thus, to him, the whole revolution consists only of this: that in the beginning both sides, crown and Parliament, overstep their bounds and go too far, until they finally find their proper equilibrium under William III and neutralize each other. M. Guizot finds it superfluous to mention that the subjection of the crown to Parliament meant subjection to the rule of a class. Nor does he think it necessary to deal with the fact that this class won the necessary power in order finally to make the crown its servant. According to him, the whole struggle between Charles I and Parliament was merely over purely political privileges. Not a word is said about why the Parliament and the class repre-

48 REVOLUTIONARY THEORY

sented in it needed these privileges. Nor does Guizot talk about
Charles I's interference with free competition, which made England's
commerce and industry increasingly impossible; nor about the dependence on Parliament into which Charles I, in his continuous need
for money, fell the more deeply the more he tried to defy it. Consequently M. Guizot explains the revolution as being merely due to the
ill will and religious fanaticism of a few troublemakers who would
not rest content with moderate freedom. Guizot is just as little able
to explain the interrelationship between the religious movement and
the development of bourgeois society. To him, of course, the Republic [Cromwell's] is likewise the work of a mere handful of
ambitious and malicious fanatics. Nowhere does he mention the attempts made to establish republics in Lisbon, Naples, and Messina at
that time—attempts following the Dutch example, as England did.

Although M. Guizot never loses sight of the French Revolution,
he does not even reach the simple conclusion that the transition from
an absolute to a constitutional monarchy can take place only after
violent struggles and passing through a republican stage, and that
even then the old dynasty, having become useless, must make way
for a usurpatory side line. Hence Guizot can say only the most trivial
commonplaces about the overthrow of the English Restoration monarchy. He does not even cite the most immediate causes: the fear on
the part of the great new landowners, who had acquired property
before the restoration of Catholicism—property robbed from the
church—which they would now have to return, meaning that seven-
tenths of England's soil would have to change hands; the aversion of
the commercial and industrial bourgeoisie to Catholicism, a religion
in no way suitable for its commerce; the nonchalance with which the
Stuarts, for their own and their courtiers' benefit, sold all of England's
industry and commerce to the French government, that is, to the
only country then in a position to offer England dangerous and often
successful competition, etc. Since M. Guizot omits the most momen-
tous points, there is nothing left for him but the highly unsatisfactory
and banal narration of mere political events.

For M. Guizot, the great mystery is the conservative nature of the
English Revolution, which he can ascribe only to the superior intelligence of the English, whereas in fact it can be found in the enduring
alliance between the bourgeoisie and a great part of the landowners,
an alliance that constitutes the major difference between it and the
French Revolution, which destroyed the great landholdings with its
parcelization policy. The English class of great landowners, allied
with the bourgeoisie—which, incidentally, had already developed
under Henry VIII—did not find itself in opposition—as did the

French feudal landowners in 1789—but rather in complete harmony with the vital requirements of the bourgeoisie. In fact, their lands were not feudal but bourgeois property. On the one hand they were able to provide the industrial bourgeoisie with the manpower necessary for manufacturing, and on the other they were able to develop agriculture to the standards consonant with industry and commerce. Thus their common interests with the bourgeoisie, thus their alliance with it.

For Guizot, English history ends with the consolidation of the constitutional monarchy. For him everything that follows is limited to a pleasant alternating game between Tories and Whigs, that is, to the great debate between M. Guizot and M. Thiers. In reality, however, the consolidation of the constitutional monarchy is only the beginning of the magnificent development and transformation of bourgeois society in England. Where M. Guizot sees only gentle calm and idyllic peace, in reality the most violent conflicts and the most penetrating revolutions are taking place. Under the constitutional monarchy, manufacturing at first expands to an extent hitherto unknown, only to make way for heavy industry, the steam engine, and the colossal factories. Whole classes of the population disappear, to be replaced by new ones, with new living conditions and new requirements. A new, more gigantic bourgeoisie comes into existence; while the old bourgeoisie fights with the French Revolution, the new one conquers the world market. It becomes so all-powerful that even before the Reform Bill gives it direct political power, it forces its opponents to enact legislation entirely in conformity with *its* interests and *its* needs. It wins direct representation in Parliament and uses it for the destruction of the last remnants of real power left to the landowners. It is, finally, at the present moment engaged in a thorough demolition of the beautiful edifice of the English Constitution, which M. Guizot so admires.

And while M. Guizot compliments the English for the fact that the reprehensible excesses of French social life, republicanism and socialism, have not destroyed the foundations of their sanctified monarchy, the class antagonisms of English society have actually reached a height not found anywhere else, and the bourgeoisie, with its incomparable wealth and productive powers, confronts a proletariat which likewise has incomparable power and concentration. The respect that M. Guizot offers to England finally adds up to the fact that, under the protection of the constitutional monarchy, more, and more radical, elements of social revolution have developed than in all other countries of the world together.

At the point where the threads of English history come together in a knot, which M. Guizot cannot even pretend to cut with mere political phrases, he takes refuge in religious catchwords, in God's armed intervention. Thus, for example, the holy spirit suddenly descends on the army and prevents Cromwell from declaring himself king. Before his conscience, Guizot saves himself through God, before his profane public, he does so through his style.

In reality, not only do *les rois s'en vont* [the kings depart] but also *les capacités de la bourgeoisie s'en vont* [the capacities of the bourgeoisie disappear].

English Prosperity—and Revolution*

WHILE THE CONTINENT in the past two years was occupied with revolutions, counterrevolutions, and the torrent of speeches inseparable from them, industrial England produced a completely different article: prosperity. Here, in due course, the commercial crisis which broke out in the fall of 1845 was twice interrupted—early in 1846 by Parliament's free-trade decisions, and early in 1848 by the February Revolution. A mass of commodities in the depressed overseas markets gradually found other outlets in the meantime. The February Revolution eliminated the competition of European industry even in the overseas markets, while English industry did not lose much more in the disrupted market of the Continent than it would have lost anyhow had the crisis continued. The February Revolution, which brought continental industry momentarily almost to a standstill, thus helped the English to weather a year of crisis quite well, contributed to the liquidation of piled-up stock in the overseas markets, and substantially made possible the new industrial upswing in the spring of 1849. This upswing, which for that matter also extended to a large part of continental industry, has reached such a degree in the past three months that manufacturers claim they have never had such a prosperous time—a claim that is always made on the eve of a crisis. The factories are overloaded with orders and operate expeditiously; they try everything to elude the ten-hour law so as to gain more working hours; masses of new factories are being built in all industrial areas and old ones are being enlarged. Cash is pouring into

---

*From Marx and Engels, "Revue," in *Neue Rheinische Zeitung. Politisch-Ökonomische Revue*, Second Issue, February, 1850.

the market, hitherto unused capital wanting to take advantage of general profits; speculation fills the discount rate, throws itself into production or on the raw materials market; and practically all articles are increasing in price, absolutely and relatively.

In short, England is blessed with "prosperity" in full bloom, and one can only inquire how long the delirium will last. Not very long, in any case. Many of the biggest markets, especially the East Indies, are already glutted; export now favors the really great markets less than the entrepôts of world commerce, whence commodities can be directed to favorable markets. Soon the colossal productive forces which English industry added to itself between 1843 and 1845, in 1846 and 1847 and especially 1849, and keeps on adding daily, will lead to a glut in the remaining markets, especially the Australian and American ones—and with the first news of this glut will come a simultaneous "panic" in speculation and production, perhaps as early as the end of the spring, or at the latest in July or August. This crisis, however, because it has to coincide with great collisions on the Continent, will have entirely different consequences from the previous ones. Hitherto every crisis has been the signal for a new advance, a new victory of the industrial bourgeoisie over landed property and over the financial bourgeoisie, but this coming one will mark the beginning of the modern English revolution, a revolution in which Cobden will take over the role of Necker.

The Character and Behavior
of Conspirators*

WE KNOW the tendency of Romance people toward conspiracies, and the role they have played in modern Spanish, Italian, and French history. After the defeat of the Spanish and Italian conspirators in the early 1820s, Lyon and especially Paris became the centers of revolutionary associations. It is known how up to 1830 the liberal bourgeois stood at the head of the conspiracies against the Restoration.[1] After the July [1830] Revolution, the republican bourgeoisie replaced them; the proletariat, already inured to conspiracy under the Restoration, came to the forefront to such a degree that the republican bourgeois became frightened by the fruitless street battles of the conspirators. The *Société des Saisons*, through which Barbès and Blanqui launched their riots in 1839, was already exclusively proletarian, and so was the *Nouvelles Saisons*, founded after the defeat and headed by Albert, and in which Chenu, La Hodde, Caussidière, etc., participated. Through its chiefs, the conspiracy was in constant contact with the petty-bourgeois elements represented in the journal *La Réforme*, but always remained very independent. These conspiracies, of course, never included the great mass of the Paris proletariat. They were confined to a relatively small, constantly fluctuating number of members, partly old, local, regular secret society conspirators, and partly newly won workers.

Of all these old conspirators, Chenu describes almost exclusively the class to which he himself belongs: the professional conspirators.

---

* Marx and Engels, review of A. Chenu's *Les Conspirateurs* (Paris, 1850), in *Neue Rheinische Zeitung. Politisch-Ökonomische Revue*, Fourth Issue, March–April, 1850.
  1. The restoration of the Bourbon dynasty after the fall of Napoleon in 1815.

54   REVOLUTIONARY THEORY

With the formation of proletarian conspiracies there came the need
for a division of labor among them; the members divided themselves
into occasional conspirators—*conspirateurs d'occasion*—workers who
practiced conspiracy as a side issue, merely attended meetings and
held themselves in readiness for the order of the chiefs to assemble
at an appointed place—and the professional conspirators, who devoted
full time to conspiracy and lived off it. The professionals formed the
middle layer between workers and chiefs, and often smuggled themselves into the two other layers.

The life style of this class of people conditions their whole character from the first. Proletarian conspiracy offers them only a limited
and uncertain existence, of course. Hence they are constantly forced
to resort to the money chests of the conspiracies. Some of them also
come into direct collision with bourgeois society in general and figure
with more or less grace in the police courts. Their precarious existence, in individual cases depending more on chance than on any
effort on their part, their irregular life, with its only fixed posts the
bistros of the *marchands de vin* [wine merchants]—which are the
rendezvous of the conspirators—their inevitable acquaintance with
all sorts of dubious types, all this places them in a circle which in
Paris is called *la bohême*. These democratic bohemians of proletarian
origin—there are also democratic bohemians of bourgeois origin, democratic tramps, and *piliers d'estaminet* [barflies]—are either workers
who have given up their work and thus became dissolute, or characters who come out of the lumpen proletariat and carry into their new
existence all the dissolute habits of that class. One can understand
how under these circumstances a couple of these *repris de justice*
[jailbirds] are entangled in nearly every conspiracy case.

The whole life of these professional conspirators bears the characteristic stamp of the bohemian. Recruiting officers of conspiracy, they
move from bistro to bistro, feel the pulse of the workers, seek out
their people, cajole them into conspiracy, and let either the association's treasury or their new friend pay for the inevitable consumption
of liters [of wine]. The bistro owner is their real host. The conspirator spends most of his time at the bistro; here he has his
rendezvous with his colleagues, with the people of his section, with
potential recruits; here, finally, the secret meetings of the sections
and section chiefs (groups) takes place.

In this undisturbed pub atmosphere, moreover, the conspirator,
like all Parisian proletarians of a convivial nature, soon develops into
a full-fledged *bambocheur* [rake]. The morose conspirator who acts
the virtuously austere spartan at his secret meetings suddenly appears
in the bistros transformed into a widely known habitué who knows

how to appreciate wine and the female sex. This bistro mood is enhanced by the constant dangers the conspirator is exposed to; at any moment he can be thrown onto the barricades and killed there; at every step the police lay traps for him which can send him to jail or even to the galleys. But it is these very dangers that give zest to his trade; the greater the peril, the more the conspirator hurries to enjoy the pleasures of the moment. At the same time the habit of danger makes him in the highest degree indifferent to life and liberty. In jail he is as much at home as in the bistro. Daily he awaits the order to break out. The desperate foolhardiness that surfaces in every Parisian insurrection is precisely what these old professional conspirators, the *hommes de coups de main* [men of surprise attack], bring with them into the fray. It is they who throw up and command the barricades, organize the resistance, plunder the arsenals, lead in the seizure of arms and munitions in homes, and in the midst of the insurrection carry out those daring coups which so often cause disarray in government ranks. In a word, they are the officers of insurrection.

It goes without saying that these conspirators do not at all confine themselves to organizing the revolutionary proletariat. Their business consists precisely in forestalling the revolutionary process, in driving it artificially toward crisis, in making a revolution extempore, without a condition for revolution. For them the only condition for revolution is the sufficient organization of their conspiracy. They are the alchemists of revolution; as we see in their rigid conceptions, they share entirely the intellectual confusion and the ignorance of the old alchemists. They seize on new discoveries which are supposed to achieve revolutionary miracles: incendiary bombs, demolition machines of magical effectiveness, riots that are to be the more miraculous and surprising the less rational ground they have. Occupied with such projects, they have no other aim than to overthrow the next government, and have the deepest contempt for theoretical elucidation of the working class and its interests. This explains their nonproletarian, but rather plebeian, anger at the *habits noirs* [black coats], the more or less educated persons who join their side of the movement as official representatives of the party, and of whom they cannot become entirely independent. The *habits noirs* must also serve them from time to time as a source of money. For the rest, it goes without saying that the conspirators must follow the development of the revolutionary party, either willingly or in spite of themselves.

The main characteristic of the conspirators' lives is their struggle with the police, to whom they have exactly the same relationship as thieves and prostitutes. The police force tolerates the conspiracies, and not merely as a necessary evil; it tolerates them as easily watched centers where the most violent revolutionary elements of society assemble, as workshops of riots which in France have become a necessary part of governmental operations as much as the police itself, and, finally, as a recruiting place for its own political *mouchards* [police spies]. Just as the most useful captors of rascals, like Vidocq and his colleagues, came out of the class of higher and lower scoundrels who have been arrested as thieves, swindlers, and fake bankrupts, and who often revert to their old calling, so also the lower political police are recruited from among the professional conspirators. The conspirators are in continuous touch with the police, and there are frequent collisions; they chase the *mouchards* just as the *mouchards* chase them. Espionage is one of their main occupations. No wonder, therefore, that goaded by misery and imprisonment, by threats and promises, men make the small jump from artisan conspirator to paid police spy so often. Hence the limitless system of suspicion in the conspiracies, blinding their members so completely that they see their best men as *mouchards*, and the real *mouchards* as their most reliable men. It is enlightening to learn that these spies, recruited from among the conspirators, often become so in good faith in order to dupe the police—until they deteriorate more and more as a consequence of their first step—and that the police are often really duped by them. For the rest, the entrapment of such a conspirator in the police net depends upon purely fortuitous circumstances and more upon a quantitative than a qualitative difference in strength of character.

Such are the conspirators whom Chenu depicts so vividly for us and whose characteristics he describes now freely, now reluctantly. Moreover, he himself is, in his not altogether clear relations with the Delessert and Marrast police, a striking portrait of the conspirator by profession.

The Secret Proletarian Societies*

AFTER THE DEFEAT of the Revolution of 1848–49, the proletarian party on the Continent lost what it had, by way of exception, possessed in that short period: freedom of the press, of speech, and the right of association, that is, the legal means for party organization. Despite the Reaction, both the bourgeois-liberal and the petty bourgeois-democratic parties found in the social position of the classes they represented the conditions which enabled them to keep more or less together and represent their common interests. For the proletarian party after 1849, as before 1848, there was only one way open—the way of *secret association*. Hence after 1849 there arose on the Continent a whole series of secret proletarian associations, exposed by the police, condemned by the courts, broken by imprisonment, but always rebuilt anew by conditions.

One segment of these secret societies aimed directly at the overthrow of the existing political system. This was justified in France, where the proletariat was defeated by the bourgeoisie and where an attack on the existing government coincided with an attack on the bourgeoisie. Another segment aimed at the creation of a proletarian party, without troubling itself about the existing governments. This was necessary in countries like Germany, where the bourgeoisie and the proletariat were equally subordinate to the semifeudal governments; hence a victorious assault on the existing governments could only help the bourgeoisie or the so-called middle classes to achieve supremacy, rather than break their power. No doubt here, too, the

---

* "The Willich-Schapper Fraction," from *Revelations About the Cologne Communist Trial*, written October–December, 1852, published in Basel in 1853.

[57]

---

members of the proletarian party would have to participate anew in a revolution against the status quo, but it was not their task to prepare that revolution, to agitate or conspire or plot for it. They could leave this preparation of revolution to general conditions and to the directly participating classes. The proletarian party had to leave it to them if it were not to renounce its own party position and the historic tasks which emerge from the general conditions of existence of the proletariat. For the proletariat, the existing governments were merely ephemeral phenomena and the status quo only a short stopping point which a petty and narrow democracy was left to to work itself off.

The "Communist League" was therefore not a conspiratorial society, but a society which was secretly to accomplish the organization of the proletarian party, because the German proletariat was officially denied, *igni et aqua*,[1] the right of publishing, speech, and association. When such a society conspires, it is only in the same sense that steam and electricity conspire against the status quo.

It goes without saying that such a secret society, which aims to construct, not a *government*, but an *opposition party of the future*, could offer little attraction for individuals who on the one hand feel their personal insignificance sprout under the theatrical cloak of conspiracy, and on the other satisfy their narrow ambitions on the day of the next revolution, but above all appear to themselves momentarily important, share in the spoils of demagogy, and want to be welcomed by the democratic charlatans.

---

1. *Igni et aqua interdictus* (excluded from fire and water) was the ostracism formula of ancient Rome.

Speech at the Anniversary of the People's Paper*

THE SO-CALLED revolutions of 1848 were but poor incidents—small fractures and fissures in the dry crust of European society. However, they revealed the abyss. Beneath the apparently solid surface they betrayed oceans of liquid matter, only needing expansion to rend into fragments continents of hard rock. Noisily and confusedly they proclaimed the emancipation of the Proletarian, i.e., the secret of the nineteenth century, and of the revolution of that century. That social revolution, it is true, was no novelty invented in 1848. Steam, electricity, and the self-acting mule were revolutionists of a rather more dangerous character than even citizens Barbès, Raspail, and Blanqui. But although the atmosphere in which we live weighs upon everyone with a 20,000-pound force, do you feel it? No more than European society before 1848 felt the revolutionary atmosphere enveloping and pressing it from all sides. There is one great fact, characteristic of this our nineteenth century, a fact which no party dares deny. On the one hand, there have started into life industrial and scientific forces which no epoch of former human history had ever suspected. On the other hand, there exist symptoms of decay far surpassing the horrors recorded of the latter times of the Roman Empire. In our days everything seems pregnant with its contrary. Machinery, gifted with the wonderful power of shortening and fructifying human

---

* Delivered April 14, 1856; published in the *People's Paper*, April 19, 1856. The *People's Paper* was a Chartist weekly, edited by Ernest Jones and published in London from 1852 to 1858. Marx wrote Engels, April 16, 1856, "The day before yesterday there was a small banquet to celebrate the anniversary of the *People's Paper*. This time . . . I accepted the invitation, the more so as I was the *only one* (as announced in the *Paper*) of the whole emigration to be invited, and I also gave the first toast . . . I gave a little speech in English. . . ."

labor, we behold starving and overworking it. The newfangled sources of wealth, by some strange weird spell, are turned into sources of want. The victories of art seem bought by the loss of character. At the same pace that mankind masters nature, man seems to become enslaved to other men or to his own infamy. Even the pure light of science seems unable to shine but on the dark background of ignorance. All our invention and progress seem to result in endowing material forces with intellectual life, and in stultifying human life into a material force. This antagonism between modern industry and science on the one hand, modern misery and dissolution on the other hand; this antagonism between the productive powers and the social relations of our epoch is a fact, palpable, overwhelming, and not to be controverted. Some parties may wail over it; others may wish to get rid of modern arts, in order to get rid of modern conflicts. Or they may imagine that so signal a progress in industry wants to be completed by as signal a regress in politics. On our part, we do not mistake the shape of the shrewd spirit that continues to mark all these contradictions. We know that to work well the newfangled forces of society, they only want to be mastered by newfangled men—and such are the workingmen. They are as much the invention of modern time as machinery itself. In the signs that bewilder the middle class, the aristocracy, and the poor prophets of regression, we do recognize our brave friend Robin Goodfellow,[1] the old mole that can work in the earth so fast, that worthy pioneer—the Revolution. The English workingmen are the first-born sons of modern industry. They will then, certainly, not be the last in aiding the social revolution produced by that industry, a revolution, which means the emancipation of their own class all over the world, which is as universal as capital rule and wages slavery. I know the heroic struggles the English working class have gone through since the middle of the last century —struggles no less glorious because they are shrouded in obscurity and burked by the middle-class historian. To revenge the misdeeds of the ruling class, there existed in the Middle Ages, in Germany, a secret tribunal called the *"Vehmgericht."* If a red cross was seen marked on a house, people knew that its owner was doomed by the *"Vehm."* All the houses of Europe are now marked with the mysterious red cross. History is the judge—its executioner, the proletarian.

---

1. A character in Shakespeare's *A Midsummer Night's Dream.*

"Political Movements": The Conquest of Power by the Proletarians*

Nota bene as to *Political Movement.*

The political movement of the working class has, naturally, as its final object the conquest of political power for itself, and this of course necessitates a previous organization of the working class developed up to a certain point, being itself an outgrowth of its economic struggles.

But on the other hand, every movement in which the working class as a *class* confronts the ruling classes and tries to vanquish them by pressure from without is a political movement. For example, an attempt in a particular factory or in a particular trade to force shorter working hours on individual capitalists through strikes, etc., is a purely economic movement; but a movement to compel the enactment of an eight-hour law, etc., is a political movement. And in this way, out of separate economic movements of the workers there grows everywhere a political movement, that is, a movement of the class, aiming to effect its interests in a general form which possesses general, socially coercive force. Although these movements presuppose a certain degree of previous organization, they are in turn equally a means for its further development.

Where the working class is not yet far enough advanced in its organization to undertake a decisive campaign against the collective power, that is, the political power, of the ruling classes, it must in any case be trained for this by constant agitation against (and a hostile attitude to) the policies of the ruling classes. Otherwise it remains a

---

* Postscript to a letter to Friedrich Bolte, in New York. London, November 23, 1871.

plaything in their hands, as the September [1870] revolution in France has shown and as is also proved to a certain degree by the game that Messrs. Gladstone & Co. still succeed in playing in England up to this hour.

Qualifying Violent Revolution*

IN THE EIGHTEENTH CENTURY the kings and the potentates were in the habit of meeting at The Hague to discuss the interests of their dynasties.

It is precisely in this place that we wanted to hold our workers' meeting, despite attempts to arouse apprehensions among us. We wanted to appear amid the most reactionary population, to reinforce the existence, propagation, and hope for the future of our great Association.[1]

When our decision became known, it was rumored that we sent emissaries to prepare the ground. Yes, we do not deny that we have such emissaries everywhere; but they are mostly unknown to us. Our emissaries in The Hague were the workers whose labor is as toilsome as that of our emissaries in Amsterdam, who are likewise workers laboring sixteen hours a day. Those are our emissaries; we have no other; and in all the countries where we recruit we find them prepared to receive us with open hearts, because they understand immediately that we strive to improve their lot.

The congress at The Hague has brought to maturity three important points:

It has proclaimed the necessity for the working class to fight the old, disintegrating society on political as well as social grounds; and

---

* Speech delivered in German and French at Amsterdam, September 8, 1872, as printed in *La Liberté*, September 15, 1872. It was published in the Dutch, Belgian, French, and German press, all the texts coinciding. The text in *Der Volksstaat* (October 2, 1872) followed that of *La Liberté* with a few small changes.

1. The International Working Men's Association, later called the First International.

we congratulate ourselves that this resolution of the London Conference will henceforth be in our Statutes.

In our midst there has been formed a group advocating the workers' abstention from political action. We have considered it our duty to declare how dangerous and fatal for our cause such principles appear to be.

Someday the worker must seize political power in order to build up the new organization of labor; he must overthrow the old politics which sustain the old institutions, if he is not to lose heaven on earth, like the old Christians who neglected and despised politics.

But we have not asserted that the ways to achieve that goal are everywhere the same.

You know that the institutions, mores, and traditions of various countries must be taken into consideration, and we do not deny that there are countries—such as America, England, and if I were more familiar with your institutions, I would perhaps also add Holland—where the workers can attain their goal by peaceful means. This being the case, we must also recognize the fact that in most countries on the Continent the lever of our revolution must be force; it is force to which we must someday appeal in order to erect the rule of labor.[2]

The Hague Congress has granted the General Councils[3] new and wider authority. In fact, at the moment when the kings are assembling in Berlin, whence are to be issued new and decisive measures of oppression against us by the mighty representatives of feudalism and of the past—precisely at that moment, when persecution is being organized, the congress of The Hague considered it proper and necessary to enlarge the authority of the General Council and to centralize all action for the approaching struggle, which would otherwise be impotent in isolation. And, moreover, where else could the authorizations of the General Council arouse disquiet if not among our enemies? Does the General Council have a bureaucracy and an armed police to compel obedience? Is not its authority entirely a moral one, and does it not submit its decisions to the judgment of the various federations entrusted with their execution? Under such conditions—without an army, without police, without courts—on the day when the kings are forced to maintain their power only with moral influence and moral authority, they will form a weak obstacle to the forward march of the revolution.

Finally, the congress of The Hague has moved the headquarters

---

2. In *Der Volksstaat*'s version this sentence was replaced by: "But not in all countries is this the case."

3. The London-based administrative body of the International Working Men's Association.

of the General Council to New York. Many, even among our friends, seem to have wondered at such a decision. Do they then forget that America will be the workers' continent par excellence, that half a million men—workers—emigrate there yearly, and that on such soil, where the worker dominates, the International is bound to strike strong roots? Moreover, the decision of the congress gives the General Council the right to employ [in Europe] any members whose collaboration it considers necessary and useful for the common welfare. Let us trust its prudence and hope it will succeed in selecting persons who will be capable of carrying out their task and who will understand how to hold up the banner of our Association in Europe with a firm hand.

Citizens, let us think of the basic principle of the International: Solidarity. Only when we have established this life-giving principle on a sound basis among the numerous workers of all countries will we attain the great final goal which we have set ourselves. The revolution must be carried out with solidarity; this is the great lesson of the French Commune, which[4] fell because none of the other centers— Berlin, Madrid, etc.—developed great revolutionary movements comparable to the mighty uprising of the Paris proletariat.

So far as I am concerned, I will continue my work and constantly strive to strengthen among all workers this solidarity that is so fruitful for the future. No, I do not withdraw from the International, and all the rest of my life will be, as have been all my efforts of the past, dedicated to the triumph of the social ideas which—you may be assured!—will lead to the world domination by the proletariat.

---

4. In *Der Volksstaat* the rest of the sentence reads: "fell only because precisely this solidarity was lacking among the workers of the other countries."

The Time Is Not Yet Ripe*

Honored Party Comrade:

The "question" before the forthcoming Zurich Congress, which you report to me, seems to me to be a blunder. What is to be done *immediately* at a given, exact moment in the future depends entirely on the historical circumstances. The question you posed exists in the land of mist; it is actually a phantom problem to which the only answer must be a critique of the question itself. We cannot solve an equation which does not include the elements of its solution in its data. For the rest, the dilemmas of a government that suddenly emerges as a result of a popular victory are in no way specifically "socialistic." Quite the contrary. The victorious bourgeois politicians feel immediately embarrassed by their "victory," while the socialist can at least proceed without embarrassment. Of one thing you can be sure—a socialist government does not come to the helm of a country without such developed conditions that it can take the necessary measures without frightening the bulk of the bourgeoisie, which is the first desideratum—time for lasting action—to be gained.

You may perhaps point out to me the example of the Paris Commune; but apart from the fact that this was merely a revolt of a city under exceptional conditions, the majority of the Commune was in no way socialistic, and could not be. Nevertheless, with a minimum quantity of common sense, it could have achieved a compromise with the Versailles government useful for the whole mass of the people—

---

*Letter to Ferdinand Domela Nieuwenhuis, February 22, 1881. In a letter of January 6, 1881, the Dutch socialist (later anarchist) leader Nieuwenhuis had asked Marx what political and social action socialists should take if they should seize power.

which was then attainable. The appropriation of the Bank of France alone would have put a fearful end to the Versailles machinations, etc., etc.

The general demands of the French bourgeoisie before 1789 were, *mutatis mutandis*, approximately as well established as the present-day demands of the proletariat in all countries with a capitalist form of production. But the way the demands of the French bourgeoisie were carried out—did any Frenchman of the eighteenth century have, *a priori*, the slightest idea about it? The doctrinal and necessarily fantastic anticipation of the action program of a revolution of the future emerges only from contemporary struggle. The dream of the imminent destruction of the world inspired the early Christians in their struggle with the Roman world empire and gave them a certainty of victory. Scientific insight into the unavoidable and continuing disintegration of the dominant order of society, constantly visible before our eyes, and the increasingly passionate whipping of the masses by the old government specters, as well as the gigantically advancing positive development of the means of production—all this serves as a guarantee that at the moment of outbreak of a real proletarian revolution its very conditions (even if surely not idyllic ones) will directly bring forth the next *modus operandi*.

According to my conviction, the critical conjunction of a new international workers' association does not yet exist; I therefore consider all labor congresses, particularly socialist congresses, insofar as they are not related directly to specific conditions in this or that nation, as useless, even harmful. They will always be dissipated in a lot of banal, chewed-over generalities.

Your most devoted,
KARL MARX

COMMUNISM AND THE
MANIFESTO

Communism— "Production of the Form of Intercourse Itself"*

COMMUNISM differs from all previous movements in that it overturns the basis of all earlier relations of production and intercourse, and for the first time consciously treats all natural premises as the creations of hitherto existing men, strips them of their natural character, and subjugates them to the power of the united individuals. Its organization is therefore essentially economic, the material production of the conditions of this unity; it turns existing conditions into conditions of unity. The reality, which communism is creating, is precisely the true basis for rendering it impossible for anything to exist independently of individuals, insofar as reality is only a product of the preceding intercourse of individuals themselves. Thus the communists in practice treat the conditions created up to now by production and intercourse as inorganic conditions, without, however, imagining that it was the plan or the destiny of previous generations to give them material, and without believing that these conditions were inorganic for the individuals creating them. The difference between the individual as a person and what is accidental to him is not a conceptual difference but a historical fact. This distinction has a different significance at different times—e.g., the estate as something accidental to the individual in the eighteenth century, the family more or less too. It is not a distinction that we have to make for each age, but one that each age makes itself from among the different elements which it finds in existence, and indeed not according to any theory, but compelled by material collisions in life. What

---

* From Marx and Engels, *The German Ideology* (1845–46), Vol. I, Part I (C). Based on a translation by the Institute of Marxism-Leninism, published by Progress Publishers, Moscow.

appears accidental to the later age as opposed to the earlier—and this applies also to the elements handed down by an earlier age—is a form of intercourse which corresponded to a definite stage of development of the productive forces. The relation of the productive forces to the form of intercourse is the relation of the form of intercourse to the occupation or activity of the individuals. (The fundamental form of this activity is, of course, material, on which depend all other forms—mental, political, religious, etc.) The various shaping of material life is, of course, in every case dependent on the needs which are already developed, and the production, as well as the satisfaction, of these needs is a historical process, which is not found in the case of a sheep or a dog (Stirner's refractory principal argument *adversus hominem*, although sheep and dogs in their present form certainly, but *malgré eux* [in spite of themselves] are products of a historical process). The conditions under which individuals have intercourse with each other, so long as the above-mentioned contradiction is absent, are conditions pertaining to their individuality, in no way external to them; conditions under which these definite individuals, living under definite relationships, can alone produce their material life and what is connected with it, are thus the conditions of their self-activity and are produced by this self-activity.[1] The definite condition under which they produce thus corresponds, as long as the contradiction has not yet appeared, to the reality of their conditioned nature, their one-sided existence, the one-sidedness of which becomes evident only when the contradiction enters on the scene and thus exists for the later individuals. Then this condition appears as an accidental fetter, and the consciousness that it is a fetter is imputed to the earlier age as well.

These various conditions, which appear first as conditions of self-activity, later as fetters upon it, form in the whole evolution of history a coherent series of forms of intercourse, the coherence of which consists in this: in the place of an earlier form of intercourse, which has become a fetter, a new one is put, corresponding to the more developed productive forces and, hence, to the advanced mode of the self-activity of individuals—a form which in its turn becomes a fetter and is then replaced by another. Since these conditions correspond at every stage to the simultaneous development of the productive forces, their history is at the same time the history of the evolving productive forces taken over by each new generation, and is therefore the history of the development of the forces of the individuals themselves.

Since this evolution takes place naturally—i.e., is not subordinated

---

1. Production of the form of intercourse itself.—K.M.

to a general plan of freely combined individuals—it proceeds from various localities, tribes, nations, branches of labor, etc., each of which to start with develops independently of the others and only gradually enters into relation with the others. Furthermore, it takes place only very slowly; the various stages and interests are never completely overcome, but only subordinated to the prevailing interest, and trail along beside the latter for centuries afterwards. It follows from this that within a nation itself the individuals, even apart from their pecuniary circumstances, have quite different developments, and that an earlier interest, the peculiar form of intercourse of which has already been ousted by that belonging to a later interest, remains for a long time afterwards in possession of a traditional power in the illusory community (state, law), which has won an existence independent of the individuals; a power which in the last resort can be broken only by a revolution. This explains why, with reference to individual points which allow of a more general summing up, consciousness can sometimes appear further advanced than the contemporary empirical relationships, so that in the struggles of a later epoch one can refer to earlier theoreticians as authorities.

On the other hand, in countries which, like North America, begin in an already advanced historical epoch, the development proceeds very rapidly. Such countries have no other natural premises than the individuals who settled there and were led to do so because the forms of intercourse of the old countries did not correspond to their wants. Thus they begin with the most advanced individuals of the old countries, and therefore with the correspondingly most advanced form of intercourse, before this form of intercourse has been able to establish itself in the old countries.[2] This is the case with all colonies, insofar as they are not mere military or trading stations. Carthage, the Greek colonies, and Iceland in the eleventh and twelfth centuries provide examples of this. A similar relationship issues from conquest, when a form of intercourse which has evolved on another soil is brought over complete to the conquered country: whereas in its home it was still encumbered with interests and relationships left over from earlier periods, here it can and must be established completely and without hindrance, if only to assure the conquerors' lasting power. (England and Naples after the Norman conquest, when they received the most perfect form of feudal organization.)

---

2. Personal energy of the individuals of various nations—Germans and Americans—energy even through cross-breeding—hence the cretinism of the Germans; in France and England, etc., foreign peoples transplanted to an already developed soil, in America to an entirely new soil; in Germany the natural population quietly stayed where it was.—K.M.

Nothing is more common than the notion that in history up till now it has only been a question of *taking*. The barbarians *take* the Roman Empire, and this fact of taking is made to explain the transition from the old world to the feudal system. In this taking by barbarians, however, the question is whether the nation which is conquered has evolved industrial productive forces, as is the case with modern peoples, or whether its productive forces are based for the most part merely on their association and on the community. Taking is further determined by the object taken. A banker's fortune, consisting of paper, cannot be taken at all without the taker's submitting to the conditions of production and intercourse of the country taken. Similarly the total industrial capital of a modern industrial country. And finally, everywhere there is very soon an end to taking, and when there is nothing more to take, you have to set about producing. From this necessity of producing, which very soon asserts itself, it follows that the form of community adopted by the settling conquerors must correspond to the stage of development of the productive forces they find in existence; or if this is not the case from the start, it must change according to the productive forces. By this, too, is explained the fact, which people profess to have noticed everywhere in the period following the migration of the peoples, namely, that the servant was master, and that the conquerors very soon took over language, culture, and manners from the conquered. The feudal system was by no means brought complete from Germany, but had its origin, as far as the conquerors were concerned, in the martial organization of the army during the actual conquest, and this evolved only after the conquest into the feudal system proper through the action of the productive forces found in the conquered countries. To what extent this form was determined by the productive forces is shown by the abortive attempts to realize other forms derived from reminiscences of ancient Rome (Charlemagne, etc.).

Thus all collisions in history have their origin, according to our view, in the contradiction between the productive forces and the form of intercourse. Incidentally, to lead to collisions in a country, this contradiction need not necessarily have reached its extreme limit in this particular country. Competition with industrially more advanced countries, brought about by the expansion of international intercourse, is sufficient to produce a similar contradiction in countries with a backward industry (e.g., the latent proletariat in Germany brought into view by the competition of English industry).

This contradiction between the productive forces and the form of intercourse—which as we saw has occurred several times in past history, without, however, endangering the basis—necessarily on each occasion burst out in a revolution, taking on at the same time various subsidiary forms, such as all-embracing collisions, collisions of various classes, contradiction of consciousness, battle of ideas, etc., political conflict, etc. From a narrow point of view one may isolate one of these subsidiary forms and consider it the basis of these revolutions; and this is all the more easy as the individuals who started the revolutions had illusions about their own activity according to their degree of culture and the stage of historical development.

The transformation, through the division of labor, of personal powers (relationships) into material powers cannot be dispelled by dismissing the general idea of it from one's mind, but can be abolished only by the individuals' again subjecting these material powers to themselves and abolishing the division of labor. This is not possible without the community.[3] Only in community has each individual the means of cultivating his gifts in all directions; only in the community, therefore, is personal freedom possible. In the previous substitutes for the community, in the state, etc., personal freedom has existed only for the individuals who developed within the relationships of the ruling class, and only insofar as they were individuals of this class. The illusory community in which individuals have up till now combined always took on an independent existence in relation to them, and was at the same time, since it was the combination of one class over against another, not only a completely illusory community, but a new fetter as well. In the real community, individuals obtain their freedom in and through their association.

It follows from all we have been saying up to now that the communal relationship into which the individuals of a class entered, and which was determined by their common interests over against a third party, was always a community to which these individuals belonged only as average individuals, only insofar as they lived within the conditions of existence of their class—a relationship in which they participated not as individuals but as members of a class. With the community of revolutionary proletarians, on the other hand, who take their conditions of existence and those of all members of society under their control, it is just the reverse; it is as individuals that the individuals participate in it. It is just this combination of individuals (assuming the advanced stage of modern productive forces, of course) which puts the conditions of the free development and movement of individuals under their control—conditions which were previously abandoned to chance and had won an

3. Marx used "community," *Gemeinde*, in the broad sense, to mean both urban municipalities and rural communities.

independent existence over against the separate individuals just because of their separation as individuals, and because of the necessity of their combination which had been determined by the division of labor, and through their separation had become a bond alien to them. Combination up till now (by no means an arbitrary one, such as is expounded for example in [Rousseau's] *Contrat social*, but a necessary one) was an agreement upon these conditions, within which the individuals were free to enjoy the freaks of fortune (compare, e.g., the formation of the North American State and the South American republics). This right to the undisturbed enjoyment, within certain conditions, of fortuity and chance has up till now been called personal freedom. These conditions of existence are, of course, only the productive forces and forms of intercourse at any particular time.

If from a *philosophical* point of view one considers this evolution of individuals in the common conditions of existence of estates and classes which followed on one another, and in the accompanying general conceptions forced upon them, it is certainly very easy to imagine that in these individuals the species, or "Man," has evolved, or that they evolved "Man"—and in this way one can give history some hard clouts on the ear. One can conceive these various estates and classes to be specific terms of the general expression, subordinate varieties of the species, or evolutionary phases of "Man."

This subsuming of individuals under definite classes cannot be abolished until a class has taken shape which has no longer any particular class interest to assert against the ruling class.

Individuals have always built on themselves, but naturally on themselves within their given historical conditions and relationships, not on the "pure" individual in the sense of the ideologists. But in the course of historical evolution, and precisely through the inevitable fact that within the division of labor social relationships take on an independent existence, there appears a division within the life of each individual, insofar as it is personal and insofar as it is determined by some branch of labor and the conditions pertaining to it. (We do not mean it to be understood from this that, for example, the *rentier* [stockholder], the capitalist, etc., cease to be persons; but their personality is conditioned and determined by quite definite class relationships, and the division appears only in their opposition to another class and, for themselves, only when they go bankrupt.) In the estate (and even more in the tribe) this is as yet concealed: for instance, a nobleman always remains a nobleman, a commoner always a commoner, apart from his other relationships, a quality inseparable from his individuality. The division between the personal and the class individual, the accidental nature of the conditions of life for the individual, appears only with the emergence of the class, which is itself a product of the bourgeoisie. This accidental character is engendered and developed only by competition and the struggle of individuals among themselves. Thus in imagination individuals seem freer under the dominance of the bourgeoisie than before, because their conditions of life seem accidental; in reality, of course, they are less free, because they are more subject to the violence of things. The difference from the estate comes out particularly in the antagonism between the bourgeoisie and the proletariat. When the estate of the urban burghers, the corporations, etc., emerged in opposition to the landed nobility, their condition of existence—movable property and craft labor, which had already existed latently before their separation from the feudal ties—appeared as something positive, which was asserted against feudal landed property, and, therefore, in its own way at first took on a feudal form. Certainly the refugee serfs treated their previous servitude as something accidental to their personality. But here they were only doing what every class that is freeing itself from a fetter does; and they did not free themselves as a class but separately. Moreover, they did not rise above the system of estates, but only formed a new estate, retaining their previous mode of labor even in their new situation, and developing it further by freeing it from its earlier fetters, which no longer corresponded to the development already attained.[4]

For the proletarians, on the other hand, the condition of their existence, labor, and with it all the conditions of existence governing modern society, have become something accidental, something over which they, as separate individuals, have no control, and over which no *social* organization can give them control. The contradiction between the individuality of each separate proletarian and labor, the condition of life forced upon him, becomes evident even to him, for he is sacrificed from youth upwards and, within his own class, has no chance of arriving at the conditions which would place him in the other class.

Thus while the refugee serfs only wished to be free to develop

---

4. N.B. It must not be forgotten that the serfs' very need of existing and the impossibility of a large-scale economy, which involved the distribution of the allotments among the serfs, very soon reduced the services of the serfs to their lord to an average of payments in kind and statute labor. This made it possible for the serf to accumulate movable property and hence facilitated his escape out of the possession of his lord and gave him the prospect of making his way as an urban citizen; it also created gradations among the serfs, so that the runaway serfs were already half burghers. It is likewise obvious that the serfs who were masters of a craft had the best chance of acquiring movable property.—K.M.

and assert those conditions of existence which were already there, and hence, in the end, only arrived at free labor, the proletarians, if they are to assert themselves as individuals, will have to abolish the very condition of their existence hitherto (which has, moreover, been that of all society up to the present), namely, labor. Thus they find themselves directly opposed to the form in which, hitherto, the individuals of which society consists have given themselves collective expression, that is, the state. In order, therefore, to assert themselves as individuals, they must overthrow the state.

Manifesto of the Communist Party

The Manifesto was written in German by Marx and Engels between December, 1847, and January, 1848. It was published anonymously in February, 1848, under the title Manifest der Kommunistischen Partei. (The twenty-three-page brochure was printed in the office of the Bildungs-Gesellschaft für Arbeiter, 46 Liverpool Street, Bishopsgate, London.) Between March and July of 1848 it was reprinted in the Deutsche Londoner Zeitung, an organ of German émigrés in London. In the same year it appeared in the Danish, Flemish, French, Italian, Polish, and Swedish languages—again anonymously. In 1850 George Julian Harney published the first English translation (by Helen MacFarlane) of the Manifesto in his Chartist publication, Red Republican, and for the first time Marx and Engels were mentioned as its authors. Since then there have been numerous editions of the Manifesto in every conceivable language.

Marx's sketch for the Manifesto, written in December, 1847, or January, 1848, is reproduced below. This is the only original sketch of the document that has been preserved. (The words in brackets were crossed out by Marx.)

For the rest we have seen:
The communists do not propose a new theory of private property. They only express the historic fact that [productions and] bourgeois production—and with it bourgeois property relationships [and] [or] [definite] of [social] the development of social forces of production are no longer [appropriate] and hence [in the development of industry itself] and in d.
But do not quarrel with us when you measure the elimination of

bourgeois property [against] from the point of view of your bourgeois ideas of freedom, education, etc. Your ideas themselves [are] [engender] [are] [corresponding to] are the products of the [existing] bourgeois production and property relationships, just as is your right, which is only the will of your class raised to the status of law. [A] A will whose content is determined by the material life conditions of your class.

[Your] The interesting conception of transforming [the] your production and property relationships from a historical [and only], transitory, definite [mature] state of development of the forces of production [forces corresponding to] corresponding to the relationships into eternal and rational natural laws, you share with all extinct ruling classes.

What you understand in the matter of feudal property, you no longer understand when it comes to bourgeois property.

And yet you cannot deny the fact that [in the course of the bourgeois] with the process of industrial development the one-sided, on—

The communists posit no new theory of property. They express a fact. You deny the most striking facts. You have to deny it. You are utopians in reverse.

The text of the Manifesto used here is based on the English translation by Samuel Moore, published, with a preface by Engels, in 1888.

A specter is haunting Europe—the specter of communism. All the powers of old Europe have entered into a holy alliance to exorcise this specter: Pope and Czar, Metternich and Guizot, French radicals and German police spies.

Where is the party in opposition that has not been decried as communistic by its opponents in power? Where the opposition that has not hurled back the branding reproach of communism, against the more advanced opposition parties, as well as against its reactionary adversaries?

Two things result from this fact.

1. Communism is already acknowledged by all European powers to be itself a power.

2. It is high time that Communists should openly, in the face of the whole world, publish their views, their aims, their tendencies, and meet this nursery tale of the specter of communism with a manifesto of the party itself.

To this end, Communists of various nationalities have assembled in London and sketched the following manifesto, to be published in the English, French, German, Italian, Flemish, and Danish languages.

I

BOURGEOIS AND PROLETARIANS

The history of all hitherto existing society is the history of class struggles.

Freeman and slave, patrician and plebeian, lord and serf, guild master and journeyman—in a word, oppressor and oppressed—stood in constant opposition to one another, carried on an uninterrupted, now hidden, now open fight, a fight that each time ended either in a revolutionary reconstitution of society at large, or in the common ruin of the contending classes.

In the early epochs of history, we find almost everywhere a complicated arrangement of society into various orders, a manifold graduation of social rank. In ancient Rome we have patricians, knights, plebeians, slaves; in the Middle Ages, feudal lords, vassals, guild masters, journeymen, apprentices, serfs; in almost all of these classes, again, subordinate gradations.

The modern bourgeois society that has sprouted from the ruins of feudal society has not done away with class antagonisms. It has but established new classes, new conditions of oppression, new forms of struggle in place of the old ones.

Our epoch, the epoch of the bourgeoisie, possesses, however, this distinctive feature: it has simplified the class antagonisms. Society as a whole is more and more splitting up into two great hostile camps, into two great classes directly facing each other: Bourgeoisie and Proletariat.

From the serfs of the Middle Ages sprang the chartered burghers of the earliest towns. From these burgesses the first elements of the bourgeoisie were developed.

The discovery of America, the rounding of the Cape, opened up fresh ground for the rising bourgeoisie. The East Indian and Chinese markets, the colonization of America, trade with the colonies, the increase in the means of exchange and in commodities generally, gave to commerce, to navigation, to industry, an impulse never before known, and thereby, to the revolutionary element in the tottering feudal society, a rapid development.

The feudal system of industry, under which industrial production was monopolized by closed guilds, now no longer sufficed for the growing wants of the new markets. The manufacturing system took its place. The guild masters were pushed to one side by the manufacturing middle class; division of labor between the different corporate guilds vanished in the face of division of labor in each single workshop.

Meantime the markets kept ever growing, the demand ever rising. Even manufacturing no longer sufficed. Thereupon steam and machinery revolutionized industrial production. The place of manufacture was taken by the giant, Modern Industry, the place of the industrial middle class by industrial millionaires, the leaders of whole industrial armies, the modern bourgeoisie.

Modern industry has established the world market for which the discovery of America paved the way. This market has given an immense development to commerce, to navigation, to communication by land. This development has, in its turn, reacted on the extension of industry; and in proportion as industry, commerce, navigation, railways extended, in the same proportion the bourgeoisie developed, increased its capital, and pushed into the background every class handed down from the Middle Ages.

We see, therefore, how the modern bourgeoisie is itself the product of a long course of development, of a series of revolutions in the modes of production and of exchange.

Each step in the development of the bourgeoisie was accompanied by a corresponding political advance of that class. An oppressed class under the sway of the feudal nobility, an armed and self-governing association in the medieval commune, here independent urban republic (as in Italy and Germany), there taxable "third estate" of the monarchy (as in France), afterwards, in the period of manufacturing proper, serving either the semifeudal or the absolute monarchy as a counterpoise against the nobility, and in fact a cornerstone of the great monarchies in general, the bourgeoisie has at last, since the establishment of Modern Industry and of the world market, conquered for itself, in the modern representative state, exclusive political sway. The executive of the modern state is but a committee for managing the common affairs of the whole bourgeoisie.

The bourgeoisie, historically, has played a most revolutionary part.

The bourgeoisie, wherever it has got the upper hand, has put an end to all feudal, patriarchal, idyllic relations. It has pitilessly torn asunder the motley feudal ties that bound man to his "natural superiors," and has left remaining no other nexus between man and man than naked self-interest, than callous "cash payment." It has drowned the most heavenly ecstasies of religious fervor, of chivalrous enthusiasm, of philistine sentimentalism, in the icy water of egotistical calculation. It has resolved personal worth into exchange value, and in place of the numberless indefeasible chartered freedoms has set up that single, unconscionable freedom—free trade. In a word, for exploitation veiled by religious and political illusions, it has substituted naked, shameless, direct, brutal exploitation.

The bourgeoisie has stripped of its halo every occupation hitherto honored and looked up to with reverent awe. It has converted the physician, the lawyer, the priest, the poet, the man of science, into its paid wage laborers.

The bourgeoisie has torn away from the family its sentimental veil, and has reduced the family relation to a mere money relation.

The bourgeoisie has disclosed how it came to pass that the brutal display of vigor in the Middle Ages, which reactionists so much admire, found its fitting complement in the most slothful indolence. It has been the first to show what man's activity can bring about. It has accomplished wonders far surpassing Egyptian pyramids, Roman aqueducts, and Gothic cathedrals; it has conducted expeditions that put in the shade all former exoduses of nations and crusades.

The bourgeoisie cannot exist without constantly revolutionizing the instruments of production, and thereby the relations of production, and with them the whole relations of society. Conservation of the old modes of production in unaltered form was, on the contrary, the first condition of existence for all earlier industrial classes. Constant revolutionizing of production, uninterrupted disturbance of all social conditions, everlasting uncertainty and agitation distinguish the bourgeois epoch from all earlier ones. All fixed, fast-frozen relations, with their train of ancient and venerable prejudices and opinions, are swept away, all newly formed ones become antiquated before they can ossify. All that is solid melts into air, all that is holy is profaned, and man is at last compelled to face with sober senses his real conditions of life, and his relations with his kind.

The need of a constantly expanding market for its products chases the bourgeoisie over the whole surface of the globe. It must nestle everywhere, settle everywhere, establish connections everywhere.

The bourgeoisie has through its exploitation of the world market given a cosmopolitan character to production and consumption in every country. To the great chagrin of reactionists, it has drawn from under the feet of industry the national ground on which it stood. All old-established national industries have been destroyed or are daily being destroyed. They are dislodged by new industries, whose introduction becomes a life-and-death question for all civilized nations, by industries that no longer work up indigenous raw material but raw material drawn from the remotest zones; industries whose products are consumed, not only at home, but in every quarter of the globe. In place of the old wants, satisfied by the productions of the country, we find new wants, requiring for their satisfaction the products of distant lands and climes. In place of the old local and national seclusion and self-sufficiency, we have intercourse in every direction, universal interdependence of nations. And as in material, so also in intellectual production. The intellectual creations of individual nations become common property. National one-sidedness and narrow-mindedness become more and more impossible, and from the numerous national and local literatures there arises a world literature.

The bourgeoisie, by the rapid improvement of all instruments of production, by the immensely facilitated means of communication, draws all, even the most barbarian, nations into civilization. The cheap prices of its commodities are the heavy artillery with which it batters down all Chinese walls, with which it forces the barbarians' intensely obstinate hatred of foreigners to capitulate. It compels all nations, on pain of extinction, to adopt the bourgeois mode of production; it compels them to introduce what it calls civilization into their midst, i.e., to become bourgeois themselves. In a word, it creates a world after its own image.

The bourgeoisie has subjected the country to the rule of the towns. It has created enormous cities, has greatly increased the urban population as compared with the rural, and has thus rescued a considerable part of the population from the idiocy of rural life. Just as it has made the country dependent on the towns, so it has made barbarian and semibarbarian countries dependent on the civilized ones, nations of peasants on nations of bourgeois, the East on the West.

The bourgeoisie keeps more and more doing away with the scattered state of the population, of the means of production, and of property. It has agglomerated population, centralized means of production, and concentrated property in a few hands. The necessary consequence of this was political centralization. Independent or but loosely connected provinces, with separate interests, laws, governments, and systems of taxation, became lumped together in one nation, with one government, one code of laws, one national class interest, one frontier, and one customs tariff.

The bourgeoisie, during its rule of scarcely one hundred years, has created more massive and more colossal productive forces than have all preceding generations together. Subjection of Nature's forces to man, machinery, application of chemistry to industry and agriculture, steam navigation, railways, electric telegraphs, clearing of whole continents for cultivation, canalization of rivers, whole populations conjured out of the ground—what earlier century had even a presentiment that such productive forces slumbered in the lap of social labor?

We see then: The means of production and of exchange on whose foundations the bourgeoisie built itself up were generated in feudal society. At a certain stage in the development of these means of production and of exchange, the conditions under which feudal society produced and exchanged, the feudal organization of agriculture and manufacturing industry—in a word, the feudal relations of property—became no longer compatible with the already developed productive forces; they became so many fetters. They had to be burst asunder; they were burst asunder.

Into their places stepped free competition, accompanied by a social and political constitution adapted to it, and by the economic and political sway of the bourgeois class.

A similar movement is going on before our own eyes. Modern bourgeois society with its relations of production, of exchange, and of property, a society that has conjured up such gigantic means of production and of exchange, is like the sorcerer who is no longer able to control the powers of the nether world whom he has called up by his spells. For many a decade past, the history of industry and commerce is but the history of the revolt of modern productive forces against modern conditions of production, against the property relations that are the condition for the existence of the bourgeoisie and of its rule. It is enough to mention the commercial crises that by their periodic return put on trial, each time more threateningly, the existence of the entire bourgeois society. In these crises a great part not only of the existing products, but also of the previously created productive forces, are periodically destroyed. In these crises there breaks out an epidemic that, in all earlier epochs, would have seemed an absurdity—the epidemic of overproduction. Society suddenly finds itself put back into a state of momentary barbarism; it appears as if a famine, a universal war of devastation, had cut off the supply of every means of subsistence; industry and commerce seem to be destroyed; and why? Because there is too much civilization, too much means of subsistence, too much industry, too much commerce. The productive forces at the disposal of society no longer tend to further the development of the conditions of bourgeois property; on the contrary, they have become too powerful for these conditions, by which they are fettered, and so soon as they overcome these fetters, they bring disorder into the whole of bourgeois society, endangering the existence of bourgeois property. The conditions of bourgeois society are too narrow to comprise the wealth created by them. And how does the bourgeoisie get over these crises? On the one hand by enforced destruction of a mass of productive forces; on the other by the conquest of new markets, and by the more thorough exploitation of the old ones. That is to say, by paving the way for more extensive and more destructive crises, and by diminishing the means whereby crises are prevented.

The weapons with which the bourgeoisie felled feudalism to the ground are now turned against the bourgeoisie itself.

But not only has the bourgeoisie forged the weapons that bring death to itself; it has also called into existence the men who are to wield those weapons—the modern working class—the proletarians.

In proportion as the bourgeoisie, i.e., capital, is developed, in the same proportion is the proletariat, the modern working class, developed, a class of laborers who live only so long as they find work, and who find work only so long as their labor increases capital. These laborers, who must sell themselves piecemeal, are a commodity, like every other article of commerce, and are consequently exposed to all the vicissitudes of competition, to all the fluctuations of the market.

Owing to the extensive use of machinery and to division of labor, the work of the proletarians has lost all individual character, and consequently all charm for the workman. He becomes an appendage of the machine, and it is only the most simple, most monotonous, and most easily acquired knack that is required of him. Hence the cost of production of a workman is restricted almost entirely to the means of subsistence that he requires for his maintenance, and for the propagation of his race. But the price of a commodity, and also of labor, is equal to its cost of production. In proportion, therefore, as the repulsiveness of the work increases, the wage decreases. Nay, more—in proportion as the use of machinery and division of labor increases, in the same proportion the burden of toil also increases, whether by prolongation of the working hours, by increase of the work done in a given time, or by increased speed of the machinery, etc.

Modern industry has converted the little workshop of the patriarchal master into the great factory of the industrial capitalist. Masses of laborers, crowded into the factory, are organized like soldiers. As privates of the industrial army they are placed under the command of a perfect hierarchy of officers and sergeants. Not only are they the slaves of the bourgeois class, and of the bourgeois state, they are daily and hourly enslaved by the machine, by the overlooker, and above all by the individual bourgeois manufacturer himself. The more openly this despotism proclaims gain to be its end and aim, the more petty, the more hateful, and the more embittering it is.

The less the skill and exertion or strength implied in manual labor —in other words, the more modern industry becomes developed— the more is the labor of men superseded by that of women. Differences of age and sex have no longer any distinctive social validity for the working class. All are instruments of labor, more or less expensive to use according to their age and sex.

No sooner is the exploitation of the laborer by the manufacturer so far at an end that he receives his wages in cash, than he is set upon by the other portions of the bourgeoisie, the landlord, the shopkeeper, the pawnbroker, etc.

The low strata of the middle class—the small tradespeople, shop-keepers, and retired tradesmen generally, the handicraftsmen and peasants—all these sink gradually into the proletariat, partly because their diminutive capital does not suffice for the scale on which Modern Industry is carried on and is swamped in the competition with the large capitalists, partly because their specialized skill is rendered worthless by new methods of production. Thus the proletariat is recruited from all classes of the population.

The proletariat goes through various stages of development. With its birth begins its struggle with the bourgeoisie. At first the contest is carried on by individual laborers, then by the workpeople of a factory, then by the operatives of one trade, in one locality, against the individual bourgeois who directly exploits them. They direct their attacks not against the bourgeois conditions of production, but against the instruments of production themselves; they destroy imported wares that compete with their labor, they smash machinery to pieces, they set factories ablaze, they seek to restore by force the vanished status of the workman of the Middle Ages.

At this stage the laborers still form an incoherent mass scattered over the whole country and broken up by their mutual competition. If anywhere they unite to form more compact bodies, this is not yet the consequence of their own active union, but of the union of the bourgeoisie, which class, in order to attain its own political ends, is compelled to set the whole proletariat in motion, and is moreover yet, for a time, able to do so. At this stage, therefore, the proletarians do not fight their enemies, but the enemies of their enemies, the remnants of absolute monarchy, the landowners, the nonindustrial bourgeoisie, the petty bourgeoisie. Thus the whole historical movement is concentrated in the hands of the bourgeoisie; every victory so obtained is a victory for the bourgeoisie.

But with the development of industry the proletariat not only increases in number, it becomes concentrated in great masses, its strength grows, and it feels that strength more. The various interests and conditions of life within the ranks of the proletariat are more and more equalized, in proportion as machinery obliterates all distinction of labor and nearly everywhere reduces wages to the same low level. The growing competition among the bourgeoisie, and the resulting commercial crises, make the wages of the worker ever more fluctuating. The unceasing improvement of machinery, ever more rapidly developing, makes their livelihood more and more precarious, the collisions between individual workmen and individual bourgeois take more and more the character of collision between two classes. Thereupon the workers begin to form combinations (trade unions) against the bourgeoisie; they club together in order to keep up the rate of wages; they found permanent associations in order to make provision beforehand for these occasional revolts. Here and there the contest breaks out into riots.

Now and then the workers are victorious, but only for a time. The real fruits of their battles lie, not in the immediate result, but in the ever expanding union of the workers. This union is helped on by the improved means of communication that are created by modern industry and that place the workers of different localities in contact with one another. It was just this contact that was needed to centralize the numerous local struggles, all of the same character, into one national struggle between classes. But every class struggle is a political struggle. And that union, to attain which the burghers of the Middle Ages, with their miserable highways, required centuries, the modern proletarians, thanks to railways, achieve in a few years.

This organization of the proletarians into a class, and consequently into a political party, is continually being upset again by the competition between the workers themselves. But it ever rises up again, stronger, firmer, mightier. It compels legislative recognition of particular interests of the workers by taking advantage of the divisions among the bourgeoisie itself. Thus the ten-hour bill in England was carried.

Altogether, collisions between the classes of the old society further in many ways the course of development of the proletariat. The bourgeoisie finds itself involved in a constant battle. At first with the aristocracy, later on with those portions of the bourgeoisie itself whose interests have become antagonistic to the progress of industry, at all times with the bourgeoisie of foreign countries. In all these battles it sees itself compelled to appeal to the proletariat, to ask for its help, and thus to drag it into the political arena. The bourgeoisie itself, therefore, supplies the proletariat with its own elements of political and general education; in other words, it furnishes the proletariat with weapons for fighting the bourgeoisie.

Further, as we have already seen, entire sections of the ruling classes are, by the advance of industry, precipitated into the proletariat, or are at least threatened in their conditions of existence. These also supply the proletariat with fresh elements of enlightenment and progress.

Finally, in times when the class struggle nears the decisive hour, the process of dissolution going on within the ruling class—in fact, within the whole range of old society—assumes such a violent, glaring character that a small section of the ruling class cuts itself adrift and joins the revolutionary class, the class that holds the future in its hands. Just as, therefore, at an earlier period, a section of the nobility went over to the bourgeoisie, so now a portion of the bourgeoisie goes over to the proletariat, and in particular, a portion of the bourgeois ideologists, who have raised themselves to the level of comprehending theoretically the historical movements as a whole.

Of all the classes that stand face to face with the bourgeoisie today, the proletariat alone is a really revolutionary class. The other classes decay and finally disappear in the face of modern industry; the proletariat is its special and essential product.

The lower middle class, the small manufacturer, the shopkeeper, the artisan, the peasant, all these fight against the bourgeoisie, to save from extinction their existence as fractions of the middle class. They are therefore not revolutionary, but conservative. Nay, more—they are reactionary, for they try to roll back the wheel of history. If by chance they are revolutionary, they are so only in view of their impending transfer into the proletariat; they thus defend not their present, but their future interests, they desert their own standpoint to place themselves at that of the proletariat.

The "dangerous class," the social scum, that passively rotting mass thrown off by the lowest layers of old society, may, here and there, be swept into the movement by a proletarian revolution; its conditions of life, however, prepare it far more for the part of a bribed tool of reactionary intrigue.

In the conditions of the proletariat, those of old society at large are already virtually swamped. The proletarian is without property; his relation to his wife and children has no longer anything in common with the bourgeois family relations; modern industrial labor, modern subjugation to capital, the same in England as in France, in America as in Germany, has stripped him of every trace of national character. Law, morality, religion are to him so many bourgeois prejudices, behind which lurk in ambush just as many bourgeois interests.

All the preceding classes that got the upper hand sought to fortify their already acquired status by subjecting society at large to their conditions of appropriation. The proletarians cannot become masters of the productive forces of society except by abolishing their own previous mode of appropriation, and thereby also every other previous mode of appropriation. They have nothing of their own to secure and to fortify; their mission is to destroy all previous securities for, and insurances of, individual property.

All previous historical movements were movements of minorities, or in the interests of minorities. The proletarian movement is the self-conscious, independent movement of the immense majority, in the interest of the immense majority. The proletariat, the lowest stratum of our present society, cannot stir, cannot raise itself up, without the whole superincumbent strata of official society being sprung into the air.

Though not in substance, yet in form, the struggle of the proletariat with the bourgeoisie is at first a national struggle. The proletariat of each country must, of course, first of all settle matters with its own bourgeoisie.

In depicting the most general phases of the development of the proletariat, we traced the more or less veiled civil war raging within existing society up to the point where that war breaks out into open revolution, and where the violent overthrow of the bourgeoisie lays the foundation for the sway of the proletariat.

Hitherto every form of society has been based, as we have already seen, on the antagonism of oppressing and oppressed classes. But in order to oppress a class, certain conditions must be assured to it under which it can at least continue its slavish existence. The serf, in the period of serfdom, raised himself to membership in the commune, just as the petty bourgeois, under the yoke of feudal absolutism, managed to develop into a bourgeois.

The modern laborer, on the contrary, instead of rising with the progress of industry, sinks deeper and deeper below the conditions of existence of his own class. He becomes a pauper, and pauperism develops more rapidly than population and wealth. And here it becomes evident that the bourgeoisie is unfit any longer to be the ruling class in society, and to impose its conditions of existence upon society as an overriding law. It is unfit to rule because it is incompetent to assure an existence to its slave within his slavery, because it cannot help letting him sink into such a state that it has to feed him, instead of being fed by him. Society can no longer live under this bourgeoisie; in other words, its existence is no longer compatible with society.

The essential condition for the existence and for the sway of the bourgeois class is the formation and augmentation of capital; the condition for capital is wage labor. Wage labor rests exclusively on competition between the laborers. The advance of industry, whose involuntary promoter is the bourgeoisie, replaces the isolation of the laborers, due to competition, by their revolutionary combination, due to association. The development of Modern Industry, therefore, cuts from under its feet the very foundation on which the bourgeoisie produces and appropriates products. What the bourgeoisie therefore produces, above all, is its own gravediggers. Its fall and the victory of the proletariat are equally inevitable.

II

PROLETARIANS AND COMMUNISTS

In what relation do the Communists stand to the proletarians as a whole?

The Communists do not form a separate party opposed to other working-class parties.

They have no interest separate and apart from those of the proletariat as a whole.

They do not set up any sectarian principles of their own, by which to shape and mold the proletarian movement.

The Communists are distinguished from the other working-class parties by this only: (1) In the national struggles of the proletarians of the different countries, they point out and bring to the front the common interests of the entire proletariat independently of all nationality. (2) In the various stages of development which the struggle of the working class against the bourgeoisie has to pass through, they always and everywhere represent the interest of the movement as a whole.

The Communists, therefore, are on the one hand, practically, the most advanced and resolute section of the working-class parties of every country, that section which pushes forward all others; on the other hand, theoretically, they have over the great mass of the proletariat the advantage of clearly understanding the line of march, the conditions, and the ultimate general results of the proletarian movement.

The immediate aim of the Communists is the same as that of all the other proletarian parties, formation of the proletariat into a class, overthrow of the bourgeois supremacy, conquest of political power by the proletariat.

The theoretical conclusions of the Communists are in no way based on ideas or principles that have been invented, or discovered, by this or that would-be universal reformer.

They merely express, in general terms, actual relations springing from an existing class struggle, from a historical movement going on under our very eyes. The abolition of existing property relations is not at all a distinctive feature of communism.

All property relations in the past have continually been subject to historical changes consequent upon the change in historical conditions.

The French Revolution, for example, abolished feudal property in favor of bourgeois property.

The distinguishing feature of communism is not the abolition of property generally, but the abolition of bourgeois property. But modern bourgeois private property is the final and most complete expression of the system of producing and appropriating products that is based on class antagonism, on the exploitation of the many by the few.

In this sense, the theory of the Communists may be summed up in the single sentence: Abolition of private property.

We Communists have been reproached with the desire of abolishing the right of personally acquiring property as the fruit of a man's own labor, which property is alleged to be the groundwork of all personal freedom, activity, and independence.

Hard-won, self-acquired, self-earned property! Do you mean the property of the petty artisan and of the small peasant, a form of property that preceded the bourgeois form? There is no need to abolish that; the development of industry has to a great extent already destroyed it, and is still destroying it daily.

Or do you mean modern bourgeois private property?

But does wage labor create any property for the laborer? Not a bit. It creates capital, i.e., that kind of property which exploits wage labor, and which cannot increase except upon condition of getting a new supply of wage labor for fresh exploitation. Property, in its present form, is based on the antagonism of capital and wage labor. Let us examine both sides of this antagonism.

To be a capitalist is to have not only a purely personal but a social status in production. Capital is a collective product, and only by the united action of many members, nay, in the last resort, only by the united action of all members of society, can it be set in motion.

Capital is therefore not a personal, it is a social power.

When, therefore, capital is converted into common property, into the property of all members of society, personal property is not thereby transformed into social property. It is only the social character of the property that is changed. It loses its class character.

Let us now take wage labor.

The average price of wage labor is the minimum wage, i.e., that quantum of the means of subsistence which is absolutely requisite to keep the laborer in bare existence as a laborer. What, therefore, the wage laborer appropriates by means of his labor merely suffices to prolong and reproduce a bare existence. We by no means intend to abolish this personal appropriation of the products of labor, an appropriation that is made for the maintenance and reproduction of human life, and that leaves no surplus wherewith to command the labor of others. All that we want to do away with is the miserable character of this appropriation, under which the laborer lives merely to increase capital, and is allowed to live only insofar as the interest of the ruling class requires it.

In bourgeois society, living labor is but a means to increase accumulated labor. In Communist society, accumulated labor is but a means to widen, to enrich, to promote the existence of the laborer.

In bourgeois society, therefore, the past dominates the present; in Communist society, the present dominates the past. In bourgeois society capital is independent and has individuality, while the living person is dependent and has no individuality.

And the abolition of this state of things is called by the bourgeois abolition of individuality and freedom! And rightly so. The abolition of bourgeois individuality, bourgeois independence, and bourgeois freedom is undoubtedly aimed at.

By freedom is meant, under the present bourgeois conditions of production, free trade, free selling and buying.

But if selling and buying disappears, free selling and buying disappears also. This talk about free selling and buying, and all the other "brave words" of our bourgeoisie about freedom in general, have a meaning, if any, only in contrast with restricted selling and buying, with the fettered traders of the Middle Ages, but have no meaning when opposed to the communistic abolition of buying and selling, of the bourgeois conditions of production, and of the bourgeoisie itself.

You are horrified at our intending to do away with private property. But in your existing society private property is already done away with for nine-tenths of the population; its existence for the few is solely due to its nonexistence in the hands of those nine-tenths. You reproach us, therefore, with intending to do away with a form of property the necessary condition for whose existence is the nonexistence of any property for the immense majority of society.

In a word, you reproach us with intending to do away with your property. Precisely so; that is just what we intend.

From the moment when labor can no longer be converted into capital, money, or rent, into a social power capable of being monopolized—i.e., from the moment when individual property can no longer be transformed into bourgeois property, into capital—from that moment, you say, individuality vanishes.

You must, therefore, confess that by "individual" you mean no other person than the bourgeois, than the middle-class owner of property. This person must indeed be swept out of the way, and made impossible.

Communism deprives no man of the power to appropriate the products of society: all that it does is to deprive him of the power to subjugate the labor of others by means of such appropriation.

It has been objected that upon the abolition of private property all work will cease, and universal laziness will overtake us.

According to this, bourgeois society ought long ago to have gone to the dogs through sheer idleness; for those of its members who work acquire nothing, and those who acquire anything do not work. The whole of this objection is but another expression of the tautology that there can no longer be any wage labor when there is no longer any capital.

All objections urged against the communistic mode of producing and appropriating material products have in the same way been urged against the communistic modes of producing and appropriating intellectual products. Just as to the bourgeois the disappearance of class property is the disappearance of production itself, so the disappearance of class culture is to him identical with the disappearance of all culture.

That culture the loss of which he laments is, for the enormous majority, a mere training to act as a machine.

But don't wrangle with us so long as you apply to our intended abolition of bourgeois property the standard of your bourgeois notions of freedom, culture, law, etc. Your very ideas are but the outgrowth of the conditions of your bourgeois production and bourgeois property, just as your jurisprudence is but the will of your class made into a law for all, a will whose essential character and direction are determined by the economic conditions of existence of your class.

The selfish misconception that induces you to transform into eternal laws of nature and of reason the social forms springing from your present mode of production and form of property—historical relations that arise and disappear in the progress of production—this misconception you share with every ruling class that has preceded you. What you see clearly in the case of ancient property, what you admit in the case of feudal property, you are of course forbidden to admit in the case of your own bourgeois form of property.

Abolition of the family! Even the most radical flare up at this infamous proposal of the Communists.

On what foundation is the present family, the bourgeois family, based? On capital, on private gain. In its completely developed form this family exists only among the bourgeoisie. But this state of things finds its complement in the practical absence of the family among the proletarians, and in public prostitution.

The bourgeois family will vanish as a matter of course when its complement vanishes, and both will vanish with the vanishing of capital.

Do you charge us with wanting to stop the exploitation of children by their parents? To this crime we plead guilty.

But, you will say, we destroy the most hallowed of relations when we replace home education by social.

And your education! Is not that also social, and determined by the social conditions under which you educate, by the intervention, direct or indirect, of society by means of schools, etc.? The Communists have not invented the intervention of society in education; they do but seek to alter the character of that intervention, and to rescue education from the influence of the ruling class.

The bourgeois claptrap about the family and education, about the hallowed co-relation of parent and child, becomes all the more disgusting, the more by the action of Modern Industry all family ties among the proletarians are torn asunder, and their children transformed into simple articles of commerce and instruments of labor.

But you Communists would introduce community of women, screams the whole bourgeoisie in chorus.

The bourgeois sees in his wife a mere instrument of production. He hears that the instruments of production are to be exploited in common, and, naturally, can come to no other conclusion than that the lot of being common to all will likewise fall to the women.

He has not even a suspicion that the real point aimed at is to do away with the status of women as mere instruments of production.

For the rest, nothing is more ridiculous than the virtuous indignation of our bourgeois at the community of women which, they pretend, is to be openly and officially established by the Communists. The Communists have no need to introduce community of women; it has existed almost from time immemorial.

Our bourgeois, not content with having the wives and daughters of their proletarians at their disposal, not to speak of common prostitutes, take the greatest pleasure in seducing each others' wives.

Bourgeois marriage is in reality a system of wives in common, and thus, at the most, what the Communists might possibly be reproached with is that they desire to introduce, in substitution for a hypocritically concealed, an openly legalized community of women. For the rest, it is self-evident that the abolition of the present system of production must bring with it the abolition of the community of women springing from that system, i.e., of prostitution both public and private.

The Communists are further reproached with desiring to abolish countries and nationalities.

The workingmen have no country. We cannot take away from them what they have not got. Since the proletariat must first of all acquire political supremacy, must rise to be the leading class of the nation, must constitute itself the nation, it is so far itself national, though not in the bourgeois sense of the word.

National differences, and antagonisms between peoples, are daily more and more vanishing, owing to the development of the bourgeoisie, to freedom of commerce, to the world market, to uniformity in the mode of production and in the conditions of life corresponding thereto.

The supremacy of the proletariat will cause them to vanish still faster. United action, of the leading civilized countries at least, is one of the first conditions for the emancipation of the proletariat.

In proportion as the exploitation of one individual by another is put an end to, the exploitation of one nation by another will also be put an end to. In proportion as the antagonism between classes within the nation vanishes, the hostility of one nation to another will come to an end.

The charges against communism made from a religious, a philosophical and, generally, from an ideological standpoint, are not deserving of serious examination.

Does it require deep intuition to comprehend that man's ideas, views, and conceptions—in a word, man's consciousness—changes with every change in the condition of his material existence, in his social relations and in his social life?

What else does the history of ideas prove than that intellectual production changes in character in proportion as material production is changed? The ruling ideas of each age have ever been the ideas of the ruling class.

When people speak of ideas that revolutionize society, they do but express the fact that within the old society the elements of a new one have been created, and that the dissolution of the old ideas keeps even pace with the dissolution of the old conditions of existence.

When the ancient world was in its last throes, the ancient religions were overcome by Christianity. When Christian ideas succumbed in the eighteenth century to rationalist ideas, feudal society fought its death battle with the then revolutionary bourgeoisie. The idea of religious liberty and freedom of conscience merely gave expression to the sway of free competition within the domain of knowledge.

"Undoubtedly," it will be said, "religious, moral, philosophical, and juridical ideas have been modified in the course of historical development. But religion, morality, philosophy, political science, and law constantly survived this change.

"There are, besides, eternal truths, such as Freedom, Justice, etc., that are common to all states of society. But communism abolishes eternal truths, it abolishes all religion and all morality, instead of constituting them on a new basis; it therefore acts in contradiction to all past historical experience."

What does this accusation reduce itself to? The history of all past society has consisted in the development of class antagonisms, antagonisms that assumed different forms at different epochs.

But whatever form they may have taken, one fact is common to all past ages, viz., the exploitation of one part of society by another. No wonder, then, that the social consciousness of past ages, despite all the multiplicity and variety it displays, moves within certain common forms, or general ideas, which cannot completely vanish except with the total disappearance of class antagonisms.

The Communist revolution is the most radical rupture with traditional property relations; no wonder that its development involves the most radical rupture with traditional ideas.

We have seen above that the first step in the revolution by the working class is to raise the proletariat to the position of ruling class, to win the battle of democracy.

The proletariat will use its political supremacy to wrest, by degrees, all capital from the bourgeoisie, to centralize all instruments of production in the hands of the state, i.e., of the proletariat organized as the ruling class; and to increase the total of productive forces as rapidly as possible.

Of course, in the beginning this cannot be effected except by means of despotic inroads on the rights of property, and on the conditions of bourgeois production, by means of measures, therefore, which appear economically insufficient and untenable, but which, in the course of the movement, outstrip themselves, necessitate further inroads upon the old social order, and are unavoidable as a means of entirely revolutionizing the mode of production.

These measures will of course be different in different countries.

Nevertheless, in the most advanced countries the following will be pretty generally applicable:

1. Abolition of property in land and application of all rents of land to public purposes.

2. A heavy progressive or graduated income tax.

3. Abolition of all right of inheritance.

4. Confiscation of the property of all emigrants and rebels.

5. Centralization of credit in the hands of the state, by means of a national bank with state capital and an exclusive monopoly.

6. Centralization of the means of communication and transport in the hands of the state.

7. Extension of factories and instruments of production owned by the state, the bringing into cultivation of wastelands, and the improvement of the soil generally in accordance with a common plan.

8. Equal liability of all to labor. Establishment of industrial armies, especially for agriculture.

9. Combination of agriculture with manufacturing industries; grad-

ual abolition of the distinction between town and country, by a more equable distribution of population over the country.

10. Free education for all children in public schools. Abolition of children's factory labor in its present form. Combination of education with industrial production, etc., etc.

When, in the course of development, class distinctions have disappeared, and all production has been concentrated in the hands of a vast association of the whole nation, the public power will lose its political character. Political power, properly so called, is merely the organized power of one class for suppressing another. If the proletariat during its contest with the bourgeoisie is compelled by the force of circumstances to organize itself as a class, if, by means of a revolution, it makes itself the ruling class and, as such, sweeps away by force the old conditions of production, then it will, along with these conditions, have swept away the conditions for the existence of class antagonisms, and of classes generally, and will thereby have abolished its own supremacy as a class.

In place of the old bourgeois society, with its classes and class antagonisms, we shall have an association in which the free development of each is the condition for the free development of all.

III

SOCIALIST AND COMMUNIST LITERATURE

1. Reactionary Socialism
2. Feudal Socialism

Owing to their historical position, it became the vocation of the aristocracies of France and England to write pamphlets against modern bourgeois society. In the French revolution of July, 1830, and in the English reform agitation, these aristocracies again succumbed to the hateful upstart. Thenceforth a serious political contest was altogether out of the question. A literary battle alone remained possible. But even in the domain of literature the old cries of the Restoration period had become impossible.

In order to arouse sympathy, the aristocracy were obliged to lose sight, apparently, of their own interests, and to formulate their indictment against the bourgeoisie in the interest of the exploited working class alone. Thus the aristocracy took their revenge by singing lampoons on their new master, and whispering in his ears sinister prophecies of coming catastrophe.

In this way arose feudal socialism; half lamentation, half lampoon;

half echo of the past, half menace of the future; at times, by its bitter, witty, and incisive criticism, striking the bourgeoisie to the very heart's core, but always ludicrous in its effect, through total incapacity to comprehend the march of modern history.

The aristocracy, in order to rally the people to them, waved the proletarian alms bag in front for a banner. But the people, so often as it joined them, saw on their hindquarters the old feudal coats of arms, and deserted with loud and irreverent laughter.

One section of the French Legitimists, and "Young England," exhibited this spectacle.

In pointing out that their mode of exploitation was different from that of the bourgeoisie, the feudalists forgot that they exploited under circumstances and conditions that were quite different, and that are now antiquated. In showing that under their rule the modern proletariat never existed, they forget that the modern bourgeoisie is the necessary offspring of their own form of society.

For the rest, so little do they conceal the reactionary character of their criticism that their chief accusation against the bourgeoisie amounts to this, that under the bourgeois regime a class is being developed which is destined to cut up root and branch the old order of society.

What they upbraid the bourgeoisie with is not so much that it creates a proletariat, as that it creates a revolutionary proletariat.

In political practice, therefore, they join in all coercive measures against the working class; and in ordinary life, despite their highfalutin phrases, they stoop to pick up the golden apples dropped from the tree of industry, and to barter truth, love, and honor for traffic in wool, beetroot sugar, and potato spirits.

As the parson has ever gone hand in hand with the landlord, so has clerical socialism with feudal socialism.

Nothing is easier than to give Christian asceticism a socialist tinge. Has not Christianity declaimed against private property, against marriage, against the state? Has it not preached, in the place of these, charity and poverty, celibacy and mortification of the flesh, monastic life and Mother Church? Christian Socialism is but the holy water with which the priest consecrates the heartburnings of the aristocrat.

Petty-Bourgeois Socialism

The feudal aristocracy was not the only class that was ruined by the bourgeoisie, not the only class whose conditions of existence pined and perished in the atmosphere of modern bourgeois society. The medieval burgesses and the small peasant bourgeoisie were the precursors of the modern bourgeoisie. In those countries which are but little developed, industrially and commercially, these two classes still vegetate side by side with the rising bourgeoisie.

In countries where modern civilization has become fully developed, a new class of petty bourgeois has been formed, fluctuating between proletariat and bourgeoisie, and ever renewing itself as a supplementary part of bourgeois society. The individual members of this class, however, are being constantly hurled down into the proletariat by the action of competition, and as modern industry develops, they can see the moment approaching when they will completely disappear as an independent section of modern society, to be replaced, in manufacture, agriculture and commerce, by overlookers, bailiffs and shopmen.

In countries like France, where the peasants constitute far more than half of the population, it was natural that writers who sided with the proletariat against the bourgeoisie should use, in their criticism of the bourgeois regime, the standard of the peasant and petty bourgeois, and from the standpoint of these intermediate classes should take up the cudgels for the working class. Thus arose petty-bourgeois socialism. Sismondi was the head of this school, not only in France but also in England.

This school of socialism dissected with great acuteness the contradictions in the conditions of modern production. It laid bare the hypocritical apologies of economists. It proved, incontrovertibly, the disastrous effects of machinery and division of labor; the concentration of capital and land in a few hands; overproduction and crises; it pointed out the inevitable ruin of the petty bourgeois and peasant, the misery of the proletariat, the anarchy in production, the crying inequalities in the distribution of wealth, the industrial war of extermination between nations, the dissolution of old moral bonds, of the old family relations, of the old nationalities.

In its positive aims, however, this form of socialism aspires either to restore the old means of production and of exchange, and with them the old property relations and the old society, or to cramp the modern means of production and of exchange within the framework of the old property relations that have been, and were bound to be exploded by those means. In either case, it is both reactionary and utopian.

Its last words are: corporate guilds for manufacture; patriarchal relations in agriculture.

Ultimately, when stubborn historical facts had dispersed all intoxicating effects of self-deception, this form of socialism ended in a miserable fit of the blues.

German or "True" Socialism

The socialist and communist literature of France, a literature that originated under the pressure of a bourgeoisie in power, and that was the expression of the struggle against this power, was introduced into Germany at a time when the bourgeoisie, in that country, had just begun its contest with feudal absolutism.

German philosophers, would-be philosophers, and *beaux esprits* eagerly seized on this literature, only forgetting that when these writings immigrated from France into Germany, French social conditions had not immigrated along with them. In contact with German social conditions, this French literature lost all its immediate practical significance and assumed a purely literary aspect. Thus to the German philosophers of the eighteenth century the demands of the first French Revolution were nothing more than the demands of "practical reason" in general, and the utterance of the will of the revolutionary French bourgeoisie signified in their eyes the laws of pure Will, of Will as it was bound to be, of true human Will generally.

The work of the German literati consisted solely in bringing the new French ideas into harmony with their ancient philosophical conscience, or rather, in annexing the French ideas without deserting their own philosophical point of view.

This annexation took place in the same way in which a foreign language is appropriated, namely by translation.

It is well known how the monks wrote silly lives of Catholic saints over the manuscripts on which the classical works of ancient heathendom had been written. The German literati reversed this process with the profane French literature. They wrote their philosophical nonsense beneath the French original. For instance, beneath the French criticism of the economic functions of money, they wrote "Alienation of Humanity," and beneath the French criticism of the bourgeois state they wrote, "Dethronement of the Category of the General," and so forth.

The introduction of these philosophical phrases at the back of the French historical criticisms they dubbed "Philosophy of Action," "True Socialism," "German Science of Socialism," "Philosophical Foundation of Socialism," and so on.

The French socialist and communist literature was thus completely emasculated. And since it ceased in the hands of the German to express the struggle of one class with the other, he felt conscious of having overcome "French onesidedness" and of representing, not true requirements, but the requirements of Truth, not the interests of the proletariat, but the interests of Human Nature, of Man in general, who belongs to no class, has no reality, who exists only in the misty realm of philosophical fantasy.

This German socialism which took its schoolboy task so seriously and solemnly, and extolled its poor stock in trade in such mountebank fashion, meanwhile gradually lost its pedantic innocence.

The fight of the German, and especially of the Prussian, bourgeoisie against feudal aristocracy and absolute monarchy—in other words, the liberal movement—became more earnest.

By this the long-wished-for opportunity was offered to "True Socialism" of confronting the political movement with the socialist demands, of hurling the traditional anathemas against liberalism, against representative government, against bourgeois competition, bourgeois freedom of the press, bourgeois legislation, bourgeois liberty and equality, and of preaching to the masses that they had nothing to gain, and everything to lose, by this bourgeois movement. German socialism forgot, in the nick of time, that the French criticism whose silly echo it was presupposed the existence of modern bourgeois society, with its corresponding economic conditions, and the political constitution adapted thereto, the very things whose attainment was the object of the pending struggle in Germany.

To the absolute governments, with their following of parsons, professors, country squires, and officials, it served as a welcome scarecrow against the threatening bourgeoisie.

It was a sweet finish after the bitter pills of floggings and bullets with which these same governments, just at that time, dosed the German working-class risings.

While this "True Socialism" thus served the government as a weapon for fighting the German bourgeoisie, it, at the same time, directly represented a reactionary interest, the interest of the German philistines. In Germany the petty-bourgeois class, a relic of the sixteenth century, and since then constantly cropping up again under various forms, is the real social basis of the existing state of things.

To preserve this class is to preserve the existing state of things in Germany. The industrial and political supremacy of the bourgeoisie threatens it with certain destruction; on the one hand, from the concentration of capital, on the other, from the rise of a revolutionary proletariat. "True Socialism" appeared to kill these two birds with one stone. It spread like an epidemic.

The robe of speculative cobwebs, embroidered with flowers of rhetoric, steeped in the dew of sickly sentiment, this transcendental robe in which the German socialists wrapped their sorry "eternal truths," all skin and bones, served to wonderfully increase the sale of their goods among such a public.

And on its part German socialism recognized, more and more, its own calling as the bombastic representative of the petty-bourgeois philistine.

It proclaimed the German nation to be the model nation, and the German petty philistine to be the typical man. To every villainous meanness of this model man it gave a hidden, higher socialistic interpretation, the exact contrary of its true character. It went to the extreme length of directly opposing the "brutally destructive" tendency of communism, and of proclaiming its supreme and impartial contempt of all class struggles. With very few exceptions, all the so-called socialist and communist publications that now (1847) circulate in Germany belong to the domain of this foul and enervating literature.

Conservative or Bourgeois Socialism

A part of the bourgeoisie is desirous of redressing social grievances, in order to secure the continued existence of bourgeois society.

To this section belong economists, philanthropists, humanitarians, improvers of the condition of the working class, organizers of charity, members of societies for the prevention of cruelty to animals, temperance fanatics, hole-and-corner reformers of every imaginable kind. This form of socialism has, moreover, been worked out into complete systems.

We may cite Proudhon's *Philosophie de la Misère* as an example of this form.

The socialistic bourgeois want all the advantages of modern social conditions without the struggles and dangers necessarily resulting therefrom. They desire the existing state of society minus its revolutionary and disintegrating elements. They wish for a bourgeoisie without a proletariat. The bourgeoisie naturally conceives the world in which it is supreme to be the best; and bourgeois socialism develops this comfortable conception into various more or less complete systems. In requiring the proletariat to carry out such a system, and thereby to march straightway into the social New Jerusalem, it but requires, in reality, that the proletariat should remain within the bounds of existing society, but should cast away all its hateful ideas concerning the bourgeoisie.

A second and more practical, but less systematic, form of this socialism sought to depreciate every revolutionary movement in the eyes of the working class by showing that no mere political reform, but only a change in the material conditions of existence, in economical relations, could be of any advantage to them. By changes in the material conditions of existence, this form of socialism, however,

by no means understands abolition of the bourgeois relations of production, an abolition that can be effected only by a revolution, but
administrative reforms, based on the continued existence of these
relations; reforms, therefore, that in no respect affect the relations
between capital and labor, but, at the best, lessen the cost, and simplify the administrative work, of bourgeois government.

Bourgeois socialism attains adequate expression when, and only
when, it becomes a mere figure of speech.

Free trade: for the benefit of the working class. Protective duties:
for the benefit of the working class. Prison reform: for the benefit of
the working class. This is the last word and the only seriously meant
word of bourgeois socialism.

It is summed up in the phrase: the bourgeois is a bourgeois—for
the benefit of the working class.

Critical-Utopian Socialism and Communism

We do not here refer to that literature which, in every great
modern revolution, has always given voice to the demands of the
proletariat: such as the writings of Babeuf and others.

The first direct attempts of the proletariat to attain its own ends
were made in times of universal excitement, when feudal society was
being overthrown. These attempts necessarily failed, owing to the
then undeveloped state of the proletariat, as well as to the absence of
the economic conditions for its emancipation, conditions that had yet
to be produced, and could be produced by the impending bourgeois
epoch alone. The revolutionary literature that accompanied these first
movements of the proletariat had necessarily a reactionary character.
It inculcated universal asceticism and social leveling in its crudest
form.

The socialist and communist systems properly so called, those of
St. Simon, Fourier, Owen, and others, spring into existence in the
early undeveloped period, described above, of the struggle between
proletariat and bourgeoisie (see Section I, Bourgeois and Proletarians).

The founders of these systems see, indeed, the class antagonisms,
as well as the action of the decomposing elements in the prevailing
form of society. But the proletariat, as yet in its infancy, offers to
them the spectacle of a class without any historical initiative or any
independent political movement.

Since the development of class antagonism keeps even pace with
the development of industry, the economic situation, as they find it,
does not as yet offer to them the material conditions for the emancipation of the proletariat. They therefore search after a new social
science, after new social laws that are to create these conditions.

Historical action is to yield to their personal inventive action, historically created conditions of emancipation to fantastic ones, and the gradual, spontaneous class organization of the proletariat to an organization of society specially contrived by these inventors. Future history resolves itself, in their eyes, into the propaganda and the practical carrying out of their social plans.

In the form of their plans they are conscious of caring chiefly for the interests of the working class, as being the most suffering class. Only from the point of view of being the most suffering class does the proletariat exist for them.

The undeveloped state of the class struggle, as well as their own surroundings, causes socialists of this kind to consider themselves far superior to all class antagonisms. They want to improve the condition of every member of society, even that of the most favored. Hence they habitually appeal to society at large, without distinction of class; nay, by preference to the ruling class. For how can people, when once they understand their system, fail to see in it the best possible plan of the best possible state of society?

Hence they reject all political, and especially all revolutionary action; they wish to attain their ends by peaceful means, and endeavor, by small experiments, necessarily doomed to failure, and by the force of example, to pave the way for the new social Gospel.

Such fantastic pictures of future society, painted at a time when the proletariat is still in a very undeveloped state, and has but a fantastic conception of its own position, correspond with the first instinctive yearnings of that class for a general reconstruction of society.

But these socialist and communist publications contain a critical element. They attack every principle of existing society. Hence they are full of the most valuable materials for the enlightenment of the working class. The practical measures proposed in them, such as the abolition of the distinction between town and country, of the family, of the carrying on of industries for the account of private individuals, and of the wage system, the proclamation of social harmony, the conversion of the functions of the state into a mere superintendence of production, all these proposals point solely to the disappearance of class antagonisms which were at that time only just cropping up, and which in these publications are recognized under their earliest, indistinct and undefined forms only. These proposals, therefore, are of a purely utopian character.

The significance of critical-utopian socialism and communism bears an inverse relation to historical development. In proportion as the modern class struggle develops and takes definite shape, this fantastic standing apart from the contest, these fantastic attacks on it, lose all practical value and all theoretical justification. Therefore, although the originators of these systems were in many respects revolutionary, their disciples have in every case formed mere reactionary sects. They hold fast to the original views of their masters, in opposition to the progressive historical development of the proletariat. They therefore endeavor, and that consistently, to deaden the class struggle and to reconcile the class antagonisms. They still dream of experimental relations of their social Utopias, of founding isolated "phalansteries," of establishing "Home Colonies," of setting up a "Little Icaria"—duodecimo editions of the New Jerusalem—and to realize all these castles in the air, they are compelled to appeal to the feelings and purses of the bourgeois. By degrees they sink into the category of the reactionary conservative socialists depicted above, differing from these only by more systematic pedantry, and by their fanatical and superstitious belief in the miraculous effects of their social science.

They therefore violently oppose all political action on the part of the working class; such action, according to them, can only result from blind unbelief in the new Gospel.

The Owenites in England and the Fourierists in France, respectively, oppose the Chartists and the "Reformists."

IV

POSITION OF THE COMMUNISTS IN RELATION TO THE VARIOUS EXISTING OPPOSITION PARTIES

Section II has made clear the relations of the Communists to the existing working-class parties, such as the Chartists in England and the Agrarian Reformers in America.

The Communists fight for the attainment of the immediate aims, for the enforcement of the momentary interests of the working class; but in the movement of the present, they also represent and take care of the future of that movement. In France the Communists ally themselves with the Social Democrats against the conservatives and radical bourgeoisie, reserving, however, the right to take up a critical position in regard to phrases and illusions traditionally handed down from the great Revolution.

In Switzerland they support the Radicals, without losing sight of the fact that this party consists of antagonistic elements, partly of democratic socialists in the French sense, partly of radical bourgeois.

In Poland they support the party that insists on an agrarian revolution as the prime condition for national emancipation, that party which fomented the insurrection of Cracow in 1846.

In Germany they fight with the bourgeoisie whenever it acts in a revolutionary way, against the absolute monarchy, the feudal squirearchy, and the petty bourgeoisie.

But they never cease, for a single instant, to instill into the working class the clearest possible recognition of the hostile antagonism between bourgeoisie and proletariat, in order that the German workers may straightway use, as so many weapons against the bourgeoisie, the social and political conditions that the bourgeoisie must necessarily introduce along with its supremacy, and in order that, after the fall of the reactionary classes in Germany, the fight against the bourgeoisie itself may immediately begin.

The Communists turn their attention chiefly to Germany because that country is on the eve of a bourgeois revolution that is bound to be carried out under more advanced conditions of European civilization, and with a more developed proletariat, than that of England was in the seventeenth, and of France in the eighteenth century, and because the bourgeois revolution in Germany will be but the prelude to an immediately following proletarian revolution.

In short, the Communists everywhere support every revolutionary movement against the existing social and political order of things.

In all these movements they bring to the front, as the leading question in each, the property question, no matter what its degree of development at the time.

Finally, they labor everywhere for the union and agreement of the democratic parties of all countries.

The Communists disdain to conceal their views and aims. They openly declare that their ends can be attained only by the forcible overthrow of all existing social conditions. Let the ruling classes tremble at a Communist revolution. The proletarians have nothing to lose but their chains. They have a world to win.

Workingmen of all countries, unite!

The Communist Party Program*

"Proletarians of all countries, unite!"

1. ALL of Germany is to be declared a united, indivisible republic.

2. Every German aged twenty-one is eligible to vote, provided he has no criminal record.

3. The representatives of the people are to be paid, so that workers shall also be able to sit in the parliament of the German people.

4. General arming of the people. In the future, the armies are to be at the same time working armies, so that the troops are no longer, as hitherto, consumers but, rather, producers of more than their maintenance cost.

This is, moreover, a means for the organization of labor.

5. The performance of justice is to be free of charge.

6. All feudal burdens, dues, socages, tithes, etc., which have hitherto burdened the country people, are abolished without any compensation.

7. Princely and other feudal landed estates, all mines, pits, etc., are transformed into state property. On those landed estates agricultural land will be cultivated on a large scale and with the most modern scientific methods for the benefit of the whole people.

8. Mortgages on peasant farms are declared to be state property. Interest on them is to be paid by the peasants to the state.

9. In the areas where tenant farming is developed, ground rent or tenure schilling is to be paid to the state as a tax.

---

* Marx and Engels, "Demands of the Communist Party in Germany," brochure written March 21–29, 1848; printed in Paris March 30, and in Cologne, September 10, 1848.

All the measures under Nos. 6, 7, 8, and 9 are conceived with a view toward diminishing the official and other burdens of the peasants and small tenant farmers, without decreasing the necessary means for the defrayal of state costs and without endangering production itself.

The landowner who is neither a peasant nor a tenant has no share in production at all. His consumption is therefore merely a misuse.

10. Private banks are to be replaced by state banks, whose paper currency is to have a legal rate of exchange.

This measure makes it possible to regulate the credit system in the interest of *all* the people and thereby undermines the domination of the big money men. As paper money by and by replaces gold and silver, it reduces the latter's value as an indispensable medium of exchange of bourgeois business and allows gold and silver to operate in foreign trade. This measure, finally, is necessary in order to tie conservative bourgeois interests to the revolution.

11. All means of transportation—railroads, canals, steamers, roads, posts, etc.—are taken over by the state. They are to be transformed into state property and put at the disposal of the impecunious class free of charge.

12. In the salary scale of all government officials there is to be no differential except that those with a family, that is, those who have greater needs, are to receive a higher salary than the others.

13. Complete separation of church and state. The clergy of all confessions are to be paid solely by their voluntary communities.

14. Limitation of the right of inheritance.

15. Introduction of heavy progressive taxes and abolition of consumer taxes.

16. Establishment of national workshops. The state guarantees all workers their existence and provides for those unable to work.

17. Universal, free education.

It is in the interest of the German proletariat, the small bourgeoisie, and the peasantry to work with all their energies for the realization of the above measures. For only through their realization will the millions of people in Germany who have hitherto been exploited by a small number, and who are in danger of further oppression, be able to attain the rights and power which belong to them as producers of all wealth.

The Committee:

KARL MARX   KARL SCHAPPER   H. BAUER   F. ENGELS

J. MOLL   W. WOLFF

Address of the Central Committee to the Communist League*

The Central Committee to the League

BROTHERS! In the two revolutionary years 1848–49 the League proved itself in double fashion: first, in that its members energetically took part in the movement in all places, that in the press, on the barricades, and on the battlefields they stood in the front ranks of the only completely revolutionary class, the proletariat. The League further proved itself in that its conception of the movement as laid down in the circulars of the congresses and of the Central Committee of 1847 as well as in the *Communist Manifesto* turned out to be the only correct one, that the expectations expressed in those documents were completely fulfilled and the conception of present-day social conditions, previously propagated only in secret by the League, is now on everyone's lips and is openly preached in the market places. At the same time the former firm organization of the League was considerably slackened. A large part of the members who directly participated in the revolutionary movement believed that the time for secret societies had gone by and that public activities alone were sufficient. The individual circles and communities allowed their connections with the Central Committee to become loose and gradually dormant. Consequently, while the Democratic party, the party of the petty bourgeoisie, organized itself more and more in Germany, the workers' party lost its only firm foothold, remained organized at the most in separate localities for local purposes, and in the general movement thus came completely under the domination and leadership of the

---

* Written in March, 1850, and published in London as a German-language leaflet. This text is based on the translation by the Institute of Marxism-Leninism, Moscow, 1966.

petty-bourgeois democrats. An end must be put to this state of affairs, the independence of all the workers must be restored. The Central Committee early realized this necessity and therefore in the winter of 1848–49 it sent an emissary, Josef Moll, to Germany for the reorganization of the League. Moll's mission, however, was without lasting effect, partly because the German workers at that time had not acquired sufficient experience and partly because it was interrupted by the insurrection of last May. Moll himself took up the musket, entered the Baden-Palatinate army, and fell on July 19[1] in the encounter at the Murg. The League lost in him one of its oldest, most active, and most trustworthy members, one who had been active in all the congresses and central committees and even prior to this had carried out a series of missions with great success. After the defeat of the revolutionary parties of Germany and France in July, 1849, almost all the members of the Central Committee came together again in London, replenished their numbers with new revolutionary forces, and set about the reorganization of the League with renewed zeal.

Reorganization can be carried out only by an emissary, and the Central Committee considers it extremely important that the emissary should leave precisely at this moment when a new revolution is impending, when the workers' party, therefore, must act in the most organized, most unanimous, and most independent fashion possible if it is not to be exploited and taken in tow again by the bourgeoisie as in 1848.

Brothers! We told you as early as 1848 that the German liberal bourgeois would soon come to power and would immediately turn their newly acquired power against the workers. You have seen how this has been fulfilled. In fact it was the bourgeois who, immediately after the March movement of 1848, took possession of the state power and used this power at once to force the workers, their allies in the struggle, back into their former oppressed position. Though the bourgeoisie was not able to accomplish this without uniting with the feudal party, which had been disposed of in March, without finally even surrendering power once again to this feudal absolutist party, still it has secured conditions for itself which in the long run, owing to the financial embarrassment of the government, would place power in its hands and would safeguard all its interests, if it were possible for the revolutionary movement now to assume a so-called peaceful development. The bourgeoisie, in order to safeguard its rule, would not even need to make itself obnoxious by violent measures against the people, since all such violent steps have already been taken by the

---

1. The date was June 29, 1849.

feudal counterrevolution. Developments, however, will not take this peaceful course. On the contrary, the revolution, which will accelerate this development, is near at hand, whether it will be called forth by an independent uprising of the French proletariat or by an invasion of the Holy Alliance against the revolutionary Babylon.

And the role, this treacherous role which the German liberal bourgeois played in 1848 against the people, will in the impending revolution be taken over by the democratic petty bourgeois, who at present occupy the same position in the opposition as the liberal bourgeois before 1848. This party, the Democratic party, which is far more dangerous to the workers than the previous liberal one, consists of three elements:

1. Of the most advanced sections of the big bourgeois, which pursue the aim of the immediate complete overthrow of feudalism and absolutism. This faction is represented by the one-time Berlin compromisers, by the tax resisters.

2. Of the democratic-constitutional petty bourgeois, whose main aim during the previous movement was the establishment of a more or less democratic federal state as striven for by their representatives, the lefts in the Frankfurt Assembly, and later by the Stuttgart parliament, and by themselves in the campaign for the Reich Constitution.

3. Of the republican petty bourgeois, whose ideal is a German federated republic after the manner of Switzerland, and who now call themselves red and social-democratic because they cherish the pious wish of abolishing the pressure of big capital on small capital, of the big bourgeois on the small bourgeois. The representatives of this faction are the members of the democratic congresses and committees, the leaders of the democratic associations, the editors of the democratic newspapers.

Now, after their defeat, all these factions call themselves republicans or reds, just as the republican petty bourgeois in France now call themselves socialists. Where, as in Württemberg, Bavaria, etc., they still find opportunity to pursue their aims constitutionally, they seize the occasion to retain their old phrases and to prove by deeds that they have not changed in the least. It is evident, moreover, that the altered name of this party does not make the slightest difference in its attitude to the workers, but merely proves that they are now obliged to turn against the bourgeois, which is united with absolutism, and to seek support in the proletariat.

The petty-bourgeois Democratic party in Germany is very powerful; it comprises not only the great majority of the bourgeois inhabitants of the towns, the small people in industry and trade and the guild masters; it numbers among its followers also the peasants and the rural proletariat, insofar as the latter has not yet found a support in the independent urban proletariat.

The relation of the revolutionary workers' party to the petty-bourgeois democrats is this: it marches with them against the faction which it aims at overthrowing, it opposes them in everything whereby they seek to consolidate their position in their own interests.

Far from desiring to revolutionize all society for the revolutionary proletarians, the democratic petty bourgeois strive for a change in social conditions by means of which existing society will be made as tolerable and comfortable as possible for them. Hence they demand, above all, diminution of state expenditure by a curtailment of the bureaucracy and shifting the chief taxes onto the big landowners and bourgeois. Further, they demand the abolition of the pressure of big capital on small, through public credit institutions and laws against usury, by which means it will be possible for them and the peasants to obtain advances, on favorable conditions, from the state instead of from the capitalists; they also demand the establishment of bourgeois property relations in the countryside by the complete abolition of feudalism. To accomplish all this they need a democratic state structure, either constitutional or republican, that will give them and their allies, the peasants, a majority; also a democratic communal structure that will give them direct control over communal property and over a series of functions now performed by the bureaucrats.

The domination and speedy increase of capital is further to be counteracted partly by restricting the right of inheritance and partly by transferring as many functions as possible to the state. As far as the workers are concerned, it remains certain above all that they are to remain wage workers as before; the democratic petty bourgeois desire only better wages and a more secure existence for the workers and hope to achieve this through partial employment by the state and through charity measures; in short, they hope to bribe the workers by more or less concealed alms and to break their revolutionary potency by making their position tolerable for the moment. The demands of the petty-bourgeois democracy here summarized are not put forward by all of its factions at the same time and only a very few members of them consider that these demands constitute definite aims in their entirety. The further separate individuals or factions among them go, the more of these demands will they make their own, and those few who see their own program in what has been outlined above might believe that thereby they have not put forward the utmost that can be demanded from the revolution. But these demands can in no wise suffice for the party of the proletariat. While the democratic petty bourgeois wish to bring the revolution to a conclusion as quickly as possible, and with the achievement, at most, of the above demands, it is our interest and our task to make the revolution permanent, until all more or less possessing classes have been forced out of their position of dominance, until the proletariat has conquered state power and the association of proletarians, not only in one country but in all the dominant countries of the world, has advanced so far that competition among the proletarians of these countries has ceased and that at least the decisive productive forces are concentrated in the hands of the proletarians. For us the issue cannot be the alteration of private property but only its annihilation, not the smoothing over of class antagonisms but the abolition of classes, not the improvement of existing society but the foundation of a new one. That during the further development of the revolution the petty-bourgeois democracy will for a moment obtain predominating influence in Germany is not open to doubt. The question therefore arises as to what the attitude of the proletariat and in particular of the League will be in relation to it:

1. During the continuance of the present conditions where the petty-bourgeois democrats are likewise oppressed.

2. In the next revolutionary struggle, which will give them the upper hand.

3. After this struggle, during the period of preponderance over the overthrown classes and the proletariat.

1. At the present moment, when the democratic petty bourgeois are everywhere oppressed, they preach in general unity and reconciliation to the proletariat, they offer it their hand and strive for the establishment of a large opposition party which will embrace all shades of opinion in the Democratic party, that is, they strive to entangle the workers in a party organization in which general social-democratic phrases predominate, behind which their special interests are concealed, and in which the particular demands of the proletariat may not be brought forward for the sake of beloved peace. Such a union would turn out solely to their advantage and altogether to the disadvantage of the proletariat. The proletariat would lose its whole independent, laboriously achieved position and once more sink down to being an appendage of official bourgeois democracy. This union must therefore be most decisively rejected. Instead of once again stooping to serve as the applauding chorus of the bourgeois democrats, the workers, and above all the League, must exert themselves to establish an independent, secret and public organization of the workers' party alongside the official democrats and make each section the central point and nucleus of workers' societies

in which the attitude and interests of the proletariat will be discussed independently of bourgeois influences. How far the bourgeois democrats are from seriously considering an alliance in which the proletarians would stand side by side with them with equal power and equal rights is shown, for example, by the Breslau democrats who in their organ, the *Neue Oder-Zeitung*, most furiously attack the independently organized workers, whom they style socialists. In the case of a struggle against a common adversary no special union is required. As soon as such an adversary has to be fought directly, the interests of both parties coincide for the moment, and as previously, so also in the future, this connection, calculated to last only for the moment, will arise of itself. It is self-evident that in the impending bloody conflicts, as in all earlier ones, it is the workers, in the main, who will have to win the victory by their courage, determination, and self-sacrifice. As previously, so also in this struggle, the mass of the petty bourgeois will as long as possible remain hesitant, undecided, and inactive, and then, as soon as the issue has been decided, will seize the victory for themselves, will call upon the workers to maintain tranquillity and return to their work, will guard against so-called excesses and bar the proletariat from the fruits of victory. It is not in the power of the workers to prevent the petty-bourgeois democrats from doing this, but it is in their power to make it difficult for them to gain the upper hand as against the armed proletariat, and to dictate such conditions to them that the rule of the bourgeois democrats will from the outset bear within it the seeds of their downfall, and that their subsequent extrusion by the rule of the proletariat will be considerably facilitated. Above all things, during the conflict and immediately after the struggle, the workers must counteract, as much as possible, the bourgeois endeavors to allay the storm, and must compel the democrats to act upon their present terrorist phrases. Their actions must be so aimed as to prevent the direct revolutionary excitement from being suppressed again immediately after the victory. On the contrary, they must keep it alive as long as possible. Far from opposing so-called excesses—instances of popular revenge against hated individuals or public buildings that are associated only with hateful recollections—such instances must not only be tolerated but the leadership of them taken in hand. During the struggle and after the struggle the workers must at every opportunity put forward their own demands alongside the demands of the bourgeois democrats. They must demand guarantees for the workers as soon as the democratic bourgeois set about taking over the government. If necessary they must obtain these guarantees by force, and in general they must see to it that the

new rulers pledge themselves to all possible concessions and promises
—the surest way to compromise them. In general, they must in
every way restrain as far as possible the intoxication of victory and
the enthusiasm for the new state of things which make their appearance after every victorious street battle, by a calm and dispassionate
estimate of the situation and by unconcealed mistrust of the new
government. Alongside the new official governments they must establish simultaneously their own revolutionary workers' governments,
whether in the form of municipal committees or municipal councils
or in the form of workers' clubs or workers' committees, so that the
bourgeois-democratic governments not only immediately lose the
support of the workers but from the outset see themselves supervised and threatened by authorities which are backed by the whole
mass of the workers. In a word, from the first moment of victory,
mistrust must be directed no longer against the conquered reactionary
party, but against the workers' previous allies, against the party that
wishes to exploit the common victory for itself alone.

2. But in order to be able energetically and threateningly to
oppose this party, whose treachery to the workers will begin from
the first hour of victory, the workers must be armed and organized.
The arming of the whole proletariat with rifles, muskets, cannon,
and munitions must be put through at once; the revival of the old
Citizens' Guard directed against the workers must be resisted. However, where the latter is not feasible the workers must attempt to
organize themselves independently as a proletarian guard with commanders elected by themselves and with a general staff of their own
choosing, and to put themselves at the command not of the state
authority but of the revolutionary community councils which the
workers will have managed to get adopted. Where workers are employed at the expense of the state they must see that they are armed
and organized in a separate corps with commanders of their own
choosing or as part of the proletarian guard. Arms and ammunition
must not be surrendered on any pretext; any attempt at disarming
must be frustrated, if necessary by force. Destruction of the influence
of the bourgeois democrats upon the workers, immediate independent
and armed organization of the workers, and the enforcement of
conditions as difficult and compromising as possible upon the inevitable momentary rule of the bourgeois democracy—these are the
main points which the proletariat and hence the League must keep
in view during and after the impending insurrection.

3. As soon as the new governments have consolidated their
positions to some extent, their struggle against the workers will
begin. Here, in order to be able to offer energetic opposition to the
democratic petty bourgeois, it is above all necessary that the

workers shall be independently organized and centralized in clubs. After the overthrow of the existing governments, the Central Committee will, as soon as it is at all possible, betake itself to Germany, immediately convene a congress, and put before the latter the necessary proposals for the centralization of the workers' clubs under a leadership established in the chief seat of the movement. The speedy organization of at least a provincial interlinking of the workers' clubs is one of the most important points for the strengthening and development of the workers' party; the immediate consequence of the overthrow of the existing governments will be the election of a national representative assembly. Here the proletariat must see to it:

a. That no groups of workers are barred on any pretext or by any kind of trickery on the part of local authorities or government commissioners.

b. That everywhere workers' candidates are put up alongside the bourgeois-democratic candidates, they consist as far as possible of members of the League, and that their election is promoted by all possible means. Even where there is no prospect whatsoever of their being elected, the workers must put up their own candidates in order to preserve their independence, to count their forces, and to bring before the public their revolutionary attitude and party standpoint. In this connection they must not allow themselves to be seduced by such arguments of the democrats as, for example, that by so doing they are splitting the Democratic party and making it possible for the reactionaries to win. The ultimate intention of all such phrases is to dupe the proletariat. The advance which the proletarian party is bound to make by such independent action is infinitely more important than the disadvantage that might be incurred by the presence of a few reactionaries in the representative body. If the democracy from the outset comes out resolutely and terroristically against the reaction, the influence of the latter in the elections will be destroyed in advance.

The first point on which the bourgeois democrats will come into conflict with the workers will be the abolition of feudalism. As in the first French Revolution, the petty bourgeois will give the feudal lands to the peasants as free property, that is to say, try to leave the rural proletariat in existence and form a petty-bourgeois peasant class which will go through the same cycle of impoverishment and indebtedness which the French peasant is now still going through.

The workers must oppose this plan in the interest of the rural proletariat and in their own interest. They must demand that the confiscated feudal property remain state property and be converted into workers' colonies cultivated by the associated rural proletariat with all the advantages of large-scale agriculture, through which the principle of common property immediately obtains a firm basis in the midst of the tottering bourgeois property relations. Just as the democrats combine with the peasants so must the workers combine with the rural proletariat. Further, the democrats will either work directly for a federated republic or, if they cannot avoid a single and indivisible republic, they will at least attempt to cripple the central government by the utmost possible autonomy and independence for the communities and provinces. The workers, in opposition to this plan, must not only strive for a single and indivisible German republic, but, also within this republic, for the most determined centralization of power in the hands of the state authority. They must not allow themselves to be misguided by the democratic talk of freedom for the communities, of self-government, etc. In a country like Germany, where there are still so many relics of the Middle Ages to be abolished, where there is so much local and provincial obstinacy to be broken, it must under no circumstances be permitted that every village, every town, and every province should put a new obstacle in the path of revolutionary activity, which can proceed with full force only from the center. It is not to be tolerated that the present state of affairs should be renewed, that Germans must fight separately in every town and in every province for one and the same advance. Least of all is it to be tolerated that a form of property, namely, communal property, which still lags behind modern private property and which everywhere is necessarily passing into the latter, together with the quarrels resulting from it between poor and rich communities, as well as communal civil law, with its trickery against the workers, that exists alongside state civil law, should be perpetuated by a so-called free communal constitution. As in France in 1793 so today in Germany it is the task of the really revolutionary party to carry through the strictest centralization.

We have seen how the democrats will come to power with the next movement, how they will be compelled to propose more or less socialistic measures. It will be asked what measures the workers ought to propose in reply. At the beginning of the movement, of course, the workers cannot yet propose any directly communistic measures. But they can:

1. Compel the democrats to interfere in as many spheres as possible of the hitherto existing social order, to disturb its regular course and to compromise themselves, as well as to concentrate the utmost possible productive forces, means of transport, factories, railways, etc., in the hands of the state.

2. They must drive the proposals of the democrats, who in any

case will not act in a revolutionary but in a merely reformist manner, to the extreme and transform them into direct attacks upon private property; thus, for example, if the petty bourgeois propose purchase of the railways and factories, the workers must demand that these railways and factories shall be simply confiscated by the state without compensation as being the property of reactionaries. If the democrats propose proportional taxes, the workers must demand progressive taxes; if the democrats themselves put forward a moderately progressive tax, the workers must insist on a tax with rates that rise so steeply that big capital will be ruined by it; if the democrats demand the regulation of state debts, the workers must demand state bankruptcy. Thus the demands of the workers must everywhere be governed by the concessions and measures of the democrats.

If the German workers are not able to attain power and achieve their own class interests without going completely through a lengthy revolutionary development, they at least know for a certainty this time that the first act of this approaching revolutionary drama will coincide with the direct victory of their own class in France and will be very much accelerated by it.

But they themselves must do the utmost for their final victory by clarifying their minds as to what their class interests are, by taking up their position as an independent party as soon as possible, and by not allowing themselves to be seduced for a single moment by the hypocritical phrases of the democratic petty bourgeois into refraining from the independent organization of the party of the proletariat. Their battle cry must be: The Revolution of Permanence.

Statutes of the Communist League*

1. THE AIM of the Communist League is the destruction of the old society—and overthrow of the bourgeoisie[1]—using all means of propaganda and political struggle; the spiritual, political, and economic emancipation of the proletariat; the carrying out of the Communist revolution. In the various stages of development which the struggle of the proletariat has to go through, the League always represents the interests of the whole movement, always attempting to unite and to organize all the revolutionary energy of the proletariat. The League remains secret and indissoluble so long as the revolution has not attained its final goal.

2. Only he can be a member who combines the following conditions:

a. Freedom from all religion, practical renunciation of every churchly association and all ceremonies not ordered by civil law.

b. Insight into the conditions, course of development, and final goal of the proletarian movement.

c. Keeping away from all associations and partial efforts inimical or obstructive to the League.

d. Ability and eagerness for propaganda, unshakable and loyal conviction, revolutionary energy.

e. Strictest secrecy about all League affairs.

3. Eligibility for membership is decided by unanimous vote of

---

* Drafted in Cologne by the Central Committee, under the direction of Marx and Engels, after the Communist split in London in September, 1850. The statutes were adopted by the London branch of the Communist League on January 5, 1851, when Marx was present.
1. Insertion by Marx.

the whole community. As a rule, new members are received by the chairman in the presence of the assembled community. Members take an oath of absolute submission to the decisions of the League.

4. He who violates the conditions of membership is excluded. Exclusion of individuals is decided by majority vote of the community. Whole communities can be excluded by the Central Authority if so instructed by the District Community. Those excluded are denounced to the whole League and are subject to surveillance like all other suspected characters.

5. The League is organized into communities, districts, a Central Authority, and a Congress.

6. Communities consist of at least three members each, of the same locality. Each community elects a chairman, who conducts the meetings, and a deputy, who acts as treasurer.

7. The communities of each country or province are under a Chief Community, a District, which is appointed by the Central Authority. The communities are in direct contact with their districts, the districts with the Central Authority.

8. The communities meet regularly at least every fourteen days; they are in at least monthly correspondence with their districts, and the district communities at least bimonthly with the Central Authority. The Central Authority reports every three months on the state of the League.

9. The chairmen and deputies of the communities and districts are chosen annually and are removable by their electors at any time. Members of the Central Authority are removable only by the Congress.

10. Every member of the League has to pay monthly dues, the minimum of which is determined by the Congress. Half of these dues go to the district and half to the Central Authority, and are used to cover administrative costs, distribution of propaganda, and the sending out of emissaries. The districts bear the cost of correspondence with their communities. Every three months the dues are sent to the district, which transmits half of the total income to the Central Authority and at the same time gives an accounting of income and expenditure to the communities. The Central Authority submits an accounting to the Congress. Extraordinary costs are met by extraordinary contributions.

11. The Central Authority is the executive organ of the whole League. It consists of at least three members, selected and recruited by the districts; its seat is determined by the Congress and it is accountable only to the Congress.

12. The Congress is the legislative organ of the whole League. It

consists of representatives of the district assemblies, which elect one deputy for every five communities.

13. The District Assembly is the representative of the districts; it meets regularly every quarter in the district center under the chairmanship of the head of the Chief Community for consultation about district affairs. Each community sends one deputy. The district assembly for the election of League representatives meets invariably in the middle of July of every year.

Art. 5 Community
Art. 6 District
Art. 7 Central Authority
Art. 8 Congress
Art. 9 Reception into the League
Art. 10 Expulsion from the League/ Money . . .[2]

14. Fourteen days after the meeting of the district election assemblies, the Congress meets at the seat of the Central Authority, if no other place has been decided upon.

15. The Congress receives from the Central Authority, which has a seat in it but no vote, an account of its whole activity and the state of the League; it declares the basic policies to be followed by the League, decides on changes in the statutes, and determines the seat of the Central Authority for the following year.

16. In urgent cases the Central Authority may call the Congress to an extraordinary session, which would then consist of the deputies elected by the districts the last time.

17. Conflicts among individual members of the same community are conclusively settled by the community; the same in districts, by the district community; and among various districts, by the Central Authority. Personal complaints about members of the Central Authority are the jurisdiction of the Congress. Conflicts among communities of the same district are decided by the district community; among communities and their district or various districts, by the Central Authority. Still, in the first instance, the convening of the district assemblies, and in the second, that of the Congress, are open as avenues for redress. The Congress also decides on all conflicts between the Central Authority and the subordinate authorities of the League.

---

2. Illegible in Marx's handwriting.

The Communist Trial in Cologne: The Prussian Press and Two London Journals*

To the Editor of the Morning Advertiser:

SIR: The undersigned call your attention to the attitude of the Prussian press, including even the most reactionary papers, such as the *Neue Preussische Zeitung*, during the pending trial of the Communists at Cologne, and to the honorable discretion they observe at the moment where scarcely a third part of the witnesses have been examined, where none of the produced documents have been verified, and not a word has fallen yet from the defense. While those papers, at the worst, represent those Cologne prisoners and the undersigned, their London friends, in accordance with the public accuser, as dangerous conspirators who alone are responsible "for the whole history of Europe of the latter four years, and for all the revolutionary commotions of 1848 and 1849"—there are in London two public organs, the *Times* and another, which have not hesitated to represent the Cologne prisoners and the undersigned as a "gang of sturdy beggars, swindlers, etc." The undersigned address to the English public the same demand which the defenders of the accused have addressed to the public in Germany—to suspend their judgment and to wait for the end of the trial. Were they to give further

---

* On October 28, 1852, Marx wrote to Engels: "In next Saturday's (October 30) *Advertiser* you will find a short statement about the infamous articles in the *Times* and the *Daily News*. It is signed: 'F. Engels, F. Freiligrath, K. Marx, W. Wolff.' The same will appear in a number of weeklies. I believe that this time the Prussian government will be exposed as never before, and will be shown that it does not deal here with democratic blockheads." The piece, written in English October 28, appeared in the *Morning Advertiser*, October 30, 1852. It was also published in the *People's Paper*, October 30; the *Spectator*, October 28; the *Examiner*, October 30; the *Leader*, October 30.

explanations at the present time, the Prussian government might obtain the means of baffling a revelation of police tricks, perjury, forgery of documents, falsification of dates, thefts, etc., unprecedented even in the records of Prussian political justice. When that revelation shall have been made in the course of the present proceedings, public opinion in England will know how to qualify the anonymous scribes of the *Times* and the other morning paper, who constitute themselves the advocates and mouthpieces of the most odious government spies.

We are, sir, your obedient servants,

F. ENGELS.
F. FREILIGRATH.
K. MARX.
W. WOLFF.

A Final Declaration on
the Recent Cologne Trials*

To the Editor of the *Morning Advertiser:*

SIR: The undersigned[1] discharge a duty to themselves and toward their new-condemned friends at Cologne by laying before the English public a statement of facts connected with the recent monster trial in that city, which have not been made sufficiently known by the London press.

Eighteen months have been wasted on the mere getting up of the evidence for this trial. During the whole of that time our friends have been kept in solitary confinement, deprived of all means of occupation and even of books; those who became ill were refused proper medical treatment, or if they obtained it the condition in which they were placed prevented them from benefiting thereby. Even after the "act of accusation" had been communicated to them, they were prohibited, in direct violation of the law, from conferring with their lawyers. And what were the pretexts for this protracted cruel imprisonment? After the lapse of the first nine months the "Chamber of Accusation" declared that there were no grounds on which a charge could be maintained, and that therefore the instruction had to be recommenced. It was recommenced. Three months later, at the opening of the assizes, the public accuser pleaded that the mass of the evidence had grown into a larger bulk than he had as yet been able to digest. And after three further months the trial was

---

* Written November 20, 1852; published in the *Morning Advertiser* November 29.

    1. The "undersigned" included four names, but Marx was the author and Engels revised the text. On November 19 Marx wrote to Engels: "Enclosed is a Declaration for the *English* press ... which you ought to *anglicize* better and conciser."

[125]

again adjourned, on the ground of the illness of one of the chief government witnesses.

The real cause of all this delay was the fear of the Prussian government to confront the meager substance of the facts with the pompously announced "unheard-of revelations." At last the government succeeded in selecting a jury such as the Rhenish provinces had never yet beheld, composed of six reactionary nobles, four members of the *haute finance*, and two members of the bureaucracy.

Now what was the evidence laid before this jury? Merely the absurd proclamations and correspondence of a set of ignorant fantasists, importance-seeking conspirators, the tools and associates at once of one Cherval, an avowed agent of the police. The greater part of those papers were formerly in the possession of a certain Oswald Dietz in London. During the Great Exhibition the Prussian police, while Dietz was absent from his home, had his drawers broken open and thus obtained the desired documents by a common theft. These papers, in the first instance, furnished the means of discovering the so-called Franco-German plot at Paris. Now the proceeding at Cologne proved that those conspirators, and Cherval, their Paris agent, were the very political opponents of the defendants and [their] undersigned London friends. But the public accuser pleaded that a mere personal quarrel had prevented the latter from taking part in the plot of Cherval and his associates. By such argumentation it was intended to prove the moral complicity of the Cologne defendants in the Paris plot; and while the accused of Cologne were thus made responsible for the acts of their very enemies, the professed friends of Cherval and his associates were produced by the government in court, not at the bar like the defendants, say, [but] in the witness box, to depose against them. This, however, appeared too bad. Public opinion forced the government to look out for less equivocal evidence. The whole of the police machinery was set to work under the direction of one Stieber, the principal government witness at Cologne, royal councilor of police and chief of the Berlin criminal police. In the sitting of October 23 Stieber announced that an extraordinary courier from London had delivered to him most important documents, proving undeniably the complicity of the accused in an alleged conspiracy with the undersigned. "Among other documents the courier had brought him the original minute book of the sittings of the secret society presided over by Dr. Marx, and with whom the defendants had been in correspondence." Stieber, however, entangled himself in discordant statements as to the date on which his courier was to have reached him. Dr.

Schneider, the leading counsel for the defense, charged him directly with perjury, upon which Stieber ventured no other reply than to fall back upon his dignity of the representative of the crown, entrusted with a most important mission from the very highest authority of state. As to the minute book, Stieber declared twice on his oath that it was the "genuine minute book of the London Communist Society," but later on, closely pressed by the defense, he admitted that it might be a mere book of votes, taken by one of his spies. At length, from his own evidence, the book was proved to be a deliberate forgery and its origin traced back to three of Stieber's London agents, Grieff, Fleury, and Hirsch. The latter has since himself admitted that he composed the book under the guidance of Fleury and Grieff. So decisive was the evidence at Cologne on the point that even the public accuser declared Stieber's important document a "most unfortunate book," a mere forgery. The same personage refused to take notice of a letter forming part of government evidence in which the handwriting of Dr. Marx had been imitated, that document too having turned out a gross and palpable forgery. In the same manner every other document brought forward in order to prove, not the revolutionary tendencies, but the activity of the accused in some distant plot, turned out a forgery of the police. So great were the government's fears of exposure that it not only caused the Post to retain all documents addressed to the counsel for the defense, but the latter to be intimidated by Stieber with a threatened prosecution for his "criminal correspondence" with the undersigned.

If now, in spite of the absence of all convincing proof, a verdict has nevertheless been obtained, that result has only become possible, at the hands even of such a jury, by the retroactive application of the new criminal code, under which the *Times* and the Peace Society themselves might at any time be tried on the formidable charge of high treason. Moreover, the trial at Cologne had assumed, by its duration, and by the extraordinary means employed on the part of the prosecution, such vast dimensions that an acquittal would have equaled a condemnation of the government; and a conviction prevailed generally in the Rhenish provinces that the immediate consequence of an acquittal would be suppression of the entire institution of the jury.

We are, sir, your most obedient servants,

> F. Engels.
> F. Freiligrath.
> K. Marx.
> W. Wolff.

The Cologne Jury*

BUT, DEAR FRIENDS, all theory is gray.[1] The "so-called social question and its solution," Saedt remarks, "has recently occupied the qualified and the unqualified." Saedt, at any rate, belongs to the qualified, for Chief Procurator Seckendorff officially "qualified" him for the study of socialism and communism three months ago. The Saedts of all times and places have always thought a Galileo "unqualified" for the investigation of celestial movements, but considered an Inquisitor, who declared him a heretic, "qualified." *E pur si muove*.[2]

In the persons of the defendants, the unarmed revolutionary proletariat confronted a jury representing the dominant classes. The defendants were therefore condemned precisely because they faced such a jury. What could have shaken the bourgeois conscience of the jurors in a moment, as it did shake public opinion, was the unmasking of government intrigue and corruption before their very eyes. But, said the jurors, if the Prussian government risked such infamous and at the same time foolhardy means against the defendants—when, so to speak, it gambled its European reputation—then the defendants, small party though they may be, must be damned dangerous and their doctrine a real force. The government has violated all the rules of the criminal code in order to protect us from the criminal monster. Let us, on our part, violate our small *point d'honneur* in order to save the honor of the government. Let us be grateful, let us condemn.

---

* Concluding remarks in *Revelations About the Cologne Communist Trial*, written October–December, 1852, published in Basel in 1853.
    1. Goethe, *Faust* (First Part).
    2. "And still it [the earth] moves": said to have been spoken by Galileo at his trial in Rome in 1633.

In pronouncing *Guilty*, the Rhenish nobility and the Rhenish bourgeoisie echoed the French bourgeoisie, which after December 2 [Louis Bonaparte's *coup d'état*] cried out: "Only theft can save property, only perjury can save religion, only bastardy can save the family, only disorder can save order!"

The whole political structure prostituted itself in France. But no other institution prostituted itself as deeply as the French courts and their juries. Let us surpass the French judges and juries, cried the jury and the court in Cologne. In the Cherval case, immediately after the *coup d'état*, the Paris jury acquitted Nette, against whom there was more evidence than against any Cologne defendant. Let us surpass the jury of the *coup d'état* of December 2. Let us condemn Roeser, Buergers, etc., subsequent to Nette.

Thus the superstitious belief in the jury system, which was still prevalent in Rhenish Prussia, has been broken forever. It has become clear that the jury system is a class court of the privileged classes, set up to bridge gaps in the law with the width of the bourgeois conscience.

Jena![3] This is the final word for a government that needs such means to maintain itself, and for a society that needs such a government for its protection. This is the last word of the Cologne Communist Trial . . . JENA!

---

3. At the battle of Jena, October 14, 1806, the Prussians were routed and forced to capitulate to Napoleon.

Personal Letters

From Wilhelm Weitling, letter to Moses Hess
BRUSSELS, MARCH 31, 1846

Dear Hess!

Last evening we met again *in pleno*. Marx brought with him a man whom he presented to us as a Russian,[1] and who never said a word throughout the whole evening. The question was: What is the best way to carry on propaganda in Germany? Seiler posed the question, but he said he could not go into further details now, since some delicate matters would have to be touched upon, etc. Marx kept on pressing him, but in vain. Both became excited, Marx violently so. In the end, the latter took up the question. His résumé was:

1. An examination must be made of the Communist party.

2. This can be achieved by criticizing the incompetent and separating them from the sources of money.

3. This examination is now the most important thing that can be done in the interest of communism.

4. He who has the power to carry authority with the moneyed men also has the means to displace the others and would probably apply it.

---

1. Present at the meeting of the Communist Correspondence Committee were: Marx and Engels, Philippe Gigot, Louis Heilberg, Sebastian Seiler, Edgar von Westphalen (Marx's brother-in-law), and Joseph Weydemeyer, as well as the Russian Annenkov, who published the report of the session in *Vyestnik Yevropy*, April, 1880, and in the *Neue Zeit*, 1883, in German.

5. "Handicraft communism" and "philosophical communism"[2] must be opposed, human feeling must be derided; these are merely obfuscations. No oral propaganda, no provision for secret propaganda, in general the word propaganda not to be used in the future.

6. The realization of communism in the near future is out of the question; the bourgeoisie must first be at the helm.

7. Marx and Engels argued vehemently against me. Weydemeyer spoke quietly. Gigot and Edgar did not say a word. Heilberg opposed Marx from an impartial viewpoint, at the very end Seiler did the same, bitterly but with admirable calm. I became vehement, Marx surpassed me, particularly at the end when everything was in an uproar, he jumping up and down in his office. Marx was especially furious at my résumé. I had said: The only thing that came out of our discussion was that he who finds the money may write what he pleases. . . .

That Marx and Engels will vehemently criticize my principles is now certain. Whether or not I will be able to defend myself as I would like to do, I don't know. Without money Marx cannot criticize and I cannot defend myself; nevertheless, in an emergency it may not matter that I have no money. I believe Marx and Engels will end by criticizing themselves through their own criticism. In Marx's brain I see nothing more than a good encyclopedia, but no genius. His influence is felt through other personalities. Rich men made him editor, *voilà tout*. Indeed, rich men who make sacrifices have a right to see or have investigations made into what they want to support. They have the power to assert this right, but the writer also has the power, no matter how poor he is, not to sacrifice his convictions for money. I am capable of sacrificing my convictions for the sake of unity. I put aside my work on my system when I received protests against it from all directions. But when I heard in Brussels that the opponents of my system intended to publish splendid systems in well-financed translations, I completed mine and made an effort to bring it to the man [Marx]. If this is not supported, then it is entirely in order to make an examination. Jackass that I was, I had hitherto believed that it would be better if we used all our own qualities against our *enemies* and encouraged especially those that bring forth persecutions in the struggle. I had thought it would be better to influence the people and, above all, to organize a portion of them for the propagation of our popular writings. But Marx and Engels do not share this view, and in this they are strengthened by their rich supporters. All

---

2. Weitling added: "These distinctions were used first by Marx, or by somebody else, not by me."

right! Very good! Splendid! I see it coming. I have often found
myself in similar circumstances, and always things turned out for the
best. . . .

Your,
WEITLING

Letter written in French to Pierre Joseph Proudhon (in Paris)
BRUSSELS, MAY 5, 1846

Dear Proudhon:

Since I left Paris I have often thought of writing to you; but circumstances beyond my control have prevented me from doing it.
Please believe me that overbusyness and vexations connected with
moving to another house are the only reasons for my silence.

And now *in medias res.* Together with two of my friends, Frederick Engels and Philippe Gigot (both of them in Brussels), I have
organized a continuing Correspondence [Committee] with German
communists and socialists not only for a discussion of scientific questions but also for a review of popular writings and socialist propaganda, as a means of using them in Germany. The main aim of our
Correspondence, however, will be to bring German socialists in contact with French and English socialists, to inform foreigners about
socialist movements in Germany and Germans in Germany about the
progress of socialism in France and England. In this way differences
of opinion can come to light, and one can attain an exchange of ideas
and impartial criticism. This is a step the socialist movement has to
take in its literary expression in order to get rid of nationalistic limitations. And at the moment of action it is certainly extremely useful
for everyone to be informed about affairs abroad as much as about
those in his own country.

In addition to the communists in Germany, our Correspondence
will also include German socialists in Paris and London. Our contacts
with the English are already established; as to France, we all believe
that we could find there no better correspondent than yourself. You
know that the English and the Germans have hitherto honored you
more than your own countrymen.

Thus you see that what is involved here is the creation of a
regular Correspondence and to secure for it the means of following
the socialist movement in various countries, to attain rich and manifold results which no individual could achieve by his own work alone.

Should you accept our proposition, the postage of the letters you will receive, as well as those which you forward to us, will be paid here, since the money collections in Germany are designed to cover the cost of the Correspondence.

The local address you would use is: M. Philippe Gigot, 8 rue Bodenbrock. This is also the address for letters sent from Brussels.

I need not add that this whole Correspondence must be kept in strictest secrecy on your part, since we have to be careful not to compromise our friends in Germany.

Please reply soon,[1] and accept the assurance of my sincere friendship.

Your devoted
KARL MARX

From letter to Joseph Weydemeyer (in New York)
LONDON, MARCH 5, 1852

Dear Weywy!

. . . Disraeli, the new Lord of the Exchequer, writes to his constituents under date of March 1: "We shall endeavor to terminate the *strife of classes* which, of late years, has exercised so pernicious an influence on the welfare of this kingdom."

To this the *Times* remarks on March 2: "If anything were ever to divide classes in this country beyond reconciliation, and leave no chance of a just and honorable peace, it would be a tax on foreign corn."

And so that not even such an ignorant "character" as Heinzen should imagine that the aristocracy is *for* and the bourgeoisie *against* the Corn Laws, that the former want "monopoly" and the latter "freedom"—only a philistine views the contradictions in such an ideological form—it is only necessary to remark that in the eighteenth century the aristocrats in England were for "freedom" (in commerce) and the bourgeois for "monopoly," the same position we see at this moment held by the two classes in Prussia in regard to corn laws. The *Neue Preussische Zeitung* is the most rabid free-trader.

Finally, in your place I would remark to the gentlemen democrats in general that they would do better first to acquaint themselves with

---

1. On May 17, 1846, Proudhon replied; he rejected the proposal that he become a member of the Correspondence Committee on the ground that he was an opponent of revolutionary methods and of communism.

the bourgeois literature before they begin to bark about contradictions. The gentlemen should study, for example, the works of Thierry, Guizot, John Wade, etc., to understand the past "history of classes." They should familiarize themselves with elementary political economy before they undertake to criticize the critiques of political economy. It suffices, for instance, merely to open Ricardo's great work to find on the first page the words with which he begins his preface:

"The produce of the earth—all that is derived from its surface by the united application of labor, machinery, and capital—is divided among *three classes* of the community; namely the proprietor of the land, the owner of the stock or capital necessary for its cultivation, and the laborers by whose industry it is cultivated."

How little bourgeois society in the United States has developed intellectually in regard to an understanding of the class struggle is most brilliantly illustrated by H. C. Carey (of Philadelphia), the only important North American economist. He attacks Ricardo, the classical representative of the bourgeoisie and the most stoical opponent of the proletariat, as a man whose work is the arsenal for anarchists, socialists, and all other enemies of the bourgeois order. He reproaches not only Ricardo but also Malthus, Mill, Say, Torrens, Wakefield, MacCulloch, Senior, Whately, R. Jones, etc.—these economic dancing masters of Europe—with tearing up society and spreading civil war by their demonstration that the economic foundations of various classes must give rise to a necessary and ever growing antagonism among them. He attempts to refute them, not, like the silly Heinzen, by linking the existence of classes with the existence of *political* privileges and *monopolies*, but by attempting to show that *economic* conditions—rents (landed property), *profit* (capital), and wages (wage labor)—instead of being conditions of struggle and antagonism, are rather conditions of association and harmony. Naturally, all he proves is that the "undeveloped" conditions in the United States are, for him, "normal conditions."

As far as I am concerned, the credit for having discovered the existence and the conflict of classes in modern society does not belong to me. Bourgeois historians presented the historical development of this class struggle, and economists showed its economic anatomy, long before I did. What I did that was new was to prove (1) that the *existence of classes* is linked to *predetermined historical phases of the development of production;* (2) that the class struggle necessarily leads to the *dictatorship of the proletariat;* and (3) that this dictatorship itself is only the transition leading to the *abolition of all classes* and the establishment of a *classless society*. Ignorant louts like

Heinzen, who deny not only the struggle but also the existence of classes, only prove that, despite all their bleeding-heart swaggering and humanistic yelping, they consider the social relationships in which the bourgeoisie rules the last product, the *ne plus ultra* of history, that they are merely the lackeys of the bourgeoisie, a servitude which is the more disgusting as these louts understand the transitory necessity of the bourgeois regime least of anyone.

From letter to Frederick Engels (in Manchester)
LONDON, JULY 27, 1854

Dear Engels:

. . . A book that has interested me very much is Thierry's *History of the Formation and Progress of the Third Estate*, 1853. It is remarkable how indignant this gentleman, *le père* of the "class struggle" in French historiography, becomes, in his preface, at the "new people" who now see an antagonism between the bourgeoisie and the proletariat, and who claim to detect traces of this antagonism even in the history of the Third Estate before 1789. He takes great pains to prove that the Third Estate includes all social ranks except nobles and clergy, and that the bourgeoisie plays its part as the representative of all the other elements. He quotes, for example, from the reports of the Venetian Embassy: *"Questi che si chiamano li stati del regno sono di tre ordini di persone, cioè del clero, della nobilità, e del restante di quelle persone che, per voce comune, si può chiamare populo"* [Those who are called the estates of the realm consist of three orders of persons, namely, the clergy, the nobility, and the rest of those persons who by common consent may be called the people]. Had Mr. Thierry read our work, he would know that the bourgeoisie's decisive opposition to the people naturally begins only when the bourgeoisie as the Third Estate ceases to be opposed to the clergy and the nobility. In regard to the "roots in history" of "an antagonism born only yesterday," his book provides the best proof that these "roots" came into existence with the Third Estate. From the *"Senatus populusque Romanus"* ["the Senate and the Roman people"] the critic, otherwise clever in his own way, ought to have concluded that in Rome there was never any other antagonism but that between the Senate and the people. What interested me was to see from the documents he quotes that the word *"catalla," "capitalia"*—capital—arises with the appearance of the communes. Moreover, he has proved despite himself that nothing did more to retard the French bourgeoisie's victory than the fact that it did not decide until 1789 to make common cause with the peasants. He describes correctly if not coherently:

1. How from the first, or at least since the rise of the towns, the French bourgeoisie gains too much influence by constituting itself the parliament, the bureaucracy, etc., and not, as happened in England, merely through commerce and industry.

2. From his account, it can well be demonstrated how class arises —when the various forms that lie at the center of gravity at different times, and the various factions that gain influence through these forms, are breaking down. In my opinion, this series of metamorphoses leading up to domination by a class has never before—at least so far as his material is concerned—been presented in this way. Unfortunately, in dealing with the *maîtrises, jurandes* [guilds, officials], etc.—in short, with the forms in which the industrial bourgeoisie developed itself— he has limited himself almost entirely to generalities, although here too he alone knows the material. What he develops and emphasizes well is the conspiratorial and revolutionary character of the municipal movement in the twelfth century. The German emperors, Frederick I and II, for example, issued edicts against these *"communiones," "conspirationes," "conjurationes"* ["communes," "conspiracies," "sworn confederacies"] quite in the spirit of the German Federal Diet.[1] For instance, in 1226 Frederick II takes it upon himself to declare all "consulates"[2] and other free municipal bodies in the cities of Provence null and void: *"Pervenit nuper ad notitiam nostram quod quarumdam civitatum, villarum, et aliorum locorum universitates ex proprio motu constituerunt juridictiones, potestates [Potestad], consulatus, regimina et alia quaedam statuta . . . et cum jam apud quadam . . . in abusum et pravam consuetudinem inoleverunt . . . nos ex imperiali auctoritate tam juridictiones, etc., atque concessiones super his, per comites Provinciae et Forcalquerii ab eis obtentas, ex certa scientia revocamus, et inania esse censemus."*[3]

Further: *"Conventiculas quoque omnes et conjurationes in civitatibus et extra . . . inter civitatem et civitatem et inter personam et*

---

1. The Diet of the German Confederation, established in 1815 and continuing until 1866; it had its seat in Frankfurt.

2. In the Middle Ages members of the municipal councils in Provence were called consuls.

3. "It has recently come to our attention that the citizenry of certain cities, market towns, and other places, have, of their own accord, constituted tribunals, authorities, consulates, administrations and certain other institutions of this kind . . . and that since in some of them . . . this has already led to abuse and malpractices . . . we hereby, by virtue of our imperial authority, revoke these tribunals, etc., and also the concessions obtained, of our sure knowledge, by the Counts of Provence and of Forcalquier, and declare them null and void."

personam, seu inter civitatem et personam, omnibus modis fieri prohibemus" (*Constitutio pacis Frederici I*).[4]

"Quod nulla civitas, nullum oppidum, communiones, constitutiones, colligationes, confederationes, vel conjurationes aliquas, quocumque nomine censeantur, facere possent; et quod nos, sine domini sui assensu, civitatibus seu oppidis in regno nostro constitutis, auctoritatem faciendi communiones, constitutiones . . . conjurationes aliquas, quaecumque nomina imponantur eisdem, non poteramus nec debegamus impertiri" (*Henrici regis sententia contra communiones civitatum*).[5]

Isn't this exactly the same stiff German professorial style which at a later period used to fulminate out of the "Central Commission of the Confederation"?[6] The *commune jurée* [sworn commune—based on oath] in Germany penetrated no further than Trier,[7] and there Emperor Frederick I put an end to it in 1161: *"Communio quoque civium trevirensium, quae et conjuratio dicitur, quam nos in civitate destruximus . . . quae et postea, sicut audivimus, reiterata est, cassetur et in irritum revocetur."*[8]

This policy of the German emperors was utilized by the French kings to give secret support to the *"conjurationes"* and *"communiones"* in Lorraine, Alsace, Dauphiné, Franche-Comté, Lyonnais, etc., and detach them from the German Empire: *"Sicut ad culminis nostri pervenit notitiam, rex Franciae . . . sinceritatem fidei vestrae molitur corrumpere"* (*Rodolphus I, epistula ad cives de Besancon*).[9]

Just the same policy as that pursued by those fellows who made the Italian cities Guelph.[10]

It is often funny to see how the word *"communio"* used to be

---

4. "We prohibit also all associations and sworn confederacies within and without the cities . . . between city and city, between person and person, or between city and person, of whatever kind they may be" (Peace Charter of Frederick I).

5. "That no city and no market town may set up communes, constitutions, unions, leagues, or sworn confederacies of any kind, no matter what they may call themselves; and that without the agreement of their lord we neither can nor ought to allow the cities and markets to establish communes, constitutions, or sworn confederacies of any kind, no matter by what name they may call themselves" (Decree of King Henry against city communes).

6. The Central Commission of Inquiry set up in Karlsbad in 1819, under Metternich's leadership, to investigate "demagogical intrigues" against German states.

7. Marx's own birthplace.

8. "The commune of the citizens of Trier, which is also called sworn confederacy, which we have abolished in the city . . . and which, as we have heard, was nevertheless later established anew, shall be dissolved and declared null and void."

9. "According to information which has reached Our Highness, the King of France . . . is seeking to undermine the sincerity of your loyalty" (Rudolph I, letter to the citizens of Besançon).

10. The Italian political party which sided with the popes against the German emperors between the twelfth and fifteenth centuries.

heaped with abuse, just as communism is today. Thus, for example, the parson Guibert de Nogent writes: "*Communio, novum ac pessimum nomen*" [Communio is a new and very bad name].

There is often something pathetic about the way the narrow-minded burghers of the twelfth century invited the peasants to flee to the cities, the *communio jurata* [sworn communes]. Thus, for example, the charter of St. Quentin says: "They [the burghers of St. Quentin] have sworn jointly each to give common aid to his confederate, to have common counsel, common responsibility, and common defense. Jointly we have determined that whoever shall enter our commune and give us his aid, whether by reason of flight or fear of his enemies or for some other offense . . . shall be allowed to enter the commune, *for the gate is open to all;* and if his lord has unjustly detained his goods and does not hold them rightfully, we shall execute justice on that account."

From letter to Engels (in Manchester)
LONDON, OCTOBER 8, 1858

Dear Frederick:
. . . With the favorable turn of world trade at this moment (although the enormous accumulations of money in the banks of London, Paris, and New York show that things are as yet far from being all right), it is at least consoling that in Russia the revolution has begun, for I regard the convocation of "Notables" at Petersburg as such a beginning. Similarly, in Prussia things are worse than in 1847, and the ridiculous delusions as to the middle-class propensities of the Prince of Prussia will be dissolved in wrath. It will do the French no harm to see that the world "mov't" (Pennsylvania English) without them. At the same time there are extraordinary movements among the Slavs, especially in Bohemia, which are indeed counterrevolutionary but nevertheless add to the ferment. The Russian war of 1854–55, lousy though it was, and little as its results harmed the Russians (Turkey, rather, was the only one harmed), has nevertheless hastened the present turn of events in Russia. The only thing that made the Germans' revolutionary movement such a complete satellite of France was Russia's attitude. With an internal movement in Muscovy this bad joke will come to an end. As soon as things there develop somewhat more clearly, we will have proof of how far the worthy State Councilor Haxthausen has allowed himself to be taken in by the "authorities" and by the peasants they have drilled.

We cannot deny that bourgeois society has experienced its sixteenth century for the second time—a sixteenth century which I hope will sound its death knell just as the first one thrust it into existence. The particular task of bourgeois society is the establishment of the world market, at least in outline, and of production based on that market. Since the world is round, this seems to have been completed by the colonization of California and Australia and the opening up of China and Japan. The difficult question for us is this: On the Continent the revolution is imminent and will also immediately assume a socialist character. Is it not bound to be crushed in this small corner, in view of the fact that in a much greater territory the movement of bourgeois society is still in the ascendant?

In regard to China specifically, I have assured myself through an exact analysis of the movement of trade since 1836, first, that the increase of English and American exports, 1844–46, proved in 1847 to be a pure fraud, and that also in the following ten years the average remained practically stationary, while the imports from China into England and America grew enormously; second, that the opening up of the Five Ports and the seizure of Hongkong only resulted in the trade moving from Canton to Shanghai. The other "emporiums" do not count. The main reason for the failure of this market seems to be the opium trade, to which indeed all increase in the export trade to China is continually confined; but added to this is the internal economic organization of the country, its miniature-scale agriculture, etc., which will take an enormous amount of time to break down. England's present treaty with China [concluded in June, 1858, after the Opium War], which in my opinion was worked out by Palmerston in conjunction with the Cabinet of Petersburg and given to Lord Elgin on his journey, is a mockery from beginning to end.

Can you give me your sources on the progress of the Russians in Central Asia? I will use the materials in any case for the *Free Press*.[1] . . .

Yours,

K.M.

---

1. Engels, "The Penetration of Russia into Central Asia," *New-York Daily Tribune*, November 3, 1858. Marx published this article, with some changes, in the *Free Press*, November 24, 1858.

Darwin, whom I have looked up again, amuses me when he says he is applying the "Malthusian" theory *also* to plants and animals, as if with Mr. Malthus the whole joke did not lie in the fact that his theory does *not* apply to plants and animals but only to people—and in geometrical progression—in contrast to plants and animals. It is remarkable how Darwin discerns among beasts and plants his English society with its division of labor, competition, opening up of new markets, "inventions," and the Malthusian "struggle for existence." It is Hobbes's *bellum omnium contra omnes* [war of all against all], and it reminds one of Hegel's phenomenology, in which civil society is described as a "spiritual animal kingdom," while in Darwin the animal kingdom figures as civil society.

Letter to Wilhelm Blos (in Hamburg)
LONDON, NOVEMBER 10, 1877

Dear Blos:

I was very glad at last to get a sign of life from *Dir* [thee]. (That *"Dir"* slipped naturally from my pen. Let us in future stick to *"Sie"* [you].) In the matter of the abominable Isolde [Kurz], I have long ago proposed a severance of relations and have vainly blustered against her.

Wherever *la Place* is written with a capital P, it always denotes the Place Vendôme, because that was the headquarters of the Commandant of the National Guard, who in Paris was then [during the Commune of 1871] the same as what we call "Town Major."

In regard to the *"suppression de l'état,"* an expression which Lissagaray himself will change in the second French edition, its meaning is no different from the one developed in my pamphlet, *The Civil War in France.* You can translate it in brief: "The elimination (or suppression) of the class state."

I "grudge not" (as Heine says[1]), nor does Engels. Neither of us gives a rap for popularity. Proof, for example, of this aversion for all

---

1. Heinrich Heine, *Lyrisches Intermezzo,* poem 18.

personality cult is that during the existence of the International I have never permitted the numerous expressions of recognition from various countries, with which I was pestered, to be publicized, and have never answered them except occasionally with a reprimand. When Engels and I first entered the secret communist society[2] we did so on condition that everything promoting a superstitious belief in authority be removed from the statutes. (Later, Lassalle acted in exactly the opposite direction.)

But events like those of the last Party Congress [at Gotha, May 27–29, 1877]—thoroughly exploited by the enemies of the party abroad—have compelled us in any case to be circumspect in our relations with "Party Comrades in Germany."

For the rest, the state of my health makes it necessary, at doctor's orders, to limit my working time to the completion of my work [*Capital*]; and Engels, who works on various major projects,[3] continues to contribute to the *Vorwärts*.[4]

I would be amused to hear more about the "experience of my connections with Father Beckx."[5]

Engels will write you one of these days.

With best regards from my wife and daughter Eleanor,

Totus tuus [all yours],

KARL MARX

---

2. The Communist League, founded in 1847, which Marx and Engels joined that year.

3. Engels was then at work on his *Anti-Düehring* and *Dialectics of Nature*.

4. The organ of the German Socialist Workers party.

5. In his letter to Marx, October 30–November 6, 1877, Blos wrote that the *Norddeutsche Allgemeine Zeitung* frequently connected Marx's International with Father Beckx's Jesuit order.

FRANCE

Chronology:
France, 1848, 1851

1848

FEBRUARY 22   *Demonstrations in Paris by workers, students, and others against the government of François Guizot, King Louis Philippe's Premier; barricades are put up and fighting begins.*

FEBRUARY 23   *Louis Philippe replaces Guizot with Count Louis-Mathieu Molé, but the workers continue fighting and by morning of February 24 become masters of Paris.*

FEBRUARY 24   *Louis Philippe abdicates in favor of his son, but a rump meeting of the Chamber of Deputies ignores the latter and chooses a provisional government of moderate republicans, which fuses with a more radical group at the Hôtel de Ville. That evening the republic is proclaimed.*

The right wing of the Provisional Government, dominated by the writer Alphonse de Lamartine, is willing to accept a moderate republic with universal suffrage; the left wing, under the influence of Louis Blanc, aims at radical social-economic reforms along the lines of Blanc's book, Organisation du Travail *(1839).*

FEBRUARY 26   *National* ateliers [*workshops*] *are set up in Paris.*

FEBRUARY 28   *Louis Blanc establishes the* Commission of the Luxemburg, *a parliament of workers and employers, to discuss common problems, but it is soon deserted by the employers. To regain control of the government, the right wing arranges for elections, brings*

[145]

troops into Paris, and attempts to win over the National Guard to the "cause of order."

MARCH 17   *The alarmed workers organize a vast demonstration, which is moved into moderate paths by Louis Blanc, but it does not succeed in quieting the middle class's fear of the "specter of communism."*

APRIL 16   *A second mass demonstration of workers in Paris fails to take power.*

APRIL 23   *Elections to the National Assembly strengthen the moderate republicans, giving them 500 seats, as against less than 100 for Louis Blanc's left wing. Legitimists (pro-Bourbon) receive around 100 seats, Orléanists about 200.*

MAY 15   *Defeated in the election, the workers organize a monster procession, invade the National Assembly, overthrow the government, and set up a new provisional government. This soon collapses, but the alarmed conservatives move to close the national workshops, now with more than 100,000 members.*

JUNE 23–26   *The workers' reply is an insurrection, resulting in bloody street fighting. The Assembly appoints General Louis Cavaignac temporary dictator, to suppress the insurrection.*

JULY–AUGUST   *In this period of reaction radical newspapers are censored and secret societies suppressed.*

NOVEMBER 4   *The National Assembly completes a new constitution providing for a single Chamber and a strong president.*

DECEMBER 10   *The presidential elections give Prince Louis Napoleon, nephew of Napoleon I, 5,327,345 votes, as against 1,879,298 for his opponents (Cavaignac, Lamartine, Thiers, and Ledru-Rollin).*

DECEMBER 20   *Louis Napoleon takes the oath as President of the Second French Republic. He promptly appoints a ministry of Orléanists, headed by Barrot, despite republican domination of the National Assembly.*

1851

DECEMBER 2   *In a coup d'état President Louis Napoleon overthrows the Republic and declares himself Emperor Napoleon III.*

The Suppression of
the June, 1848, Revolution[*]

THE PARIS WORKERS are crushed by superior force, they did not surrender. They are *beaten*, but their opponents are *defeated*. The momentary triumph of brute force is bought with the destruction of all the illusions and imaginings of the February Revolution, with the dissolution of the whole old-republican party, with the splitting of the French nation into two nations—a nation of owners and a nation of workers. The tricolor republic now has only one color, the color of the beaten, the *color of blood*. She has become a *red republic*.

No reputable republicans, whether *National* or *Réforme*, were on the side of the people! Without other leaders and without other means than indignation itself, the people withstood the combined bourgeoisie and soldiery longer than any French regime, equipped with all the military apparatus, had ever been able to resist the people with a fraction of the bourgeoisie on their side. So that the last illusion of the people could vanish and thereby lead to a complete break with the past, the usual poetic trimmings of French uprisings —the enthusiastic bourgeois youth, the students of the École Polytechnique, the tricorns—all had to stand side by side with the bourgeoisie. The pupils of the medical faculty had to deny the help of science to the wounded plebeians. Science does not exist for the plebeians who committed the unspeakable and unheard-of crime of risking a fight for their own existence, instead of that of Louis Philippe or M. Marrast.

The last official residue of the February Revolution, the Executive Commission, has drifted away like a misty apparition under the

* From "Die Junirevolution," in *Neue Rheinische Zeitung*, June 29, 1848.

gravity of events. Lamartine's star shells were transformed into Cavaignac's incendiary rockets.

The *fraternité*, the brotherhood of the opposing classes, of which the one exploits the other, this *fraternité*, proclaimed in February, written in big letters on the face of Paris, on every jail and on every barracks—has for its true, unadulterated, prosaic expression: *civil war*, civil war in its most frightful aspect, war of labor against capital. This brotherhood flamed from all the windows of Paris on the evening of June 25, illuminating the Paris of the bourgeoisie while the Paris of the proletariat burned, bled, and moaned.

The brotherhood lasted only so long as the interest of the bourgeoisie fraternized with the interest of the proletariat. Pedants of the old revolutionary tradition of 1793; socialist system builders who begged the bourgeoisie for the people and who were allowed to deliver long sermons and to compromise themselves only so long as the proletarian lion had to be lulled to sleep; republicans who yearned for the whole old bourgeois order after the departure of the crowned head; dynastic [pro-Orléans] oppositionists, for whom the fall of a dynasty was subordinate to the chance of getting a ministerial post; Legitimists [pro-Bourbons], who did not want to throw away the livery but only to change its style—all these were the allies with whom the people made their February revolution. What the people instinctively hated in Louis Philippe was not Louis Philippe but the crowned rule of a class, capital on the throne. But generous as always, it imagined that it had destroyed its enemy after it had toppled the *common* enemy, the enemy of its enemies.

The February Revolution was the beautiful revolution, the revolution of universal sympathy, while the contradictions that burst forth against the monarchy remained undeveloped and slumbered side by side in harmony, while the social conflict which formed its background had won only a tenuous existence, the existence of the phrase, the word. The June Revolution is the ugly revolution, the repulsive revolution, because reality took the place of the phrase, because the republic bared the head of the monster itself when it knocked off its sheltering and secret crown.

Order! was Guizot's war cry. *Order!* cried Sébastiani, the Guizot henchman, when Warsaw became Russian. *Order!* cried Cavaignac, the brutal voice of the French National Assembly and of the republican bourgeoisie.

Order! thundered the grapeshot as it tore the bodies of the proletariat.

None of the numerous revolutions of the French bourgeoisie since 1789 was an attempt against *order*, because each left intact the rule of the class, the slavery of the workers, and the bourgeois order, no matter how often the political form of that rule and that slavery changed. June had laid hands on that order. Woe to that June!

Under the Provisional Government it was respectable—more than that, it was *necessary*, politically as well as ideologically—to preach to the workers, who, as thousands of official placards proclaimed, "put at the disposal of the Republic three months of misery," that the February Revolution was made in their own interest, that it concerned itself only with the *interests of the workers*. With the opening of the National Assembly, one became factual. It now was a matter, in the words of Minister Trélat, of "restoring labor to its old conditions." In other words, the workers fought in February only in order to be thrown into an industrial crisis.

The business of the National Assembly consisted of undoing February, at least for the workers, and throwing them back into the old relationships. But this did not happen, because it is as little in the power of the assembly as in that of a king to call out to an industrial crisis of universal character and say: *No further!* The National Assembly, in its brutal eagerness to put an end to the vexing February speeches, did not itself understand the measures that were possible in the framework of the old relationships. It pressed Paris workers, aged seventeen to twenty-five, into the army or threw them into the streets; it expelled foreigners from Paris to Sologne without giving them the termination pay that was owed them; it guaranteed adult Parisians the bread of charity in the militarily organized workshops, under the condition that they would not participate in people's meetings, that is, that they would cease to be republicans. Neither the sentimental rhetoric of February nor the brutal legislature of May 15 was sufficient now. Decisions had to be made factually and practically. Do you have a rabble that made the revolution for *you* or for *us?* The bourgeoisie put the question in such a way that in June it had to be answered—with grapeshot and barricades.

And yet, as a representative of the people [François-Joseph Ducoux] said on June 25, stupor has affected the whole National Assembly. It is bewildered, as question and answer drench the pavements of Paris in blood—some are bewildered because their illusions have vanished in powder smoke, others because they cannot understand how the people dared to represent their very own interests *independently*, by themselves. They take recourse to *Russian money*, *English money, Bonapartist eagle, the fleur-de-lis*, and amulets of all sorts to explain this extraordinary event. But both sides of the Assembly feel that an immeasurable chasm separates them from the people. Neither dares to speak up for the people.

As soon as stupor is over, rage breaks out, and the majority rightly hisses those miserable utopians and hypocrites who commit the anachronism of mouthing the word *fraternité*, brotherhood. What is involved here is the abolition of this word and the illusions concealed in its manifold womb. . . .

The deep abyss which has opened before us, should it mislead the democrats and lead us to imagine that the struggles for political forms are without content, illusory, void?

Only weak and cowardly spirits can raise such a question. The collisions produced by the conditions of bourgeois society itself must be fought out, they cannot be imagined away. The best political form is the one in which the social contradictions are neither obliterated nor violently and artificially, and therefore superficially, fettered. The best political form is the one that permits free struggle and hence leads to a solution.

We will be asked whether we have no tears, no sighs, no word for the victims who fell before the fury of the people, for the National Guard, the Mobile Guard, the Republican Guard, the rank and file.

The state will take care of their widows and orphans, decrees will glorify them, solemn funeral processions will inter their remains, the official press will declare them immortal, the European press will pay them homage from East to West.

But the plebeians, torn by hunger, reviled by the press, abandoned by the physicians, cursed by the respectable thieves as firebrands and galley slaves, their women and children plunged into boundless misery, their best survivors deported overseas—for them the laurels on the darkling brow, that is the *privilege*, that is the *right of the democratic press.*

The Paris *Réforme* on French Conditions[*]

Cologne, November 2

EVEN *before* the June uprisings, we repeatedly exposed the illusions of the republicans of the tradition of 1793, the republicans of *La Réforme* (of Paris). The June Revolution and the movement that grew out of it are gradually forcing these utopian republicans to open their eyes.

An editorial in the October 29 issue of *La Réforme* shows us how this party is struggling between its old fancies and the new facts.

La Réforme says: "For a long time, the struggles, which with us had as their aim the control of the government, have been *class struggles:* struggles of the bourgeoisie and the people against the nobility at the outset of the First Republic; surrender of the armed people abroad, rule of the bourgeoisie at home, under the Empire; attempts at restoration of feudalism under the old-line Bourbons; finally, the triumph and rule of the bourgeoisie in 1830—such is our history."

La Réforme adds with a sigh: "It is, surely, with regret that we speak of *classes,* of godless and hateful differences; but we cannot ignore the fact that these differences exist."

This means: *La Réforme*'s republican optimism has hitherto seen only "*citoyens*"; history has moved in on it so directly that it can no longer talk away the division of these "*citoyens*" into "bourgeois" and "proletarians."

La Réforme continues: "In February bourgeois despotism was broken. What did the people demand? Justice for all, and equality. This was their first call, their first wish. The bourgeoisie, awakened

* *Neue Rheinische Zeitung,* November 3, 1848.

by the lightning that had struck it, had at first no wish different from that of the people."

La Réforme still judges the character of the February Revolution according to the February proclamations. Far from being broken, bourgeois despotism was really consummated by the February Revolution. The crown, the last feudal halo which hid the rule of the bourgeois class, was knocked down. The rule of capital came clearly to the fore. Bourgeois and proletariat fought a common enemy in the February Revolution. As soon as the common enemy was eliminated, the two hostile classes faced each other alone on the battlefield, and the decisive war between them had to begin. If, it will be asked, the February Revolution consummated the rule of the bourgeoisie, why did the bourgeoisie revert to royalism? Nothing is simpler. The bourgeoisie yearns for the period when it ruled without being responsible for its rule; when a fictitious power, standing between it and the people, acted for it and at the same time had to serve as its shield; when it possessed, so to speak, a substantial scapegoat which the proletariat could strike at whenever it wanted to aim at the bourgeoisie—a scapegoat against which the latter allied with the proletariat as soon as it became burdensome and wanted to take power for itself. In the King the bourgeoisie had a lightning conductor for the people; in the people, a lightning conductor for the King.

La Réforme misunderstood the partly hypocritical and partly well-meant fancies which prevailed on the day after Louis Philippe's defeat; for in reality, after the February days the movement appears to it to be a series of mistakes and unfortunate incidents which could have been avoided by a great man meeting the needs of the situation. As if Lamartine had been a will-o'-the-wisp, rather than the real man of the situation!

The real man, the great man, still does not appear, La Réforme complains, and the situation worsens daily: "On the one hand, the industrial and commercial crisis grows. On the other hand, the hate grows, and everyone pursues opposing ends. Those who were suppressed before February 24 seek an ideal of happiness and freedom in the conception of a new society. Those who ruled under the monarchy think only of winning back their power so as to wield it with redoubled severity."

How, then, does La Réforme step between the harshly opposing classes? Does it rise to even the suspicion that class antagonisms and class struggles will disappear only with the disappearance of the classes themselves?

No! It has only admitted the existence of class antagonisms. But class antagonisms rest on economic grounds, on the hitherto existing material means of production and the relationships springing from them. *La Réforme* knows no other way of changing and abolishing them than to look away from this actual basis and its material relationships, and to thrust itself back to the hazy blue sky of republican ideology, that is, to the poetic February period from which the June Revolution violently ejected it. One hears only: "The saddest thing about these internal dissensions is the extinction, the loss, of patriotic national feeling"; that is, precisely that enthusiasm which both classes whitewashed with patriotism and nationalism to cover their specific interests and life conditions. When they did that in 1789, the actual antagonism had not yet developed. What was then the corresponding expression of the situation is today a flight from the situation. What was then a body is today a relic.

"Clearly," *La Réforme* concludes, "it is a deep-rooted evil from which France suffers; but it is not incurable. It has its origins in the confusion of ideas and manners, in the neglect of justice and equality in social relationships, in the corruption of individualistic education. In this orbit one must seek the means of reorganization. Instead, however, one finds refuge in material means."

La Réforme shoves the matter into "conscience," and now this moral twaddle is supposed to help in all emergencies. Thus the antagonism between the bourgeoisie and the proletariat derives from the ideas of these two classes. But whence do these ideas derive? From the social relationships. And whence these relationships? From the material, the economic life conditions of hostile classes. According to *La Réforme*, both are helped when they *lose the consciousness* of their actual situation and their actual antagonism and intoxicate themselves with the opium of "patriotic" feelings and the rhetoric of 1793. What helplessness!

The Class Struggles in France, 1848-50

*This work appeared originally as a series of articles in the Neue Rhein-
ische Zeitung. Politisch-Ökonomische Revue, a journal founded by Marx
and Engels in London in December, 1849, and published (in Hamburg) until November, 1850. The articles were in four issues in 1850:
I (January), II (February), III (March), and V–VI (May–October).*

*After Marx's death Engels brought out the articles in abridged form
in Die Neue Zeit, Vol. II, Nos. 27 and 28 (1894–1895), and in book
form—Die Klassenkämpfe in Frankreich 1848, bis 1850—in Berlin in
1895. In his introduction to the book, Engels wrote, "The work here
republished was Marx's first attempt to explain a section of contemporary history by means of his materialist conception, on the basis of
the given economic situation. In the Communist Manifesto, the theory
was applied in broad outline to the whole of modern history. . . . Here,
on the other hand, the question was to demonstrate the inner causal
connection in the course of a development which extended over some
years . . . to trace political events back to effects of what were, in the
final analysis, economic causes."*

*Except for some minor changes, especially in the footnotes, the text
used here is a translation prepared by the Institute of Marxism-Leninism
and published by Progress Publishers, Moscow, in 1969. It is based on
the Engels edition of 1895.*

With the exception of only a few chapters, every important part
of the revolutionary annals from 1848 to 1849 bear the heading: *Defeat
of the revolution!*

What succumbed in these defeats was not the revolution. It
was the prerevolutionary traditional appendages, results of social re-

lationships which had not yet come to the point of sharp class antagonisms—persons, illusions, conceptions, projects from which the revolutionary party before the February Revolution was not free, from which it could be freed not by the victory of February, but only by a series of defeats.

In a word: The revolution made progress, forged ahead, not by its immediate tragicomic achievements but, on the contrary, by the creation of a powerful, united counterrevolution, by the creation of an opponent in combat with whom the party of overthrow ripened into a really revolutionary party.

To prove this is the task of the following pages.

I

THE DEFEAT OF JUNE, 1848

After the July Revolution, when the liberal banker Laffitte led his companion, the Duke of Orléans, in triumph to the Hôtel de Ville, he let fall the words: *"From now on the bankers will rule."* Laffitte had betrayed the secret of the revolution.

It was not the French bourgeoisie that ruled under Louis Philippe, but one faction of it: bankers, stock-exchange kings, railway kings, owners of coal and iron mines and forests, a part of the landed proprietors associated with them—the so-called *finance aristocracy.* It sat on the throne, it dictated laws in the Chambers, it distributed public offices, from cabinet portfolios to tobacco bureau posts.

The *industrial bourgeoisie* proper formed part of the official opposition, that is, it was represented only as a minority in the Chambers. Its opposition was expressed all the more resolutely the more unalloyed the autocracy of the finance aristocracy became, and the more it imagined that its domination over the working class was insured after the revolts of 1832, 1834, and 1839, which had been drowned in blood. Grandin, a Rouen manufacturer and the most fanatical instrument of bourgeois reaction in the Constituent as well as in the Legislative National Assembly, was the most violent opponent of Guizot in the Chamber of Deputies. Léon Faucher, later known for his impotent efforts to climb into prominence as the Guizot of the French counterrevolution, in the last days of Louis Philippe waged a war of the pen for industry against speculation and its train bearer, the government. Bastiat agitated in the name of Bordeaux and the whole of wine-producing France against the ruling system.

The petty bourgeoisie of all gradations, and the peasantry also, were completely excluded from political power. Finally, in the official opposition or entirely outside the *pays légal* [electorate], there were the ideological representatives and spokesmen of the above classes, their savants, lawyers, doctors, etc., in a word, their so-called men of talent.

Owing to its financial straits, the July Monarchy was dependent from the beginning on the big bourgeoisie, and its dependence on the big bourgeoisie was the inexhaustible source of increasing financial straits. It was impossible to subordinate the administration of the state to the interests of national production without balancing the budget, without establishing a balance between state expenditures and revenues. And how was this balance to be established without limiting state expenditures—that is, without encroaching on interests which were so many props of the ruling system—and without redistributing taxes—that is, without shifting a considerable share of the burden of taxation onto the shoulders of the big bourgeoisie itself?

On the contrary, the faction of the bourgeoisie that ruled and legislated through the Chambers had a *direct interest* in the indebtedness of the state. The state deficit was really the main object of its speculation and the chief source of its enrichment. At the end of each year a new deficit. After the lapse of four or five years a new loan. And every new loan offered new opportunities to the finance aristocracy for defrauding the state, which was kept artificially on the verge of bankruptcy—it had to negotiate with the bankers under the most unfavorable conditions. Each new loan gave a further opportunity, that of plundering the public which invested its capital in state bonds by means of stock-exchange manipulations, the secrets of which the government and the majority in the Chambers were privy to. In general, the instability of state credit and the possession of state secrets gave the bankers and their associates in the Chambers and on the throne the possibility of evoking sudden, extraordinary fluctuations in the quotations of government securities, the result of which was always bound to be the ruin of a mass of smaller capitalists and the fabulously rapid enrichment of the big gamblers. As the state deficit was in the direct interest of the ruling faction of the bourgeoisie, it is clear why the extraordinary state expenditure in the last years of Louis Philippe's reign was far more than double the extraordinary state expenditure under Napoleon, indeed reached a yearly sum of nearly 400,000,000 francs, whereas the whole average annual export of France seldom attained a volume amounting to 750,000,000 francs. The enormous sums which in this way flowed through the hands of the state facilitated, moreover, swindling contracts for deliveries, bribery, defalcations, and all kinds of roguery.

The defrauding of the state, practiced wholesale in connection with loans, was repeated retail in public works. What occurred in the relations between Chamber and government became multiplied in the relations between individual departments and individual entrepreneurs.

The ruling class exploited the building of railways in the same way it exploited state expenditures in general and state loans. The Chambers piled the main burdens on the state, and secured the golden fruits to the speculating finance aristocracy. One recalls the scandals in the Chamber of Deputies when by chance it leaked out that all the members of the majority, including a number of ministers, had been interested as shareholders in the very railway constructions which as legislators they had carried out afterward at the cost of the state.

On the other hand, the smallest financial reform was wrecked through the influence of the bankers. For example, the postal reform. Rothschild protested. Was it permissible for the state to curtail sources of revenue out of which interest was to be paid on its ever increasing debt?

The July Monarchy was nothing other than a joint stock company for the exploitation of France's national wealth, whose dividends were divided among ministers, Chambers, 240,000 voters, and their adherents. Louis Philippe was the director of this company— Robert Macaire[1] on the throne. Trade, industry, agriculture, shipping, the interests of the industrial bourgeoisie, were bound to be continually endangered and prejudiced under this system. Cheap government, *gouvernement à bon marché*, was what it had inscribed on its banner in the July days.

Since the finance aristocracy made the laws, was at the head of the administration of the state, had command of all the organized public authorities, dominated public opinion through the actual state of affairs and through the press, the same prostitution, the same shameless cheating, the same mania to get rich was repeated in every sphere, from the court to the Café Borgne,[2] to get rich not by production, but by pocketing the already available wealth of others. Clashing every moment with the bourgeois laws themselves, an unbridled assertion of unhealthy and dissolute appetites manifested itself, particularly at the top of bourgeois society—lusts wherein wealth derived from gambling naturally seeks its satisfaction, where pleasure becomes debauched, where money, filth, and blood commingle. The finance aristocracy, in its mode of acquisition as well as

---

1. Robert Macaire, a swindler, is a character in *Robert and Bertrand*, a comedy by B. Antier and F. Lemaître (1834).
2. A term applied to cafés of dubious reputation.

in its pleasures, is nothing but the *rebirth of the lumpen proletariat on the heights of bourgeois society*.

And the nonruling factions of the French bourgeoisie cried: *Corruption!* The people cried: *À bas les grands voleurs! À bas les assassins!* [Down with the big thieves! Down with the assassins!] when in 1847, on the most prominent stages of bourgeois society, the same scenes were publicly enacted that regularly lead the lumpen proletariat to brothels, to workhouses and lunatic asylums, to the bar of justice, to the dungeon, and to the scaffold. The industrial bourgeoisie saw its interests endangered, the petty bourgeoisie was filled with moral indignation, the imagination of the people was offended, Paris was flooded with pamphlets—"The Rothschild Dynasty," "Usurers Kings of the Epoch," etc.—in which the rule of the finance aristocracy was denounced and stigmatized with greater or less wit.

Rien pour la gloire! [Nothing for glory!] Glory brings no profit! *La paix partout et toujours!* [Peace everywhere and always!] War depresses the quotations of the 3 and 4 percents which the France of the Bourse jobbers had inscribed on her banner. Her foreign policy was therefore lost in a series of mortifications to French national sentiment, which reacted all the more vigorously when the rape of Poland was brought to its conclusion with the incorporation of Cracow by Austria, and when Guizot came out actively on the side of the Holy Alliance in the Swiss *Sonderbund* war. The victory of the Swiss liberals in this mimic war raised the self-respect of the bourgeois opposition in France; the bloody uprising of the people in Palermo worked like an electric shock on the paralyzed masses of the people and awoke their great revolutionary memories and passions.

The eruption of the general discontent was finally accelerated and the mood for revolt ripened by two economic world events.

The potato blight and the crop failures of 1845 and 1846 increased the general ferment among the people. The famine of 1847 called forth bloody conflicts in France as well as on the rest of the Continent. As against the shameless orgies of the finance aristocracy, the struggle of the people for the prime necessities of life! At Buzançais, hunger rioters executed; in Paris, oversatiated *escrocs* [swindlers] snatched from the courts by the royal family!

The second great economic event that hastened the outbreak of the revolution was a general commercial and industrial crisis in England. Already heralded in the autumn of 1845 by the wholesale reverses of the speculators in railway shares, staved off during 1846 by a number of incidents such as the impending abolition of the Corn Laws, the crisis finally burst in the autumn of 1847 with the bankruptcy of the London wholesale grocers, on the heels of which followed the insolvencies of the land banks and the closing of the factories in the English industrial districts. The aftereffect of this crisis on the Continent had not yet spent itself when the February Revolution broke out.

The devastation of trade and industry caused by the economic epidemic made the autocracy of the finance aristocracy still more unbearable. Throughout the whole of France the bourgeois opposition agitated at banquets for an electoral reform which should win for it the majority in the Chambers and overthrow the Ministry of the Bourse. In Paris the industrial crisis had, moreover, the particular result of throwing a multitude of manufacturers and big traders, who under the existing circumstances could no longer do any business in the foreign market, onto the home market. They set up large establishments, the competition of which ruined the small *épiciers* [grocers] and *boutiquiers* [shopkeepers] en masse. Hence the innumerable bankruptcies among this section of the Paris bourgeoisie, and hence their revolutionary action in February. It is well known how Guizot and the Chambers answered the reform proposals with an unambiguous challenge, how Louis Philippe too late resolved on a ministry led by Barrot, how things went as far as hand-to-hand fighting between the people and the army, how the army was disarmed by the passive conduct of the National Guard, how the July Monarchy had to give way to a provisional government.

The Provisional Government which emerged from the February barricades necessarily mirrored in its composition the different parties which shared in the victory. It could not be anything but a compromise between the different classes which together had overturned the July throne, but whose interests were mutually antagonistic. The great majority of its members consisted of representatives of the bourgeoisie. The republican petty bourgeoisie was represented by Ledru-Rollin and Flocon, the republican bourgeoisie by the people from the *National*,[3] the dynastic opposition by Crémieux, Dupont de l'Eure, etc. The working class had only two representatives, Louis Blanc and Albert. Finally, Lamartine in the Provisional Government; this was at first no real interest, no definite class; this was the February Revolution itself, the common uprising with its illusions, its poetry, its visionary content, and its phrases. For the rest, the spokesman of the February Revolution, by his position and his views, belonged to the bourgeoisie.

If Paris, as a result of political centralization, rules France, the workers, in moments of revolutionary earthquakes, rule Paris. The

---

3. *Le National*, a liberal Paris daily.

first act in the life of the Provisional Government was an attempt to escape from this overpowering influence by an appeal from intoxicated Paris to sober France. Lamartine disputed the right of the barricade fighters to proclaim a republic on the ground that only the majority of Frenchmen had that right; they must await their votes, the Paris proletariat must not besmirch its victory by a usurpation. The bourgeoisie allows the proletariat only one usurpation—that of fighting.

Up to noon of February 25 the republic had not yet been proclaimed; on the other hand, all the ministries had already been divided among the bourgeois elements of the Provisional Government and among the generals, bankers, and lawyers of the *National*. But the workers were determined this time not to put up with any bamboozlement like that of July, 1830. They were ready to take up the fight anew and to get a republic by force of arms. With this message, Raspail betook himself to the Hôtel de Ville. In the name of the Paris proletariat he commanded the Provisional Government to proclaim a republic; if this order of the people were not fulfilled within two hours, he would return at the head of 200,000 men. The bodies of the fallen were scarcely cold, the barricades were not yet disarmed, and the only force that could be opposed to them was the National Guard. Under these circumstances the doubts born of considerations of state policy and the juristic scruples of conscience entertained by the Provisional Government suddenly vanished. The time limit of two hours had not yet expired when all the walls of Paris were resplendent with the gigantic historical words: *République française! Liberté, Egalité, Fraternité!*

Even the memory of the limited aims and motives which drove the bourgeoisie into the February Revolution was extinguished by the proclamation of the republic on the basis of universal suffrage. Instead of only a few factions of the bourgeoisie, all classes of French society were suddenly hurled into the orbit of political power, forced to leave the boxes, the stalls, and the gallery and to act in person upon the revolutionary stage! With the constitutional monarchy vanished also the semblance of a state power independently confronting bourgeois society, as well as the whole series of subordinate struggles which this semblance of power called forth!

By dictating the republic to the Provisional Government, and through the Provisional Government to the whole of France, the proletariat immediately stepped into the foreground as an independent party, but at the same time challenged the whole of bourgeois France to enter the lists against it. What it won was the terrain for the fight for its revolutionary emancipation, but by no means this emancipation itself.

The first thing the February Republic had to do was, rather, to complete the rule of the bourgeoisie by allowing, besides the finance aristocracy, all the propertied classes to enter the orbit of political power. The majority of the great landowners, the Legitimists, were emancipated from the political nullity to which they had been condemned by the July Monarchy. Not for nothing had the *Gazette de France* agitated in common with the opposition papers; not for nothing had La Rochejaquelein taken the side of the revolution in the session of the Chamber of Deputies on February 24. The nominal proprietors, the *peasants*, who form the great majority of the French people, were put by universal suffrage in the position of arbiters of the fate of France. The February Republic finally brought the rule of the bourgeoisie clearly into view, since it struck off the crown behind which capital had kept itself concealed.

Just as the workers in the July days had fought for and won the bourgeois monarchy, so in the February days they fought for and won the bourgeois republic. Just as the July Monarchy had to proclaim itself a monarchy surrounded by republican institutions, so the February Republic was forced to proclaim itself a republic surrounded by social institutions. The Paris proletariat compelled this concession, too.

Marche, a worker, dictated the decree by which the newly formed Provisional Government pledged itself to guarantee the workers a livelihood by means of labor, to provide work for all citizens, etc. And when a few days later it forgot its promises and seemed to have lost sight of the proletariat, a mass of 20,000 workers marched on the Hôtel de Ville with the cry: Organize labor! Form a special Ministry of Labor! Reluctantly and after long debate, the Provisional Government nominated a permanent special commission charged with *finding* means of improving the lot of the working classes! This commission consisted of delegates from the corporations [guilds] of Paris artisans and was presided over by Louis Blanc and Albert. The Luxembourg Palace was assigned to it as its meeting place. In this way the representatives of the working class were banished from the seat of the Provisional Government, the bourgeois part of which retained the real state power and the reins of administration exclusively in its hands; and side by side with the ministries of finance, trade, and public works, side by side with the Bank and the Bourse, there arose a socialist synagogue whose high priests, Louis Blanc and Albert, had the task of discovering the promised land, of preaching the new gospel, and of providing work for the Paris proletariat. Unlike any profane state power, they had no budget, no executive authority at their disposal. They were supposed to break the pillars of bourgeois society by dashing their heads against them. While the Luxembourg sought the philosopher's stone, in the Hôtel de Ville they minted the current coinage.

And yet the claims of the Paris proletariat, so far as they went beyond the bourgeois republic, could win no other existence than the nebulous one of the Luxembourg.

In common with the bourgeoisie the workers had made the February Revolution, and alongside the bourgeoisie they sought to secure the advancement of their interests, just as they had installed a worker in the Provisional Government itself alongside the bourgeois majority. Organize labor! But wage labor, that is the existing, the bourgeois organization of labor. Without it there is no capital, no bourgeoisie, no bourgeois society. A special Ministry of Labor! But the ministries of finance, of trade, of public works—are not these the *bourgeois* ministries of labor? And alongside these a proletariat Ministry of Labor had to be a ministry of impotence, a ministry of pious wishes, a Luxembourg Commission. Just as the workers thought they would be able to emancipate themselves side by side with the bourgeoisie, so they thought they would be able to consummate a proletarian revolution within the national walls of France, side by side with the remaining bourgeois nations. But French relations of production are conditioned by the foreign trade of France, by her position on the world market and the laws thereof; how was France to break them without a European revolutionary war, which would strike back at the despot of the world market, England?

As soon as it has risen up, a class in which the revolutionary interests of society are concentrated finds the content and the material for its revolutionary activity directly in its own situation: foes to be laid low, measures dictated by the needs of the struggle to be taken; the consequences of its own deeds drive it on. It makes no theoretical inquiries into its own task. The French working class had not attained this level; it was still incapable of accomplishing its own revolution.

The development of the industrial proletariat is, in general, conditioned by the development of the industrial bourgeoisie. Only under its rule does the proletariat gain that extensive national existence which can raise its revolution to a national one, and only thus does the proletariat itself create the modern means of production, which become just so many means of its revolutionary emancipation. Only bourgeois rule tears up the material roots of feudal society and levels the ground on which alone a proletarian revolution is possible. French industry is more developed and the French bourgeoisie more revolutionary than that of the rest of the Continent. But was not the

February Revolution aimed directly against the finance aristocracy? This fact proved that the industrial bourgeoisie did not rule France. The industrial bourgeoisie can rule only where modern industry shapes all property relations to suit itself, and industry can win this power only where it has conquered the world market, for national bounds are inadequate for its development. But French industry, to a great extent, maintains its command even of the national market only through a more or less modified system of prohibitive duties. While, therefore, the French proletariat, at the moment of a revolution, possesses in Paris actual power and influence which spur it on to a drive beyond its means, in the rest of France it is crowded into separate, scattered industrial centers, almost lost in the superior number of peasants and petty bourgeois. The struggle against capital in its developed, modern form—in its decisive aspect, the struggle of the industrial wage worker against the industrial bourgeois—is in France a partial phenomenon, which after the February days could so much the less supply the national content of the revolution, since the struggle against capital's secondary modes of exploitation, that of the peasant against usury and mortgages or of the petty bourgeois against the wholesale dealer, banker, and manufacturer—in a word, against bankruptcy—was still hidden in the general uprising against the finance aristocracy. Nothing is more understandable, then, than that the Paris proletariat sought to secure the advancement of its own interests side by side with those of the bourgeoisie, instead of enforcing them as the revolutionary interests of society itself, that it let the red flag be lowered to the tricolor. The French workers could not take a step forward, could not touch a hair of the bourgeois order, until the course of the revolution had aroused the mass of the nation, peasants and petty bourgeois, standing between the proletariat and the bourgeoisie, against this order, against the rule of capital, and had forced it to attach itself to the proletarians as its protagonists. The workers could buy this victory only through the tremendous defeat in June.

The Luxembourg Commission, this creation of the Paris workers, must be given the credit of having disclosed, from a Europe-wide tribune, the secret of the revolution of the nineteenth century: *the emancipation of the proletariat*. The *Moniteur* blushed when it had to propagate officially the "wild ravings" which up to that time had lain buried in the apocryphal writings of the socialists and reached the ear of the bourgeoisie only from time to time as remote, half-terrifying, half-ludicrous legends. Europe awoke astonished from its bourgeois doze. Therefore, in the minds of the proletarians, who confused the finance aristocracy with the bourgeoisie in general; in the imagination of the good old republicans who denied the very existence of classes or, at most, admitted them as a result of the constitutional monarchy; in the hypocritical phrases of the factions of the bourgeoisie which up to now had been excluded from power, the rule of the bourgeoisie was abolished with the introduction of the republic. At that time all the royalists were transformed into republicans and all the millionaires of Paris into workers. The phrase which corresponded to this imaginary abolition of class relations was *fraternité*, universal fraternization and brotherhood. This pleasant abstraction from class antagonisms, this sentimental reconciliation of contradictory class interests, this visionary elevation above the class struggle, this *fraternité*, was the real catchword of the February Revolution. The classes were divided by a mere misunderstanding, and on February 24 Lamartine christened the Provisional Government *"un gouvernement qui suspende ce malentendu terrible qui existe entre les différentes classes"* [a government that removes this terrible misunderstanding which exists between the different classes]. The Paris proletariat reveled in this magnanimous intoxication of fraternity.

The Provisional Government, for its part, once it was compelled to proclaim the republic, did everything to make it acceptable to the bourgeoisie and to the provinces. The bloody terror of the first French republic was disavowed by the abolition of the death penalty for political offenses; the press was opened to all opinions; the army, the courts, the administration remained with a few exceptions in the hands of their old dignitaries; none of the July Monarchy's great offenders was brought to book. The bourgeois republicans of the *National* amused themselves by exchanging monarchist names and costumes for old republican ones. To them the republic was only a new ball dress for the old bourgeois society. The young republic sought its chief merit not in frightening, but rather in constantly taking fright itself, and in winning existence and disarming resistance by soft compliance and nonresistance. At home to the privileged classes, abroad to the despotic powers, it was loudly announced that the republic was of a peaceful nature. Live and let live was its professed motto. In addition to that, shortly after the February Revolution the Germans, Poles, Austrians, Hungarians, and Italians revolted, each people in accordance with its immediate situation. Russia and England—the latter itself agitated, the former cowed—were not prepared. The republic, therefore, had no *national* enemy to face. Consequently there were no great foreign complications which could fire the energies, hasten the revolutionary process, drive the Provisional Government forward or throw it overboard. The Paris proletariat, which looked upon the republic as its own creation, naturally acclaimed each act of the Provisional Government which facilitated the firm emplacement of the latter in bourgeois society. It willingly allowed itself to be employed on police service by Caussidière in order to protect property in Paris, just as it allowed Louis Blanc to arbitrate wage disputes between workers and masters. It made it a *point d'honneur* to preserve the bourgeois honor of the republic unblemished in the eyes of Europe.

The republic encountered no resistance either abroad or at home. This disarmed it. Its task was no longer the revolutionary transformation of the world, but consisted only in adapting itself to the relations of bourgeois society. As to the fanaticism with which the Provisional Government undertook this task there is no more eloquent testimony than its financial measures.

Public credit and private credit were naturally shaken. Public credit rests on confidence that the state will allow itself to be exploited by the wolves of finance. But the old state had vanished and the revolution was directed above all against the finance aristocracy. The vibrations of the last European commercial crisis had not yet ceased. Bankruptcy still followed bankruptcy.

Private credit was therefore paralyzed, circulation restricted, production at a standstill before the February Revolution broke out. The revolutionary crisis increased the commercial crisis. And if private credit rests on confidence that bourgeois production in the entire scope of its relations—the bourgeois order—will not be touched, will remain inviolate, what effect must a revolution have had which questioned the basis of bourgeois production, the economic slavery of the proletariat, which set up against the Bourse the sphinx of the Luxembourg? The uprising of the proletariat is the abolition of bourgeois credit, for it is the abolition of bourgeois production and its order. Public credit and private credit are the economic thermometer by which the intensity of a revolution can be measured. The more they fall, the more the fervor and generative power of the revolution rises.

The Provisional Government wanted to strip the republic of its antibourgeois appearance. And so it had, above all, to try to peg the exchange value of this new form of state, its quotation on the Bourse. Private credit necessarily rose again, together with the current Bourse quotation of the republic.

In order to allay the very suspicion that it would not or could not honor the obligations assumed by the monarchy, in order to build up confidence in the republic's bourgeois morality and capacity to pay, the Provisional Government took refuge in braggadocio as undignified as it was childish. *In advance* of the legal date of payment it paid out the interest on the 5-percent, 4½-percent and 4-percent bonds to the state creditors. The bourgeois aplomb, the self-assurance of the capitalists, suddenly awoke when they saw the anxious haste with which this government sought to buy their confidence.

The financial embarrassment of the Provisional Government was naturally not lessened by a theatrical stroke which robbed it of its stock of ready cash. The financial pinch could no longer be concealed and petty bourgeois, domestic servants, and workers had to pay for the pleasant surprise which had been prepared for the state creditors.

It was announced that no more money could be drawn on savings bank books for an amount of over a hundred francs. The sums deposited in the savings banks were confiscated and by decree transformed into an irredeemable state debt. This embittered the already hard-pressed petty bourgeois against the republic. Since he received state debt certificates in place of his savings bank books, he was forced to go to the Bourse in order to sell them and thus deliver himself directly into the hands of the Bourse jobbers against whom he had made the February Revolution.

The finance aristocracy, which ruled under the July Monarchy, had its high church in the Bank. Just as the Bourse governs state credit, the Bank governs commercial credit.

Directly threatened not only in its rule but in its very existence by the February Revolution, the Bank tried from the outset to discredit the republic by making the lack of credit general. It suddenly stopped the credits of the bankers, the manufacturers, and the merchants. As it did not immediately call forth a counterrevolution, this maneuver necessarily reacted on the Bank itself. The capitalists drew out the money they had deposited in the vaults of the Bank. The possessors of bank notes rushed to the pay office in order to exchange them for gold and silver.

The Provisional Government could have forced the Bank into bankruptcy without forcible interference, in a legal manner; it would have had only to remain passive and leave the Bank to its fate. The bankruptcy of the Bank would have been the deluge which in an instant would have swept from French soil the finance aristocracy, the most powerful and dangerous enemy of the republic, the golden pedestal of the July Monarchy. And once the Bank was bankrupt, the bourgeoisie itself would have had to regard it as a last desperate attempt at rescue, if the government had formed a national bank and subjected national credit to the control of the nation.

The Provisional Government, on the contrary, fixed a compulsory quotation for the notes of the Bank. It did more. It transformed all provincial banks into branches of the Banque de France and allowed it to cast its net over the whole of France. Later it pledged the state forests to the Bank as a guarantee for a loan contracted from it. In this way the February Revolution directly strengthened and enlarged the bankocracy which it should have overthrown.

Meanwhile the Provisional Government was writhing under the incubus of a growing deficit. In vain it begged for patriotic sacrifices. Only the workers threw it their alms. Recourse had to be had to a heroic measure, to the imposition of a new tax. But who was to be taxed? The Bourse wolves, the bank kings, the state creditors, the *rentiers*, the industrialists? That was not the way to ingratiate the republic with the bourgeoisie. That would have meant, on the one hand, to endanger state credit and commercial credit, while on the other, attempts were made to purchase them with such great sacrifices and humiliations. But someone had to fork over the cash. Who was sacrificed to bourgeois credit? *Jacques le bonhomme,* the peasant.

The Provisional Government imposed an additional tax of 45 centimes to the franc on the four direct taxes. The government press cajoled the Paris proletariat into believing that this tax would fall chiefly on the big landed proprietors, on the possessors of the milliard granted by the Restoration. But in truth it hit the peasant class above all, that is, the large majority of the French people. *They had to pay the costs of the February Revolution;* in them the counterrevolution gained its main material. The 45-centime tax was a question of life and death for the French peasant; he made it a life-and-death question for the republic. From that moment the *republic* meant to the French peasant the *45-centime tax,* and he saw in the Paris proletariat the spendthrift who did himself well at his expense.

Whereas the Revolution of 1789 began by shaking the feudal burdens off the peasants, the Revolution of 1848 announced itself to the rural population by the imposition of a new tax, in order not to endanger capital and to keep its state machine going.

There was only one means by which the Provisional Government could set aside all these inconveniences and jerk the state out of its old rut—a declaration of state bankruptcy. Everyone recalls how Ledru-Rollin in the National Assembly subsequently described the virtuous indignation with which he repudiated this presumptuous proposal of the Bourse wolf Fould, now French Finance Minister. Fould had handed him the apple from the tree of knowledge.

By honoring the bills drawn on the state by the old bourgeois society, the Provisional Government succumbed to the latter. It had become the hard-pressed debtor of bourgeois society instead of confronting it as the pressing creditor that had to collect the revolutionary debts of many years. It had to consolidate the shaky bourgeois relationships in order to fulfill obligations which are only to be fulfilled within these relationships. Credit became a condition of life for it, and the concessions to the proletariat, the promises made to it, became so many fetters which had to be struck off. The emancipation of the workers—even as a phrase—became an unbearable danger to the new republic, for it was a standing protest against the restoration of credit, which rests on undisturbed and untroubled recognition of the existing economic class relations. Therefore, it was necessary to have done with the workers.

The February Revolution had cast the army out of Paris. The National Guard, that is, the bourgeoisie in its different gradations, constituted the sole power. Alone, however, it did not feel itself a match for the proletariat. Moreover, it was forced gradually and piecemeal to open its ranks and admit armed proletarians, albeit after the most tenacious resistance and after setting up a hundred different obstacles. There consequently remained but one way out: *to play off one part of the proletariat against the other.*

For this purpose the Provisional Government formed twenty-four battalions of Mobile Guards, each a thousand strong, composed of young men from fifteen to twenty years old. They belonged for the most part to the lumpen proletariat, which in all big towns forms a mass sharply differentiated from the industrial proletariat, a recruiting ground for thieves and criminals of all kinds living on the crumbs of society, people without a definite trade, vagabonds, *gens sans feu et sans aveu* [men without hearth or home], varying according to the degree of civilization of the nation to which they belong, but never renouncing their *lazzaroni* character; at the youthful age at which the Provisional Government recruited them, thoroughly malleable, as capable of the most heroic deeds and the most exalted sacrifices as of the basest banditry and the foulest corruption. The Provisional Government paid them 1 franc 50 centimes a day; that is, it bought them. It gave them their own uniform; that is, it made them outwardly distinct from the blouse-wearing workers. In part it assigned officers from the standing army as their leaders; in part they themselves elected young sons of the bourgeoisie whose rodomontades about death for the fatherland and devotion to the republic captivated them.

And so the Paris proletariat was confronted with an army, drawn from its own midst, of 24,000 young, strong, foolhardy men. It gave cheers for the Mobile Guard on its marches through Paris. It acknowledged it to be its foremost fighters on the barricades. It regarded it as the proletarian guard in contradistinction to the bourgeois National Guard. Its error was pardonable.

Besides the Mobile Guard, the government decided to rally around itself an army of industrial workers. A hundred thousand workers, thrown on the streets by the crisis and the revolution, were enrolled by the Minister Marie in so-called national *ateliers* [workshops]. Under this grandiose name was hidden nothing else than the employment of the workers on tedious, monotonous, unproductive earthworks at a wage of 23 sous. English workhouses in the open—that is what these national *ateliers* were. The Provisional Government believed that it had formed, in them, a second proletarian army against the workers themselves. This time the bourgeoisie was mistaken in the national *ateliers*, just as the workers were mistaken in the Mobile Guard. It had created an *army for mutiny*.

But one purpose was achieved.

National *ateliers* was the name of the people's workshops which Louis Blanc preached in the Luxembourg Palace. Marie's *ateliers*, devised in direct antagonism to the Luxembourg, offered occasion, thanks to the common label, for a comedy of errors worthy of the Spanish servant farce. The Provisional Government itself surreptitiously spread the report that these national *ateliers* were the discovery of Louis Blanc, and this seemed the more plausible because Louis Blanc, the prophet of the national *ateliers*, was a member of the Provisional Government. And in the half-naïve, half-intentional confusion of the Paris bourgeoisie, in the artificially molded opinion of France, of Europe, these workhouses were the first realization of socialism, which was put in the pillory with them.

In their appellation, though not in their content, the national *ateliers* were the embodied protest of the proletariat against bourgeois industry, bourgeois credit, and the bourgeois republic. The whole hate of the bourgeoisie was therefore turned upon them. It had found in them, simultaneously, the point against which it could direct the attack, as soon as it was strong enough to break openly with the February illusions. All the discontent, all the ill humor of the petty bourgeois too was directed against these national *ateliers*, the common target. With real fury they totted up the money the proletarian loafers swallowed up while their own situation was becoming daily more unbearable. A state pension for sham labor, so that's socialism! they grumbled to themselves. They sought the reason for their misery in the national *ateliers*, the declamations of the Luxembourg, the processions of the workers through Paris. And no one was more fanatic about the alleged machinations of the communists than the petty bourgeoisie, who hovered hopelessly on the brink of bankruptcy.

Thus in the approaching mêlée between bourgeoisie and proletariat, all the advantages, all the decisive posts, all the middle strata of society were in the hands of the bourgeoisie, at the same time as the waves of the February Revolution rose high over the whole Continent, and each new post brought a new bulletin of revolution, now from Italy, now from Germany, now from the remotest parts of southeastern Europe, and maintained the general ecstasy of the people, giving it constant testimony of a victory that it had already forfeited.

March 17 and April 16 were the first skirmishes in the big class struggle which the bourgeois republic hid under its wing.

March 17 revealed the proletariat's ambiguous situation, which permitted no decisive act. Its demonstration originally pursued the purpose of pushing the Provisional Government back onto the path of revolution, of effecting the exclusion of its bourgeois members, according to circumstances, and of compelling the postponement of the elections for the National Assembly and the National Guard. But on March 16 the bourgeoisie represented in the National Guard staged a hostile demonstration against the Provisional Government. With the cry *À bas Ledru-Rollin!* it surged to the Hôtel de Ville. And the people were forced, on March 17, to shout: Long live Ledru-Rollin! Long live the Provisional Government! They were forced to take sides *against* the bourgeoisie in support of the bourgeois republic, which seemed to them to be in danger. They strengthened the Provisional Government, instead of subordinating it to themselves. March 17 went off in a melodramatic scene, and whereas the Paris proletariat on this day once more displayed its giant body, the bourgeoisie both inside and outside the Provisional Government was all the more determined to smash it.

April 16 was a misunderstanding engineered by the Provisional Government in alliance with the bourgeoisie. The workers had gathered in great numbers in the Champ de Mars and in the Hippodrome to choose their nominees to the general staff of the National Guard. Suddenly throughout Paris, from one end to the other, a rumor spread as quick as lightning, to the effect that the workers had met armed in the Champ de Mars, under the leadership of Louis Blanc, Blanqui, Cabet, and Raspail, in order to march thence on the Hôtel de Ville, overthrow the Provisional Government, and proclaim a communist government. The general alarm is sounded—Ledru-Rollin, Marrast, and Lamartine later contended for the honor of having initiated this—and in an hour 100,000 men are under arms; the Hôtel de Ville is occupied at all points by the National Guard; the cry Down with the Communists! Down with Louis Blanc, with Blanqui, with Raspail, with Cabet! thunders throughout Paris. Innumerable deputations pay homage to the Provisional Government, all ready to save the fatherland and society. When the workers finally appear before the Hôtel de Ville, in order to hand over to the Provisional Government a patriotic collection they had made in the Champ de Mars, they learn to their amazement that bourgeois Paris has defeated their shadow in a very carefully calculated sham battle. The terrible attempt of April 16 furnished the excuse for recalling the army to Paris—the real purpose of the clumsily staged comedy— and for the reactionary federalist demonstrations in the provinces.

On May 4 the National Assembly,[4] the result of the direct general elections, convened. Universal suffrage did not possess the magic power which republicans of the old school had ascribed to it. They saw in the whole of France, at least in the majority of Frenchmen, *citoyens* with the same interests, the same understanding, etc. This was their *cult of the people*. Instead of their imaginary people, the elections brought the real people to the light of day; that is, representatives of the different classes into which it falls. We have seen why peasants and petty bourgeois had to vote under the leadership of a bourgeoisie spoiling for a fight and of big landowners frantic for restoration. But if universal suffrage was not the miracle-working magic wand the republican worthies had taken it for, it possessed the incomparably higher merit of unchaining the class struggle, of letting the various middle strata of bourgeois society rapidly get over their illusions and disappointments, of tossing all the sections of the exploiting class at one throw to the apex of the state, and thus tearing from them their deceptive mask, whereas the monarchy with its property qualifications had let only certain factions of the bourgeoisie compromise themselves, allowing the others to lie hidden behind the scenes and surrounding them with the halo of a common opposition.

In the Constituent National Assembly, which met on May 4, the bourgeois republicans, the republicans of the *National*, had the upper hand. Even Legitimists and Orléanists at first dared to show themselves only under the mask of bourgeois republicanism. The fight against the proletariat could be undertaken only in the name of the republic.

The republic dates from May 4, not from February 25—that is, the republic recognized by the French people; it is not the republic which the Paris proletariat thrust upon the Provisional Government, not the republic with social institutions, not the vision that hovered before the fighters on the barricades. The republic proclaimed by the National Assembly, the sole legitimate republic, is a republic which is no revolutionary weapon against the bourgeois order, but rather its political reconstitution, the political reconsolidation of bour-

---

4. The Constituent National Assembly, in power from May 4, 1848, to May, 1849.

geois society; in a word, *a bourgeois republic*. This contention re-sounded from the tribune of the National Assembly, and in the entire republican and antirepublican bourgeois press it found its echo.

And we have seen how the February Republic in reality was not and could not be other than a bourgeois republic; how the Provisional Government, nevertheless, was forced by the immediate pressure of the proletariat to announce it as a republic with social institutions; how the Paris proletariat was still incapable of going beyond the bourgeois republic otherwise than in its fancy, in imagination; how everywhere the republic acted in the service of the bourgeoisie when it really came to action; how the promises made to it became an un-bearable danger for the new republic; how the whole life process of the Provisional Government was comprised in a continuous fight against the demands of the proletariat.

In the National Assembly all France sat in judgment upon the Paris proletariat. The Assembly broke immediately with the social illusions of the February Revolution; it roundly proclaimed the bour-geois republic, nothing but the bourgeois republic. It at once ex-cluded the representatives of the proletariat, Louis Blanc and Albert, from the Executive Commission it had appointed; it threw out the proposal of a special Labor Ministry and received with acclamation the statement of Minister Trélat: "The question now is merely one of *bringing labor back to its old conditions.*"

But all this was not enough. The February Republic was won by the workers with the passive support of the bourgeoisie. The prole-tarians rightly regarded themselves as the victors of February, and they made the arrogant claims of victors. They had to be vanquished in the streets, they had to be shown that they were worsted as soon as they did not fight *with* the bourgeoisie, but *against* the bourgeoisie. Just as the February Republic, with its socialist concessions, required a battle of the proletariat, united with the bourgeoisie, against the monarchy, so a second battle was necessary to sever the republic from socialist concessions, to officially work out the bourgeois republic as dominant. The bourgeoisie had to refute, arms in hand, the demands of the proletariat. And the real birthplace of the bourgeois republic is not the *February victory;* it is the *June defeat.*

The proletariat hastened the decision when, on the fifteenth of May, it pushed its way into the National Assembly, sought in vain to recapture its revolutionary influence, and only delivered its energetic leaders to the jailers of the bourgeoisie. *Il faut en finir!* This situation must end! With this cry the National Assembly gave vent to its determination to force the proletariat into a decisive struggle. The Executive Commission issued a series of provocative decrees, such as that prohibiting congregations of people, etc. The workers were directly provoked, insulted, and derided from the tribune of the Constituent National Assembly. But the real point of the attack was, as we have seen, the national *ateliers*. The Constituent Assembly imperiously pointed these out to the Executive Commission, which waited only to hear its own plan proclaimed the command of the National Assembly.

The Executive Commission began by making admission to the national *ateliers* more difficult, by turning the day wage into a piece wage, by banishing workers not born in Paris to the Sologne, ostensibly for the construction of earthworks. These earthworks were only a rhetorical formula with which to embellish their exile, as the workers, returning disillusioned, announced to their comrades. Finally, on June 21, a decree appeared in the *Moniteur* which ordered the forcible expulsion of all unmarried workers from the national *ateliers* or their enrollment in the army.

The workers were left no choice; they had to starve or let fly. They answered on June 22 with the tremendous insurrection in which the first great battle was fought between the two classes that split modern society. It was a fight for the preservation or annihilation of the bourgeois order. The veil that shrouded the republic was torn asunder.

It is well known how the workers, with unexampled bravery and ingenuity, without leaders, without a common plan, without means and, for the most part, lacking weapons, held in check for five days the army, the Mobile Guard, the Paris National Guard, and the National Guard that streamed in from the provinces. It is well known how the bourgeoisie compensated itself for the mortal anguish it suffered by unheard-of brutality, massacring over 3,000 prisoners.

The official representatives of French democracy were steeped in republican ideology to such an extent that it was only some weeks later that they began to have an inkling of the significance of the June fight. They were stupefied by the gunpowder smoke in which their fantastic republic dissolved.

The immediate impression which the news of the June defeat made on us, the reader will allow us to describe in the words of the *Neue Rheinische Zeitung*.[5]

Woe to that June! reechoes Europe.

The Paris proletariat was *forced* into the June insurrection by the bourgeoisie. This sufficed to mark its doom. Its immediate, avowed

---

5. Marx's article, in the *Neue Rheinische Zeitung* of June 29, 1848, from which he quotes here, appears on pages 147–150.

needs did not drive it to engage in a fight for the forcible overthrow of the bourgeoisie, nor was it equal to this task. The *Moniteur* had to inform it officially that the time was past when the republic saw any occasion to bow and scrape to its illusions, and only its defeat convinced it of the truth that the slightest improvement in its position remains a utopia within the bourgeois republic, a utopia that becomes a crime as soon as it wants to become a reality. In place of the demands, exuberant in form but still limited and even bourgeois in content, whose concession the proletariat wanted to wring from the February Republic, there appeared the bold slogan of revolutionary struggle: *Overthrow of the bourgeoisie! Dictatorship of the working class!*

By making its burial place the birthplace of the bourgeois republic, the proletariat compelled the latter to come out forthwith in its pure form as the state whose admitted object it is to perpetuate the rule of capital, the slavery of labor. Having constantly before its eyes the scarred, irreconcilable, invincible enemy—invincible because his existence is the condition of its own life—bourgeois rule, freed from all fetters, was bound to turn immediately into *bourgeois terrorism*. With the proletariat removed for the time being from the stage and bourgeois dictatorship recognized officially, the middle strata of bourgeois society, the petty bourgeoisie and the peasant class, had to adhere more and more closely to the proletariat as their position became more unbearable and their antagonism to the bourgeoisie more acute. Just as earlier they had to find the cause of their distress in its upsurge, so now in its defeat.

If the June insurrection raised the self-assurance of the bourgeoisie all over the Continent, and caused it to league itself openly with the feudal monarchy against the people, who was the first victim of this alliance? The continental bourgeoisie itself. The June defeat prevented it from consolidating its rule and from bringing the people, half satisfied and half out of humor, to a standstill at the lowest stage of the bourgeois revolution.

Finally, the defeat of June divulged to the despotic powers of Europe the secret that France must maintain peace abroad at any price in order to be able to wage civil war at home. Thus the peoples who had begun the fight for their national independence were abandoned to the superior power of Russia, Austria, and Prussia, but at the same time the fate of these national revolutions was made subject to the fate of the proletarian revolution, and they were robbed of their apparent autonomy, their independence of the great social revolution. The Hungarian shall not be free, nor the Pole, nor the Italian, as long as the worker remains a slave!

Finally, with the victories of the Holy Alliance, Europe has taken on a form that makes every fresh proletarian upheaval in France directly coincide with a *world war*. The new French revolution is forced to leave its national soil forthwith and conquer the European terrain, on which alone the social revolution of the nineteenth century can be accomplished.

Thus only the June defeat has created all the conditions under which France can seize the initiative of the European revolution. Only after being dipped in the blood of the June insurgents did the tricolor become the flag of the European revolution—the *red flag!*

And we exclaim: *The revolution is dead! Long live the revolution!*

II

JUNE 13, 1849

February 25, 1848, granted the republic to France, June 25 thrust the revolution upon her. And revolution, after June, meant: *overthrow of bourgeois society*, whereas before February it meant: *overthrow of the form of government*.

The June fight was led by the republican faction of the bourgeoisie; with victory political power necessarily fell to its share. The state of siege laid gagged Paris unresisting at its feet, and in the provinces there prevailed a moral state of siege, the threatening, brutal arrogance of victory of the bourgeoisie and the unleashed property fanaticism of the peasants. No danger, therefore, from below!

The crash of the revolutionary might of the workers was simultaneously a crash of the political influence of the democratic republicans; that is, of the republicans in the sense of the petty bourgeoisie, represented in the Executive Commission by Ledru-Rollin, in the Constituent National Assembly by the party of the *Montagne* and in the press by the *Réforme*. Together with the bourgeois republicans they had conspired on April 16 against the proletariat, together with them they had warred against it in the June days. Thus they themselves blasted the background against which their party stood out as a power, for the petty bourgeoisie can preserve a revolutionary attitude toward the bourgeoisie only as long as the proletariat stands behind it. The proletarians were dismissed. The sham alliance concluded with them reluctantly and with mental reservations during the epoch of the Provisional Government and the Executive Commission was openly broken by the bourgeois republicans. Spurned and repulsed as allies, they sank down to subordinate henchmen of the tricolor men, from whom they could not wring any concessions but

whose domination they had to support whenever it, and with it the
republic, seemed to be put in jeopardy by the antirepublican bourgeois
factions. Lastly, these factions, the Orléanists and the Legitimists,
were from the very beginning in a minority in the Constituent National Assembly. Before the June days they dared to react only under
the mask of bourgeois republicanism; the June victory allowed for a
moment the whole of bourgeois France to greet its savior in Cavaignac;
and when, shortly after the June days, the antirepublican party regained independence, the military dictatorship and the state of siege
in Paris permitted it to put out its antennae only very timidly and
cautiously.

Since 1830 the bourgeois republican faction, in the person of its
writers, its spokesmen, its men of talent and ambition, its deputies,
generals, bankers, and lawyers, had grouped itself around a Parisian
journal, the *National*. In the provinces this journal had its branch
newspapers. The coterie of the *National* was the dynasty of the tricolor republic. It immediately took possession of all state offices—of
the ministries, the prefecture of police, the post-office directorship, the
prefectures, the higher army officers' posts—which had now become
vacant. At the head of the executive power stood its general,
Cavaignac; its editor in chief, Marrast, became permanent president of
the Constituent National Assembly. As master of ceremonies he at
the same time did the honors, in his salons, of the respectable republic.

Even revolutionary French writers, awed, as it were, by the
republican tradition, have strengthened the mistaken belief that the
royalists dominated the Constituent National Assembly. On the contrary, after the June days, the Constituent Assembly remained the
exclusive representative of bourgeois republicanism, and it empha-
sized this aspect all the more resolutely, the more the influence of the
tricolor republicans collapsed outside the Assembly. If the question
was one of maintaining the *form* of the bourgeois republic, then the
Assembly had the votes of the democratic republicans at its disposal;
if one of maintaining the *content*, then even its mode of speech no
longer separated it from the royalist bourgeois factions, for it is the
interests of the bourgeoisie, the material conditions of its class rule and
class exploitation, that form the content of the bourgeois republic.

Thus it was not royalism but bourgeois republicanism that was
realized in the life and work of this Constituent Assembly, which in
the end did not die, nor was killed, but decayed.

For the entire duration of its rule, for as long as it gave its grand
performance of state on the proscenium, an unbroken sacrificial feast
was being staged in the background—the continual sentencing by
courts-martial of the captured June insurgents or their deportation

without trial. The Constituent Assembly had the tact to admit that in the June insurgents it was not judging criminals but wiping out enemies.

The first act of the Constituent National Assembly was to set up a commission of inquiry into the events of June and of May 15, and into the part played by the socialist and democratic party leaders during these days. The inquiry was directly aimed at Louis Blanc, Ledru-Rollin, and Caussidière. The bourgeois republicans burned with impatience to rid themselves of these rivals. They could have entrusted the venting of their spleen to no more suitable object than M. Odilon Barrot, the former chief of the dynastic opposition, the incarnation of liberalism, the *nullité grave,* the thoroughly shallow person who not only had a dynasty to revenge, but even had to settle accounts with the revolutionists for thwarting his premiership. A sure guarantee of his relentlessness. This Barrot was therefore appointed chairman of the commission of inquiry, and he constructed a complete legal process against the February Revolution which may be summarized thus: March 17, *demonstration;* April 16, *conspiracy;* May 15, *attempt;* June 23, *civil war!* Why did he not stretch his erudite criminologist's researches as far back as February 24? the *Journal des Débats* inquired; that is, to the foundation of Rome. The origin of states gets lost in a myth that one may believe but may not discuss. Louis Blanc and Caussidière were handed over to the courts. The National Assembly completed the work of purging itself which it had begun on May 15.

The plan formed by the Provisional Government, and again taken up by Goudchaux, of taxing capital—in the form of a mortgage tax— was rejected by the Constituent Assembly; the law that limited the working day to ten hours was repealed; imprisonment for debt was once more introduced; the large section of the French population that can neither read nor write was excluded from jury service. Why not from the franchise also? Journals again had to deposit caution money. The right of association was restricted.

No one had fought more fanatically in the June days for the salvation of property and the restoration of credit than the Parisian petty bourgeois—keepers of cafés and restaurants, *marchands de vins,* small traders, shopkeepers, handicraftsmen, etc. The shopkeeper had pulled himself together and marched against the barricades in order to restore the traffic which leads from the streets into the shop. But behind the barricade stood the customers and the debtors; before it the creditors of the shop. And when the barricades were thrown down and the workers were crushed and the shopkeepers, drunk with victory, rushed back to their shops, they found the entrance barred by a savior of property, an official agent of credit, who presented them

with threatening notices: Overdue promissory note! Overdue house
rent! Overdue bond! Doomed shop! Doomed shopkeeper!

Salvation of property! But the house they lived in was not their
property; the shop they kept was not their property; the commodities
they dealt in were not their property. Neither their business, nor the
plate they ate from, nor the bed they slept on belonged to them any
longer. It was precisely from them that this property had to be saved
—for the houseowner who let the house, for the banker who discounted the promissory note, for the capitalist who made the advances
in cash, for the manufacturer who entrusted the sale of his commodities to these retailers, for the wholesale dealer who had credited the
raw materials to these handicraftsmen. *Restoration of credit!* But
credit, having regained strength, proved itself a vigorous and jealous
god; it turned the debtor who could not pay out of his four walls,
together with wife and child, surrendered his sham property to capital,
and threw the man himself into the debtors' prison, which had once
more reared its head threateningly over the corpses of the June
insurgents.

The petty bourgeois saw with horror that by striking down the
workers they had delivered themselves without resistance into the
hands of their creditors. Their bankruptcy, which since February had
been dragging on in chronic fashion and had apparently been ignored, was openly declared after June.

Their nominal property had been left unassailed as long as it was
of consequence to drive them to the battlefield in the name of property. Now that the great issue with the proletariat had been settled,
the small matter of the *épicier* could in turn be settled. In Paris the
mass of overdue paper amounted to over 21,000,000 francs; in the
provinces to over 11,000,000. The proprietors of more than 7,000
Paris firms had not paid their rent since February.

While the National Assembly had instituted an inquiry into political guilt, going as far back as the end of February, the petty bourgeois on their part now demanded an inquiry into civil debts up to
February 24. They assembled en masse in the Bourse hall and threateningly demanded, on behalf of every businessman who could prove
that his insolvency was due solely to the stagnation caused by the
revolution and that his business had been in good condition on
February 24, an extension of the term of payment by order of a
commerce court and the compulsory liquidation of creditors' claims
in consideration of a moderate percentage payment. As a legislative
proposal, this question was dealt with in the National Assembly in
the form of *concordats à l'amiable* [amicable agreements]. The Assembly vacillated; then it suddenly learned that at the same time, at

the Porte St. Denis, thousands of wives and children of the insurgents had prepared an amnesty petition.

In the presence of the resurrected specter of June, the petty bourgeoisie trembled and the National Assembly retrieved its implacability. The *concordats à l'amiable*, the amicable settlements between debtor and creditor, were rejected in their most essential points.

Thus long after the democratic representatives of the petty bourgeois had been repulsed within the National Assembly by the republican representatives of the bourgeoisie, this parliamentary breach received its bourgeois, its real economic meaning by the petty bourgeois as debtors being handed over to the bourgeois as creditors. A large part of the former were completely ruined and the remainder were allowed to continue their businesses only under conditions which made them absolute serfs of capital. On August 22, 1848, the National Assembly rejected the *concordats à l'amiable;* on September 19, 1848, in the midst of the state of siege, Prince Louis Bonaparte and the prisoner of Vincennes, the Communist Raspail, were elected representatives of Paris. The bourgeoisie, however, elected the usurious moneychanger and Orléanist Fould. From all sides at once, therefore, open declaration of war against the Constituent National Assembly, against bourgeois republicanism, against Cavaignac.

It needs no argument to show how the mass bankruptcy of the Paris petty bourgeois was bound to produce aftereffects far transcending the circle of its immediate victims, and to convulse bourgeois commerce once more, while the state deficit was swollen anew by the costs of the June insurrection, and state revenues sank continuously through the hold-up of production, the restricted consumption, and the decreasing imports. Cavaignac and the National Assembly could have recourse to no other expedient than a new loan, which forced them still further under the yoke of the finance aristocracy.

While the petty bougeois had harvested bankruptcy and liquidation by order of court as the fruit of the June victory, Cavaignac's Janissaries, the Mobile Guards, found their reward in the soft arms of the courtesans, and as "the youthful saviors of society" they received all kinds of homage in the salons of Marrast, the knight of the tricolor, who served simultaneously as the Amphitryon and the troubadour of the respectable republic. Meantime, this social favoritism and the disproportionately higher pay of the Mobile Guard embittered the army, while all those national illusions with which bourgeois republicanism, through its journal, the *National*, had been able to attach to itself a part of the army and peasant class under Louis Philippe vanished at the same time. The role of mediator which Cavaignac and the National Assembly played in North Italy in order, together with England, to betray it to Austria—this one day of rule destroyed eighteen years of opposition on the part of the *National*. No government was less national than that of the *National*, none more dependent on England, and, under Louis Philippe, the *National* lived by paraphrasing daily Cato's dictum: *Carthaginem esse delendam* [Carthage must be destroyed]; none was more servile toward the Holy Alliance, and from a Guizot the *National* had demanded the tearing up of the Treaties of Vienna. The irony of history made Bastide, the ex-editor for foreign affairs of the *National*, Minister of Foreign Affairs of France, so that he might refute every one of his articles in every one of his dispatches.

For a moment, the army and the peasant class had believed that, simultaneously with the military dictatorship, war abroad and *gloire* had been placed on the order of the day in France. But Cavaignac was not the dictatorship of the saber over bourgeois society; he was the dictatorship of the bourgeoisie by the saber. And of the soldier they now required only the gendarme. Under the stern features of antique-republican resignation Cavaignac concealed humdrum submission to the humiliating conditions of his bourgeois office. *L'argent n'a pas de maître!* Money has no master! He, as well as the Constituent Assembly in general, idealized this old election cry of the Third Estate by translating it into political speech: The bourgeoisie has no king; the true form of its rule is the republic.

And the "great organic work" of the Constituent National Assembly consisted in working out this form, in producing a republican constitution. The rechristening of the Christian calendar as a republican one, of the saintly Bartholomew as the saintly Robespierre, made no more change in the wind and weather than this constitution made or was supposed to make in bourgeois society. Where it went beyond a change of costume, it put on record the existing facts. Thus it solemnly registered the fact of the republic, the fact of universal suffrage, the fact of a single sovereign National Assembly in place of two limited constitutional chambers. Thus it registered and regulated the fact of the dictatorship of Cavaignac by replacing the stationary, irresponsible hereditary monarchy with an ambulatory, responsible, elective monarchy, with a quadrennial presidency. Thus it elevated no less to an organic law the fact of the extraordinary powers with which the National Assembly, after the horrors of May 15 and June 25, had prudently invested its president in the interest of its own security. The remainder of the constitution was a work of terminology. The royalist labels were torn off the mechanism of the old monarchy and republican labels stuck on. Marrast, former editor in chief of the *National*, now editor in chief of the constitution, acquitted himself of this academic task not without talent.

The Constituent Assembly resembled the Chilean official who wanted to regulate property relations in land more firmly by a cadastral survey just at the moment when subterranean rumblings announced the volcanic eruption that was to hurl away the land from under his very feet. While in theory it accurately marked off the forms in which the rule of the bourgeoisie found republican expression, in reality it held its own only by the abolition of all formulas, by force *sans phrase*, by the *state of siege*. Two days before it began its work on the constitution, it proclaimed an extension of the state of siege. Formerly constitutions had been made and adopted as soon as the social process of revolution had reached a point of rest, the newly formed class relationships had established themselves, and the contending factions of the ruling class had had recourse to a compromise which allowed them to continue the struggle among themselves and at the same time to keep the exhausted masses of the people out of it. This constitution, on the contrary, did not sanction any social revolution; it sanctioned the momentary victory of the old society over the revolution.

The first draft of the constitution, made before the June days, still contained the *droit au travail*, the right to work, the first clumsy formula wherein the revolutionary demands of the proletariat are summarized. It was transformed into the *droit à l'assistance*, the right to public relief, and what modern state does not feed its paupers in some form or other? The right to work is, in the bourgeois sense, an absurdity, a miserable, pious wish. But behind the right to work stands the power over capital; behind the power over capital, the appropriation of the means of production, their subjection to the associated working class, and therefore the abolition of wage labor, of capital, and of their mutual relations. Behind the "right to work" stood the June insurrection. The Constituent Assembly, which in fact put the revolutionary proletariat *hors la loi*, outside the law, had on principle to throw the proletariat's formula out of the constitution, the law of laws; had to pronounce its anathema upon the "right to work." But it did not stop there. As Plato banned the poets from his republic, so it banished forever from its republic—*the progressive tax*. And the progressive tax is not only a bourgeois measure, which can be carried out within the existing relations of production to a greater or less degree; it was the only means of binding the middle strata of bourgeois society to the "respectable" republic, of reducing the state debt, of holding the antirepublican majority of the bourgeoisie in check.

In the matter of the *concordats à l'amiable*, the tricolor republicans had actually sacrificed the petty bourgeoisie to the big bourgeoisie. They elevated this isolated fact to a principle by the legal prohibition

182

of a progressive tax. They put bourgeois reform on the same level as proletarian revolution. But what class then remained as the mainstay of their republic? The big bourgeoisie. And its mass was antirepublican. While it exploited the republicans of the *National* in order to consolidate again the old relations of economic life, it thought, on the other hand, of exploiting the once more consolidated social relations in order to restore the political forms that corresponded to them. As early as the beginning of October, Cavaignac felt compelled to make Dufaure and Vivien, previously ministers of Louis Philippe, ministers of the republic, however much the brainless puritans of his own party growled and blustered.

While the tricolor constitution rejected every compromise with the petty bourgeoisie and was unable to win the attachment of any new social element to the new form of government, it hastened, on the other hand, to restore its traditional inviolability to a body that constituted the most hard-bitten and fanatical defender of the old state. It raised the irremovability of judges, which had been questioned by the Provisional Government, to an organic law. The one king whom it had removed rose again, by the score, in these irremovable inquisitors of legality.

The French press has analyzed from numerous aspects the contradictions of M. Marrast's constitution; for example, the coexistence of two sovereigns, the National Assembly and the President, etc., etc.

The comprehensive contradiction of this constitution, however, consists in the following: The classes whose social slavery the constitution is to perpetuate—proletariat, peasantry, petty bourgeoisie—it puts in possession of political power through universal suffrage. And from the class whose old social power it sanctions, the bourgeoisie, it withdraws the political guarantees of this power. It forces the political rule of the bourgeoisie into democratic conditions, which at every moment help the hostile classes to victory and jeopardize the very foundations of bourgeois society. From the first group it demands that they should not go forward from political to social emancipation; from the others that they should not go back from social to political restoration.

These contradictions perturbed the bourgeois republicans little. To the extent that they ceased to be indispensable—and they were indispensable only as the protagonists of the old society against the revolutionary proletariat—they fell, a few weeks after their victory, from the position of a party to that of a coterie. And they treated the constitution as a big intrigue. What was to be constituted in it was, above all, the rule of the coterie. The President was to be a protracted Cavaignac; the Legislative Assembly a protracted Constituent Assembly. They hoped to reduce the political power of the masses of the people to a semblance of power, and to be able to make sufficient play with this sham power itself to keep continually hanging over the majority of the bourgeoisie the dilemma of the June days: realm of the *National* or realm of anarchy.

The work on the constitution, which was begun on September 4, was finished on October 23. On September 2 the Constituent Assembly had decided not to dissolve until the organic laws supplementing the constitution were enacted. Nonetheless, it now decided to bring to life the creation that was most peculiarly its own, the President, on December 10, long before the circle of its own activity was closed. So sure was it of hailing, in the homunculus of the constitution, the son of his mother. As a precaution it was provided that if none of the candidates received two million votes, the election should pass over from the nation to the Constituent Assembly.

Futile provisions! The first day of the realization of the constitution was the last day of the rule of the Constituent Assembly. In the abyss of the ballot box lay its sentence of death. It sought the "son of his mother" and found the "nephew of his uncle." Saul Cavaignac slew one million votes, but David Napoleon slew six million. Saul Cavaignac was beaten six times over.

December 10, 1848, was the day of the *peasant insurrection*. Only from this day does the February of the French peasants date. The symbol that expressed their entry into the revolutionary movement, clumsily cunning, knavishly naïve, doltishly sublime, a calculated superstition, a pathetic burlesque, a cleverly stupid anachronism, a world-historic piece of buffoonery and an indecipherable hieroglyphic for the understanding of the civilized—this symbol bore the unmistakable physiognomy of the class that represents barbarism within civilization. The republic had announced itself to this class with the tax collector; it announced itself to the republic with the emperor. Napoleon was the only man who had exhaustively represented the interests and the imagination of the peasant class, newly created in 1789. By writing his name on the frontispiece of the republic, it declared war abroad and the enforcing of its class interests at home. Napoleon was to the peasants not a person but a program. With banners, with beat of drums and blare of trumpets, they marched to the polling booths shouting: *Plus d'impôts, à bas les riches, à bas la république, vive l'Empereur!* No more taxes, down with the rich, down with the republic, long live the emperor! Behind the emperor was hidden the peasant war. The republic that they voted down was the *republic of the rich.*

December 10 was the *coup d'état* of the peasants, which overthrew the existing government. And from that day on, when they had taken a government from France and given a government to her, their eyes were fixed steadily on Paris. For a moment active heroes of the revolutionary drama, they could no longer be forced back into the inactive and spineless role of the chorus.

The other classes helped to complete the election victory of the peasants. To the proletariat, the election of Napoleon meant the deposition of Cavaignac, the overthrow of the Constituent Assembly, the dismissal of bourgeois republicanism, the cessation of the June victory. To the petty bourgeoisie, Napoleon meant the rule of the debtor over the creditor. For the majority of the big bourgeoisie, the election of Napoleon meant an open breach with the faction of which it had had to make use, for a moment, against the revolution, but which became intolerable to it as soon as this faction sought to consolidate the position of the moment into a constitutional position. Napoleon in place of Cavaignac meant to this majority the monarchy in place of the republic, the beginning of the royalist restoration, a sly hint at Orléans, the fleur-de-lis hidden beneath the violet. Lastly, the army voted for Napoleon against the Mobile Guard, against the peace idyll, for war.

Thus it happened, as the *Neue Rheinische Zeitung* stated, that the most simple-minded man in France acquired the most multifarious significance. Just because he was nothing, he could signify everything save himself. Meanwhile, different as the meaning of the name Napoleon might be in the mouths of the different classes, with this name each wrote on his ballot: Down with the party of the *National*, down with Cavaignac, down with the Constituent Assembly, down with the bourgeois republic. Minister Dufaure publicly declared in the Constituent Assembly: December 10 is a second February 24.

Petty bourgeoisie and proletariat had voted en bloc *for* Napoleon, in order to vote *against* Cavaignac and, by pooling their votes, to wrest the final decision from the Constituent Assembly. The more advanced sections of the two classes, however, put forward their own candidates. Napoleon was the *collective name* of all parties in coalition against the bourgeois republic; Ledru-Rollin and Raspail were the *proper names,* the former of the democratic petty bourgeoisie, the latter of the revolutionary proletariat. The votes for Raspail—the proletarians and their socialist spokesmen declared it loudly—were to be merely a demonstration, so many protests against any presidency, that is, against the constitution itself, so many votes against Ledru-Rollin, the first act by which the proletariat, as an independent political party, declared its separation from the democratic party. This party, on the other hand—the democratic petty bourgeoisie and its parliamentary representative, the *Montagne*[6]—treated the candidature of Ledru-Rollin with all the seriousness with which it is in the habit of solemnly duping itself. For the rest, this was its last attempt to set itself up as an independent party, as against the proletariat. Not only the republican bourgeois party, but also the democratic petty bourgeoisie and its *Montagne* were beaten on December 10.

France now possessed a Napoleon side by side with a *Montagne*, proof that both were only the lifeless caricatures of the great realities whose names they bore. Louis Napoleon, with the emperor's hat and the eagle, parodied the old Napoleon no more miserably than the *Montagne*, with its phrases borrowed from 1793 and its demagogic poses, parodied the old *Montagne*. Thus the traditional 1793 superstition was stripped off at the same time as the traditional Napoleon superstition. The revolution had come into its own only when it had won its *own*, its *original* name, and it could do that only when the modern revolutionary class, the industrial proletariat, came dominatingly into its foreground. One can say that December 10 dumfounded the *Montagne* and caused it to grow confused in its own mind, if for no other reason than because that day laughingly cut short with a contemptuous peasant jest the classical analogy to the old revolution.

On December 20 Cavaignac laid down his office and the Constituent Assembly proclaimed Louis Napoleon President of the Republic. On December 19, the last day of its sole rule, it rejected the proposal of amnesty for the June insurgents. Would revoking the decree of June 27, under which it had condemned 15,000 insurgents to deportation without judicial sentence, not have meant revoking the June battle itself?

Odilon Barrot, the last minister of Louis Philippe, became the first minister of Louis Napoleon. Just as Louis Napoleon dated his rule, not from December 10, but from a decree of the Senate of 1804, so he found a prime minister who did not date his ministry from December 20, but from a royal decree of February 24. As the legitimate heir of Louis Philippe, Louis Napoleon mollified the change of government by retaining the old ministry, which, moreover, had not had time to be worn out, since it had not found time to embark upon life.

The leaders of the royalist bourgeois factions advised him in this choice. The head of the old dynastic opposition, who had

6. The Jacobins, who sat in the "Mountain," or raised seats, in the French National Convention, which met in Paris in September, 1792.

unconsciously constituted the transition to the republicans of the *National,* was still more fitted to constitute with full consciousness the transition from the bourgeois republic to the monarchy.

Odilon Barrot was the leader of the one old opposition party which, always fruitlessly struggling for ministerial portfolios, had not yet been used up. In rapid succession the revolution hurled all the old opposition parties to the top of the state, so that they would have to deny, to repudiate their old phrases not only in deeds but even in words, and might finally be flung all together, combined in a repulsive commixture, on the dung heap of history by the people. And no apostasy was spared this Barrot, this incarnation of bourgeois liberalism, who for eighteen years had hidden the rascally vacuity of his mind behind the serious demeanor of his body. If at certain moments the far too striking contrast between the thistles of the present and the laurels of the past startled the man himself, one glance in the mirror gave him back his ministerial composure and human self-admiration. What beamed at him from the mirror was Guizot, whom he had always envied, who had always mastered him, Guizot himself, but Guizot with the Olympian forehead of Odilon. What he overlooked were the ears of Midas.

The Barrot of February 24 first became manifest in the Barrot of December 20. Associated with him, the Orléanist and Voltairean, was the Legitimist and Jesuit Falloux, as Minister of Public Worship.

A few days later, the Ministry of Home Affairs was given to Léon Faucher, the Malthusian. Law, religion, and political economy! The ministry of Barrot contained all this and, in addition, a combination of Legitimists and Orléanists. Only the Bonapartist was lacking. Bonaparte still hid his longing to signify Napoleon, for Soulouque did not yet play Toussaint L'Ouverture.

The party of the *National* was immediately relieved of all the higher posts, where it had entrenched itself. The prefecture of police, the post-office directorship, the procuratorship general, the *mairie* [mayor's office] of Paris were all filled with old creatures of the monarchy. Changarnier, the Legitimist, received the unified supreme command of the National Guard of the Department of the Seine, of the Mobile Guard and the troops of the line of the first military division; Bugeaud, the Orléanist, was appointed commander in chief of the Alpine Army. This change of officials continued uninterrupted under the Barrot government. The first act of his ministry was the restoration of the old royalist administration. The official scene was at once transformed—scenery, costumes, speech, actors, supers, mutes, prompters, the position of the parties, the theme of the drama, the content of the conflict, the whole situation. Only the premundane

Constituent Assembly remained in its place. But from the hour when the National Assembly had installed Bonaparte, Bonaparte Barrot, and Barrot Changarnier, France stepped out of the period of republican constitution into the period of the constituted republic. And what place was there for a Constituent Assembly in a constituted republic? After the earth had been created, there was nothing else for its creator to do but flee to heaven. The Constituent Assembly was determined not to follow his example; the National Assembly was the last asylum of the party of the bourgeois republicans. If all levers of executive power had been wrested from it, was there not left to it constituent omnipotence? Its first thought was to hold under all circumstances the position of sovereignty it occupied, and thence to reconquer the lost ground. Once the Barrot Ministry was displaced by a ministry of the *National*, the royalist personnel would have to vacate the palaces of the administration forthwith and the tricolor personnel would triumphantly move in again. The National Assembly resolved on the overthrow of the ministry and the ministry itself offered an opportunity for the attack, a better one than the Constituent Assembly itself could have invented.

It will be remembered that for the peasants Louis Bonaparte signified: No more taxes! Six days he sat in the President's chair, and on the seventh, on December 27, his ministry proposed the retention of the salt tax, whose abolition the Provisional Government had decreed. The salt tax shares with the wine tax the privilege of being the scapegoat of the old French financial system, particularly in the eyes of the countryfolk. The Barrot Ministry could not have put into the mouth of the peasants' choice a more mordant epigram on his electors than the words: *Restoration of the salt tax!* With the salt tax, Bonaparte lost his revolutionary salt—the Napoleon of the peasant insurrection dissolved like an apparition, and nothing remained but the great unknown of royalist bourgeois intrigue. And not without intention did the Barrot Ministry make this act of tactlessly rude disillusionment the first governmental act of the President.

The Constituent Assembly, for its part, eagerly seized the double opportunity of overthrowing the ministry and, as against the elected choice of the peasantry, setting itself up as the representative of peasant interests. It rejected the proposal of the finance minister, reduced the salt tax to a third of its former amount, thus increasing by sixty millions a state deficit of five hundred and sixty millions, and, after this vote of no confidence, calmly awaited the resignation of the ministry. So little did it comprehend the new world that surrounded it and its own changed position. Behind the ministry stood the President and behind the President stood six millions who had placed in the ballot box as many votes of no confidence in the Constituent Assembly. The Constituent Assembly gave the nation back its no-confidence vote. Absurd exchange! It forgot that its votes were no longer legal tender. The rejection of the salt tax only matured the decision of Bonaparte and his ministry to finish the Constituent Assembly. There began that long duel which lasted the entire latter half of the life of the Constituent Assembly. January 29, March 21, and May 8 are the *journées,* the great days of this crisis, just so many forerunners of June 13.

Frenchmen, for example Louis Blanc, have construed January 29 as the date of the emergence of a constitutional contradiction, the contradiction between a sovereign, indissoluble National Assembly born of universal suffrage and a President who, to go by the wording, was responsible to the Assembly, but who, to go by reality, was not only similarly sanctioned by universal suffrage and in addition united in his own person all the votes that were split up a hundred times and distributed among the individual members of the National Assembly, but who was also in full possession of the whole executive power, above which the National Assembly hovered as a merely moral force. This interpretation of January 29 confuses the language of the struggle on the platform, through the press, and in the clubs with its real content. Louis Bonaparte as against the Constituent National Assembly—that was not one unilateral constitutional power as against another; that was not the executive power as against the legislative. That was the constituted bourgeois republic itself as against the intrigues and ideological demands of the revolutionary faction of the bourgeoisie that had founded it and was now amazed to find that its constituted republic looked like a restored monarchy, and now desired forcibly to prolong the constituent period with its conditions, its illusions, its language, and its personages and to prevent the mature bourgeois republic from emerging in its complete and peculiar form. As the Constituent National Assembly represented Cavaignac, who had fallen back into its midst, so Bonaparte represented the Legislative National Assembly that had not yet been divorced from him, that is, the National Assembly of the constituted bourgeois republic.

The election of Bonaparte could become explicable only by putting in the place of the one name its manifold meanings, by repeating itself in the election of the new National Assembly. The mandate of the old was annulled by December 10. Thus on January 29 it was not the President and the National Assembly of the same republic that were face to face; it was the National Assembly of the republic that was coming into being and the President of the republic that had come into being, two powers that embodied quite different periods in the life process of the republic; the one, the small republican faction of the bourgeoisie that alone could proclaim the republic, wrest it from the revolutionary proletariat by street fighting and a reign of terror, and draft its ideal basic features in the constitution; and the other, the whole royalist mass of the bourgeoisie that alone could rule in this constituted bourgeois republic, strip the constitution of its ideological trimmings, and realize by its legislation and administration the indispensable conditions for the subjugation of the proletariat.

The storm which broke on January 29 gathered its elements during the whole month of January. The Constituent Assembly wanted to drive the Barrot Ministry to resign by its no-confidence vote. The Barrot Ministry, on the other hand, proposed to the Constituent Assembly that it should give itself a definitive no-confidence vote, decide on suicide, and decree its own dissolution. On January 6, Rateau, one of the most obscure deputies, at the order of the ministry brought this motion before the Constituent Assembly that in August had determined not to dissolve until it had enacted a whole series of organic laws supplementing the constitution. Fould, the ministerialist, bluntly declared to it that its dissolution was necessary "for the restoration of the deranged credit." And did it not derange credit when it prolonged the provisional stage and, with Barrot, again called Bonaparte in question, and, with Bonaparte, the constituted republic? Barrot the Olympian became a raving Roland at the prospect of seeing the premiership he had finally pocketed, which the republicans had already withheld from him for ten months, again torn from him after scarcely two weeks' enjoyment of it— Barrot, confronting this wretched Assembly, out-tyrannized the tyrant. His mildest words were, "No future is possible with it." And actually it did represent only the past. "It is incapable," he added ironically, "of providing the republic with the institutions which are necessary for its consolidation." Incapable indeed! Its bourgeois energy was broken simultaneously with its exceptional antagonism to the proletariat, and with its antagonism to the royalists its republican exuberance lived anew. Thus it was doubly incapable of consolidating the bourgeois republic, which it no longer comprehended, by means of the corresponding institutions.

Simultaneously with Rateau's motion the ministry evoked a storm of petitions throughout the land, and from all corners of France came flying daily at the head of the Constituent Assembly bundles of billets-doux in which it was more or less categorically requested to dissolve and make its will. The Constituent Assembly, on its side, called forth counterpetitions in which it caused itself to be requested to remain alive. The election struggle between Bonaparte and Cavaignac was renewed as a petition struggle for and against the dissolution of the National Assembly; the petitions were to be belated commentaries on December 10. This agitation continued during the whole of January.

In the conflict between the Constituent Assembly and the President, the former could not refer back to the general election as its origin, for the appeal was from the Assembly to universal suffrage. It could base itself on no regularly constituted power, for the issue was the struggle against the legal power. It could not overthrow the ministry by no-confidence votes, as it again essayed to do on January 6 and 26, for the ministry did not ask for its confidence. Only one possibility was left to it, that of insurrection. The fighting forces of the insurrection were the republican part of the National Guard, the Mobile Guard, and the centers of the revolutionary proletariat, the clubs. The Mobile Guard, those heroes of the June days, in December formed the organized fighting force of the republican faction of the bourgeoisie, just as before June the national *ateliers* had formed the organized fighting force of the revolutionary proletariat. As the Executive Commission of the Constituent Assembly directed its brutal attack on the national *ateliers*, when it had to put an end to the now unbearable pretensions of the proletariat, so the ministry of Bonaparte directed its attack on the Mobile Guard, when it had to put an end to the now unbearable pretensions of the republican faction of the bourgeoisie. It ordered the disbanding of the Mobile Guard. One half of it was dismissed and thrown on the street, the other was organized on monarchist instead of democratic lines, and its pay was reduced to the usual pay of troops of the line. The Mobile Guard found itself in the position of the June insurgents and every day the press carried public confessions in which it admitted its blame for June and implored the proletariat to forgive it.

And the clubs? From the moment when the Constituent Assembly in the person of Barrot called in question the President, and in the person of the President the constituted bourgeois republic, and in the person of the constituted bourgeois republic the bourgeois republic in general, all the constituent elements of the February Republic necessarily ranged themselves around it—all the parties that wished to overthrow the existing republic and by a violent retrograde process to transform it into a republic of their class interests and principles. The scrambled eggs were unscrambled, the crystallizations of the revolutionary movement had again become fluid, the republic that was being fought for was again the indefinite republic of the

February days, the defining of which each party reserved to itself. For a moment the parties again took up their old February positions, without sharing the illusions of February. The tricolor republicans on the *National* again leaned on the democratic republicans of the *Réforme* and pushed them as protagonists into the foreground of the parliamentary struggle. The democratic republicans again leaned on the socialist republicans—on January 27 a public manifesto announced their reconciliation and union—and prepared their insurrectional background in the clubs. The ministerial press rightly treated the tricolor republicans of the *National* as the resurrected insurgents of June. In order to maintain themselves at the head of the bourgeois republic, they called in question the bourgeois republic itself. On January 26 Minister Faucher proposed a law on the right of association, the first paragraph of which read: "Clubs are forbidden." He moved that this bill immediately be discussed as urgent. The Constituent Assembly rejected the motion of urgency, and on January 27 Ledru-Rollin put forward a proposition, with 230 signatures appended to it, to impeach the ministry for violation of the constitution. The impeachment of the ministry at times when such an act was a tactless disclosure of the impotence of the judge, to wit, the majority of the Chamber, or an impotent protest of the accuser against this majority itself—that was the great revolutionary trump that the latter-day *Montagne* played from now on at each high spot of the crisis. Poor *Montagne!* crushed by the weight of its own name!

On May 15 Blanqui, Barbès, Raspail, etc., had attempted to break up the Constituent Assembly by forcing an entrance into its hall at the head of the Paris proletariat. Barrot prepared a moral May 15 for the same Assembly when he wanted to dictate its self-dissolution and close the hall. The same Assembly had commissioned Barrot to make the inquiry against the May accused, and now, at the moment when he appeared before it like a royalist Blanqui, when it sought for allies against him in the clubs, among the revolutionary proletarians, in the party of Blanqui—at this moment the relentless Barrot tormented it with the proposal to withdraw the May prisoners from the Court of Assizes with its jury and hand them over to the High Court, the *haute cour* devised by the party of the *National*. Remarkable how wild fear for a ministerial portfolio could pound out of the head of a Barrot points worthy of a Beaumarchais! After much vacillation the National Assembly accepted his proposal. As against the makers of the May attempt, it reverted to its normal character.

If the Constituent Assembly, as against the President and the ministers, was driven to insurrection, the President and the ministers, as against the Constituent Assembly, were driven to a *coup d'état,* for they had no legal means of dissolving it. But the Constituent Assembly was the mother of the constitution and the constitution was the mother of the President. With the *coup d'état* the President tore up the constitution and extinguished his republican legal title. He was then forced to pull out his imperial legal title, but the imperial legal title woke up the Orléanist legal title and both paled before the Legitimist legal title. The downfall of the legal republic could shoot to the top only its extreme antipode, the Legitimist monarchy, at a moment when the Orléanist party was still only the vanquished of February and Bonaparte was still only the victor of December 10, when both could oppose to republican usurpation only their likewise usurped monarchist titles. The Legitimists were aware of the propitiousness of the moment; they conspired openly. They could hope to find their monk in General Changarnier. The imminence of the white monarchy was as openly announced in their clubs as was that of the red republic in the proletarian clubs.

The ministry would have escaped all difficulties by a happily suppressed rising. "Legality is the death of us," cried Odilon Barrot. A rising would have allowed it, under the pretext of *salut public* [public safety], to dissolve the Constituent Assembly, to violate the constitution in the interests of the constitution itself. The brutal behavior of Odilon Barrot in the National Assembly, the motion for the dissolution of the clubs, the tumultuous removal of fifty tricolor prefects and their replacement by royalists, the dissolution of the Mobile Guard, the ill treatment of their chiefs by Changarnier, the reinstatement of Lerminier, the professor who was impossible even under Guizot, the toleration of the Legitimist braggadocio—all these were just so many provocations to mutiny. But the mutiny remained mute. It expected its signal from the Constituent Assembly and not from the ministry.

Finally came January 29, the day the decision was to be taken on the motion of Mathieu (de la Drôme) for unconditional rejection of Rateau's motion. Legitimists, Orléanists, Bonapartists, Mobile Guard, *Montagne*, clubs—all conspired on this day, each just as much against the ostensible enemy as against the ostensible ally. Bonaparte, on horseback, mustered a part of the troops on the Place de la Concorde; Changarnier play-acted with a display of strategic maneuvers; the Constituent Assembly found its building occupied by the military. This Assembly, the center of all the conflicting hopes, fears, expectations, ferments, tensions, and conspiracies, this lionhearted Assembly did not falter for a moment when it came nearer to the *Weltgeist* [world spirit] than ever. It was like the fighter who not only feared to make use of his own weapons but also felt himself obliged to maintain the weapons of his opponent unimpaired. Scorning death, it signed its own death warrant and rejected the unconditional rejection of the Rateau motion. Itself in a state of siege, it set limits to a constituent activity whose necessary frame had been the state of siege of Paris. It revenged itself worthily when on the following day it instituted an inquiry into the fright that the ministry had given it on January 29. In this great comedy of intrigues the *Montagne* showed its lack of revolutionary energy and political understanding by allowing itself to be used by the party of the *National* as the crier in the contest. The party of the *National* had made its last attempt to continue to maintain, in the constituted republic, the monopoly of rule it had possessed during the inchoate period of the bourgeois republic. It was shipwrecked.

While in the January crisis it was a question of the existence of the Constituent Assembly, in the crisis of March 21 it was a question of the existence of the constitution—there of the personnel of the *National* party, here of its ideal. There is no need to point out that the respectable republicans surrendered the exaltation of their ideology more cheaply than the worldly enjoyment of governmental power.

On March 21 Faucher's bill against the right of association—the suppression of the clubs—was on the order of the day in the National Assembly. Article 8 of the constitution guarantees to all Frenchmen the right to associate. The prohibition of the clubs was therefore an unequivocal violation of the constitution, and the Constituent Assembly itself was to canonize the profanation of its holy of holies. But the clubs—these were the gathering points, the conspiratorial seats of the revolutionary proletariat. The National Assembly had itself forbidden the coalition of the workers against its bourgeois. And the clubs—what were they but a coalition of the whole working class against the whole bourgeois class, the formation of a workers' state against the bourgeois state? Were they not just so many constituent assemblies of the proletariat and just so many military detachments of revolt in fighting trim? What the constitution was to constitute above all else was the rule of the bourgeoisie. By the right of association the constitution, therefore, could manifestly mean only associations that harmonized with the rule of the bourgeoisie, that is, with bourgeois order. If for reasons of theoretical propriety it expressed itself in general terms, were not the government and the National Assembly there to interpret and apply it in a special case? And if in the primeval epoch of the republic the clubs actually were forbidden by the state of siege, had they not to be forbidden in the ordered, constituted republic by the law? The tricolor republicans had nothing to oppose to this prosaic interpretation of the constitution but the high-flown phraseology of the constitution. A section of them, Pagnerre, Duclerc, etc., voted for the ministry and thereby gave it a majority. The others, with the archangel Cavaignac and the father of the church Marrast at their head, retired, after the article on the prohibition of the clubs had gone through, to a special committee room, jointly with Ledru-Rollin and the *Montagne*—"and held a council." The National Assembly was paralyzed; it no longer had a quorum. At the right time, M. Crémieux remembered in the committee room that the way from here led directly to the street and that it was no longer February, 1848, but March, 1849. The party of the *National*, suddenly enlightened, returned to the National Assembly's hall of session, behind it the *Montagne*, duped once more. The latter, constantly tormented by revolutionary longings, just as constantly clutched at constitutional possibilities, and still felt itself more in place behind the bourgeois republicans than in front of the revolutionary proletariat. Thus the comedy was played. And the Constituent Assembly itself had decreed that the violation of the letter of the constitution was the only appropriate realization of its spirit.

There was only one point left to settle, the relation of the constituted republic to the European revolution, its *foreign policy*. On May 8, 1849, unwonted excitement prevailed in the Constituent Assembly, whose term of life was due to end in a few days. The attack of the French army on Rome, its repulse by the Romans, its political infamy and military disgrace, the foul assassination of the Roman republic by the French republic—the first Italian campaign of the second Bonaparte—was on the order of the day. The *Montagne* had once more played its great trump; Ledru-Rollin had laid on the President's table the inevitable bill of impeachment against the ministry, and this time also against Bonaparte, for violation of the constitution.

The motive of May 8 was repeated later as the motive of June 13. Let us get clear about the expedition to Rome.

As early as the middle of November, 1848, Cavaignac had sent a battle fleet to Civitavecchia in order to protect the Pope, to take him on board and ship him over to France. The Pope was to consecrate the respectable republic, and to insure the election of Cavaignac as President. With the Pope, Cavaignac wanted to angle for the priests, with the priests for the peasants, and with the peasants for the presidency. The expedition of Cavaignac, an election advertisement in its immediate purpose, was at the same time a protest and a threat against the Roman revolution. It contained in embryo France's intervention in favor of the Pope.

This intervention on behalf of the Pope, in association with Austria and Naples against the Roman republic, was decided at the first meeting of Bonaparte's ministerial council, on December 23. Falloux in the ministry—that meant the Pope in Rome—and in the Rome of the Pope. Bonaparte no longer needed the Pope in order to become the President of the peasants; but he needed the conservation of the Pope in order to conserve the peasants of the President. Their credulity had made him President. With faith they would lose credulity, and with the Pope, faith. And the Orléanists and Legitimists in coalition, who ruled in Bonaparte's name! Before the king was restored, the power that consecrates kings had to be restored. Apart from their royalism: without the old Rome, subject to his temporal rule, no Pope; without the Pope, no Catholicism; without Catholicism, no French religion; and without religion, what would become of the old French society? The mortgage the peasant has on heavenly possessions guarantees the mortgage the bourgeois has on peasant possessions. The Roman revolution was therefore an attack on property, on the bourgeois order, dreadful as the June Revolution. Reestablished bourgeois rule in France required the restoration of papal rule in Rome. Finally, to smite the Roman revolutionists was to smite the allies of the French revolutionists; the alliance of the counterrevolutionary classes in the constituted French republic was necessarily supplemented by the alliance of the French republic with the Holy Alliance, with Naples and Austria.

The decision of the ministerial council on December 23 was no secret to the Constituent Assembly. On January 8 Ledru-Rollin had interpellated the ministry about it; the ministry had denied it and the National Assembly had proceeded to the order of the day. Did it trust the word of the ministry? We know it spent the whole month of January giving the ministry no-confidence votes. But if it was part of the ministry's role to lie, it was part of the National Assembly's role to feign belief in its lie and thereby save republican *dehors* [face].

Meanwhile Piedmont was beaten, Charles-Albert had abdicated, and the Austrian army knocked at the gates of France. Ledru-Rollin vehemently interpellated. The ministry proved that it had only continued in North Italy the policy of Cavaignac and Cavaignac only the policy of the Provisional Government, that is, of Ledru-Rollin. This time it even reaped a vote of confidence from the National Assembly and was authorized to occupy temporarily a suitable point in Upper Italy to give support to peaceful negotiations with Austria concerning the integrity of Sardinian territory and the question of Rome. It is known that the fate of Italy is decided on the battlefields of North Italy. Hence Rome would fall with Lombardy and Piedmont, or France would have to declare war on Austria and thereby on the European counterrevolution. Did the National Assembly suddenly take the Barrot Ministry for the old Committee of Public Safety? Or itself for the Convention? Why, then, the military occupation of a point in Upper Italy? This transparent veil covered the expedition against Rome.

On April 14, 14,000 men sailed under Oudinot for Civitavecchia; on April 16 the National Assembly voted the ministry a credit of 1,200,000 francs for the maintenance of a fleet of intervention in the Mediterranean Sea for three months. Thus it gave the ministry every means of intervening against Rome, while it adopted the pose of letting it intervene against Austria. It did not see what the ministry did; it only heard what it said. Such faith was not found in Israel; the Constituent Assembly had fallen into the position of not daring to know what the constituted republic had to do.

Finally, on May 8, the last scene of the comedy was played; the Constituent Assembly urged the ministry to take swift measures to bring the Italian expedition back to the aim set for it. Bonaparte that same evening inserted a letter in the *Moniteur* in which he lavished the greatest appreciation on Oudinot. On May 11 the National Assembly rejected the bill of impeachment against this same Bonaparte and his ministry. And the *Montagne*, which instead of tearing this web of deceit to pieces took the parliamentary comedy tragically in order to play in it the role of Fouquier-Tinville, did not betray its natural petty-bourgeois calf's hide under the borrowed lion's skin of the Convention!

The latter half of the life of the Constituent Assembly is summarized thus: On January 29 it admits that the royalist bourgeois factions are the natural superiors of the republic constituted by it; on March 21, that the violation of the constitution is its realization; and on May 11, that the bombastically proclaimed passive alliance of the French republic with the struggling peoples means its active alliance with the European counterrevolution.

This miserable Assembly left the stage after it had given itself the satisfaction, two days before its first birthday, May 4, of rejecting the motion of amnesty for the June insurgents. Its power shattered, held in deadly hatred by the people, repulsed, maltreated, contemptuously thrown aside by the bourgeoisie, whose tool it was, forced in the second half of its life to disavow the first, robbed of its republican illusions, without having created anything great in the past, without hope in the future, and with its living body dying bit by bit, it was able to galvanize its own corpse into life only by continually recalling and living through the June victory over and over again, affirming itself by constantly repeated damnation of the damned. A vampire living on the blood of the June insurgents!

It left behind a state deficit increased by the costs of the June insurrection, by the loss of the salt tax, by the compensation it paid the plantation owners for abolishing Negro slavery, by the costs of the Roman expedition, by the loss of the wine tax, whose abolition it resolved upon when already at its last gasp—a malicious old man, happy to impose on his laughing heir a compromising debt of honor.

With the beginning of March the agitation for the election of the Legislative National Assembly had commenced. Two main groups opposed each other, the party of Order and the democratic-socialist, or Red, party; between the two stood the Friends of the Constitution, under which name the tricolor republicans of the *National* sought to put forward a party. The party of Order was formed directly after the June days; only after December 10 had allowed it to cast off the coterie of the *National*, of the bourgeois republicans, was the secret of its existence, the coalition of Orléanists and Legitimists into one party, disclosed. The bourgeois class fell apart into two big factions which alternately—the big landed proprietors under the restored monarchy and the finance aristocracy and the industrial bourgeoisie under the July Monarchy —had maintained a monopoly of power. Bourbon was the royal name for the predominant influence of the interests of the one faction, Orléans the royal name for the predominant influence of the interests of the other faction—the nameless realm of the republic was the only one in which both factions could maintain with equal power the common class interest without giving up their mutual rivalry. If the bourgeois republic could not be anything but the perfected and clearly expressed rule of the whole bourgeois class, could it be anything but the rule of the Orléanists supplemented by the Legitimists, and of the Legitimists supplemented by the Orléanists, the synthesis of the Restoration and the July Monarchy? The bourgeois republicans of the *National* did not represent any large faction of their class resting on economic foundations. They possessed only the importance and the historical claim of having asserted, under the monarchy, as against the two bourgeois factions that understood only their particular regime, the general regime of the bourgeois class, the nameless realm of the republic, which they idealized and embellished with antique arabesques, but in which above all they hailed the rule of their coterie. If the party of the *National* grew confused in its own mind when it descried the royalists in coalition at the top of the republic founded by it, these royalists deceived themselves no less concerning the fact of their united rule. They did not comprehend that if each of their factions, regarded separately, by itself, was royalist, the product of their chemical combination had necessarily to be republican, that the white and the blue monarchy had to neutralize each other in the tricolor republic. Forced by antagonism to the revolutionary proletariat and the transition classes thronging more and more around it as their center to summon their united strength and to conserve the organization of this united strength, each faction of the party of Order had to assert, as against the desire for restoration and the overweening presumption of the other, their joint rule, that is, the republican form of bourgeois rule. Thus we find these royalists in the beginning believing in an immediate restoration, later preserving the republican form with foaming rage and deadly invective against it on their lips, and finally confessing that they can endure each other only in the republic and postponing the restoration indefinitely. The enjoyment of the united rule itself strengthened each of the two factions, and made each of them still more unable and unwilling to subordinate itself to the other, that is, to restore the monarchy.

The party of Order directly proclaimed in its election program the rule of the bourgeois class, that is, the preservation of the life conditions of its rule: property, family, religion, order! Naturally it represented its class rule and the conditions of its class rule as the rule of civilization and as the necessary conditions of material production as well as of the relations of social intercourse arising from it. The party of Order had enormous money resources at its command; it organized its branches throughout France; it had all the ideologists of the old society in its pay; it had the influence of the existing governmental power at its disposal; it possessed an army of unpaid vassals in the whole mass of petty bourgeois and peasants, who, still removed from the revolutionary movement, found in the high dignitaries of property the natural representatives of their petty prejudices. This party, represented throughout the country by countless petty kings, could punish the rejection of their candidates as insurrection, dismiss the rebellious workers, the recalcitrant farm hands, domestic servants, clerks, railway officials, copyists, all the functionaries civilly subordinate to it. Finally, here and there it could maintain the delusion that the republican Constituent Assembly had prevented the Bonaparte of December 10 from manifesting his wonderworking powers. We have not mentioned the Bonapartists in connection with the party of Order. They were not a serious faction of the bourgeois class, but a collection of old, superstitious invalids and young, unbelieving soldiers of fortune. The party of Order was victorious in the elections; it sent a large majority to the Legislative Assembly.

As against the coalesced counterrevolutionary bourgeois class, the sections of the petty bourgeoisie and peasant class already revolutionized naturally had to ally themselves with the high dignitary of revolutionary interests, the revolutionary proletariat. We have seen how the democratic spokesmen of the petty bourgeoisie in parliament, that is, the *Montagne*, were driven by parliamentary defeats to the socialist spokesmen of the proletariat, and how the actual petty bourgeoisie, outside of parliament, was driven by the *concordats à l'amiable*, by the brutal enforcement of bourgeois interests, and by bankruptcy to the actual proletarians. On January 27 *Montagne* and the socialists had celebrated their reconciliation; at the great banquet of February, 1849, they repeated their act of union. The social and the democratic party, the party of the workers and that of the petty bourgeois, united to form the *social-democratic party*, that is, the *Red* party.

Paralyzed for a moment by the agony that followed the June days, the French republic had lived through a continuous series of feverish excitements since the raising of the state of siege, since October 19. First the struggle for the presidency, then the struggle between the President and the Constituent Assembly; the struggle for the clubs; the trial of Bourges which, in contrast with the petty figures of the President, the coalesced royalists, the respectable republicans, the democratic *Montagne*, and the socialist doctrines of the proletariat, caused the proletariat's real revolutionists to appear as primordial monsters such as only a deluge leaves behind on the surface of society, or such as could only precede a social deluge; the election agitation; the execution of the Bréa murderers; the continual proceedings against the press; the violent interference of the government with the banquets by police action; the insolent royalist provocations; the exhibition of the portraits of Louis Blanc and Caussidière on the pillory; the unbroken struggle between the constituted republic and the Constituent Assembly, which each moment drove the revolution back to its starting point, which each moment made the victors the vanquished and the vanquished the victors and in an instant changed around the positions of the parties and the classes, their separations and connections; the rapid march of the European counterrevolution; the glorious Hungarian fight; the armed uprisings in Germany; the Roman expedition; the ignominious defeat of the French army before Rome—in this vortex of the movement, in this torment of historical unrest, in this dramatic ebb and flow of revolutionary passions, hopes, and disappointments, the different classes of French society had to count their epochs of development in weeks when they had previously counted them in half-centuries. A considerable part of the peasants and of the provinces was revolutionized. Not only were they disappointed in Napoleon, but the Red party offered them, instead of the name, the content, instead of illusory freedom from taxation, repayment of the milliard paid to the Legitimists, the adjustment of mortgages, and the abolition of usury.

The army itself was infected with the revolutionary fever. In voting for Bonaparte it had voted for victory, and he gave it defeat. In him it had voted for the Little Corporal behind whom the great revolutionary general is concealed, and he once more gave it the great generals behind whom the pipe-clay corporal shelters himself. There was no doubt that the Red party, that is, the coalesced democratic party, was bound to celebrate, if not victory, still, great triumphs; that Paris, the army, and a great part of the provinces would vote for it. Ledru-Rollin, the leader of the *Montagne*, was elected by five departments; no leader of the party of Order carried off such a victory, no candidate belonging to the proletarian party proper. This election reveals to us the secret of the democratic-socialist party. If, on the one hand, the *Montagne*, the parliamentary champion of the democratic petty bourgeoisie, was forced to unite with the socialist doctrinaires of the proletariat—the proletariat, forced by the terrible material defeat of June to raise itself up again through intellectual victories and not yet enabled through the development of the remaining classes to seize the revolutionary dictatorship, had to throw itself into the arms of the doctrinaires of its emancipation, the founders of socialist sects—the revolutionary peasants, the army, and the provinces, on the other hand, ranged themselves behind the *Montagne*, which thus became lord and master in the revolutionary army camp and through the understanding with the socialists eliminated every antagonism in the revolutionary party. In the latter half of the life of the Constituent Assembly it represented the Assembly's republican fervor and caused to be buried in oblivion its sins during the Provisional Government, during the Executive Commission, during the June days. In the same measure as the party of the *National*, in accordance with its half-and-half nature, had allowed itself to be put down by the royalist ministry, the party of the Mountain, which had been brushed aside during the omnipotence of the *National*, rose and asserted itself as the parliamentary representative of the revolution. In fact, the party of the *National* had nothing to oppose to the other, royalist factions but ambitious personalities and idealistic humbug. The party of the Mountain, on the contrary, represented a mass hovering between the bourgeoisie and the proletariat, a mass whose material interests demanded democratic institutions. In comparison with the Cavaignacs and the Marrasts, Ledru-Rollin and the *Montagne*, therefore, represented the true revolution, and from the consciousness of this important situation they drew the greater courage the more the expression of revolutionary energy limited itself to parliamentary attacks, bringing in bills of impeachment, threats, raised voices, thundering speeches, and extremes which were pushed only as far as phrases. The peasants were in about the same position as the petty bourgeoisie; they had more or less the same social demands to put forward. All the middle strata of society, so far as they were driven into the revolutionary movement, were therefore bound to find their hero in Ledru-Rollin. Ledru-Rollin was the personage of the democratic petty bourgeoisie. As against the party of Order, the half-conservative, half-revolutionary, and wholly utopian reformers of this order had first to be pushed to the forefront.

The party of the *National*, "the Friends of the Constitution *quand même*," the *républicains purs et simples*, were completely defeated in the elections. A tiny minority of them was sent into the Legislative Chamber; their most noted leaders vanished from the stage, even Marrast, the editor in chief and the Orpheus of the respectable republic.

On May 28 the Legislative Assembly convened; on June 11 the collision of May 8 was renewed and, in the name of the *Montagne*, Ledru-Rollin brought in a bill of impeachment against the President and the ministry for violation of the constitution, for the bombardment of Rome. On June 12 the Legislative Assembly rejected the bill of impeachment, just as the Constituent Assembly had rejected it on May 11, but the proletariat this time drove the *Montagne* onto the streets—not to a street battle, however, but only to a street procession. It is enough to say that the *Montagne* was at the head of this movement to know that the movement was defeated, and that June, 1849, was a caricature, as ridiculous as it was vile, of June, 1848. The great retreat of June 13 was eclipsed only by the still greater battle report of Changarnier, the great man that the party of Order improvised. Every social epoch needs its great men, and when it does not find them, it invents them, as Helvétius says.

On December 20 only one half of the constituted bourgeois republic was in existence: the President; on May 28 it was completed by the other half, the Legislative Assembly. In June, 1848, the constituent bourgeois republic, by an unspeakable battle against the proletariat, and in June, 1849, the constituted bourgeois republic, by an unutterable comedy with the petty bourgeoisie, engraved their names in the birth register of history. June, 1849, was the nemesis of June, 1848. In June, 1849, it was not the workers that were vanquished; it was the petty bourgeois, who stood between them and the revolution, that were felled. June, 1849, was not a bloody tragedy between wage labor and capital, but a prison-filling and lamentable play of debtors and creditors. The party of Order had won, it was all-powerful; it had now to show what it was.

III
CONSEQUENCES OF JUNE 13, 1849

On December 20 the Janus head of the constitutional republic had still shown only one face, the executive face with the indistinct, plain features of L. Bonaparte; on May 28, 1849, it showed its second face, the legislative, pitted with the scars that the orgies of the Restoration and the July Monarchy had left behind. With the Legislative National Assembly the phenomenon of the constitutional republic was completed, that is, the republican form of government in which the rule of the bourgeois class is constituted, the common rule, therefore, of the two great royalist factions that form the French bourgeoisie, the coalesced Legitimists and Orléanists, the party of Order. While the French republic thus became the property of the coalition of the royalist parties, the European coalition of the counterrevolutionary powers embarked simultaneously upon a general crusade against the last places of refuge of the March revolutions. Russia invaded Hungary; Prussia marched against the army defending the Reich constitution; and Oudinot bombarded Rome. The European crisis was evidently approaching a decisive turning point; the eyes of all Europe were turned on Paris, and the eyes of all Paris on the Legislative Assembly.

On June 11 Ledru-Rollin mounted its tribune. He made no speech; he formulated an indictment of the ministers, naked, unadorned, factual, concentrated, forceful.

The attack on Rome is an attack on the constitution; the attack on the Roman republic is an attack on the French republic. Article 5 of the constitution reads: "The French republic never employs its forces against the liberty of any people whatsoever"—and the President employs the French army against Roman liberty. Article 54 of the constitution forbids the executive power to declare any war whatsoever without the consent of the National Assembly. The Constituent Assembly's resolution of May 8 expressly commands the ministers to make the Rome expedition conform with the utmost speed to its original mission; it therefore just as expressly prohibits war on Rome—and Oudinot bombards Rome. Thus Ledru-Rollin called the constitution itself as a witness for the prosecution against Bonaparte and his ministers. At the royalist majority of the National Assembly, he, the tribune of the constitution, hurled the threatening declaration: "The republicans will know how to command respect for the constitution by every means, be it even by force of arms!" *"By force of arms!"* came the hundredfold echo of the *Montagne*. The majority answered with a terrible tumult; the President of the National Assembly called Ledru-Rollin to order; Ledru-Rollin repeated the challenge, and finally laid on the President's table a motion for the impeachment of Bonaparte and his ministers. By 361 votes to 203, the National Assembly resolved to pass on from the bombardment of Rome to the next item on the agenda.

Did Ledru-Rollin believe he could beat the National Assembly by means of the constitution, and the President by means of the National Assembly?

To be sure, the constitution forbade any attack on the liberty of foreign peoples, but what the French army attacked in Rome was, according to the ministry, not "liberty" but the "despotism of anarchy." Had the *Montagne* still not comprehended, all experiences in the Constituent Assembly notwithstanding, that the interpretation of the constitution did not belong to those who had made it, but only to those who had accepted it? That its wording must be construed in its viable meaning and that the bourgeois meaning was its only viable meaning? That Bonaparte and the royalist majority of the National Assembly were the authentic interpreters of the constitution, as the priest is the authentic interpreter of the Bible, and the judge the authentic interpreter of the law? Should the National Assembly, freshly emerged from the general elections, feel itself bound by the testamentary provisions of the dead Constituent Assembly, whose will an Odilon Barrot had broken while it was alive? When Ledru-Rollin cited the Constituent Assembly's resolution of May 8, had he forgotten that the same Constituent Assembly on May 11 had rejected his first motion for the impeachment of Bonaparte and the ministers; that it had acquitted the President and the ministers; that it had thus sanctioned the attack on Rome as "constitutional"; that he only lodged an appeal against a judgment already delivered; that he, lastly, appealed from the republican Constituent Assembly to the royalist Legislative Assembly? The constitution itself calls insurrection to its aid by summoning, in a special article, every citizen to protect it. Ledru-Rollin based himself on this article. But at the same time, are not the public authorities organized for the defense of the constitution, and does not the violation of the constitution begin only from the moment when one of the constitutional public authorities rebels against the other? And the President of the republic, the ministers of the republic, and the National Assembly of the republic were in the most harmonious agreement.

What the *Montagne* attempted on June 11 was *"an insurrection within the limits of pure reason,"* that is, a purely *parliamentary insurrection*. The majority of the Assembly, intimidated by the prospect of an armed rising of the popular masses, was, in Bonaparte and the ministers, to destroy its own power and the significance of its own election. Had not the Constituent Assembly similarly attempted to annul the election of Bonaparte, when it insisted so obstinately on the dismissal of the Barrot-Falloux Ministry?

Neither were there lacking from the time of the Convention models for parliamentary insurrections which had suddenly transformed completely the relation between the majority and the minority—and should the young *Montagne* not succeed where the old had succeeded?—nor did relations at the moment seem unfavorable for such an undertaking. Popular unrest in Paris had reached an alarmingly high point; the army, according to its vote at the election, did not seem favorably inclined toward the government; the legislative majority itself was still too young to have become consolidated, and in addition it consisted of old gentlemen. If the *Montagne* were successful in a parliamentary insurrection, the helm of state would fall directly into its hands. The democratic petty bourgeoisie, for its part, wished, as always, for nothing more fervently than to see the battle fought out in the clouds over its head between the departed spirits of parliament. Finally, both of them, the democratic petty bourgeoisie and its representatives, the *Montagne*, would, through a parliamentary insurrection, achieve their great purpose, that of breaking the power of the bourgeoisie without unleashing the proletariat or letting it appear otherwise than in perspective; the proletariat would have been used without becoming dangerous.

After the vote of the National Assembly on June 11, a conference took place between some members of the *Montagne* and delegates of the secret workers' societies. The latter urged that the attack be started the same evening. The *Montagne* decisively rejected this plan. On no account did it want to let the leadership slip out of its hands; its allies were as suspect to it as its antagonists, and rightly so. The memory of June, 1848, surged through the ranks of the Paris proletariat more vigorously than ever. Nevertheless it was chained to the alliance with the *Montagne*. The latter represented the largest part of the departments; it had increased its influence in the army; it had at its disposal the democratic section of the National Guard; it had the moral power of the shopkeepers behind it. To begin the revolution at this moment against the will of the *Montagne* would have meant for the proletariat, decimated moreover by cholera and driven out of Paris in considerable numbers by unemployment, to repeat uselessly the June days of 1848, without the situation which had forced this desperate struggle. The proletarian delegates did the only rational thing. They obligated the *Montagne* to compromise itself, that is, to come out beyond the confines of the parliamentary struggle, in the event that its bill of impeachment was rejected. During the whole of June 13 the proletariat maintained this same skeptically watchful attitude, and awaited a seriously engaged irrevocable mêlée between the democratic National Guard and the army, in order then to plunge into the fight and push the revolution forward beyond the petty-bourgeois aim set for it. In the event of victory a proletarian commune was already formed which would take its place beside the official government. The Parisian workers had learned in the bloody school of June, 1848.

On June 12 Minister Lacrosse himself brought forward in the Legislative Assembly the motion to proceed at once to the discussion of the bill of impeachment. During the night the government had made every provision for defense and attack; the majority of the National Assembly was determined to drive the rebellious minority out into the streets; the minority itself could no longer retreat; the die was cast; the bill of impeachment was rejected by 377 votes to 8. The "Mountain," which had abstained from voting, rushed resentfully into the propaganda halls of the "pacific democracy," the newspaper offices of the *Démocratie Pacifique*.

Its withdrawal from the parliament building broke its strength as withdrawal from the earth broke the strength of Antaeus, her giant son. Samsons in the precincts of the Legislative Assembly, the *Montagnards* were only Philistines in the precincts of the "pacific democracy." A long, noisy, rambling debate ensued. The *Montagne* was determined to compel respect for the constitution by every means, *"only not by force of arms."* In this decision it was supported by a manifesto and by a deputation of "Friends of the Constitution." "Friends of the Constitution" was what the wreckage of the coterie of the *National*, the bourgeois-republican party, called itself. While six of its remaining parliamentary representatives had voted against, the others in a body voting for, the rejection of the bill of impeachment, while Cavaignac placed his saber at the disposal of the party of Order, the larger, extraparliamentary part of the coterie greedily seized the opportunity to emerge from its position of a political pariah and to press into the ranks of the democratic party. Did they not appear as the natural shield bearers of this party, which hid itself behind their shield, behind their *principles*, behind the *constitution?*

Till break of day the "Mountain" was in labor. It gave birth to "a proclamation to the people," which on the morning of June 13 occupied a more or less shamefaced place in two socialist journals. It declared the President, the ministers, and the majority of the Legislative Assembly *"outside the constitution"* and summoned the National Guard, the army, and finally also the people "to arise." *"Long live the Constitution!"* was the slogan it put forward, a slogan that signified nothing other than *"Down with the revolution!"*

In conformity with the constitutional proclamation of the Mountain, there was a so-called peaceful demonstration of the petty bourgeois on June 13, that is, a street procession from the Château d'Eau through the Boulevards, 30,000 strong, mainly National Guardsmen, unarmed, with an admixture of members of the secret workers' sections, moving along with the cry: *"Long live the Constitution!"* which was uttered mechanically, icily, and with a bad conscience by the members of the procession itself, and thrown back ironically by the echo of the people that surged along the sidewalks, instead of swelling up like thunder. From the many-voiced song the chest notes were missing. And when the procession swung by the meeting hall of the "Friends of the Constitution" and a hired herald of the constitution appeared on the housetop, violently cleaving the air with his claquer hat and from tremendous lungs letting the catchcry *"Long live the Constitution!"* fall like hail on the heads of the pilgrims, they themselves seemed overcome for a moment by the comedy of the situation. It is known how the procession, having arrived at the termination of the Rue de la Paix, was received in the Boulevards by the dragoons and chasseurs of Changarnier in an altogether unparliamentary way, how in a trice it scattered in all directions, and how it threw behind it a few shouts of "To arms" only in order that the parliamentary call to arms of June 11 might be fulfilled.

The majority of the *Montagne* assembled in the Rue du Hasard scattered when this violent dispersion of the peaceful procession, the muffled rumors of murder of unarmed citizens on the Boulevards, and the growing tumult in the streets seemed to herald the approach of a rising. Ledru-Rollin at the head of a small band of deputies saved the honor of the Mountain. Under the protection of the Paris Artillery, which had assembled in the Palais National, they betook themselves to the Conservatoire des Arts et Métiers, where the fifth and sixth legions of the National Guard were to arrive. But the *Montagnards* waited in vain for the fifth and sixth legions; these discreet National Guards left their representatives in the lurch; the Paris Artillery itself prevented the people from throwing up barricades; chaotic disorder made any decision impossible; the troops of the line advanced with fixed bayonets; some of the representatives were taken prisoner, while others escaped. Thus ended June 13.

If June 23, 1848, was the insurrection of the revolutionary proletariat, June 13, 1849, was the insurrection of the democratic petty bourgeois, each of these two insurrections being the classically pure expression of the class which had been its vehicle.

Only in Lyon did it come to an obstinate, bloody conflict. Here, where the industrial bourgeoisie and the industrial proletariat stand directly opposed to one another, where the workers' movement is not, as in Paris, included in and determined by the general movement, June 13, in its repercussion, lost its original character. Wherever else it broke out in the provinces it did not kindle fire—a cold lightning flash.

June 13 closes the first period in the life of the constitutional republic, which had attained its normal existence on May 28, 1849, with the meeting of the Legislative Assembly. The whole period of this prologue is filled with vociferous struggle between the party of Order and the *Montagne*, between the big bourgeoisie and the petty bourgeoisie, which strove in vain against the consolidation of the bourgeois republic, for which it had itself continuously conspired in the Provisional Government and in the Executive Commission, and for which, during the June days, it had fought fanatically against the proletariat. The thirteenth of June breaks its resistance and makes the legislative dictatorship of the united royalists a *fait accompli*. From this moment the National Assembly is only a Committee of Public Safety of the party of Order.

Paris had put the President, the ministers, and the majority of the National Assembly in a "state of impeachment"; they put Paris in a "state of siege." The Mountain had declared the majority of the Legislative Assembly "outside the constitution"; for violation of the constitution the majority handed over the Mountain to the *haute cour* and proscribed everything in it that still had vital force. It was decimated to a rump without head or heart. The minority had gone so far as to attempt a parliamentary insurrection; the majority elevated its parliamentary despotism to law. It decreed new "standing orders," which annihilate the freedom of the tribune and authorize the president of the National Assembly to punish representatives for violation of the standing orders with censure, with fines, with stoppage of their salaries, with suspension of membership, with incarceration. Over the rump of the Mountain it hung the rod instead of the sword. The remainder of the deputies of the Mountain owed it to their honor to make a mass exit. By such an act the dissolution of the party of Order would have been hastened. It would have had to break up into its original component parts the moment not even the semblance of an opposition would hold it together any longer.

Simultaneously with their parliamentary power, the democratic petty bourgeois were robbed of their armed power through the dissolution of the Paris Artillery and the eighth, ninth, and twelfth legions of the National Guard. On the other hand, the legion of high finance, which on June 13 had raided the print shops of Boulé and Roux, demolished the presses, played havoc with the offices of the republican journals, and arbitrarily arrested editors, compositors, printers, shipping clerks, and errand boys, received encouraging approval from the tribune of the National Assembly. All over France the disbanding of National Guards suspected of republicanism was repeated.

A new press law, a new law of association, a new law on the state of siege, the prisons of Paris overflowing, the political refugees driven out, all the journals that go beyond the limits of the *National* suspended, Lyon and the five departments surrounding it abandoned to the brutal persecution of military despotism, the courts ubiquitous, and the army of officials, so often purged, purged once more—these were the inevitable, the constantly recurring commonplaces of victorious reaction, worth mentioning after the massacres and the deportations of June only because this time they were directed not only against Paris but also against the departments, not only against the proletariat but, above all, against the middle classes.

The repressive laws by which the declaration of a state of siege was left to the discretion of the government, the press still more firmly muzzled, and the right of association annihilated, absorbed the whole of the legislative activity of the National Assembly during the months of June, July, and August.

However, this epoch is characterized not by the exploitation of victory in fact, but in principle; not by the resolutions of the National Assembly, but by the grounds advanced for these resolutions; not by the thing but by the phrase; not by the phrase but by the accent and the gesture which enliven the phrase. The brazen, unreserved expression of royalist sentiments, the contemptuously aristocratic insults to the republic, the coquettishly frivolous babbling of restoration aims— in a word, the boastful violation of republican decorum—give its peculiar tone and color to this period. Long live the Constitution! was the battle cry of the *vanquished* of June 13. The *victors* were therefore absolved from the hypocrisy of constitutional, that is, republican, speech. The counterrevolution subjugated Hungary, Italy, and Germany, and they believed that the restoration was already at the gates of France. Among the masters of ceremonies of the factions of Order there ensued a real competition to document their royalism in the *Moniteur*, and to confess, repent, and crave pardon before God and man for liberal sins perchance committed by them under the monarchy. No day passed without the February Revolution being declared a national calamity from the tribune of the National Assembly, without some Legitimist provincial cabbage-Junker solemnly stating that he had never recognized the republic, without one of the cowardly deserters of and traitors to the July Monarchy relating the belated deeds of heroism in the performance of which only the philanthropy of Louis Philippe or other misunderstandings had hindered him. What was admirable in the February days was not the magnanimity of the victorious people, but the self-sacrifice and moderation of the royalists, who had allowed it to be victorious. One Representative of the People proposed to divert part of the money destined for the relief of those wounded in February to the Municipal Guards, who alone in those days had deserved well of the fatherland. Another wanted to have an equestrian statue decreed to the Duke of Orléans in the Place du Carrousel. Thiers called the constitution a dirty piece of paper. There appeared in succession on the tribune Orléanists, to repent of their conspiracy against the legitimate monarchy; Legitimists, who reproached themselves with having hastened the overthrow of monarchy in general by resisting the illegitimate monarchy; Thiers, who repented of having intrigued against Molé; Molé, who repented of having intrigued against Guizot; Barrot, who repented of having intrigued against all three. The cry "Long live the Social-Democratic Republic!" was declared unconstitutional; the cry "Long live the Republic!" was prosecuted as social-democratic. On the anniversary of the Battle of Waterloo, a representative declared: "I fear an invasion of the Prussians less than the entry of the revolutionary refugees into France." To the complaints about the terrorism organized in Lyon and the neighboring departments, Baraguay d'Hilliers answered: "I prefer the white terror to the red terror." And the Assembly applauded frantically every time an epigram against the republic, against the revolution, against the constitution, for the monarchy, or for the Holy Alliance fell from the lips of its orators. Every infringement of the minutest republican formality—for example, that of addressing the representatives as *citoyens*—filled the knights of order with enthusiasm.

The by-elections in Paris on July 8, held under the influence of the state of siege and of the abstention of a great part of the proletariat from the ballot box, the taking of Rome by the French army, the entry into Rome of the red eminences and, in their train, of inquisition and monkish terrorism, added fresh victories to the victory of June and increased the intoxication of the party of Order.

Finally, in the middle of August, half with the intention of attending the Department Councils just assembled, half through exhaustion from the tendentious orgy of many months, the royalists decreed a two-month recess of the National Assembly. With transparent irony they left behind a commission of twenty-five representatives, the cream of the Legitimists and the Orléanists, a Molé and a Changarnier, as proxies for the National Assembly and as guardians of the republic. The irony was more profound than they suspected. They, condemned by history to help to overthrow the monarchy they loved, were destined by it to conserve the republic they hated.

The second period in the life of the constitutional republic, its royalist period of sowing wild oats, closes with the recess of the Legislative Assembly.

The state of siege in Paris had again been raised, the activities of the press had again begun. During the suspension of the social-democratic papers, during the period of repressive legislation and royalist bluster, the *Siècle*, the old literary representative of the monarchist-constitutional petty bourgeois, republicanized itself; the *Presse*, the old literary exponent of the bourgeois reformers, democratized itself; while the *National*, the old classic organ of the republican bourgeois, socialized itself.

The secret societies grew in extent and intensity in the same degree that the public clubs became impossible. The workers' industrial co-operatives, tolerated as purely commercial societies, while of no account economically, became politically so many means of cementing the proletariat. June 13 had struck off the official heads of the various semirevolutionary parties; the masses that remained won a head of their own. The knights of order had practiced intimidation by prophecies of the terror of the red republic; the base excesses, the hyperborean atrocities of the victorious counterrevolution in Hungary, in Baden, and in Rome washed the "red republic" white. And the malcontent intermediate classes of French society began to prefer the promises of the red republic with its problematic terrors to the terrors of the red monarchy with its actual hopelessness. No socialist in France spread more revolutionary propaganda than Haynau. *À chaque capacité selon ses œuvres!* [To each man of talent according to his work!]

In the meantime Louis Bonaparte exploited the recess of the National Assembly to make princely tours of the provinces, the most hot-blooded Legitimists made pilgrimages to Ems, to the grandchild of the saintly Louis, and the mass of the popular representatives on the side of order intrigued in the Department Councils, which had just met. It was necessary to make them pronounce what the majority of the National Assembly did not yet dare pronounce, an urgent motion for immediate revision of the constitution. According to the constitution, it could not be revised before 1852, and then only by a

National Assembly called together expressly for this purpose. If, however, the majority of the Department Councils expressed themselves to this effect, was not the National Assembly bound to sacrifice the virginity of the constitution to the voice of France? The National Assembly entertained the same hopes in regard to these provincial assemblies as the nuns in Voltaire's *Henriade* entertained in regard to the pandours. But, some exceptions apart, the Potiphars of the National Assembly had to deal with just so many Josephs of the provinces. The vast majority did not want to understand the importunate insinuation. The revision of the constitution was frustrated by the very instruments which were to have called it into being, by the votes of the Department Councils. The voice of France, and indeed of bourgeois France, had spoken and had spoken against revision.

At the beginning of October the Legislative National Assembly met once more—*tantum mutatus ab illo*.[7] Its physiognomy was completely changed. The unexpected rejection of revision on the part of the Department Councils had put it back within the limits of the constitution and indicated the limits of its term of life. The Orléanists had become mistrustful because of the pilgrimages of the Legitimists to Ems; the Legitimists had grown suspicious because of the Orléanists' negotiations with London; the journals of the two factions had fanned the fire and weighed the reciprocal claims of their pretenders. Orléanists and Legitimists grumbled in unison at the machinations of the Bonapartists, which showed themselves in the princely tours, in the more or less transparent emancipatory attempts of the President, in the presumptuous language of the Bonapartist newspapers; Louis Bonaparte grumbled at a National Assembly which found only the Legitimist-Orléanist conspiracy legitimate, at a ministry which betrayed him continually to this National Assembly. Finally, the ministry was itself divided on the Roman policy and on the income tax proposed by Minister Passy, decried as socialistic by the conservatives.

One of the first bills of the Barrot Ministry in the reassembled Legislative Assembly was a demand for a credit of 300,000 francs for the payment of a widow's pension to the Duchess of Orléans! The National Assembly granted it and added to the list of debts of the French nation a sum of seven million francs. Thus while Louis Philippe continued to play successfully the role of the *pauvre honteux*, the shamefaced beggar, the ministry dared not move an increase of salary for Bonaparte nor did the Assembly appear inclined to grant it. And Louis Bonaparte, as ever, vacillated in the dilemma: *Aut Caesar aut Clichy!*[8]

---

7. How great the change since then (Virgil, *Aeneid*).
8. *Either Caesar or Clichy*. Clichy was a debtors' prison in Paris.

The minister's second demand for a credit, one of nine million francs for the costs of the Rome expedition, increased the tension between Bonaparte on the one hand and the ministers and the National Assembly on the other. Louis Bonaparte had inserted a letter to his military aide, Edgar Ney, in the *Moniteur*, in which he bound the papal government to constitutional guarantees. The Pope, on his part, had published an address, *motu proprio* [in his own words], in which he rejected any limitation of his restored rule. Bonaparte's letter, with studied indiscretion, raised the curtain on his cabinet in order to expose himself to the eyes of the gallery as a benevolent genius who was, however, misunderstood and shackled in his own house. It was not the first time that he had coquetted with the "furtive flights of a free soul."[9] Thiers, the reporter of the commission, completely ignored Bonaparte's flight and contented himself with translating the papal allocution into French. It was not the ministry but Victor Hugo who sought to save the President through an order of the day in which the National Assembly was to express its agreement with Napoleon's letter. *Allons donc! Allons donc!* With this disrespectful, frivolous interjection the majority buried Hugo's motion. The policy of the President? The letter of the President? The President himself? *Allons donc! Allons donc!* Who the devil takes Monsieur Bonaparte seriously? Do you believe, Monsieur Victor Hugo, that we believe you that you believe in the President? *Allons donc! Allons donc!*

Finally, the breach between Bonaparte and the National Assembly was hastened by the discussion on the recall of the Orléans and the Bourbons. In default of the ministry, the President's cousin [Joseph Bonaparte], son of the ex-king of Westphalia, had put forward this motion, which had no other purpose than to push the Legitimist and the Orléanist pretenders down to the same level, or rather a *lower* level than the Bonapartist pretender, who at least stood in fact at the pinnacle of the state.

Napoleon Bonaparte was disrespectful enough to make the recall of the expelled royal families and the amnesty of the June insurgents parts of one and the same motion. The indignation of the majority compelled him to apologize immediately for this sacrilegious concatenation of the holy and the impious, of the royal races and the proletarian brood, of the fixed stars of society and of its swamp lights, and to assign each of the two motions to its proper place. The majority energetically rejected the recall of the royal family, and Berryer, the Demosthenes of the Legitimists, left no doubt about the

---

9. From Georg Herwegh, *"Aus den Bergen"* ("From the Mountains").

meaning of the vote. The civic degradation of the pretenders, that is what is intended! It is desired to rob them of their halo, of the last majesty that is left to them, the majesty of exile! What, cried Berryer, would the pretenders think of the President, who, forgetting his august origin, came here to live as a simple private individual? It could not have been more clearly intimated to Louis Bonaparte that he had not gained the day by his presence, that whereas the royalists in coalition needed him here in France as a "neutral man" in the presidential chair, the serious pretenders to the throne had to be kept out of profane sight by the fog of exile.

On November 1, Louis Bonaparte answered the Legislative Assembly with a message which in quite brusque words announced the dismissal of the Barrot Ministry and the formation of a new ministry. The Barrot-Falloux Ministry was the ministry of the royalist coalition, the Hautpoul Ministry was the ministry of Bonaparte, the organ of the President as against the Legislative Assembly, the ministry of the clerks.

Bonaparte was no longer the merely neutral man of December 10, 1848. His possession of the executive power had grouped a number of interests around him, the struggle with anarchy forced the party of Order itself to increase his influence, and if he was no longer popular, the party of Order was unpopular. Could he not hope to compel the Orléanists and the Legitimists, through their rivalry as well as through the necessity of some sort of monarchist restoration, to recognize the neutral pretender?

From November 1, 1849, dates the third period in the life of the constitutional republic, a period which closes with March 10, 1850. The regular game, so much admired by Guizot, of the constitutional institutions, the wrangling between executive and legislative power, now begins. More, as against the hankering for restoration on the part of the united Orléanists and Legitimists, Bonaparte defends his title to his actual power, the republic; as against the hankering for restoration on the part of Bonaparte, the party of Order defends its title to its common rule, the republic; as against the Orléanists, the Legitimists, and as against the Legitimists, the Orléanists, defend the status quo, the republic. All these factions of the party of Order, each of which has its own king and its own restoration *in petto* [secretly], mutually enforce, as against their rivals' hankering for usurpation and revolt, the common rule of the bourgeoisie, the form in which the special claims remain neutralized and reserved—*the republic*.

Just as Kant makes the republic, so these royalists make the monarchy the only rational form of state, a postulate of practical reason whose realization is never attained, but whose attainment must always be striven for and mentally adhered to as the goal.

Thus the constitutional republic had gone forth from the hands of the bourgeois republicans as a hollow ideological formula to become a form full of content and life in the hands of the royalists in coalition. And Thiers spoke more truly than he suspects when he said: "We, the royalists, are the true pillars of the constitutional republic."

The overthrow of the ministry of the coalition and the appearance of the ministry of the clerks has a second significance. Its Finance Minister was Fould. Fould as Finance Minister signifies the official surrender of France's national wealth to the Bourse, the management of the state's property by the Bourse and in the interests of the Bourse. With the nomination of Fould, the finance aristocracy announced its restoration in the *Moniteur*. This restoration necessarily supplemented the other restorations, which form just so many links in the chain of the constitutional republic.

Louis Philippe had never dared to make a genuine *loup-cervier* [stock-exchange wolf] finance minister. Just as his monarchy was the ideal name for the rule of the big bourgeoisie, so in his ministries the privileged interests had to bear ideologically disinterested names. The bourgeois republic everywhere pushed into the forefront what the different monarchies, Legitimist as well as Orléanist, had kept concealed in the background. It made earthly what they had made heavenly. In place of the names of the saints it put the bourgeois proper names of the dominant class interests.

Our whole exposition has shown how the republic, from the first day of its existence, did not overthrow but consolidated the finance aristocracy. But the concessions made to it were a fate to which submission was made without the desire to bring it about. With Fould, the initiative in the government returned to the finance aristocracy.

The question will be asked how the coalesced bourgeoisie could bear and suffer the rule of finance, which under Louis Philippe depended on the exclusion or subordination of the remaining bourgeois factions.

The answer is simple.

First of all, the finance aristocracy itself forms a weighty, authoritative part of the royalist coalition, whose common governmental power is denominated republic. Are not the spokesmen and leading lights among the Orléanists the old confederates and accomplices of the finance aristocracy? Is it not itself the golden phalanx of Orléanism? As far as the Legitimists are concerned, under Louis Philippe they had already participated in practice in all the orgies of the

Bourse, mine, and railway speculations. In general, the combination of large landed property with high finance is a normal fact. Proof: England; proof: even Austria.

In a country like France, where the volume of national production stands at a disproportionately lower level than the amount of the national debt, where government bonds form the most important subject of speculation and the Bourse the chief market for the investment of capital that wants to turn itself to account in an unproductive way —in such a country a countless number of people from all bourgeois or semibourgeois classes must have an interest in the state debt, in the Bourse gamblings, in finance. Do not all these interested subalterns find their natural mainstays and commanders in the faction which represents this interest in its vastest outlines, which represents it as a whole?

What conditions the accrual of state property to high finance? The constantly growing indebtedness of the state. And the indebtedness of the state? The constant excess of its expenditure over its income, a disproportion which is simultaneously the cause and effect of the system of state loans.

In order to escape from this indebtedness, the state must (1) restrict its expenditure, that is, simplify and curtail the government organism, govern as little as possible, employ as few personnel as possible, enter as little as possible into relations with bourgeois society. This path was impossible for the party of Order, whose means of repression, official interference in the name of the state, and ubiquity through organs of state were bound to increase in the same measure as the number of quarters increased from which its rule and the conditions for the existence of its class were threatened. The gendarmerie cannot be reduced in the same measure as attacks on persons and property increase.

Or (2) the state must seek to evade the debts and produce an immediate but transitory balance in its budget by putting extraordinary taxes on the shoulders of the wealthiest classes. But was the party of Order to sacrifice its own wealth on the altar of the fatherland to stop the national wealth from being exploited by the Bourse? *Pas si bête!* [Not so stupid!]

Therefore, without a complete revolution in the French state, no revolution in the French state budget. Along with this state budget necessarily goes the lordship of the trade in state debts, of the state creditors, the bankers, the money dealers, and the wolves of the Bourse. Only one faction of the party of Order was directly concerned in the overthrow of the finance aristocracy—the manufacturers. We are not speaking of the middle, of the smaller people en-

gaged in industry; we are speaking of the reigning princes of the
manufacturing interests, who had formed the broad basis of the
dynastic opposition under Louis Philippe. Their interest is indubitably
reduction of the costs of production and hence reduction of the taxes,
which enter into production, and hence reduction of the state debts,
the interest on which enters into the taxes, hence the overthrow of the
finance aristocracy.

In England—and the largest French manufacturers are petty bourgeois compared with their English rivals—we actually find the manufacturers, a Cobden, a Bright, at the head of the crusade against the
bank and the stock-exchange aristocracy. Why not in France? In
England industry predominates; in France, agriculture. In England
industry requires free trade; in France, protective tariffs, national
monopoly alongside the other monopolies. French industry does not
dominate French production; the French industrialists, therefore, do
not dominate the French bourgeoisie. In order to secure the advancement of their interests as against the remaining factions of the bourgeoisie, they cannot, like the English, take the lead of the movement
and simultaneously push their class interests to the fore; they must
follow in the train of the revolution, and serve interests which are
opposed to the collective interests of their class. In February they
had misunderstood their position; February sharpened their wits. And
who is more directly threatened by the workers than the employer,
the industrial capitalist? The manufacturer, therefore, of necessity became in France the most fanatical member of the party of Order. The
reduction of his profit by finance, what is that compared with the
abolition of profit by the proletariat?

In France, the petty bourgeois does what normally the industrial
bourgeois would have to do; the worker does what normally would
be the task of the petty bourgeois; and the task of the worker, who
accomplishes that? No one. In France it is not accomplished; in France
it is proclaimed. It is not accomplished anywhere within the national
boundaries. The class war within French society turns into a world
war, in which the nations confront one another. Accomplishment
begins only at the moment when, through the world war, the proletariat is pushed to the van of the people that dominates the world
market, to the van of England. The revolution, which finds here not
its end, but its organizational beginning, is no short-lived revolution.
The present generation is like the Jews whom Moses led through the
wilderness. It not only has a new world to conquer, it must go under
in order to make room for the men who are able to cope with a new
world.

Let us return to Fould.

On November 14, 1849, Fould mounted the tribune of the National Assembly and expounded his system of finance: an apology for the old system of taxes! Retention of the wine tax! Abandonment of Passy's income tax!

Passy, too, was no revolutionist; he was an old minister of Louis Philippe's. He belonged to the puritans of the Dufaure brand and to the most intimate confidants of Teste,[10] the scapegoat of the July Monarchy. Passy, too, had praised the old tax system and recommended the retention of the wine tax, but he had at the same time torn the veil from the state deficit. He had declared the necessity for a new tax, the income tax, if the bankruptcy of the state was to be avoided. Fould, who had recommended state bankruptcy to Ledru-Rollin, recommended the state deficit to the Legislative Assembly. He promised economies, the secret of which later revealed itself in that, for example, expenditures diminished by sixty millions while the floating debt increased by two hundred millions—conjurers' tricks in the grouping of figures, in the drawing up of accounts, which all finally amounted to new loans.

Alongside the other jealous bourgeois factions, the finance aristocracy naturally did not act in so shamelessly corrupt a manner under Fould as under Louis Philippe. But once it existed, the system remained the same: constant increase in the debts, masking of the deficit. And in time the old Bourse swindling came out more openly. Proof: the law concerning the Avignon Railway; the mysterious fluctuations in government securities, for a brief time the topic of the day throughout Paris; finally, the ill-starred speculations of Fould and Bonaparte on the elections of March 10.

With the official restoration of the finance aristocracy, the French people soon had to stand again before a February 24.

The Constituent Assembly, in an attack of misanthropy against its heir, had abolished the wine tax for the year of our Lord 1850. New debts could not be paid with the abolition of old taxes. Creton, a cretin of the party of Order, had moved the retention of the wine tax even before the Legislative Assembly recessed. Fould took up this motion in the name of the Bonapartist ministry and on December 20, 1849, the anniversary of the day Bonaparte was proclaimed President, the National Assembly decreed the restoration of the wine tax.

---

10. On July 8, 1847, before the Chamber of Peers in Paris, began the trial of Parmentier and General Cubières for bribery of officials with a view to obtaining a salt works concession, and of the then Minister of Public Works, Teste, for accepting such money bribes. The latter, during the trial, attempted to commit suicide. All were sentenced to pay heavy fines, Teste, in addition, to three years' imprisonment.—Note by Engels to the 1895 edition.

The sponsor of this restoration was not a financier; it was the Jesuit chief Montalembert. His argument was strikingly simple: Taxation is the maternal breast on which the government is suckled. The government is the instruments of repression; it is the organs of authority; it is the army; it is the police; it is the officials, the judges, the ministers; it is the *priests*. An attack on taxation is an attack by the anarchists on the sentinels of order, who safeguard the material and spiritual production of bourgeois society from the inroads of the proletarian vandals. Taxation is the fifth god, side by side with property, the family, order, and religion. And the wine tax is incontestably taxation and, moreover, not ordinary, but traditional, monarchically disposed, respectable taxation. *Vive l'impôt des boissons!* [Long live the tax on drinks!] Three cheers and one cheer more!

When the French peasant paints the devil he paints him in the guise of a tax collector. From the moment when Montalembert elevated taxation to a god, the peasant became godless, atheist, and threw himself into the arms of the devil, of *socialism*. The religion of order had forfeited him; the Jesuits had forfeited him; Bonaparte had forfeited him. December 20, 1849, had irrevocably compromised December 20, 1848. The "nephew of his uncle" was not the first of his family whom the wine tax defeated, this tax which, in Montalembert's phrase, heralds the revolutionary storm. The real, the great Napoleon declared on St. Helena that the reintroduction of the wine tax had contributed more to his downfall than all else, since it had alienated from him the peasants of Southern France. As far back as under Louis XIV the favorite object of the hatred of the people (see the writings of Boisguillebert and Vauban), abolished by the first revolution, it was reintroduced by Napoleon in a modified form in 1808. When the Restoration entered France, there trotted before it not only the Cossacks, but also the promises to abolish the wine tax. The *gentilhommerie* [gentry] naturally did not need to keep its word to the *gens taillables à merci et miséricorde* [people taxed pitilessly]. The year 1830 promised the abolition of the wine tax. It was not its way to do what it said or say what it did. The year 1848 promised the abolition of the wine tax, just as it promised everything. Finally, the Constituent Assembly, which promised nothing, made, as already mentioned, a testamentary provision whereby the wine tax was to disappear on January 1, 1850. And just ten days before January 1, 1850, the Legislative Assembly introduced it once more, so that the French people perpetually pursued it, and when they had thrown it out the door saw it come in again through the window.

The popular hatred of the wine tax is explained by the fact that it unites in itself all the odiousness of the French system of taxation.

The mode of its collection is odious, the mode of its distribution aristocratic, for the rates of taxation are the same for the commonest as for the costliest wines; it increases, therefore, in geometrical progression as the wealth of the consumers decreases, an inverted progressive tax. It accordingly directly provokes the poisoning of the laboring classes by putting a premium on adulterated and imitation wines. It lessens consumption, since it sets up *octrois* [toll houses] before the gates of all towns of over four thousand inhabitants and transforms each such town into a foreign country with a protective tariff against French wine. The big wine merchants, but still more the small ones, the *marchands de vins*, whose livelihood directly depends on the consumption of wine, are so many avowed enemies of the wine tax. And finally, by lessening consumption the wine tax curtails the producers' market. While it renders the urban workers incapable of paying for wine, it renders the wine growers incapable of selling it. And France has a wine-growing population of about twelve million. One can therefore understand the hatred of the people in general; one can in particular understand the fanaticism of the peasants against the wine tax. And in addition they saw in its restoration no isolated, more or less accidental event. The peasants have a kind of historical tradition of their own, which is handed down from father to son, and in this historical school it is muttered that whenever any government wants to dupe the peasants, it promises the abolition of the wine tax, and as soon as it has duped the peasants, it retains or reintroduces the wine tax. In the wine tax the peasant tests the bouquet of the government, its tendency. The restoration of the wine tax on December 20 meant: Louis Bonaparte is like the rest. But he was not like the rest; he was a *peasant discovery*, and in the petitions carrying millions of signatures against the wine tax they took back the votes that they had given a year before to the "nephew of his uncle."

The countryfolk—over two-thirds of the total French population —consist for the most part of so-called free landowners. The first generation, gratuitously freed by the Revolution of 1789 from its feudal burdens, had paid no price for the soil. But the following generations paid, under the form of the price of land, what their semiserf forefathers had paid in the form of rent, tithes, *corvée*, etc. The more, on the one hand, the population grew and the more, on the other hand, the partition of the soil increased, the higher became the price of the parcels, for the demand for them increased with their smallness. But in proportion as the price the peasant paid for his parcel rose, whether he bought it directly or whether he had it accounted as capital by his co-heirs, necessarily the indebtedness of the peasant, that is, the mortgage, also rose. The claim to a debt encumbering the land is termed a mortgage, a pawn ticket in respect of the land. Just as privileges accumulated on the medieval estate, mortgages accumulate on the modern small allotment. On the other hand, under the system of parcelization the soil is purely an instrument of production for its proprietor. Now the fruitfulness of land diminishes in the same measure as land is divided. The application of machinery to the land, the division of labor, major soil-improvement measures, such as cutting drainage and irrigation canals and the like, become more and more impossible, while the unproductive costs of cultivation increase in the same proportion as the division of the instrument of production itself. All this, regardless of whether the possessor of the small allotment possesses capital or not. But the more the division increases, the more does the parcel of land with its utterly wretched inventory form the entire capital of the small allotment peasant, the more does investment of capital in the land diminish, the more does the peasant lack land, money, and education for making use of the progress in agronomy, and the more does the cultivation of the soil retrogress. Finally, the net proceeds diminish in the same proportion as the gross consumption increases, as the whole family of the peasant is kept back from other occupations through its holding and yet is not enabled to live by it.

In the measure, therefore, that the population and, with it, the division of the land increases, does the instrument of production, the soil, become more expensive and its fertility decrease, does agriculture decline and the peasant become loaded with debt. And what was the effect becomes, in its turn, the cause. Each generation leaves behind another more deeply in debt; each new generation begins under more unfavorable and more aggravating conditions; mortgaging begets mortgaging, and when it becomes impossible for the peasant to offer his small holding as security for new debts, that is, to encumber it with new mortgages, he falls a direct victim to usury, and usurious interest rates become so much the more exorbitant.

Thus it came about that the French peasant cedes to the capitalist, in the form of interest on the mortgages encumbering the soil and in the form of interest on the advances made by the usurer without mortgages, not only ground rent, not only the industrial profit—in a word, not only the whole net profit—but even a part of the wages, and that therefore he has sunk to the level of the Irish tenant farmer —all under the pretense of being a private proprietor.

This process was accelerated in France by the ever growing burden of taxes, by court costs called forth in part directly by the formalities with which French legislation encumbers the ownership of land, in part by the innumerable conflicts over parcels everywhere bounding and crossing each other, and in part by the litigiousness of the peasants, whose enjoyment of property is limited to the fanatical assertion of their title to their fancied property, their property rights.

According to a statistical statement of 1840, the gross production of French agriculture amounted to 5,237,178,000 francs. Of this the costs of cultivation came to 3,552,000,000 francs, including consumption by the persons working. There remained a net product of 1,685,178,000 francs, from which 550,000,000 had to be deducted for interest on mortgages, 100,000,000 for law officials, 350,000,000 for taxes, and 107,000,000 for registration money, stamp duty, mortgage fees, etc. There was left one-third of the net product or 538,000,000; when distributed over the population, not 25 francs per head net product. Naturally, neither usury outside of mortgage nor lawyers' fees, etc., are included in this calculation.

The condition of the French peasants, when the republic had added new burdens to their old ones, is comprehensible. It can be seen that their exploitation differs only in form from the exploitation of the industrial proletariat. The exploiter is the same: *capital.* The individual capitalists exploit the individual peasants through mortgages and usury; the capitalist class exploits the peasant class through the state taxes. The peasant's title to property is the talisman by which capital held him hitherto under its spell, the pretext under which it set him against the industrial proletariat. Only the fall of capital can raise the peasant; only an anticapitalist, a proletarian government can break his economic misery, his social degradation. The constitutional republic is the dictatorship of his united exploiters; the social-democratic, the red republic, is the dictatorship of his allies. And the scale rises or falls according to the votes the peasant casts into the ballot box. He himself has to decide his fate. So spoke the socialists in pamphlets, almanacs, calendars, and leaflets of all kinds. This language became more understandable to him through the counter-writings of the party of Order, which for its part turned to him, and which by gross exaggeration, by its brutal conception and representation of the intentions and ideas of the socialists, struck the true peasant note and overstimulated his lust after forbidden fruit. But most understandable was the language of the actual experience that the peasant class had gained from the use of the suffrage, were the disillusionments overwhelming him, blow upon blow, with revolutionary speed. *Revolutions are the locomotives of history.*

The gradual revolutionizing of the peasants was manifested by various symptoms. It early revealed itself in the elections to the Legislative Assembly; it was revealed in the state of siege in the five departments bordering Lyon; it was revealed a few months after

June 13 in the election of a *Montagnard* in place of the former president of the *Chambre introuvable*[11] by the Department of the Gironde; it was revealed on December 20, 1849, in the election of a red in place of a deceased Legitimist deputy in the Department du Gard, that promised land of the Legitimists, the scene of the most frightful infamies committed against the republicans in 1794 and 1795 and the center of the white terror in 1815, when liberals and Protestants were publicly murdered. This revolutionizing of the most stationary class is most clearly evident since the reintroduction of the wine tax. The governmental measures and the laws of January and February, 1850, are directed almost exclusively against the departments and the peasants. The most striking proof of their progress.

The Hautpoul circular, by which the gendarme was appointed inquisitor of the prefect, of the subprefect, and, above all, of the mayor, and by which espionage was organized even in the hidden corners of the remotest village community; the law against the schoolteachers, by which they (the men of talent, the spokesmen, the educators and interpreters of the peasant class) were subjected to the arbitrary power of the prefect—they, the proletarians of the learned class, were chased like hunted beasts from one community to another; the bill against the mayors, by which the Damocles sword of dismissal was hung over their heads, and they, the presidents of the peasant communities, were every moment set in opposition to the President of the Republic and the party of Order; the ordinance which transformed the seventeen military districts of France into four pashaliks and forced the barracks and the bivouac on the French as their national salon; the education law, by which the party of Order proclaimed unconsciousness and the forcible stupefaction of France as the condition of its life under the regime of universal suffrage— what were all these laws and measures? Desperate attempts to reconquer the departments and the peasants of the departments for the party of Order.

Regarded as repression, they were wretched methods that wrung the neck of their own purpose. The big measures, like the retention of the wine tax, of the 45-centime tax, the scornful rejection of peasant petitions for the repayment of the milliard, etc., all these legislative thunderbolts struck the peasant class all at once, wholesale, from the center; the laws and measures cited made attack and resistance general, the topic of the day in every hut; they inoculated

---

11. This is the name given by history to the fanatically ultraroyalist and reactionary Chamber of Deputies elected immediately after the second overthrow of Napoleon, in 1815.—Note by Engels to the 1895 edition.

every village with revolution; they *localized and peasantized the revolution.*

On the other hand, do not these proposals of Bonaparte and their acceptance by the National Assembly prove the unity of the two powers of the constitutional republic, so far as it is a question of repression of anarchy—that is, of all the classes that rise against the bourgeois dictatorship? Did not Soulouque [Louis Bonaparte], directly after his brusque message, assure the Legislative Assembly of his *dévouement* [devotion] to order, through the immediately following message of Carlier, that dirty, mean caricature of Fouché, as Louis Bonaparte himself was the shallow caricature of Napoleon?

The education law shows us the alliance of the young Catholics with the old Voltaireans. Could the rule of the united bourgeois be anything else but the coalesced despotism of the pro-Jesuit Restoration and the make-believe free-thinking July Monarchy? Had not the weapons that the one bourgeois faction had distributed among the people against the other faction, in their mutual struggle for supremacy, again been torn from it, the people, since the latter was confronting their united dictatorship? Nothing has aroused the Paris shopkeeper more than this coquettish *étalage* [display] of Jesuitism, not even the rejection of the *concordats à l'amiable.*

Meanwhile the collisions between the different factions of the party of Order, as well as between the National Assembly and Bonaparte, continued. The National Assembly was far from pleased that Bonaparte, immediately after his *coup d'état,* after appointing his own, Bonapartist ministry, summoned before him the invalids of the monarchy, newly appointed prefects, and made their unconstitutional agitation for his reelection as President the condition of their appointment; that Carlier celebrated his inauguration with the closing of a Legitimist club, or that Bonaparte founded a journal of his own, *Le Napoléon,* which betrayed the secret longings of the President to the public, while his ministers had to deny them from the tribune of the Legislative Assembly. The latter was far from pleased by the defiant retention of the ministry, notwithstanding its various votes of no confidence; far from pleased by the attempt to win the favor of the noncommissioned officers by an extra pay of four sous a day and the favor of the proletariat by a plagiarization of Eugène Sue's *Mystères* by an honor loan bank; far from pleased, finally, by the effrontery with which the ministers were made to move the deportation of the remaining June insurgents to Algiers, in order to heap unpopularity on the Legislative Assembly *en gros,* while the President reserved popularity for himself *en détail,* by individual grants of pardon. Thiers let fall threatening words about *coups d'état* and *coups de tête* [rash acts], and the Legislative Assembly revenged itself on Bonaparte by rejecting every proposed law that he put forward for his own benefit, and by inquiring with noisy mistrust, in every instance when he made a proposal in the common interest, whether he did not aspire, through increase of the executive power, to augment the personal power of Bonaparte. In a word, it revenged itself by a conspiracy of contempt.

The Legitimist party, on its part, saw with vexation the more capable Orléanists once more occupying almost all posts and centralization increasing, while it sought its salvation principally in decentralization. And so it was. The counterrevolution centralized forcibly, that is, it prepared the mechanism of the revolution. It even centralized the gold and silver of France in the Paris Bank through the compulsory quotation of bank notes, and so created the ready war chest of the revolution.

Lastly, the Orléanists saw with vexation the emergent principle of legitimacy contrasted with their bastard principle, and themselves every moment snubbed and maltreated as the bourgeois *mésalliance* of a noble spouse.

Little by little we have seen peasants, petty bourgeois, the middle classes in general, stepping alongside the proletariat, driven into open antagonism to the official republic and treated by it as antagonists. *Revolt against bourgeois dictatorship, need of a change of society, adherence to democratic-republican institutions as organs of their movement, grouping around the proletariat as the decisive revolutionary power*—these are the common characteristics of the so-called party of social democracy, the party of the red republic. This party of anarchy, as its opponents christened it, is no less a coalition of different interests than the party of Order. From the smallest reform of the old social disorder to the overthrow of the old social order, from bourgeois liberalism to revolutionary terrorism—as far apart as this lie the extremes that form the starting point and the finishing point of the party of "anarchy."

Abolition of the protective tariff—socialism! For it strikes at the monopoly of the *industrial* faction of the party of Order. Regulation of the state budget—socialism! For it strikes at the monopoly of the *financial* faction of the party of Order. Free admission of foreign meat and corn—socialism! For it strikes at the monopoly of the third faction of the party of Order, *large landed property*. The demands of the free-trade party, that is, of the most advanced English bourgeois party, appear in France as so many socialist demands. Voltaireanism—socialism! For it strikes at a fourth faction of the party of Order, the *Catholic*. Freedom of the press, right of association, universal public education—socialism, socialism! They strike at the general monopoly of the party of Order.

So swiftly had the march of the revolution ripened conditions that the friends of reform of all shades, the most moderate claims of the middle classes, were compelled to group themselves around the banner of the most extreme party of revolution, around the red flag.

Yet manifold as the socialism of the different large sections of the party of anarchy was, according to the economic conditions and the total revolutionary requirements of the class or fraction of a class arising out of these, in one point it is in harmony: in proclaiming itself *the means of emancipating the proletariat* and the emancipation of the latter as its *object*. Deliberate deception on the part of some; self-deception on the part of the others, who promote the world transformed according to their own needs as the best world for all, as the realization of all revolutionary claims and the elimination of all revolutionary collisions.

Behind the general socialist phrases of the *party of anarchy*, which sound rather alike, there is concealed the socialism of the *National*, of the *Presse*, and of the *Siècle*, which more or less consistently wants to overthrow the rule of the finance aristocracy and to free industry and trade from their hitherto existing fetters. This is the socialism of industry, of trade, and of agriculture, whose bosses in the party of Order deny these interests, insofar as they no longer coincide with their private monopolies. Petty-bourgeois socialism, socialism par excellence, is distinct from this bourgeois socialism, to which, as to every variety of socialism, sections of the workers and petty bourgeois naturally rally. Capital hounds this class chiefly as its creditor, so it demands credit institutions; capital crushes it by competition, so it demands associations supported by the state; capital overwhelms it by concentration, so it demands progressive taxes, limitations on inheritance, taking over of large construction projects by the state, and other measures that forcibly stem the growth of capital. Since it dreams of the peaceful achievement of its socialism—allowing, perhaps, for a second February Revolution lasting a brief day or so—the coming historical process naturally appears to it as an application of systems which the thinkers of society, whether in companies or as individual inventors, devise or have devised. Thus they become the eclectics or adepts of the existing socialist systems, of doctrinaire socialism, which was the theoretical expression of the proletariat only as long as it had not yet developed further into a free historical movement of its own.

While this utopian doctrinaire socialism, which subordinates the total movement to one of its stages, which puts in place of common social production the brainwork of individual pedants and, above all, in fantasy does away with the revolutionary struggle of the classes and its requirements by small conjurers' tricks or great sentimentality; while this doctrinaire socialism, which at bottom only idealizes present society, takes a picture of it without shadows, and wants to achieve its ideal athwart the realities of present society; while the proletariat surrenders this socialism to the petty bourgeoisie; while the struggle of the different socialist leaders among themselves sets forth each of the so-called systems as a pretentious adherence to one of the transit points of the social revolution as against another—the proletariat rallies more and more around revolutionary socialism, around communism, for which the bourgeoisie has itself invented the name of Blanqui. This socialism is the *declaration of the permanence of the revolution*, the *class dictatorship* of the proletariat as the necessary transit point to the *abolition of class distinctions generally*, to the abolition of all the relations of production on which they rest, to the abolition of all the social relations that correspond to these relations of production, to the revolutionizing of all the ideas that result from these social relations.

The scope of this exposition does not permit of developing the subject further.

We have seen that just as in the party of Order the finance aristocracy necessarily took the lead, so in the party of "anarchy" the proletariat. While the different classes, united in a revolutionary league, grouped themselves around the proletariat, while the departments became ever more unsafe and the Legislative Assembly itself ever more morose toward the pretensions of the French Soulouque, the long deferred and delayed by-election of substitutes for the *Montagnards*, proscribed after June 13, drew near.

The government, scorned by its foes, maltreated and daily humiliated by its alleged friends, saw only one means of emerging from this repugnant and untenable position—a *revolt*. A revolt in Paris would have permitted the proclamation of a state of siege in Paris and the departments and thus the control of the elections. On the other hand, the friends of order, in face of a government that had gained victory over anarchy, were constrained to make concessions, if they did not want to appear as anarchists themselves.

The government set to work. At the beginning of February, 1850, provocation of the people by chopping down the trees of liberty. In vain. If the trees of liberty lost their place, the government itself lost its head and fell back, frightened by its own provocation. The National Assembly, however, received this clumsy attempt at emancipation on the part of Bonaparte with ice-cold mistrust. The removal of the wreaths of immortelles from the July column was no more successful. It gave part of the army an opportunity for revolutionary demonstrations and the National Assembly the occasion for a more or less veiled vote of no confidence in the ministry. In vain the government press threatened the abolition of universal suffrage and the invasion of the Cossacks. In vain was Hautpoul's direct challenge, issued to the Left in the Legislative Assembly itself, to betake itself to the streets, and his declaration that the government was ready to receive it. Hautpoul received nothing but a call to order from the President, and the party of Order, with silent, malicious joy, allowed a deputy of the Left to mock Bonaparte's usurpatory longings. In vain, finally, was the prophecy of a revolution on February 24. The government caused February 24 to be ignored by the people.

The proletariat did not allow itself to be provoked to *revolt*, because it was on the point of making a *revolution*.

Unhindered by the provocations of the government, which only heightened the general exasperation at the existing situation, the election committee, wholly under the influence of the workers, put forward three candidates for Paris: Deflotte, Vidal, and Carnot. Deflotte was a June deportee, amnestied through one of Bonaparte's popularity-seeking ideas; he was a friend of Blanqui and had taken part in the attempt of May 15. Vidal, known as a communist writer through his book *Concerning the Distribution of Wealth*, was formerly secretary to Louis Blanc in the Luxembourg Commission. Carnot, son of the man of the Convention who had organized the victory, the least compromised member of the *National* party, Minister of Education in the Provisional Government and the Executive Commission, was through his democratic public education bill a living protest against the education law of the Jesuits. These three candidates represented the three allied classes: at the head, the June insurgent, the representative of the revolutionary proletariat; next to him the doctrinaire socialist, the representative of the socialist petty bourgeoisie; finally, the third, the representative of the republican bourgeois party whose democratic formulas had gained a socialist significance vis-à-vis the party of Order and had long lost their own significance. This was a general coalition against the bourgeoisie and the government, as in February. But this time *the proletariat was at the head of the revolutionary league*.

In spite of all efforts the socialist candidates won. The army itself voted for the June insurgent against its own War Minister La Hitte. The party of Order was thunderstruck. The elections in the departments did not solace them; the departments gave a majority to the *Montagnards*.

The election of March 10, 1850! It was the revocation of June, 1848: the butchers and deporters of the June insurgents returned to the National Assembly but returned, bowed down, in the train of the deported, and with their principles on their lips. *It was the revocation of June 13, 1849:* the *Montagne*, proscribed by the National Assembly, returned to the National Assembly, but as advance trumpeters of the revolution, no longer as its commanders. *It was the revocation of December 10:* Napoleon had lost out with his Minister La Hitte. The parliamentary history of France knows only one analogy: the rejection of d'Haussez, minister of Charles X, in 1830. Finally, the election of March 10, 1850, *was the cancellation of the election of May 13,* which had given the party of Order a majority. The election of March 10 protested against the majority of May 13. March 10 was a revolution. Behind the ballots lie the paving stones.

"The vote of March 10 means war," shouted Ségur d'Aguesseau, one of the most advanced members of the party of Order.

With March 10, 1850, the constitutional republic entered a new phase, the phase of its dissolution. The different factions of the majority are again united among themselves and with Bonaparte; they are again the saviors of order; he is again their neutral man. If they remember that they are royalists, it happens only from despair of the possibility of a bourgeois republic; if he remembers that he is a pretender, it happens only because he despairs of remaining President.

At the command of the party of Order, Bonaparte answers the election of Deflotte, the June insurgent, by appointing Baroche Minister of Internal Affairs, Baroche, the accuser of Blanqui and Barbès, of Ledru-Rollin and Guinard. The Legislative Assembly answers the election of Carnot by adopting the education law, the election of Vidal by suppressing the socialist press. The party of Order seeks to blare away its own fears by the trumpet blasts of its press. "The sword is holy," cries one of its organs; "the defenders of order must take the offensive against the Red party," cries another; "between socialism and society there is a duel to the death, a war without surcease or mercy; in this duel of desperation one or the other must go under; if society does not annihilate socialism, socialism will annihilate society," crows a third cock of Order. Throw up the barricades of order, the barricades of religion, the barricades of the family! An end must be made of the 127,000 voters of Paris! A Bartholomew's Night for the socialists! And the party of Order believes for a moment in its own certainty of victory.

Their organs hold forth most fanatically of all against the *"boutiquiers* of Paris." The June insurgent of Paris elected by the shopkeepers of Paris as their representative! This means that a second

June, 1848, is impossible; this means that a second June 13, 1849, is impossible; this means that the moral influence of capital is broken; this means that the bourgeois assembly now represents only the bourgeoisie; this means that big property is lost, because its vassal, small property, seeks its salvation in the camp of the propertyless.

The party of Order naturally returns to its inevitable commonplace. "More repression," it cries, "tenfold repression!" But its power of repression has diminished tenfold, while resistance has increased a hundredfold. Must not the chief instrument of repression, the army, itself be repressed? And the party of Order speaks its last word: "The iron ring of suffocating legality must be broken. The constitutional republic is impossible. We must fight with our true weapons; since February, 1848, we have fought the revolution with its weapons and on its terrain; we have accepted its institutions; the constitution is a fortress which safeguards only the besiegers, not the besieged! By smuggling ourselves into holy Ilion in the belly of the Trojan horse, we have, unlike our forefathers, the *Grecs,* not conquered the hostile town, but made prisoners of ourselves."[12]

The foundation of the constitution, however, is universal suffrage. *Annihilation of universal suffrage*—such is the last word of the party of Order, of the bourgeois dictatorship.

On May 4, 1848, on December 20, 1848, on May 13, 1849, and on July 8, 1849, universal suffrage admitted that they were right. On March 10, 1850, universal suffrage admitted that it had itself been wrong. Bourgeois rule as the outcome and result of universal suffrage, as the express act of the sovereign will of the people—that is the meaning of the bourgeois constitution. But has the constitution any further meaning from the moment that the content of this suffrage, of this sovereign will, is no longer bourgeois rule? Is it not the duty of the bourgeoisie so to regulate the suffrage that it wills the reasonable, its rule? By ever and anon putting an end to the existing state power and creating it anew out of itself, does not universal suffrage put an end to all stability, does it not every moment question all the powers that be, does it not annihilate authority, does it not threaten to elevate anarchy itself to the position of authority? After March 10, 1850, who would still doubt it?

By repudiating universal suffrage, with which it hitherto draped itself and from which it sucked its omnipotence, the bourgeoisie openly confesses, "*Our dictatorship has hitherto existed by the will of the people; it must now be consolidated against the will of the*

---

12. A play on words: Greeks, but also professional cheats.—Note by Engels to the 1895 edition.

people." And, consistently, it seeks its props no longer within France, but without, in foreign countries, in *invasion.*

With the invasion, this second Coblenz,[13] its seat established in France itself, rouses all the national passions against itself. With the attack on universal suffrage it provides a general pretext for the new revolution, and the revolution requires such a pretext. Every special pretext would divide the factions of the revolutionary league, and give prominence to their differences. The general pretext stuns the semirevolutionary classes; it permits them to deceive themselves concerning the definite character of the coming revolution, concerning the consequences of their own act. Every revolution requires a question for discussion at banquets. Universal suffrage is the banquet question of the new revolution.

The bourgeois factions in coalition, however, are already condemned, since they take flight from the only possible form of their united power, from the most potent and complete form of their class rule, the constitutional republic, back to the subordinate, incomplete, weaker form of monarchy. They resemble the old man who in order to regain his youthful strength fetched out his boyhood garments and suffered torment trying to get his withered limbs into them. Their republic had the sole merit of being the hothouse of the revolution.

March 10, 1850, bears the inscription: *Après moi le déluge!*

IV

THE ABOLITION OF UNIVERSAL SUFFRAGE IN 1850[14]

The same symptoms have shown themselves in France since 1849, and particularly since the beginning of 1850. The Parisian industries are abundantly employed and the cotton factories of Rouen and Mulhouse are also doing pretty well, although here, as in England, the high prices of the raw material have exercised a retarding influ-

13. Coblenz was the center of the counterrevolutionary émigrés during the French Revolution.
14. The continuation of the three foregoing chapters is found in the *Revue* in the fifth and sixth double issue of the *Neue Rheinische Zeitung* [*Politisch-Ökonomische Revue*], the last to appear. Here, after the great commercial crisis that broke out in England in 1847 had first been described and the coming to a head of the political complications on the European continent in the revolutions of February and March, 1848, had been explained by its reactions there, it is then shown how the prosperity of trade and industry that again set in during the course of 1848 and increased still further in 1849 paralyzed the revolutionary upsurge and made possible the simultaneous victories of the reaction. With special reference to France, it is then said:—Written by Engels for the 1895 edition, as an introductory paragraph to Section IV.

ence. The development of prosperity in France was, in addition, especially promoted by the comprehensive tariff reform in Spain and by the reduction of the duties on various luxury articles in Mexico; the export of French commodities to both markets has considerably increased. The growth of capital in France led to a series of speculations, for which the exploitation of the California gold mines on a large scale served as a pretext. A swarm of companies have sprung up; the low denomination of their shares and their socialist-colored prospectuses appeal directly to the purses of the petty bourgeois and the workers, but all and sundry result in that sheer swindling which is characteristic of the French and Chinese alone. One of these companies is even patronized directly by the government. The import duties in France during the first nine months of 1848 amounted to 63,000,000 francs, of 1849 to 95,000,000 francs, and of 1850 to 93,000,000 francs. Moreover, in the month of September, 1850, they again rose by more than a million compared with the same month of 1849. Exports also rose in 1849, and still more in 1850.

The most striking proof of restored prosperity is the Bank's reintroduction of specie payment by the law of August 6, 1850. On March 15, 1848, the Bank had been authorized to suspend specie payment. Its note circulation, including that of the provincial banks, amounted at that time to 373,000,000 francs (£14,920,000). On November 2, 1849, this circulation amounted to 482,000,000 francs, or £19,280,000, an increase of £4,360,000, and on September 2, 1850, to 496,000,000 francs, or £19,840,000, an increase of about £5,000,000. This was not accompanied by any depreciation of the notes; on the contrary, the increased circulation of the notes was accompanied by the steadily increasing accumulation of gold and silver in the vaults of the Bank, so that in the summer of 1850 its metallic reserve amounted to about £14,000,000, an unprecedented sum in France. That the Bank was thus placed in a position to increase its circulation and therewith its active capital by 123,000,000 francs, or £5,000,000, is striking proof of the correctness of our assertion in an earlier issue that the finance aristocracy has not only not been overthrown by the revolution, but has even been strengthened. This result becomes still more evident from the following survey of French bank legislation during the last few years. On June 10, 1847, the Bank was authorized to issue notes of 200 francs; hitherto the smallest denomination had been 500 francs. A decree of March 15, 1848, declared the notes of the Bank of France legal tender and relieved it of the obligation of redeeming them in specie. Its note issue was limited to 350,000,000 francs. It was simultaneously authorized to issue notes of 100 francs. A decree of April 27 prescribed the merging of the departmental banks in the Bank of France; another decree, of May 2, 1848, increased the latter's note issue to 442,000,000 francs. A decree of December 22, 1849, raised the maximum of the note issue to 525,000,000 francs. Finally, the law of August 6, 1850, reestablished the exchangeability of notes for specie. These facts, the continual increase in the circulation, the concentration of the whole of French credit in the hands of the Bank, and the accumulation of all French gold and silver in the Bank's vaults led M. Proudhon to the conclusion that the Bank must now shed its old snakeskin and metamorphose itself into a Proudhonist people's bank. He did not even need to know the history of the English bank restriction from 1797 to 1819; he only needed to direct his glance across the Channel to see that this fact, for him unprecedented in the history of bourgeois society, was nothing more than a very normal bourgeois event, which only now occurred in France for the first time. One sees that the allegedly revolutionary theoreticians who, after the Provisional Government, talked big in Paris were just as ignorant of the nature and the results of the measures taken as the gentlemen of the Provisional Government themselves.

In spite of the industrial and commercial prosperity that France momentarily enjoys, the mass of the people, the twenty-five million peasants, suffer from a great depression. The good harvests of the past few years have forced the prices of corn much lower even than in England, and the position of the peasants under such circumstances, in debt, sucked dry by usury and crushed by taxes, must be anything but splendid. The history of the past three years has, however, provided sufficient proof that this class of the population is absolutely incapable of any revolutionary initiative.

Just as the period of crisis began later on the Continent than in England, so also did prosperity. The process originated in England, which is the demiurge of the bourgeois cosmos. On the Continent the various phases of the cycle repeatedly experienced by bourgeois society assume a secondary and tertiary form. First, the Continent exports to England disproportionately more than to any other country. This export to England, however, depends on the latter's position, especially in regard to the overseas market. England exports disproportionately more to overseas countries than to the whole Continent, so that the quantity of continental exports to those countries is always dependent on England's foreign trade. Hence when crises on the Continent produce revolutions there first, the bases for them are always laid in England. Violent outbreaks naturally erupt sooner at the extremities of the bourgeois body than in its heart, because in the latter the possibilities of accommodation are greater than in the

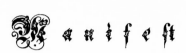

Manifest

ber

Kommunistischen Partei.

Veröffentlicht im Februar 1848.

Proletarier aller Länder vereinigt Euch!

London.

Gedruckt in der Office der „Bildungs-Gesellschaft für Arbeiter"
von J. E. Burghard.

46, LIVERPOOL STREET, BISHOPSGATE.

The first edition of The Communist Manifesto, *by Karl Marx and Frederick Engels, as published in London in 1848.*

(Top) Karl Marx in the 1870s. This photograph, by Mayall, hung in Stalin's office. (Bottom, left) Ferdinand Lassalle. (Bottom, right) Frederick Engels in the 1840s.

(Top, left) Georg Weerth, poet and friend of Marx. (Top, right) Wilhelm Wolff. (Bottom, left) Wilhelm Stieber, Prussian police spy. (Bottom, right) Wilhelm Liebknecht.

(Top, left) Joseph Bonaparte, King of Spain. (Top, right) Isabel II, Queen of Spain. (Bottom, left) Maria Christina, the Regent. (Bottom, right) Francisco Serrano, Duke de la Torre.

(Top, left) Marshal Narvaez, Duke of Valencia. (Top, right) Manuel Godoy. (Bottom, left) General Rafael del Riego. (Bottom, right) The guerrilla leader Juan Martín, "El Empecinado."

(Above) The French Provisional Government of 1848. Seated, Arago, Ledru-Rollin, Dupont, Marie, Lamartine; standing, Blanc, Crémieux, Marrast, Albert, Garnier-Pagès. (Below) William I of Prussia proclaimed Emperor, Versailles, 1871.

The French writer and politician Pierre Joseph Proudhon, author of La Philosophie de la Misère *and other early socialist works. From a painting done in 1853 by Gustave Courbet.*

Armand Barbès in prison, after the Revolution of 1848. Drawing by Traviès.

Caussidière, Police Prefect of Paris. Caricature by Tony Johannot.

(Top, left) Lamartine, Minister of Foreign Affairs in the Provisional Government. (Top, right) Ledru-Rollin, Minister of Interior. (Bottom, left) Thiers, head of Versailles Government. (Bottom, right) General Cavaignac. Paintings by Ary Scheffer, Mme. Mongez, Paul Delaroche, Ary Scheffer.

Blanqui, a leader of the Revolution of 1848 and, although a prisoner of Thiers, a spiritual leader of the Paris Commune. Repeatedly imprisoned, Blanqui held to his socialist principles, including advocacy of the dictatorship of the prole-tariat. From a painting by his wife.

Paul Lafargue, a Cuban-born Marxist organizer in France and Spain, and a leader of the Lyon revolt at the time of the Commune. Lafargue was married to Marx's daughter Laura.

Leaders of the Commune. (Clockwise) Assi, member of the Central Committee of the National Guard; Grousset, Delegate for Foreign Affairs; Trinquet, Committee of Police; Rigault, Chairman of the Committee of Public Safety.

(Clockwise) Ferré, member of the Commune's Committee of Police; Jourde, Chairman of the Finance Committee; Dombrowski, Polish revolutionary, Commander of the Armed Forces; Flourens, a Commander and Assistant Mayor.

Delescluze, revolutionist and Communard. Delescluze and Dombrowski died on the barricades. Assi, Grousset, Trinquet, and Jourde were exiled. Rigault, Ferré, and Flourens were shot by the Versailles Government.

Leading German-language theorists of Marxism in the generation after Marx.
Left, Eduard Bernstein (1850-1932); right, Karl Kautsky (1854-1938).

former. On the other hand, the degree to which continental revolutions affect England is at the same time the thermometer that indicates to what extent these revolutions really put into question bourgeois life conditions, and to what extent they touch only their political formations.

Given this general prosperity, wherein the productive forces of bourgeois society are developing as luxuriantly as it is possible for them to do within bourgeois relationships, a real revolution is out of the question. Such a revolution is possible only in periods when both of these factors—the *modern forces of production* and the *bourgeois forms of production*—come into *opposition* with each other. The various bickerings in which representatives of the individual factions of the continental party of Order presently engage and compromise each other, far from providing an occasion for revolution, are, on the contrary, possible only because the bases of relationships are momentarily so secure and—what the reactionaries do not know—so *bourgeois*. On this all the reactionary attempts to hold back bourgeois development will rebound just as much as will all the ethical indignation and all the enraptured proclamations of the democrats. *A new revolution is only a consequence of a new crisis. The one, however, is as sure to come as the other.*

Let us now turn to France.

The victory that the people, in conjunction with the petty bourgeois, had won in the elections of March 10 was annulled by the people itself when it provoked the new election of April 28. Vidal was elected not only in Paris, but also in the Lower Rhine. The Paris Committee, in which the *Montagne* and the petty bourgeoisie were strongly represented, induced him to accept for the Lower Rhine. The victory of March 10 ceased to be a decisive one; the date of the decision was once more postponed; the tension of the people was relaxed; it became accustomed to legal triumphs instead of revolutionary ones. The revolutionary meaning of March 10, the rehabilitation of the June insurrection, was finally completely annihilated by the candidature of Eugène Sue, the sentimental petty-bourgeois social-fantast, which the proletariat could at best accept as a joke to please the grisettes. As against this well-meaning candidature, the party of Order, emboldened by the vacillating policy of its opponents, put up a candidate who was to represent the June victory. This comic candidate was the Spartan *paterfamilias* Leclerc, from whose person, however, the heroic armor was torn piece by piece by the press, and who experienced a brilliant defeat in the election. The new election victory on April 28 put the *Montagne* and the petty bourgeoisie in high feather. They already exulted in the thought of being able to arrive at

the goal of their wishes in a purely legal way and without again pushing the proletariat into the foreground through a new revolution;
they reckoned positively on bringing Ledru-Rollin into the presidential chair and a majority of *Montagnards* into the Assembly through
universal suffrage in the new elections of 1852. The party of Order,
rendered perfectly certain by the prospective elections, by Sue's candidature, and by the mood of the *Montagne* and the petty bourgeoisie,
that the latter were resolved to remain quiet no matter what happened, answered the two election victories with an election law
which abolished universal suffrage.

The government took good care not to make this legislative
proposal on its own responsibility. It made an apparent concession to
the majority by entrusting the working out of the bill to the high
dignitaries of this majority, the seventeen burgraves. Thus it was not
the government that proposed the repeal of universal suffrage to the
Assembly; the majority of the Assembly proposed it to itself.

On May 8 the project was brought into the Chamber. The entire
social-democratic press rose as one man in order to preach to the
people dignified bearing, *calme majestueux*, passivity, and trust in its
representatives. Every article of these journals was a confession that a
revolution would, above all, annihilate the so-called revolutionary
press, and that therefore it was now a question of its self-preservation.
The allegedly revolutionary press betrayed its whole secret. It signed
its own death warrant.

On May 21 the *Montagne* put the preliminary question to debate
and moved the rejection of the whole project on the ground that it
violated the constitution. The party of Order answered that the
constitution would be violated if it were necessary; there was, however, no need for this at present, because the constitution was capable
of every interpretation, and because the majority alone was competent
to decide on the correct interpretation. To the unbridled, savage
attacks of Thiers and Montalembert the *Montagne* opposed a decorous
and refined humanism. It took its stand on the ground of law; the
party of Order referred it to the ground on which the law grows, to
bourgeois property. The *Montagne* whimpered: Did they really want,
then, to conjure up revolutions by main force? The party of Order
replied: One would await them.

On May 22 the preliminary question was settled by 462 votes to
227. The same men who had proved with such solemn profundity
that the National Assembly and every individual deputy would be renouncing his mandate if he renounced the people, his mandator, now
stuck to their seats and suddenly sought to let the country act, through
petitions at that, instead of acting themselves, and still sat there un-

moved when, on May 31, the law went through in splendid fashion. They sought to revenge themselves by a protest in which they recorded their innocence of the rape of the constitution, a protest which they did not even submit openly, but smuggled into the President's pocket from the rear.

An army of 150,000 men in Paris, the long deferment of the decision, the appeasing attitude of the press, the pusillanimity of the *Montagne* and of the newly elected representatives, the majestic calm of the petty bourgeois, but above all, the commercial and industrial prosperity, prevented any attempt at revolution on the part of the proletariat.

Universal suffrage had fulfilled its mission. The majority of the people had passed through the school of development, which is all that universal suffrage can serve for in a revolutionary period. It had to be set aside by a revolution or by the reaction.

The *Montagne* developed a still greater display of energy on an occasion that arose soon afterward. From the tribune War Minister Hautpoul had termed the February Revolution a baneful catastrophe. The orators of the *Montagne*, who, as always, distinguished themselves by their morally indignant bluster, were not allowed by the President, Dupin, to speak. Girardin proposed to the *Montagne* that it should walk out at once en masse. Result: The *Montagne* remained seated, but Girardin was cast out from its midst as unworthy.

The election law still needed one thing to complete it, a new press law. This was not long in coming. A proposal of the government, made many times more drastic by amendments of the party of Order, increased the caution money, put an extra stamp on *feuilleton* fiction (answer to the election of Eugène Sue), taxed all publications appearing weekly or monthly up to a certain number of sheets, and finally provided that every article of a journal must bear the signature of the author. The provisions concerning the caution money killed the so-called revolutionary press; the people regarded its extinction as satisfaction for the abolition of universal suffrage. However, neither the tendency nor the effect of the new law extended only to this section of the press. As long as the newspaper press was anonymous, it appeared as the organ of a numberless and nameless public opinion; it was the third power in the state. Through the signature of every article, a newspaper became a mere collection of literary contributions from more or less known individuals. Every article sank to the level of an advertisement. Hitherto the newspapers had circulated as the paper money of public opinion; now they were resolved into more or less bad solo bills, whose worth and circulation depended on the credit not only of the drawer but also of the endorser. The press of the party of Order had incited not only for the repeal of universal suffrage but also for the most extreme measures against the bad press. However, in its sinister anonymity even the good press was irksome to the party of Order and still more to its individual provincial representatives. As for itself, it demanded only the paid writer, with name, address, and description. In vain the good press bemoaned the ingratitude with which its services were rewarded. The law went through; the provision about the giving of names hit it hardest of all. The names of republican journalists were rather well known; but the respectable firms of the *Journal des Débats*, the *Assemblée Nationale*, the *Constitutionnel*, etc., etc., cut a sorry figure in their high protestations of state wisdom when the mysterious company all at once disintegrated into purchasable penny-a-liners of long practice, who had defended all possible causes for cash, like Granier de Cassagnac, or into old milksops who called themselves statesmen, like Capefigue, or into coquettish fops, like M. Lemoinne of the *Débats*.

In the debate on the press law the *Montagne* had already sunk to such a level of moral degeneracy that it had to confine itself to applauding the brilliant tirades of an old notable of Louis Philippe's time, M. Victor Hugo.

With the election law and the press law the revolutionary and democratic party exits from the official stage. Before their departure home, shortly after the end of the session, the two factions of the *Montagne*, the socialist democrats and the democratic socialists, issued two manifestoes, two *testimonia paupertatis* [certificates of pauperism] in which they proved that while power and success were never on their side, they nonetheless had ever been on the side of eternal justice and all the other eternal truths.

Let us now consider the party of Order. The *Neue Rheinische Zeitung* had said: "As against the hankering for restoration on the part of the united Orléanists and Legitimists, Bonaparte defends his title to his actual power, the republic; as against the hankering for restoration on the part of Bonaparte, the party of Order defends its title to its common rule, the republic; as against the Orléanists, the Legitimists, and as against the Legitimists, the Orléanists, defend the status quo, the republic. All these factions of the party of Order, each of which has its own king and its own restoration *in petto*, mutually enforce, as against their rivals' hankering for usurpation and revolt, the common rule of the bourgeoisie, the form in which the special claims remain neutralized and reserved—the republic. . . . And Thiers spoke more truly than he suspects when he said: 'We, the royalists, are the true pillars of the constitutional republic.' "

This comedy of the *républicains malgré eux* [republicans in spite of themselves], the antipathy to the status quo and the constant consolidation of it; the incessant friction between Bonaparte and the National Assembly; the ever renewed threat of the party of Order to split into its separate component parts, and the ever repeated conjugation of its factions; the attempt of each faction to transform each victory over the common foe into a defeat for its temporary allies; the mutual petty jealousy, chicanery, harassment, the tireless drawing of swords that ever and again ends with a *baiser Lamourette*[15]—this whole unedifying comedy of errors never developed more classically than during the past six months.

The party of Order regarded the election law at the same time as a victory over Bonaparte. Had not the government abdicated when it handed over the editing of and responsibility for its own proposal to the Commission of Seventeen? And did not the chief strength of Bonaparte as against the Assembly lie in the fact that he was the chosen of six millions? Bonaparte, on his part, treated the election law as a concession to the Assembly, with which he claimed to have purchased harmony between the legislative and executive powers. As reward, the vulgar adventurer demanded an increase of three millions in his civil list. Dared the National Assembly enter into a conflict with the executive at a moment when it had excommunicated the great majority of Frenchmen? It was roused to anger; it appeared to want to go to extremes; its commission rejected the motion; the Bonapartist press threatened, and referred to the disinherited people, deprived of its franchise; numerous noisy attempts at an arrangement took place, and the Assembly finally gave way in fact, but at the same time revenged itself in principle. Instead of increasing the civil list in principle by three millions per annum, it granted Bonaparte an accommodation of 2,160,000 francs. Not satisfied with this, it made even this concession only after it had been supported by Changarnier, the general of the party of Order and the protector thrust upon Bonaparte. Therefore it really granted the two millions not to Bonaparte, but to Changarnier.

This sop, thrown to him *de mauvaise grâce* [with bad grace], was accepted by Bonaparte quite in the spirit of the donor. The Bonapartist press blustered anew against the National Assembly. When in the debate on the press law the amendment was made on the signing of names—which, in turn, was directed especially against the less important papers—the representatives of the private interests of Bonaparte, the principal Bonapartist paper, the *Pouvoir*, published an open

---

15. Lamourette's kiss. On July 7, 1792, Bishop Adrien Lamourette, a deputy in the Legislative Assembly, proposed that party dissensions be ended with a fraternal kiss. The deputies enthusiastically embraced each other then, but the fraternal embrace was soon forgotten. French wits came to use the expression to denote a trivial love affair.

and vehement attack on the National Assembly. The ministers had to disavow the paper before the Assembly; the *gérant* [manager] of the *Pouvoir* was summoned before the bar of the National Assembly and sentenced to pay the highest fine, 5,000 francs. Next day the *Pouvoir* published a still more insolent article against the Assembly, and as the revenge of the government, the public prosecutor promptly prosecuted a number of Legitimist journals for violating the constitution.

Finally there came the question of proroguing the Assembly. Bonaparte desired this in order to be able to operate unhindered by the Assembly. The party of Order desired it partly for the purpose of carrying on its factional intrigues, partly for the pursuit of the private interests of the individual deputies. Both needed it in order to consolidate and push further the victories of reaction in the provinces. The Assembly therefore adjourned from August 11 until November 11. Since, however, Bonaparte in no way concealed that his only concern was to get rid of the irksome surveillance of the National Assembly, the Assembly imprinted on the vote of confidence itself the stamp of lack of confidence in the President. All Bonapartists were kept off the permanent commission of twenty-eight members who stayed on during the recess as guardians of the virtue of the republic. In their stead, even some republicans of the *Siècle* and the *National* were elected to it, in order to prove to the President the attachment of the majority to the constitutional republic.

Shortly before, and especially immediately after the recess, the two big factions of the party of Order, the Orléanists and the Legitimists, appeared to want to be reconciled, and this by a fusion of the two royal houses under whose flags they were fighting. The papers were full of reconciliation proposals that were said to have been discussed at the sickbed of Louis Philippe at St. Leonards, when the death of Louis Philippe suddenly simplified the situation. Louis Philippe was the usurper, Henry V the dispossessed; the Count of Paris, on the other hand, owing to the childlessness of Henry V, was his lawful heir to the throne. Every pretext for objecting to a fusion of the two dynastic interests was now removed. But precisely now the two factions of the bourgeoisie first discovered that it was not zeal for a definite royal house that divided them, but that it was rather their divided class interests that kept the two dynasties apart. The Legitimists, who had made a pilgrimage to the residence of Henry V at Wiesbaden just as their competitors had to St. Leonards, received there the news of Louis Philippe's death. Forthwith they formed a ministry *in partibus infidelium*,[16] which consisted mostly of members

---

16. In the realms of the unbelievers; referring to the non-Christian dioceses to which Catholic bishops were assigned by the Early Church.

of that commission of guardians of the virtue of the republic and which on the occasion of a squabble in the bosom of the party came out with the most outspoken proclamation of right by the grace of God. The Orléanists rejoiced over the compromising scandal that this manifesto called forth in the press, and did not conceal for a moment their open enmity to the Legitimists.

During the adjournment of the National Assembly, the Councils of the departments met. The majority of them declared for a more or less qualified revision of the constitution; that is, they declared for a not definitely specified monarchist restoration, for a "solution," and confessed at the same time that they were too incompetent and too cowardly to find this solution. The Bonapartist faction at once construed this desire for revision in the sense of a prolongation of Bonaparte's presidency.

The constitutional solution, the retirement of Bonaparte in May, 1852, the simultaneous election of a new President by all the electors of the land, the revision of the constitution by a Chamber of Revision during the first months of the new presidency, is utterly inadmissible for the ruling class. The day of the new presidential election would be the day of rendezvous for all the hostile parties, the Legitimists, the Orléanists, the bourgeois republicans, the revolutionists. It would have to come to a violent decision between the different factions. Even if the party of Order should succeed in uniting around the candidature of a neutral person outside the dynastic families, he would still be opposed by Bonaparte. In its struggle with the people, the party of Order is compelled constantly to increase the power of the executive. Every increase of the executive's power increases the power of its bearer, Bonaparte. In the same measure, therefore, as the party of Order strengthens its joint might, it strengthens the fighting resources of Bonaparte's dynastic pretensions, it strengthens his chance of frustrating a constitutional solution by force on the day of the decision. He will then have, as against the party of Order, no more scruples about the one pillar of the constitution than that party had, as against the people, about the other pillar in the matter of the election law. He would, seemingly even against the Assembly, appeal to universal suffrage. In a word, the constitutional solution questions the entire political status quo and behind the jeopardizing of the status quo the bourgeois sees chaos, anarchy, civil war. He sees his purchases and sales, his promissory notes, his marriages, his agreements duly acknowledged before a notary, his mortgages, his ground rents, house rents, profits, all his contracts and sources of income called in question on the first Sunday in May, 1852, and he cannot expose himself to this risk. Behind the jeopardizing of the political status quo lurks the danger of the collapse of the entire bourgeois society. The only possible solution in the framework of the bourgeoisie is the post-ponement of the solution. It can save the constitutional republic only by a violation of the constitution, by the prolongation of the power of the President. This is also the last word of the press of Order, after the protracted and profound debates on the "solutions" in which it indulged after the session of the general councils. The high and mighty party of Order thus finds itself, to its shame, compelled to take seriously the ridiculous, commonplace, and, to it, odious person of the pseudo Bonaparte.

This dirty figure likewise deceived himself about the causes that clothed him more and more with the character of the indispensable man. While his party had sufficient insight to ascribe the growing im-portance of Bonaparte to circumstances, he believed that he owed it solely to the magic power of his name and his continual caricaturing of Napoleon. He became more enterprising every day. To offset the pilgrimages to St. Leonards and Wiesbaden, he made his round trips through France. The Bonapartists had so little faith in the magic effect of his personality that they sent with him everywhere as claquers people from the Society of December 10, that organization of the Paris lumpen proletariat, packed en masse into railway trains and post chaises. They put speeches into the mouth of their marionette which, according to the reception in the different towns, proclaimed republican resignation or perennial tenacity as the keynote of the President's policy. In spite of all maneuvers these journeys were any-thing but triumphal processions.

When Bonaparte believed he had thus made the people enthusiastic, he set out to win the army. He caused great reviews to be held on the plain of Satory, near Versailles, at which he sought to buy the soldiers with garlic sausages, champagne, and cigars. Whereas the genuine Napoleon, amid the hardships of his campaigns of conquest, knew how to cheer up his weary soldiers with outbursts of patriarchal famili-arity, the pseudo Napoleon believed it was in gratitude that the troops shouted: *Vive Napoléon, vive le saucisson!* that is, Hurrah for the *Wurst* [sausage], hurrah for the *Hanswurst* [buffoon]!

These reviews led to the outbreak of the long suppressed dissen-sion between Bonaparte and his War Minister Hautpoul, on the one hand, and Changarnier, on the other. In Changarnier the party of Order had found its real neutral man, in whose case there could be no question of his own dynastic claims. It had designated him Bona-parte's successor. In addition, Changarnier had become the great gen-eral of the party of Order through his conduct on January 29 and June 13, 1849, the modern Alexander whose brutal intervention had, in the eyes of the timid bourgeois, cut the Gordian knot of the revolution. At bottom just as ridiculous as Bonaparte, he had thus become a power in the very cheapest manner and was set up by the National Assembly to watch the President. He himself coquetted, for example, in the matter of the salary grant, with the protection that he gave Bonaparte, and rose up ever more overpoweringly against him and the ministers. When, on the occasion of the election law, an insurrection was expected, he forbade his officers to take any orders whatever from the War Minister or the President. The press was also instrumental in magnifying the figure of Changarnier. With the complete absence of great personalities, the party of Order naturally found itself compelled to endow a single individual with the strength lacking in its class as a whole and so puff up this individual to a prodigy. Thus arose the myth of Changarnier, the "bulwark of society." The arrogant charlatanry, the secretive air of importance with which Changarnier condescended to carry the world on his shoulders, forms the most ridiculous contrast to the events during and after the [last] Satory review, which irrefutably proved that it needed only a stroke of the pen by Bonaparte, the infinitely little, to bring this fantastic offspring of bourgeois fear, the colossus Changarnier, back to the dimensions of mediocrity and transform him, society's heroic savior, into a pensioned general.

Bonaparte had for some time been revenging himself on Changarnier by provoking the War Minister to disputes in matters of discipline with the irksome protector. The last review at Satory finally brought the old animosity to a climax. The constitutional indignation of Changarnier knew no bounds when he saw the cavalry regiments file past with the unconstitutional cry: *Vive l'Empereur!* In order to forestall any unpleasant debate on this cry in the coming session of the Chamber, Bonaparte removed War Minister Hautpoul by appointing him governor of Algiers. In his place he put a reliable old general of the time of the Empire, one who was fully a match for Changarnier in brutality. But so that the dismissal of Hautpoul might not appear as a concession to Changarnier, he simultaneously transferred General Neumayer, the right hand of the great savior of society, from Paris to Nantes. It was Neumayer who at the last review had induced the whole of the infantry to file past the successor of Napoleon in icy silence. Changarnier, himself attacked in the person of Neumayer, protested and threatened. To no purpose. After two days' negotiations, the decree transferring Neumayer appeared in the *Moniteur,* and there was nothing left for the hero of Order but to submit to discipline or resign.

Bonaparte's struggle with Changarnier is the continuation of his struggle with the party of Order. The reopening of the National Assembly on November 11 will therefore take place under threatening auspices. It will be a storm in a teacup. In essence the old game must go on. Meanwhile the majority of the party of Order will, despite the clamor of the sticklers for principle in its different factions, be compelled to prolong the power of the President. Similarly, Bonaparte, already humbled by lack of money, will, despite all preliminary protestations, accept this prolongation of power from the hands of the National Assembly as simply delegated to him. Thus the solution is postponed; the status quo continued; one faction of the party of Order compromised, weakened, made unworkable by the other; the repression of the common enemy, the mass of the nation, extended and exhausted—until the economic relations themselves have again reached the point of development where a new explosion blows into the air all these squabbling parties with their constitutional republic.

For the peace of mind of the bourgeois it must be said, however, that the scandal between Bonaparte and the pary of Order has the result of ruining a multitude of small capitalists on the Bourse and putting their assets into the pockets of the big wolves of the Bourse.

The Eighteenth Brumaire of
Louis Napoleon*

PREFACE TO THE SECOND EDITION

My friend Joseph Weydemeyer, whose death was so untimely, intended to publish a political weekly in New York starting from January 1, 1852. He invited me to provide this weekly with a history of the *coup d'état*. Down to the middle of February, I accordingly wrote him weekly articles under the title *The Eighteenth Brumaire of Louis Bonaparte*. Meanwhile, Weydemeyer's original plan had fallen through. Instead, in the spring of 1852 he began to publish a monthly, *Die Revolution*, whose first number consists of my *Eighteenth Brumaire*. A few hundred copies of this found their way into Germany at that time, without, however, getting into the actual book market. A German bookseller of extremely radical pretensions to whom I offered the sale of my book was most virtuously horrified at a "presumption" so "contrary to the times."

From the above facts it will be seen that the present work took shape under the immediate pressure of events and its historical material does not extend beyond the month of February, 1852. Its republication now is due in part to the demand of the book trade, in part to the urgent requests of my friends in Germany.

Of the writings dealing with the same subject at approximately the same time as mine, only two deserve notice: Victor Hugo's

---

* Written from December, 1851, to February, 1852. The original title as it appeared in the New York German-language monthly, *Die Revolution*, was *The Eighteenth Brumaire of Louis Napoleon*. Later editions, including the second one, brought out in Hamburg in 1869, used the title, *The Eighteenth Brumaire of Louis Bonaparte*. The eighteenth Brumaire in the Revolutionary Calendar—November 9, 1799—was the day Napoleon Bonaparte made himself dictator by a *coup d'état*.

Napoléon le Petit and Proudhon's *Coup d'État.* Victor Hugo confines himself to bitter and witty invective against the responsible producer of the *coup d'état.* The event itself appears in his work like a bolt from the blue. He sees in it only the violent act of a single individual. He does not notice that he makes this individual great instead of little by ascribing to him a personal power of initiative unparalleled in world history. Proudhon, for his part, seeks to represent the *coup d'état* as the result of an antecedent historical development. Inadvertently, however, his historical construction of the *coup d'état* becomes a historical apologia for its hero. Thus he falls into the error of our so-called objective historians. I, on the contrary, demonstrate how the *class struggle* in France created circumstances and relationships that made it possible for a grotesque mediocrity to play a hero's part.

A revision of the present work would have robbed it of its particular coloring. Accordingly, I have confined myself to mere correction of printer's errors and to striking out allusions now no longer intelligible.

The concluding words of my work: "But when the imperial mantle finally falls on the shoulders of Louis Bonaparte, the bronze statue of Napoleon will come crashing down from the top of the Vendôme Column," have already been fulfilled. Colonel Charras opened the attack on the Napoleon cult in his work on the campaign of 1815. Subsequently, and especially in the past few years, French literature has made an end of the Napoleon legend with the weapons of historical research, criticism, satire, and wit. Outside France, this violent breach with the traditional popular belief, this tremendous mental revolution, has been little noticed and still less understood.

Lastly, I hope that my work will contribute toward eliminating the school-taught phrase now current, particularly in Germany, of so-called Caesarism. In this superficial historical analogy the main point is forgotten, namely, that in ancient Rome the class struggle took place only within a privileged minority, between the free rich and the free poor, while the great productive mass of the population, the slaves, formed the purely passive pedestal for these combatants. People forget Sismondi's significant saying: The Roman proletariat lived at the expense of society, while modern society lives at the expense of the proletariat. With so complete a difference between the material, economic conditions of the ancient and the modern class struggles, the political figures produced by them can likewise have no more in common with one another than the Archbishop of Canterbury has with the High Priest Samuel.

London, June 23, 1869

I*

Hegel remarks somewhere that all great world-historic facts and personages appear, so to speak, twice. He forgot to add: the first time as tragedy, the second time as farce. Caussidière for Danton, Louis Blanc for Robespierre, the *Montagne* of 1848 to 1851 for the *Montagne* of 1793 to 1795, the nephew for the uncle. And the same caricature occurs in the circumstances of the second edition of the Eighteenth Brumaire.

Men make their own history, but they do not make it as they please; they do not make it under self-selected circumstances, but under circumstances existing already, given and transmitted from the past. The tradition of all dead generations weighs like an Alp on the brains of the living. And just as they seem to be occupied with revolutionizing themselves and things, creating something that did not exist before, precisely in such epochs of revolutionary crisis they anxiously conjure up the spirits of the past to their service, borrowing from them names, battle slogans, and costumes in order to present this new scene in world history in this time-honored disguise and this borrowed language. Thus Luther put on the mask of the Apostle Paul, the Revolution of 1789–1814 draped itself alternately in the guise of the Roman Republic and the Roman Empire, and the Revolution of 1848 knew nothing better to do than to parody, now 1789, now the revolutionary tradition of 1793–95. In like manner, the beginner who has learned a new language always translates it back into his mother tongue, but he assimilates the spirit of the new language and expresses himself freely in it only when he moves in it without recalling the old and when he forgets his native tongue.

When we think about this conjuring up of the dead of world history, a salient difference reveals itself. Camille Desmoulins, Danton, Robespierre, St. Just, Napoleon, the heroes as well as the parties and the masses of the old French Revolution, performed the task of their time—that of unchaining and establishing modern bourgeois society —in Roman costumes and with Roman phrases. The first one destroyed the feudal foundation and cut off the feudal heads that had grown on it. The other created inside France the only conditions under which free competition could be developed, parceled-out land properly used, and the unfettered productive power of the nation employed; and beyond the French borders it swept away feudal

* Part I and Part VII are translated by the editor from the German edition of 1869; the rest of the translation, Parts II to VI, is based on the third edition, prepared by Engels (1885), as translated and published by Progress Publishers, Moscow, 1937.

institutions everywhere, to provide, as far as necessary, bourgeois society in France with an appropriate up-to-date environment on the
European continent. Once the new social formation was established,
the antediluvian colossi disappeared and with them also the resurrected
Romanism—the Brutuses, the Gracchi, the publicolas, the tribunes,
the senators, and Caesar himself. Bourgeois society in its sober reality
bred its own true interpreters and spokesmen in the Says, Cousins,
Royer-Collards, Benjamin Constants, and Guizots; its real military
leaders sat behind the office desk and the hog-headed Louis XVIII
was its political chief. Entirely absorbed in the production of wealth
and in peaceful competitive struggle, it no longer remembered that the
ghosts of the Roman period had watched over its cradle. But unheroic
though bourgeois society is, it nevertheless needed heroism, sacrifice,
terror, civil war, and national wars to bring it into being. And in the
austere classical traditions of the Roman Republic the bourgeois gladi-
ators found the ideals and the art forms, the self-deceptions, that they
needed to conceal from themselves the bourgeois-limited content of
their struggles and to keep their passion on the high plane of great
historic tragedy. Similarly, at another stage of development a century
earlier, Cromwell and the English people had borrowed from the Old
Testament the speech, emotions, and illusions for their bourgeois revolution. When the real goal had been achieved and the bourgeois transformation of English society had been accomplished, Locke supplanted
Habakkuk.

Thus the awakening of the dead in those revolutions served the
purpose of glorifying the new struggles, not of parodying the old; of
magnifying the given task in the imagination, not recoiling from its
solution in reality; of finding once more the spirit of revolution, not
making its ghost walk again.

From 1848 to 1851, only the ghost of the old revolution circulated
—from Marrast, the republican in yellow [kid] gloves who disguised
himself as old Bailly, down to the adventurer who hides his trivial
and repulsive features behind the iron death mask of Napoleon. A
whole nation, which thought it had acquired an accelerated power of
motion by means of a revolution, suddenly finds itself set back into a
defunct epoch, and to remove any doubt about the relapse, the old
dates arise again—the old chronology, the old names, the old edicts,
which had long since become a subject of antiquarian scholarship, and
the old minions of the law who had seemed long dead. The nation
feels like the mad Englishman in Bedlam who thinks he is living in
the time of the old Pharaohs and daily bewails the hard labor he must
perform in the Ethiopian gold mines, immured in this subterranean
prison, a pale lamp fastened to his head, the overseer of the slaves

behind him with a long whip, and at the exits a confused welter of barbarian war slaves who understand neither the forced laborers nor each other, since they speak no common language. "And all this," sighs the mad Englishman, "is expected of me, a freeborn Briton, in order to make gold for the Pharaohs." "In order to pay the debts of the Bonaparte family," sighs the French nation. The Englishman, so long as he was not in his right mind, could not get rid of his *idée fixe* of mining gold. The French, so long as they were engaged in revolution, could not get rid of the memory of Napoleon, as the election of December 10 proved. They longed to return from the perils of revolution to the fleshpots of Egypt, and December 2, 1851, was the answer. Now they have not only a caricature of the old Napoleon, but the old Napoleon himself, caricatured as he would have to be in the middle of the nineteenth century.

The social revolution of the nineteenth century cannot take its poetry from the past but only from the future. It cannot begin with itself before it has stripped away all superstition about the past. The former revolutions required recollections of past world history in order to smother their own content. The revolution of the nineteenth century must let the dead bury their dead in order to arrive at its own content. There the phrase went beyond the content; here the content goes beyond the phrase.

The February Revolution was a surprise attack, a seizing of the old society unawares, and the people proclaimed this unexpected stroke a deed of world importance, ushering in a new epoch. On December 2 the February Revolution is conjured away as a cardsharp's trick, and what seems overthrown is no longer the monarchy but the liberal concessions that had been wrung from it through centuries of struggle. Instead of society having conquered a new content for itself, it seems that the state has only returned to its oldest form, to a shamelessly simple rule by the sword and the monk's cowl. This is the answer to the *coup de main* of February, 1848, given by the *coup de tête* of December, 1851. Easy come, easy go. Meantime, the interval did not pass unused. During 1848–51 French society, by an abbreviated because revolutionary method, caught up with the studies and experiences which in a regular, so to speak, textbook course of development would have preceded the February Revolution, if the latter were to be more than a mere ruffling of the surface. Society seems now to have retreated to behind its starting point; in truth, it has first to create for itself the revolutionary point of departure—the situation, the relations, the conditions under which alone modern revolution becomes serious.

Bourgeois revolutions like those of the eighteenth century storm more swiftly from success to success, their dramatic effects outdo each other, men and things seem set in sparkling diamonds, ecstasy is the order of the day; but they are short-lived, soon they have reached their zenith, and a long *Katzenjammer* [crapulence] takes hold of society before it learns to assimilate the results of its storm-and-stress period soberly. On the other hand, proletarian revolutions like those of the nineteenth century constantly criticize themselves, constantly interrupt themselves in their own course, return to the apparently accomplished, in order to begin anew; they deride with cruel thoroughness the half-measures, weaknesses, and paltriness of their first attempts, seem to throw down their opponents only so the latter may draw new strength from the earth and rise before them again more gigantic than ever, recoil constantly from the indefinite colossalness of their own goals—until a situation is created which makes all turning back impossible, and the conditions themselves call out: *Hic Rhodus, hic salta!*[1]

For the rest, every fair observer, even if he had not followed the course of French developments step by step, must have had a presentiment of the imminence of an unheard-of disgrace for the revolution. It was enough to hear the complacent yelps of victory with which the democrats congratulated each other on the expectedly gracious consequences of the second Sunday in May, 1852. In their minds that second Sunday of May had become an *idée fixe*, a dogma, like the day of Christ's reappearance and the beginning of the millennium in the minds of the chiliasts. As always, weakness had taken refuge in a belief in miracles, believed the enemy to be overcome when he was only conjured away in imagination, and lost all understanding of the present in an inactive glorification of the future that was in store for it and the deeds it had in mind but did not want to carry out yet. Those heroes who seek to disprove their demonstrated incapacity by offering each other their sympathy and getting together in a crowd had tied up their bundles, collected their laurel wreaths in advance, and occupied themselves with discounting on the exchange market the republics *in partibus* for which they had already providently organized the government personnel with all the calm of their unassuming disposition. December 2 struck them like a thunderbolt from a clear sky, and those who in periods of petty depression gladly let their inner fears be drowned by the loudest ranters will

---

1. Here is the rose, here dance! From Aesop's fable, "The Swaggerer," referring to one who boasted that he had made a gigantic leap in Rhodes (which also means "rose" in Greek) and was challenged: "Here is Rhodes, here leap!" Marx's paraphrase, "Here is the rose, here dance," is from the quotation used by Hegel in the preface to his book *Outlines of the Philosophy of Right* (1821).

perhaps have convinced themselves that the times are past when the cackle of geese could save the Capitol.

The constitution, the National Assembly, the dynastic parties, the blue and red republicans, the heroes of Africa, the thunder from the platform, the sheet lightning of the daily press, the entire literature, the political names and the intellectual reputations, the civil law and the penal code, *liberté, égalité, fraternité,* and the second Sunday in May, 1852—all have vanished like a phantasmagoria before the spell of a man whom even his enemies do not make out to be a sorcerer. Universal suffrage seems to have survived only for the moment, so that with its own hand it may make its last will and testament before the eyes of all the world and declare in the name of the people itself: "All that exists deserves to perish."[2]

It is not enough to say, as the French do, that their nation was taken unawares. Nations and women are not forgiven the unguarded hour in which the first adventurer who came along could violate them. Such turns of speech do not solve the riddle but only formulate it differently. It remains to be explained how a nation of thirty-six millions can be surprised and delivered without resistance into captivity by three knights of industry.

Let us recapitulate in general outline the phases that the French Revolution went through from February 24, 1848, to December, 1851.

Three main periods are unmistakable: *the February period; the period of the constitution of the republic or the Constituent National Assembly*—May 4, 1848, to May 28, 1849; and *the period of the constitutional republic or the Legislative National Assembly*—May 28, 1849, to December 2, 1851.

The first period—from February 24, the overthrow of Louis Philippe, to May 4, 1848, the meeting of the Constituent Assembly— the February period proper, may be designated as the prologue of the revolution. Its character was officially expressed in the fact that the government it improvised itself declared that it was *provisional,* and like the government, everything that was mentioned, attempted, or enunciated during this period proclaimed itself to be only provisional. Nobody and nothing ventured to lay any claim to the right of existence and of real action. All the elements that had prepared or determined the revolution—the dynastic opposition, the republican bourgeoisie, the democratic-republican petty bourgeoisie, and the social-democratic workers, provisionally found their place in the February government.

It could not be otherwise. The February days originally intended

---

2. From Goethe's *Faust,* Part One.

an electoral reform by which the circle of the politically privileged among the possessing class itself was to be widened and the exclusive domination of the aristocracy of finance overthrown. When it came to the actual conflict, however—when the people mounted the barricades, the National Guard maintained a passive attitude, the army offered no serious resistance, and the monarchy ran away—the republic appeared to be a matter of course. Every party construed it in its own way. Having secured it arms in hand, the proletariat impressed its stamp upon it and proclaimed it to be a *social republic*. There was thus indicated the general content of the modern revolution, a content which was in most singular contradiction to everything that, with the material available, with the degree of education attained by the masses, under the given circumstances and relations, could be immediately realized in practice. On the other hand, the claims of all the remaining elements that had collaborated in the February Revolution were recognized by the lion's share they obtained in the government. In no period, therefore, do we find a more confused mixture of high-flown phrases and actual uncertainty and clumsiness, of more enthusiastic striving for innovation and more deeply rooted domination of the old routine, of more apparent harmony of the whole of society and more profound estrangement of its elements. While the Paris proletariat still reveled in the vision of the wide prospects that had opened before it and indulged in seriously meant discussions of social problems, the old powers of society had grouped themselves, assembled, reflected, and found unexpected support in the mass of the nation, the peasants and petty bourgeois, who all at once stormed onto the political stage after the barriers of the July Monarchy had fallen.

The second period, from May 4, 1848, to the end of May, 1849, is the period of the *constitution*, the *foundation, of the bourgeois republic*. Immediately after the February days not only had the dynastic opposition been surprised by the republicans and the republicans by the socialists, but all France by Paris. The National Assembly, which met on May 4, 1848, had emerged from the national elections and represented the nation. It was a living protest against the pretensions of the February days and was to reduce the results of the revolution to the bourgeois scale. In vain the Paris proletariat, which immediately grasped the character of this National Assembly, attempted on May 15, a few days after it met, to negate its existence forcibly, to dissolve it, to disintegrate again into its constituent parts the organic form in which the proletariat was threatened by the reacting spirit of the nation. As is known, May 15 had no other result but that of removing Blanqui and his comrades—that is, the real leaders of the proletarian party—from the public stage for the entire duration of the cycle we are considering.

The bourgeois monarchy of Louis Philippe can be followed only by a bourgeois republic; that is to say, whereas a limited section of the bourgeoisie ruled in the name of the king, the whole of the bourgeoisie will now rule in the name of the people. The demands of the Paris proletariat are utopian nonsense, to which an end must be put. To this declaration of the Constituent National Assembly the Paris proletariat replied with the June insurrection, the most colossal event in the history of European civil wars. The bourgeois republic triumphed. On its side stood the aristocracy of finance, the industrial bourgeoisie, the middle class, the petty bourgeois, the army, the lumpen proletariat organized as the Mobile Guard, the intellectual lights, the clergy, and the rural population. On the side of the Paris proletariat stood none but itself. More than three thousand insurgents were butchered after the victory, and fifteen thousand were deported without trial. With this defeat the proletariat passes into the background on the revolutionary stage. It attempts to press forward again on every occasion, as soon as the movement appears to make a fresh start, but with ever decreased expenditure of strength and always slighter results. As soon as one of the social strata above it gets into revolutionary ferment, the proletariat enters into an alliance with it and so shares all the defeats that the different parties suffer, one after another. But these subsequent blows become the weaker, the greater the surface of society over which they are distributed. The more important leaders of the proletariat in the Assembly and in the press successively fall victim to the courts, and ever more equivocal figures come to head it. In part it throws itself into *doctrinaire experiments, exchange banks and workers' associations, hence into a movement in which it renounces the revolutionizing of the old world by means of the latter's own great, combined resources, and seeks, rather, to achieve its salvation behind society's back, in private fashion, within its limited conditions of existence, and hence necessarily suffers shipwreck.* It seems to be unable either to rediscover revolutionary greatness in itself or to win new energy from the connections newly entered into, until *all classes* with which it contended in June themselves lie prostrate beside it. But at least it succumbs with the honors of the great, world-historic struggle; not only France, but all Europe trembles at the June earthquake, while the ensuing defeats of the upper classes are so cheaply bought that they require barefaced exaggeration by the victorious party to be able to pass for events at all, and become the more ignominious the further the defeated party is removed from the proletarian party.

The defeat of the June insurgents, to be sure, had now prepared, had leveled the ground on which the bourgeois republic could be founded and built, but it had shown at the same time that in Europe the questions at issue are other than that of "republic or monarchy." It had revealed that here "bourgeois republic" signifies the unlimited despotism of one class over other classes. It had proved that in countries with an old civilization, with a developed formation of classes, with modern conditions of production, and with an intellectual consciousness in which all traditional ideas have been dissolved by the work of centuries, *the republic signifies in general only the political form of revolution of bourgeois society and not its conservative form of life*—as, for example, in the United States of North America, where, though classes already exist, they have not yet become fixed, but continually change and interchange their elements in constant flux, where the modern means of production, instead of coinciding with a stagnant surplus population, rather compensate for the relative deficiency of heads and hands, and where, finally, the feverish, youthful movement of material production, which has to make a new world of its own, has neither time nor opportunity left for abolishing the old world of ghosts.

During the June days all classes and parties had united in the party of Order against the proletarian class as the party of anarchy, of socialism, of communism. They had "saved" society from "the enemies of society." They had given out the watchwords of the old society, "property, family, religion, order," to their army as passwords and had proclaimed to the counterrevolutionary crusaders: "In this sign thou shalt conquer!" From that moment, as soon as one of the numerous parties which gathered under this sign against the June insurgents seeks to hold the revolutionary battlefield in its own class interest, it goes down before the cry: "Property, family, religion, order." Society is saved just as often as the circle of its rulers contracts, as a more exclusive interest is maintained against a wider one. Every demand of the simplest bourgeois financial reform, of the most ordinary liberalism, of the most formal republicanism, of the most shallow democracy, is simultaneously castigated as an "attempt on society" and stigmatized as "socialism." And finally the high priests of "religion and order" themselves are driven with kicks from their Pythian tripods, hauled out of their beds in the darkness of night, put in prison vans, thrown into dungeons or sent into exile; their temple is razed to the ground, their mouths are sealed, their pens broken, their law torn to pieces in the name of religion, of property, of the family, of order. Bourgeois fanatics for order are shot down on their balconies by mobs of drunken soldiers, their domestic sanctuaries profaned, their houses bombarded for amusement—in the name of property, of the family, of religion, and of order. Finally, the scum of bourgeois society forms the holy phalanx of order and the hero Crapulinski installs himself in the Tuileries as the "savior of society."

II

Let us pick up the threads of the development once more.

The history of the Constituent National Assembly since the June days is the history of the domination and the disintegration of the republican faction of the bourgeoisie, of the faction known by the names of tricolor republicans, pure republicans, political republicans, formalist republicans, etc.

Under the bourgeois monarchy of Louis Philippe it had formed the official republican opposition and consequently a recognized component part of the political world of the day. It had its representatives in the Chambers and a considerable sphere of influence in the press. Its Paris organ, the *National*, was considered just as respectable in its way as the *Journal des Débats*. Its character corresponded to this position under the constitutional monarchy. It was not a faction of the bourgeoisie held together by great common interests and marked off by specific conditions of production. It was a clique of republican-minded bourgeois, writers, lawyers, officers, and officials that owed its influence to the personal antipathies of the country to Louis Philippe, to memories of the old republic, to the republican faith of a number of enthusiasts, above all, however, to *French nationalism*, whose hatred of the Vienna treaties and of the alliance with England it stirred up perpetually. A large part of the following the *National* had under Louis Philippe was due to this concealed imperialism, which could consequently confront it later, under the republic, as a deadly rival in the person of Louis Bonaparte. It fought the aristocracy of finance, as did all the rest of the bourgeois opposition. Polemics against the budget, which in France were closely connected with fighting the aristocracy of finance, procured popularity too cheaply and material for puritanical leading articles too plentifully not to be exploited. The industrial bourgeoisie was grateful to it for its slavish defense of the French protectionist system, which it accepted, however, more on national grounds than on grounds of national economy; the bourgeoisie as a whole, for its vicious denunciation of communism and socialism. For the rest, the party of the *National* was *purely republican;* that is, it demanded a republican instead of a monarchist form of bourgeois rule and, above all, the lion's share of this rule. About the conditions of this transformation it was by no means clear in its own mind. On the other hand, what was clear as daylight to it, and was publicly acknowledged at the reform banquets in the last days of Louis Philippe, was its unpopularity with the democratic petty bourgeois, and in particular with the revolutionary proletariat. These pure republicans, as is indeed the way with pure republicans, were already at the point of contenting themselves in the first instance with a regency of the Duchess of Orléans when the February Revolution broke out and assigned their best-known representatives a place in the Provisional Government. From the start they naturally had the confidence of the bourgeoisie and a majority in the Constituent National Assembly. The *socialist* elements of the Provisional Government were excluded forthwith from the Executive Commission which the National Assembly formed when it met, and the party of the *National* took advantage of the outbreak of the June insurrection to discharge the Executive Commission also, and therewith to get rid of its closest rivals, the petty-bourgeois, or democratic, republicans (Ledru-Rollin, etc.). Cavaignac, the general of the bourgeois-republican party who commanded the June massacre, took the place of the Executive Commission with a sort of dictatorial power. Marrast, former editor in chief of the *National,* became the perpetual president of the Constituent National Assembly, and the ministries, as well as all other important posts, fell to the portion of the pure republicans.

The republican bourgeois faction, which had long regarded itself as the legitimate heir of the July Monarchy, thus found its fondest hopes exceeded; it attained power, however, not as it had dreamed under Louis Philippe, through a liberal revolt of the bourgeoisie against the throne, but through a rising of the proletariat against capital, a rising laid low with grapeshot. What it had conceived as the *most revolutionary* event turned out in reality to be the *most counterrevolutionary.* The fruit fell into its lap, but it fell from the tree of knowledge, not from the tree of life.

The exclusive rule of the bourgeois republicans lasted only from June 24 to December 10, 1848. It is summed up in the drafting of a republican constitution and in the state of siege of Paris.

The new constitution was at bottom only the republicanized edition of the constitutional Charter of 1830. The narrow electoral qualification of the July Monarchy, which excluded even a large part of the bourgeoisie from political rule, was incompatible with the existence of the bourgeois republic. In lieu of this qualification, the February Revolution had at once proclaimed direct universal suffrage. The bourgeois republicans could not undo this event. They had to content themselves with adding the limiting proviso of a six months' residence in the constituency. The old organization of the administration, the municipal system, the judicial system, the army, etc., continued to exist inviolate, or, where the constitution changed them, the change concerned the table of contents, not the contents; the name, not the subject matter.

The inevitable general staff of the liberties of 1848, personal liberty, liberty of the press, of speech, of association, of assembly, of education and religion, etc., received a constitutional uniform which made them invulnerable. For each of these liberties is proclaimed as the absolute right of the French *citoyen*, but always with the marginal note that it is unlimited so far as it is not limited by the "equal rights of others and the public safety" or by "laws" which are intended to mediate just this harmony of the individual liberties with one another and with the public safety. For example: "The citizens have the right of association, of peaceful and unarmed assembly, of petition and of expressing their opinions, whether in the press or in any other way. *The enjoyment of these rights has no limit save the equal rights of others and the public safety.*" "Education is free. Freedom of education shall be *enjoyed* under the conditions fixed by law and under the supreme control of the state." "The home of every citizen is inviolable *except* in the forms prescribed by law." The constitution, therefore, constantly refers to future *organic* laws which are to put into effect those marginal notes and regulate the enjoyment of these unrestricted liberties in such manner that they will collide neither with one another nor with the public safety. And later these organic laws were brought into being by the friends of order and all those liberties regulated in such manner that the bourgeoisie in its enjoyment of them finds itself unhindered by the equal rights of the other classes. Where it forbids these liberties entirely to "the others," or permits enjoyment of them under conditions that are just so many police traps, this always happens solely in the interest of "public safety"—that is, the safety of the bourgeoisie—as the constitution prescribes. In the sequel, both sides accordingly appeal with complete justice to the constitution: the friends of order, who abrogated all these liberties, as well as the democrats, who demanded all of them. For each paragraph of the constitution contains its own antithesis, its own upper and lower house, namely, liberty in the general phrase, abrogation of liberty in the marginal note. Thus so long as the *name* of freedom was respected and only its actual realization prevented, of course in a legal way, the constitutional existence of liberty remained intact, inviolate, however mortal the blows dealt to its existence in actual life.

This constitution, made inviolable in so ingenious a manner, was nevertheless, like Achilles, vulnerable in one point—not in the heel, but in the head, or rather in the two heads it wound up with: the *Legislative Assembly* on the one hand, the *President* on the other. Glance through the constitution and you will find that only the paragraphs in which the relationship of the President to the Legislative Assembly is defined are absolute, positive, noncontradictory, and cannot be distorted. For here it was a question of the bourgeois republicans safeguarding themselves. Articles 45–70 of the Constitution are so worded that the National Assembly can remove the President constitutionally, whereas the President can remove the National Assembly only unconstitutionally, only by setting aside the constitution itself. Here, therefore, it challenges its forcible destruction. It not only sanctifies the division of powers, like the Charter of 1830, it widens it into an intolerable contradiction. The play of the constitutional powers, as Guizot termed the parliamentary squabble between the legislative and executive power, is in the constitution of 1848 continually played *va-banque* [staking all]. On one side are seven hundred and fifty representatives of the people, elected by universal suffrage and eligible for reelection; they form an uncontrollable, indissoluble, indivisible National Assembly, a National Assembly that enjoys legislative omnipotence, decides in the last instance on war, peace, and commercial treaties, alone possesses the right of amnesty, and, by its permanence, perpetually holds the front of the stage. On the other side is the President, with all the attributes of royal power, with authority to appoint and dismiss his ministers independently of the National Assembly, with all the resources of the executive power in his hands, bestowing all posts and disposing thereby in France of the livelihoods of at least a million and a half people, for so many depend on the five hundred thousand officials and officers of every rank. He has the whole of the armed forces behind him. He enjoys the privilege of pardoning individual criminals, of suspending National Guards, of discharging, with the concurrence of the Council of State, general, cantonal, and municipal councils elected by the citizens themselves. Initiative and direction are reserved to him in all treaties with foreign countries. While the Assembly constantly performs on the boards and is exposed to daily public criticism, he leads a secluded life in the Elysian Fields, and that with Article 45 of the constitution before his eyes and in his heart, crying to him daily: "*Frère, il faut mourir!*" ["Brother, one must die!"] Your power ceases on the second Sunday of the lovely month of May in the fourth year after your election! Then your glory is at an end, the piece is not played twice, and if you have debts, look to it quickly that you pay them off with the 600,000 francs granted you by the constitution, unless, perchance, you prefer to go to Clichy on the second Monday of the lovely month of May! Thus, whereas the constitution assigns power to the President, it seeks to secure moral power for the National Assembly. Apart from the fact that it is impossible to create a moral power by paragraphs of law, the constitution here abrogates itself once more by having the President elected by all Frenchmen through direct suffrage. While the votes of France are split up among the seven hundred and fifty members of the National Assembly, they are here, on the contrary, concentrated on a single individual. While each separate representative of the people represents only this or that party, this or that town, this or that bridgehead, or even only the mere necessity of electing someone as the seven hundred and fiftieth, without examining too closely either the cause or the man, *he* is the elect of the nation and the act of his election is the trump that the sovereign people plays once every four years. The elected National Assembly stands in a metaphysical relation, but the elected President in a personal relation, to the nation. The National Assembly, indeed, exhibits in its individual representatives the manifold aspects of the national spirit, but in the President this national spirit finds its incarnation. As against the Assembly, he possesses a sort of divine right; he is President by the grace of the people.

Thetis, the sea goddess, prophesied to Achilles that he would die in the bloom of youth. The constitution, which, like Achilles, had its weak spot, also had, like Achilles, a presentiment that it must go to an early death. It was sufficient for the constitution-making pure republicans to cast a glance from the lofty heaven of their ideal republic at the profane world to perceive how the arrogance of the royalists, the Bonapartists, the democrats, the communists, as well as their own discredit, grew daily in the same measure as they approached the completion of their great legislative work of art, without Thetis on this account having to leave the sea and communicate the secret to them. They sought to cheat destiny by a catch in the constitution, through Article 111, according to which every motion for a revision of the constitution must be supported by at least three-quarters of the votes, cast in three successive debates with an entire month between each, with the added proviso that not less than five hundred members of the National Assembly must vote. Thereby they merely made the impotent attempt to continue exercising a power—when only a parliamentary minority, as which they already saw themselves prophetically in their mind's eye—a power which at that time, when they commanded a parliamentary majority and all the resources of governmental authority, was daily slipping more and more from their feeble hands.

Finally the constitution, in a melodramatic paragraph, entrusts itself "to the vigilance and the patriotism of the whole French people and every single Frenchman," after it has previously entrusted in another paragraph the "vigilant" and "patriotic" to the tender, most painstaking care of the High Court of Justice, the *haute cour* it invented for the purpose.

Such was the Constitution of 1848, which on December 2, 1851, was not overthrown by a head, but fell down at the touch of a mere hat; this hat, to be sure, was a three-cornered Napoleonic hat.

While the bourgeois republicans in the Assembly were busy devising, discussing, and voting this constitution, Cavaignac outside the Assembly maintained the state of siege of Paris. The state of siege of Paris was the midwife of the Constituent Assembly in its travail of republican creation. If the constitution is subsequently put out of existence by bayonets, it must not be forgotten that it was likewise by bayonets, and these turned against the people, that it had to be protected in its mother's womb and by bayonets that it had to be brought into existence. The forefathers of the "respectable republicans" had sent their symbol, the tricolor, on a tour around Europe. They themselves in turn produced an invention that of itself made its way over the whole Continent, but returned to France with ever renewed love until it has now become naturalized in half her departments—the state of siege. A splendid invention, periodically employed in every ensuing crisis in the course of the French Revolution. But barrack and bivouac, which were thus periodically laid on French society's head to compress its brain and render it quiet; saber and musket, which were periodically allowed to act as judges and administrators, as guardians and censors, to play policeman and do night watchman's duty; mustache and uniform, which were periodically trumpeted forth as the highest wisdom of society and as its rector— were not barrack and bivouac, saber and musket, mustache and uniform finally bound to hit upon the idea of instead saving society once and for all by proclaiming their own regime as the highest and freeing civil society completely from the trouble of governing itself? Barrack and bivouac, saber and musket, mustache and uniform were bound to hit upon this idea all the more as they might then also expect better cash payment for their higher services, whereas from the merely periodic state of siege and the transient rescues of society at the bidding of this or that bourgeois faction, little of substance was gleaned save some killed and wounded and some friendly bourgeois grimaces. Should not the military at last one day play state of siege in their own interest and for their own benefit, and at the same time besiege the citizens' purses? Moreover, be it noted in passing, one must not forget that Colonel Bernard, the same military commission president who under Cavaignac had fifteen thousand insurgents deported without trial, is at this moment again at the head of the military commissions active in Paris.

Whereas with the state of siege in Paris, the respectable, the pure republicans planted the nursery in which the praetorians of December 2, 1851, were to grow up, they on the other hand deserve praise for the reason that, instead of exaggerating the national sentiment as under Louis Philippe, they now, when they had command of the national power, crawled before foreign countries, and instead of setting Italy free, let her be reconquered by Austrians and Neapolitans. Louis Bonaparte's election as President on December 10, 1848, put an end to the dictatorship of Cavaignac and to the Constituent Assembly.

In Article 44 of the Constitution it is stated: "The President of the French Republic must never have lost his status of French citizen." The first President of the French Republic, L. N. Bonaparte, had not merely lost his status of French citizen, had not only been an English special constable, he was even a naturalized Swiss.

I have worked out elsewhere the significance of the election of December 10. I will not revert to it here. It is sufficient to remark here that it was a *reaction of the peasants*, who had had to pay the costs of the February Revolution, against the remaining classes of the nation; a reaction of the country against the town. It met with great approval in the army, for which the republicans of the *National* had provided neither glory nor additional pay; among the big bourgeoisie, which hailed Bonaparte as a bridge to monarchy; among the proletarians and petty bourgeois, who hailed him as a scourge for Cavaignac. I shall have an opportunity later of going more closely into the relationship of the peasants to the French Revolution.

The period from December 20, 1848, until the dissolution of the Constituent Assembly in May, 1849, comprises the history of the downfall of the bourgeois republicans. After having founded a republic for the bourgeoisie, driven the revolutionary proletariat out of the field, and reduced the democratic petty bourgeoisie to silence for the time being, they are themselves thrust aside by the mass of the bourgeoisie, which justly impounds this republic as its property. This bourgeois mass was, however, royalist. One section of it, the large landowners, had ruled during the Restoration and was accordingly Legitimist. The other, the aristocrats of finance and big industrialists, had ruled during the July Monarchy and was consequently Orléanist. The high dignitaries of the army, the university, the church, the bar, the academy, and the press were to be found on either side, though in various proportions. Here, in the bourgeois republic, which bore neither the name Bourbon nor the name Orléans, but the name *capital*, they had found the form of state in which they could rule conjointly. The June insurrection had already united them in the party of Order. Now it was necessary, in the first place, to remove the coterie of bourgeois republicans who still occupied the seats of the National Assembly. Just as brutal as these pure republicans had been in their misuse of physical force against the people, just as cowardly, mealy-mouthed, broken-spirited, and incapable of fighting were they now in their retreat, when it was a question of maintaining their republicanism and their legislative rights against the executive power and the royalists. I need not relate here the ignominious history of their dissolution. They did not succumb; they passed out of existence. Their history has come to an end forever, and, both inside and outside the Assembly, they figure in the following period only as memories, memories that seem to regain life whenever the mere name republic is once more the issue and as often as the revolutionary conflict threatens to sink down to the lowest level. I may remark in passing that the journal which gave its name to this party, the *National*, was converted to socialism in the following period.

Before we finish with this period we must still cast a retrospective glance at the two powers, one of which annihilated the other on December 2, 1851, whereas from December 20, 1848, until the exit of the Constituent Assembly, they had lived in conjugal relations. We mean Louis Bonaparte, on the one hand, and the party of the coalesced royalists, the party of Order, of the big bourgeoisie, on the other. On acceding to the presidency, Bonaparte at once formed a ministry of the party of Order, at the head of which he placed Odilon Barrot, the old leader, *notabene*, of the most liberal faction of the parliamentary bourgeoisie. M. Barrot had at last secured the ministerial portfolio whose image had haunted him since 1830, and what is more, the premiership in the ministry; but not, as he had imagined under Louis Philippe, as the most advanced leader of the parliamentary opposition, but with the task of putting a parliament to death, and as the confederate of all his archenemies, Jesuits and Legitimists. He brought the bride home at last, but only after she had been prostituted. Bonaparte seemed to efface himself completely. This party acted for him.

The very first meeting of the council of ministers resolved on the expedition to Rome, which, it was agreed, should be undertaken behind the back of the National Assembly and the means for which were to be wrested from it under false pretenses. Thus they began by swindling the National Assembly and secretly conspiring with the absolutist powers abroad against the revolutionary Roman republic.

In the same manner and with the same maneuvers Bonaparte prepared his *coup* of December 2 against the royalist Legislative Assembly and its constitutional republic. Let us not forget that the same party which formed Bonaparte's ministry on December 20, 1848, formed the majority of the Legislative National Assembly on December 2, 1851.

In August the Constituent Assembly had decided to dissolve only after it had worked out and promulgated a whole series of organic laws that were to supplement the constitution. On January 6, 1849, the party of Order had a deputy named Rateau move that the Assembly should let the organic laws go and rather decide on its *own dissolution*. Not only the ministry, with Odilon Barrot at its head, but all the royalist members of the National Assembly told it in bullying accents then that its dissolution was necessary for the restoration of credit, for the consolidation of order, for putting an end to the indefinite provisional arrangements and establishing a definitive state of affairs; that it hampered the productivity of the new government and sought to prolong its existence merely out of malice; that the country was tired of it. Bonaparte took note of all this invective against the legislative power, learned it by heart, and proved to the parliamentary royalists, on December 2, 1851, that he had learned from them. He repeated their own catchwords against them.

The Barrot Ministry and the party of Order went further. They caused petitions to the National Assembly to be made throughout France, in which this body was politely requested to decamp. They thus led the unorganized popular masses into the fire of battle against the National Assembly, the constitutionally organized expression of the people. They taught Bonaparte to appeal against the parliamentary assemblies to the people. At length, on January 29, 1849, the day had come on which the Constituent Assembly was to decide concerning its own dissolution. The National Assembly found the building where its sessions were held occupied by the military; Changarnier, the general of the party of Order, in whose hands the supreme command of the National Guard and troops of the line had been united, held a great military review in Paris, as if a battle were impending, and the royalists in coalition threateningly declared to the Constituent Assembly that force would be employed if it should prove unwilling. It was willing, and only bargained for a very short extra term of life. What was January 29 but the *coup d'état* of December 2, 1851, only carried out by the royalists with Bonaparte against the republican National Assembly? The gentlemen did not observe, or did not wish to observe, that Bonaparte availed himself of January 29, 1849, to have a portion of the troops march past him in front of the Tuileries.

and seized with avidity on just this first public summoning of the military power against the parliamentary power to foreshadow Caligula. They, to be sure, saw only their Changarnier.

A motive that particularly actuated the party of Order in forcibly cutting short the duration of the Constituent Assembly's life was the organic laws supplementing the constitution, such as the law on education, the law on religious worship, etc. To the royalists in coalition it was most important that they themselves should make these laws and not let them be made by the republicans, who had grown mistrustful. Among these organic laws, however, was also a law on the responsibility of the President of the Republic. In 1851 the Legislative Assembly was occupied with the drafting of just such a law, when Bonaparte anticipated this *coup* with the *coup* of December 2. What would the royalists in coalition not have given in their winter election campaign of 1851 to have found the Responsibility Law ready to hand, and drawn up, at that, by a mistrustful, hostile, republican Assembly!

After the Constituent Assembly had itself shattered its last weapon on January 29, 1849, the Barrot Ministry and the friends of order hounded it to death, left nothing undone that could humiliate it, and wrested from the impotent, self-despairing Assembly laws that cost it the last remnant of respect in the eyes of the public. Bonaparte, occupied with his fixed Napoleonic idea, was brazen enough to exploit publicly this degradation of the parliamentary power. For when on May 8, 1849, the National Assembly passed a vote of censure of the ministry because of the occupation of Civitavecchia by Oudinot, and ordered it to bring back the Roman expedition to its alleged purpose, Bonaparte published the same evening in the *Moniteur* a letter to Oudinot in which he congratulated him on his heroic exploits and, in contrast to the ink-slinging parliamentarians, already posed as the generous protector of the army. The royalists smiled at this. They regarded him simply as their dupe. Finally, when Marrast, the President of the Constituent Assembly, believed for a moment that the safety of the National Assembly was endangered and, relying on the constitution, requisitioned a colonel and his regiment, the colonel declined, cited discipline in his support, and referred Marrast to Changarnier, who scornfully refused him with the remark that he did not like *baïonnettes intelligentes* [intellectual bayonets]. In November, 1851, when the royalists in coalition wanted to begin the decisive struggle with Bonaparte, they sought to put through in their notorious Quaestors' Bill the principle of the direct requisition of troops by the President of the National Assembly. One of their generals, Le Flô, had signed the bill. In vain did Changarnier vote for it and Thiers pay homage to the farsighted wisdom of the former Constituent Assembly. The War Minister, Saint-Arnaud, answered him as Changarnier had answered Marrast—and to the acclamation of the *Montagne!*

Thus the party of Order, when it was not yet the National Assembly, when it was still only the ministry, had itself stigmatized the parliamentary regime. And it makes an outcry when December 2, 1851, banishes this regime from France!

We wish it a happy journey.

III

On May 28, 1849, the Legislative National Assembly met. On December 2, 1851, it was dispersed. This period covers the span of life of the *constitutional, or parliamentary, republic.*

In the first French Revolution the rule of the Constitutionalists is followed by the rule of the Girondists and the rule of the Girondists by the rule of the Jacobins. Each of these parties relies on the more progressive party for support. As soon as it has brought the revolution far enough to be unable to follow it further, still less to go ahead of it, it is thrust aside by the bolder ally that stands behind it and sent to the guillotine. The revolution thus moves along an ascending line.

It is the reverse with the Revolution of 1848. The proletarian party appears as an appendage of the petty-bourgeois-democratic party. It is betrayed and dropped by the latter on April 16, May 15, and in the June days. The democratic party, in its turn, leans on the shoulders of the bourgeois-republican party. The bourgeois republicans no sooner believe themselves well established than they shake off the troublesome comrade and support themselves on the shoulders of the party of Order. The party of Order hunches its shoulders, lets the bourgeois republicans tumble, and throws itself on the shoulders of armed force. It fancies it is still sitting on those shoulders when one fine morning it perceives that the shoulders have transformed themselves into bayonets. Each party kicks from behind at the one driving forward, and leans over in front toward the party which presses backward. No wonder that in this ridiculous posture it loses its balance and, having made the inevitable grimaces, collapses with curious gyrations. The revolution thus moves in a descending line. It finds itself in this state of retrogressive motion before the last February barricade has been cleared away and the first revolutionary authority constituted.

The period that we have before us comprises the most motley

mixture of crying contradictions: constitutionalists who conspire openly against the constitution; revolutionists who are confessedly constitutional; a National Assembly that wants to be omnipotent and always remains parliamentary; a *Montagne* that finds its vocation in patience and counters its present defeats by prophesying future victories; royalists who form the *patres conscripti* [elders] of the republic and are forced by the situation to keep the hostile royal houses they adhere to abroad, and the republic, which they hate, in France; an executive power that finds its strength in its very weakness and its respectability in the contempt that it calls forth; a republic that is nothing but the combined infamy of two monarchies, the Restoration and the July Monarchy, with an imperial label—alliances whose first proviso is separation; struggles whose first law is indecision; wild, inane agitation in the name of tranquillity, most solemn preaching of tranquillity in the name of revolution; passions without truth, truths without passion; heroes without heroic deeds, history without events; development, whose sole driving force seems to be the calendar, wearying with constant repetition of the same tensions and relaxations; antagonisms that periodically seem to work themselves up to a climax only to lose their sharpness and fall away without being able to resolve themselves; pretentiously paraded exertions and philistine terror at the danger of the world's coming to an end, and at the same time the pettiest intrigues and court comedies played by the world redeemers, who in their *laisser aller* [letting things take their course] remind us less of the Day of Judgment than of the times of the Fronde[3]—the official collective genius of France brought to naught by the artful stupidity of a single individual; the collective will of the nation, as often as it speaks through universal suffrage, seeking its appropriate expression through the inveterate enemies of the interests of the masses, until at length it finds it in the self-will of a filibuster. If any section of history has been painted gray on gray, it is this. Men and events appear as reverse Schlemihls, as shadows that have lost their bodies. The revolution itself paralyzes its own bearers and endows only its adversaries with passionate forcefulness. When the "red specter," continually conjured up and exorcised by the counterrevolutionaries finally appears, it appears not with the Phrygian cap of anarchy on its head, but in the uniform of order, in red breeches.

We have seen that the ministry which Bonaparte installed on December 20, 1848, on his Ascension Day, was a ministry of the party of Order, of the Legitimist and Orléanist coalition. This Barrot-Falloux Ministry had outlived the republican Constituent Assembly,

---

3. An antiroyalist movement of 1648–53.

whose term of life it had more or less violently cut short, and found itself still at the helm. Changarnier, the general of the allied royalists, continued to unite in his person the general command of the First Army Division and of the National Guard of Paris. Finally, the general elections had secured the party of Order a large majority in the National Assembly. Here the deputies and peers of Louis Philippe encountered a hallowed host of Legitimists, for whom many of the nation's ballots had become transformed into admission cards to the political stage. The Bonapartist representatives of the people were too sparse to be able to form an independent parliamentary party. They appeared merely as the *mauvaise queue* [evil appendage] of the party of Order. Thus the party of Order was in possession of the governmental power, the army and the legislative body, in short, of the whole of the state power; it had been morally strengthened by the general elections, which made its rule appear as the will of the people, and by the simultaneous triumph of the counterrevolution on the whole continent of Europe.

Never did a party open its campaign with greater resources or under more favorable auspices.

The shipwrecked pure republicans found that they had melted down to a clique of about fifty men in the Legislative National Assembly, the African generals Cavaignac, Lamoricière, and Bedeau at their head. The great opposition party, however, was formed by the *Montagne*. The social-democratic party had given itself this parliamentary baptismal name. It commanded more than two hundred of the seven hundred and fifty votes of the National Assembly and was consequently at least as powerful as any one of the three factions of the party of Order taken by itself. Its numerical inferiority compared with the entire royalist coalition seemed compensated by special circumstances. Not only did the elections in the departments show that it had gained a considerable following among the rural population. It counted in its ranks almost all the deputies from Paris; the army had made a confession of democratic faith by the election of three noncommissioned officers; and the leader of the *Montagne*, Ledru-Rollin, in contradistinction to all the representatives of the party of Order, had been raised to the parliamentary peerage by five departments, which had pooled their votes for him. In view of the inevitable clashes of the royalists among themselves and of the whole party of Order with Bonaparte, the *Montagne* thus seemed to have all the elements of success before it on May 28, 1849. A fortnight later it had lost everything, honor included.

Before we pursue parliamentary history further, some remarks are necessary to avoid common misconceptions regarding the whole character of the epoch that lies before us. Looked at with the eyes of democrats, the period of the Legislative National Assembly is concerned with what the period of the Constituent Assembly was concerned with: the simple struggle between republicans and royalists. The movement itself, however, they sum up in the one shibboleth: *"reaction"*—night, in which all cats are gray and which permits them to reel off their night watchman's commonplaces. And to be sure, at first sight the party of Order reveals a maze of different royalist factions which not only intrigue against each other—each seeking to elevate its own pretender to the throne and exclude the pretender of the opposing faction—but also all unite in common hatred of, and common onslaughts on, the "republic." In opposition to this royalist conspiracy the *Montagne*, for its part, appears as the representative of the "republic." The party of Order appears to be perpetually engaged in a "reaction," directed against press, association, and the like, neither more nor less than in Prussia, and, as in Prussia, carried out in the form of brutal police intervention by the bureaucracy, the gendarmerie, and the law courts. The *Montagne*, for its part, is just as continually occupied in warding off these attacks and thus defending the "eternal rights of man" as every so-called people's party has done, more or less, for a century and a half. If one looks at the situation and the parties more closely, however, this superficial appearance, which veils the *class struggle* and the peculiar physiognomy of this period, disappears.

Legitimists and Orléanists, as we have said, formed the two great factions of the party of Order. Was what held these factions fast to their pretenders and kept them apart from each other nothing but fleur-de-lis and tricolor, House of Bourbon and House of Orléans, different shades of royalism—was it at all the confession of faith of royalism? Under the Bourbons, *big landed property* had governed, with its priests and lackeys; under Orléans, high finance, large-scale industry, large-scale trade, that is, *capital,* with its retinue of lawyers, professors, and smooth-tongued orators. The Legitimate Monarchy was merely the political expression of the hereditary rule of the lords of the soil, as the July Monarchy was only the political expression of the usurped rule of the bourgeois parvenus. What kept the two factions apart, therefore, was not any so-called principles, it was their material conditions of existence, two different kinds of property; it was the old contrast between town and country, the rivalry between capital and landed property. That at the same time old memories, personal enmities, fears and hopes, prejudices and illusions, sympathies and antipathies, convictions, articles of faith and principles bound them to one or the other royal house, who denies this? Upon the different forms of property, upon the social conditions of existence, rises an entire superstructure of distinct and peculiarly formed sentiments, illusions, modes of thought, and views of life. The entire class creates and forms them out of its material foundations and out of the corresponding social relations. The single individual, who derives them through tradition and upbringing, may imagine that they form the real motives and the starting point of his activity. While each faction, Orléanists and Legitimists, sought to make itself and the other believe that it was loyalty to the two royal houses which separated them, facts later proved that it was rather their divided interests which forbade the uniting of the two royal houses. And as in private life one differentiates between what a man thinks and says of himself and what he really is and does, so in historical struggles one must distinguish still more the phrases and fancies of parties from their real organism and their real interests, their conception of themselves from their reality. Orléanists and Legitimists found themselves side by side in the republic, with equal claims. If each side wished to effect the restoration of its own royal house against the other, that merely signified that each of the two great interests into which the bourgeoisie is split—landed property and capital—sought to restore its own supremacy and the subordination of the other. We speak of two interests of the bourgeoisie, for large landed property, despite its feudal coquetry and pride of race, has been rendered thoroughly bourgeois by the development of modern society. Thus the Tories in England long imagined that they were enthusiastic about monarchy, the church, and the beauties of the old English Constitution, until the day of danger wrung from them the confession that they are enthusiastic only about ground rent.

The royalists in coalition carried on their intrigues against one another in the press, in Ems, in Claremont, outside parliament. Behind the scenes they donned their old Orléanist and Legitimist liveries again and once more engaged in their old tourneys. But on the public stage, in their grand performances of state as a great parliamentary party, they put off their respective royal houses with mere obeisances and adjourn the restoration of the monarchy *in infinitum*. They do their real business as the party of Order, that is, under a *social*, not under a *political* title; as representatives of the bourgeois world order, not as knights of errant princesses; as the bourgeois class against other classes, not as royalists against the republicans. And as the party of Order they exercised more unrestricted and sterner domination over the other classes of society than ever previously under the Restoration or under the July Monarchy, a domination which, in general, was possible only under the form of the parliamentary republic, for only under this form could the two great divisions of the French bourgeoisie unite, and thus put the rule of their class instead of the regime of a privileged faction of it on the order of the day. If they nevertheless, as the party of Order, also insulted the republic and expressed their repugnance to it, this happened not merely from royalist memories. Instinct taught them that the republic, true enough, makes their political rule complete, but at the same time undermines its social foundation, since they must now confront the subjugated classes and contend against them without mediation, without the concealment afforded by the crown, without being able to divert the national interest by their subordinate struggles among themselves and with the monarchy. It was a feeling of weakness that caused them to recoil from the pure conditions of their own class rule and to yearn for the former more incomplete, more undeveloped, and precisely on that account less dangerous forms of this rule. On the other hand, every time the royalists in coalition come in conflict with the pretender who confronts them, with Bonaparte, every time they believe their parliamentary omnipotence endangered by the executive power—every time, therefore, that they must produce their political title to their rule—they come forward as *republicans* and not as *royalists*, from the Orléanist Thiers, who warns the National Assembly that the republic divides them least, to the Legitimist Berryer, who on December 2, 1851, as a tribune swathed in a tricolored sash, harangues the people assembled before the town hall of the Tenth Arrondissement in the name of the republic. To be sure, a mocking echo calls back to him: Henry V! Henry V!

As against the coalesced bourgeoisie, a coalition between petty bourgeois and workers had been formed, the so-called Social-Democratic party. The petty bourgeois saw that they were badly rewarded after the June days of 1848, that their material interests were imperiled, and that the democratic guarantees which were to insure the effectuation of these interests were called in question by the counterrevolution. Accordingly they came closer to the workers. On the other hand, their parliamentary representation, the *Montagne*, thrust aside during the dictatorship of the bourgeois republicans, had in the last half of the life of the Constituent Assembly reconquered its lost popularity through the struggle with Bonaparte and the royalist ministers. It had concluded an alliance with the socialist leaders. In February, 1849, banquets celebrated the reconciliation. A joint program was drafted, joint election committees were set up and joint candidates put forward. The revolutionary point was broken off and a democratic turn given to the social demands of the proletariat; the purely political form was stripped off the democratic claims of the petty bourgeoisie and their socialist point thrust forward. Thus arose *social-democracy*. The new *Montagne*, the result of this combination, contained, apart from some supernumeraries from the working class and some socialist sectarians, the same elements as the old *Montagne*, but numerically stronger. However, in the course of development it had changed with the class that it represented. The peculiar character of social-democracy is epitomized in the fact that democratic-republican institutions are demanded as a means, not of doing away with two extremes, capital and wage labor, but of weakening their antagonism and transforming it into harmony. However different the means proposed for the attainment of this end may be, however much it may be trimmed with more or less revolutionary notions, the content remains the same. This content is the transformation of society in a democratic way, but a transformation within the bounds of the petty bourgeoisie. Only one must not get the narrow-minded notion that the petty bourgeoisie, on principle, wishes to enforce an egoistic class interest. Rather, it believes that the special conditions of its emancipation are the general conditions within whose frame alone modern society can be saved and the class struggle avoided. Just as little must one imagine that the democratic representatives are indeed all shopkeepers or enthusiastic champions of shopkeepers. According to their education and their individual position they may be as far apart as heaven and earth. What makes them representatives of the petty bourgeoisie is the fact that in their minds they do not get beyond the limits which the latter do not get beyond in life, that they are consequently driven, theoretically, to the same problems and solutions to which material interest and social position drive the latter practically. This is, in general, the relationship between the political and literary representatives of a class and the class they represent.

After this analysis it is obvious that if the *Montagne* continually contends with the party of Order for the republic and the so-called rights of man, neither the republic nor the rights of man are its final end, any more than an army which one wants to deprive of its weapons and which resists has taken the field in order to remain in possession of its own weapons.

Immediately, as soon as the National Assembly met, the party of Order provoked the *Montagne*. The bourgeoisie now felt the necessity of making an end of the democratic petty bourgeois, just as a year before it had realized the necessity of settling with the revolutionary proletariat. But the situation of the adversary was different. The strength of the proletarian party lay in the streets, that of the petty bourgeois in the National Assembly itself. It was therefore a question of decoying them out of the National Assembly into the streets and causing them to smash their parliamentary power themselves, before time and circumstances could consolidate it. The *Montagne* rushed headlong into the trap.

The bombardment of Rome by the French troops was the bait that was thrown. It violated Article 5 of the constitution, which forbids the French Republic to employ its military forces against the freedom of another people. In addition to this, Article 54 prohibited any declaration of war by the executive power without the assent of the National Assembly, and by its resolution of May 8 the Constituent Assembly had disapproved of the Roman expedition. On these grounds Ledru-Rollin brought in a bill of impeachment against Bonaparte and his ministers on June 11, 1849. Exasperated by the wasp stings of Thiers, he actually let himself be carried away to the point of threatening that he would defend the constitution by every means, even with arms in hand. The *Montagne* rose to a man and repeated this call to arms. On June 12 the National Assembly rejected the bill of impeachment, and the *Montagne* left the parliament. The events of June 13 are known: the proclamation issued by a section of the *Montagne* declaring Bonaparte and his ministers "outside the constitution"; the street procession of the democratic National Guard, who, unarmed as they were, dispersed on encountering the troops of Changarnier, etc., etc. A part of the *Montagne* fled abroad; another part was arraigned before the High Court at Bourges; and a parliamentary regulation subjected the remainder to the schoolmasterly surveillance of the President of the National Assembly. Paris was again declared in a state of siege and the democratic part of its National Guard dissolved. Thus the influence of the *Montagne* in parliament and the power of the petty bourgeois in Paris were broken.

Lyon, where June 13 had given the signal for a bloody insurrection of the workers, was, along with the five surrounding departments, likewise declared in a state of siege, a condition that has continued up to the present moment.

The bulk of the *Montagne* had left its vanguard in the lurch, having refused to subscribe to its proclamation. The press had deserted, only two journals having dared to publish the pronunciamento. The petty bourgeois betrayed their representatives in that the National Guard either stayed away or, where they appeared, hindered the building of barricades. The representatives had duped the petty bourgeois in that the alleged allies from the army were nowhere to be seen. Finally, instead of gaining an accession of strength from it, the democratic party had infected the proletariat with its own weakness and, as usual with the great deeds of democrats, the leaders had the satisfaction of being able to charge their "people" with desertion, and the people the satisfaction of being able to charge its leaders with humbugging it.

Seldom had an action been announced with more noise than the impending campaign of the *Montagne,* seldom had an event been trumpeted with greater certainty or longer in advance than the inevitable victory of the democracy. Most assuredly the democrats believe in the trumpets before whose blasts the walls of Jericho fell down. And as often as they stand before the ramparts of despotism, they seek to imitate the miracle. If the *Montagne* wished to triumph in parliament it should not have called to arms. If it called to arms in parliament it should not have acted in parliamentary fashion in the streets. If the peaceful demonstration was meant seriously, then it was folly not to foresee that it would be given a warlike reception. If a real struggle was intended, then it was a queer idea to lay down the weapons with which it would have to be waged. But the revolutionary threats of the petty bourgeois and their democratic representatives are mere attempts to intimidate the antagonist. And when they have run into a blind alley, when they have sufficiently compromised themselves to make it necessary to activate their threats, then this is done in an ambiguous fashion that avoids nothing so much as the means to the end and tries to find excuses for succumbing. The blaring overture that announced the contest dies away in a pusillanimous snarl as soon as the struggle has to begin, the actors cease to take themselves *au sérieux,* and the action collapses completely, like a pricked bubble.

No party exaggerates its means more than the democratic, none deludes itself more light-mindedly over the situation. Since a section of the army had voted for it, the *Montagne* was now convinced that the army would revolt for it. And on what occasion? On an occasion which, from the standpoint of the troops, had no other meaning than that the revolutionists took the side of the Roman soldiers against the French soldiers. On the other hand, the recollections of June, 1848, were still too fresh to allow of anything but a profound aversion on the part of the proletariat toward the National Guard and a thoroughgoing mistrust of the democratic chiefs on the part of the chiefs of the secret societies. To iron out these differences, it was necessary for great common interests to be at stake. The violation of an abstract paragraph of the constitution could not provide these interests. Had not the constitution been repeatedly violated, according to the assurance of the democrats themselves? Had not the most popular journals branded it as counterrevolutionary botchwork? But the democrat, because he represents the petty bourgeoisie—that is, a *transition class,* in which the interests of two classes are simultaneously mutually blunted—imagines himself elevated above class antagonism generally. The democrats concede that a privileged class confronts them, but they, along with all the rest of the nation, form the *people*. What they represent is the people's rights; what interests them is the people's interests. Accordingly, when a struggle is impending they do not need to examine the interests and positions of the different classes. They do not need to weigh their own resources too critically. They have merely to give the signal and the people, with all its inexhaustible resources, will fall upon the oppressors. Now if in the performance their interests prove to be uninteresting and their potency impotence, then either the fault lies with pernicious sophists, who split the indivisible people into different hostile camps, or the army was too brutalized and blinded to comprehend that the pure aims of democracy are the best thing for it, or the whole thing has been wrecked by a detail in its execution, or else an unforeseen accident has this time spoiled the game. In any case, the democrat comes out of the most disgraceful defeat just as immaculate as he was innocent when he went into it, with the newly won conviction that he is bound to win, not that he himself and his party have to give up the old standpoint, but, on the contrary, that conditions have to ripen to suit him.

Therefore one must not imagine the *Montagne*, decimated and broken though it was, and humiliated by the new parliamentary regulation, as being particularly miserable. If June 13 had removed its chiefs, it made room, on the other hand, for men of lesser caliber, whom this new position flattered. If their impotence in parliament could no longer be doubted, they were entitled now to confine their actions to outbursts of moral indignation and blustering declamation. If the party of Order affected to see embodied in them, as the last official representatives of the revolution, all the terrors of anarchy, they could in reality be all the more insipid and modest. They consoled themselves, however, for June 13 with the profound utterance: but if they dare to attack universal suffrage, well then—then we'll show them what we are made of! *Nous verrons!* [We shall see!]

So far as the *Montagnards* who fled abroad are concerned, it is sufficient to remark here that Ledru-Rollin, because in barely a fortnight he had succeeded in ruining irretrievably the powerful party at whose head he stood, now found himself called upon to form a French government *in partibus;* that to the extent that the level of the revolution sank and the official bigwigs of official France became more dwarflike, his figure in the distance, removed from the scene of action, seemed to grow in stature; that he could figure as the republican pretender for 1852, and that he issued periodical circulars to the Wallachians and other peoples in which the despots of the Continent were threatened with the deeds of himself and his confederates. Was

Proudhon altogether wrong when he cried to these gentlemen: *"Vous n'êtes que des blagueurs"* ["you are nothing but windbags"]?

On June 13 the party of Order had not only broken the *Montagne*, it had effected the *subordination of the constitution to the majority decisions of the National Assembly*. And it understood the republic thus: that the bourgeoisie rules here in parliamentary forms, without, as in a monarchy, encountering any barrier such as the veto power of the executive or the right to dissolve parliament. This was a *parliamentary republic*, as Thiers termed it. But whereas on June 13 the bourgeoisie secured its omnipotence within the house of parliament, did it not afflict parliament itself, as against the executive authority and the people, with incurable weakness by expelling its most popular part? By surrendering numerous deputies without further ado on the demand of the courts, it abolished its own parliamentary immunity. The humiliating regulations to which it subjected the *Montagne* exalted the President of the Republic in the same measure as it degraded the individual representatives of the people. By branding an insurrection for the protection of the constitutional charter an anarchic act aiming at the subversion of society, it precluded the possibility of its appealing to insurrection should the executive authority violate the constitution in relation to it. And by the irony of history, the general who on Bonaparte's instructions bombarded Rome and thus provided the immediate occasion for the constitutional revolt of June 13, that very Oudinot had to be the man offered by the party of Order imploringly and unavailingly to the people as general on behalf of the constitution against Bonaparte on December 2, 1851. Another hero of June 13, Vieyra, who was lauded from the tribune of the National Assembly for the brutalities he committed in the democratic newspaper offices at the head of a gang of National Guards belonging to high finance circles—this same Vieyra had been initiated into Bonaparte's conspiracy and he contributed substantially to depriving the National Assembly in the hour of its death of any protection by the National Guard.

June 13 had still another meaning. The *Montagne* had wanted to force the impeachment of Bonaparte. Its defeat was therefore a direct victory for Bonaparte, his personal triumph over his democratic enemies. The party of Order gained the victory; Bonaparte had only to cash in on it. He did so. On June 14 a proclamation could be read on the walls of Paris in which the President, reluctantly, against his will, compelled as it were by the sheer force of events, comes forth from his cloistered seclusion and, posing as misunderstood virtue, complains of the calumnies of his opponents and, while he seems to identify his person with the cause of order, rather identifies the cause of order with his person. Moreover, the National Assembly had, it is true, subsequently approved the expedition against Rome, but Bonaparte had taken the initiative in the matter. After having reinstalled the High Priest Samuel in the Vatican, he could hope to enter the Tuileries as King David. He had won the priests over to his side.

The revolt of June 13 was confined, as we have seen, to a peaceful street procession. No war laurels were therefore to be won against it. Nevertheless, at a time as poor as this in heroes and events, the party of Order transformed this bloodless battle into a second Austerlitz. Platform and press praised the army as the power of order, in contrast to the popular masses representing the impotence of anarchy, and extolled Changarnier as the "bulwark of society," a deception in which he himself finally came to believe. Surreptitiously, however, the corps that seemed doubtful were transferred from Paris, the regiments which had shown the most democratic sentiments in the elections were banished from France to Algiers; the turbulent spirits among the troops were relegated to penal detachments; and finally the isolation of the press from the barracks and of the barracks from bourgeois society was systematically carried out.

Here we have reached the decisive turning point in the history of the French National Guard. In 1830 it was decisive in the overthrow of the Restoration. Under Louis Philippe every rebellion miscarried in which the National Guard stood on the side of the troops. When in the February days of 1848 it evinced a passive attitude toward the insurrection and an equivocal one toward Louis Philippe, he gave himself up for lost and actually was lost. Thus the conviction took root that the revolution could not be victorious without the National Guard, nor the army against it. This was the superstition of the army in regard to civilian omnipotence. The June days of 1848, when the entire National Guard, with the troops of the line, put down the insurrection, had strengthened the superstition. After Bonaparte's assumption of office, the position of the National Guard was to some extent weakened by the unconstitutional union, in the person of Changarnier, of the command of its forces with the command of the First Army Division.

Just as the command of the National Guard appeared here as an attribute of the military commander in chief, so the National Guard itself appeared as only an appendage of the troops of the line. Finally, on June 13 its power was broken, and not only by its partial disbandment, which from this time on was periodically repeated all over France, until mere fragments of it were left behind. The demonstration of June 13 was, above all, a demonstration of the democratic National Guards. They had not, to be sure, borne their arms, but had worn their uniforms against the army; precisely in this uniform, however, lay the talisman. The army convinced itself that this uniform was a piece of woolen cloth like any other. The spell was broken. In the June days of 1848, bourgeoisie and petty bourgeoisie had united as the National Guard with the army against the proletariat; on June 13, 1849, the bourgeoisie let the petty-bourgeois National Guard be dispersed by the army; on December 2, 1851, the National Guard of the bourgeoisie itself had vanished, and Bonaparte merely registered this fact when he subsequently signed the decree for its disbandment. Thus the bourgeoisie had itself smashed its last weapon against the army; the moment the petty bourgeoisie no longer stood behind it as a vassal, but before it as a rebel, it had to smash it as in general it was bound to destroy all its means of defense against absolutism with its own hand as soon as it had itself become absolute.

Meanwhile, the party of Order celebrated the reconquest of a power that seemed lost in 1848 only to be found again, freed from its restraints, in 1849, celebrated by means of invectives against the republic and the constitution, of curses on all future, present, and past revolutions, including that which its own leaders had made, and in laws by which the press was muzzled, association destroyed, and the state of siege regulated as an organic institution. The National Assembly then adjourned from the middle of August to the middle of October, after having appointed a permanent commission for the period of its absence. During this recess the Legitimists intrigued with Ems, the Orléanists with Claremont, Bonaparte by means of princely tours, and the Departmental Councils in deliberations on a revision of the constitution: incidents which regularly recur in the periodic recesses of the National Assembly and which I propose to discuss only when they become events. Here it may merely be remarked, in addition, that it was impolitic for the National Assembly to disappear from the stage for considerable intervals and leave only a single, albeit a sorry, figure to be seen at the head of the republic, that of Louis Bonaparte, while to the scandal of the public the party of Order fell asunder into its royalist component parts and followed its conflicting desires for restoration. As often as the confused noise of parliament grew silent during these recesses and its body dissolved into the nation, it became unmistakably clear that only one thing was still lacking to complete the true form of this republic: to make the former's recess permanent and replace the latter's inscription, *Liberté, Égalité, Fraternité*, with the unambiguous words: infantry, cavalry, artillery!

IV

In the middle of October, 1849, the National Assembly met once more. On November 1 Bonaparte surprised it with a message in which he announced the dismissal of the Barrot-Falloux Ministry and the formation of a new ministry. No one has ever sacked lackeys with less ceremony than Bonaparte his ministers. The kicks that were intended for the National Assembly were given in the meantime to Barrot & Co.

The Barrot Ministry, as we have seen, had been composed of Legitimists and Orléanists; it was a ministry of the party of Order. Bonaparte had needed it to dissolve the republican Constituent Assembly, to bring about the expedition against Rome, and to break the Democratic party. Behind this ministry he had seemingly effaced himself, surrendered governmental power into the hands of the party of Order, and donned the modest character mask that the responsible editor of a newspaper wore under Louis Philippe, the mask of the *homme de paille* [straw man]. He now threw off a mask which was no longer the light veil behind which he could hide his physiognomy, but an iron mask which prevented him from displaying a physiognomy of his own. He had appointed the Barrot Ministry in order to blast the republican National Assembly in the name of the party of Order; he dismissed it in order to declare his own name independent of the National Assembly of the party of Order.

Plausible pretexts for this dismissal were not lacking. The Barrot Ministry neglected even the decencies that would have let the President of the Republic appear as a power side by side with the National Assembly. During the recess of the National Assembly Bonaparte published a letter to Edgar Ney in which he seemed to disapprove of the illiberal attitude of the Pope, just as in opposition to the Constituent Assembly he had published a letter in which he commended Oudinot for the attack on the Roman republic. When the National Assembly now voted the budget for the Roman expedition, Victor Hugo, out of alleged liberalism, brought up this letter for discussion. The party of Order with scornfully incredulous outcries stifled the idea that Bonaparte's ideas could have any political importance. Not one of the ministers took up the gauntlet for him. On another occasion Barrot, with his well-known hollow rhetoric, let fall from the platform words of indignation concerning the "abominable intrigues" that, according to his assertion, went on in the immediate entourage of the President. Finally, while the ministry obtained from the National Assembly a widow's pension for the Duchess of Orléans it rejected any proposal to increase the Civil List of the President. And in Bonaparte the imperial pretender was so intimately bound up with the adventurer down on his luck that the one great idea, that he was called to restore the empire, was always supplemented by the other, that it was the mission of the French people to pay his debts.

The Barrot-Falloux Ministry was the first and last *parliamentary ministry* that Bonaparte brought into being. Its dismissal forms, accordingly, a decisive turning point. With it the party of Order lost, never to reconquer it, an indispensable position for the maintenance of the parliamentary regime, the lever of executive power. It is immediately obvious that in a country like France, where the executive power commands an army of officials numbering more than half a million individuals and therefore constantly maintains an immense mass of interests and livelihoods in the most absolute dependence; where the state enmeshes, controls, regulates, superintends, and tutors civil society from its most comprehensive manifestations of life down to its most insignificant stirrings, from its most general modes of being to the private existence of individuals; where through the most extraordinary centralization this parasitic body acquires a ubiquity, an omniscience, a capacity for accelerated mobility, and an elasticity which finds a counterpart only in the helpless dependence, the loose shapelessness of the actual body politic—it is obvious that in such a country the National Assembly forfeits all real influence when it loses command of the ministerial posts, if it does not at the same time simplify the administration of the state, reduce the army of officials as far as possible, and, finally, let civil society and public opinion create organs of their own, independent of the governmental power. But it is precisely with the maintenance of that extensive state machine in its numerous ramifications that the *material interests* of the French bourgeoisie are interwoven in the closest fashion. Here it finds posts for its surplus population and makes up in the form of state salaries for what it cannot pocket in the form of profit, interest, rents, and honorariums. On the other hand, its *political interests* compelled it to increase daily the repressive measures and therefore the resources and the personnel of the state power, while at the same time it had to wage an uninterrupted war against public opinion and mistrustfully mutilate, cripple, the independent organs of the social movement, where it did not succeed in amputating them entirely. Thus the French bourgeoisie was compelled by its class position to annihilate, on the one hand, the vital conditions of all parliamentary power, and therefore, likewise, of its own, and to render irresistible, on the other hand, the executive power hostile to it.

The new ministry was called the Hautpoul Ministry. Not in the sense that General Hautpoul had received the rank of Prime Minister. Rather, simultaneously with Barrot's dismissal, Bonaparte abolished this dignity, which, true enough, condemned the President of the Republic to the status of the legal nonentity of a constitutional monarch, but of a constitutional monarch without throne or crown, without scepter or sword, without freedom from responsibility, without imprescriptible possession of the highest state dignity, and worst of all, without a Civil List. The Hautpoul Ministry contained only one man of parliamentary standing, the moneylender Fould, one of the most notorious of the high financiers. To his lot fell the Ministry of Finance. Look up the quotations on the Paris Bourse and you will find that from November 1, 1849, onward the French *fonds* [government securities] rise and fall with the rise and fall of Bonapartist stocks. While Bonaparte had thus found his ally in the Bourse, he at the same time took possession of the police by appointing Carlier police prefect of Paris.

Only in the course of development, however, could the consequences of the change of ministers come to light. To begin with, Bonaparte had taken a step forward only to be driven backward all the more conspicuously. His brusque message was followed by the most servile declaration of allegiance to the National Assembly. As often as the ministers dared to make a diffident attempt to introduce his personal fads as legislative proposals, they themselves seemed to carry out, against their will and compelled by their position, comical commissions whose fruitlessness they were persuaded of in advance. As often as Bonaparte blurted out his intentions behind the ministers' backs and played with his *"idées napoléoniennes,"* his own ministers disavowed him from the tribune of the National Assembly. His usurpatory longings seemed to make themselves heard only in order that the malicious laughter of his opponents might not be muted. He behaved like an unrecognized genius, whom all the world takes for a simpleton. Never did he enjoy the contempt of all classes in fuller measure than during this period. Never did the bourgeoisie rule more absolutely, never did it display more ostentatiously the insignia of domination.

I need not write here the history of its legislative activity, which is summarized during this period in two laws: in the law reestablishing the wine tax and the education law abolishing unbelief. If wine drinking was made harder for the French, they were presented all the more plentifully with the water of true life. If in the law on the wine tax the bourgeoisie declared the old, hateful French tax system to be inviolable, it sought through the education law to insure among the masses the old state of mind that put up with the tax system. One is astonished to see the Orléanists, the liberal bourgeois, these old apostles of Voltaireanism and eclectic philosophy, entrust to their hereditary enemies, the Jesuits, the superintendence of the French mind. However Orléanists and Legitimists could part company in regard to the pretenders to the throne, they understood that securing their united rule necessitated the uniting of the means of repression of two epochs, that the means of subjugation of the July Monarchy had to be supplemented and strengthened by the means of subjugation of the Restoration.

The peasants, disappointed in all their hopes, crushed more than ever by the low level of grain prices on the one hand, and by the growing burden of taxes and mortgage debts on the other, began to bestir themselves in the departments. They were answered by a drive against the schoolmasters, who were made subject to the clergy, by a drive against the mayors, made subject to the prefects, and by a system of espionage to which all were made subject. In Paris and the large towns reaction itself has the physiognomy of its epoch and challenges more than it strikes down. In the countryside it becomes dull, coarse, petty, tiresome, and vexatious, in a word, the gendarme. One comprehends how three years of the regime of the gendarme, consecrated by the regime of the priest, were bound to demoralize immature masses.

Whatever amount of passion and declamation might be employed by the party of Order against the minority from the tribune of the National Assembly, its speech remained as monosyllabic as that of the Christians, whose words were to be: Yea, yea; nay, nay! As monosyllabic on the platform as in the press. Flat as a riddle whose answer is known in advance. Whether it was a question of the right of petition or the tax on wine, freedom of the press or free trade, the clubs or the municipal charter, protection of personal liberty or regulation of the state budget, the watchword constantly recurs, the theme remains always the same, the verdict is ever ready and invariably reads: "Socialism!" Even bourgeois liberalism is declared socialistic, bourgeois enlightenment socialistic, bourgeois financial reform socialistic. It was socialistic to build a railway where a canal already existed, and it was socialistic to defend oneself with a cane when one was attacked with a rapier.

This was not merely a figure of speech, fashion, or party tactics. The bourgeoisie had a true insight into the fact that all the weapons it had forged against feudalism turned their points against itself, that all the means of education it had produced rebelled against its own civilization, that all the gods it had created had fallen away from it. It understood that all the so-called bourgeois liberties and organs of progress attacked and menaced its *class rule* at its social foundation and its political summit simultaneously, and had therefore become "socialistic." In this menace and this attack it rightly discerned the secret of socialism, whose import and tendency it judges more correctly than so-called socialism knows how to judge itself; the latter can, accordingly, not comprehend why the bourgeoisie callously hardens its heart against it, whether it sentimentally bewails the sufferings of mankind, or in Christian spirit prophesies the millennium and universal brotherly love, or in humanistic style twaddles about mind, education, and freedom, or in doctrinaire fashion invents a system for the conciliation and welfare of all classes. What the bourgeoisie did not grasp, however, was the logical conclusion that its own parliamentary regime, its political rule in general, was now also bound to meet with the general verdict of condemnation as being socialistic. As long as the rule of the bourgeois class had not been completely organized, as long as it had not acquired its pure political expression, the antagonism of the other classes likewise could not appear in its pure form, and where it did appear could not take the dangerous turn that transforms every struggle against the state power into a struggle against capital. If in every stirring of life in society it saw "tranquillity" imperiled, how could it want to maintain at the head of society a regime of unrest, its own regime, the parliamentary regime, this regime that, according to the expression of one of its spokesmen, lives in struggle and by struggle? The parliamentary regime lives by discussion; how shall it forbid discussion? Every interest, every social institution, is here transformed into general ideas, debated as ideas; how shall any interest, any institution, sustain itself above thought and impose itself as an article of faith? The struggle of the orators on the platform evokes the struggle of the scribblers of the press; the debating club in parliament is necessarily supplemented by debating clubs in the salons and the bistros; the representatives, who constantly appeal to public opinion, give public opinion the right to speak its real mind in petitions. The parliamentary regime leaves everything to the decision of majorities; how shall the great majorities outside parliament not want to decide? When you play the fiddle at the top of the state, what else is to be expected but that those down below dance?

Thus by now stigmatizing as "socialistic" what it had previously extolled as "liberal," the bourgeoisie confesses that its own interests dictate that it should be delivered from the danger of its *own rule;* that to restore tranquillity in the country its bourgeois parliament must, first of all, be given its quietus; that to preserve its social power intact its political power must be broken; that the individual bourgeois can continue to exploit the other classes and to enjoy undisturbed property, family, religion, and order only on condition that their class be condemned along with the other classes to like political nullity; that in order to save its purse it must forfeit the crown, and the sword that is to safeguard it must at the same time be hung over its own head as a sword of Damocles.

In the domain of the interests of the general citizenry, the National Assembly showed itself so unproductive that, for example, the discussions on the Paris-Avignon railway, which began in the winter of 1850, were still not ripe for conclusion on December 2, 1851. Where it did not repress or pursue a reactionary course it was stricken with incurable barrenness.

While Bonaparte's ministry partly took the initiative in framing laws in the spirit of the party of Order, and partly even outdid that party's harshness in their execution and administration, he, on the other hand, sought by childishly silly proposals to win popularity, to bring out his opposition to the National Assembly, and to hint at a secret reserve that was only temporarily prevented by conditions from making its hidden treasures available to the French people. Such was the proposal to decree an increase in pay of four sous a day to the noncommissioned officers. Such was the proposal of an honor-system loan bank for the workers. Money as a gift and money as a loan, it was with prospects such as these that he hoped to lure the masses. Donations and loans—the financial science of the lumpen proletariat, whether of high degree or low, is restricted to this. Such were the only springs Bonaparte knew how to set in action. Never has a pretender speculated more stupidly on the stupidity of the masses.

The National Assembly flared up repeatedly over these unmistakable attempts to gain popularity at its expense, over the growing danger that this adventurer, whom his debts spurred on and no established reputation held back, would venture a desperate *coup*. The discord between the party of Order and the President had taken on a threatening character when an unexpected event threw him back repentant into its arms. We mean the by-elections of March 10, 1850. These elections were held for the purpose of filling the representatives' seats that after June 13 had been rendered vacant by imprisonment or exile. Paris elected only social-democratic candidates. It even concentrated most of the votes on an insurgent of June, 1848, on De Flotte. Thus did the Parisian petty bourgeoisie, in alliance with the proletariat, revenge itself for its defeat on June 13, 1849. It seemed to have disappeared from the battlefield at the moment of danger only to reappear there on a more propitious occasion with more numerous fighting forces and with a bolder battle cry. One circumstance seemed to heighten the peril of this election victory. The army voted in Paris for the June insurgent against La Hitte, a minister of Bonaparte's, and in the departments largely for the *Montagnards,* who here too, though indeed not so decisively as in Paris, maintained the ascendancy over their adversaries.

Bonaparte saw himself suddenly confronted with revolution once more. As on January 29, 1849, as on June 13, 1849, so on March 10, 1850, he disappeared behind the party of Order. He made obeisance, he pusillanimously begged pardon, he offered to appoint any ministry it pleased at the behest of the parliamentary majority, he even implored the Orléanist and Legitimist party leaders, the Thiers, the Berryers, the Broglies, the Molés, in brief, the so-called burgraves, to take the helm of state themselves. The party of Order proved unable to take advantage of this opportunity that would never return. Instead of boldly possessing itself of the power offered, it did not even compel Bonaparte to reinstate the ministry dismissed on November 1; it contented itself with humiliating him by its forgiveness and adjoining M. Baroche to the Hautpoul Ministry. As public prosecutor this Baroche had stormed and raged before the High Court at Bourges, the first time against the revolutionists of May 15, the second time against the democrats of June 13, both times because of an attempt on the life of the National Assembly. None of Bonaparte's ministers subsequently contributed more to the degradation of the National Assembly, and after December 2, 1851, we meet him once more as the comfortably installed and highly paid vice president of the Senate. He had spat in the revolutionists' soup in order that Bonaparte might eat it up.

The social-democratic party, for its part, seemed only to look for pretexts to put its own victory once again in doubt and to blunt its point. Vidal, one of the newly elected representatives of Paris, had been elected simultaneously in Strasbourg. He was induced to decline the election for Paris and accept it for Strasbourg. And so, instead of making its victory at the polls conclusive and thereby compelling the party of Order to contest it in parliament at once, instead of thus forcing the adversary to fight at the moment of popular enthusiasm and favorable mood in the army, the democratic party wearied Paris during the months of March and April with a new election campaign, let the aroused popular passions wear themselves out in this repeated provisional election game, let the revolutionary energy satiate itself with constitutional successes, dissipate itself in petty intrigues, hollow declamations, and sham movements, let the bourgeoisie rally and make its preparations, and, lastly, weakened the significance of the March elections by a sentimental commentary in the April by-election, the election of Eugène Sue. In a word, it made an April Fool of March 10.

The parliamentary majority understood the weakness of its antagonist. Its seventeen burgraves—for Bonaparte had left to it the direction of and responsibility for the attack—drew up a new electoral law, the introduction of which was entrusted to M. Faucher, who solicited this honor for himself. On May 8 he introduced the law

The Eighteenth Brumaire of Louis Napoleon

bnby which universal suffrage was to be abolished, a residence of three
years in the locality of the election to be imposed as a condition on
the electors, and finally, the proof of this residence made dependent
in the case of workers on a certificate from their employers.

Just as the democrats had, in revolutionary fashion, raged and
agitated during the constitutional election contest, so now, when it
was requisite to prove the serious nature of that victory arms in hand,
did they in constitutional fashion preach order, *calme majestueux*,
lawful action, that is to say, blind subjection to the will of the counterrevolution, which imposed itself as the law. During the debate the
"Mountain" put the party of Order to shame by asserting, against the
latter's revolutionary passion, the dispassionate attitude of the philistine
who keeps within the law, and by felling that party to earth with the
fearful reproach that it was proceeding in a revolutionary manner.
Even the newly elected deputies were at pains to prove by their
decorous and discreet action what a misconception it was to decry
them as anarchists and construe their election as a victory for revolution. On May 31 the new electoral law went through. The *Montagne*
contented itself with smuggling a protest into the President's pocket.
The electoral law was followed by a new press law, by which the
revolutionary newspaper press was entirely suppressed. It had deserved its fate. The *National* and *La Presse*, two bourgeois organs,
were left after this deluge as the most advanced outposts of the
revolution.

We have seen how during March and April the democratic leaders
had done everything to embroil the people of Paris in a sham fight,
how after May 8 they did everything to restrain them from a real
fight. In addition to this, we must not forget that the year 1850 was
one of the most splendid years of industrial and commercial prosperity, and the Paris proletariat was therefore fully employed. But
the election law of May 31, 1850, excluded it from any participation
in political power. It cut the proletariat off from the very arena of
the struggle. It threw the workers back into the position of pariahs
which they had occupied before the February Revolution. By letting
themselves be led by the democrats in the face of such an event and
forgetting the revolutionary interests of their class for momentary
ease and comfort, they renounced the honor of being a conquering
power, surrendered to their fate, proved that the defeat of June, 1848,
had put them out of the fight for years and that the historical process
would for the present again have to go on over their heads. As for the
petty-bourgeois democracy, which on June 13 had cried, "But if
once universal suffrage is attacked, then we'll show them," it now
consoled itself with the contention that the counterrevolutionary
blow which had struck it was no blow and the law of May 31 no

law. On the second Sunday in May, 1852, every Frenchman would appear at the polling place with ballot in one hand and sword in the other. With this prophecy it rested content. Lastly, the army was disciplined by its superior officers for the elections of March and April, 1850, just as it had been disciplined for those of May 28, 1849. This time, however, it said decidedly: "The revolution shall not dupe us a third time."

The law of May 31, 1850, was the *coup d'état* of the bourgeoisie. All its conquests over the revolution hitherto had only a provisional character and were endangered as soon as the existing National Assembly retired from the stage. They depended on the hazards of a new general election, and the history of elections since 1848 irrefutably proved that the bourgeoisie's moral sway over the mass of the people was lost in the same measure as its actual domination developed. On March 10 universal suffrage declared itself directly against the domination of the bourgeoisie; the bourgeoisie answered by outlawing universal suffrage. The law of May 31 was therefore one of the necessities of the class struggle. On the other hand, the constitution required a minimum of two million votes to make an election of the President of the Republic valid. If none of the candidates for the presidency received this minimum, the National Assembly was to choose the President from among the three candidates to whom the largest number of votes would fall. At the time when the Constituent Assembly made this law, ten million electors were registered on the rolls of voters. In its view, therefore, a fifth of the people entitled to vote was sufficient to make the presidential election valid. The law of May 31 struck at least three million votes off the electoral rolls, reduced the number of people entitled to vote to seven million, and nevertheless retained the legal minimum of two million for the presidential election. It therefore raised the legal minimum from a fifth to nearly a third of the effective votes; that is, it did everything to smuggle the election of the President out of the hands of the people and into the hands of the National Assembly. Thus through the electoral law of May 31 the party of Order seemed to have made its rule doubly secure, by surrendering the election of the National Assembly and that of the President of the Republic to the stationary section of society.

V

As soon as the revolutionary crisis had been weathered and universal suffrage abolished, the struggle between the National Assembly and Bonaparte broke out again.

The constitution had fixed Bonaparte's salary at 600,000 francs. Barely six months after his installation he succeeded in increasing this sum to twice as much, for Odilon Barrot wrung from the Constituent National Assembly an extra allowance of 600,000 francs a year for so-called representation moneys. After June 13 Bonaparte had caused similar requests to be voiced, this time without eliciting response from Barrot. Now, after May 31, he at once availed himself of the favorable moment and had his ministers propose a Civil List of three millions in the National Assembly. A long life of adventurous vagabondage had endowed him with the most developed antennae for feeling out the weak moments when he might squeeze money from his bourgeois. He practiced *chantage* [blackmail] regularly. The National Assembly had violated the sovereignty of the people with his assistance and his cognizance. He threatened to denounce its crime to the tribunal of the people unless it loosened its purse strings and purchased his silence with three million a year. It had robbed three million Frenchmen of their franchise. He demanded, for every Frenchman out of circulation, a franc in circulation, precisely three million francs. He, the elect of six millions, claimed damages for the votes which he said he had retrospectively been cheated out of. The Commission of the National Assembly refused the importunate man. The Bonapartist press threatened. Could the National Assembly break with the President of the Republic at a moment when in principle it had definitely broken with the mass of the nation? It rejected the annual Civil List, it is true, but it granted, for this once, an extra allowance of 2,160,000 francs. It thus rendered itself guilty of the double weakness of granting the money and of showing at the same time by its vexation that it granted it unwillingly. We shall see later for what purpose Bonaparte needed the money. After this vexatious aftermath, which followed on the heels of the abolition of universal suffrage and in which Bonaparte exchanged his humble attitude during the crisis of March and April for challenging impudence to the usurpatory parliament, the National Assembly adjourned for three months, from August 11 to November 11. In its place it left behind a Permanent Commission of twenty-eight members, which contained no Bonapartists but did contain some moderate republicans. The Permanent Commission of 1849 had included only Order men and Bonapartists. But at that time the party of Order declared itself permanently against the revolution. This time the parliamentary republic declared itself permanently against the President. After the law of May 31, this was the only rival that still confronted the party of Order.

When the National Assembly met once more in November, 1850,

it seemed that, instead of the petty skirmishes it had hitherto had with the President, a great and ruthless struggle, a life-and-death struggle between the two powers, had become inevitable.

As in 1849 so during this year's parliamentary recess—the party of Order had broken up into its separate factions, each occupied with its own restoration intrigues, which had obtained fresh nutriment through the death of Louis Philippe. The Legitimist king, Henry V, had even nominated a formal ministry which resided in Paris and in which members of the Permanent Commission held seats. Bonaparte, in his turn, was therefore entitled to make tours of the French departments, and according to the disposition of the town he favored with his presence, now more or less covertly, now more or less overtly, to divulge his own restoration plans and canvass votes for himself. On these processions, which the great official *Moniteur* and the little private *Moniteurs* of Bonaparte naturally had to celebrate as triumphal processions, he was constantly accompanied by persons affiliated with the Society of December 10. This society dates from the year 1849. On the pretext of founding a benevolent society, the lumpen proletariat of Paris had been organized into secret sections, each section led by Bonapartist agents, with a Bonapartist general at the head of the whole. Alongside decayed roués with dubious means of subsistence and of dubious origin, alongside ruined and adventurous offshoots of the bourgeoisie, were vagabonds, discharged soldiers, discharged jailbirds, escaped galley slaves, swindlers, mountebanks, *lazzaroni*, pickpockets, tricksters, gamblers, *maquereaux* [pimps], brothel keepers, porters, literati, organ grinders, ragpickers, knife grinders, tinkers, beggars—in short, the whole indefinite, disintegrated mass, thrown hither and thither, which the French call *la bohème;* from this kindred element Bonaparte formed the core of the Society of December 10. A "benevolent society"—insofar as, like Bonaparte, all its members felt the need of benefiting themselves at the expense of the laboring nation. This Bonaparte, who constitutes himself chief of the lumpen proletariat, who here alone rediscovers in mass form the interests which he personally pursues, who recognizes in this scum, offal, refuse of all classes the only class upon which he can base himself unconditionally, is the real Bonaparte, the Bonaparte *sans phrase*. An old, crafty roué, he conceives the historical life of the nations and their performances of state as comedy in the most vulgar sense, as a masquerade in which the grand costumes, words, and postures merely serve to mask the pettiest knavery. Thus his expedition to Strasbourg, where the trained Swiss vulture played the part of the Napoleonic eagle. For his irruption into Boulogne he puts some London lackeys into French uniforms. They represent the army. In his Society of December 10 he assembles ten thousand rascals who are to play the part of the people as Nick Bottom[4] that of the lion. At a moment when the bourgeoisie itself played the most complete comedy, but in the most serious manner in the world, without infringing any of the pedantic conditions of French dramatic etiquette, and was itself half deceived, half convinced of the solemnity of its own performance of state, the adventurer, who took the comedy as plain comedy, was bound to win. Only when he has eliminated his solemn opponent, when he himself now takes his imperial role seriously and under the Napoleonic mask imagines he is the real Napoleon, does he become the victim of his own conception of the world, the serious buffoon who no longer takes world history for a comedy but his comedy for world history. What the national *ateliers* were for the socialist workers, what the Mobile Guards were for the bourgeois republicans, the Society of December 10 was for Bonaparte, the party fighting force peculiar to him. On his journeys the detachments of this society packing the railways had to improvise a public for him, stage popular enthusiasm, roar *Vive l'Empereur*, insult and thrash republicans, under police protection, of course. On his return journeys to Paris they had to form the advance guard, forestall counterdemonstrations or disperse them. The Society of December 10 belonged to him, it was his work, his very own idea. Whatever else he appropriates is put into his hands by the force of circumstances; whatever else he does, the circumstances do for him or he is content to copy from the deeds of others. But Bonaparte with official phrases about order, religion, family, and property in public, before the citizens, and with the secret society of the Schufterles and Spiegelbergs, the society of disorder, prostitution, and theft, behind him—that is Bonaparte himself as the original author, and the history of the Society of December 10 is his own history.

Now it had happened by way of exception that people's representatives belonging to the party of Order came under the cudgels of the Decembrists. Still more. Yon, the police commissioner assigned to the National Assembly and charged with watching over its safety, acting on the deposition of a certain Allais, advised the Permanent Commission that a section of the Decembrists had decided to assassinate General Changarnier and Dupin, the President of the National Assembly, and had already designated the individuals who were to perpetrate the deed. One comprehends the terror of M. Dupin. A parliamentary inquiry into the Society of December 10—that is, the profanation of the Bonapartist secret world—seemed inevitable. Just before the meeting of the National Assembly Bonaparte providently

---

4. A character in Shakespeare's *Midsummer Night's Dream*.

disbanded his society, naturally only on paper, for in a detailed memoir at the end of 1851 Police Prefect Carlier still sought in vain to move him to really break up the Decembrists.

The Society of December 10 was to remain the private army of Bonaparte until he succeeded in transforming the public army into a Society of December 10. Bonaparte made the first attempt at this shortly after the adjournment of the National Assembly, and precisely with the money just wrested from it. As a fatalist, he lives in the conviction that there are certain higher powers which man, and the soldier in particular, cannot withstand. Among these powers he counts, first and foremost, cigars and champagne, cold poultry and garlic sausage. Accordingly, to begin with, he treats officers and noncommissioned officers in his Élysée apartments to cigars and champagne, cold poultry and garlic sausage. On October 3 he repeats this maneuver with the mass of the troops at the St. Maur review, and on October 10 the same maneuver on a still larger scale at the Satory army parade. The uncle remembered the campaigns of Alexander in Asia, the nephew the triumphal marches of Bacchus in the same land. Alexander was a demigod, to be sure. But Bacchus was a god and moreover the tutelary deity of the Society of December 10.

After the review of October 3, the Permanent Commission summoned War Minister Hautpoul. He promised that these breaches of discipline would not recur. We know how on October 10 Bonaparte kept Hautpoul's word. As commander in chief of the Paris army, Changarnier had commanded at both reviews. At once a member of the Permanent Commission, chief of the National Guard, the "savior" of January 29 and June 13, the "bulwark of society," the candidate of the party of Order for presidential honors, the suspected monk of two monarchies, he had hitherto never acknowledged himself as the subordinate of the War Minister, had always openly derided the republican constitution, and had pursued Bonaparte with an ambiguous lordly protection. Now he was consumed with zeal for discipline against the War Minister and for the constitution against Bonaparte. While on October 10 a section of the cavalry raised the shout: "*Vive Napoléon! Vivent les saucissons!*" Changarnier arranged that at least the infantry marching past under the command of his friend Neumayer should preserve an icy silence. As a punishment, the War Minister relieved General Neumayer of his post in Paris at Bonaparte's instigation, on the pretext of appointing him commanding general of the Fourteenth and Fifteenth divisions. Neumayer refused this exchange of posts and so had to resign. Changarnier, for his part, published an order of the day on November 2 in which he forbade the troops to indulge in political outcries or demonstrations of any kind while under arms. The Élysée newspapers attacked Changarnier; the papers of the party of Order attacked Bonaparte; the Permanent Commission held repeated secret sessions in which it was repeatedly proposed to declare the country in danger; the army seemed divided into two hostile camps, with two hostile general staffs, one in the Élysée, where Bonaparte resided, the other in the Tuileries, the quarters of Changarnier. It seemed that only the meeting of the National Assembly was needed to give the signal for battle. The French public judged this friction between Bonaparte and Changarnier like the English journalist who characterized it in these words: "The political housemaids of France are sweeping away the glowing lava of the revolution with old brooms and wrangle with one another while they do their work."

Meanwhile, Bonaparte hastened to remove the War Minister Hautpoul, to pack him off in all haste to Algiers, and to appoint General Schramm War Minister in his place. On November 12 he sent to the National Assembly a message of American prolixity, overloaded with detail, redolent of order, desirous of reconciliation, constitutionally acquiescent, treating of all and sundry, but not of the *questions brûlantes* [burning questions] of the moment. As if in passing, he made the remark that according to the express provisions of the constitution the President alone could dispose of the army. The message closed with the following words of great solemnity: "Above all things, France demands tranquillity. . . . But bound by an oath, I shall keep within the narrow limits that it has set for me. . . . As far as I am concerned, elected by the people and owing my power to it alone, I shall always bow to its lawfully expressed will. Should you resolve at this session on a revision of the constitution, a Constituent Assembly will regulate the position of the executive power. If not, then the people will solemnly pronounce its decision in 1852. But whatever the solutions of the future may be, let us come to an understanding, so that passion, surprise, or violence may never decide the destiny of a great nation. . . . What occupies my attention, above all, is not who will rule France in 1852, but how to employ the time which remains at my disposal so that the intervening period may pass by without agitation or disturbance. I have opened my heart to you with sincerity; you will answer my frankness with your trust, my good endeavors with your cooperation, and God will do the rest."

The respectable, hypocritically moderate, virtuously commonplace language of the bourgeoisie reveals its deepest meaning in the mouth of the autocrat of the Society of December 10 and the picnic hero of St. Maur and Satory.

The burgraves of the party of Order did not delude themselves for a moment concerning the trust that this opening of the heart deserved. About oaths they had long been blasé; they numbered in their midst veterans and virtuosos of political perjury. Nor had they failed to hear the passage about the army. They observed with annoyance that in its discursive enumeration of lately enacted laws the message passed over the most important law, the electoral law, in studied silence, and moreover, in the event of there being no revision of the constitution, left the election of the President in 1852 to the people. The electoral law was the lead ball chained to the feet of the party of Order, which prevented it from walking and so much the more from storming forward! Moreover, by the official disbandment of the Society of December 10 and the dismissal of War Minister Hautpoul, Bonaparte had with his own hand sacrificed the scapegoats on the altar of the country. He had blunted the edge of the expected collision. Finally, the party of Order itself anxiously sought to avoid, to mitigate, to gloss over any decisive conflict with the executive power. For fear of losing their conquests over the revolution, they allowed their rival to carry off the fruits thereof. "Above all things, France demands tranquillity." This was what the party of Order had cried to the revolution since February, this was what Bonaparte's message cried to the party of Order. "Above all things, France demands tranquillity." Bonaparte committed acts that aimed at usurpation, but the party of Order committed "unrest" if it raised a row about these acts and construed them hypochondriacally. The sausages of Satory were quiet as mice when no one spoke of them. "Above all things, France demands tranquillity." Bonaparte demanded, therefore, that he be left in peace to do as he liked and the parliamentary party was paralyzed by a double fear, the fear of again evoking revolutionary unrest and the fear of itself appearing as the instigator of unrest in the eyes of its own class, in the eyes of the bourgeoisie. Consequently, since France demanded tranquillity above all things, the party of Order dared not answer "war" after Bonaparte had talked "peace" in his message. The public, which had anticipated scenes of great scandal at the opening of the National Assembly, was cheated of its expectations. The opposition deputies, who demanded the submission of the Permanent Commission's minutes on the October events, were outvoted by the majority. On principle, all debates that might cause excitement were eschewed. The proceedings of the National Assembly during November and December, 1850, were without interest.

At last, toward the end of December, guerrilla warfare began over a number of prerogatives of parliament. The movement got bogged down in petty squabbles about the prerogatives of the two powers, since the bourgeoisie had done away with the class struggle for the moment by abolishing universal suffrage.

A judgment for debt had been obtained from the court against Mauguin, one of the people's representatives. In answer to the inquiry of the president of the court, the Minister of Justice, Rouher, declared that a capias should be issued against the debtor without further ado. Mauguin was thus thrown into debtors' prison. The National Assembly flared up when it learned of the assault. Not only did it order his immediate release, but it even had him fetched forcibly from Clichy the same evening, by its clerk. In order, however, to confirm its faith in the sanctity of private property and with the idea at the back of its mind of opening, in case of need, a place of safekeeping for *Montagnards* who had become troublesome, it declared imprisonment of people's representatives for debt permissible when its consent had been previously obtained. It forgot to decree that the President might also be locked up for debt. It destroyed the last semblance of the immunity that enveloped the members of its own body.

It will be remembered that, acting on the information given by a certain Allais, Police Commissioner Yon had denounced a section of the Decembrists for planning the murders of Dupin and Changarnier. In reference to this, at the very first session the quaestors made the proposal that parliament should form a police force of its own, paid out of the private budget of the National Assembly and absolutely independent of the police prefect. The Minister of the Interior, Baroche, protested against this invasion of his domain. A miserable compromise on this matter was concluded, according to which, true, the police commisioner of the Assembly was to be paid out of its private budget and to be appointed and dismissed by its quaestors, but only after previous agreement with the Minister of the Interior. Meanwhile the government had started criminal proceedings against Alais, and here it was easy to represent his information as a hoax and through the mouth of the public prosecutor to cast ridicule upon Dupin, Changarnier, Yon, and the whole National Assembly. Thereupon, on December 29, Minister Baroche writes a letter to Dupin in which he demands Yon's dismissal. The bureau of the Assembly, alarmed by its violence in the Mauguin affair and accustomed when it has ventured a blow at the executive power to receive two blows from it in return, does not sanction this decision. It dismisses Yon as a reward for his official zeal and robs itself of a parliamentary prerogative indispensable against a man who does not decide by night in order to execute by day, but decides by day and executes by night.

We have seen how on great and striking occasions during the months of November and December the National Assembly avoided or quashed the struggle with the executive power. Now we see it compelled to take up the struggle on the pettiest occasions. In the Mauguin affair it confirms the principle of imprisoning people's representatives for debt, but reserves the right to have it applied only to representatives obnoxious to itself and wrangles over this infamous privilege with the Minister of Justice. Instead of availing itself of the alleged murder plot to decree an inquiry into the Society of December 10 and irredeemably unmasking Bonaparte before France and Europe in his true character of chief of the Paris lumpen proletariat, it lets the conflict be degraded to a point where the only issue between it and the Minister of the Interior is which of them has the authority to appoint and dismiss a police commissioner. Thus during the whole of this period we see the party of Order compelled by its equivocal position to dissipate and disintegrate its struggle with the executive power in petty jurisdictional squabbles, pettifoggery, legalistic hairsplitting, and delimitational disputes, and to make the most ridiculous matters of form the substance of its activity. It does not dare take up the conflict at the moment when this has significance from the standpoint of principle, when the executive power has really exposed itself and the cause of the National Assembly would be the cause of the nation. By so doing it would give the nation its marching orders, and it fears nothing more than that the nation should move. On such occasions it accordingly rejects the motions of the *Montagne* and proceeds to the order of the day. The question at issue in its large aspects having thus been dropped, the executive power calmly waits for the time when it can again take up the same question on petty and insignificant occasions, when this is, so to speak, of only local parliamentary interest. Then the repressed rage of the party of Order breaks out, then it tears the curtain away from the coulisses, then it denounces the President, then it declares the republic in danger, but then, also, its fervor appears absurd and the occasion for the struggle seems a hypocritical pretext or altogether not worth fighting about. The parliamentary storm becomes a storm in a teacup, the fight becomes an intrigue, the conflict a scandal. While the revolutionary classes gloat with malicious joy over the humiliation of the National Assembly, for they are just as enthusiastic about the parliamentary prerogatives of this Assembly as the latter is about the public liberties, the bourgeoisie outside parliament does not understand how the bourgeoisie inside parliament can waste time over such petty squabbles and imperil tranquillity by such pitiful rivalries with the President. It becomes confused by a strategy that makes peace at the moment when all the world is expecting battles, and attacks at the moment when all the world believes peace has been made.

On December 20 Pascal Duprat interpellated the Minister of the Interior concerning the Gold Bars Lottery. This lottery was a "daughter of Elysium." Bonaparte with his faithful followers had brought her into the world and Police Prefect Carlier had placed her under his official protection, although French law forbids all lotteries except raffles for charitable purposes. Seven million lottery tickets at a franc apiece, the profits ostensibly to be devoted to shipping Parisian vagabonds to California. On the one hand, golden dreams were to supplant the socialist dreams of the Paris proletariat, the seductive prospect of the first prize the doctrinaire right to work. Naturally the Paris workers did not recognize in the glitter of the California gold bars the inconspicuous francs that were enticed out of their pockets. In the main, however, the matter was nothing short of a downright swindle. The vagabonds who wanted to open California gold mines without troubling to leave Paris were Bonaparte himself and his debt-ridden Round Table. The three millions voted by the National Assembly had been squandered in riotous living; in one way or another coffers had to be replenished. In vain had Bonaparte opened a national subscription for the building of so-called *cités ouvrières* [workers' cities], and headed the list himself with a considerable sum. The hardhearted bourgeois waited mistrustfully for him to pay up his share, and since this naturally did not ensue, the speculation in socialist castles in the air immediately fell to the ground. The gold bars proved a better draw. Bonaparte & Co. were not content to pocket part of the excess of the seven millions over the bars to be alloted in prizes; they manufactured false lottery tickets; they issued ten, fifteen, and even twenty tickets with the same number —a financial operation in the spirit of the Society of December 10! Here the National Assembly was confronted not with the fictitious President of the Republic but with Bonaparte in the flesh. Here it could catch him in the act, in conflict not with the constitution but with the *Code pénal*. If after Duprat's interpellation it proceeded to the order of the day, this did not happen merely because Girardin's motion that it should declare itself "satisfied" reminded the party of Order of its own systematic corruption. The bourgeois, and above all the bourgeois inflated into a statesman, supplements his practical meanness by theoretical extravagance. As a statesman he becomes, like the state power that confronts him, a higher being that can be fought only in a higher, consecrated fashion.

Bonaparte, who precisely because he was a bohemian, a princely lumpen proletarian, had the advantage over a rascally bourgeois in that he could conduct the struggle meanly, now saw, after the Assembly guided him with its own hand across the slippery ground of the military banquets, the reviews, the Society of December 10, and finally the *Code pénal*, that the moment had come when he could pass from an apparent defensive to the offensive. The minor defeats mean-while sustained by the Minister of Justice, the Minister of War, the Minister of the Navy, and the Minister of Finance, through which the National Assembly signified its snarling displeasure, troubled him little. He not only prevented the ministers from resigning and thus recognizing the sovereignty of parliament over the executive power, but could now consummate what he had begun during the recess of the National Assembly: the severance of the military power from parliament, the *removal of Changarnier.*

An Élysée paper published an order of the day alleged to have been addressed during the month of May to the First Army Division, and therefore proceeding from Changarnier, in which the officers were urged, in the event of an insurrection, to give no quarter to the traitors in their own ranks, but to shoot them immediately, and to refuse troops to the National Assembly if it should requisition them. On January 3, 1851, the cabinet was interpellated concerning this order of the day. For the investigation of this matter it requests a breathing space, first of three months, then of a week, finally of only twenty-four hours. The Assembly insists on an immediate explanation. Changarnier rises and declares that there never was such an order of the day. He adds that he will always hasten to comply with the de-mands of the National Assembly and that in case of a clash it can count on him. It receives his declaration with indescribable applause and passes a vote of confidence in him. It abdicates, it decrees its own impotence and the omnipotence of the army by placing itself under the private protection of a general; but the general deceives himself when he puts at its command against Bonaparte a power that he holds only as a fief from the same Bonaparte, and when, in his turn, he expects to be protected by this parliament, his own protégé in need of protection. Changarnier, however, believes in the mysterious power with which the bourgeoisie has endowed him since January 29, 1849. He considers himself the third power, existing side by side with both the other state powers. He shares the fate of the rest of this epoch's heroes, or rather saints, whose greatness consists precisely in the biased great opinion of them that their party creates in its own in-terests and who shrink to everyday figures as soon as circumstances call on them to perform miracles. Unbelief is, in general, the mortal enemy of these reputed heroes who are really saints. Hence their majestically moral indignation at the dearth of enthusiasm displayed by wits and scoffers.

That same evening the ministers were summoned to the Élysée. Bonaparte insists on the dismissal of Changarnier; five ministers refuse to sign; the *Moniteur* announces a ministerial crisis, and the press of the party of Order threatens to form a parliamentary army under Changarnier's command. The party of Order had constitutional authority to take this step. It merely had to appoint Changarnier president of the National Assembly and requisition any number of troops it pleased for its protection. It could do so all the more safely as Changarnier still actually stood at the head of the army and the Paris National Guard and was only waiting to be requisitioned together with the army. The Bonapartist press did not as yet even dare to question the right of the National Assembly to requisition troops directly, a legal scruple that in the given circumstances did not look promising. That the army would have obeyed the order of the National Assembly is probable when one bears in mind that Bonaparte had to search all Paris for eight days in order, finally, to find two generals—Baraguay d'Hilliers and Saint-Jean d'Angély—who declared themselves ready to countersign Changarnier's dismissal. That the party of Order, however, would have found in its own ranks and in parliament the necessary number of votes for such a resolution is more than doubtful, when one considers that eight days later two hundred and eighty-six votes detached themselves from the party and that in December, 1851, at the last hour of decision, the *Montagne* still rejected a similar proposal. Nevertheless, the burgraves might, perhaps, still have succeeded in spurring the mass of their party to a heroism that consisted in feeling themselves secure behind a forest of bayonets and accepting the services of an army that had deserted to their camp. Instead of this, on the evening of January 6, Messrs. the Burgraves betook themselves to the Élysée to make Bonaparte desist from dismissing Changarnier by using statesmanlike phrases and urging considerations of state. Whomever one seeks to persuade, one acknowledges as master of the situation. On January 12, Bonaparte, assured by this step, appoints a new ministry in which the leaders of the old ministry, Fould and Baroche, remain. Saint-Jean d'Angély becomes War Minister, the *Moniteur* publishes the decree dismissing Changarnier, and his command is divided between Baraguay d'Hilliers, who receives the First Army Division, and Perrot, who receives the National Guard. The bulwark of society has been discharged, and while this does not cause any tiles to fall from the roofs, quotations on the Bourse are, on the other hand, going up.

By repulsing the army, which places itself in the person of Changarnier at its disposal, and so surrendering the army irrevocably to the President, the party of Order declares that the bourgeoisie has forfeited its vocation to rule. A parliamentary ministry no longer existed. Having now indeed lost its grip on the army and the National Guard, what forcible means remained to it with which simultaneously to maintain the usurped authority of parliament over the people and its constitutional authority against the President? None. Only the appeal to impotent principles remained to it now, to principles that it had itself always interpreted merely as general rules, which one prescribes for others in order to be able to move all the more freely oneself. The dismissal of Changarnier and the falling of the military power into Bonaparte's hands closes the first part of the period we are considering, the period of struggle between the party of Order and the executive power. War between the two powers has now been openly declared, is openly waged, but only after the party of Order has lost both arms and soldiers. Without the ministry, without the army, without the people, without public opinion, after its electoral law of May 31 no longer the representative of the sovereign nation, *sans* eyes, *sans* ears, *sans* teeth, *sans* everything, the National Assembly had undergone a gradual transformation into an ancient French parliament that has to leave action to the government and content itself with growling remonstrances *post festum* [belatedly].

The party of Order receives the new ministry with a storm of indignation. General Bedeau recalls to mind the mildness of the Permanent Commission during the recess, and the excessive consideration it showed by waiving the publication of its minutes. The Minister of the Interior himself now insists on the publication of these minutes, which by this time have naturally become as dull as ditch water, disclose no fresh facts, and have not the slightest effect on the blasé public. Upon Rémusat's proposal the National Assembly retires into its office and appoints a "Committee for Extraordinary Measures." Paris departs the less from the rut of its everyday routine because at this moment trade is prosperous, factories are busy, corn prices low, foodstuffs overflowing, and the savings banks receiving fresh deposits daily. The "extraordinary measures" that parliament has announced with so much noise fizzle out on January 18 in a no-confidence vote against the ministry without General Changarnier ever being mentioned. The party of Order was forced to frame its motion in this way to secure the votes of the republicans, since of all the ministry's measures, Changarnier's dismissal was precisely the only one the republicans approved of, while the party of Order was in fact not in a position to censure the other ministerial acts, which it had itself dictated.

The no-confidence vote of January 18 was passed by four hundred and fifteen votes to two hundred and eighty-six. Thus, it was carried only by a coalition of the extreme Legitimists and Orléanists with the pure republicans and the *Montagne*. Thus it proved that the party of Order had lost in conflicts with Bonaparte not only the ministry, not only the army, but also its independent parliamentary majority; that a squad of representatives had deserted its camp, out of fanaticism for conciliation, out of fear of the struggle, out of lassitude, out of family regard for the state salaries so near and dear to them, out of speculation about ministerial posts becoming vacant (Odilon Barrot), out of sheer egoism, which makes the ordinary bourgeois always inclined to sacrifice the general interest of his class for this or that private motive. From the first, the Bonapartist representatives adhered to the party of Order only in the struggle against revolution. The leader of the Catholic party, Montalembert, had already at that time thrown his influence into the Bonapartist scale, since he despaired of the parliamentary party's prospects of life. Lastly, the leaders of this party, Thiers and Berryer, the Orléanist and the Legitimist, were compelled openly to proclaim themselves republicans, to confess that their hearts were royalist but their heads republican, that the parliamentary republic was the sole possible form for the rule of the bourgeoisie as a whole. Thus they were compelled, before the eyes of the bourgeois class itself, to stigmatize the restoration plans, which they continued indefatigably to pursue behind parliament's back, as an intrigue as dangerous as it was brainless.

The no-confidence vote of January 18 hit the ministers and not the President. But it was not the ministry, it was the President who had dismissed Changarnier. Should the party of Order impeach Bonaparte himself? Because of his restoration desires? The latter merely supplemented their own. Because of his conspiracy in connection with the military reviews and the Society of December 10? They had buried these themes long since under routine orders of the day. Because of the dismissal of the hero of January 29 and June 13, the man who in May, 1850, threatened to set fire to all four corners of Paris in the event of a rising? Their allies of the *Montagne* and Cavaignac did not even allow them to raise the fallen bulwark of society by means of an official attestation of sympathy. They themselves could not deny the President the constitutional authority to dismiss a general. They only raged because he made an unparliamentary use of his constitutional right. Had they not continually made an unconstitutional use of their parliamentary prerogative, particularly in regard to the abolition of universal suffrage? They were therefore reduced to moving within strictly parliamentary limits. And it took that peculiar malady which since 1848 has raged all over the Continent, *parliamentary cretinism*, which holds those infected by it fast in an imaginary world and robs them of all sense, all memory, all understanding of the rude external world—it took this parliamentary cretinism for those who had destroyed all the conditions of parliamentary power with their own hands, and were bound to destroy them in their struggle with the other classes, still to regard their parliamentary victories as victories and to believe they hit the President by striking at his ministers. They merely gave him the opportunity to humiliate the National Assembly afresh in the eyes of the nation. On January 20 the *Moniteur* announced that the resignation of the entire ministry had been accepted. On the pretext that no parliamentary party any longer had a majority—as the vote of January 18, this fruit of the coalition between *Montagne* and royalists, proved—and pending the formation of a new ministry, of which not one member was an Assembly representative, all being absolutely unknown and insignificant individuals; a ministry of mere clerks and copyists. The party of Order could now work to exhaustion playing with these marionettes; the executive power no longer thought it worth while to be seriously represented in the National Assembly. The more his ministers were pure dummies, the more obviously Bonaparte concentrated the whole executive power in his own person and the more scope he had to exploit it for his own ends.

In coalition with the *Montagne*, the party of Order revenged itself by rejecting the grant to the President of 1,800,000 francs which the chief of the Society of December 10 had compelled his ministerial clerks to propose. This time a majority of only a hundred and two votes decided the matter; thus twenty-seven fresh votes had fallen away since January 18; the dissolution of the party of Order was progressing. At the same time, so there might not for a moment be any mistake about the meaning of its coalition with the *Montagne*, it scorned even to consider a proposal signed by a hundred and eighty-nine members of the *Montagne* calling for a general amnesty of political offenders. It sufficed for the Minister of the Interior, a certain Vaïsse, to declare that the tranquillity was only apparent, that in secret great agitation prevailed, that in secret ubiquitous societies were being organized, the democratic papers were preparing to come out again, the reports from the departments were unfavorable, the Geneva refugees were directing a conspiracy spreading by way of Lyon all over the South of France, France was on the verge of an industrial and commercial crisis, the manufacturers of Roubaix had reduced working hours, the prisoners of Belle Isle were in revolt—it sufficed for even a mere Vaïsse to conjure up the red specter and the party of Order rejected without discussion a motion that would certainly have won the National Assembly immense popularity and thrown Bonaparte back into its arms. Instead of letting itself be intimidated by the executive power with the prospect of fresh disturbances, it ought rather to have allowed the class struggle a little elbow room, so as to keep the executive power dependent on it. But it did not feel equal to the task of playing with fire.

Meanwhile the so-called transition ministry continued to vegetate until the middle of April. Bonaparte wearied and befooled the National Assembly with continual new ministerial combinations. Now he seemed to want to form a republican ministry with Lamartine and Billault, now a parliamentary one with the inevitable Odilon Barrot, whose name is never missing when a dupe is necessary, then a Legitimist ministry with Vatimesnil and Benoit d'Azy, and then again an Orléanist one with Maleville. While he thus kept the different factions of the party of Order in tension against one another, and alarmed them as a whole by the prospect of a republican ministry and the consequent inevitable restoration of universal suffrage, he at the same time engendered in the bourgeoisie the conviction that his honest efforts to form a parliamentary ministry were being frustrated by the irreconcilability of the royalist factions. The bourgeoisie, however, cried out all the louder for a "strong government"; it found it all the more unpardonable to leave France "without administration," the more a general commercial crisis seemed now to be approaching, and won recruits for socialism in the towns just as the ruinously low price of corn did in the countryside. Trade daily became slacker, the number of unemployed increased perceptibly; ten thousand workers, at least, were breadless in Paris; innumerable factories stood idle in Rouen, Mulhouse, Lyon, Roubaix, Tourcoing, St. Étienne, Elbeuf, etc. Under these circumstances Bonaparte could venture, on April 11, to restore the ministry of January 18: Messrs. Rouher, Fould, Baroche, etc., reinforced by M. Léon Faucher, whom the Constituent Assembly during its last days had, with the exception of five votes cast by ministers, unanimously stigmatized by a vote of no confidence for sending out false telegrams. The National Assembly had therefore gained a victory over the ministry on January 18, had struggled with Bonaparte for three months, only to have Fould and Baroche on April 11 admit the puritan Faucher as a third party into their ministerial alliance.

In November, 1849, Bonaparte had contented himself with an unparliamentary ministry, in January, 1851, with an extraparliamentary one, and on April 11 he felt strong enough to form an antiparliamentary ministry, which harmoniously combined in itself the no-confidence votes of both Assemblies, the Constituent and the Legislative, the republican and the royalist. This gradation of ministries was the thermometer with which parliament could measure the decrease of its own vital heat. By the end of April the latter had fallen so low that Persigny, in a personal interview, could urge Changarnier to go over to the camp of the President. Bonaparte, he assured him, regarded the influence of the National Assembly as completely destroyed, and the proclamation was already prepared that was to be published after the *coup d'état*, which was kept steadily in view but was by chance again postponed. Changarnier informed the leaders of the party of Order of the obituary notice, but who believes that bedbug bites are fatal? And parliament, stricken, disintegrated, and death-tainted as it was, could not prevail upon itself to see in its duel with the grotesque chief of the Society of December 10 anything but a duel with a bedbug. But Bonaparte answered the party of Order as Agesilaus did King Agis: "*I seem to thee an ant, but one day I shall be a lion.*"[5]

VI

The coalition with the *Montagne* and the pure republicans, to which the party of Order saw itself condemned in its unavailing efforts to maintain posssession of the military power and to reconquer supreme control of the executive power, proved incontrovertibly that it had forfeited its independent parliamentary majority. On May 28 the mere power of the calendar, of the hour hand of the clock, gave the signal for its complete disintegration. With May 28, the last year of the life of the National Assembly began. It now had to decide for continuing the constitution unaltered or for revising it. But revision of the constitution—that implied not only rule of the bourgeoisie or of the petty-bourgeois democracy, democracy or proletarian anarchy, parliamentary republic or Bonaparte, it implied at the same time Orléans or Bourbon! Thus fell in the midst of parliament the apple of discord that was bound to inflame openly the conflict of interests which split the party of Order into hostile factions. The party of Order was a combination of heterogeneous social substances. The question of revision generated a political temperature at which the product again decomposed into its original components.

The Bonapartists' interest in a revision was simple. For them it was above all a question of abolishing Article 45, which forbade Bonaparte's reelection and the prolongation of his authority. No less simple appeared the position of the republicans. They unconditionally rejected any revision; they saw in it a universal conspiracy against the republic. Since they commanded more than a quarter of the votes in the National Assembly, and according to the constitution three-quarters of the votes were required for a resolution for revision to be

---

5. Paraphrase of a story by the Greek writer Athenaeus (*ca.* second century A.D.) in his book, *Deipnosophistae*.

legally valid and for the convocation of a revising Assembly, they needed only to count their votes to be sure of victory. And they were sure of victory.

As against these clear positions, the party of Order found itself inextricably caught in contradictions. If it should reject revision, it would imperil the status quo, since it would leave Bonaparte only one way out, that of force; and since on the second Sunday in May, 1852, at the decisive moment, it would be surrendering France to revolutionary anarchy, with a President who had lost his authority, with a parliament which for a long time had not possessed it, and with a people that meant to reconquer it. If it voted for constitutional revision, it knew that it voted in vain and would be bound to fail constitutionally because of the republicans' veto. If it unconstitutionally declared a simple majority vote to be binding, it could hope to dominate the revolution only if it subordinated itself unconditionally to the sovereignty of the executive power; then it would make Bonaparte master of the constitution, of its revision, and of the party itself. A partial revision, which would prolong the authority of the President, would pave the way for imperial usurpation. A general revision, which would shorten the existence of the republic, would bring the dynastic claims into unavoidable conflict, for the conditions of a Bourbon and an Orléanist restoration were not only different, they were mutually exclusive.

The parliamentary republic was more than the neutral territory on which the two factions of the French bourgeoisie, Legitimists and Orléanists, large landed property and industry, could dwell side by side with equality of rights. It was the unavoidable condition of their common rule, the sole form of state in which their general class interest subjected to itself at the same time both the claims of their particular factions and all the remaining classes of society. As royalists they fell back into their old antagonism, into the struggle for the supremacy of landed property or of money, and the highest expression of this antagonism, its personification, was their kings themselves, their dynasties. Hence the resistance of the party of Order to the recall of the Bourbons.

The Orléanist and people's representative Creton had in 1849, 1850, and 1851 periodically introduced a motion for the revocation of the decree exiling the royal families. Just as regularly, parliament presented the spectacle of an Assembly of royalists that obdurately barred the gates through which their exiled kings might return home. Richard III murdered Henry VI, remarking that he was too good for this world and belonged in heaven. The royalists declared France too bad to possess her kings again. Constrained by force of circumstances, they had become republicans and repeatedly sanctioned the popular decision that banished their kings from France.

A revision of the constitution—and circumstances compelled taking that into consideration—called in question, along with the republic, the common rule of the two bourgeois factions, and revived, with the possibility of a monarchy, the rivalry of the interests which the monarchy had predominantly represented by turns, the struggle for the supremacy of one faction over the other. The diplomats of the party of Order believed they could settle the struggle by an amalgamation of the two dynasties, by a so-called fusion of the royalist parties and their royal houses. The real fusion of the Restoration and the July Monarchy was the parliamentary republic, in which Orléanist and Legitimist colors were obliterated and the various species of bourgeois disappeared into the bourgeois as such, the bourgeois genus. Now, however, Orléanist was to become Legitimist and Legitimist Orléanist. Royalty, in which their antagonism was personified, was to embody their unity, the expression of their exclusive factional interests was to become the expression of their common class interest; the monarchy was to do what only the abolition of two monarchies, the republic, could do and had done. This was the philosopher's stone, to produce which the doctors of the party of Order racked their brains. As if the Legitimist monarchy could ever become the monarchy of the industrial bourgeois or the bourgeois monarchy ever become the monarchy of the hereditary landed aristocracy. As if landed property and industry could fraternize under one crown, when the crown could descend to only one head, the head of the elder brother or of the younger. As if industry could come to terms with landed property at all, so long as landed property itself does not decide to become industrial. If Henry V should die tomorrow, the Count of Paris would not on that account become the king of the Legitimists unless he ceased to be the king of the Orléanists. The philosophers of fusion, however, who became more vociferous in proportion as the question of revision came to the fore, who had provided themselves with an official daily organ in the *Assemblée Nationale*, and who are again at work even at this very moment (February, 1852), considered the whole difficulty to be due to the opposition and rivalry of the two dynasties. The attempts to reconcile the Orléans family with Henry V, begun since the death of Louis Philippe, but, like the dynastic intrigues generally, played at only while the National Assembly was in recess, during the entr'actes, behind the scenes—sentimental coquetry with the old superstition rather than seriously meant business—now became grand performances of state, enacted by the party of Order on the public stage, instead of in amateur theatricals as before. The couriers sped from Paris to Venice, from Venice to Claremont, from Claremont to Paris. The Count of Chambord issues a manifesto in which "with the help of all the members of his family" he announces not his, but the "national" restoration. The Orléanist Salvandy throws himself at the feet of Henry V. The Legitimist chiefs, Berryer, Benoit d'Azy, Saint-Priest, travel to Claremont to persuade the Orléans set, but in vain. The fusionists perceive too late that the interests of the two bourgeois factions neither lose exclusiveness nor gain pliancy when they become accentuated in the form of family interests, the interests of two royal houses. If Henry V were to recognize the Count of Paris as his heir—the sole success that the fusion could achieve at best—the House of Orléans would not win any claim that the childlessness of Henry V had not already secured to it, but it would lose all the claims it had gained through the July Revolution. It would waive its original claims, all the titles it had wrested from the older branch of the Bourbons in almost a hundred years of struggle; it would barter away its historical prerogative, the prerogative of the modern kingdom, for the prerogative of its genealogical tree. The fusion, therefore, would be nothing but a voluntary abdication of the House of Orléans, its resignation to Legitimacy, repentant withdrawal from the Protestant state church into the Catholic. A withdrawal, moreover, that would not even bring it to the throne it had lost, but to the steps of the throne where it had been born. The old Orléanist ministers, Guizot, Duchâtel, etc., who likewise hastened to Claremont to advocate the fusion, in fact represented merely the *Katzenjammer* over the July Revolution, the despair about the bourgeois kingdom and the kingliness of the bourgeois, the superstitious belief in Legitimacy as the last charm against anarchy. Imagining themselves mediators between Orléans and Bourbons, they were in reality merely Orléanist renegades, and the Prince of Joinville received them as such. On the other hand, the viable, bellicose section of the Orléanists, Thiers, Baze, etc., convinced Louis Philippe's family all the more easily that if any directly monarchist restoration presupposed the fusion of the two dynasties, and if any such fusion presupposed abdication of the House of Orléans, it was, on the contrary, wholly in accord with the tradition of their forefathers to recognize the republic for the moment and wait until events permitted the conversion of the presidential chair into a throne. Rumors of Joinville's candidature were circulated, public curiosity was kept in suspense, and a few months later, in September, after the rejection of revision, his candidature was publicly proclaimed.

The attempt at a royalist fusion of Orléanists with Legitimists had thus not only failed; it had destroyed their parliamentary fusion, their common republican form, and had broken up the party of Order into its original component parts; but the more the estrangement between Claremont and Venice grew, the more their settlement collapsed and the Joinville agitation gained ground, so much the more eager and earnest became the negotiations between Bonaparte's minister Faucher and the Legitimists.

The disintegration of the party of Order did not stop at its original elements. Each of the two great factions, in its turn, decomposed all over again. It was as if all the old shadings that had formerly fought and jostled one another within each of the two circles, whether Legitimist or Orléanist, had thawed out again like dry Infusoria on contact with water, as if they had acquired anew sufficient vital energy to form groups of their own and independent antagonisms. The Legitimists dreamed they were back among the controversies between the Tuileries and the Pavillon Marsan, between Villèle and Polignac. The Orléanists relived the golden days of the tourney between Guizot, Molé, Broglie, Thiers, and Odilon Barrot.

The section of the party of Order that was eager for revision, but was divided again on the limits to revision—a section composed of the Legitimists led by Berryer and Falloux, on the one hand, and by La Rochejaquelein, on the other, and of the conflict-weary Orléanists led by Molé, Broglie, Montalembert and Odilon Barrot—agreed with the Bonapartist representatives on the following indefinite and broadly framed motion: "With the object of restoring to the nation the full exercise of its sovereignty, the undersigned representatives move that the constitution be revised."

At the same time, however, they unanimously declared through their reporter Tocqueville that the National Assembly had no right to move the abolition of the republic, that this right was vested solely in the Revising Chamber. For the rest, the constitution might be revised only in a "legal" manner, hence only if the constitutionally prescribed three-quarters of the number of votes were cast in favor of revision. On July 19, after six days of stormy debate, revision was rejected, as was to be anticipated. Four hundred and forty-six votes were cast for it, but two hundred and seventy-eight against. The extreme Orléanists, Thiers, Changarnier, etc., voted with the republicans and the *Montagne*.

Thus the majority of parliament declared against the constitution, but this constitution itself declared for the minority and that its vote was binding. But had not the party of Order subordinated the constitution to the parliamentary majority on May 31, 1850, and on June 13, 1849? Up to now, was not its whole policy based on the subordination of the paragraphs of the constitution to the decisions of the parliamentary majority? Had it not left to the democrats the antediluvian superstitious belief in the letter of the law, and castigated the democrats for it? At the present moment, however, revision of the constitution meant nothing but continuation of the presidential authority, just as continuation of the constitution meant nothing but Bonaparte's deposition. Parliament had declared for him, but the constitution declared against parliament. He therefore acted in the sense of parliament when he tore up the constitution and acted in the sense of the constitution when he adjourned parliament.

Parliament had declared the constitution and, with the latter, its own rule to be "beyond the majority"; by its vote it had abolished the constitution and prolonged the term of presidential power, while declaring at the same time that neither could the one die nor the other live so long as the Assembly itself continued to exist. Those who were to bury it were standing at the door. While it debated on revision, Bonaparte removed General Baraguay d'Hilliers, who had proved irresolute, from the command of the First Army Division and appointed in his place General Magnan, the victor of Lyon, the hero of the December days, one of his creatures, who under Louis Philippe had already more or less compromised himself in Bonaparte's favor on the occasion of the Boulogne expedition.

The party of Order proved by its decision on revision that it knew neither how to rule nor how to serve; neither how to live nor how to die; neither how to suffer the republic nor how to overthrow it; neither how to uphold the constitution nor how to throw it overboard; neither how to cooperate with the President nor how to break with him. To whom, then, did it look for the solution of all the contradictions? To the calendar, to the course of events. It ceased to presume to sway them. It therefore challenged events to assume sway over it, and thereby challenged the power to which, in the struggle against the people, it had surrendered one attribute after another until it stood impotent before this power. In order that the head of the executive power might be able the more undisturbedly to draw up his plan of campaign against it, strengthen his means of attack, select his tools, and fortify his positions, it resolved precisely at this critical moment to retire from the stage and adjourn for three months, from August 10 to November 4.

The parliamentary party was not only dissolved into its two great factions, each of these factions was not only split up within itself, but the party of Order in parliament had fallen out with the party of Order *outside* parliament. The spokesmen and scribes of the bourgeoisie, its platform and its press—in short, the ideologists of the bourgeoisie and the bourgeoisie itself, the representatives and the represented—faced one another in estrangement and no longer understood one another.

The Legitimists in the provinces, with their limited horizon and unlimited enthusiasm, accused their parliamentary leaders, Berryer and Falloux, of deserting to the Bonapartist camp and of defection from Henry V. Their fleur-de-lis minds believed in the fall of man, but not in diplomacy.

Far more fateful and decisive was the breach of the commercial bourgeoisie with its politicians. It reproached them not as the Legitimists reproached theirs, with having abandoned their principles, but on the contrary, with clinging to principles that had become useless.

I have indicated above that since Fould's entry into the ministry the section of the commercial bourgeoisie which had held the lion's share of power under Louis Philippe, namely, the aristocracy of finance, had become Bonapartist. Fould not only represented Bonaparte's interests in the Bourse, he represented at the same time the interests of the Bourse before Bonaparte. The position of the aristocracy of finance is most strikingly depicted in a passage from its European organ, the London *Economist*. In the issue of February 1, 1851, its Paris correspondent writes: "Now we have it stated from numerous quarters that above all things France demands tranquillity. The President declares it in his message to the Legislative Assembly; it is echoed from the tribune; it is asserted in the journals; it is announced from the pulpit; it is demonstrated by the sensitiveness of the public funds at the least prospect of disturbance, and their firmness the instant it is made manifest that the executive is victorious."

In its issue of November 29, 1851, the *Economist* declares in its own name: "The President is the guardian of order, and is now recognized as such on every stock exchange of Europe."

The aristocracy of finance, therefore, condemned the parliamentary struggle of the party of Order with the executive power as a disturbance of order, and celebrated every victory of the President over its ostensible representatives as a victory of order. By the aristocracy of finance must here be understood not merely the great loan promoters and speculators in public funds, in regard to whom it is immediately obvious that their interests coincide with the interests of the state power. All modern finance, the whole of the banking business, is interwoven in the closest fashion with public credit. A part of their business capital is necessarily invested and put out at interest in quickly convertible public funds. Their deposits, the capital placed at their disposal and distributed by them among merchants and industrialists, are partly derived from the dividends of holders of government securities. If in every epoch the stability of the state power signified Moses and the prophets to the entire money market and to the priests of this money market, why not all the more so today, when every deluge threatens to sweep away the old states, and the old state debts with them?

The industrial bourgeoisie too, in its fanaticism for order, was angered by the squabbles of the parliamentary party of Order with the executive power. After their vote of January 18 on the occasion of Changarnier's dismissal, Thiers, Anglès, Sainte-Beuve, etc., received from their constituents, in precisely the industrial districts, public reproofs in which their coalition with the *Montagne* was especially scourged as high treason to order. If, as we have seen, the boastful taunts, the petty intrigues which marked the struggle of the party of Order with the President merited no better reception, then on the other hand this bourgeois party, which required its representatives to allow the military power to pass from its own parliament to an adventurous pretender without offering resistance, was not even worth the intrigues that were squandered in its interests. It proved that the struggle to maintain its public interests, its own class interests, its political power, only troubled and upset it, as it disturbed private business.

With barely an exception the bourgeois dignitaries of the departmental towns, the municipal authorities, the judges of the commercial courts, etc., everywhere received Bonaparte on his tours in the most servile manner, even when, as in Dijon, he made an unrestrained attack on the National Assembly, and especially on the party of Order.

When trade was good, as it still was at the beginning of 1851, the commercial bourgeoisie raged against any parliamentary struggle, lest trade be put out of humor. When trade was bad, as it continually was from the end of February, 1851, the commercial bourgeoisie accused the parliamentary struggles of being the cause of stagnation and cried out for them to stop so that trade could start again. The revision debates came on just in this bad period. Since the question here was whether the existing form of state was to be or not to be, the bourgeoisie felt all the more justified in demanding from its representatives the ending of this torturous provisional arrangement and at the same time the maintenance of the status quo. There was no contradiction in this. By the end of the provisional arrangement it understood precisely its continuation, the postponement to a distant future of the moment when a decision had to be reached. The status quo could be maintained in only two ways: prolongation of Bonaparte's authority or his constitutional retirement and the election of Cavaignac. A section of the bourgeoisie desired the latter solution and knew no better advice to give its representatives than to keep silent and leave the burning question untouched. They were of the opinion that if their representatives did not speak, Bonaparte would not act. They wanted an ostrich parliament that would hide its head in order to remain unseen. Another section of the bourgeoisie desired, because Bonaparte was already in the presidential chair, to leave him sitting in it, so that everything could remain in the same old rut. They were indignant because their parliament did not openly infringe the constitution and abdicate without ceremony.

The Department Councils, those provincial representative bodies of the big bourgeoisie, which met from August 25 on during the recess of the National Assembly, declared almost unanimously for revision, and thus against parliament and in favor of Bonaparte.

Still more unequivocally than in its falling out with its parliamentary representatives, the bourgeoisie displayed its wrath against its literary representatives, its own press. The sentences to ruinous fines and shameless terms of imprisonment, on the verdicts of bourgeois juries, for every attack of bourgeois journalists on Bonaparte's usurpationist desires, for every attempt of the press to defend the political rights of the bourgeoisie against the executive power, astonished not merely France, but all Europe.

While the parliamentary party of Order, by its clamor for tranquillity, as I have shown, committed itself to quiescence, while it declared the political rule of the bourgeoisie to be incompatible with the safety and existence of the bourgeoisie—by destroying with its own hands, in the struggle against the other classes of society, all the conditions for its own regime, the parliamentary regime—the extraparliamentary mass of the bourgeoisie, on the other hand, by its servility toward the President, by its vilification of parliament, by its brutal maltreatment of its own press, invited Bonaparte to suppress and annihilate its speaking and writing section, its politicians and its literati, its platform and its press, so it would then be able to pursue its private affairs with full confidence in the protection of a strong and unrestricted government. It declared unequivocally that it longed to get rid of its own political rule in order to get rid of the troubles and dangers of ruling.

And this extraparliamentary bourgeoisie, which had already rebelled against the purely parliamentary and literary struggle for the rule of its own class, and had betrayed the leaders of this struggle, now dares after the event to indict the proletariat for not having risen in a bloody struggle, a life-and-death struggle on its behalf! This bourgeoisie, which every moment sacrificed its general class interests, that is, its political interests, to the narrowest and most sordid private interests, and demanded a similar sacrifice from its representatives, now moans that the proletariat has sacrificed its ideal political interests to its material interests. It poses as a lovely creature that has been misunderstood and deserted in the decisive hour by the proletariat, misled by socialists. And it finds a general echo in the bourgeois world. Naturally, I do not speak here of German shyster politicians and riffraff of the same persuasion. I refer, for example, to the already quoted *Economist*, which as late as November 29, 1851, that is, four days prior to the *coup d'état*, declared Bonaparte to be the "guardian of order" but Thiers and Berryer to be "anarchists," and on December 27, 1851, after Bonaparte had quieted these "anarchists," is already vociferous about the treason to "the skill, knowledge, discipline, spiritual insight, intellectual resources, and moral weight of the middle and upper ranks" committed by the masses of "ignorant, untrained, and stupid *proletaires*." The stupid, ignorant, and vulgar mass was none other than the bourgeois mass itself.

In the year 1851, France, to be sure, had passed through a kind of minor trade crisis. The end of February showed a decline in exports compared with 1850; in March trade suffered and factories closed down; in April the position of the industrial departments appeared as desperate as after the February days; in May business had still not revived; as late as June 28 the holdings of the Bank of France showed, by the enormous growth of deposits and the equally great decrease in advances on bills of exchange, that production was at a standstill, and it was not until the middle of October that a progressive improvement of business again set in. The French bourgeoisie attributed this trade stagnation to purely political causes, to the struggle between parliament and the executive power, to the precariousness of a merely provisional form of state, to the terrifying prospect of the second Sunday in May of 1852. I will not deny that all these circumstances had a depressing effect on some branches of industry in Paris and the departments. But in any case the influence of political conditions was only local and inconsiderable. Does this require further proof than the fact that the improvement of trade set in toward the middle of October, at the very moment when the political situation grew worse, the political horizon darkened, and a thunderbolt from Elysium was expected at any moment? For the rest, the French bourgeois, whose "skill, knowledge, spiritual insight, and intellectual resources" reach no further than his nose, could throughout the period of the Industrial Exhibition in London have found the cause of his commercial misery right under his nose. While in France factories were closed down, in England commercial bankruptcies broke out. While in April and May the industrial panic reached a

climax in France, in April and May the commercial panic reached a
climax in England. Like the French woolen industry, the English
woolen industry suffered, and as French silk manufacture, so did
English silk manufacture. True, the English cotton mills continued
working, but no longer at the same profits as in 1849 and 1850. The
only difference was that the crisis in France was industrial, in England commercial; that while in France the factories stood idle, in
England they extended operations, but under less favorable conditions than in preceding years; that in France it was exports, in England imports which were hardest hit. The common cause, which is
naturally not to be sought within the bounds of the French political
horizon, was obvious. The years 1849 and 1850 were years of the
greatest material prosperity and of an overproduction that appeared
as such only in 1851. At the beginning of this year it was given a
further special impetus by the prospect of the Industrial Exhibition.
In addition there were the following special circumstances: first, the
partial failure of the cotton crop in 1850 and 1851, then the certainty
of a bigger cotton crop than had been expected; first the rise, then
the sudden fall—in short, the fluctuations in the price of cotton. The
crop of raw silk, in France at least, had turned out to be even below
the average yield. Woolen manufacture, finally, had expanded so
much since 1848 that the production of wool could not keep pace
with it and the price of raw wool rose out of all proportion to the
price of woolen manufactures. Here, then, in the raw material of
three industries for the world market, we already have threefold
material for a stagnation in trade. Apart from these special circumstances, the apparent crisis of 1851 was nothing else but the halt
which overproduction and overspeculation invariably make in completing the industrial cycle, before they summon all their strength in
order to rush feverishly through the final phase of this cycle and
arrive once more at their starting point, the *general trade crisis.* During such intervals in the history of trade, commercial bankruptcies
break out in England, while in France industry itself is reduced to
idleness, partly forced into retreat by the competition, just then
becoming intolerable, of the English in all markets, and partly singled
out for attack as a luxury industry by every business stagnation. Thus
besides the general crisis France goes through national trade crises of
her own, which are nevertheless determined and conditioned far more
by the general state of the world market than by French local influences. It will not be without interest to contrast the judgment of the
English bourgeois with the prejudice of the French bourgeois. In its
annual trade report for 1851, one of the largest Liverpool houses
writes: "Few years have more thoroughly belied the anticipations

formed at their commencement than the one just closed; instead of the great prosperity which was almost unanimously looked for it has proved one of the most discouraging that has been seen for the last quarter of a century—this, of course, refers to the mercantile, not to the manufacturing classes. And yet there certainly were grounds for anticipating the reverse at the beginning of the year—stocks of produce were moderate, money was abundant, and food was cheap, a plentiful harvest well secured, unbroken peace on the Continent, and no political or fiscal disturbances at home; indeed, the wings of commerce were never more unfettered. . . . To what source, then, is this disastrous result to be attributed? We believe to overtrading in both imports and exports. Unless our merchants will put more stringent limits to their freedom of action, nothing but a triennial panic can keep us in check."

Now picture to yourself the French bourgeois, how in the throes of this business panic his trade-crazy brain is tortured, set in a whirl, and stunned by rumors of *coups d'état* and the restoration of universal suffrage, by the struggle between parliament and the executive power, by the Fronde war between Orléanists and Legitimists, by the communist conspiracies in the south of France, by alleged *Jacqueries* in the departments of Nièvre and Cher, by the advertisements of the different candidates for the presidency, by the cheapjack solutions offered by the journals, by the threats of the republicans to uphold the constitution and universal suffrage by force of arms, by the gospel-preaching émigré heroes *in partibus*, who announced that the world would come to an end on the second Sunday in May, 1852— think of all this and you will comprehend why in this unspeakable, deafening chaos of fusion, revision, prorogation, constitution, conspiration, coalition, emigration, usurpation, and revolution, the bourgeois madly snorts at his parliamentary republic: *"Rather an end with terror than terror without end!"*

Bonaparte understood this cry. His power of comprehension was sharpened by the growing turbulence of creditors, who with each sunset which brought settling day, the second Sunday in May, 1852, nearer, saw a movement of the stars protesting their earthly bills of exchange. They had become veritable astrologers. The National Assembly had blighted Bonaparte's hopes of a constitutional prolongation of his authority; the candidature of the Prince of Joinville forbade further vacillation.

If ever an event has, well in advance of its coming, cast its shadow before, it was Bonaparte's *coup d'état*. As early as January 29, 1849, barely a month after his election, he had made a proposal about it to Changarnier. In the summer of 1849 his own Prime Minister, Odilon

Barrot, had covertly denounced the policy of *coups d'état;* in the winter of 1850 Thiers had openly done so. In May, 1851, Persigny had sought once more to win Changarnier for the *coup;* the *Messager de l'Assemblée* had published an account of these negotiations. During every parliamentary storm the Bonapartist journals threatened a *coup d'état,* and the nearer the crisis drew, the louder their tone became. In the orgies that Bonaparte kept up every night with men and women of the "swell mob," as soon as the hour of midnight approached and copious potations had loosened tongues and fired imaginations, the *coup d'état* was fixed for the following morning. Swords were drawn, glasses clinked, the representatives were thrown out the window, the imperial mantle fell upon Bonaparte's shoulders, until the following morning banished the ghost once more and astonished Paris learned, from vestals of little reticence and from indiscreet paladins, of the danger it had once again escaped. During the months of September and October rumors of a *coup d'état* followed fast, one after the other. Simultaneously the shadow took on color, like a variegated daguerreotype. Look up the September and October copies of the organs of the European daily press and you will find, word for word, intimations like the following: "Paris is full of rumors of a *coup d'état.* The capital is to be filled with troops during the night, and the next morning is to bring decrees which will dissolve the National Assembly, declare the Department of the Seine in a state of siege, restore universal suffrage, and appeal to the people. Bonaparte is said to be seeking ministers for the execution of these illegal decrees." The dispatches that bring these tidings always end with the fateful word "postponed." The *coup d'état* was ever the fixed idea of Bonaparte. With this idea he had again set foot on French soil. He was so obsessed by it that he continually betrayed it and blurted it out. He was so weak that, just as continually, he gave it up again. The shadow of the *coup d'état* had become so familiar to the Parisians as a specter that they were not willing to believe in it when it finally appeared in the flesh. What allowed the *coup d'état* to succeed was therefore neither the reticent reserve of the chief of the Society of December 10 nor the fact that the National Assembly was caught unawares. If it succeeded, it succeeded despite *his* indiscretion and with *its* foreknowledge, a necessary, inevitable result of antecedent developments.

On October 10 Bonaparte announced to his ministers his decision to restore universal suffrage; on the sixteenth they handed in their resignations; on the twenty-sixth Paris learned of the formation of the Thorigny Ministry. Police Prefect Carlier was simultaneously replaced by Maupas; the head of the First Military Division, Magnan, concentrated the most reliable regiments in the capital. On November

4 the National Assembly resumed its sessions. It had nothing better to do than to recapitulate in a short, succinct form the course it had gone through and to prove that it was buried only after it had died.

The first post it forfeited in the struggle with the executive power was the ministry. It had solemnly to admit this loss by accepting at full value the Thorigny Ministry, a mere shadow cabinet. The Permanent Commission had received M. Giraud with laughter when he presented himself in the name of the new ministers. Such a weak ministry for such strong measures as the restoration of universal suffrage! Yet the precise object was to get nothing through in parliament, but everything against parliament.

On the very first day of its reopening, the National Assembly received the message from Bonaparte in which he demanded the restoration of universal suffrage and the abolition of the law of May 31, 1850. The same day his ministers introduced a decree to this effect. The National Assembly at once rejected the ministry's motion of urgency and rejected the law itself on November 13 by three hundred and fifty-five votes to three hundred and forty-eight. Thus, it tore up its mandate once more; it once more confirmed the fact that it had transformed itself from the freely elected representatives of the people into the usurpatory parliament of a class; it acknowledged once more that it had itself cut in two the muscles which connected the parliamentary head with the body of the nation.

If by its motion to restore universal suffrage the executive power appealed from the National Assembly to the people, the legislative power appealed by its Quaestors' Bill from the people to the army. This Quaestors' Bill was to establish its right of directly requisitioning troops, of forming a parliamentary army. While it thus designated the army as the arbitrator between itself and the people, between itself and Bonaparte, while it recognized the army as the decisive state power, it had to confirm, on the other hand, the fact that it had long given up its claim to dominate this power. By debating its right to requisition troops, instead of requisitioning them at once, it betrayed its doubts about its own powers. By rejecting the Quaestors' Bill, it made public confession of its impotence. This bill was defeated, its proponents lacking a hundred and eight votes of a majority. The *Montagne* thus decided the issue. It found itself in the position of Buridan's ass—not, indeed, between two bundles of hay with the problem of deciding which was the more attractive, but between two showers of blows with the problem of deciding which was the harder. On the one hand, there was the fear of Changarnier; on the other, the fear of Bonaparte. It must be confessed that the position was not a heroic one.

On November 18 an amendment was moved to the law on

municipal elections introduced by the party of Order, to the effect that instead of three years', one year's domicile should suffice for municipal electors. The amendment was lost by a single vote, but this one vote immediately proved to be a mistake. By splitting up into its hostile factions, the party of Order had long ago forfeited its independent parliamentary majority. It showed now that there was no longer any majority at all in parliament. The National Assembly had become *incapable of transacting business*. Its atomic constituents were no longer held together by any force of cohesion; it had drawn its last breath; it was dead.

Finally, a few days before the catastrophe, the extraparliamentary mass of the bourgeoisie was solemnly to confirm once more its breach with the bourgeoisie in parliament. Thiers, as a parliamentary hero infected more than the rest with the incurable disease of parliamentary cretinism, had, after the death of parliament, hatched out, together with the Council of State, a new parliamentary intrigue, a Responsibility Law by which the President was to be firmly held within the limits of the constitution. Just as, on laying the foundation stone of the new market halls in Paris on September 15, Bonaparte, like a second Masaniello, had enchanted the *dames des halles*, the fishwives—to be sure, one fishwife outweighed seventeen burgraves in real power—just as after the introduction of the Quaestors' Bill he enraptured the lieutenants whom he regaled in the Élysée, so now, on November 25, he swept off their feet the industrial bourgeoisie, which had gathered at the circus to receive at his hands prize medals for the London Industrial Exhibition.

I shall give the significant portion of his speech as reported in the *Journal des Débats:* " 'With such unhoped-for successes, I am justified in reiterating how great the French Republic would be if it were permitted to pursue its real interests and reform its institutions, instead of being constantly disturbed by demagogues, on the one hand, and by monarchist hallucinations, on the other.' (Loud, stormy and repeated applause from every part of the amphitheater.) 'The monarchist hallucinations hinder all progress and all important branches of industry. In place of progress nothing but struggle. One sees men who were formerly the most zealous supporters of the royal authority and prerogative become partisans of a Convention merely in order to weaken the authority that has sprung from universal suffrage.' (Loud and repeated applause.) 'We see men who have suffered most from the Revolution, and have deplored it most, provoke a new one, and merely in order to fetter the nation's will. . . . I promise you tranquillity for the future,' etc., etc. (Bravo, bravo, a storm of bravos.)"

Thus the industrial bourgeoisie applauds with servile bravos the *coup d'état* of December 2, the annihilation of parliament, the downfall of its own rule, the dictatorship of Bonaparte. The thunder of applause on November 25 had its answer in the thunder of cannon on December 4, and it was on the house of Monsieur Sallandrouze, who had clapped most, that they clapped most of the bombs.

Cromwell, when he dissolved the Long Parliament, went alone into its midst, took out his watch so that it should not continue to exist a minute after the time limit he had fixed, and drove out each one of the members of Parliament with hilariously humorous taunts. Napoleon, smaller than his prototype, at least betook himself on the eighteenth Brumaire to the legislative body and read out to it, though in a faltering voice, its sentence of death. The second Bonaparte, who, moreover, found himself in possession of an executive power very different from that of Cromwell or Napoleon, sought his model not in the annals of world history but in the annals of the Society of December 10, in the annals of the criminal courts. He robs the Bank of France of twenty-five million francs, buys General Magnan with a million, the soldiers with fifteen francs apiece and liquor, comes together with his accomplices secretly like a thief in the night, has the houses of the most dangerous parliamentary leaders broken into, and Cavaignac, Lamoricière, Le Flô, Changarnier, Charras, Thiers, Baze, etc., dragged from their beds and put in prison, the chief squares of Paris and the parliamentary building occupied by troops, and cheapjack placards posted early in the morning on all the walls, proclaiming the dissolution of the National Assembly and the Council of State, the restoration of universal suffrage, and the placing of the Seine Department in a state of siege. In like manner he inserted a little later in the *Moniteur* a false document which asserted that influential parliamentarians had grouped themselves around him and formed a state *consulta*.

The rump parliament, assembled in the *mairie* building of the Tenth Arrondissement and consisting mainly of Legitimists and Orléanists, votes the deposition of Bonaparte amid repeated cries of "Long live the Republic," unavailingly harangues the gaping crowds before the building, and is finally led off in the custody of African sharpshooters, first to the d'Orsay barracks, and later packed into prison vans and transported to the prisons of Mazas, Ham, and Vincennes. Thus ended the party of Order, the Legislative Assembly, and the February Revolution. Before hastening to close, let us briefly summarize the latter's history:

1. *First period.* From February 24 to May 4, 1848. February period. Prologue. Universal-brotherhood swindle.

316 FRANCE

2. *Second period.* Period of constituting the republic and of the Constituent National Assembly.

a. May 4 to June 25, 1848. Struggle of all classes against the proletariat. Defeat of the proletariat in the June days.

b. June 25 to December 10, 1848. Dictatorship of the pure bourgeois republicans. Drafting of the constitution. Proclamation of a state of siege in Paris. The bourgeois dictatorship set aside on December 10 by the election of Bonaparte as President.

c. December 20, 1848, to May 28, 1849. Struggle of the Constituent Assembly with Bonaparte and with the party of Order in alliance with him. Passing of the Constituent Assembly. Fall of the republican bourgeoisie.

3. *Third period.* Period of the constitutional republic and of the Legislative National Assembly.

a. May 28, 1849, to June 13, 1849. Struggle of the petty bourgeoisie with the bourgeoisie and with Bonaparte. Defeat of the petty-bourgeois democracy.

b. June 13, 1849, to May 31, 1850. Parliamentary dictatorship of the party of Order. It completes its rule by abolishing universal suffrage, but loses the parliamentary ministry.

c. May 31, 1850, to December 2, 1851. Struggle between the parliamentary bourgeoisie and Bonaparte.

(1) May 31, 1850, to January 12, 1851. The Assembly loses the supreme command of the army.

(2) January 12 to April 11, 1851. It is worsted in its attempts to regain the administrative power. The party of Order loses its independent parliamentary majority. It forms a coalition with the republicans and the *Montagne.*

(3) April 11, 1851, to October 9, 1851. Attempts at revision, fusion, prorogation. The party of Order decomposes into its separate constituents. The breach between the bourgeois parliament and press and the mass of the bourgeoisie becomes definite.

(4) October 9 to December 2, 1851. Open breach between parliament and the executive power. The Assembly performs its dying act and succumbs, left in the lurch by its own class, by the army, and by all the remaining classes. Passing of the parliamentary regime and of bourgeois rule. Victory of Bonaparte. Parody of restoration of empire.

VII

The *social republic* appeared as a phrase, as a prophecy, on the threshold of the February Revolution. In the June days of 1848, it was drowned in the blood of the Paris proletariat, but it haunts the subsequent acts of the drama like a ghost. The *democratic republic* announces its appearance. It is dissipated on June 13, 1849, together with its deserting petty bourgeois, but in its flight it redoubles its boastfulness. The *parliamentary republic* together with the bourgeoisie takes possession of the entire state; it enjoys its existence to the full, but December 2, 1851, buries it to the accompaniment of the anguished cry of the coalesced royalists: "Long live the Republic!"

The French bourgeoisie balked at the domination of the working proletariat; it has brought the lumpen proletariat to domination, with the Chief of the Society of December 10 at the head. The bourgeoisie kept France in breathless fear of the future terrors of red anarchy; Bonaparte discounted this future for it when, on December 4, he had the eminent bourgeois of the Boulevard Montmartre and the Boulevard des Italiens shot down at their windows by the drunken army of law and order. The bourgeoisie apotheosized the sword; the sword rules it. It destroyed the revolutionary press; its own press is destroyed. It placed popular meetings under police surveillance; its salons are placed under police supervision. It disbanded the democratic National Guard; its own National Guard is disbanded. It imposed a state of siege; a state of siege is imposed upon it. It supplanted the juries by military commissions; its juries are supplanted by military commissions. It subjected public education to the sway of the priests; the priests subject it to their own education. It jailed people without trial; it is being jailed without trial. It suppressed every stirring in society by means of state power; every stirring in its society is suppressed by means of state power. Out of enthusiasm for its moneybag, it rebelled against its own politicians and literary men; its politicians and literary men are swept aside, but its moneybag is being plundered now that its mouth has been gagged and its pen broken. The bourgeoisie never tired of crying out to the revolution what St. Arsenius cried out to the Christians: "*Fuge, tace, quiesce!*" ["Flee, be silent, keep still!"] Bonaparte cries to the bourgeoisie: "*Fuge, tace, quiesce!*"

The French bourgeoisie had long ago found the solution to Napoleon's dilemma: "In fifty years Europe will be republican or Cossack." It solved it in the "Cossack republic." No Circe using black magic has distorted that work of art, the bourgeois republic, into a monstrous shape. That republic has lost nothing but the semblance of respectability. Present-day France was already contained in the parliamentary republic. It required only a bayonet thrust for the bubble to burst and the monster to leap forth before our eyes.

Why did the Paris proletariat not rise in revolt after December 2?

The overthrow of the bourgeoisie had as yet been only decreed; the decree was not carried out. Any serious insurrection of the proletariat would at once have put new life into the bourgeoisie, reconciled it with the army, and insured a second June defeat for the workers.

On December 4 the proletariat was incited by bourgeois and shopkeeper to fight. On the evening of that day several legions of the National Guard promised to appear, armed and uniformed, on the scene of battle. For the bourgeois and the shopkeeper had learned that in one of his decrees of December 2 Bonaparte had abolished the secret ballot and had ordered them to put a "yes" or "no" after their names on the official registers. The resistance of December 4 intimidated Bonaparte. During the night he had placards posted on all the street corners of Paris announcing the restoration of the secret ballot. The bourgeois and the shopkeeper believed they had gained their objective. Those who failed to appear next morning were the bourgeois and the shopkeeper.

By a *coup de main* the night of December 1–2 Bonaparte had robbed the Paris proletariat of its leaders, the barricade commanders. An army without officers, averse to fighting under the banner of the *Montagnards* because of the memories of June, 1848 and 1849, and May, 1850, it left to its vanguard, the secret societies, the task of saving the insurrectionary honor of Paris, which the bourgeoisie had surrendered to the military so unresistingly that, subsequently, Bonaparte could disarm the National Guard with the sneering motive of his fear that its weapons would be turned against it by the anarchists!

"This is the complete and final triumph of socialism!" Thus Guizot characterized December 2. But if the overthrow of the parliamentary republic contains within itself the germ of the triumph of the proletarian revolution, its immediate and obvious result was *Bonaparte's victory over parliament, of the executive power over the legislative power, of force without phrases over the force of phrases.* In parliament the nation made its general will the law; that is, it made the law of the ruling class its general will. It renounces all will of its own before the executive power and submits itself to the superior command of an alien, of authority. The executive power, in contrast to the legislative one, expresses the heteronomy of a nation in contrast to its autonomy. France therefore seems to have escaped the despotism of a class only to fall back under the despotism of an individual, and what is more, under the authority of an individual without authority. The struggle seems to be settled in such a way that all classes, equally powerless and equally mute, fall on their knees before the rifle butt.

But the revolution is thoroughgoing. It is still traveling through purgatory. It does its work methodically. By December 2, 1851, it had completed half of its preparatory work; now it is completing the other half. It first completed the parliamentary power in order to be able to overthrow it. Now that it has achieved this, it completes the executive power, reduces it to its purest expression, isolates it, sets it up against itself as the sole target, in order to concentrate all its forces of destruction against it. And when it has accomplished this second half of its preliminary work, Europe will leap from its seat and exult: Well burrowed, old mole![6]

The executive power with its enormous bureaucratic and military organization, with its wide-ranging and ingenious state machinery, with a host of officials numbering half a million, besides an army of another half million—this terrifying parasitic body which enmeshes the body of French society and chokes all its pores sprang up in the time of the absolute monarchy, with the decay of the feudal system which it had helped to hasten. The seignorial privileges of the landowners and towns became transformed into so many attributes of the state power, the feudal dignitaries into paid officials, and the motley patterns of conflicting medieval plenary powers into the regulated plan of a state authority whose work is divided and centralized as in a factory.

The first French Revolution, with its task of breaking all separate local, territorial, urban, and provincial powers in order to create the civil unity of the nation, was bound to develop what the monarchy had begun, centralization, but at the same time the limits, the attributes, and the agents of the governmental power. Napoleon completed this state machinery. The Legitimate Monarchy and the July Monarchy added nothing to it but a greater division of labor, increasing at the same rate as the division of labor inside the bourgeois society created new groups of interests, and therefore new material for the state administration. Every common interest was immediately severed from the society, countered by a higher, general interest, snatched from the activities of society's members themselves and made an object of government activity—from a bridge, a schoolhouse, and the communal property of a village community, to the railroads, the national wealth, and the national university of France. Finally the parliamentary republic, in its struggle against the revolution, found itself compelled to strengthen the means and the centralization of governmental power with repressive measures. All revolutions perfected this machine instead of breaking it. The parties, which alter-

---

6. A paraphrase from Shakespeare's *Hamlet*, Act I, Scene 5: "Well said, old mole!"

nately contended for domination, regarded the possession of this huge state structure as the chief spoils of the victor.

But under the absolute monarchy, during the first Revolution, and under Napoleon the bureaucracy was only the means of preparing the class rule of the bourgeoisie. Under the Restoration, under Louis Philippe, under the parliamentary republic, it was the instrument of the ruling class, however much it strove for power of its own.

Only under the second Bonaparte does the state seem to have made itself completely independent. The state machinery has so strengthened itself vis-à-vis civil society that the Chief of the Society of December 10 suffices for its head—an adventurer dropped in from abroad, raised on the shoulders of a drunken soldiery which he bought with whisky and sausages and to which he has to keep throwing more sausages. Hence the low-spirited despair, the feeling of monstrous humiliation and degradation that oppresses the breast of France and makes her gasp. She feels dishonored.

And yet the state power is not suspended in the air. Bonaparte represented a class, and the most numerous class of French society at that, the *small-holding peasants*.

Just as the Bourbons were the dynasty of the big landed property and the Orléans the dynasty of money, so the Bonapartes are the dynasty of the peasants, that is, the French masses. The chosen of the peasantry is not the Bonaparte who submitted to the bourgeois parliament but the Bonaparte who dismissed the bourgeois parliament. For three years the towns had succeeded in falsifying the meaning of the December 10 election and in cheating the peasants out of the restoration of the Empire. The election of December 10, 1848, has been consummated only by the *coup d'état* of December 2, 1851.

The small-holding peasants form an enormous mass whose members live in similar conditions but without entering into manifold relations with each other. Their mode of production isolates them from one another instead of bringing them into mutual intercourse. The isolation is furthered by France's poor means of communication and the poverty of the peasants. Their field of production, the small holding, permits no division of labor in its cultivation, no application of science, and therefore no multifariousness of development, no diversity of talent, no wealth of social relationships. Each individual peasant family is almost self-sufficient, directly produces most of its consumer needs, and thus acquires its means of life more through an exchange with nature than in intercourse with society. A small holding, the peasant and his family; beside it another small holding, another peasant and another family. A few score of these constitute a village, and a few score villages constitute a department. Thus the great mass of the French nation is formed by the simple addition of homonymous magnitudes, much as potatoes in a sack form a sack of potatoes. Insofar as millions of families live under conditions of existence that separate their mode of life, their interests, and their culture from those of the other classes, and put them in hostile opposition to the latter, they form a class. Insofar as there is merely a local interconnection among these small-holding peasants, and the identity of their interests forms no community, no national bond, and no political organization among them, they do not constitute a class. They are therefore incapable of asserting their class interest in their own name, whether through a parliament or a convention. They cannot represent themselves, they must be represented. Their representative must at the same time appear as their master, as an authority over them, an unlimited governmental power which protects them from the other classes and sends them rain and sunshine from above. The political influence of the small-holding peasants, therefore, finds its final expression in the executive power which subordinates society to itself.

Historical tradition gave rise to the French peasants' belief in the miracle that a man named Napoleon would bring all glory back to them. And there turned up an individual who claims to be that man because he bears the name Napoleon, in consequence of the Code Napoléon, which decrees: "Inquiry into paternity is forbidden." After a twenty-year vagabondage and a series of grotesque adventures the legend is consummated, and the man becomes Emperor of the French. The *idée fixe* of the nephew was realized because it coincided with the *idée fixe* of the most numerous class of the French people.

But, it may be objected, what about the peasant uprisings in half of France, the raids of the army on the peasants, the mass incarceration and transportation of the peasants?

Since Louis XIV, France has experienced no similar persecution of the peasants "on account of demagogic agitation."

But let us not misunderstand. The Bonaparte dynasty represents not the revolutionary, but the conservative peasant; not the peasant who strikes out beyond the condition of his social existence, the small holding, but rather one who wants to consolidate his holding; not the countryfolk who in alliance with the towns want to overthrow the old order through their own energies, but on the contrary those who, in solid seclusion within this old order, want to see themselves and their small holdings saved and favored by the ghost of the Empire. It represents not the enlightenment but the superstition of the peasant; not his judgment but his prejudice; not his future but his past; not his modern Cevennes[7] but his modern Vendée.[8]

---

7. A peasant uprising in the Cevennes mountains in 1702–1705.
8. A peasant-backed uprising against the French Revolution in the French province of Vendée, in 1793.

The three years' stern rule of the parliamentary republic freed a part of the French peasants from the Napoleonic illusion and revolutionized them, even though superficially; but the bourgeoisie violently repulsed them as often as they set themselves in motion. Under the parliamentary republic the modern and the traditional consciousness of the French peasant contended for mastery. The process took the form of an incessant struggle between the schoolmasters and the priests. The bourgeoisie struck down the schoolmasters. The peasants for the first time made efforts to behave independently vis-à-vis the government. This was shown in the continual conflict between the mayors and the prefects. The bourgeoisie deposed the mayors. Finally, during the period of the parliamentary republic, the peasants of different localities rose against their own offspring, the army. The bourgeoisie punished these peasants with sieges and executions. And this same bourgeoisie now cries out against the stupidity of the masses, the vile multitude that betrayed it to Bonaparte. The bourgeoisie itself has violently strengthened the imperialism of the peasant class; it has preserved the conditions that form the birthplaces of this species of peasant religion. The bourgeoisie, in truth, is bound to fear the stupidity of the masses so long as they remain conservative, and the insight of the masses as soon as they become revolutionary.

In the uprisings after the *coup d'état*, a part of the French peasants protested, arms in hand, against their own vote of December 10, 1848. The school they had gone to since 1848 had sharpened their wits. But they had inscribed themselves in the historical underworld; history held them to their word, and the majority was still so implicated that precisely in the reddest departments the peasant population voted openly for Bonaparte. In their view, the National Assembly had hindered his progress. He has now merely broken the fetters that the towns had imposed on the will of the countryside. In some parts the peasants even entertained the grotesque notion of a convention with Napoleon.

After the first Revolution had transformed the semifeudal peasants into freeholders, Napoleon confirmed and regulated the conditions in which they could exploit undisturbed the soil of France which they had only just acquired, and could slake their youthful passion for property. But what is now ruining the French peasant is his small holding itself, the division of the land and the soil, the property form which Napoleon consolidated in France. It is exactly these material conditions which made the feudal peasant a small-holding peasant and Napoleon an emperor. Two generations sufficed to produce the unavoidable result: progressive deterioration of agriculture and progressive indebtedness of the agriculturist. The "Napoleonic" property form, which at the beginning of the nineteenth century was the condition of the emancipation and enrichment of the French countryfolk, has developed in the course of this century into the law of their enslavement and their pauperism. And just this law is the first of the "Napoleonic ideas" which the second Bonaparte has to uphold. If he still shares with the peasants the illusion that the cause of their ruin is to be sought not in the small holdings themselves but outside them— in the influence of secondary circumstances—his experiments will shatter like soap bubbles when they come in contact with the relations of production.

The economic development of small-holding property has radically changed the peasants' relations with the other social classes. Under Napoleon the fragmentation of the land in the countryside supplemented free competition and the beginning of big industry in the towns. The peasant class was the ubiquitous protest against the recently overthrown landed aristocracy. The roots that small-holding property struck in French soil deprived feudalism of all nourishment. The landmarks of this property formed the natural fortification of the bourgeoisie against any surprise attack by its old overlords. But in the course of the nineteenth century the urban usurer replaced the feudal one, the mortgage replaced the feudal obligation, bourgeois capital replaced aristocratic landed property. The peasant's small holding is now only the pretext that allows the capitalist to draw profits, interest, and rent from the soil, while leaving it to the agriculturist himself to see to it how he can extract his wages. The mortgage debt burdening the soil of France imposes on the French peasantry an amount of interest equal to the annual interest on the entire British national debt. Small-holding property, in this enslavement by capital toward which its development pushes it unavoidably, has transformed the mass of the French nation into troglodytes. Sixteen million peasants (including women and children) dwell in caves, a large number of which have but one opening, others only two and the most favored only three. Windows are to a house what the five senses are to the head. The bourgeois order, which at the beginning of the century set the state to stand guard over the newly emerged small holdings and fertilized them with laurels, has become a vampire that sucks the blood from their hearts and brains and casts them into the alchemist's caldron of capital. The Code Napoléon is now nothing but the codex of distraints, of forced sales and compulsory auctions. To the four million (including children, etc.) officially recognized paupers, vagabonds, criminals, and prostitutes in France must be added another five million who hover on the margin of existence and either have their haunts in the countryside itself or, with their rags and their children, continually desert the countryside for the towns and the towns for the countryside. Therefore the interests of the peasants are no longer, as under Napoleon, in accord with, but are now in opposition to bourgeois interests, to capital. Hence they find their natural ally and leader in the *urban proletariat*, whose task it is to overthrow the bourgeois order. But "strong and unlimited government"—and this is the second "Napoleonic idea" that the second Napoleon has to carry out—is called upon to defend this "material order" by force. This "material order" also serves, in all Bonaparte's proclamations, as the slogan against the rebellious peasants.

In addition to the mortgage which capital imposes on it, the small holding is burdened by *taxes*. Taxes are the life source of the bureaucracy, the army, the priests, and the court—in short, of the entire apparatus of the executive power. Strong government and heavy taxes are identical. By its very nature, small-holding property forms a basis for an all-powerful and numberless bureaucracy. It creates a uniform level of personal and economic relationships over the whole extent of the country. Hence it also permits uniform action from a supreme center on all points of this uniform mass. It destroys the aristocratic intermediate steps between the mass of the people and the power of the state. On all sides, therefore, it calls forth the direct intrusion of this state power and the interposition of its immediate organs. Finally, it produces an unemployed surplus population which can find no place either on the land or in the towns and which perforce reaches out for state offices as a sort of respectable alms, and provokes the creation of additional state positions. By the new markets which he opened with bayonets, and by the plundering of the Continent, Napoleon repaid the compulsory taxes with interest. These taxes were a spur to the industry of the peasant, whereas now they rob his industry of its last resources and complete his defenselessness against pauperism. An enormous bureaucracy, well gallooned and well fed, is the "Napoleonic idea" which is most congenial to the second Bonaparte. How could it be otherwise, considering that alongside the actual classes of society, he is forced to create an artificial caste for which the maintenance of his regime becomes a bread-and-butter question? Hence one of his first financial operations was the raising of officials' salaries to their old level and the creation of new sinecures.

Another "Napoleonic idea" is the domination of the priests as an instrument of government. But while at the time of their emergence the small-holding owners, in their accord with society, in their dependence on natural forces and submission to the authority which protected them from above, were naturally religious, now that they are ruined by debts, at odds with society and authority, and driven beyond their own limitations, they have become naturally irreligious.

Heaven was quite a pleasing addition to the narrow strip of land just won, especially as it makes the weather; it becomes an insult as soon as it is thrust forward as a substitute for the small holding. The priest then appears as only the anointed bloodhound of the earthly police —another "Napoleonic idea." The expedition against Rome will take place in France itself next time, but in a sense opposite from that of M. de Montalembert.

Finally, the culminating "Napoleonic idea" is the ascendancy of the army. The army was the "point of honor" of the small-holding peasants, it was they themselves transformed into heroes, defending their new possessions against the outer world, glorifying their recently won nationhood, plundering and revolutionizing the world. The uniform was their own state costume; war was their poetry; the small holding, enlarged and rounded off in imagination, was their fatherland, and patriotism the ideal form of the sense of property. But the enemies whom the French peasant now has to defend his property against are not the Cossacks; they are the *huissiers* [bailiffs] and the tax collectors. The small holding no longer lies in the so-called fatherland but in the registry of mortgages. The army itself is no longer the flower of the peasant youth; it is the swamp flower of the peasant lumpen proletariat. It consists largely of replacements, of substitutes, just as the second Bonaparte is himself only a replacement, the substitute for Napoleon. It now performs its deeds of valor by hounding the peasants in masses like chamois, by doing gendarme duty; and if the natural contradictions of his system chase the Chief of the Society of December 10 across the French border, his army, after some acts of brigandage, will reap, not laurels, but thrashings.

It is clear: *All "Napoleonic ideas" are ideas of the undeveloped small holding in the freshness of its youth;* they are a contradiction to the outlived holdings. They are only the hallucinations of its death struggle, words transformed into phrases, spirits transformed into ghosts. But the parody of imperialism was necessary to free the mass of the French nation from the weight of tradition and to work out in pure form the opposition between state power and society. With the progressive deterioration of small-holding property, the state structure erected upon it collapses. The centralization of the state that modern society requires arises only on the ruins of the military-bureaucratic government machinery which was forged in opposition to feudalism.

The condition of the French peasants provides us with the answer to the riddle of the general elections of December 20 and 21, which bore the second Bonaparte up Mount Sinai, not to receive laws but to give them.

Obviously the bourgeoisie now had no choice but to elect Bonaparte. When the puritans of the Council of Constance [1414–18] complained of the dissolute lives of the popes and wailed about the necessity for moral reform, Cardinal Pierre d'Ailly thundered at them: "Only the devil in person can still save the Catholic Church, and you ask for angels." Similarly, after the *coup d'état* the French bourgeoisie cried out: Only the Chief of the Society of December 10 can still save bourgeois society! Only theft can still save property; only perjury, religion; bastardy, the family; disorder, order!

As the executive authority which has made itself independent, Bonaparte feels it to be his task to safeguard "bourgeois order." But the strength of this bourgeois order lies in the middle class. He poses, therefore, as the representative of the middle class and issues decrees in this sense. Nevertheless, he is somebody solely because he has broken the power of that middle class, and keeps on breaking it daily. He poses, therefore, as the opponent of the political and literary power of the middle class. But by protecting its material power he revives its political power. Thus the cause must be kept alive, but the effect, where it manifests itself, must be done away with. But this cannot happen without small confusions of cause and effect, since in their interaction both lose their distinguishing marks. New decrees obliterate the border line. Bonaparte knows how to pose at the same time as the representative of the peasants and of the people in general, as a man who wants to make the lower classes happy within the framework of bourgeois society. New decrees cheat the "true socialists" of their governmental skill in advance. But above all, Bonaparte knows how to pose as the Chief of the Society of December 10, as the representative of the lumpen proletariat to which he himself, his entourage, his government, and his army belong, and whose main object is to benefit itself and draw California lottery prizes from the state treasury. And he confirms himself as Chief of the Society of December 10 with decrees, without decrees, and despite decrees.

This contradictory task of the man explains the contradictions of his government, the confused groping which tries now to win, now to humiliate, first one class and then another, and uniformly arrays all of them against him; whose uncertainty in practice forms a highly comical contrast to the imperious, categorical style of the government decrees, a style slavishly copied from the uncle.

Industry and commerce, hence the business affairs of the middle class, are to prosper in hothouse fashion under the strong government: the grant of innumerable railroad concessions. But the Bonapartist lumpen proletariat is to enrich itself: those in the know play *tripotage* [underhand dealings] on the Exchange with the railroad concessions. But no capital is forthcoming for the railroads: obligation of the Bank to make advances on railroad shares. But at the same time the Bank is to be exploited for personal gain and therefore must be cajoled: release the Bank from the obligation to publish its report weekly; leonine[9] agreement of the Bank with the government. The people are to be given employment: initiation of public works. But the public works increase the people's tax obligations: hence reduction of taxes by an attack on the *rentiers,* by conversion of the 5-percent bonds into 4½-percent. But the middle class must again receive a sweetening: hence a doubling of the wine tax for the people, who buy wine retail, and a halving of the wine tax for the middle class, which drinks it wholesale; dissolution of the actual workers' associations, but promises of miraculous future associations. The peasants are to be helped: mortgage banks which hasten their indebtedness and accelerate the concentration of property. But these banks are to be used to make money out of the confiscated estates of the House of Orléans; no capitalist wants to agree to this condition, which is not in the decree, and the mortgage bank remains a mere decree, etc., etc.

Bonaparte would like to appear as the patriarchal benefactor of all classes. But he cannot give to one without taking from another. Just as it was said of the Duke de Guise in the time of the Fronde that he was the most obliging man in France because he gave all his estates to his followers, with feudal obligations to him, so Bonaparte would like to be the most obliging man in France and turn all the property and all the labor of France into a personal obligation to himself. He would like to steal all of France in order to make a present of it to France, or rather in order to buy France anew with French money, for as the Chief of the Society of December 10 he must buy what ought to belong to him. And to the Institution of Purchase belong all the state institutions, the Senate, the Council of State, the Assembly, the Legion of Honor, the military medals, the public laundries, the public works, the railroads, the general staff, the officers of the National Guard, the confiscated estates of the House of Orléans. The means of purchase is obtained by selling every place in the army and the government machinery. But the most important feature of this process, by which France is taken in order to give to her, are the percentages that find their way into the pockets of the head and the members of the Society of December 10 during the turnover. The witticism with which Countess L., the

---

9. From Aesop's fable about the lion who made a contract in which one partner got all the profits and the other all the disadvantages.

mistress of M. de Morny, characterized the confiscation of the Orléans estates—"It is the first *vol* [the word means both "flight" and "theft"] of the eagle"—is applicable to every flight of this eagle, who is more like a raven. He and his followers call out to one another like that Italian Carthusian admonishing the miser who ostentatiously counted the goods on which he could still live for years: *"Tu fai conto sopra i beni, bisogna prima far il conto sopra gli anni"* ["Thou countest thy goods, thou shouldst first count thy years"]. In order not to make a mistake in the years, they count the minutes. At the court, in the ministries, at the head of the administration and the army, a gang of blokes of whom the best that can be said is that one does not know whence they come—these noisy, disreputable, rapacious bohemians who crawl into galMoned coats with the same grotesque dignity as the high dignitaries of Soulouque—elbow their way forward. One can visualize clearly this upper stratum of the Society of December 10 if one reflects that Veron-Crevel[10] is its preacher of morals and Granier de Cassagnac its thinker. When Guizot, at the time of his ministry, turned this Granier of an obscure newspaper into a dynastic opponent, he used to boast of him with the quip: *"C'est le roi des drôles"* ["He is the king of buffoons"]. It would be wrong to recall either the Regency or Louis XV in connection with Louis Bonaparte's court and clique. For "often before France has experienced a government of mistresses, but never before a government of kept men."[11]

Driven by the contradictory demands of his situation, and being at the same time, like a juggler, under the necessity of keeping the public gaze on himself, as Napoleon's successor, by springing constant surprises—that is to say, under the necessity of arranging a *coup d'état* in miniature every day—Bonaparte throws the whole bourgeois economy into confusion, violates everything that seemed inviolable to the Revolution of 1848, makes some tolerant of revolution and makes others lust for it, and produces anarchy in the name of order, while at the same time stripping the entire state machinery of its halo, profaning it and making it at once loathsome and ridiculous. The cult of the Holy Tunic of Trier[12] he duplicates in Paris in the cult of the Napoleonic imperial mantle. But when the imperial mantle finally falls on the shoulders of Louis Bonaparte, the bronze statue of Napoleon will come crashing down from the top of the Vendôme Column.

---

10. A dissolute philistine character in Balzac's novel *Cousin Bette*.
11. Quoted from Mme. de Girardin.—K.M.
12. A Catholic relic, allegedly taken from Christ when he was dying, preserved in the cathedral of Marx's native city.

Chronology:
France, 1870–71

1870

JANUARY 10   *About 100,000 people demonstrate against the Empire on the occasion of the funeral of Victor Noir, a republican journalist killed by the Emperor's cousin, Pierre Bonaparte.*

MAY 8   *A national plebiscite votes confidence in the Empire by 7,358,786 "ayes" against 1,571,939 "nays."*

JULY 19   *After a diplomatic struggle over the Hohenzollern (Prussian) candidacy to the Spanish throne, France declares war on Prussia.*

AUGUST 4, 6   *Crown Prince Frederick, commanding one of three German armies invading France, defeats French Marshal MacMahon at Wörth and Weissenburg, pushes him out of Alsace, surrounds Strasbourg, and drives on Nancy. The other two German armies surround Marshal Bazaine's forces in Metz.*

AUGUST 16, 18   *Bazaine's efforts to break through the German lines are bloodily defeated at Mars-la-Tour and Gravelotte. The Germans advance on Châlons.*

SEPTEMBER 1   *Battle of Sedan. MacMahon, attempting to relieve Bazaine at Metz and finding the road closed, fights and is defeated at Sedan.*

SEPTEMBER 2   *The French army, together with Emperor Napoleon III, capitulates at Sedan.*

SEPTEMBER 4   *At the news of Sedan, a Paris mob invades the*

[329]

Palais Bourbon and forces the Legislative Assembly to proclaim the fall of the Empire. That evening, at the Hôtel de Ville, the Third Republic is proclaimed, and a Provisional Government of National Defense is set up under the leadership of Louis Jules Trochu, as President, and Léon Gambetta.

SEPTEMBER 19   *Two German armies besiege Paris. The Provisional Government sends a delegation to Tours, soon to be joined by Gambetta (who escapes from Paris in a balloon), to organize resistance in the provinces.*

OCTOBER 27   *Marshal Bazaine surrenders at Metz with 173,000 men.*

OCTOBER 31   *A socialist and radical attempt to set up a Commune in Paris, after the model of 1792, fails. Besieged Paris has only a week's supply of food left.*

1871

JANUARY 28   *Paris capitulates. By the armistice agreement with Bismarck, an election of a representative Assembly is to determine either a continuation of war or terms of peace.*

FEBRUARY 8   *Elections held in France.*

FEBRUARY 13   *The National Assembly meets at Bordeaux; two-thirds of the members are conservatives and wish to end the war.*

FEBRUARY 16   *The Assembly elects Adolphe Thiers chief executive.*

FEBRUARY 28   *Thiers introduces to the Assembly a peace treaty, which he and Jules Favre have negotiated with Bismarck, providing the cession of Alsace and part of Lorraine to Germany and an indemnity of five billion francs. After attacks on the treaty by Louis Blanc, Gambetta, Clemenceau, and others, it is accepted on March 1 by a vote of 546 to 107.*

MARCH 1–3   *After four months of suffering, besieged Parisians, angry and humiliated by the entry of German troops and fearful of the republic, begin to take action. The National Guard organizes a Central Committee and prepares for conflict.*

MARCH 11   *The Assembly adjourns, to meet again at Versailles on March 20.*

MARCH 18   *Thiers sends regular French troops to Paris, but they fraternize with the crowd. The mob executes Generals Claude Martin Lecomte and Jacques Léonard Clément Thomas; the French army withdraws, and Paris is left in the hands of the radicals.*

MARCH 26   *A municipal council—the Commune—is elected under the auspices of the central committee of the National Guard. The members of the Commune consist of radical and moderate republicans, followers of radicals like Proudhon and Blanqui, and members of Marx's First International.*

APRIL   *The Commune, with its diverse and clashing viewpoints, attempts to decentralize national power, substitute the National Guard for a standing army, and separate church from state. But it soon becomes involved in armed struggle with the government of the National Assembly now sitting in Versailles.*

APRIL 2   *The Versailles troops take the offensive against the Paris Commune.*

MAY 10   *The peace treaty is signed at Frankfurt.*

MAY 21–28 *In the face of bitter but poorly organized resistance behind barricades, the Versailles troops enter Paris and indulge in a "bloody week" of slaughter. Thousands of Communards and other Parisians, including innocent civilians, are summarily executed; numerous others are imprisoned and deported.*

The Civil War in France

ADDRESS OF THE GENERAL COUNCIL OF
THE INTERNATIONAL WORKING MEN'S ASSOCIATION

Written by Marx in April–May, 1871, The Civil War in France was published in English as a brochure in June, 1871. (The title page stated: "Printed and Published for the Council by Edward Truelove, 256 High Holborn, 1871. Price Twopence.") It was also published in German, in Der Volksstaat, a Social-Democratic organ which appeared in Leipzig twice (later, three times) weekly, June 28 to July 29, 1871. A new German edition, with an introduction by Engels, appeared in Berlin in 1891 (Verlag der Expedition des Vorwärts, Berliner Volksblatt, 1891). A Russian edition, edited by Lenin, came out in Odessa in 1905. Communists consider The Civil War in France "a most important work of scientific communism."

TO ALL THE MEMBERS OF THE ASSOCIATION
IN EUROPE AND THE UNITED STATES

I

On the fourth of September, 1870, when the workingmen of Paris proclaimed the republic, which was almost instantaneously acclaimed throughout France, without a single voice of dissent, a cabal of place-hunting barristers, with Thiers for their statesman and Trochu for their general, took hold of the Hôtel de Ville. At that time they were imbued with such fanatical faith in the mission of Paris to represent France in all epochs of historical crisis that, to legitimate their usurped titles as governors of France, they thought it quite sufficient to produce their lapsed mandates as representatives of Paris. In our second address on the later war, five days after the rise of these men, we told you who they were.[1] Yet in the turmoil of surprise, with the real leaders of the working class still shut up in Bonapartist prisons and the Prussians already marching upon Paris, Paris bore with their assumption of power on the express condition that it was to be wielded for the single purpose of national defense. Paris, however, could not be seriously defended (was not defensible) without arming the working class, organizing it into a National Guard, and training it by the experience of war itself. But Paris armed was the revolution armed. A victory of Paris over the Prussian aggressor would have been a victory of the French workman over the French capitalist and his state parasites. In this conflict between national duty and class interest, the Government of National Defense did not hesitate a moment to turn into a Government of National Defection.

The first step they took was to send Thiers on a roving tour to all the courts of Europe, there to beg mediation by offering to barter the republic for a king. Four months after the commencement of the siege, when they thought the opportune moment had come for breaking the news of the capitulation, Trochu, in the presence of Jules Favre and other colleagues, addressed the assembled mayors of Paris in these terms: "The first question put to me by my colleagues on the very evening of the fourth of September was this: Paris, can it with any chance of success stand a siege by the Prussian army? I did not hesitate to answer in the negative. Some of my colleagues here present will warrant the truth of my words and the persistence of my opinion. I told them, in these very terms, that, under the existing state of things, the attempt of Paris to hold out against a siege by the Prussian army would be a folly. Without doubt, I added, it would be an heroic folly; but that would be all. . . . The events" (managed by himself) "have not given the lie to my prevision."

This nice little speech of Trochu was afterwards published by M. Corbon, one of the mayors present.

Thus on the very evening of the proclamation of the republic, Trochu's "plan" was known to his colleagues to be the capitulation of Paris. If national defense had been more than a pretext for the personal government of Thiers, Favre, & Co., the upstarts of the fourth of September would have abdicated on the fifth—would have initiated the people of Paris into Trochu's "plan" and called

---

1. "The Second Address of the General Council," September 6–9, 1870.

upon them to surrender at once, or to take their own fate into their own hands. Instead of this, the infamous impostors resolved upon curing the heroic folly of Paris by a regimen of famine and broken heads, and to dupe her in the meantime by ranting manifestoes holding forth that Trochu, "the governor of Paris, will never capitulate," and Jules Favre, the Foreign Minister, will "not cede an inch of our territory, nor a stone of our fortresses." In a letter to Gambetta that very same Jules Favre avows that what they were "defending" against were not the Prussian soldiers, but the workingmen of Paris. During the whole continuance of the siege the Bonapartist cutthroats, whom Trochu had wisely entrusted with the command of the Paris army, exchanged, in their intimate correspondence, ribald jokes at the well-understood mockery of defense. (See, for instance, the correspondence of Alphonse Simon Guiod, supreme commander of the artillery of the Army of Defense of Paris and Grand Cross of the Legion of Honor, to Susane, general of division of artillery, a correspondence published by the *Journal Officiel* of the Commune.) The mask of imposture was at last dropped on January 28, 1871. With the true heroism of utter self-debasement, the Government of National Defense, in their capitulation, came out as the government of France by Bismarck's prisoners—a part so base that Louis Bonaparte himself had, at Sedan, shrunk from accepting it. After the events of the eighteenth of March, on their wild flight to Versailles, the *capitulards* left in the hands of Paris the documentary evidence of their treason, to destroy which, as the Commune says in its manifesto to the provinces, "those men would not recoil from battering Paris into a heap of ruins washed by a sea of blood."

To be eagerly bent upon such a consummation, some of the leading members of the Government of Defense had, besides, most peculiar reasons of their own.

Shortly after the conclusion of the armistice, M. Millière, one of the representatives of Paris to the National Assembly, now shot by express order of Jules Favre, published a series of authentic legal documents in proof that Jules Favre, living in concubinage with the wife of a drunkard resident at Algiers, had, by a most daring concoction of forgeries, spread over many years, contrived to grasp, in the name of the children of his adultery, a large succession, which made him a rich man, and that in a lawsuit undertaken by the legitimate heirs he escaped exposure only with the connivance of the Bonapartist tribunals. As these dry legal documents were not to be got rid of by any amount of rhetorical horsepower, Jules Favre for the first time in his life held his tongue, quietly awaiting the outbreak of the civil war, in order then frantically to denounce the people of Paris as a band of escaped convicts in utter revolt against family, religion, order, and property. This same forger had hardly got into power, after the fourth of September, when he sympathetically let loose upon society Pic and Taillefer, convicted, even under the Empire, of forgery, in the scandalous affair of the *Étendard*."[2] One of these men, Taillefer, having dared to return to Paris under the Commune, was at once reinstated in prison; and then Jules Favre exclaimed, from the tribune of the National Assembly, that Paris was setting free all her jailbirds!

Ernest Picard, the Joe Miller of the government of National Defense, who appointed himself Finance Minister of the republic after having in vain striven to become the Home Minister of the Empire, is the brother of one Arthur Picard, an individual expelled from the Paris Bourse as a blackleg (see report of the Prefecture of Police, dated July 13, 1867), and convicted, on his own confession, of a theft of 300,000 francs, while manager of one of the branches of the Société Générale, Rue Palestro No. 5 (see report of the Prefecture of Police, December 11, 1868). This Arthur Picard was made by Ernest Picard the editor of his paper *l'Électeur Libre*. While the common run of stockjobbers were led astray by the official lies of this finance office paper, Arthur was running backwards and forwards between the finance office and the Bourse, there to discount the disasters of the French army. The whole financial correspondence of that worthy pair of brothers fell into the hands of the Commune.

Jules Ferry, a penniless barrister before the fourth of September, contrived, as mayor of Paris during the siege, to job a fortune out of famine. The day on which he would have to give an account of his maladministration would be the day of his conviction.

These men, then, could find their tickets-of-leave only in the ruins of Paris: they were the very men Bismarck wanted. With the help of some shuffling of cards, Thiers, hitherto the secret prompter of the government, now appeared at its head, with the ticket-of-leave men for his ministers.

Thiers, that monstrous gnome, has charmed the French bourgeoisie for almost half a century, because he is the most consummate intellectual expression of their own class corruption. Before he became a statesman he had already proved his lying powers as a historian. The chronicle of his public life is the record of the misfortunes of France. Banded, before 1830, with the republicans, he slipped into office under Louis Philippe by betraying his protector Laffitte, ingratiating himself with the king by exciting mob riots against the clergy, during

---

2. A Bonapartist newspaper.

which the church of St. Germain l'Auxerrois and the Archbishop's palace were plundered, and by acting the minister-spy upon, and the jail-*accoucheur* of, the Duchess de Berry. The massacre of the republicans in the rue Transnonain, and the subsequent infamous laws of September against the press and the right of association were his work. Reappearing as the chief of the cabinet in March, 1840, he astonished France with his plan of fortifying Paris. To the republicans who denounced this plan as a sinister plot against the liberty of Paris, he replied from the tribune of the Chamber of Deputies: "What! to fancy that any works of fortification could ever endanger liberty! And first of all you calumniate any possible government in supposing that it could some day attempt to maintain itself by bombarding the capital; . . . but that government would be a hundred times more impossible after its victory than before."

Indeed, no government would ever have dared to bombard Paris from the forts but that government which had previously surrendered these forts to the Prussians.

When King Bomba tried his hand at Palermo, in January, 1848, Thiers, then long since out of office, again rose in the Chamber of Deputies: "You know, gentlemen, what is happening at Palermo. You, all of you, shake with horror" (in the parliamentary sense) "on hearing that during forty-eight hours a large town has been bombarded—by whom? Was it by a foreign enemy exercising the rights of war? No, gentlemen, it was by its own government. And why? Because that unfortunate town demanded its rights. Well, then, for the demand of its rights it has got forty-eight hours of bombardment . . . Allow me to appeal to the opinion of Europe. It is doing a service to mankind to arise, and to make reverberate, from what is perhaps the greatest tribune in Europe, some words" (indeed words) "of indignation against such acts . . . When the Regent Espartero, who had rendered services to his country" (which M. Thiers never did), "intended bombarding Barcelona, in order to suppress its insurrection, there arose from all parts of the world a general outcry of indignation."

Eighteen months afterwards, M. Thiers was among the fiercest defenders of the bombardment of Rome by a French army. In fact the fault of King Bomba seems to have consisted in this only, that he limited his bombardment to forty-eight hours.

A few days before the Revolution of February, fretting at the long exile from place and pelf to which Guizot had condemned him, and sniffing in the air the scent of an approaching popular commotion, Thiers, in that pseudo-heroic style which won him the nickname of Mirabeau *mouche* [Mirabeau the fly], declared to the Chamber of

Deputies: "I am of the party of revolution, not only in France, but in Europe. I wish the government of the revolution to remain in the hands of moderate men . . . but if that government should fall into the hands of ardent minds, even into those of radicals, I shall, for all that, not desert my cause. I shall always be of the party of the revolution."

The Revolution of February came. Instead of displacing the Guizot cabinet by the Thiers cabinet, as the little man had dreamed, it superseded Louis Philippe by the republic. On the first day of the popular victory he carefully hid himself, forgetting that the contempt of the workingmen screened him from their hatred. Still, with his legendary courage, he continued to shy the public stage, until the June massacres had cleared it for his sort of action. Then he became the leading mind of the "party of Order" and its parliamentary republic, that anonymous interregnum in which all the rival factions of the ruling class conspired together to crush the people, and conspired against each other to restore each of them its own monarchy. Then, as now, Thiers denounced the republicans as the only obstacle to the consolidation of the republic; then, as now, he spoke to the republic as the hangman spoke to Don Carlos: "I shall assassinate thee, but for thy own good." Now, as then, he will have to exclaim on the day after his victory: "*L'Empire est fait*"—the Empire is consummated. Despite his hypocritical homilies about necessary liberties and his personal grudge against Louis Bonaparte, who had made a dupe of him, and kicked out parliamentarism—and outside of its factitious atmosphere the little man is conscious of withering into nothingness—he had a hand in all the infamies of the Second Empire, from the occupation of Rome by French troops to the war with Prussia, which he incited by his fierce invective against German unity, not as a cloak of Prussian despotism, but as an encroachment upon the vested right of France in German disunion. Fond as he was of brandishing, with his dwarfish arms, in the face of Europe the sword of the first Napoleon, whose historical shoeblack he had become, his foreign policy always culminated in the utter humiliation of France, from the London convention of 1840 to the Paris capitulation of 1871, and the present civil war, where he hounds on the prisoners of Sedan and Metz against Paris by special permission of Bismarck. Despite his versatility of talent and shiftiness of purpose, this man has his whole lifetime been wedded to the most fossil routine. It is self-evident that to him the deeper undercurrents of modern society remained forever hidden; but even the most palpable changes on its surface were abhorrent to a brain all of whose vitality had fled to the tongue. Thus he never tired of denouncing as a sacrilege any deviation from the old French protective system. When a minister of Louis Philippe, he railed at railways as a wild chimera; and when in opposition under Louis Bonaparte, he branded as a profanation every attempt to reform the rotten French army system. Never in his long political career has he been guilty of a single— even the smallest—measure of any practical use. Thiers was consistent only in his greed for wealth and his hatred of the men that produce it. Having entered his first ministry under Louis Philippe poor as Job, he left it a millionaire. His last ministry under the same king (of March 1, 1840) exposed him to public taunts of peculation in the Chamber of Deputies, to which he was content to reply with tears— a commodity he deals in as freely as Jules Favre, or any other crocodile. At Bordeaux his first measure for saving France from impending financial ruin was to endow himself with three millions a year, the first and the last word of the "Economical Republic," the vista of which he had opened to his Paris electors in 1869. One of his former colleagues of the Chamber of Deputies of 1830, himself a capitalist and, nevertheless, a devoted member of the Paris Commune, M. Beslay, lately addressed Thiers thus in a public placard: "The enslavement of labor by capital has always been the cornerstone of your policy, and from the very day you saw the Republic of Labor installed at the Hôtel de Ville, you have never ceased to cry out to France: 'These are criminals!' "

A master in small state roguery, a virtuoso in perjury and treason, a craftsman in all the petty stratagems, cunning devices, and base perfidies of parliamentary party warfare; never scrupling, when out of office, to fan a revolution, and to stifle it in blood when at the helm of the state; with class prejudices standing him in the place of ideas, and vanity in the place of a heart; his private life as infamous as his public life is odious—even now, when playing the part of a French Sulla, he cannot help setting off the abomination of his deeds by the ridicule of his ostentation.

The capitulation of Paris, by surrendering to Prussia not only Paris, but all France, closed the long-continued intrigues of treason with the enemy, which the usurpers of the fourth of September had begun, as Trochu himself said, on that very same day. On the other hand, it initiated the civil war they were now to wage, with the assistance of Prussia, against the republic and Paris. The trap was laid in the very terms of the capitulation. At that time above onethird of the territory was in the hands of the enemy, the capital was cut off from the provinces, all communications were disorganized. To elect under such circumstances a real representation of France was impossible, unless ample time were given for preparation. In view of this, the capitulation stipulated that a National Assembly must be elected within eight days; so that in many parts of France the news of the impending election arrived only on its eve. This assembly, moreover, was, by an express clause of the capitulation, to be elected for the sole purpose of deciding on peace or war, and, eventually, to conclude a treaty of peace. The population could not but feel that the terms of the armistice rendered the continuation of the war impossible, and that for sanctioning the peace imposed by Bismarck, the worst men in France were the best. But not content with these precautions, Thiers, even before the secret of the armistice had been broached to Paris, set out for an electioneering tour through the provinces, there to galvanize back into life the Legitimist party, which now, along with the Orléanists, had to take the place of the then impossible Bonapartists. He was not afraid of them. Impossible as a government of modern France, and therefore contemptible as rivals, what party were more eligible as a tool of counterrevolution than the party whose action, in the words of Thiers himself (Chamber of Deputies, January 5, 1833), "had always been confined to the three resources of foreign invasion, civil war, and anarchy"?

They verily believed in the advent of their long-expected retrospective millennium. There were the heels of foreign invasion trampling upon France; there was the downfall of an empire and the captivity of a Bonaparte; and there they were themselves. The wheel of history had evidently rolled back to stop at the *"Chambre introuvable"* of 1816. In the assemblies of the republic, 1848–51, they had been represented by their educated and trained parliamentary champions; it was the rank-and-file of the party which now rushed in—all the Pourceaugnacs[3] of France.

As soon as this Assembly of "Rurals" had met at Bordeaux, Thiers made it clear to them that the peace preliminaries must be assented to at once, without even the honors of a parliamentary debate, as the only condition on which Prussia would permit them to open the war against the republic and Paris, its stronghold. The counterrevolution had, in fact, no time to lose. The Second Empire had more than doubled the national debt, and plunged all the large towns into heavy municipal debts. The war had fearfully swelled the liabilities and mercilessly ravaged the resources of the nation. To complete the ruin, the Prussian Shylock was there with his bond for the keep of half a million of his soldiers on French soil, his indemnity of five milliards, and interest at 5 percent on the unpaid installments thereof. Who was to pay the bill? It was only by the violent overthrow of the republic that the appropriators of wealth

---

3. A narrow-minded member of the petty landed gentry; from Molière's comedy of that name.

could hope to shift onto the shoulders of its producers the cost of a war which they, the appropriators, had themselves originated. Thus the immense ruin of France spurred on these patriotic representatives of land and capital, under the very eyes and patronage of the invader, to graft upon the foreign war a civil war—a slaveholders' rebellion.

There stood in the way of this conspiracy one great obstacle—Paris. To disarm Paris was the first condition of success. Paris was therefore summoned by Thiers to surrender its arms. Then Paris was exasperated by the frantic antirepublican demonstrations of the "Rural" Assembly and by Thiers' own equivocations about the legal status of the republic; by the threat to decapitate and decapitalize Paris; the appointment of Orléanist ambassadors; Dufaure's laws on overdue commercial bills and house rents, inflicting ruin on the commerce and industry of Paris; Pouyer-Quertier's tax of two centimes upon every copy of every imaginable publication; the sentences of death against Blanqui and Flourens; the suppression of the republican journals; the transfer of the National Assembly to Versailles; the renewal of the state of siege declared by Palikao, and expired on the fourth of September; the appointment of Vinoy, the Decembrist, as governor of Paris—of Valentin, the imperialist gendarme, as its prefect of police—and of Aurelle de Paladines, the Jesuit general, as the commander in chief of its National Guard.

And now we have to address a question to M. Thiers and the men of national defense, his understrappers. It is known that through the agency of M. Pouyer-Quertier, his finance minister, Thiers had contracted a loan of two milliards. Now is it true, or not,

1. That the business was so managed that a consideration of several hundred millions was secured for the private benefit of Thiers, Jules Favre, Ernest Picard, Pouyer-Quertier, and Jules Simon and—

2. That no money was to be paid down until after the "pacification" of Paris?

At all events, there must have been something very pressing in the matter, for Thiers and Jules Favre, in the name of the majority of the Bordeaux Assembly, unblushingly solicited the immediate occupation of Paris by Prussian troops. Such, however, was not the game of Bismarck, as he sneeringly, and in public, told the admiring Frankfurt philistines on his return to Germany.

II

Armed Paris was the only serious obstacle in the way of the counterrevolutionary conspiracy. Paris was therefore to be disarmed.

On this point the Bordeaux Assembly was sincerity itself. If the roaring rant of its Rurals had not been audible enough, the surrender of Paris by Thiers to the tender mercies of the triumvirate of Vinoy the Decembrist, Valentin the Bonapartist gendarme, and Aurelle de Paladines the Jesuit general, would have cut off even the last subterfuge of doubt. But while insultingly exhibiting the true purpose of the disarmament of Paris, the conspirators asked her to lay down her arms on a pretext which was the most glaring, the most barefaced of lies. The artillery of the Paris National Guard, said Thiers, belonged to the state, and to the state it must be returned. The fact was this: From the very day of the capitulation, by which Bismarck's prisoners had signed the surrender of France, but reserved to themselves a numerous bodyguard for the express purpose of cowing Paris, Paris stood on the watch. The National Guard reorganized themselves and entrusted their supreme control to a Central Committee elected by their whole body, save some fragments of the old Bonapartist formations. On the eve of the Prussians' entrance into Paris, the Central Committee took measures for the removal to Montmartre, Belleville, and La Villette of the cannon and *mitrailleuses* treacherously abandoned by the *capitulards* in and about the very quarters the Prussians were to occupy. That artillery had been furnished by the subscriptions of the National Guard. As their private property it was officially recognized in the capitulation of the twenty-eighth of January, and on that very title exempted from the general surrender into the hands of the conqueror of arms belonging to the government. And Thiers was so utterly destitute of even the flimsiest pretext for initiating the war against Paris that he had to resort to the flagrant lie of the artillery of the National Guard being state property!

The seizure of her artillery was evidently but to serve as the preliminary to the general disarmament of Paris, and, therefore, of the Revolution of the Fourth of September. But that revolution had become the legal status of France. The republic, its work, was recognized by the conqueror in the terms of the capitulation. After the capitulation, it was acknowledged by all the foreign powers, and in its name the National Assembly had been summoned. The Paris workingmen's revolution of the fourth of September was the only legal title of the National Assembly seated at Bordeaux, and of its executive. Without it, the National Assembly would at once have to give way to the *Corps Législatif* elected in 1869 by universal suffrage under French, not under Prussian, rule, and forcibly dispersed by the arm of the revolution. Thiers and his ticket-of-leave men would have had to capitulate for safe conducts signed by Louis Bonaparte, to save them from a voyage to Cayenne. The National

Assembly, with its power of attorney to settle the terms of peace with Prussia, was but an incident of that revolution, the true embodiment of which was still armed Paris, which had initiated it, undergone for it a five months' siege, with its horrors of famine, and made her prolonged resistance, despite Trochu's plan, the basis of an obstinate war of defense in the provinces. And Paris was now either to lay down her arms at the insulting behest of the rebellious slaveholders of Bordeaux, and acknowledge that her Revolution of the Fourth of September meant nothing but a simple transfer of power from Louis Bonaparte to his royal rivals; or she had to stand forward as the self-sacrificing champion of France, whose salvation from ruin and whose regeneration were impossible without the revolutionary overthrow of the political and social conditions that had engendered the Second Empire, and, under its fostering care, matured into utter rottenness. Paris, emaciated by a five months' famine, did not hesitate one moment. She heroically resolved to run all the hazards of a resistance against the French conspirators, even with Prussian cannon frowning upon her from her own forts. Still, in its abhorrence of the civil war into which Paris was to be goaded, the Central Committee continued to persist in a merely defensive attitude, despite the provocations of the Assembly, the usurpations of the Executive, and the menacing concentration of troops in and around Paris.

Thiers opened the civil war by sending Vinoy, at the head of a multitude of *sergents-de-ville* and some regiments of the line, upon a nocturnal expedition against Montmartre, there to seize, by surprise, the artillery of the National Guard. It is well known how this attempt broke down before the resistance of the National Guard and the fraternization of the line with the people. Aurelle de Paladines had printed beforehand his bulletin of victory, and Thiers held ready the placards announcing his measures of *coup d'état*. Now these had to be replaced by Thiers' appeals, imparting his magnanimous resolve to leave the National Guard in the possession of their arms, with which, he said, he felt sure they would rally round the government against the rebels. Out of 300,000 National Guards only 300 responded to this summons to rally round little Thiers against themselves. The glorious workingmen's revolution of the eighteenth of March took undisputed sway of Paris. The Central Committee was its provisional government. Europe seemed, for a moment, to doubt whether its recent sensational performances of state and war had any reality in them, or whether they were the dreams of a long bygone past.

From the eighteenth of March to the entrance of the Versailles troops into Paris, the proletarian revolution remained so free from the acts of violence in which the revolutions, and still more the counterrevolutions, of the "better classes" abound, that no facts were left to its opponents to cry out about but the execution of generals Lecomte and Clément Thomas, and the affair of the Place Vendôme.

One of the Bonapartist officers engaged in the nocturnal attempt against Montmartre, General Lecomte, had four times ordered the 81st line regiment to fire at an unarmed gathering in the Place Pigalle, and on their refusal fiercely insulted them. Instead of shooting women and children, his own men shot him. The inveterate habits acquired by the soldiery under the training of the enemies of the working class are, of course, not likely to change the very moment these soldiers change sides. The same men executed Clément Thomas.

"General" Clément Thomas, a malcontent ex-quartermaster sergeant, had, in the latter times of Louis Philippe's reign, enlisted at the office of the republican newspaper *National*, there to serve in the double capacity of responsible manager and of dueling bully for that very combative journal. After the Revolution of February the men of the *National*, having got into power, metamorphosed this old quartermaster sergeant into a general on the eve of the butchery of June, of which he, like Jules Favre, was one of the sinister plotters and became one of the most dastardly executioners. Then he and his generalship disappeared for a long time, to again rise to the surface on November 1, 1870. The day before, the Government of Defense, caught at the Hôtel de Ville, had solemnly pledged their parole to Blanqui, Flourens, and other representatives of the working class to abdicate their usurped power into the hands of a commune to be freely elected by Paris. Instead of keeping their word, they let loose on Paris the Bretons of Trochu, who now replaced the Corsicans of Bonaparte. General Tamisier alone, refusing to sully his name by such a breach of faith, resigned the commandership in chief of the National Guard, and in his place Clément Thomas for once became again a general. During the whole of his tenure of command, he made war, not upon the Prussians, but upon the Paris National Guard. He prevented their general armament, pitted the bourgeois battalions against the workingmen's battalions, weeded out the officers hostile to Trochu's "plan," and disbanded, under the stigma of cowardice, the very same proletarian battalions whose heroism has now astonished their most inveterate enemies. Clément Thomas felt quite proud of having reconquered his June preeminence as the personal enemy of the working class of Paris. Only a few days before the eighteenth of March, he laid before the War Minister, Le Flô, a plan of his own for "finishing off *la fine fleur* [the cream] of the Paris *canaille.*" After Vinoy's rout, he must needs appear upon the scene of action in the quality of an amateur spy. The Central Committee and the Paris workingmen were as much responsible for the killing of Clément Thomas and Lecomte as the Princess of Wales was for the fate of the people crushed to death on the day of her entrance into London.

The massacre of unarmed citizens in the Place Vendôme is a myth which M. Thiers and the Rurals persistently ignored in the Assembly, intrusting its propagation exclusively to the servants' hall of European journalism. The "men of order," the reactionaries of Paris, trembled at the victory of the eighteenth of March. To them it was the signal of popular retribution at last arriving. The ghosts of the victims assassinated at their hands from the days of June, 1848, down to January 22, 1871, arose before their faces. Their panic was their only punishment. Even the *sergents-de-ville*, instead of being disarmed and locked up, as ought to have been done, had the gates of Paris flung wide open for their safe retreat to Versailles. The men of order were not only left unharmed, but allowed to rally and quietly to seize more than one stronghold in the very center of Paris. This indulgence of the Central Committee—this magnanimity of the armed workingmen—so strangely at variance with the habits of the party of Order, the latter misinterpreted as mere symptoms of conscious weakness. Hence their silly plan to try, under the cloak of an unarmed demonstration, what Vinoy had failed to perform with his cannon and *mitrailleuses.* On March 22 a riotous mob of swells started from the quarters of luxury, all the *petits crevés* [fast young fellows] in their ranks, and at their head the nortorious familiars of the Empire—the Heckeren, Coëtlogon, Henri de Pène, etc. Under the cowardly pretense of a pacific demonstration, this rabble, secretly armed with the weapons of the bravo, fell into marching order, ill treated and disarmed the detached patrols and sentries of the National Guard they met with on their progress, and, on debouching from the rue de la Paix, with the cry of "Down with the Central Committee! Down with the assassins! The National Assembly forever!" attempted to break through the line drawn up there, and thus to carry by surprise the head-quarters of the National Guard in the Place Vendôme. In reply to their pistol shots, the regular *sommations* (the French equivalent of the English Riot Act) were made, and when they proved ineffective, fire was commanded by the general of the National Guard [Bergeret]. One volley dispersed into wild flight the silly coxcombs, who expected that the mere exhibition of their "respectability" would have the same effect upon the Revolution of Paris as Joshua's trumpets upon the wall of Jericho. The runaways left behind them two National Guards killed, nine severely wounded (among them a member of the Central Committee [Maljournal]), and the whole scene of their exploit strewn with revolvers, daggers, and sword canes, in evidence of the "unarmed" character of their "pacific" demonstration. When on June 13, 1849, the National Guard made a really pacific demonstration in protest against the felonious assault of French troops upon Rome, Changarnier, then general of the party of Order, was acclaimed by the National Assembly, and especially by M. Thiers, as the savior of society, for having launched his troops from all sides upon these unarmed men, to shoot and saber them down and to trample them under their horses' feet. Paris then was placed under a state of siege. Dufaure hurried through the Assembly new laws of repression. New arrests, new proscriptions—a new Reign of Terror set in. But the lower orders manage these things otherwise. The Central Committee of 1871 simply ignored the heroes of the "pacific demonstration"; so much so that only two days later they were enabled to muster under Admiral Saisset for that *armed* demonstration, crowned by the famous stampede to Versailles. In their reluctance to continue the civil war opened by Thiers' burglarious attempt on Montmartre, the Central Committee made itself, this time, guilty of a decisive mistake in not at once marching upon Versailles, then completely helpless, and thus putting an end to the conspiracies of Thiers and his Rurals. Instead of this, the party of Order was again allowed to try its strength at the ballot box, on the twenty-sixth of March, the day of the election of the Commune. Then, in the *mairies* of Paris, they exchanged bland words of conciliation with their too generous conquerors, muttering in their hearts solemn vows to exterminate them in due time.

Now look at the reverse of the medal. Thiers opened his second campaign against Paris at the beginning of April. The first batch of Parisian prisoners brought into Versailles were subjected to revolting atrocities, while Ernest Picard, with his hands in his trousers pockets, strolled about jeering them, and while Mesdames Thiers and Favre, in the midst of their ladies of honor (?), applauded, from the balcony, the outrages of the Versailles mob. The captured soldiers of the line were massacred in cold blood; our brave friend General Duval, the iron founder, was shot without any form of trial. Galliffet, the kept man of his wife, so notorious for her shameless exhibitions at the orgies of the Second Empire, boasted in a proclamation of having commanded the murder of a small troop of National Guards, with their captain and lieutenant, surprised and disarmed by his Chasseurs. Vinoy, the runaway, was awarded by Thiers the Grand Cross of the Legion of Honor for his general order to shoot down every soldier of the line taken in the ranks of the Federals. Desmarêt, the gendarme, was decorated for the treacherous butcherlike chopping in pieces of the high-souled and chivalrous Flourens, who had saved the heads of the Government of Defense on October 31, 1870. The "encouraging particulars" of his assassination were triumphantly expatiated upon by Thiers in the National Assembly. With the elated vanity of a parliamentary Tom Thumb permitted to play the part of a Tamerlane, he denied the rebels against his littleness every right of civilized warfare, up to the right of neutrality for ambulances. Nothing more horrid than that monkey, allowed for a time to give full fling to his tigerish instincts, as foreseen by Voltaire.[4]

After the decree of the Commune of April 7 ordering reprisals and declaring it to be its duty "to protect Paris against the cannibal exploits of the Versailles banditti, and to demand an eye for an eye, a tooth for a tooth," Thiers did not stop the barbarous treatment of prisoners, moreover insulting them in his bulletins as follows: "Never have more degraded countenances of a degraded democracy met the afflicted gazes of honest men"—honest like Thiers himself and his ministerial ticket-of-leave men. Still, the shooting of prisoners was suspended for a time. Hardly, however, had Thiers and his Decembrist generals become aware that the communal decree of reprisals was but an empty threat, that even their gendarme spies caught in Paris under the disguise of National Guards, that even *sergents-de-ville* taken with incendiary shells upon them, were spared—when the wholesale shooting of prisoners was resumed and carried on uninterruptedly to the end. Houses to which National Guards had fled were surrounded by gendarmes, inundated with petroleum (which here occurs for the first time in this war), and then set fire to, the charred corpses being afterwards brought out by the ambulance of the press at the Ternes. Four National Guards, having surrendered to a troop of mounted Chasseurs at Belle Epine, on April 25, were afterwards shot down, one after another, by the captain, a worthy man of Galliffet's. One of his four victims left for dead, Scheffer, crawled back to the Parisian outposts and deposed to this fact before a commission of the Commune. When Tolain interpellated the War Minister upon the report of this commission, the Rurals drowned his voice and forbade Le Flô to answer. It would be an insult to their "glorious" army to speak of its deeds. The flippant tone in which Thiers' bulletins announced the bayoneting of the Federals surprised asleep at Moulin Saquet, and the wholesale fusillades at Clamart, shocked the nerves of even the not oversensitive London *Times*. But it would be ludicrous today to attempt recounting the merely preliminary atroci-

---

4. In *Candide*, Chapter 22.

ties committed by the bombarders of Paris and the fomenters of a slaveholders' rebellion protected by foreign invasion. Amidst all these horrors, Thiers, forgetful of his parliamentary laments on the terrible responsibility weighing down his dwarfish shoulders, boasts in his bulletin that *l'Assemblée siège paisiblement* [the Assembly continues meeting in peace], and proves by his constant carousals, now with Decembrist generals, now with German princes, that his digestion is not troubled in the least, not even by the ghosts of Lecomte and Clément Thomas.

III

On the dawn of the eighteenth of March, Paris arose to the thunderburst of *"Vive la Commune!"* What is the Commune, that sphinx so tantalizing to the bourgeois mind?

"The proletarians of Paris," said the Central Committee in its manifesto of March 18, "amidst the failures and treasons of the ruling classes, have understood that the hour has struck for them to save the situation by taking into their own hands the direction of public affairs. . . . They have understood that it is their imperious duty and their absolute right to render themselves masters of their own destinies, by seizing upon the governmental power."

But the working class cannot simply lay hold of the ready-made state machinery and wield it for its own purposes.

The centralized state power, with its ubiquitous organs of standing army, police, bureaucracy, clergy, and judiciary—organs wrought after the plan of a systematic and hierarchic division of labor—originates from the days of absolute monarchy, serving nascent middle-class society as a mighty weapon in its struggles against feudalism. Still, its development remained clogged by all manner of medieval rubbish, seignorial rights, local privileges, municipal and guild monopolies, and provincial constitutions. The gigantic broom of the French Revolution of the eighteenth century swept away all these relics of bygone times, thus clearing simultaneously the social soil of its last hindrances to the superstructure of the modern state edifice raised under the First Empire, itself the offspring of the coalition wars of old semifeudal Europe against modern France. During the subsequent regimes the government, placed under parliamentary control—that is, under the direct control of the propertied classes—not only became a hotbed of huge national debts and crushing taxes; with its irresistible allurements of place, pelf, and patronage, it not only became the bone of contention between the rival factions and adventurers of the ruling classes; but its political character changed simultaneously with the economic changes of society. At the same pace at which the progress of modern industry developed, widened, intensified the class antagonism between capital and labor, the state power assumed more and more the character of the national power of capital over labor, of a public force organized for social enslavement, of an engine of class despotism. After every revolution marking a progressive phase in the class struggle, the purely repressive character of the state power stands out in bolder and bolder relief. The Revolution of 1830, resulting in the transfer of government from the landlords to the capitalists, transferred it from the more remote to the more direct antagonists of the workingmen. The bourgeois republicans who, in the name of the Revolution of February, took the state power, used it for the June massacres, in order to convince the working class that "social" republic meant the republic insuring their social subjection, and in order to convince the royalist bulk of the bourgeois and landlord class that they might safely leave the cares and emoluments of government to the bourgeois "republicans." However, after their one heroic exploit of June, the bourgeois republicans had, from the front, to fall back to the rear of the party of Order—a combination formed by all the rival fractions and factions of the appropriating class in their now openly declared antagonism to the producing classes. The proper form of their joint-stock government was the parliamentary republic, with Louis Bonaparte for its President. Theirs was a regime of avowed class terrorism and deliberate insult toward the "vile multitude." If the parliamentary republic, as M. Thiers said, "divided them" (the different fractions of the ruling class) "least," it opened an abyss between that class and the whole body of society outside their spare ranks. The restraints by which their own divisions had under former regimes still checked the state power were removed by their union; and in view of the threatening upheaval of the proletariat, they now used that state power mercilessly and ostentatiously as the national war engine of capital against labor. In their uninterrupted crusade against the producing masses they were, however, bound not only to invest the executive with continually increased powers of repression, but at the same time to divest their own parliamentary stronghold—the National Assembly —one by one, of all its own means of defense against the Executive. The Executive, in the person of Louis Bonaparte, turned them out. The natural offspring of the party of Order republic was the Second Empire.

The Empire, with the *coup d'état* for its certificate of birth, universal suffrage for its sanction, and the sword for its scepter, professed to rest upon the peasantry, the large mass of producers not directly involved in the struggle of capital and labor. It professed to save the working class by breaking down parliamentarism, and with it the undisguised subserviency of government to the propertied classes. It professed to save the propertied classes by upholding their economic supremacy over the working class; and finally it professed to unite all classes by reviving for all the chimera of national glory. In reality, it was the only form of government possible at a time when the bourgeoisie had already lost, and the working class had not yet acquired, the faculty of ruling the nation. It was acclaimed throughout the world as the savior of society. Under its sway, bourgeois society, freed from political cares, attained a development unexpected even by itself. Its industry and commerce expanded to colossal dimensions; financial swindling celebrated cosmopolitan orgies; the misery of the masses was set off by a shameless display of gorgeous, meretricious, and debased luxury. The state power, apparently soaring high above society, was at the same time itself the greatest scandal of that society and the very hotbed of all its corruptions. Its own rottenness, and the rottenness of the society it had saved, were laid bare by the bayonet of Prussia, herself eagerly bent upon transferring the supreme seat of that regime from Paris to Berlin. Imperialism is at the same time the most prostitute and the ultimate form of the state power which nascent middle-class society had commenced to elaborate as a means of its own emancipation from feudalism, and which full-grown bourgeois society had finally transformed into a means for the enslavement of labor by capital.

The direct antithesis to the Empire was the Commune. The cry of "social republic" with which the Revolution of February was ushered in by the Paris proletariat did but express a vague aspiration after a republic that was not only to supersede the monarchical form of class rule, but class rule itself. The Commune was the positive form of that republic.

Paris, the central seat of the old governmental power, and at the same time the social stronghold of the French working class, had risen in arms against the attempt of Thiers and the Rurals to restore and perpetuate that old governmental power bequeathed to them by the Empire. Paris could resist only because, in consequence of the siege, it had got rid of the army and replaced it by a National Guard, the bulk of which consisted of workingmen. This fact was now to be transformed into an institution. The first decree of the Commune, therefore, was the suppression of the standing army and the substitution for it of the armed people.

The Commune was formed of the municipal councilors, chosen by universal suffrage in the various wards of the town, responsible and revocable at short terms. The majority of its members were naturally workingmen, or acknowledged representatives of the working class. The Commune was to be a working, not a parliamentary, body, executive and legislative at the same time. Instead of continuing to be the agent of the central government, the police was at once stripped of its political attributes and turned into the responsible and at all times revocable agent of the Commune. So were the officials of all other branches of the administration. From the members of the Commune downwards, the public service had to be done at *workmen's wages*. The vested interests and the representation allowances of the high dignitaries of state disappeared along with the high dignitaries themselves. Public functions ceased to be the private property of the tools of the central government. Not only municipal administration, but the whole initiative hitherto exercised by the state was laid into the hands of the Commune.

Having once got rid of the standing army and the police, the physical-force elements of the old government, the Commune was anxious to break the spiritual force of repression, the "parson power," by the disestablishment and disendowment of all churches as proprietary bodies. The priests were sent back to the recesses of private life, there to feed upon the alms of the faithful in imitation of their predecessors, the Apostles. The whole of the educational institutions were opened to the people gratuitously, and at the same time cleared of all interference of church and state. Thus not only was education made accessible to all, but science itself freed from the fetters which class prejudice and governmental force had imposed upon it.

The judicial functionaries were to be divested of that sham independence which had but served to mask their abject subserviency to all succeeding governments to which, in turn, they had taken, and broken, the oaths of allegiance. Like the rest of public servants, magistrates and judges were to be elective, responsible, and revocable.

The Paris Commune was, of course, to serve as a model to all the great industrial centers of France. The communal regime once established in Paris and the secondary centers, the old centralized government would in the provinces, too, have to give way to the self-government of the producers. A rough sketch of national organization, which the Commune had no time to develop, states clearly that the Commune was to be the political form of even the smallest country hamlet, and that in the rural districts the standing army was to be replaced by a national militia, with an extremely short term of service. The rural communes of every district were to administer their common affairs by an assembly of delegates in the central town, and these district assemblies were again to send deputies to the National Delegation in

Paris, each delegate to be at any time revocable and bound by the *mandat impératif* [formal instructions] of his constituents. The few but important functions which would still remain for a central government were not to be suppressed, as has been intentionally misstated, but were to be discharged by communal, and therefore strictly responsible, agents. The unity of the nation was not to be broken but, on the contrary, to be organized by the communal constitution and to become a reality by the destruction of the state power which claimed to be the embodiment of that unity independent of, and superior to, the nation itself, from which it was but a parasitic excrescence. While the merely repressive organs of the old governmental power were to be amputated, its legitimate functions were to be wrested from an authority usurping preeminence over society itself, and restored to the responsible agents of society. Instead of deciding once in three or six years which member of the ruling class was to misrepresent the people in parliament, universal suffrage was to serve the people, constituted in communes, as individual suffrage serves every other employer in the search for the workmen and managers in his business. And it is well known that companies, like individuals, in matters of real business generally know how to put the right man in the right place, and, if they for once make a mistake, to redress it promptly. On the other hand, nothing could be more foreign to the spirit of the Commune than to supersede universal suffrage by hierarchic investiture.

It is generally the fate of completely new historical creations to be mistaken for the counterpart of older and even defunct forms of social life, to which they may bear a certain likeness. Thus this new Commune, which breaks the modern state power, has been mistaken for a reproduction of the medieval communes, which first preceded, and afterwards became the substratum of, that very state power. The communal constitution has been mistaken for an attempt to break up into a federation of small states, as dreamed of by Montesquieu and the Girondins, that unity of great nations which, if originally brought about by political force, has now become a powerful coefficient of social production. The antagonism of the Commune against the state power has been mistaken for an exaggerated form of the ancient struggle against overcentralization. Peculiar historical circumstances may have prevented the classical development, as in France, of the bourgeois form of government, and may have allowed, as in England, completion of the great central state organs by corrupt vestries, jobbing councilors, and ferocious poor-law guardians in the towns, and virtually hereditary magistrates in the counties. The communal constitution would have restored to the social body all the forces hitherto absorbed by the state parasite feeding upon, and clogging the free movement of, society. By this one act it would have initiated the re-generation of France. The provincial French middle class saw in the Commune an attempt to restore the sway their order had held over the country under Louis Philippe and which, under Louis Napoleon, was supplanted by the pretended rule of the country over the towns. In reality, the communal constitution brought the rural producers under the intellectual lead of the central towns of their districts, and these secured to them, in the workingmen, the natural trustees of their interests. The very existence of the Commune involved, as a matter of course, local municipal liberty, but no longer as a check upon the now superseded state power. It could only enter into the head of a Bismarck, who, when not engaged in his intrigues of blood and iron, always likes to resume his old trade, so befitting his mental caliber, of contributor to *Kladderadatsch* (the Berlin *Punch*)—it could only enter into such a head to ascribe to the Paris Commune aspirations after that caricature of the old French municipal organization of 1791, the Prussian municipal constitution which degrades the town gov-ernments to mere secondary wheels in the police machinery of the Prussian state. The Commune made that catchword of bourgeois revolutions, cheap government, a reality, by destroying the two greatest sources of expenditure—the standing army and state func-tionarism. Its very existence presupposed the nonexistence of mon-archy, which, in Europe at least, is the normal incumbrance and indispensable cloak of class rule. It supplied the republic with the basis of really democratic institutions. But neither cheap government nor the "true republic" was its ultimate aim; they were its mere concomitants.

The multiplicity of interpretations to which the Commune has been subjected, and the multiplicity of interests which construed it in their favor, show that it was a thoroughly expansive political form, while all previous forms of government had been emphatically repres-sive. Its true secret was this: It was essentially a working-class government, the produce of the struggle of the producing against the appropriating class, the political form at last discovered under which to work out the economic emancipation of labor.

Except on this last condition, the communal constitution would have been an impossibility and a delusion. The political rule of the producer cannot coexist with the perpetuation of his social slavery. The Commune was therefore to serve as a lever for uprooting the economic foundations upon which rests the existence of classes, and therefore of class rule. With labor emancipated, every man becomes a workingman, and productive labor ceases to be a class attribute.

It is a strange fact. In spite of all the tall talk and all the immense literature, for the past sixty years, about Emancipation of Labor, no sooner do the workingmen anywhere take the subject into their own hands with a will, than up rises at once all the apologetic phraseology of the mouthpieces of present society with its two poles of Capital and Wage Slavery (the landlord now is but the sleeping partner of the capitalist), as if capitalist society were still in its purest state of virgin innocence, with its antagonisms still undeveloped, with its delusions still unexploded, with its prostitute realities not yet laid bare. The Commune, they exclaim, intends to abolish property, the basis of all civilization! Yes, gentlemen, the Commune intended to abolish that class property which makes the labor of the many the wealth of the few. It aimed at the expropriation of the expropriators. It wanted to make individual property a truth by transforming the means of production, land and capital, now chiefly the means of enslaving and exploiting labor, into mere instruments of free and associated labor. But this is communism, "impossible" communism! Why, those members of the ruling classes who are intelligent enough to perceive the impossibility of continuing the present system—and they are many— have become the obtrusive and full-mouthed apostles of cooperative production. If cooperative production is not to remain a sham and a snare; if it is to supersede the capitalist system; if united cooperative societies are to regulate national production upon a common plan, thus taking it under their own control, and putting an end to the constant anarchy and periodical convulsions which are the fatality of capitalist production—what else, gentlemen, would it be but communism, "possible" communism?

The working class did not expect miracles from the Commune. They have no ready-made utopias to introduce *par décret du peuple*. They know that in order to work out their own emancipation, and along with it that higher form to which present society is irresistibly tending by its own economic agencies, they will have to pass through long struggles, through a series of historic processes, transforming circumstances and men. They have no ideals to realize but to set free the elements of the new society with which old collapsing bourgeois society itself is pregnant. In the full consciousness of their historic mission, and with the heroic resolve to act up to it, the working class can afford to smile at the coarse invective of the gentlemen's gentlemen with the pen and inkhorn, and at the didactic patronage of well-wishing bourgeois doctrinaires, pouring forth their ignorant platitudes and sectarian crotchets in the oracular tone of scientific infallibility.

When the Paris Commune took the management of the revolution in its own hands; when plain workingmen for the first time dared to infringe upon the governmental privilege of their "natural superiors," and, under circumstances of unexampled difficulty, performed their work modestly, conscientiously, and efficiently—performed it at salaries the highest of which barely amounted to one-fifth of what, according to high scientific authority,[5] is the minimum required for a secretary to a certain metropolitan school board—the old world writhed in convulsions of rage at the sight of the red flag, the symbol of the Republic of Labor, floating over the Hôtel de Ville.

And yet this was the first revolution in which the working class was openly acknowledged as the only class capable of social initiative, even by the great bulk of the Paris middle class—shopkeepers, tradesmen, merchants—the wealthy capitalists alone excepted. The Commune had saved them by a sagacious settlement of that ever recurring cause of dispute among the middle classes themselves—the debtor and creditor accounts. The same portion of the middle class, after they had assisted in putting down the workingmen's insurrection of June, 1848, had been at once unceremoniously sacrificed to their creditors by the then Constituent Assembly. But this was not their only motive for now rallying round the working class. They felt that there was but one alternative—the Commune, or the Empire—under whatever name it might reappear. The Empire had ruined them economically by the havoc it made of public wealth, by the wholesale financial swindling it fostered, by the props it lent to the artificially accelerated centralization of capital, and the concomitant expropriation of their own ranks. It had suppressed them politically, it had shocked them morally by its orgies, it had insulted their Voltaireanism by handing over the education of their children to the *frères Ignorantins*, it had revolted their national feeling as Frenchmen by precipitating them headlong into a war which left only one equivalent for the ruins it made—the disappearance of the Empire. In fact, after the exodus from Paris of the high Bonapartist and capitalist *bohême*, the true middle-class party of Order came out in the shape of the "Union Républicaine," enrolling themselves under the colors of the Commune and defending it against the willful misconstruction of Thiers. Whether the gratitude of this great body of the middle class will stand the present severe trial, time must show.

The Commune was perfectly right in telling the peasants that its victory was their only hope. Of all the lies hatched at Versailles and reechoed by the glorious European penny-a-liners one of the most tremendous was that the Rurals represented the French peasantry. Think only of the love of the French peasant for the men to whom, after 1815, he had to pay the milliard of indemnity. In the eyes of

---

5. Professor Huxley.—Note to the German edition of 1871.

the French peasant, the very existence of a great landed proprietor is
in itself an encroachment on his conquests of 1789. The bourgeois in
1848 had burdened the peasant's plot of land with the additional tax
of 45 centimes on the franc, but then he did so in the name of the
revolution; while now he had fomented a civil war against the revolution, to shift onto the peasant's shoulders the chief load of the five
milliards of indemnity to be paid to the Prussian. The Commune, on
the other hand, in one of its first proclamations, declared that the true
originators of the war would be made to pay its cost. The Commune
would have delivered the peasant of the blood tax—would have given
him a cheap government, transformed his present bloodsuckers, the
notary, advocate, executor, and other judicial vampires, into salaried
communal agents, elected by, and responsible to, himself. It would
have freed him of the tyranny of the *garde champêtre*, the gendarme,
and the prefect; would have put enlightenment by the schoolmaster in
the place of stultification by the priest. And the French peasant is,
above all, a man of reckoning. He would find it extremely reasonable
that the pay of the priest, instead of being extorted by the tax collector, should depend only upon the spontaneous action of the
parishioners' religious instincts. Such were the great immediate boons
which the rule of the Commune—and that rule alone—held out to the
French peasantry. It is therefore quite superfluous here to expatiate
upon the more complicated but vital problems which the Commune
alone was able, and at the same time compelled, to solve in favor of
the peasant, viz., the hypothecary debt, living like an incubus upon
his parcel of soil, the *prolétariat foncier* [rural proletariat] daily
growing upon it, and his expropriation from it enforced, at a more
and more rapid rate, by the very development of modern agriculture
and the competition of capitalist farming.

The French peasant had elected Louis Bonaparte President of the
Republic, but the party of Order created the Empire. What the
French peasant really wants he commenced to show in 1849 and
1850, by opposing his *maire* to the government's prefect, his schoolmaster to the government's priest, and himself to the government's
gendarme. All the laws made by the party of Order in January and
February, 1850, were avowed measures of repression against the
peasant. The peasant was a Bonapartist because the great Revolution,
with all its benefits to him, was, in his eyes, personified in Napoleon.
This delusion, rapidly breaking down under the Second Empire (and
in its very nature hostile to the Rurals), this prejudice of the past,
how could it have withstood the appeal of the Commune to the living
interests and urgent wants of the peasantry?

The Rurals—this was, in fact, their chief apprehension—knew that
three months' free communication of Communal Paris with the prov-

inces would bring about a general rising of the peasants, and hence their anxiety to establish a police blockade around Paris, so as to stop the spread of the rinderpest.

If the Commune was thus the true representative of all the healthy elements of French society, and therefore the truly national government, it was, at the same time, as a workingmen's government, as the bold champion of the emancipation of labor, emphatically international. Within sight of the Prussian army, which had annexed to Germany two French provinces, the Commune annexed to France the working people all over the world.

The Second Empire had been the jubilee of cosmopolitan black-legism, the rakes of all countries rushing in at its call for a share in its orgies and in the plunder of the French people. Even at this moment the right hand of Thiers is Ganesco, the foul Wallachian, and his left hand is Markovsky, the Russian spy. The Commune admitted all foreigners to the honor of dying for an immortal cause. Between the foreign war lost by their treason, and the civil war fomented by their conspiracy with the foreign invader, the bourgeoisie had found the time to display their patriotism by organizing police hunts upon the Germans in France. The Commune made a German workingman [Leo Frankel] its Minister of Labor. Thiers, the bourgeoisie, the Second Empire, had continually deluded Poland by loud professions of sympathy, while in reality betraying her to, and doing the dirty work of, Russia. The Commune honored the heroic sons of Poland [Wróblewski and Dombrowski] by placing them at the head of the defenders of Paris. And to broadly mark the new era of history it was conscious of initiating, under the eyes of the conquering Prussians on the one side, and of the Bonapartist army, led by Bonapartist generals, on the other, the Commune pulled down that colossal symbol of martial glory, the Vendôme Column.

The great social measure of the Commune was its own working existence. Its special measures could but betoken the tendency of a government of the people by the people. Such were the abolition of the night work of journeymen bakers; the prohibition, under penalty, of the employers' practice of reducing wages by levying upon their workpeople fines under manifold pretexts—a process in which the employer combines in his own person the parts of legislator, judge, and executor, and filches the money to boot. Another measure of this class was the surrender, to associations of workmen, under reserve of compensation, of all closed workshops and factories, no matter whether the respective capitalists had absconded or preferred to strike work.

The financial measures of the Commune, remarkable for their sagacity and moderation, could only be such as were compatible with the state of a besieged town. Considering the colossal robberies committed upon the city of Paris by the great financial companies and contractors, under the protection of Haussmann, the Commune would have had an incomparably better title to confiscate their property than Louis Napoleon had against the Orléans family. The Hohenzollerns and the English oligarchs, who both have derived a good deal of their estates from church plunder, were, of course, greatly shocked at the Commune clearing but 8,000 francs out of secularization.

While the Versailles Government, as soon as it had recovered some spirit and strength, used the most violent means against the Commune; while it put down the free expression of opinion all over France, even to the forbidding of meetings of delegates from the large towns; while it subjected Versailles and the rest of France to an espionage far surpassing that of the Second Empire; while its gendarme inquisitors burned all papers printed at Paris and sifted all correspondence from and to Paris; while in the National Assembly the most timid attempts to put in a word for Paris were howled down in a manner unknown even to the *Chambre introuvable* of 1816; with the savage warfare of Versailles outside and its attempts at corruption and conspiracy inside Paris—would the Commune not have shamefully betrayed its trust by affecting to keep up all the decencies and appearances of liberalism as in a time of profound peace? Had the government of the Commune been akin to that of M. Thiers, there would have been no more occasion to suppress party of Order papers at Paris than there was to suppress Communal papers at Versailles.

It was irritating indeed to the Rurals that at the very same time they declared the return to the church to be the only means of salvation for France, the infidel Commune unearthed the peculiar mysteries of the Picpus nunnery, and of the Church of St. Laurent. It was a satire upon M. Thiers that, while he showered grand crosses upon the Bonapartist generals in acknowledgment of their mastery in losing battles, signing capitulations, and rolling cigarettes at Wilhelmshöhe, the Commune dismissed and arrested its generals whenever they were suspected of neglecting their duties. The expulsion from, and arrest by, the Commune of one of its members [Blanchet] who had slipped in under a false name, and had undergone at Lyon six days' imprisonment for simple bankruptcy, was it not a deliberate insult hurled at the forger, Jules Favre, then still the Foreign Minister of France, still selling France to Bismarck, and still dictating his orders to that paragon government of Belgium? But indeed the Commune did not pretend to infallibility, the invariable attribute of all governments of the old stamp. It published its doings and sayings, it initiated the public into all its shortcomings.

In every revolution there intrude, at the side of its true agents, men of a different stamp; some of them survivors of and devotees to past revolutions, without insight into the present movement, but preserving popular influence by their known honesty and courage, or by the sheer force of tradition; others mere bawlers, who, by dint of repeating year after year the same set of stereotyped declamations against the government of the day, have sneaked into the reputation of revolutionists of the first water. After the eighteenth of March, some such men did also turn up, and in some cases contrived to play preeminent parts. As far as their power went, they hampered the real action of the working class, exactly as men of that sort have hampered the full development of every previous revolution. They are an unavoidable evil: with time they are shaken off; but time was not allowed to the Commune.

Wonderful, indeed, was the change the Commune had wrought in Paris! No longer any trace of the meretricious Paris of the Second Empire. No longer was Paris the rendezvous of British landlords, Irish absentees, American ex-slaveholders and shoddy men, Russian ex-serfowners, and Wallachian boyards. No more corpses at the morgue, no nocturnal burglaries, scarcely any robberies; in fact, for the first time since the days of February, 1848, the streets of Paris were safe, and that without any police of any kind. "We," said a member of the Commune, "no longer hear of assassination, theft, and personal assault; it seems indeed as if the police had dragged along with it to Versailles all its conservative friends."

The cocottes had refound the scent of their protectors—the absconding men of family, religion, and, above all, of property. In their stead, the real women of Paris showed again at the surface—heroic, noble, and devoted, like the women of antiquity. Working, thinking, fighting, bleeding Paris—almost forgetful, in its incubation of a new society, of the cannibals at its gates—radiant in the enthusiasm of its historic initiative!

Opposed to this new world at Paris, behold the old world at Versailles—that assembly of the ghouls of all defunct regimes, Legitimists and Orléanists, eager to feed upon the carcass of the nation—with a tail of antediluvian republicans, sanctioning, by their presence in the Assembly, the slaveholders' rebellion, relying for the maintenance of their parliamentary republic upon the vanity of the senile mountebank at its head, and caricaturing 1789 by holding their ghastly meetings in the Jeu de Paume.[6] There it was, this Assembly, the representative of everything dead in France, propped up to the semblance of life by

---

6. The tennis court in Versailles where, on June 20, 1789, members of the National Assembly met and took an oath to stay until a constitution was granted.

nothing but the swords of the generals of Louis Bonaparte. Paris all truth, Versailles all lie; and that lie vented through the mouth of Thiers.

Thiers tells a deputation of the mayors of the Seine-et-Oise, "You may rely upon my word, which I have *never* broken!"

He tells the Assembly itself that it is "the most freely elected and most liberal Assembly France ever possessed"; he tells his motley soldiery that it is "the admiration of the world, and the finest army France ever possessed"; he tells the provinces that the bombardment of Paris by him is a myth: "If some cannon shots have been fired, it is not the deed of the army of Versailles, but of some insurgents trying to make believe that they are fighting, while they dare not show their faces."

He again tells the provinces that "the artillery of Versailles does not bombard Paris, but only cannonades it."

He tells the Archbishop of Paris that the pretended executions and reprisals (!) attributed to the Versailles troops are all moonshine. He tells Paris that he is only anxious "to free it from the hideous tyrants who oppress it," and that, in fact, the Paris of the Commune is "but a handful of criminals."

The Paris of M. Thiers was not the real Paris of the "vile multitude," but a phantom Paris, the Paris of the *francs-fileurs* [absconders], the Paris of the Boulevards, male and female—the rich, the capitalist, the gilded, the idle Paris, now thronging with its lackeys, its blacklegs, its literary *bohême*, and its cocottes at Versailles, St. Denis, Rueil, and St. Germain; considering the civil war but an agreeable diversion, eyeing the battle going on through telescopes, counting the rounds of cannon, and swearing by their own honor and that of their prostitutes that the performance was far better got up than it used to be at the Porte St. Martin. The men who fell were really dead; the cries of the wounded were cries in good earnest; and besides, the whole thing was so intensely historical.

This is the Paris of M. Thiers, as the emigration of Coblenz was the France of M. de Calonne.

IV

The first attempt of the slaveholders' conspiracy to put down Paris by getting the Prussians to occupy it was frustrated by Bismarck's refusal. The second attempt, that of the eighteenth of March, ended in the rout of the army and the flight to Versailles of the government, which ordered the whole administration to break up and follow in its track. By the semblance of peace negotiations with Paris,

Thiers found the time to prepare for war against it. But where to find
an army? The remnants of the line regiments were weak in number
and unsafe in character. His urgent appeal to the provinces to succor
Versailles, by their National Guards and volunteers, met with a flat
refusal. Brittany alone furnished a handful of Chouans fighting under
a white flag, every one of them wearing on his breast the heart of
Jesus in white cloth, and shouting *"Vive le Roi!"* Thiers was therefore compelled to collect in hot haste a motley crew of sailors,
marines, Pontifical Zouaves, Valentin's gendarmes, and Pietri's *sergents-
de-ville* and *mouchards*. This army, however, would have been ridiculously ineffective without the installments of imperialist war prisoners
which Bismarck granted in numbers just sufficient to keep the civil
war agoing and keep the Versailles government in abject dependence
on Prussia. During the war itself the Versailles police had to look
after the Versailles army, while the gendarmes had to drag it on by
exposing themselves at all posts of danger. The forts which fell were
not taken, but bought. The heroism of the Federals convinced Thiers
that the resistance of Paris was not to be broken by his own strategic
genius and the bayonets at his disposal.

Meanwhile, his relations with the provinces became more and
more difficult. Not one single address of approval came in to gladden
Thiers and his Rurals. Quite the contrary. Deputations and addresses
demanding, in a tone anything but respectful, conciliation with Paris
on the basis of the unequivocal recognition of the republic, the acknowledgment of the communal liberties, and the dissolution of the
National Assembly, whose mandate was extinct, poured in from all
sides, and in such numbers that Dufaure, Thiers' Minister of Justice,
in his circular of April 23 to the public prosecutors, commanded
them to treat "the cry of conciliation" as a crime! In view, however,
of the hopeless prospect held out by his campaign, Thiers resolved to
shift his tactics by ordering municipal elections to take place all over
the country on the thirtieth of April, on the basis of the new
municipal law dictated by himself to the National Assembly. What
with the intrigues of his prefects, what with police intimidation, he
felt quite sanguine of imparting, by the verdict of the provinces, to
the National Assembly that moral power it had never possessed, and
of getting at last from the provinces the physical force required for
the conquest of Paris.

His banditti warfare against Paris, exalted in his own bulletins,
and the attempts of his ministers at the establishment throughout
France of a reign of terror, Thiers was from the beginning anxious
to accompany with a little byplay of conciliation, which had to
serve more than one purpose. It was to dupe the provinces, to inveigle

the middle-class element in Paris, and above all to afford the professed republicans in the National Assembly the opportunity of hiding their treason against Paris behind their faith in Thiers. On March 21, when still without an army, he had declared to the Assembly: "Come what may, I will not send an army to Paris."

On March 27 he rose again: "I have found the republic an accomplished fact, and I am firmly resolved to maintain it."

In reality, he put down the revolution at Lyon and Marseilles in the name of the republic, while the roars of his Rurals drowned the very mention of its name at Versailles. After this exploit he toned down the "accomplished fact" into a hypothetical fact. The Orléans princes, whom he had cautiously warned off Bordeaux, were now, in flagrant breach of the law, permitted to intrigue at Dreux. The concessions held out by Thiers in his interminable interviews with the delegates from Paris and the provinces, although constantly varied in tone and color according to time and circumstances, did in fact never come to more than the prospective restriction of revenge to the "handful of criminals implicated in the murder of Lecomte and Clément Thomas," on the well-understood premise that Paris and France were unreservedly to accept M. Thiers himself as the best of all possible republics, as he, in 1830, had done with Louis Philippe. Even these concessions he not only took care to render doubtful by the official comments put upon them in the Assembly through his ministers. He had his Dufaure to act. Dufaure, this old Orléanist lawyer, had always been the justiciary of the state of siege, as now in 1871 under Thiers, so in 1839 under Louis Philippe, and in 1849 under Louis Bonaparte's presidency. While out of office he made a fortune by pleading for the Paris capitalists, and made political capital by pleading against the laws he had himself originated. He now hurried through the National Assembly not only a set of repressive laws which were, after the fall of Paris, to extirpate the last remnants of republican liberty in France; he foreshadowed the fate of Paris by abridging the, for him, too slow procedure of courts-martial, and by a newfangled, Draconic code of deportation. The Revolution of 1848, abolishing the penalty of death for political crimes, had replaced it with deportation. Louis Bonaparte did not dare, at least not in theory, to reestablish the regime of the guillotine. The Rural Assembly, not yet bold enough even to hint that the Parisians were not rebels, but assassins, had therefore to confine its prospective vengeance against Paris to Dufaure's new code of deportation. Under all these circumstances Thiers himself could not have gone on with his comedy of conciliation had it not, as he intended it to do, drawn forth shrieks of rage from the Rurals, whose ruminating minds understood neither the play nor its necessities of hypocrisy, tergiversation, and procrastination.

In sight of the impending municipal elections of April 30, Thiers enacted one of his great conciliation scenes on the twenty-seventh. Amidst a flood of sentimental rhetoric, he exclaimed from the tribune of the Assembly: "There exists no conspiracy against the republic but that of Paris, which compels us to shed French blood. I repeat it again and again. Let those impious arms fall from the hands which hold them, and chastisement will be arrested at once by an act of peace excluding only the small number of criminals."

To the violent interruption of the Rurals he replied: "Gentlemen, tell me, I implore you, am I wrong? Do you really regret that I could have stated the truth that the criminals are only a handful? Is it not fortunate in the midst of our misfortunes that those who have been capable of shedding the blood of Clément Thomas and General Lecomte are but rare exceptions?"

France, however, turned a deaf ear to what Thiers flattered himself to be a parliamentary siren's song. Out of 700,000 municipal councilors returned by the 35,000 communes still left to France, the united Legitimists, Orléanists, and Bonapartists did not carry 8,000. The supplementary elections which followed were still more decidedly hostile. Thus instead of getting from the provinces the badly needed physical force, the National Assembly lost even its last claim to moral force, that of being the expression of the universal suffrage of the country. To complete the discomfiture, the newly chosen municipal councils of all the cities of France openly threatened the usurping Assembly at Versailles with a counter Assembly at Bordeaux.

Then the long-expected moment of decisive action had at last come for Bismarck. He peremptorily summoned Thiers to send to Frankfurt plenipotentiaries for the definitive settlement of peace. In humble obedience to the call of his master, Thiers hastened to despatch his trusty Jules Favre, backed by Pouyer-Quertier. Pouyer-Quertier, an "eminent" Rouen cotton spinner, a fervent and even servile partisan of the Second Empire, had never found any fault with it save its commercial treaty with England, prejudicial to his own shop interest. Hardly installed at Bordeaux as Thiers' Minister of Finance, he denounced that "unholy" treaty, hinted at its near abrogation, and even had the effrontery to try, although in vain (having counted without Bismarck), the immediate enforcement of the old protective duties against Alsace, where, he said, no previous international treaties stood in the way. This man, who considered counterrevolution as a means to put down wages at Rouen, and the surrender of French provinces as a means to bring up the price of his wares in France, was he not *the one* predestined to be picked out by Thiers as the helpmate of Jules Favre in his last and crowning treason?

On the arrival at Frankfurt of this exquisite pair of plenipotentiaries, bully Bismarck at once met them with the imperious alternative: either the restoration of the Empire, or the unconditional acceptance of my own peace terms! These terms included a shortening of the intervals in which the war indemnity was to be paid and the continued occupation of the Paris forts by Prussian troops until Bismarck should feel satisfied with the state of things in France; Prussia thus being recognized as the supreme arbiter in internal French politics! In return for this he offered to let loose, for the extermination of Paris, the captive Bonapartist army, and to lend them the direct assistance of Emperor Wilhelm's troops. He pledged his good faith by making payment of the first installment of the indemnity dependent on the "pacification" of Paris. Such a bait was, of course, eagerly swallowed by Thiers and his plenipotentiaries. They signed the treaty of peace on May 10, and had it endorsed by the Versailles Assembly on the eighteenth.

In the interval between the conclusion of peace and the arrival of the Bonapartist prisoners, Thiers felt the more bound to resume his comedy of conciliation, as his Republican tools stood in sore need of a pretext for blinking their eyes at the preparations for the carnage of Paris. As late as the eighth of May he replied to a deputation of middle-class conciliators: "Whenever the insurgents make up their minds for capitulation, the gates of Paris shall be flung wide open during a week for all except the murderers of Generals Clément Thomas and Lecomte."

A few days afterwards, when violently interpellated on these promises by the Rurals, he refused to enter into any explanations; not, however, without giving them this significant hint: "I tell you there are impatient men among you, men who are in too great a hurry. They must have another eight days; at the end of these eight days there will be no more danger, and the task will be proportionate to their courage and to their capacities."

As soon as MacMahon was able to assure him that he could shortly enter Paris, Thiers declared to the Assembly that "he would enter Paris with the laws in his hands, and demand a full expiation from the wretches who had sacrificed the lives of soldiers and destroyed public monuments."

As the moment of decision drew near he said—to the Assembly, "I shall be pitiless!"; to Paris, that it was doomed; and to his Bonapartist banditti, that they had state license to wreak vengeance upon

Paris to their hearts' content. At last, when treachery had opened
the gates of Paris to General Douay on May 21, Thiers, on the
twenty-second, revealed to the Rurals the "goal" of his conciliation
comedy, which they had so obstinately persisted in not understanding.
"I told you a few days ago that we were approaching our goal;
today I come to tell you the goal is reached. The victory of order,
justice, and civilization is at last won!"

So it was. The civilization and justice of bourgeois order comes
out in its lurid light whenever the slaves and drudges of that order
rise against their masters. Then this civilization and justice stand
forth as undisguised savagery and lawless revenge. Each new crisis
in the class struggle between the appropriator and the producer
brings out this fact more glaringly. Even the atrocities of the bourgeois in June, 1848, vanish before the ineffable infamy of 1871. The
self-sacrificing heroism with which the population of Paris—men,
women, and children—fought for eight days after the entrance of the
Versaillais, reflects as much the grandeur of their cause as the infernal
deeds of the soldiery reflect the innate spirit of that civilization of
which they are the mercenary vindicators. A glorious civilization
indeed, the great problem of which is how to get rid of the heaps
of corpses it made after the battle was over!

To find a parallel for the conduct of Thiers and his bloodhounds
we must go back to the times of Sulla and the two Triumvirates of
Rome. The same wholesale slaughter in cold blood; the same dis-
regard, in massacre, of age and sex; the same system of torturing
prisoners; the same proscriptions, but this time of a whole class; the
same savage hunt after concealed leaders, lest one might escape; the
same denunciations of political and private enemies; the same indifference for the butchery of entire strangers to the feud. There is but
this difference, that the Romans had no *mitrailleuses* for the dispatch,
in the lump, of the proscribed, and that they had not "the law in their
hands," nor on their lips the cry of "civilization."

And after those horrors, look upon the other, still more hideous
face of that bourgeois civilization as described by its own press.

"With stray shots," writes the Paris correspondent of a London
Tory paper, "still ringing in the distance, and untended wounded
wretches dying amid the tombstones of Père Lachaise—with 6,000
terror-stricken insurgents wandering in an agony of despair in the
labyrinth of the catacombs, and wretches hurried through the streets
to be shot down in scores by the *mitrailleuses*—it is revolting to see
the cafés filled with the votaries of absinthe, billiards, and dominoes,
female profligacy perambulating the boulevards, and the sound of
revelry disturbing the night from the *cabinets particuliers* of fashionable restaurants."

M. Édouard Hervé writes in the *Journal de Paris*, a Versaillist journal suppressed by the Commune: "The way in which the population of Paris manifested its satisfaction yesterday was rather more than frivolous, and we fear it will grow worse as time progresses. Paris has now a fête-day appearance, which is sadly out of place; and unless we are to be called the *Parisiens de la décadence*, this sort of thing must come to an end."

And then he quotes the passage from Tacitus: "Yet on the morrow of that horrible struggle, even before it was completely over, Rome—degraded and corrupt—began once more to wallow in the voluptuous slough which was destroying its body and polluting its soul—*alibi proelia et vulnera; alibi balnea popinaeque* [here fights and wounds, there baths and restaurants]."

M. Hervé only forgets to say that the "population of Paris" he speaks of is but the population of the Paris of M. Thiers—the *francs-fileurs* returning in throngs from Versailles, St. Denis, Rueil, and St. Germain—the Paris of the "Decline."

In all its bloody triumphs over the self-sacrificing champions of a new and better society, that nefarious civilization, based upon the enslavement of labor, drowns the moans of its victims in a hue-and-cry of calumny, reverberated by a worldwide echo. The serene workingmen's Paris of the Commune is suddenly changed into a pandemonium by the bloodhounds of "order." And what does this tremendous change prove to the bourgeois mind of all countries? Why, that the Commune has conspired against civilization! The Paris people die enthusiastically for the Commune in numbers unequaled in any battle known to history. What does that prove? Why, that the Commune was not the people's own government but the usurpation of a handful of criminals! The women of Paris joyfully give up their lives at the barricades and on the place of execution. What does this prove? Why, that the demon of the Commune has changed them into Megæras and Hecates! The moderation of the Commune during two months of undisputed sway is equaled only by the heroism of its defense. What does that prove? Why, that for months the Commune carefully hid, under a mask of moderation and humanity, the bloodthirstiness of its fiendish instincts, to be let loose in the hour of its agony!

The workingmen's Paris, in the act of its heroic self-holocaust, involved in its flames buildings and monuments. While tearing to pieces the living body of the proletariat, its rulers must no longer expect to return triumphantly into the intact architecture of their abodes. The government of Versailles cries, "Incendiarism!" and whispers this cue to all its agents, down to the remotest hamlet, to hunt up its enemies everywhere as suspect of professional incendiarism. The bourgeoisie of the whole world, which looks complacently upon the wholesale massacre after the battle, is convulsed by horror at the desecration of brick and mortar!

When governments give state licenses to their navies to "kill, burn, and destroy," is that a license for incendiarism? When the British troops wantonly set fire to the Capitol at Washington and to the Summer Palace of the Chinese Emperor, was that incendiarism? When the Prussians, not for military reasons, but out of the mere spite of revenge, burned down, with the help of petroleum, towns like Châteaudun and innumerable villages, was that incendiarism? When Thiers, during six weeks, bombarded Paris, under the pretext that he wanted to set fire only to those houses in which there were people, was that incendiarism? In war, fire is an arm as legitimate as any. Buildings held by the enemy are shelled to set them on fire. If their defenders have to retire, they themselves light the flames to prevent the attack from making use of the buildings. To be burned down has always been the inevitable fate of all buildings situated in the front of battle of all the regular armies of the world. But in the war of the enslaved against their enslavers, the only justifiable war in history, this is by no means to hold good! The Commune used fire strictly as a means of defense. They used it to stop up to the Versailles troops those long, straight avenues which Haussmann had expressly opened to artillery fire; they used it to cover their retreat, in the same way as the Versaillais, in their advance, used their shells which destroyed at least as many buildings as the fire of the Commune. It is a matter of dispute, even now, which buildings were set fire to by the defense, and which by the attack. And the defense resorted to fire only then, when the Versailles troops had already commenced their wholesale murdering of prisoners. Besides, the Commune had long before given full public notice that, if driven to extremities, they would bury themselves under the ruins of Paris and make Paris a second Moscow, as the Government of Defense, but only as a cloak for its treason, had promised to do. For this purpose Trochu had found them the petroleum. The Commune knew that its opponents cared nothing for the lives of the Paris people, but cared much for their own Paris buildings. And Thiers, on the other hand, had given them notice that he would be implacable in his vengeance. No sooner had he got his army ready on one side, and the Prussians shutting up the trap on the other, than he proclaimed: "I shall be pitiless! The expiation will be complete, and justice will be stern!" If the acts of the Paris workingmen were vandalism, it was the vandalism of defense in despair, not the vandalism of triumph, like that which the Christians perpetrated upon the really priceless art treasures of heathen antiquity; and even that vandalism has been justified by the historian as an unavoidable and comparatively trifling concomitant to the titanic struggle between a new society arising and an old one breaking down. It was still less the vandalism of Haussmann, razing historic Paris to make place for the Paris of the sightseer!

But the execution by the Commune of the sixty-four hostages, with the Archbishop of Paris at their head! The bourgeoisie and its army in June, 1848, reestablished a custom which had long disappeared from the practice of war—the shooting of their defenseless prisoners. This brutal custom has since been more or less strictly adhered to by the suppressors of all popular commotions in Europe and India, thus proving that it constitutes a real "progress of civilization"! On the other hand, the Prussians, in France, had reestablished the practice of taking hostages—innocent men who were to answer to them with their lives for the acts of others. When Thiers, as we have seen, from the very beginning of the conflict, enforced the humane practice of shooting down the Communal prisoners, the Commune, to protect their lives, was obliged to resort to the Prussian practice of securing hostages. The lives of the hostages had been forfeited over and over again by the continued shooting of prisoners on the part of the Versaillais. How could they be spared any longer after the carnage with which MacMahon's praetorians celebrated their entrance into Paris? Was even the last check upon the unscrupulous ferocity of bourgeois governments—the taking of hostages—to be made a mere sham of? The real murderer of Archbishop Darboy is Thiers. The Commune again and again had offered to exchange the archbishop, and ever so many priests in the bargain, against the single Blanqui, then in the hands of Thiers. Thiers obstinately refused. He knew that with Blanqui he would give the Commune a head, while the archbishop would serve his purpose best in the shape of a corpse. Thiers acted upon the precedent of Cavaignac. In June, 1848, did not Cavaignac and his men of order raise shouts of horror by stigmatizing the insurgents as the assassins of Archbishop Affre! They knew perfectly well that the archbishop had been shot by the soldiers of order. M. Jacquemet, the archbishop's vicar general, present on the spot, had immediately afterwards handed them his evidence to that effect.

All this chorus of calumny, which the party of Order in its orgies of blood never fails to raise against its victims, only proves that the bourgeois of our day considers himself the legitimate successor to the baron of old, who thought every weapon in his own hand fair against the plebeian, while in the hands of the plebeian a weapon of any kind constituted in itself a crime.

The conspiracy of the ruling class to break down the revolution

by a civil war carried on under the patronage of the foreign invader
—a conspiracy which we have traced from the very fourth of
September down to the entrance of MacMahon's praetorians through
the gate of St. Cloud—culminated in the carnage of Paris. Bismarck
gloats over the ruins of Paris, in which he saw perhaps the first installment of that general destruction of great cities he had prayed
for when still a simple Rural in the Prussian *Chambre introuvable* of
1849. He gloats over the cadavers of the Paris proletariat. For him
this is not only the extermination of revolution, but the extinction
of France, now decapitated in reality, and by the French Government
itself. With the shallowness characteristic of all successful statesmen,
he sees but the surface of this tremendous historic event. Whenever
before has history exhibited the spectacle of a conqueror crowning
his victory by turning into, not only the gendarme, but the hired
bravo of the conquered government? There existed no war between
Prussia and the Commune of Paris. On the contrary, the Commune
had accepted the peace preliminaries, and Prussia had announced her
neutrality. Prussia was therefore no belligerent. She acted the part
of a bravo—a cowardly bravo because incurring no danger; a hired
bravo because stipulating beforehand the payment of her blood
money of 500 millions on the fall of Paris. And thus at last came
out the true character of the war, ordained by Providence as a
chastisement of godless and debauched France by pious and moral
Germany! And this unparalleled breach of the law of nations, even as
understood by the old-world lawyers, instead of arousing the "civilized" governments of Europe to declare the felonious Prussian Government, the mere tool of the St. Petersburg Cabinet, an outlaw
among nations, only incites them to consider whether the few victims
who escape the double cordon around Paris are not to be given up
to the hangman at Versailles!

That, after the most tremendous war of modern times, the conquering and the conquered hosts should fraternize for the common
massacre of the proletariat—this unparalleled event does indicate,
not, as Bismarck thinks, the final repression of a new society up-
heaving, but the crumbling into dust of bourgeois society. The highest heroic effort of which old society is still capable is national war;
and this is now proved to be a mere governmental humbug, intended
to defer the struggle of classes and to be thrown aside as soon
as that class struggle bursts out into civil war. Class rule is no longer
able to disguise itself in a national uniform; the national governments
are *one* as against the proletariat!

After Whitsunday, 1871, there can be neither peace nor truce
possible between the workingmen of France and the appropriators

of their produce. The iron hand of a mecenary soldiery may for a time keep both classes tied down in common oppression. But the battle must break out again and again in ever growing dimensions, and there can be no doubt as to who will be the victor in the end—the appropriating few, or the immense working majority. And the French working class is only the advance guard of the modern proletariat.

While the European governments thus testify, before Paris, to the international character of class rule, they cry down the International Working Men's Association—the international counter-organization of labor against the cosmopolitan conspiracy of capital—as the fountainhead of all these disasters. Thiers denounced it as the despot of labor, pretending to be its liberator. Picard ordered that all communications between the French Internationals and those abroad should be cut off; Count Jaubert, Thiers' mummified accomplice of 1835, declares it the great problem of all civilized governments to weed it out. The Rurals roar against it, and the whole European press joins the chorus. An honorable French writer [Robinet], completely foreign to our Association, speaks as follows: "The members of the Central Committee of the National Guard, as well as the greater part of the members of the Commune, are the most active, intelligent, and energetic minds of the International Working Men's Association . . . men who are thoroughly honest, sincere, intelligent, devoted, pure, and fanatical in the *good* sense of the word."

The police-tinged bourgeois mind naturally figures to itself the International Working Men's Association as acting in the manner of a secret conspiracy, its central body ordering, from time to time, explosions in different countries. Our Association is, in fact, nothing but the international bond between the most advanced workingmen in the various countries of the civilized world. Wherever, in whatever shape, and under whatever conditions the class struggle obtains any consistency, it is but natural that members of our Association should stand in the foreground. The soil out of which it grows is modern society itself. It cannot be stamped out by any amount of carnage. To stamp it out, the governments would have to stamp out the despotism of capital over labor—the condition of their own parasitical existence.

Workingmen's Paris, with its Commune, will be forever celebrated as the glorious harbinger of a new society. Its martyrs are enshrined in the great heart of the working class. Its exterminators history has already nailed to that eternal pillory from which all the prayers of their priests will not avail to redeem them.

NOTES

I

"The column of prisoners halted in the Avenue Uhrich, and was drawn up, four or five deep, on the footway facing to the road. General Marquis de Galliffet and his staff dismounted and commenced an inspection from the left of the line. Walking down slowly and eying the ranks, the General stopped here and there, tapping a man on the shoulder or beckoning him out of the rear ranks. In most cases, without further parley, the individual thus selected was marched out into the center of the road, where a small supplementary column was, thus, soon formed. . . . It was evident that there was considerable room for error. A mounted officer pointed out to General Galliffet a man and woman for some particular offense. The woman, rushing out of the ranks, threw herself on her knees, and, with outstretched arms, protested her innocence in passionate terms. The general waited for a pause, and then with most impassible face and unmoved demeanor, said, 'Madame, I have visited every theater in Paris, your acting will have no effect on me' ('*ce n'est pas la peine de jouer la comédie*'). . . . It was not a good thing on that day to be noticeably taller, dirtier, cleaner, older, or uglier than one's neighbors. One individual in particular struck me as probably owing his speedy release from the ills of this world to his having a broken nose. . . . Over a hundred being thus chosen, a firing party told off, and the column resumed its march, leaving them behind. A few minutes afterwards a dropping fire in our rear commenced, and continued for over a quarter of an hour. It was the execution of these summarily convicted wretches."—Paris correspondent, *Daily News*, June 8.

This Galliffet, "the kept man of his wife, so notorious for her shameless exhibitions at the orgies of the Second Empire," went, during the war, by the name of the French "Ensign Pistol."

"The *Temps*, which is a careful journal, and not given to sensation, tells a dreadful story of people imperfectly shot and buried before life was extinct. A great number were buried in the square around St. Jacques-la-Boucherie; some of them very superficially. In the daytime the roar of the busy streets prevented any notice being taken; but in the stillness of the night the inhabitants of the houses in the neighborhood were roused by distant moans, and in the morning a clenched hand was seen protruding through the soil. In consequence of this, exhumations were ordered to take place. . . . That many wounded have been buried alive I have not the slightest doubt. One case I can vouch for. When Brunel was shot with his mistress on the 24th ult. in the courtyard of a house in the Place Vendôme, the bodies lay there until the afternoon of the 27th. When the burial party came to remove the corpses, they found the woman living still and took her to an ambulance. Though she had received four bullets she is now out of danger."—Paris correspondent, *Evening Standard*, June 8.

II

The following letter appeared in the London *Times* of June 13:
"To the Editor of the *Times:*
"Sir: On June 6, 1871, M. Jules Favre issued a circular to all the European powers, calling upon them to hunt down the International Working Men's Association. A few remarks will suffice to characterize that document.

"In the very preamble of our statutes it is stated that the International was founded 'September 28, 1864, at a public meeting held at St. Martin's Hall, Long Acre, London.' For purposes of his own Jules Favre puts back the date of its origin behind 1862.

"In order to explain our principles, he professes to quote 'their' (the International's) 'sheet of the 25th of March, 1869.' And then what does he quote? The sheet of a society which is not the International. This sort of maneuver he already recurred to when, still a comparatively young lawyer, he had to defend the *National* newspaper, prosecuted for libel by Cabet. Then he pretended to read extracts from Cabet's pamphlets while reading interpolations of his own—a trick exposed while the court was sitting, and which, but for the indulgence of Cabet, would have been punished by Jules Favre's expulsion from the Paris bar. Of all the documents quoted by him as documents of the International, not one belongs to the International. He says, for instance: ' "The Alliance declares itself atheist," says the General Council, constituted in London in July 1869.'

"The General Council never issued such a document. On the contrary, it issued a document[7] which quashed the original statutes of [Bakunin's] 'Alliance'—L'Alliance de la Démocratie Socialiste, at Geneva—quoted by Jules Favre.

"Throughout his circular, which pretends in part also to be directed against the Empire, Jules Favre repeats against the International but the police inventions of the public prosecutors of the Empire, which broke down miserably even before the law courts of that Empire.

"It is known that in its two addresses" (of July and September

---

7. "The International Working Men's Association and the Alliance of Socialist Democracy."

last) "on the late war, the General Council of the International denounced the Prussian plans of conquest against France. Later on, Mr. Reitlinger, Jules Favre's private secretary, applied, though of course in vain, to some members of the General Council for getting up by the Council a demonstration against Bismarck, in favor of the Government of National Defense; they were particularly requested not to mention the republic. The preparations for a demonstration with regard to the expected arrival of Jules Favre in London were made—certainly with the best of intentions—in spite of the General Council, which, in its address of the 9th of September, had distinctly forewarned the Paris workmen against Jules Favre and his colleagues.

"What would Jules Favre say if, in its turn, the International were to send a circular on Jules Favre to all the cabinets of Europe, drawing their particular attention to the documents published at Paris by the late M. Millière?

"I am, sir, your obedient servant,

"John Hales,

"Secretary to the General Council of the International Working Men's Association.

*256 High Holborn, London
Western Central, June 12*"

In an article on "The International Society and Its Aims," that pious informer, the London *Spectator* (June 24), among other similar tricks, quotes, even more fully than Jules Favre has done, the above document of the "Alliance" as the work of the International, and that eleven days after the refutation has been published in the *Times*. We do not wonder at this. Frederick the Great used to say that of all Jesuits the worst are the Protestant ones.

Report on France*

THE LETTERS had been posted outside the line by Lafargue; they had therefore been delayed by rail: both the French and the Prussian governments sifted the letters. Most of the information they contained was old but there were a few facts which the papers had not given. It was stated that the provinces knew as little what was going on in Paris as during the siege. Except where the fighting was going on it had never been so quiet. A great part of the middle class had joined the National Guards of Belleville. The great capitalists had run away and the small tradespeople went with the working class. No one could have an idea of the enthusiasm of the people and the National Guards, and the people at Versailles must be fools if they believed that they could enter Paris. Paris did not believe in a rising in the provinces and knew that superior forces were brought against it but there was no fear on that account, but there was fear of the Prussian intervention and want of provisions. The decrees about rent and commercial bills were two master strokes: without them three-fourths of the tradespeople would have become bankrupt. The murder of Duval and Flourens had excited a sentiment of vengeance. The family of Flourens and the Commune had sent a legal officer to have the cause of their death certain, but in vain. Flourens had been killed in a house.

About the fabrication of telegrams there was some information. When Brutto had gone through the accounts of the Government of National Defense he had discovered that money had been paid for

---

* Remarks (in English) at the meeting of the General Council of the International, April 25, 1871.

the construction of an improved portable guillotine. The guillotine had been found and publicly burned by order of the Commune. The gas company had owed the municipality more than a million but had not shown any willingness to refund till their goods had been seized; then a bill to the amount had been given on the Bank of France. The telegrams and correspondents gave altogether different versions of these things. The greatest eyesore was that the Commune governed so cheap. The highest officials only received at the rate of 6,000 francs [per] year, the others only workman's wages.

The address was to be ready at the next meeting.

"The Principles of the Commune
Were Eternal..."*

CITIZEN MARX explained that he had been ill, and had not been able to finish the address upon which he was engaged, but he hoped to have it ready by Tuesday next. In reference to the struggle in Paris he said he was afraid the end was near, but if the Commune was beaten, the struggle would only be deferred. The principles of the Commune were eternal and could not be crushed; they would assert themselves again and again until the working classes were emancipated. The Commune of Paris was being crushed by the aid of the Prussians, they were acting as gendarmes for Thiers. The plot for its destruction was concocted between Bismarck, Thiers, and Favre; Bismarck stated at Frankfurt that Thiers and Favre had asked him to interfere. The result showed that he was willing to do anything he could to assist them, short of risking the lives of German soldiers —not that he valued life when there was anything to be got, but he wished to see France sink still lower so that he might be able to exact the more. He had allowed Thiers to have more soldiers than was stipulated in the convention, and had only allowed food to go into Paris in limited quantities. It was only the old story. The upper classes always united to keep down the working class. In the eleventh century there was a war between some French knights and Norman knights, and the peasants rose in insurrection; the knights immediately forgot their differences and coalesced to crush the movement of the peasants. To show how Prussians have been doing police work, it might be mentioned that 500 were arrested

---

* Remarks (in English) at the meeting of the General Council of the International, May 23, 1871. The minutes of the meeting were written by the Secretary, John Hales.

[375]

at Rouen, which is occupied by the Prussians—upon the plea that they belonged to the International. The International was feared. In the French Assembly the other day, Count Jaubert—a dried-up mummy, a minister of 1834, a man noted for supporting measures against the press—made a speech in which he said that after order was restored, the first duty of the government must be to inquire into the working of the International, and put it down.

"Infamous Lies" About the Commune*

CITIZEN MARX said the Council must disclaim all connection with [Bakunin's] so-called International Democratic Association, as it was started in opposition to the International Working Men's Association, which had to bear the responsibilities of its acts, absurd as they sometimes were. Another thing to which he wished to call the attention of the Council was the infamous lies circulated about the Commune by the English press. They were lies fabricated by the French and Prussian police. They were afraid lest the truth should be known. It was asserted that Millière was one of the most furious members of the Commune. Now it was a fact that he never was a member of the Commune, but as he had been a deputy for Paris it was necessary to have an excuse for shooting him. The English press acted as police and bloodhounds of Thiers. Slanders against the Commune and against the International were invented to serve his bloody policy. The press knew full well the objects and principles of the International. It had given reports of the prosecutions against it in Paris under the Empire. It had had representatives at the various congresses held by the Association, and had reported their proceedings, and yet it circulated reports to the effect that the Association included the Fenian Brotherhood,[1] the Carbonari[2] (ceased to exist 1830), the Marianne[3] (ditto 1854), and other secret societies, and asked if Colonel Henderson knew of the whereabouts of the General

---

* Remarks (in English) at the meeting of the General Council of the International, June 6, 1871. The minutes of the meeting were written by the Secretary, John Hales.

  1. A secret organization founded in the 1850s among Irish immigrants in America and later extended to Ireland.

  2. A secret Italian society active in the first three decades of the nineteenth century.

  3. A secret French republican society founded in 1850.

Council which was said to sit in London. These things were simply invented to justify any action taken against the International. The upper classes were afraid of the principles of the International.

He wished also to call attention to the fact that Mazzini had written in the *Contemporary Review* [June, 1871] denouncing the Commune. It was not so well known as it ought to be, but Mazzini had always been opposed to the workmen's movements. He denounced the insurgents of June, 1848, when Louis Blanc, who then had more courage than he has now, answered him.

When Pierre Leroux—who had a large family—obtained employment in London, Mazzini was the man to denounce him. The fact was, Mazzini with his old-fashioned republicanism knew nothing and accomplished nothing. In Italy he had created a military despotism by his cry for Nationality. With him the state—which was an imaginary thing—was everything, and society—which was a reality —was nothing. The sooner the people repudiated such men the better.

Attack on Jules Favre and Odger*

CITIZEN MARX said there was one other subject to which he wished to allude. It appeared that at a meeting of the Land and Labour League a Mr. Shipton—whom he did not know—had been criticizing the address on the *Civil War in France* and had said that he (Dr. Marx) had repudiated the Council. Such a remark only showed Mr. Shipton's ignorance: "Because he had avowed himself the author of the charges contained in the address, he had repudiated the Council!" Why, that avowal was made by the sanction of the Council, so that men like Mr. Odger, who were apologists for Mr. Thiers and Favre, should no longer have the power to say they did not know whether the charges were true or not. The men charged were distinctly challenged to indict him for libel, so that the matter might be tested in a court of law, but it did not serve their purpose to do so, as they knew well what the result would be. Of course it was to be easily understood why Mr. Odger was not satisfied. He had exhibited an amount of ignorance in dealing with foreign politics that would not have been creditable to any ordinary reader of newspapers. He had said the character of Jules Favre was irreproachable. Why, it was well known that he had been all his life the bitter opponent of the French working class and of all labor movements; he was the principal instigator of the massacres of June, 1848; he was the author of the expedition to Rome in 1849; he was the man who obtained the expulsion of Louis Blanc from France, and was one of the men who brought back Bonaparte; and yet Mr. Odger unblushingly stood up and

---

* Remarks (in English) at the meeting of the General Council of the International, August 1, 1871.

said nothing could be said against the character of Jules Favre. Why, if Mr. Odger, who claimed to have been one of the foremost men of the International, had attended to his duties as a member, he must have known such a statement had no ground whatever to rest upon. It was either made with a knowledge that it was false, or it betrayed an inexcusable ignorance. Mr. Odger knew nothing of the International for the last five years, as he had never attended to the duties. The office of President was abolished by the Congress because it was found to be a sham. Mr. Odger was the first and only President of the International; he never attended to his duties—the Council got on quite as well without—therefore the office was abolished.

Personal Letters

ON THE FRANCO-PRUSSIAN WAR

From letter to Frederick Engels (in Manchester)
LONDON, JULY 20, 1870

Dear Fred:
Enclosed is a letter from Kugelmann, which will enlighten you significantly on the mysteries of the current war. He is right in criticizing the appeal for a Brunswick assembly,[1] a few copies of which I am enclosing. In addition, I am sending you *Réveil*.[2] You will find in it the first half of the Act of Accusation before the High Court of Blois; how pitiable appear the French conspirators, who, without any reason, turn into *mouchards*, compared to the Fenians! But the paper is also interesting because of the leading article by old Delescluze. Although he opposes the government, [his article] is the most complete expression of chauvinism, *"car la France est le seul pays de l'idée"* ["for only France is the country of ideas"]—that is, of ideas it has about itself. The only thing that annoys these chauvinistic republicans is that the real expression of their idol—L. Bonaparte with the long nose of a stock-exchange shark—does not correspond to their fancy picture. The French need a thrashing. If the Prussians win, the centralization of state power will be useful for the centralization of the German working class. German predominance would also transfer the center of gravity of the workers' movement in Western Europe from France to Germany, and one has only to compare the movement in the two countries from 1866 until now to see that the German working class is superior to the French both theoretically and organizationally. Their predominance over the French on the world stage would mean at the same time the predominance of *our* theory over Proudhon's, etc.

Your

K.M.

---

1. On July 16, 1870, a committee of the German Social-Democratic Workers' party issued a call for a popular assembly in Brunswick.
2. A left-wing republican weekly edited by Delescluze.

Letter written in English to Paul and Laura Lafargue (in Paris)
LONDON, JULY 28, 1870

My dear children,
You must excuse the long delay of my answer. You know I cannot stand heat. It weighs down my energies. On the other hand, I was
overwhelmed with business, the German "friends" firing at me a
mitrailleuse of letters which, under present circumstances, I could not
decline answering at once.

You want of course to hear something of the war. So much is sure
that L. Bonaparte has already missed his first opportunity. You understand that his first plan was to take the Prussians unawares and get
the better of them by surprise. It is, in point of fact, much easier to
get the French army—a mere soldiers' army till now—ready than the
Prussian one, which consists largely of the civilian element forming
the *Landwehr*. Hence, if Bonaparte, as he at first intended, had made
a dash even with half-collected forces, he might have succeeded to
surprise the fortress of Mayence, to push simultaneously forward in
the direction of Würzburg, thus to separate northern from southern
Germany, and so throw consternation amidst the camp of his adversaries. However, he has allowed this opportunity to slip. He saw
unmistakable signs of the *national* character of the war in Germany
and was stunned by the unanimous, quick, immediate adhesion of
Southern Germany to Prussia. His habitude of hesitation, so much
adapted to his old trade of conspirator planning *coups d'état* and
plebiscites, got the upper hand, but this method will not do for war,
which demands quick and unwavering resolution. He let his first plan
slip and resolved to collect his full forces. Thus he *lost his advantage
of a first start*, of surprise, while the Prussians have *gained* all the
time necessary for mobilizing their forces. Hence you may say that
Bonaparte has already lost his first campaign.

Whatever may now be the first incidents of the war, it will become extremely serious. Even a first great French victory would
decide nothing, because the French army will now find on its way
three great fortresses, Mayence, Coblenz, and Cologne, ready for a
protracted defense. In the long run, Prussia has greater military forces
to her disposal than Bonaparte. It may even be that on one side or the
other she will be able to cross the French frontier and make "*le sol
sacré de la patrie*"—according to the chauvinists of the *Corps Législatif* this *sol sacré* is situated only on the French side of the Rhine—
the theater of war!

Both nations remind me of the anecdote of the two Russian noblemen accompanied by two Jews, their serfs. Nobleman A strikes the Jew of Nobleman B, and B answers: *"Schlägst Du meinen Jud, schlag ich deinen Jud"* ["If you beat my Jew, I will beat your Jew"]. So both nations seem reconciled to their despots by being allowed, each of them, to strike at the despot of the other nation.

In Germany the war is considered as a *national* war, because it is a war of defense. The middle class (not to speak of the *Krautjunkertum*) overdoes itself in manifestations of loyalty. One believes himself taken back to the times of 1812, *"für Gott, König, und Vaterland,"* with the old donkey Arndt's *"Was ist des Teutschen Vaterland!"*

The singing of the *"Marseillaise"* at the bidding of the man of December is of course a parody, like the whole history of the Second Empire. Still it shows that he feels that *"Partant pour la Syrie"*[1] would not do for the occasion. On the other hand, that dammed old ass Wilhelm *"Annexander"*[2] sings *"Jesus meine Zuversicht,"*[3] flanked on the one side by *larron* [thief] Bismarck and on the other by the *policier* Stieber!

On both sides it is a disgusting exhibition.

Still there is this consolation, that the workmen protest in Germany as in France. In point of fact the war of classes in both countries is too far developed to allow any political war whatever to roll back for a long time the wheel of history. I believe, on the contrary, that the present war will produce results not at all expected by the "officials" on both sides.

I enclose two cuts from Liebknecht's *Volksstaat*. You will see that he and Bebel behaved exceedingly well in the Reichstag.

For my own part, I should like that both, Prussians and French, thrashed each other alternately, and that—as I believe will be the case—the Germans got *ultimately* the better of it. I wish this because the definite defeat of Bonaparte is likely to provoke revolution in France, while the definite defeat of the Germans would only protract the present state of things for twenty years.

The English upper classes are full of moral indignation against Bonaparte, at whose feet they have fawned for eighteen years. Then they wanted him as the savior of their privileges, of rents and profits. At the same time, they know the man to be seated on a volcano, the which unpleasant position forces him to trouble peace periodically, and makes him—besides his parvenuship—an unpleasant bedfellow.

---

1. "On to Syria," an early nineteenth-century Bonapartist song, became the official song at Napoleon III's imperial celebrations.

2. A double pun on annexation and Alexander the Great.

3. "Jesus Is My Shepherd."

Now they hope that to solid Prussia, Protestant Prussia, Prussia backed by Russia, will fall the part of keeping down revolution in Europe. It would for them be a safer and more respectable policeman.

As to the English workmen, they hate Bonaparte more than Bismarck, principally because he is the aggressor. At the same time they say: "The plague on both your houses," and if the English oligarchy, as it seems very inclined, should take part in the war against France, there will be a "tuck" at London. For my own part, I do everything in my power, through the means of the International, to stimulate this "neutrality" spirit and to baffle the *"paid"* (paid by the "respectables") leaders of the English working class who strain every nerve to mislead them.

I hope the measures as to the houses within the fortification *rayon* [radius] will not hurt you. Thousand kisses to my sweet little Schnaps.

Yours devotedly,

OLD NICK

From letter to Engels (in Manchester)
LONDON, JULY 28, 1870

Dear Fred:

. . . The singing of the *"Marseillaise"* in France is a parody, as is the whole Second Empire. But at least the dog [Napoleon III] feels that the song, *"Partant pour la Syrie,"* would not do. In Prussia, on the other hand, such buffooneries are not necessary. "Jesus Is My Shepherd!" sung by Wilhelm I, with Bismarck on his right and Stieber on his left, is the German *"Marseillaise"!* As in 1812. The German philistine seems to be downright enchanted that now he can unrestrainedly give vent to his innate servility. Who would have considered it possible that twenty-two years after 1848, a national war would possess such a theoretical expression!

Fortunately, the whole demonstration proceeds entirely from the middle class. The working class, with the exception of Schweitzer's immediate followers, takes no part in it. Fortunately, the war of classes in both countries, France and Germany, has developed so far that war abroad could seriously reverse the wheel of history. . . .

Greetings.

Your

K.M.

From letter to Engels (*in Manchester*)
LONDON, AUGUST 1, 1870

(IN ALL HASTE)
Dear Fred:
. . . The local oligarchy desires the British to join Prussia in the war. After they have crawled before Bonaparte for eighteen years and used him properly as the savior of rents and profits, they now believe they would find in God-fearing monarchist Prussia a more respectable and safer policeman of the Continent.[1] But the fellows had better take care. Among the people here there is a general watchword: That damned German dynasty of ours wants to involve us in the continental war for family reasons![2]

Figaro here, a typical copy of which I gave Dupont, is an *English* paper, established by the French Embassy.

Bismarck, on his part, has duly bought up among the English press, etc., *Lloyd's* and *Reynold's!* The latter, in yesterday's issue, demands the dismemberment of France. This swine *ne ménage pas les transitions* [doesn't shrink from changing flags]. The fellow who had always cursed the Germans and eulogized the French has suddenly been transformed into a kind of Blind.

As for that lad [Blind], he hopes, through his patriotic clamor and noisy "suspension" of his republicanism on the altar of patriotism, to be elected deputy to the next Reichstag. . . .
Greetings.

Your
K.M.

From letter to Engels (*in Manchester*)
LONDON, AUGUST 8, 1870

Dear Fred:
I am leaving only tomorrow (delayed by business of the International), but for Ramsgate and not Brighton, because, according to the latest news, it is too hot in the former and, in addition, Arnold Winkelried Ruge makes that place too unsafe.

---

1. The preceding nine words were written in English.
2. The last three words were written in English.

The Empire is made, i.e., the German Empire. It seems as if all the trickery that has been perpetrated since the Second Empire has finally resulted in carrying out, by hook and crook, though neither by the path intended nor in the way imagined, the "national" aims of 1848—Hungary, Italy, Germany! It seems to me that this sort of movement will only come to an end as soon as the Prussians and the Russians come to blows. This is by no means improbable. The press of the Muscovite party (I have seen a lot of it at Borkheim's) has attacked the Russian government just as violently for its friendly attitude to Prussia as the French papers representing Thiers' point of view attacked Boustrapa[1] in 1866 for his flirtation with Prussia. Only the Czar, the German-Russian party, and the official St. Petersburg *Journal* sounded a note hostile to France. But the last thing they expected was such a decided Prussian-German success. Like Bonaparte in 1866, they thought the belligerent powers would weaken each other by a long struggle so that Holy Russia could intervene as supreme arbiter and dictate to them.

But now! If Alexander does not want to be poisoned, something must be done to appease the national party. Russia's prestige will obviously be even more "injured" by a German-Prussian Empire than the prestige of the Second Empire was by the North German Confederation.

Russia therefore—just as Bonaparte did in 1866–70—will intrigue with Prussia in order to get concessions in regard to Turkey, and all this trickery, despite the Russian religion of the Hohenzollerns, will end in *war between the cheaters.* However silly German Michael may be, his newly fortified national sentiment will hardly allow him to be pressed into the service of Russia without any remaining reason whatever, or so much as a pretext (especially now when he can no longer be lectured into putting up with everything in order that German unity may first be achieved). *Qui vivra verra* [Who lives longest will see most]. If our Handsome William[2] lives on for a bit we may yet witness his proclamations to the Poles. When God wants to do something especially great, says old Carlyle, he always chooses the stupidest people for it.

What troubles me at the moment is the state of affairs in France itself. The next great battle can hardly fail to turn against the French. And then? If the defeated army retreats to Paris, under the leadership of Boustrapa, the result will be a peace of the most humiliating kind, perhaps with the restoration of the Orléans. If a revolution

---

1. Emperor Napoleon III.
2. Emperor William I.

breaks out in Paris, the question is whether they have the means and the leadership to offer a serious resistance to the Prussians. One cannot conceal from oneself that twenty years of the Bonapartist farce have produced enormous demoralization. One is hardly justified in reckoning on revolutionary heroism. What do you think about it?. . . .

Your

K.M.

Letter to Engels (in Manchester)
LONDON, SEPTEMBER 6, 1870

Dear Fred:

I was on the verge of sitting down and writing to you when Serraillier came and informed me that tomorrow morning he leaves London for Paris, to remain there only a few days, however. Main purpose: to arrange there (*Conseil Fédéral de Paris*) matters with the International. This is the more necessary as today the whole French Branch[1] leaves for Paris in order to commit there stupidities in the name of the International. "They" want to overthrow the provisional government, establish a commune in Paris, appoint Pyat French Ambassador to London, etc.

Today I received from the *Conseil Fédéral* a Proclamation to the German people (which I am sending you tomorrow), together with an urgent plea to the General Council to issue a new Manifesto to the German people. I had already intended to propose it this evening.[2] Be so good as to send me as quickly as possible notes in English on the military aspect of Alsace-Lorraine to be used in the Manifesto.

I have already replied *comprehensively* to the *Conseil Fédéral* today, and have had at the same time the unpleasant task of opening their eyes to the real state of affairs.

I received from Brunswick [seat of the Social-Democratic Committee] the reply that it will act exactly according to my instructions.

Apropos. On Sunday, Longuet telegraphed me the Proclamation of the Republic. I received the telegram at four o'clock in the morning.

Jules Favre,[3] although a notorious scoundrel and June [1848] man,

---

1. The French Branch of the International was established in London in the fall of 1865.
2. At the request of the International's General Council, Marx wrote "The Second Address of the General Council on the Franco-German War" between September 6 and 9, 1870.
3. Favre was the Foreign Minister of Thiers' Government of National Defense

is good *pour le moment* as Foreign Minister. He always fought against the old Thiers policy and came out in favor of Italian and German unity.

I only regret that Rochefort is a member of the same government as the infamous Garnier-Pagès. But he could not very well have refused to join the Defense Committee.

Thanks for the money. What claims I have on half of your honorarium God only knows.

Salut.

Your

K.M.

Paul, Laura, and Schnappy have luckily arrived at Bordeaux on September 2. This is the more fortunate since under present circumstances Lafargue could never have left Paris.

Here a veritable flood of *réfugiés qui on sauvé la caisse* [refugees who have brought their money to safety]. As I have written you, gentlemen's lodgings are rising in price.

Do you not believe that if the weather, which is now abominable in France, continues, the Prussians, after this extraordinary long drought, might see reason; the more so as an Anglo-Russian-Austrian alliance threatens?

Dupont, who has been in correspondence with Pigott, is supposed to have written that animal a rough letter in the name of the French Republic. Urge him to it.

Letter to Ludwig Kugelmann (in Hanover)
LONDON, DECEMBER 13, 1870

Dear Kugelmann:

You must account for my long silence on the ground that during this war, which drew most of the foreign correspondents of the General Council to France, I had to carry on practically the whole correspondence of the International, which is no trifle. Furthermore, in the "press freedom" that now prevails, particularly in the North

---

(1870–71), which negotiated with the Germans the capitulation of Paris. Of him Marx wrote to Hermann Jung on January 18, 1871: "The disgraceful decree of June 27, 1848, by which thousands of Paris workers who had been jailed during the June insurrection were transported to Algeria, etc., without legal proceedings, was issued by Jules Favre. Later he stubbornly refused to agree to the amnesty proposals introduced from time to time by the republican party in the Constituent Assembly. Jules Favre was one of the most notorious tools of the reign of terror imposed on the French working class by General Cavaignac after the June insurrection."

German Bund, and most "particularly" in Hanover, it would be dangerous for my German correspondents, if not for me, to express my views on the war, and what else can one write about at this moment?

You ask me, for example, to send you our first Address on the war. I did send it to you. It has obviously been intercepted. Today I am enclosing both Addresses printed in one pamphlet, as well as Professor Beesly's article in the *Fortnightly Review*[1] and today's *Daily News*. Since this is a pro-Prussian paper, the things will be permitted to pass through. Professor Beesly is a Comteist and as such he feels obliged to assert all kinds of crotchets, but is otherwise a very able and brave man. He is professor of history at the University of London.

It seems that not only Bonaparte, his generals, and his army are captive in Germany, but with him also the whole imperialism with all its defects has acclimatized itself in the land of the oak and the linden.

As for the German bourgeois, his conquest-drunkenness does not surprise me in any way. First, *accaparation* [monopolizing, grabbing] is the life principle of all the bourgeoisie, and taking foreign provinces is still "taking." Furthermore, the German citizen had submissively received so many kicks from his sovereigns, especially the Hohenzollerns, that for him it must be a genuine pleasure to apply the same kicks to the foreigner for a change.

At any rate, this war has liberated us from the "bourgeois republicans." Through terror, it put an end to this tribe. And that is a significant result. It gave our professors the best opportunity to expose themselves to the world as servile pedants. The conditions which will follow from this will be the best propaganda for our principles.

Here in England, at the beginning of the war public opinion was ultra-Prussian; it is now reversed. In the *café chantants*, for example, German songs with their *"Wi-Wa-Wacht am Rhein"* are hissed, while French songs are accompanied by the chorus of the *"Marseillaise."* Apart from the decisive sympathies of the masses for the Republic and the anger of the respectability[2] at the alliance between Prussia and Russia, which is now crystal-clear, and the shameless tone of Prussian diplomacy since its military successes, the manner of its war conduct—the system of requisitions, the burning of villages, the shooting of *francs-tireurs* [volunteers], the taking of hostages, and

---

1. "The International Working Men's Association," November 1, 1870.
2. The word is in English.

similar practices from the Thirty Years' War—has created universal indignation. Of course the English did the same in India, Jamaica, etc., but the French are neither Hindus nor Negroes, and the Prussians are no heaven-born Englishmen! It is a purely Hohenzollern idea that a nation commits a crime when it continues to defend itself after its standing army has been defeated. In reality, the Prussian national war against Napoleon I was a real thorn in the flesh of the gallant Frederick William III, as one can see in Professor Pertz's story of Gneisenau, who through his decree levying a militia created a system of war by volunteers.[3] It annoyed Frederick William III that the people fought on their own, independently of the order from the Most High.

Still, not every day is night. The war in France can still take an *"öklich"* [disgusting] turn. The resistance of the Army of the Loire[4] was beyond expectations, and the present dispersion of German forces right and left is designed merely to instill terror, but in reality has no other consequence than to call forth the defensive forces at all points and to weaken the offensive ones. Even the threatened bombardment of Paris is merely a trick. According to all rules of probability, it can have no appreciable effect on the city of Paris itself. Even if a few outer fortifications are shot down and breaches are made, of what use is it when the number of the besieged is greater than the besiegers? And when the besieged fight exceptionally well in the sorties, while the enemy are defending themselves behind entrenchments, are not the roles reversed?

Starving out Paris is the only effective means. But should this be dragged out long enough for the building up of armies and the development of a national war in the provinces, then nothing is gained by it except a change in the center of gravity. Furthermore, even after the capitulation of Paris, which cannot be kept in order with a mere handful, a large number of the invaders would be tied up.

However the war ends, it has trained the French proletariat in the use of arms, and this is the best guarantee for the future.

The shameless tone that Russia and Prussia take toward England can have entirely unexpected and unpleasant consequences for them. The matter rests simply on this: In the Paris Peace Treaty of 1856, England *disarmed herself.* She is a sea power, and can throw only the means of sea warfare into the scales against the great continental

3. By an edict of April 21, 1813, during the War of Liberation against Napoleon, Prussia created a *Landsturm* (militia).
4. The Army of the Loire, organized by General Aurelle de Paladines on November 15, 1870, successfully fought the Germans in the Orléans area.

military powers. Here the infallible method is the temporary destruction—that is, the shutting down—of the overseas commerce of the continentals. This rests mainly on enforcing the basic principle—the seizure of enemy goods in neutral ships. This maritime right (along with similar other rights) the English have given up in their so-called Declaration, annexed to the Paris Treaty. Clarendon did that at the secret order of the pro-Russian Palmerston. Nevertheless, the Declaration does not constitute an inherent part of the Treaty itself and has *never* been legally sanctioned in England. The Russians and Prussians are reckoning without their host when they imagine that the influence of the Queen, who is Prussianized out of family interests, and the bourgeois imbecility of a Gladstone would prevent John Bull in a crucial moment from casting overboard the self-imposed "gracious impediment." And then he can make hash of the Russian-German overseas commerce in a few weeks. Then we will have occasion to study the long faces of the Petersburg and Berlin diplomats and the even longer faces of the "power patriots." *Que vivra, verra.*

My best compliments to Madame la Comtesse and Fränzchen,

Your

K.M.

Apropos. Can you send me the various Reichstag speeches of Windthorst?

From letter to Ludwig Kugelmann (in Hanover)
LONDON, FEBRUARY 4, 1871

Dear Kugelmann:

I was sorry to learn from your last letter that your state of health has again become worse. In the autumn and winter months mine was tolerable, although the cough I contracted during my last stay in Hanover is still troubling me.

I sent you the *Daily News* containing my letter. Obviously it has been confiscated, as were the other things I sent you. Today I am enclosing the clipping, as well as the first Address of the General Council [on the Franco-Prussian War]. The letter actually contains nothing but facts, but was effective because of that.

You know my views of the middle-class heroes. M. Jules Favre (notorious from the days of the Provisional Government and Cavaignac & Co.) have, however, surpassed my expectations. First they allowed the *"sabre orthodoxe,"* the *"crétin militaire"*—as

Blanqui properly characterizes Trochu—to carry out his "plan." This plan consisted simply in prolonging the *passive resistance* of Paris to the utmost, that is, to the starvation point, while confining the offensive to sham maneuvers and *"des sorties platoniques."* What I am saying is not merely supposition. I know the contents of a letter that Jules Favre himself wrote to Gambetta in which he complains that he and other members of that part of the government cringing in Paris vainly sought to goad Trochu to serious offensive measures. Trochu always answered that that would give the upper hand to *Parisian demagogy.* Gambetta replied: *"Vous avez prononcé votre propre condamnation!"* ["You have pronounced your own condemnation!"] Trochu considered it much more important to keep down the reds with the help of his Breton bodyguard—who rendered him the same services the Corsicans rendered L. Bonaparte—than to defeat the Prussians. This is the real secret of the defeats not only at Paris but throughout France, where the bourgeoisie, in agreement with the majority of the local authorities, has acted on the same principle.

After Trochu's plan had been carried out to its climax—to the point where Paris had to surrender or starve—Jules Favre & Co. merely had to follow the example of the commander of the fortress of Toul. He did not surrender. He simply explained to the Prussians that he was compelled through lack of food to abandon the defense and open the gates of the fortress. They could now do what they liked.

But Jules Favre is not content with signing a formal capitulation. Having declared himself, his associates in the government, and Paris the prisoners of war of the King of Prussia, he has the brazenness to act in the name of the whole of France. What did he know of the situation in France outside Paris? Absolutely nothing, except what Bismarck was gracious enough to tell him.

More. These *Messieurs les prisonniers du roi de Prusse* go further and declare that the part of the French government still free in Bordeaux[1] has forfeited its authority and can act only in agreement with them—the prisoners of war of the Prussian king. Since as prisoners of war they can act only at the dictate of their war lord, they thereby proclaim the King of Prussia *de facto* the highest authority in France.

Even Louis Bonaparte, after he surrendered and was taken prisoner at Sedan, was less shameless. To Bismarck's proposals he replied that

---

1. Part of the Government of National Defense, formed in Paris on September 4, 1870, moved to Bordeaux on December 6, 1870; it was headed by Léon Gambetta.

he could not enter upon negotiations because as a Prussian prisoner he had ceased to exercise any authority in France.

At the most, J. Favre could have accepted a conditional armistice for the whole of France, namely, with the proviso that the agreement should be sanctioned by the Bordeaux government, which alone had the right and was competent to agree with the Prussians upon the clauses of such an armistice. At any rate, they would not have allowed the latter to exclude the eastern theater of war from the armistice. They would not have allowed the Prussians to round off their line of occupation so advantageously for themselves.

Made insolent by the usurpation of his prisoners of war, who in that capacity continue to play at being the French government, Bismarck is now interfering in internal French affairs *sans gêne* [without embarrassment]. He protests, noble soul, against Gambetta's decree on the general elections for the Assembly because, according to him, it prejudices the freedom of elections. Indeed! Gambetta should answer with a protest against the state of siege and other conditions in Germany which annihilate the freedom of elections to the Reichstag.

I hope Bismarck sticks to his conditions of peace. Four hundred million pounds sterling as war indemnity—half the English national debt! Even the French bourgeois will understand that! Perhaps they will realize at last that by continuing the war they could at worst *only gain.*

The mob, high class and low, judges by appearances, the façade, the immediate result. During the past twenty years it has, all over the world, apotheosized L. Bonaparte. I have always exposed him, even at his apogee, as a *mediocre scoundrel.* This is also my opinion of the Junker Bismarck. Still, I do not consider Bismarck as dumb as he would have been if his diplomacy had been freely his own. The man is strangled in a net of the Russian Chancellery which only a lion could tear apart, and he is no lion.

For example, Bismarck's demand that France hand over to him twenty of her best battleships and Pondichéry in the East Indies! Such an idea could not come out of a real Prussian diplomat. He would have known that a Prussian Pondichéry would be merely a pawn in English hands, since England could at will seize the twenty battleships before they reached the Eastern Ocean, and that from the Prussian viewpoint such demands could only have the absurd purpose of making John Bull mistrustful before the Prussians are out of the French woods. But it is in Russia's interest to bring forth exactly such a result, the more to secure Prussia's vassalage. In fact, those demands have produced a complete turnabout in the opinion even of England's peace-loving middle class. They now all call for war. This provocation of England

and this endangerment of her interests enrage even the bourgeoisie. It is more than probable that, thanks to this Prussian "wisdom," Gladstone & Co. will be kicked out of office and supplanted by a ministry declaring war against Prussia. . . .

Yours,

K.M.

ON THE PARIS COMMUNE

From letter to Ludwig Kugelmann (in Hanover)

LONDON, MARCH 3, 1869

Dear Kugelmann:

The damned photographer has again pulled me by the nose for weeks and has not yet delivered the additional copies. But I will no longer postpone my reply to you because of this. . . .

A very interesting movement is going on in France.

The Parisians are making a regular study of their latest revolutionary past, in order to prepare themselves for the business of the impending new revolution. First, the *origin of the Empire*—then the *coup d'état of December*. This had been completely forgotten, just as the reaction in Germany had also managed completely to extirpate the memory of 1848-49.

Hence Ténot's books on the *coup d'état* attracted such enormous attention in Paris and in the provinces that in a short time they went through ten printings. They were followed by dozens of other books on the same period. *C'était la rage* [It was the rage], and hence soon became a speculative business for the book dealers.

These books came from the *opposition*—Ténot, for example, is an *homme du "Siècle"* [man of the "Century"] (I mean the liberal bourgeois paper, not our century). All the liberal and illiberal scoundrels who belong to the official opposition favor this movement. Also the republican democrats, men, for example, like Delescluze, who was formerly Ledru-Rollin's adjutant, and now, as a republican patriarch, is the editor of the Paris *Réveil*.

Up to now, everybody has been reveling in these posthumous disclosures or rather reminiscences—everybody who is not Bonapartist.

But then came *le revers de la médaille* [the other side of the medal].

First the French government itself got the renegade Hippolyte Castille to publish *The Massacres of June 1848*. This was a fist blow

---

* See also Marx in the First International Vol. II of this series.

to Thiers, Falloux, Marie, Jules Favre, Jules Simon, Pelletan, etc., in short, to the leaders of what is called in France *"L'Union Libérale,"* who want to filch the next elections, the infamous old hounds!

Then, however, came the socialist party, which "exposed" the opposition and the republican democrats of the old ilk.

Among others, Vermorel: *The Men of 1848* and *The Opposition.* Vermorel is a Proudhonist.

Finally come the Blanquists; for example, G. Tridon: *The Gironde and the Girondists.*

And so the whole historical witches' cauldron is bubbling.

When will *our country* get that far!

To show you how well the French police are served:

I intended to go to Paris at the beginning of next week to see my daughter.

Last Saturday a police agent inquired at Lafargue's whether M. Marx had arrived yet. He said he had a message for him. Forewarned!

My most cordial greetings to your dear wife and Fränzchen.

How is Madame Tenge?

> *Yours,*
> K.M.

Letter written in English to Edward Spencer Beesly (in London)
LONDON, OCTOBER 19, 1870

Dear Sir:

Deak is against the workers. He is in reality the Hungarian edition of an English Whig.

As to Lyon,[1] I have received letters not fit for publication. At first everything went well. Under the pressure of the "International" section, the republic was proclaimed before Paris had taken that step. A revolutionary government was at once established—*La Commune*—composed partly of workmen belonging to the International, partly of radical middle-class republicans. The *octrois* were at once abolished, and rightly so. The Bonapartist and clerical intriguers were intimidated. Energetic means were taken to arm the whole people. The middle class began, if not really to sympathize with, at least to experience quietly, the new order of things. The action of Lyon was at once felt at Marseilles and Toulouse, where the International sections are strong.

But the asses Bakunin and Cluseret arrived at Lyon and spoiled

---

1. On September 4, 1870, an insurrection broke out in Lyon, and Michael Bakunin attempted to transform it into an anarchist movement.

everything. Since they both belonged to the International they had, unfortunately, influence enough to mislead our friends. The Hôtel de Ville was seized for a short time—a most foolish decree on the *abolition de l'état* and similar nonsense were issued. You understand that the very fact of a Russian—represented by the middle-class papers as an agent of Bismarck—pretending to impose himself as the leader of a *Comité du Salut de la France* [Committee of Safety of France] was quite sufficient to turn the balance of public opinion. As to Cluseret, he behaved as both a fool and a coward. These two men have left Lyon after their failure.

At Rouen, as in most industrial towns of France, the sections of the International, following the example of Lyon, have enforced the official admission into the "committees of defense" of the working-class element.

Still, I must tell you that according to all information I receive from France, the middle class on the whole prefers Prussian conquest to the victory of a republic with socialist tendencies.

Your devoted

KARL MARX

Letter written in English to Paul Lafargue (in Bordeaux)
LONDON, FEBRUARY 4, 1871

Dear Paul,

Il faut créer des nouveaux défenseurs à la France. [One must create new defenders for France.] You and Laura seem seriously and successfully engaged in that patriotic business. The whole family was delighted to hear that our dear Laura has passed victoriously through the critical juncture und we hope the progress will prove no les favorable.

Embrace little Schnappy on my part and tell him that Old Nick feels highly elated at the two photograms of his successor. In the "serious" copy the stern qualities of the little man protrude, while in his attitude as *franc-tireur* there is a charming expression of humor und *espièglerie* [roguishness].

You know my low opinion of middle-class heroes. Still, Jules Favre & Co. have contrived to surpass my worst anticipations. When Trochu had carried out his mysterious "plan," that is to say, when that *"sabre orthodoxe,"* that *"crétin militaire,"* had pushed the passive resistance of Paris to the point where there remained only the alternatives of starvation or capitulation—Jules Favre & Co. might have followed the precedent of the Governor of Toul. When his power of resistance had altogether broken down, he did not *capitulate*. He simply informed the Prussians of the real state of things, declared that he could not any longer go on with the defense, being deprived of provisions, and that they might now do as they liked. He made them no concession at all. He simply recognized a *fait accompli*. Favre & Co., on the contrary, not only sign a formal capitulation. They have the impudence to act on behalf of *all* France, although in complete ignorance of the state of affairs *en dehors de Paris*, in regard to which they were strictly confined to the disinterested information Bismarck condescended to vouchsafe them. Moreover, having capitulated, having become *Messieurs les prisonniers du roi de Prusse*, they go further and declare that the Bordelais delegation has lost its power and must only act in union with *Messieurs les prisonniers du roi de Prusse*. Why, even Louis Bonaparte, after his capitulation and surrender at Sedan, declared to Bismarck he could enter into no negotiations with him, because he had ceased to be a free agent, and because, by the very fact of his being a Prussian *prisoner*, he had ceased to hold any authority over France!

Thus even L. Bonaparte was less shameless than Favre & Co!

The only condition which Favre could have accepted conditionally, that is to say under the reserve of his act being assented to by the Bordelais delegation, was the armistice. Yet to settle the terms of that armistice he must have left to the men who were not prisoners of *le roi de Prusse*. They would certainly not have allowed the Prussians to exclude from that armistice the eastern theater of war, and would not have allowed the Prussians to improve, on the plea of the armistice, the whole outlines of their military occupation, rounding it off in the way most profitable to themselves.

Emboldened by the dastardly servilism of the Paris delegation who presume to participate in the government of France, after having become *Messieurs les capitulards et les prisonniers du roi de Prusse*, Bismarck considers himself and acts already as the *de facto* supreme authority in France. He protests against Gambetta's decree[1] relating to the general elections as interfering with their "liberty." He dictates the terms on which the general assembly ought to be chosen. Why! Gambetta might reply by protesting against the conditions under which at this very moment the general elections for the Reichstag are carried on in Germany. He might insist that to render these elections free, Bismarck ought above all things to abolish or at least to suspend the state of siege maintained through a great part of Prussia. To give you one instance of the liberty of election in Germany. At Frankfurt (on the Main) a workmen's candidate (not residing in

---

1. A January, 1871, decree excluding certain types of persons from the suffrage.

Frankfurt) is proposed and opens his electoral campaign in that town. What do the Prussian authorities resort to? To the expulsion of that candidate from Frankfurt by the police force!

I hope the Prussians will insist on their modest demand of 400 million pounds sterling war contribution by France! This may rouse even the French middle class whose maneuvers together with the intrigues of the local administration (which Gambetta has allowed to a great part to rest in the hands of Bonapartists, Orléanists, etc.) are the true key to the till now reverses of the war. Even the middle class may at last become aware that they will lose more by giving in than by fighting!

At the same time, if France holds still out for some time, the foreign relations will become much more favorable to her cause.

In England the Gladstone Ministry is seriously endangered. It may soon be kicked out. The public opinion here is now again warlike to the highest degree. This change has been worked by Prussia's demands, mainly by her asking Pondichéry and the twenty first-rate French men-of-war. John Bull sees in this a menace against England and a Russian intrigue (and these demands have indeed been suggested to Prussia by the St. Petersburg cabinet). In Russia itself a great change seems imminent. Since the assumption of the Imperial title by the King of Prussia, the anti-German party, the so-called Muscovite party, led by the Prince successor, has again got the upper hand. It is very probable that the present Emperor will either have to accept its dictates and a consequent change of his foreign policy, or that he will share the fate of his predecessors and by some means or other be released of his "mortal body." If such a convulsion in Russia takes place, Prussia, whose frontiers on the Russian and Austrian sides are quite denuded of troops, quite exposed and defenseless, will prove unable to keep up her present forces in France. She will at once lower her tone and become quite tractable.

Hence if France holds out, if she improves the armistice to repair her forces, if she understands at last that in order to carry on a revolutionary war, revolutionary measures and revolutionary energy are wanted, she may still be saved. Bismarck knows perfectly that he is in a fix. He hopes to get out of it by "bullying." He confides in the cooperation of all reactionary elements of France.

Yours,

OLD NICK

P.S. The master who now employs Dupont has received a letter from a house at Bordeaux which wants an agent at Manchester. Behind the back of his master—a most infamous and brutal parvenu—Dupont would like to ascertain whether *he* would get that agency. He therefore requests you to obtain informations about this point. The address of the house in question is: Labadie et Co. (Vins et esprits), rue des Terres de Bordes, Bordeaux.

What is Prudhomme doing? Has his health improved?

From letter to Wilhelm Liebknecht (in Leipzig)
LONDON, APRIL 6, 1871

Dear Liebknecht:

The news of your and Bebel's, as well as the Brunswickers', release from prison was received with great jubilation in the General Council here.

It appears that the Parisians are defeated. It is their own fault, but a fault which really arose from their too great *honnêteté* [decency]. The Central Committee and later the Commune gave the mischievous abortion Thiers time to concentrate hostile forces: First, because they stupidly did not want to start civil war—as if Thiers had not started it by his attempt at the forcible disarming of Paris, as if the National Assembly, which had been summoned only to decide the question of war or peace with the Prussians, had not immediately declared war on the republic! Second, in order to avoid the appearance of having usurped power, they lost precious moments (they should have advanced on Versailles immediately after the defeat of the reactionaries in Paris) by the election of the Commune, the organization of which, etc., cost yet more time.

You must not believe a word of all the stuff you may see in the papers about internal events in Paris. It is all lies and fraud. Never has the vileness of bourgeois journalism displayed itself more splendidly.

It is highly characteristic that the German Unity-Emperor, Unity-Empire, and Unity-Parliament in Berlin do not seem to exist at all to the outside world. Every breath of wind in Paris stirs more interest.

You must follow carefully the events in the Danubian principalities. If the revolution in France is temporarily defeated—the movement there can be suppressed only for a short time—a new war situation will open for Europe from the East, and Rumania will offer the orthodox Czar the first pretext for it. So keep an eye out there. . . .

Your

K.M.

Letter to Ludwig Kugelmann (*in Hanover*)
LONDON, APRIL 12, 1871

Dear Kugelmann:
Your "medical" advice has been effective in that I consulted my
Dr. Maddison and put myself into his charge for the time being.
Still, he declared that my lungs are in best shape and that my cough
is connected with bronchitis, etc. That will have an effect on the liver.
Yesterday we received the by no means reassuring news that
Lafargue (not Laura) is now in Paris.
If you look through the last chapter of my *Eighteenth Brumaire*
you will find that I discuss the next stage of the French revolution
as being, not, as hitherto, a transfer of the bureaucratic-military
machine from one hand to another, but as being its *destruction*,
which is the precondition of every real popular revolution on the
Continent. What elasticity, what historical initiative, what capacity for
sacrifice on the part of those Parisians! After six months of famine
and ruin, through internal treason more than through the external
enemy, they rise, in the face of Prussian bayonets, as if there were
no war between France and Germany and as if the enemy did not
stand before the gates of Paris! History shows no example of comparable grandeur! If they succumb, it is only because of their "good
nature." They should have immediately marched on Versailles, after
Vinoy and then the reactionary part of the National Guard had abandoned the field. The right moment was lost through scruples of
conscience. They did not want to *start a civil war*—as if that mischievous abortion Thiers had not already started a civil war with his
disarmament attempt before Paris! The second mistake: The Central
Committee gave up its power too soon, in order to make place for
the Commune.[1] Again out of too "honorable" a scrupulousness! However the case may be, the present rebellion of Paris—even if they
succumb to the wolves, swine, and common dogs of the old society
—is the most glorious act of our party since the Paris June [1848]
insurrection. Compare these heaven-stormers of Paris with the heaven-
slaves of the German-Prussian Holy Roman Empire and their posthumous masquerades, smelling of barracks, church, country bumpkins,
and above all philistinism.

---

1. On March 18, 1871, the Central Committee of the National Guard took over
power in Paris; ten days later it handed over its authority to the Council of the
Commune, elected on March 26.

"Liberty Guiding the People," detail from a painting by Eugène Delacroix commemorating the Paris revolt of July 28, 1830.

(Above) "The Firing Party" *(the executions by the French, Madrid, May 3, 1808), a painting by Goya. (Below)* "Tampoco"—"Not This," *from Goya's series of etchings,* The Disasters of War.

From Goya's Disasters of War. *(Above)* "Por una Navaja"—"*For a Knife.*"
(Below) "Qué Valor!"—"*What Courage!*"

(Above) On the barricades in Frankfurt, Germany, during the Revolution of 1848. *(Below)* The attack on the Royal Palace, in Paris, during the Revolution.

(Above) "Flight of the King," 1848, by Arnout and Adam. (Below) "The Judgment of Paris"—presidential candidates Louis Napoleon, Cavaignac and Lamartine, Thiers and Ledru-Rollin.

RÉPUBLIQUE FRANÇAISE.

LIBERTÉ, ÉGALITÉ, FRATERNITÉ.

AU NOM DU PEUPLE FRANÇAIS,

LE GOUVERNEMENT PROVISOIRE, convaincu que la grandeur d'âme est la suprême politique, et que chaque révolution opérée par le Peuple français doit au Monde la consécration d'une vérité philosophique de plus;

Considérant qu'il n'y a pas de plus sublime principe que l'inviolabilité de la vie humaine;

Considérant que, dans les mémorables journées où nous sommes, le Gouvernement provisoire a constaté avec orgueil que pas un cri de vengeance ou de mort n'est sorti de la bouche du Peuple;

DÉCLARE que, dans sa pensée, la peine de mort est abolie en matière politique, et qu'il présentera ce vœu à la ratification définitive de l'Assemblée nationale.

Le Gouvernement provisoire a une si ferme conviction de la vérité qu'il proclame au nom du Peuple français, que si les hommes coupables qui viennent de faire couler le sang de la France étaient dans les mains du Peuple, il y aurait à ses yeux un châtiment plus exemplaire à les dégrader qu'à les frapper.

> **DUPONT** (DE L'EURE),
> **LAMARTINE**,
> **GARNIER-PAGÈS**,
> **ARAGO**,
> **MARIE**,
> **LEDRU-ROLLIN**,
> **CRÉMIEUX**,
> **LOUIS BLANC**,
> **MARRAST**,
> **FLOCON**,
> **ALBERT, ouvrier.**

IMPRIMERIE NATIONALE. — 26 Février 1848.

An affiche—*placard, handbill—of February 28, 1848. The Provisional Government abolishes the death penalty for all political offenses.*

Citoyens
DE PARIS

L'ordre est donné partout de suspendre le feu.

Nous venons d'être chargés par le **Roi** de former un nouveau ministère.

La chambre va être dissoute. Un appel est fait au pays.

Le général Lamoricière est nommé commandant en chef de la garde nationale de Paris.

MM. ODILLON BARROT, THIERS, LAMORICIÈRE DUVERGIER DE HAURANNE sont nommés ministres.

Liberté, Ordre, Réforme.

ODILLON BARROT et A. THIERS.

Imprimerie Lange Levy et comp., rue du Croissant,

A handbill of February 24, 1848. The Thiers-Barrot Ministry demands a cease-fire and dissolves the National Assembly in the name of "Order."

"*Proudhon as Robert Macaire*," *a caricature by Bertail deriding Proudhon's social and economic ideas.*

A typical poster of the time of the Provisional Government of 1848.

French newspapers like these flourished after the Provisional Government's freedom of the press decree on March 4, 1848.

AU NOM DU PEUPLE FRANÇAIS.

LE PRÉSIDENT DE LA RÉPUBLIQUE

DÉCRÈTE:

Art. 1.

L'Assemblée nationale est dissoute.

Art. 2.

Le Suffrage universel est rétabli. La loi du 31 mai est abrogée.

Art. 3.

Le Peuple français est convoqué dans ses comices à partir du 14 décembre jusqu'au 21 décembre suivant.

Art. 4.

L'état de siége est décrété dans l'étendue de la I" division militaire.

Art. 5.

Le Conseil d'État est dissous.

Art. 6.

Le Ministre de l'intérieur est chargé de l'exécution du présent décret.

Fait au Palais de l'Élysée, le 2 décembre 1851.

LOUIS-NAPOLÉON BONAPARTE.

Le Ministre de l'Intérieur,

DE MORNY.

IMPRIMERIE NATIONALE. — Décembre 1851.

A handbill of December 2, 1851, Louis Napoleon's coup d'état. The Assembly is dissolved and a "state of siege" announced.

A café meeting of a "Red Republican" club in April, 1871, during the Paris Commune.

(Above) The Commune is proclaimed. (Below) Parisians seize guns from the National Guard.

*(Above) Communard prisoners executed by Versailles Government troops.
(Below) The execution of Generals Thomas and Lecomte.*

The suppression of the Paris Commune. (Above) Communards fight "à la mort." (Below) The last hours of the Commune.

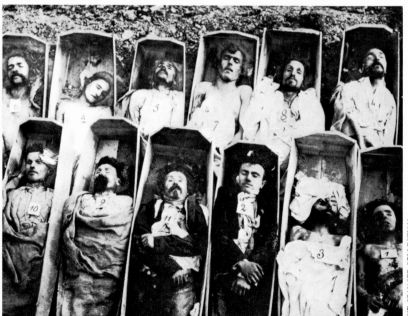

(Above) The Vendôme statue of Napoleon I pulled down by the Communards (Courbet is indicated by an X). (Below) Bodies of unidentified Communards.

Apropos. In the official publication regarding those subsidized directly by L. Bonaparte's treasury, there is the notation that Vogt received 40,000 francs in August, 1859! I have reported this fact to Liebknecht for further use.

You can send me the Haxthausen [publication], since recently I have received various brochures not only from Germany but also from Petersburg, undamaged.

Thank you for sending me the various newspapers (I ask for more, since I want to write something about Germany, the Reichstag, etc.).

Best regards for Frau Countess and little kitten.

Your

K.M.

Mrs. Karl Marx, letter to Wilhelm Liebknecht (in Leipzig)
LONDON, APRIL, 1871*

I cannot begin to tell you in what a state of agitation, fear, and despair we all find ourselves in our house. Since the June [1870] battle, we have not experienced anything like it. I fear very much that the communist movement, the first silver ray in the darkness, is lost and with it all our best and most loyal friends. Above all, the death of Gustave Flourens has shocked us most deeply. We were personal friends. You will recall that about a year ago there appeared in the *Marseillaise* some articles on the vile treatment of the Fenians. They attracted the greatest attention in France and England. Through these articles, which originated with us, we came in contact with Rochefort and Flourens, the latter of whom immediately became an ardent champion of O'Donovan Rossa. Flourens, now assassinated by one of the Bonapartist myrmidons who are now performing the barbaric service for the monster Thiers, was a noble soul through and through. Audacious to the point of rashness, knightly, humane, compassionate, gentle to the point of weakness (nothing human was alien to him), he had a richly developed mind, being himself a scholar and a representative of modern science; young, rich and endowed with fine, courteous manners, he had a warm and impulsive nature that made him turn toward the poor, the oppressed, the disinherited, not only the embattled and struggling in his own country—no, no, his great heart beat for every nation, every race, every tribe.

---

* Liebknecht had this letter printed in the *Volksstaat* of April 15, 1871.

Hence his adventurous campaigns in country after country, where there was something to fight and struggle for. Even his enemies could say nothing else about him except: "Bold like a warrior, learned like a lexicon." The bourgeoisie saw in him the personification of the red specter and they pursued him with furious rage. Hence the fanatical jubilation in Versailles, the smile of victory of Picard, as they bore away the tall, slender figure of the first victim.

Draft of a letter to Leo Frankel and Louis-Eugène Varlin (in Paris)
LONDON, MAY 13, 1871

Worthy Citizens Frankel and Varlin:
I have had meetings with the bearer.[1]
Would it not be useful to find a secure hiding place for the papers that compromise the Versailles riffraff? Such a measure of caution can never be harmful.

In a letter from Bordeaux I am informed that in the latest communal elections four members of the International were elected. The provinces are beginning to ferment. Unfortunately, their action is limited to localities and is "pacific."

I have sent several hundred letters in your behalf to every corner of the world where we have sections.[2] In any case, the working class has been for the Commune from the beginning.

Even the bourgeois newspapers of England have abated their savagery. I manage from time to time to smuggle favorable articles into them.

The Commune seems to me to lose too much time on trifles and personal wranglings. One sees that there are other influences there than those of the workers. All this would do no harm if you had time to make up for lost time.

It is altogether necessary to do quickly everything you can outside of Paris, in England and elsewhere. The Prussians, to be sure, are not going to deliver the forts to the Versailles Government, but after the final peace treaty (on May 26)[3] they will permit it to

---

1. Probably Eilau.
2. At the end of April, 1871, Frankel had written to Marx: "It would be most desirable for me if you would help me with your advice, as I am presently alone so to speak, but am also solely responsible for all labor reforms that I am to, and will, institute."
3. The preliminary peace treaty was concluded by Thiers in Versailles on February 26, and the final one in Frankfurt on May 10, 1871.

besiege Paris with their gendarmes. Since, as you know, Thiers & Co. conceded a big gratuity[4] in the treaty concluded by Pouyer-Quertier, they hesitated to accept the help of German bankers which Bismarck offered. In this instance the Germans lost the gratuity. Since a condition was the capture of Paris, the French begged Bismarck for a delay in the payment of the first installment until the siege of Paris. Bismarck accepted this condition. As Prussia itself is in urgent need of money, it will give the Versaillais all possible relief in order to hasten the siege of Paris. Thus be on guard!

Letter to Edward Spencer Beesly (in London)
LONDON, JUNE 12, 1871

Dear Sir:

Lafargue, his family, and my daughter are in the Pyrenees on the Spanish frontier, but on the French side. Since Lafargue was born in Cuba, he could obtain a Spanish passport. I wish he would definitely settle on the Spanish side, since he played a conspicuous role in Bordeaux.

Despite my admiration for your articles in the *Bee-Hive*[1]—you will excuse my remark that as a party man I take a completely inimical position toward Comteism and as a man of science I have but a scant opinion of him, but I consider you the only Comteist, in England as well as in France, who treats historical crises not as a sectarian but as a historian in the best sense of the term—I regret to find your name in that newspaper. The *Bee-Hive* pretends to be a labor paper, but is in reality an organ of renegades, sold to Sam. Morley & Co. During the recent Franco-Prussian War the General Council of the International was forced to break all relations with that sheet and to declare publicly that it is a sham labor paper. But the big London newspapers declined to print that statement, with the exception of the local London *Eastern Post*. Under these circumstances, your contribution to the *Bee-Hive* sacrifices the good cause even further.

A lady friend of mine is leaving for Paris in three or four days. I am giving her regular passports for some members of the Commune who are still in hiding in Paris. If you or your friends have any commissions for Paris, please write to me.

4. A loan of 300,000,000 francs.
1. Articles on the Paris Commune, which appeared March 25, April 1, 15, 22, May 20, 27, June 3, 10, 1871.

What consoles me is the nonsense which the *"petite presse"* [penny papers] publishes daily about my writings and my contacts with the Commune, and which is sent to me daily from Paris. It shows that the Versailles police badly need to acquire genuine documents. My contacts with the Commune were maintained through a German businessman who traveled between Paris and London in that year. Everything was arranged verbally, with two exceptions:

In reply to its inquiry, I sent a letter to the members of the Commune—through the same intermediary—on how it could trade certain securities on the London Stock Exchange.

Secondly, on May 11, ten days before the catastrophe, I sent through the same intermediary all the details of the secret agreement between Bismarck and Favre in Frankfurt.

I received the information from Bismarck's right hand—a man [Miquel] who once (from 1848 to 1853) belonged to the secret society [the Communist League] of which I was the leader. This man knows that I still have in my possession all the reports sent me from Germany. He depends on my discretion. Hence his efforts to convince me of his good intentions. He is the same man who, as I told you, transmitted to me the warning that Bismarck was determined to have me arrested if I should again visit Dr. Kugelmann in Hanover this year.[2]

If only the Commune had heeded my warning! I advised its members to fortify the northern heights, the Prussian side, of Montmartre, and they still had time to do it; I told them in advance that they would otherwise fall into a mousetrap; I denounced Pyat, Grousset, and Vésinier to them; I urged them to send immediately to London all the papers that compromised the members of the National Defense, in order to checkmate to a certain extent the savagery of the enemies of the Commune—to frustrate in part the plans of the Versaillais.

If the Versaillais had known those documents were available, they would not have published forged ones.

The "Address" of the International will not appear before Wednesday. I will then immediately send you a copy. Material for four to five sheets was printed in two sheets. Hence the many corrections, revisions, and typos. Hence also the delay.

Your faithful

KARL MARX

---

2. On April 15, 1871, Kugelmann informed Marx that Berlin was alerted to Marx's expected visit to Hanover.

Mrs. Karl Marx, letter to Peter Imandt (in Dundee)
LONDON, JUNE 13, 1871

My dear Mr. Imandt:

I have just received your note and hasten to tell you right away that Mohr[1] is "all right." These are all police lies which Stieber and the French scoundrels are now trumping up.[2] Today you will receive copies of the Address of the International. Perhaps you can get some of it into the press. The girls are with Laura for the past six weeks. First they were in Bordeaux. That, however, became too hot for Lafargue. They moved from there and are now close to the Spanish border; safe, we hope.

Your brother wrote yesterday a few lines about the arrest of Mohr; please inform him what you know. I have my hands full today.

You cannot imagine, dear Mr. Imandt, what grief and rage we have gone through in the past few weeks. It took more than twenty years to raise such gallant, able, heroic men, and now they are practically all gone. About some there is still hope; the best have been murdered, Varlin, Jaclard, Rigault, Tridon, etc., etc.; but above all, the true heroes who for eight days have fought without a leader in Villette, Belleville, and St. Antoine: Workingmen and workingwomen!! etc., etc. The vulgar ranters of the Félix Pyat type will probably get away. Others are still in hiding, but I fear the bloodhounds will smell them out yet.

Most cordial greetings from

Your
JENNY MARX

---

1. "The Moor," Marx's favorite family nickname.
2. European newspapers, among them London's *Pall Mall Gazette* of June 7, 1871, printed a story that Marx had been arrested in Holland. In a letter to the *Pall Mall Gazette*, June 9, 1871, Marx branded it as "one of the numerous sensational stories on the International which the Franco-Prussian police has been tirelessly fabricating in the past two months."

From letter to Engels (in London)
MANCHESTER, MAY 31, 1873

Dear Fred:

. . . The French catastrophe[1] pleased me insofar as it included the disgrace of Thiers and his toadies; displeased me because in reverse circumstances I should have hoped to see various individuals absent from London, in addition to the fact that from a personal and party point of view, I regard any violent catastrophe in France as untimely now.

Still, I am by no means convinced that the *événement* [event] will lead to a restoration. The Rurals surely took into consideration that there was something insurrectionary in Paris, Lyon, Marseilles, but particularly in Paris. In that case they could have had a go at it, arrested a portion of the radical left, etc., in short, created a situation which, *d'une manière ou d'une autre* [one way or another], would have to end with a restoration, and quickly. Bonaparte himself, in his attempt to carry out his *coup d'état*, that is, to achieve a result, had seen himself crippled on the first day by the mere passive resistance of the Parisians, and he knew very well that if this lasted six to eight more days, the *coup* failed, and irretrievably so. Hence the signal to begin the various assassinations on the boulevards, etc., without any provocation, to improvise a terror. Specifically, M. Morny, the real manager, later unembarrassedly admitted himself to be the author of this plan of operations.

For this the Rurals lacked pluck; but it would have been dubious too, even if they had had one instead of three pretenders. On the contrary, these fellows rather hoped that events would free them from the Buridan Dilemma.[2]

Now, on the other hand, when they find themselves in a purely parliamentary situation, a brawl is beginning directly in their own ranks. Everyone hopes to seize for himself as much of the neighboring fraction, that is, the left center, as possible, in order to blow up his rivals. But in regard to MacMahon, this philistine, in my

1. On May 24, 1873, the royalist majority of the French National Assembly forced the resignation of Louis-Adolphe Thiers and elected the monarchist Marshal MacMahon President of the Republic.

2. The French medieval logician Jean Buridan (or Buridanus) is said to have illustrated the "unfreedom" of the will by the dilemma of a hungry donkey standing exactly in the middle between two bundles of hay and, unable to decide which to eat, starving to death.

opinion, will never act on his own. There is still another circumstance that will hasten the decomposition of this composition. The only thing that holds them together is God, that is, Catholicism. The more vehement and "more honorable" men of the Right will absolutely demand a show of colors vis-à-vis the Pope and Spain, and it seems to me that entirely apart from domestic resistance, regard for Mr. Bismarck must prevent any action in that direction. But the Jesuit Fathers, who have in reality directed the whole maneuver of the Rurals up to now, and also the old hag, the wife of MacMahon, will not let themselves be put off with fair words. Under such circumstances a new *changement de décoration* could well take place in the National Assembly as rapidly as last time. It was, after all, only a shifting of nine votes that disabled the *homme nécessaire* [necessary man; Thiers], thereby, it may be remarked in passing, showing that, contrary to Hegel, necessity does not include its possibility....

Yours,

K.M.

GERMANY

Chronology:
Germany, 1848-78

Aside from Austria and its Empire, the German-speaking part of Europe at mid–nineteenth century consisted of countless sovereignties. There were six kingdoms—Baden, Bavaria, Hesse, Prussia, Saxony, and Württemberg; five grand duchies; thirteen duchies and principalities; three free cities; and hundreds of sovereign mini-mini-states. Many of them were loosely affiliated with the Germanic Confederation, which had been founded in 1815 to replace the ancient and obsolete Holy Roman Empire.

In the confused revolutionary struggles of 1848–49 two main currents crossed and clashed with each other: (1) internal political reform, including radical demands by workers, and (2) unification of all German states in a national government. The German problem was really the fundamental question: Who should unite what under which form of government—democratic or autocratic, republican or monarchical?

Prussia, the most powerful and militarily the most important of the German monarchies, played a leading role. It led in both the movement for unification and the suppression of radicalism. 1848 was the year of revolution all over Europe. There were outbreaks in Austria, Belgium, France, Hungary, and Poland, but they were particularly widespread in Germany.

1848

FEBRUARY	*At the news of the February Revolution in Paris, popular demonstrations occur in Berlin and other German cities suffering from unemployment and hunger due to a drought in 1847.*
FEBRUARY 27	*A revolution breaks out in Baden.*
MARCH 3	*5,000 workers demonstrate in Cologne, where Marx is living.*

GERMANY

MARCH 13   *Revolution in Vienna; demands include popular representation, freedom of the press, and political reform. Prince Clemens von Metternich, Chancellor for thirty-three years, flees to England.*

MARCH 15   *Barricades up in Berlin; soldiers attempting to clear the streets.*

MARCH 18   *A demonstration before the royal palace in Berlin demands: withdrawal of the military, an armed National Guard, freedom of the press, and convocation of a United Landtag (Diet).*

MARCH 19   *King Frederick William IV of Prussia grants the demands.*

MARCH 21   *The King issues a proclamation promising to merge Prussia with the rest of Germany, and parades through the streets wearing the revolutionary tricolor: black-red-gold.*

MARCH 26   *A Berlin mass meeting of 20,000 workers demands: (1) shorter working hours; (2) free public school education; (3) care of the sick; (4) universal male suffrage; (5) a ministry of labor to represent the interest of workers.*

MARCH 29   *The King appoints a bourgeois ministry, with the Cologne banker Ludolf Camphausen as Prime Minister and the industrialist David Justus Hansemann as Finance Minister.*

MARCH 31   *A national Vorparlament (Preliminary Parliament), meeting in Frankfurt, orders elections for a National Assembly.*

LATE MARCH   *Revolutionary movements among poor peasants and agricultural workers in Mecklenburg, Prussia, Saxony, and Thuringia demand higher wages, tax reduction, and land. In the cities more than thirty labor strikes take place between March and May.*

APRIL 13   *In Cologne, at the initiative of the Bund der Kommunisten (Communist League), a Workers' Association is organized, with Karl Marx as a member (and, in October, its temporary president).*

APRIL 25   *In Cologne a Democratic Society, of which Marx is a member, is organized to direct the revolutionary elements.*

MAY 17   *Kaiser Francis Joseph I flees from Vienna to Innsbruck.*

MAY 18   *The National Assembly meets at Frankfurt. Despite powerful labor unrest, there are no proletarian or working-class representatives, except Wilhelm Wolff, who does not become a member until May, 1849, when the Assembly is already dying.*

MAY 22   *The Prussian Constituent Assembly, consisting of 400 middle-class members, meets in Berlin, and continues its sessions through the summer.*

JUNE 1   *In Cologne the* Neue Rheinische Zeitung, *a radical-revolutionary newspaper under Marx's editorship, publishes its first issue; hounded by Prussian government censorship, it is finally suppressed on May 19, 1849.*

JUNE 14   *In Berlin workers storm the arsenal and seize weapons.*

JUNE 14-16   *A congress of democratic and labor associations, with 234 delegates representing 89 organizations, meets in Frankfurt.*

JUNE 25   *In Berlin, the King appoints a new Prime Minister, Rudolf von Auerswald, with Hansemann remaining as Finance Minister.*

JUNE 28   *The Frankfurt parliament suspends the Diet of the Germanic Confederation and appoints Archduke John of Austria Imperial Vice-Regent, but without military power or political authority.*

NOVEMBER 9   *King Frederick William IV exiles the Prussian Constituent Assembly from Berlin to Brandenburg.*

NOVEMBER 10   *A Prussian army under General Count Friedrich Heinrich von Wrangel enters Berlin, meeting no resistance from the city militia.*

NOVEMBER 12   *The King declares a state of siege in Berlin.*

DECEMBER 5   *The Brandenburg Ministry dissolves the Constituent Assembly and issues a constitution, satisfactory to the middle-class, providing for a future bicameral legislature—a* Herrenhaus (*House of Lords*) *and a* Landtag (*Diet*)—*and retaining the authority of the King.*

1849

MARCH 27   *The Frankfurt Assembly adopts a national constitution providing for a federal state under a hereditary "Emperor of the Germans," a bicameral legis-*

414   GERMANY

lature, and a Supreme Court for the whole realm. Rejected by the large states, it was never put into effect.

MARCH 28   *The Frankfurt Assembly elects Frederick William IV "Emperor of the Germans," but the Prussian "divine right" monarch finally rejects the offer (April 21).*

SPRING–   *A revolution in Hungary against Austria is sup-*
SUMMER   *pressed in August with the help of Czarist Russian troops.*

APRIL 21   *Most Germanic states withdraw their representatives from the Frankfurt parliament.*

MAY 2   *A Provisional Government based on the Reich Constitution is established in the Palatinate.*

MAY 3–8   *Insurrections in Dresden and Leipzig, led by workers, against the Saxon king's refusal to accept the Reich Constitution, are militarily suppressed.*

MAY 11   *A revolt breaks out in the Prussian fortress of Rastatt; the soldiers free their imprisoned comrades and force the officers to leave.*

MAY 13   *A mass demonstration in Baden, where the army goes over to the people, leads to the establishment of a Provisional Government based on the Reich Constitution.*

MAY 30   *In Frankfurt the remaining 130 representatives of the parliament vote to hold their sessions in Stuttgart.*

JUNE 12   *Prussian troops assault the revolutionary forces in Baden and the Palatinate. After several battles and skirmishes the revolutionists, supported by volunteers from the rest of Germany as well as France, Hungary, Poland, and Switzerland, including Frederick Engels (who was wounded), are finally defeated by July 12.*

The "rump parliament" of Frankfurt, in Stuttgart since June 6, is dispersed by soldiers.

JUNE 29   *By royal decree, all political associations and meetings in Prussia are put under police supervision.*

JULY 23   *Rastatt, the last center of revolutionary resistance, capitulates to the Prussian army.*

The German revolutions of 1848–49 were thus defeated everywhere. The attempt to unite Germany under a parliamentary system ended in failure. In the next two decades it was the Prussian monarchy and its powerful military system that took steps for unification. Radicalism was suppressed, and the labor movement became temporarily dormant in Germany.

1852

OCTOBER 4– *Eleven members of the Communist League, former*
NOVEMBER 12 *associates of Karl Marx (then living in London), are tried in Cologne. The police, as Marx later showed in* Enthüllungen über den Kommunisten Prozess zu Köln *(Revelations of the Cologne Communist Trial), use forged evidence. Three of the accused—journalist Heinrich Bürgers, tailor Peter Nothjung, and cigar maker Peter Gerhard Röser— are sentenced to six years in a fortress. Three— journalist Hermann Heinrich Becker, chemist Karl Wunibald Otto, and Wilhelm Joseph Reiff—receive five-year prison sentences. One, Friedrich Lessner, a tailor who later became a close associate of Marx in London, got off with one year.*

1860

JANUARY 1 *Publication in Hamburg of the first issue of* Nordstern, *a weekly under the editorship of a former communist, Karl von Bruhn; in 1863 the* Nordstern *became an organ of Ferdinand Lassalle's* Allgemeiner Deutscher Arbeiterverein (General German Labor Association).

1862

AUGUST *After a royal amnesty for political exiles, Wilhelm Liebknecht, a German revolutionary friend and follower of Marx in London, returns to Germany and becomes active as newspaper editor and labor organizer.*

SEPTEMBER 24 *Otto von Bismarck becomes Prussian Prime Minister.*

1863

MAY 23 *The* Allgemeiner Deutscher Arbeiterverein (*ADAV*), Germany's *first national workers' association, is founded in Leipzig under the leadership of Ferdinand Lassalle. By August it had 1,000 members.*

1864

MARCH 12 *Tried for high treason in Berlin, Lassalle attacks the liberal bourgeoisie, defends the Prussian Government as a "people's monarchy," and advocates an alliance between it and the workers against the middle class.*

MAY 21 *In Berlin, at the first anniversary of the founding of the ADAV, Liebknecht espouses Marx and attacks the growing Lassalle personality cult among workers.*

AUGUST 31 *Lassalle dies in Geneva after a duel over a love affair. The leadership of the ADAV, with around 4,600 members, more than half of them in the Rhineland, is taken over by Bernhard Becker.*

SEPTEMBER 28 *Marx helps to found the International Working Men's Association—the First International—in London.*

1865

JANUARY 4 Der Sozial-Demokrat, *published three times weekly in Berlin, becomes the organ of the ADAV. Marx contributes an article on the death of Proudhon.*

FEBRUARY 23 *Marx and Engels, objecting to the* Sozial-Demokrat's *Lassallean policies, inform the editors they will no longer contribute to the paper.*

JULY 2 *Liebknecht, expelled from Berlin, moves to Leipzig, where he and August Bebel become active in labor organizing.*

1866

JUNE 16 *Outbreak of the Austro-Prussian War for the domination of Germany.*

JULY 3 *The Prussians defeat the Austrians in the Battle of Sadowa (Königgrätz).*

AUGUST 16 *At Prussia's demand, sixteen North German states and the three free cities join a North German Confederation.*

AUGUST 23 *The Austro-Prussian War ends with the Treaty of Prague.*

1867

FEBRUARY 12   *August Bebel, candidate of the Saxon People's party, becomes the first revolutionary labor leader elected to the North German Diet.*

APRIL 16   *The North German Confederation, consisting of twenty-two middle and small states, adopts a Bismarck-prepared constitution providing for a bicameral legislature—a* Bundesrat *(Federal Council) and a* Reichstag *(Diet)—under the presidency of the King of Prussia, who controls its armed forces.*

JUNE–JULY 8   *The North German Confederation, under Bismarck's leadership, makes customs agreements with four of the big South German States: Baden, Bavaria, Hesse, and Württemberg.*

AUGUST 31   *Four Saxon People's party candidates—August Bebel, Ferdinand Götz, Wilhelm Liebknecht, and Reinhold Heinrich Schraps—are elected to the Diet.*

OCTOBER 17   *In the Diet Bebel and Liebknecht attack the Prussian military system and propose instead a three-year universal service.*

NOVEMBER 22   *At the general congress of ADAV in Berlin 20 delegates, representing 3,408 members, have as their agenda: (1) Prussia and the German question; (2) universal suffrage; (3) abolition of the usury laws; (4) woman labor; (5) food adulteration; (6) British factory laws; (7) an eight-hour workday. J. B. von Schweitzer is reelected president.*

1868

JANUARY 8   *Publication in Leipzig of the first issue of Liebknecht's* Demokratisches Wochenblatt *(Democratic Weekly); it becomes the organ of the Union of German Workers' Educational Associations and the People's party.*

APRIL 27– MAY 3   *Meeting of the first* Zollparlament *(Customs Parliament) in Berlin. This is a genuine all-German Assembly, although still limited to customs questions.*

AUGUST 22–26   *The general congress of the ADAV in Hamburg, with 36 delegates representing 7,274 members from 83 organizations, shows the rapid growth of German trade unionism. The congress discusses political free-*

*dom, Lassalle, the working day, the international
character of the labor movement, and the work of
Marx, whom von Schweitzer had invited as an
honorary guest (he did not accept).*

SEPTEMBER
5–7
*Under the leadership of Bebel, the congress of the
Union of German Labor Associations in Nuremberg,
115 delegates representing 13,000 members, votes,
69 to 46, to accept a revolutionary labor program
based on the statutes of the First International.*

SEPTEMBER 16
*The police close the headquarters of the ADAV in
Leipzig.*

OCTOBER 10
*With police approval, von Schweitzer moves ADAV
headquarters to Berlin.*

1869

MARCH 28–
APRIL
*At the ADAV congress in Elberfeld, Barmen, with
57 delegates representing 12,000 members, Bebel and
Liebknecht attack von Schweitzer's pro-Bismarck
policies, but the latter wins a vote of confidence.*

AUGUST 7–9
*At a historic congress 262 labor and trade union
delegates, representing some 10,000 members, meet
in Eisenach and, under the leadership of Bebel and
Liebnecht, found the* Sozialdemokratische Arbeiter
Partei *(SDAP)* (Social-Democratic Labor party),
Germany's first nation-wide socialist party.

1870

JANUARY 23–
24
*At a meeting in Augsburg, Bavarian members break
away from von Schweitzer's ADAV and form their
own German Social-Democratic Labor party.*

JUNE 4–7
*At the SDAP congress in Stuttgart, with 70 delegates
representing 13,000 members in 110 localities, it is
resolved that the socialist party will use its membership in parliament as a platform for the proletariat.*

JULY 19
*Napoleon III declares war on Prussia to prevent
German unification, and thereby makes it a war of
German national defense.
During the first days of the Franco-Prussian War
the SDAP, at meetings in Berlin, Breslau, Dresden,
etc., declares the solidarity of German workers with
French workers and condemns the war policies of
the dynasts.*

JULY 21   *In the Diet, Bebel and Liebknecht refuse to vote for a war loan, which is supported by the ADAV.*

SEPTEMBER 1–2   *The Germans, under the leadership of Prussian Count Helmuth von Moltke, decisively defeat the French in the Battle of Sedan.*

SEPTEMBER 5   *The Brunswick committee of the SDAP issues a manifesto inspired by Marx and Engels calling for immediate peace with the French Republic.*

SEPTEMBER 9   *At the order of the Prussian Governor-General of North Germany, the SDAP Brunswick committee is imprisoned in the Boyen fortress in East Prussia, where they remain until March 30, 1871.*

SEPTEMBER 19   *Two German armies besiege Paris.*

NOVEMBER 26–28   *At a tumultuous meeting of the Diet, Bebel and Liebknecht again refuse to vote for war credits, attack the Prussian plans of conquest, and announce their solidarity with the French people.*

EARLY DE-CEMBER   *SDAP branches in Augsburg, Fürth, Munich, and Nuremberg proclaim their solidarity with Bebel and Liebknecht.*

DECEMBER 17   *The editors of the Leipzig Social-Democratic weekly, Der Volksstaat—Bebel, Adolf Hepner, and Liebknecht—are arrested for "preparation for high treason" and kept in prison until March 28, 1871.*

1871

JANUARY 18   *In the Hall of Mirrors at Versailles, the triumphant Germans, led by Bismarck, proclaim Prussian King William I Emperor of Germany.*

FEBRUARY 26   *Conclusion of the preliminary peace treaty between the German Empire and France, the latter to cede Alsace and most of Lorraine and to pay five billion francs indemnity.*

MARCH 3   *In elections to the Reichstag taking place, in the words of Bebel, amidst "the pealing of bells and the thundering of cannon," the SDAP wins only two deputies out of 317.*

APRIL 14   *The new Reichstag adopts a remodeled constitution to fit the new empire, twenty-five formerly independent states plus Alsace-Lorraine, under the domination of Prussia.*

MAY 10　　　The *final peace treaty with France is concluded in Frankfurt.*

MAY 18–25　At the *ADAV congress in Berlin, Wilhelm Hasenclever, another Lassallean, replaces von Schweitzer in the presidency.*

1872

MARCH 11–26　Bebel, *Hepner, and Liebknecht tried for high treason in Leipzig. Hepner is acquitted, Bebel and Liebknecht sentenced to two years in a fortress. Bebel was in Schloss Hubertusburg from July 8, 1872, to April, 1874, and Liebknecht from mid-June, 1872, to April 15, 1874.*

JULY 6　　　The *Leipzig district court revokes Bebel's seat in the Reichstag and sentences him to an additional nine months' imprisonment for* lèse majesté.

1873

JANUARY 20　In *a by-election in Leipzig the imprisoned Bebel is reelected to the Reichstag with more votes than he received in 1871.*

1874

JANUARY 10　In *the Reichstag elections the SDAP wins 6 out of 361 seats.*

JUNE 25　　A *court order temporarily suspends the ADAV in Berlin.*

1875

MAY 22–27　At *a congress in Gotha, where 56 SDAP delegates join 73 ADAV delegates, the two separate labor parties, both threatened by Bismarck's policies, unite to form the Socialist Labor party. Marx sent programmatic suggestions to the Gotha Congress, but this newly united socialist party adopted an essentially Lassallean policy.*

1876

OCTOBER 1　Publication *of the first issue of* Vorwärts, *central organ of Germany's Socialist Labor party, in Leip-*

zig, three times weekly, under the editorship (until
1878) of Liebknecht and Hasenclever.

1877

JANUARY 10   In the Reichstag elections the Socialist Labor party
receives more than 10 percent of the vote and wins
12 deputies out of 345.

JUNE 12   Bebel is sentenced to nine months' (later reduced to
six) imprisonment for insult to Bismarck.

1878

MAY 11   An unemployed tinsmith, Emil Max Hödel, tries to
assassinate the Emperor.

MAY 20   Bismarck introduces in the Reichstag a law for the
suppression of socialist meetings, clubs, and publications.

MAY 24   The Reichstag, by a vote of 251 to 57, defeats the
Bismarck law.

JUNE 2   Another attempt on the life of William I is made
by a deranged radical, Dr. Karl Eduard Nobiling;
the Emperor is gravely wounded.

JUNE 11   Bismarck has the Bundesrat dissolve the Reichstag
and call for new elections.

JULY 30   In the new Reichstag elections, the Socialist Labor
party loses both votes and seats. Its vote is reduced
to 437,158 (from 493,447 in 1877) and its seats from
12 (in 1877) to 9.

OCTOBER 19   The Reichstag, by a vote of 221 to 149, passes a
"Law Against the Dangerous Efforts of the Social-
Democracy," outlawing publications, meetings,
money collections, etc., by radicals aiming to "overthrow the existing order of state or society."

For the next dozen years, socialism in Germany was driven under-
ground, although socialist deputies were permitted in the Reichstag.
In subsequent elections to the Reichstag, the Socialist Labor party,
indeed, steadily increased its vote: 1884, 549,990 votes, 24 deputies;
1887, 763,128 votes, 11 deputies; 1890, 1,427,298 votes, 35 deputies;
1893, 1,786,738 votes, 44 deputies.
In the Reichstag elections of January 12, 1912, on the eve of
World War I, Germany's Social Democratic party—successor to the
Socialist Labor party—polled 4,250,400 votes, 31 percent of the total,
winning 110 deputies out of 345.

A Radical German Revolution*

A *radical* German revolution, however, is confronted with a major difficulty.

For revolutions require a *passive* element, a *material* basis. Theory is actualized in a people only insofar as it actualizes their needs. But will the enormous discrepancy between the demands of German thought and the answers of German reality correspond to a similar discrepancy between civil society and the state and within civil society itself? Will theoretical needs be directly practical needs? It does not suffice that thought should press for actualization; reality must itself press toward thought.

But Germany has not risen to the intermediate states of political emancipation at the same time as modern nations. It has not yet reached in practice even the stages it has surmounted in theory. How could it clear with a *salto mortale* [mortal leap] not only its own limitations but at the same time those of modern nations—limitations which it must actually attain and experience as an emancipation from its own actual limitations? A radical revolution can only be a revolution of radical needs, whose preconditions and birthplaces seem to be lacking.

But though Germany followed the development of modern nations only through the abstract activity of thought, without taking an active part in the real struggles of that development, it did, nevertheless, share the *sufferings* of that development even without sharing its enjoyment or partial satisfaction. Abstract activity on one side cor-

---

* From "Toward the Critique of Hegel's Philosophy of Law: Introduction," written at the end of 1843 and early 1844; published in *Deutsch-Französische Jahrbücher*, 1844.

[422]

responds to abstract suffering on the other. One fine day Germany will find itself at the level of European decay before ever having reached the level of European emancipation. One will then be able to compare it to a fetishist wasting away from the diseases of Christianity.

If next we consider *German governments*, we find that, owing to the conditions of the time, the position of Germany, the standpoint of German education, and finally, driven by their own fortunate instinct, these governments combine the civilized deficiencies of the modern political order, whose advantages we [Germans] do not possess, with the barbaric deficiencies of the *ancien régime*, which we enjoy in full measure; consequently Germany must participate more and more, if not in the sense at least in the non-sense, in the political forms transcending its own status quo.

Is there, for example, another country in the world which shares so naïvely all the illusions of a constitutional system without sharing its realities, as does so-called constitutional Germany? And was it not, necessarily, a German government's brainstorm to combine the tortures of censorship with the tortures of the French September laws [1835] which presuppose freedom of the press? Just as the gods of all nations were found in the Roman pantheon, so one can find the sins of all forms of state in the Holy Roman Empire of the German nation. That this eclecticism will reach an unprecedented height is especially guaranteed by the politico-aesthetic gourmanderie of a German king [Frederick William IV], who plans to play all the roles of kingship—feudal as well as bureaucratic, absolute as well as constitutional, autocratic as well as democratic—if not in the person of the people at least in his own person, if not for the people, at least for himself. Germany, as a political system lacking the political reality of the present, will not be able to shed the specific German limitations without shedding the general limitations of the political present.

It is not radical revolution, or universal human emancipation, that is a utopian dream for Germany, but rather the partial, the *merely* political revolution that would leave the pillars of the house standing. What is the basis of a partial, a merely political revolution? It is part of civil society emancipating itself and attaining universal supremacy; it is a particular class undertaking a general emancipation of society by virtue of its special situation. This class emancipates the whole of society, but only on condition that the whole of society finds itself in the same situation as this class; for example, that it has or can easily acquire money and education.

No class of civil society can play this role without arousing an impulse of enthusiasm in itself and in the masses, an impulse in which it fraternizes and merges with society in general, identifies itself with it, and is felt and recognized as its general representative—an impulse in which its claims and rights are truly the rights and claims of society itself, in which it is actually the social head and the social heart. Only in the name of general rights of society can a particular class claim general authority. Revolutionary energy and intellectual self-confidence are not by themselves sufficient for the seizure of this emancipatory position and thereby of the political control of all spheres of society in the interest of its own sphere. For a *popular revolution* and the *emancipation of a particular class* of civil society to coincide, for *one* class to stand for the whole society, all the defects of society must conversely be concentrated in another class; a particular class must be the class of general compulsion and must incorporate the general limitation. In addition, a particular social sphere must stand for the notorious crime of the whole society, so that the emancipation of this sphere appears as general self-emancipation. For one class to be the class of emancipation par excellence, conversely another one must be the obvious class of oppression. The negative-general significance of the French nobility and the French clergy determined the positive-general significance of the adjoining and opposing bourgeois class.

But in Germany every class lacks not only the consistency, penetration, courage, and ruthlessness which could stamp it as the negative representation of society, but also that breadth of soul which identifies itself, if only momentarily, with the soul of the people—lacks that genius for inspiring material force toward political power, that revolutionary audacity which hurls at its opponent the defiant words: *I am nothing, and I should be everything.* The main feature of German morality and honor, in classes as well as individuals, is rather that modest egoism which asserts its narrowness and lets others do the same against it. The relationship of different spheres of German society is therefore not dramatic but epic. Each of them begins to be aware of itself and place itself beside the others, not as soon as it is oppressed but as soon as circumstances, without its initiative, create a social underpinning on which it can exert pressure in turn. Even the moral self-esteem of the German middle class rests only on its awareness of being the general representative of the philistine mediocrity of all the other classes. Hence not only do German kings ascend their throne *mal à propos,* but every section of civil society goes through a defeat before it celebrates victory, develops its own obstacles before it overcomes those facing it, asserts its narrow-minded nature before it can assert its generous one, so that even the opportunity of playing a great role is always gone before it has actually existed and each class is involved in a struggle with the class beneath it as soon as it begins a struggle with the class above it. Thus the princely domain struggles against the monarchy, the bureaucrat against the aristocracy, and the bourgeoisie against them all, while the proletariat is already beginning to find itself in a struggle against the bourgeois. The middle class hardly dares to conceive, from its own standpoint, the idea of emancipation, and the development of social conditions, as well as the progress of political theory, show that standpoint to be already antiquated or at least problematical.

In France it is enough that one be something in order to be everything. In Germany no one can be anything unless he renounces everything. In France partial emancipation is the basis of universal emancipation. In Germany universal emancipation is the *sine qua non* of any partial emancipation. In France it is the reality, in Germany the impossibility, of gradual emancipation which must give birth to complete freedom. In France every class in the nation is politically idealistic and experiences itself first of all not as a particular class but as a representative of the social needs of society in general. Hence the role of emancipator passes successively and dramatically to different classes of people until it finally reaches the class which actualizes social freedom, no longer assuming certain conditions which are external to man and yet are created by human society, but rather organizing all the conditions of human existence on the hypothesis of social freedom. By contrast, in Germany, where practical life is as mindless as intellectual life is impractical, no class of civil society has any need or capacity for general emancipation until it is forced to it by its immediate condition, by the material necessity, by its *very chains*.

Where, then, is the positive possibility of German emancipation?

Answer: In the formation of a class with *radical chains*, a class in civil society that is not a class of civil society, a class which is the dissolution of all classes, a sphere of society which has a universal character because of its universal suffering and which claims no particular right because no particular wrong but simply general wrong is perpetrated on it, which can no longer invoke a *historical* but only a *human* title, which does not one-sidedly oppose the consequences but totally opposes the premises of the German political system—a sphere, finally, which cannot emancipate itself without emancipating itself from all the other spheres of society and thereby emancipating all the other spheres of society; a sphere, in short, that is the *complete loss* of humanity and can redeem itself only through the *complete redemption of society*. This dissolution of society as a particular class is the *proletariat*.

The proletariat began to appear in Germany only as a result of the emerging industrial movement; for it is not naturally induced poverty but only artificially produced poverty, not the masses mechanically oppressed by the weight of society but the masses arising from the acute disintegration of society—preferably of the middle class—which produces the proletariat, although, needless to say, naturally induced poverty and Christian-Germanic serfdom gradually also enter its ranks.

When it heralds the *dissolution of the existing world order*, the proletariat merely expresses the secret of its own existence, because it *is* the factual dissolution of this world order. When the proletariat demands the *negation of private property*, it merely raises to the principle of society that which society has raised to its principle, what the proletariat already embodies in *itself* as the negative result of society without any assistance from it. The proletarian then finds himself in the same relation to the emerging world as the German King finds himself in relation to the existing world when the King calls the people *his* people or a horse *his* horse. In declaring the people to be his private property, he merely proclaims that the private property owner is king.

As philosophy finds its material weapons in the proletariat, so the proletariat finds in philosophy its intellectual weapons, and once the lightning of thought has struck deeply in this unsophisticated soil of the people, the emancipation of the Germans to become men will be realized.

Let us summarize the result:

The only possible practical emancipation of Germany is emancipation based on the theory proclaiming man as the highest essence of humanity. In Germany, emancipation from the Middle Ages is possible only with emancipation at the same time from the partial victories over the Middle Ages. In Germany *no* sort of bondage can be broken without *every* sort of bondage being broken. Thorough-minded Germany cannot make a revolution without making a fundamental revolution. The *emancipation of the German is the emancipation of mankind.* The *head* of this emancipation is philosophy, its *heart* is the *proletariat.* Philosophy cannot actualize itself without the elevation of the proletariat; the proletariat cannot raise itself without the actualization of philosophy.

When all the inner conditions are fulfilled, the day of German resurrection will be heralded by the crowing of the Gallic rooster.

Demands of the Communist Party in Germany*

"Proletarians of all countries, unite!"

1. All of Germany is declared to be a united, indivisible republic.

2. Every German aged twenty-one is a voter and eligible for office, provided that he has no criminal record.

3. The representatives of the people are to be paid, so that workers too may sit in the parliament of the German nation.

4. General arming of the people. In the future, armies are to be worker armies, so that they will not be mere consumers but will produce more than their cost of maintenance.

This is, moreover, a means of organizing labor.

5. The administration of justice is to be free.

6. All feudal dues, all tributes, all villeinage, tithes, etc., which have hitherto weighed on the peasantry, are to be abolished without any compensation.

7. Princely and other feudal estates, all mines, quarries, etc., are to be transformed into national property. On these estates, large-scale agriculture is to be pursued with the most modern techniques of science for the benefit of the community.

8. Mortgages on peasant holdings are to be declared state property. Interest on those mortgages is to be paid to the state by the peasants.

9. In districts with a developed leasehold system, ground rents or tenant dues are to be paid to the state as taxes.

All the measures mentioned under 6, 7, 8, and 9 are designed to lessen the public and other burdens of the peasants and small tenants,

---

* Written in Paris by Marx and Engels March 21–29, 1848, for the Communist League. Published as a handbill in Paris on March 30, and in Cologne on September 10, 1848.

[427]

428

without reducing the means necessary to defray state costs and without endangering production.

The actual landowner, who is neither a peasant nor a tenant, has no share in production. His consumption, therefore, is a mere abuse.

10. In place of all private bankers, there is to be one state bank, whose paper currency is to be legal tender.

This measure makes it possible to regulate the credit system in the interest of the *whole* nation and thereby undermines the rule of the big money men. While it gradually replaces gold and silver with paper money, it cheapens the indispensable instrument of bourgeois commerce—the universal means of exchange—and permits gold and silver to be issued for other purposes. This measure is necessary in the end to connect the interests of the conservative bourgeois to the Revolution.

11. All means of transportation—railroads, canals, steamers, roads, posts, etc.—are to be taken over by the state. They are to be transformed into state property and put at the disposal of the propertyless classes free of charge.

12. In the salaries of the civil servants, the only differential is to be that those with a family, that is, those who have greater needs, are to receive higher pay than the others.

13. Complete separation of church and state. The clergy of all confessions are to be paid only by their voluntary communities.

14. Limitation on the right of inheritance.

15. Establishment of steep progressive taxation and elimination of consumer taxes.

16. Establishment of national workshops. The state guarantees all workers their livelihood and takes care of those unable to work.

17. Universal popular education, free of charge.

It is to the interest of the German proletariat, the small bourgeoisie, and the peasantry to work with all their energies to put through the above measures. For only through their realization can the millions, who have hitherto been exploited and oppressed in Germany by a small number who will try to continue to keep them under oppression, attain their rights and achieve the power which properly belongs to them as the producers of all wealth.

The Committee:

KARL MARX   KARL SCHAPPER   H. BAUER

F. ENGELS   J. MOLL   W. WOLFF

Hüser*

Cologne, May 31

In MAINZ, Herr Hüser, with the help of old fortress regulations and antediluvian federal laws, has discovered a new method of making Prussians and other Germans even more slaves than they were before May 22, 1815.[1] We advise Herr Hüser to take out a patent on his new invention, which would in any case be very lucrative. According to this method, one sends out two or more drunken soldiers, who naturally start a fight with citizens. The public authority steps in and arrests the soldiers; this becomes sufficient for the commander of any fortress to declare the city to be in a state of siege, so that all arms can be confiscated and the inhabitants exposed to the mercy of the brutal soldiery. This plan is the more profitable in that Germany has more fortresses aimed against the interior than the exterior; it is particularly lucrative because any local commandant who is paid by the people—a Hüser, a Roth von Schreckenstein, or any similar feudal name—may dare more than a king or a kaiser, since he can suppress freedom of the press, since he can, for example, forbid the people of Mainz, who are not Prussians, to express their antipathies for the King of Prussia and the Prussian political system.

Herr Hüser's project is only a part of reactionary Berlin's great plan, which strives to disarm all civil guards, especially on the Rhine, as soon as possible, to destroy gradually the whole arming of the people now developing, and to deliver us defenselessly into the hands of an army consisting mostly of foreign elements either easily assembled or already prepared.

This is what has actually happened in Aachen, in Trier, in Mannheim, in Mainz, and it can happen elsewhere.

---

* Published June 1, 1848, this was Marx's first article in the *Neue Rheinische Zeitung*.

1. On May 22, 1815, the Prussian King issued a decree for the establishment of provisional popular assemblies, with a promise for a constitution.

A United German State*

A CONSTITUENT National Assembly must above all be an *active*, a revolutionary-active Assembly. The Assembly in Frankfurt engages in schoolboy parliamentary exercises and leaves action to the governments. Granted that this learned council, after the most mature deliberations, will succeed in concocting the best agenda and the best constitution, but of what use are the best agenda and the best constitution when the governments in the meantime use bayonets as their agenda?

The German National Assembly, apart from the fact that it is the product of an indirect election, suffers from a peculiarly Germanic illness. It resides in Frankfurt am Main, and Frankfurt am Main is an ideal central point in regard to ideals of the past, that is, ideals of the imaginary unity of Germany. Nor is Frankfurt am Main a metropolis with a big revolutionary population that would stand behind the National Assembly, partly protecting and partly prodding. For the first time in world history a constituent assembly of a great nation sits in a small town. The German development up to now has brought this about. With French and English national assemblies taking place on fiery ground—Paris and London—the German National Assembly had to consider itself fortunate to find a *neutral* ground, a neutral ground where it could think about the best constitution and the best agenda in comfortable peace of mind.

Nevertheless, Germany's present condition offered an opportunity to overcome the country's unfortunate material situation. The Assembly had only to confront dictatorially the encroachments of obsolete

---

* From Marx and Engels, "The Program of the Radical-Democratic Party and the Left at Frankfurt," in *Neue Rheinische Zeitung*, June 7, 1848.

governments everywhere and it would have won for itself a power in public opinion on which all the bayonets and rifle butts would have been splintered. Instead of that, it left Mainz, before its very eyes, to the despotism of the soldiery and left other Germans to the chicanery of Frankfurt philistines. The Assembly simply bores the German nation, instead of exciting it or being excited by it. In its eyes, to be sure, there is a *public*, which temporarily observes with good-natured humor the burlesque movements of the Holy Roman Empire revived by the German Parliamentary ghost, but in its eyes there exists no *nation* in whose life it could rediscover its own life. Far from being the central organ of the revolutionary movement, the Assembly has hitherto not been even its echo.

Should the National Assembly produce from its womb a central authority, in view of its present composition and after it has let favorable moments pass unused, little comfort could be expected from such a provisional government. If it creates no central authority, then it has signed its own abdication and will be blown away in all directions by the slightest revolutionary breeze.

The program of the left, as also of the radicals, has the merit of having grasped this necessity. Both programs also call out, with Heine:

> *Bedenk' ich die Sache ganz genau,*
> *So brauchen wir gar keinen Kaiser.*[1]

And the difficulty as to *"who* is to be the Kaiser"—the many good arguments in favor of an elective Kaiser and the equally good arguments in favor of a hereditary one—will force the conservative majority of the Assembly to cut the Gordian knot and elect *no Kaiser at all.*

It is a mystery how the so-called Radical-Democratic party could have proclaimed as Germany's final constitution a federation composed of constitutional monarchies, little principalities, and small republics, all these heterogeneous elements making up a federal state with a republican government at the top.

There is no doubt that, moreover, Germany's central government as created by the National Assembly must arise *alongside* the still actually existing governments. But with the existence of the national government, a struggle against the individual governments must begin, and in such a struggle either the national government and German unity or the individual governments with their constitutional princes and petty little republics must perish.

---

1. From Heine's *"Deutschland. Ein Wintermärchen."* Freely translated: "It would be wiser/To have no kaiser."

GERMANY

We do not propose the utopian demand that a *unitary*, *indivisible German republic* be proclaimed *a priori*, but we ask the so-called Radical-Democratic party not to confuse the starting point of the struggle and the revolutionary movement with their end goal. German unity, like a German constitution, can emerge only as a result of a movement wherein the inner conflicts, as well as the problem of war with the East, will be driven to resolutions. The definitive constitutionalization cannot be decreed; it merges with the development we have to go through. It is therefore not a question either of the actualization of this or that opinion, of this or that political idea; it is a question of insight into the course of development. The National Assembly has only to take the next immediate practical step.

Nothing could be more confusing than the notion of the editor of the democratic Manifesto—even though he assures us that "every man is glad to get rid of his confusion"—to take the North American federal union as the model for a German constitution!

Apart from the fact that they are homogeneous, the United States of North America stretch over an area as big as civilized Europe. Their analogy could be found only in a European federation. And for Germany to federate with other countries, it must first of all become *a* country. In Germany, the struggle between centralization and federalization is the struggle between modern culture and feudalism. Germany had declined into a bourgeois version of feudalism at the moment when the great European monarchies emerged, but it was also excluded from the world market at the moment when that market opened up Western Europe for itself. Germany became impoverished while those monarchies grew rich. Germany became countrified while they became metropolitan. Even if Russia were not knocking on Germany's gates, national economic conditions alone should force the country into the most rigid centralization. Viewed even from the bourgeois standpoint alone, the consistent unity of Germany is the first condition for rescuing it from the existing misery and for creating national wealth. And, moreover, how can one expect to solve modern social problems in a territory splintered into 39 little states?

For the rest, the editor of the democratic program seems to have no need to go into the question of the underlying material economic conditions. In his motivation, he adheres to the concept of federation. Federation is *a union of the free and equal*. Hence Germany must become a *federal state*. Cannot the German states federate into *a* great state without trespassing on the concept of a union of the free and equal?

The Fall of the Camphausen Ministry*

Cologne, June 22

No matter how beautifully the sun may shine,
Sooner or later it must decline.[1]

And the sun that was dyed in the hot Polish blood of March 30[2] had also declined.

The Camphausen Ministry has shed the liberal-bourgeois garment of the counterrevolution. The counterrevolution feels itself strong enough to throw off the inconvenient mask.

A popular but untenable left-center ministry may possibly follow the Ministry of March 30 for a few days. Its real successor is the Ministry of the Prince of Prussia. Camphausen has the honor of having provided him, the natural chief of the absolutist-feudal party, as a successor to it and to himself.

Why pamper the bourgeois guardians much longer?

Do the Russians not stand on the eastern frontier and the Prussian troops on the western? Are the Poles not won over by shrapnel and *lapis infernalis* to Russian propaganda?

Have not measures been arranged to repeat the bombardment of Prague in practically all Rhineland cities?

Did the army not have all the time needed, during the Danish and Polish wars and in small conflicts between the military and the people, to train itself into a brutal soldiery?

Is the bourgeoisie not tired of revolution? And does there not

---

* Published in *Neue Rheinische Zeitung*, June 23, 1848.
  1. "*Scheint die Sonne noch so schön,/Einmal muss sie untergehn,*" from Ferdinand Raimund, *Das Mädchen aus der Feenwelt oder der Bauer als Millionär* [*The Girl from the Fairy World or the Peasant as Millionaire*], Act II, Scene 6.
  2. It was under the Camphausen Ministry, which began on March 30, 1848, that the Polish uprising in Posen was crushed.

GERMANY

rise in the ocean the rock on which the counterrevolution will build its church—*England?*

The Camphausen Ministry seeks to snatch a few more pennies' worth of popularity, to arouse public sympathy by the assurance that it left the political stage as a dupe. And certainly it is a trickster tricked. In the service of the big bourgeoisie, it had to cheat the democratic revolution of its fruits; in the struggle with the democracy, it had to ally with the aristocratic party and to become the tool of its lust for counterrevolution. The later is now sufficiently strengthened to be able to throw its protector overboard. *Herr Camphausen sowed reaction in the bourgeois sense, he will reap it in the aristocratic and absolutist sense.* This was the man's good intention, this was his bad luck. A penny's worth of popularity for the disappointed man.

A penny's worth of popularity!

No matter how beautifully the sun may shine,
Sooner or later it must decline!

But in the *East* it rises again.

Prussia's Feudal Reforms*

Cologne, June 24

IN THE constituent session of the twentieth of this month, that fateful session in which Camphausen's sun set and the ministerial crisis set in, Herr Patow submitted a memorandum on the main principles that were to regulate the elimination of feudalism on the land.

When one reads this memorandum, one cannot understand how a peasant war has not broken out long ago in the Old Prussian provinces. What a confused mass of performances, tributes, and deliverings; what a jumble of medieval names, one crazy one after another! Loan suzerainty, decease, capitation, Elector's metes, blood tithe, patronage money, Walpurgis rent, bees' rent, wax lease, meadow right, tithes. *Laudemiums*,[1] additional rentals—all this has remained until now in the "best-administered state in the world," and would have continued unto eternity if the French had not made their revolution in February!

Yes, most of these exactions, and especially the most oppressive among them, would have continued unto eternity if Herr Patow had had his way. It was precisely Herr Patow who was assigned this department, to spare the bumpkin-Junkers in the Marches, in Pomerania, in Silesia as much as possible, and to cheat the peasants of the fruits of the Revolution as much as possible!

The Berlin Revolution made all these feudal relations forever impossible. The peasants, naturally, immediately did away with them in practice. There was nothing left for the government to do

---

* "Patow's Commutation Memorandum," in *Neue Rheinische Zeitung*, June 25, 1848.
1. In Roman law, 2 percent of the price paid the owner for his consent to sell.

[435]

but to put in legal form the *actually existing abolition of all feudal burdens by the will of the people*.

But before the nobility decided on its Fourth of August,[2] its castles were in flames. The government, here represented by an aristocrat, declared for the aristocracy. It put a memorandum before the Assembly demanding that it betray the peasant revolution, which had broken out all over Germany in March, to the aristocracy. The government is responsible for the consequences that the application of Patow's principles would have on the land.

For Herr Patow wants the peasants to pay compensation for all the feudal exactions abolished, even the *Laudemiums*. The only exactions to be abolished without compensation are those that flow from serfdom, from the old tax system and the patrimonial jurisdiction, or those that are worthless to the feudal lord (how generous!); that is, in general the exactions that are the least part of the whole feudal burden.

On the other hand, all feudal commutations arrived at by agreement or judicial decision are final. That is: the peasants who settled their exactions under the reactionary and proaristocratic laws enacted since 1816 and particularly since 1840, and have been swindled of their property by bribed officials in favor of feudal lords, receive no compensation.

Rent banks are to be established, to throw sand into the eyes of the peasants.

If Herr Patow had his way, the feudal exactions would be eliminated under his law as little as they were under the old law of 1807.

The correct title for Herr Patow's essay is: Memorandum on the Maintenance of Feudal Exactions Forever by Means of Their Commutation.

The government is provoking a peasant war. Perhaps Russia will not "shy away" from a "momentary loss of Silesia."

---

2. On the night of August 4, 1789, the French National Assembly, under growing peasant pressure, formally abolished a whole series of feudal burdens on the peasantry, which the latter had already done away with in reality.

Conflict with the Monarchy*

THE CRISIS in Berlin has advanced one more step: *The conflict with the monarchy*, which until yesterday could still be considered avoidable, has *now really begun*. . . .

Every provisional government after a revolution necessitates a dictatorship, and an energetic dictatorship at that. From the very beginning we have reproached Camphausen for not acting dictatorially and for not immediately destroying and removing the remnants of the old institutions. While Herr Camphausen rocked himself in the cradle of constitutional dreams, the defeated party strengthened its position in the bureaucracy and in the army, and indeed, here and there ventured into open battle. The Assembly, convened to arrange a constitution, made its appearance by the side of the monarchy as its equal. Two equal powers in one provisional government! Herr Camphausen's attempt to share authority "in order to save freedom" was precisely what led to collisions in the provisional government. Behind the monarchy lurked the counter-revolutionary camarilla of the aristocracy, the military, and the bureaucracy. Behind the majority of the Assembly stood the bourgeoisie. The ministry tried to mediate. Too weak to represent effectively the interests of the bourgeoisie and the peasantry, and to destroy the power of the nobility, the bureaucracy, and the army leaders in one blow, too inept to avoid hurting the financial arrangements of the bourgeoisie everywhere—its efforts came to nothing more than making itself unpopular with all parties and bringing about the very collision it wished to avoid.

* From "The Crisis and the Counterrevolution," in *Neue Rheinische Zeitung*, September 14, 1848.

In every nonconstitutional state, what is decisive is not this or that principle, but only the *salut public*, the public weal. The ministry could have avoided the collision between the Assembly and the crown only if it alone had claimed to represent the principle of the public welfare, even if it had to do so at the risk of *itself* coming into collision with the crown. But the ministry preferred to make itself "acceptable" in Potsdam. It never hesitated to take dictatorial measures against the democracy in the name of public safety. . . .

But against the counterrevolution the ministry was very careful not to take action—in the name of public safety! . . .

To sum up: The unavoidable collision between two equal authorities in one provisional government has now begun. The ministry did not know how to run the government energetically; it neglected to take the necessary measures for the public safety. The Assembly only carried out its obligation when it demanded that the ministry do its duty. The ministry regards this as an injury to the crown, which it compromises at the moment of its abdication. Monarchy and Assembly confront each other. The policy of "unity" has led to separation and to conflict. Perhaps only arms will decide.

Whoever has the most courage and consistency will win.

Freedom of Deliberations
in Berlin*

Cologne, September 16

SINCE THE BEGINNING of the crisis, it has been constantly asserted in the counterrevolutionary press that the Berlin Assembly does not deliberate freely. Specifically, Correspondent G. of the *Kölnische Zeitung*, who continues in his job in "the interim until a successor is named," has pointed with unmistakable anxiety to "8,000 to 10,000 boxing-club members" who "morally" support their leftist friends in the little chestnut glade.[1] The *Vossiche, Spenersche*, and other newspapers have raised similar complaints, and on the seventh of this month Herr Reichensperger even proposed removing the Assembly from Berlin (perhaps to Charlottenburg?).

The *Berliner Zeitungs-Halle* publishes a long article in which it tries to refute these charges. It explains that the great leftist majority was by no means inconsistent with the former wavering position of the Assembly. It can be proven "that the vote of the seventh, even on the part of those who had formerly voted with the ministry, could occur without contradiction to the previous attitude; yes, viewed from the standpoint of those members, it was fully in accord with it . . ." Those who moved over from the center "had lived in a delusion; they had imagined that the ministers were the executors of the people's will; in the efforts of the ministers to restore law and order, they thought they saw the expression of the will of the majority and did not perceive that the ministers could admit the will of the people only when it was not contrary to the will of the crown, not where it opposed it."

---

* From *Neue Rheinische Zeitung*, September 17, 1848.
1. The National Assembly met in the Singing Academy, in a small chestnut glade in Berlin.

[439]

Thus the *Zeitungs-Halle* "explains" the striking phenomenon of the sudden revulsion in the minds of so many members against their previous notions and delusions. The matter could not have been stated more innocently.

Nevertheless, the paper admits that there have been intimidations. But it believes that "if outside influences have had any effect, it was that of keeping the clever ministerial shams and deceptions somewhat in balance, and thus enabling many weak and dependent members to follow . . . their natural instinct for survival."

The reasons that caused the *Zeitungs-Halle* morally to defend before the public the wavering members of the center in this way were evident: the article was written more for these gentlemen of the center than for the public at large. For us, who have the privilege of speaking out frankly and who support representatives of a party only so long and so far as they act as revolutionaries—for us these reasons do not exist.

Why should we not say it? On the seventh of this month the centrists indeed let themselves be intimidated by the popular masses; whether their fear was justified or not remains to be seen.

The right of the democratic popular masses to exert a moral effect on the attitude of constituent assemblies by their presence is an old revolutionary right of the people which, since the English and French revolutions, cannot be dispensed with in stormy times. To this right history is indebted for practically all the energetic steps taken by such assemblies. If, therefore, the occupiers of the "ground of legality" and the scared and philistinish friends of "freedom of deliberations" yammer against it, they do so for no other reason than that they do not want any energetic decisions to be taken.

"Freedom of deliberations"! There is no more hollow phrase than this. On the one side "freedom of deliberations" is injured by freedom of the press, by freedom of assembly and of speech, by freedom of the people to arm. It is injured on the other by the existing public authority, which rests in the hands of the crown and its ministers: by the army, the police, and the so-called independent judges, who are in reality dependent on promotion and political change.

At all times freedom of deliberations is a phrase which means nothing more than independence of every influence not recognized by law. These recognized influences—bribery, promotion, private interests, fear of a dissolution of the chamber, etc.—are what actually make the deliberations "free." But in revolutionary times this phrase is completely meaningless. Where two powers and two parties confront each other prepared for battle, and where the battle may break out at any moment, the deputies have only one choice: Either they place themselves *under the protection of the people* and put up with a small scolding from time to time, or they place themselves *under the protection of the crown*, move to some small town, deliberate under the protection of bayonets and cannon or even under a state of siege—and then they cannot complain when the crown and the bayonets prescribe their decisions for them.

Intimidation by the unarmed people or intimidation by the armed soldiery—the Assembly must choose.

The French Constituent Assembly [of 1789] moved from Versailles to Paris. It is properly indicative of the whole character of the German Revolution that its Confederate Assembly moves from Berlin to Charlottenburg.

Revolution in Vienna*

Cologne, October 11

In its first issue (June 1), the *Neue Rheinische Zeitung* reported from Vienna a revolution there (May 25). Today, in our first reappearance after suspension during the state of siege in Cologne, we bring the news of the incomparably more important Vienna Revolution of October 6 and 7. The detailed reports of the events in Vienna oblige us to omit all editorial articles today. Hence only a few words, and those only on the Vienna Revolution. Our readers will see from the reports of the Vienna correspondent [Eduard von Müller-Tellering] that this revolution is in danger of being wrecked, or at least crippled in its development, by the bourgeoisie's mistrust of the working class. Be that as it may, its setback in Hungary, Italy, and Germany thwarts the entire campaign of the counterrevolution. The flight of the Kaiser and the Czech deputies from Vienna compels the Vienna bourgeoisie, if it is not to surrender advantageously or disadvantageously, to continue the struggle. The Frankfurt Assembly, which is now occupied with granting us Germans

A NATIONAL PRISON AND A COMMON WHIP,[1]

will be frightened out of its dreams and the Berlin Ministry disconcerted in its universal panacea, the state of siege, by the event in Vienna. Like the Revolution, the state of siege has made a tour around the world. They tried to apply the experiment on a large scale to an entire country, Hungary. It was this experiment in Hungary, rather than the counterrevolution, that occasioned the revolution in Vienna. The state of siege will never recover from this reverse. The state of siege is compromised forever. It is an irony of

* *Neue Rheinische Zeitung,* October 12, 1848.
1. From Heinrich Heine, *"Der Tannhäuser."*

fate that, at the same time as Jellachich, the western hero of the state of siege, Cavaignac, has also become the target of attacks by all those he saved in June with grapeshot. Only by decisively joining the Revolution can he still make himself acceptable for a time.

Following the reports from Vienna, we are printing a few more dispatches from October 5, because they are an echo of the Viennese hopes and fears about the fate of Hungary.

The "Cologne Revolution"*

Cologne, October 12

THE "Cologne Revolution" of September 25 was a carnival, the *Kölnische Zeitung* tells us, and the *Kölnische Zeitung* is right. The "Cologne military command" introduced Cavaignac on September 26. And the *Kölnische Zeitung* admires the wisdom and moderation of the "Cologne military command." But who is the most comical—the workers who built the barricades on September 25, or Cavaignac, who on September 26 most solemnly pronounced a state of siege, suspended journals, disarmed the civil guard, and prohibited association?

Poor *Kölnische Zeitung!* The Cavaignac of the "Cologne Revolution" is not one cubit bigger than the "Cologne Revolution" itself. Poor *Kölnische Zeitung!* It must take the "Revolution" jokingly and the "Cavaignac" of this gay revolution seriously. Vexatious, thankless, disagreeable theme!

We do not waste words on the rights of the military command. D'Ester has exhausted this subject.[1] For the rest, we consider the military command as a subordinate tool. The actual authors of this strange tragedy were the *"right-minded citizens,"* the Dumonts & Co. Hence it is no wonder that Herr Dumont was instrumental in peddling the Address against d'Ester, Borchardt, and Kyll. What they had to defend, these "right-minded" ones, was not the action of the military command but their own action.

The Cologne event wandered through the Sahara Desert of the German press in the form given it by the Cologne *Journal des Débats.* Sufficient ground to return to this.

---

* *Neue Rheinische Zeitung,* October 13, 1848.
1. On September 29, 1848, Dr. d'Ester, a communist deputy in the Prussian National Assembly, demanded the suspension of the state of siege in Cologne.

Moll, one of the most beloved leaders of the Workers' Association,[2] was to be arrested. Schapper and Becker were already arrested. To carry out these arrests, they chose a *Monday*, a day when everyone knows most of the workers are free. Hence the authorities must have known that the arrests would stir up a great ferment among the workers and could even be the cause of violent resistance. Strange coincidence, that these arrests occurred precisely on a Monday! The excitement was the more easily to be foreseen as, on the occasion of Stein's motion against the army order,[3] and after Wrangel's Proclamation[4] and Pfuel's appointment as Prime Minister, a decisive counterrevolutionary blow, hence a revolution, was expected in Berlin. The workers therefore had to view the arrests, not as legal but as *political* measures. In the procurator they saw only a counterrevolutionary authority. They believed they were being robbed of their leaders on the eve of important events. They were determined at all costs to keep Moll from being arrested. And they left the field of battle only after they achieved their aim. The barricades were built only when the workers assembled on the Old Market Place discovered that the military was moving to an attack from all directions. The workers were not attacked; hence they did not have to defend themselves. Furthermore, it became known to them that no important news had arrived from Berlin. Thus they withdrew, after having vainly waited for the enemy throughout most of the night.

Hence nothing is more ridiculous than the reproach of cowardice that has been made against the Cologne workers.

But other reproaches have been made against them, in order to justify the state of siege and to trim down the Cologne event to a small June Revolution. Their actual plan was supposed to have been the plundering of the good city of Cologne. The charge derives from the alleged plundering of *one* clothing shop. As if every city did not have its contingent of thieves, who naturally take advantage of days of public excitement. Or does one understand by plundering the plundering of arms stores? If so, one should send the Cologne *parquet* [law court] to Berlin to help prepare the case against the March Revolution. Without the plundered arms stores, perhaps we would never have had the satisfaction of seeing Herr Hansemann transformed into a bank director and Herr Müller into a state secretary.

---

2. The Workers' Association was founded by communists in Cologne on April 13, 1848.

3. On August 9, Deputy Stein made a motion protesting against an attack by Prussian troops in Schweidnitz which killed fourteen men.

4. On September 17, 1848, General Wrangel issued a proclamation in Berlin in defense of "public order."

446   GERMANY

Enough of the Cologne workers. Let us come to the so-called democrats. What do the *Kölnische Zeitung*, the *Deutsche Zeitung*, the *Augsburger Allgemeine Zeitung*, and whatever the names of the other "right-minded" papers are, reproach them with?

The heroic Brüggemanns, the Bassermanns, etc., called for blood, and the soft-hearted democrats, out of *cowardice*, did not agree to bloodshed.

The fact, however, is this: The democrats declared in the Kranz (on the Old Market Place), in the Eiser Hall, and on the workers' barricades that under no circumstances did they want any *Putsch*. But at that point, when there was no important question to drive the whole population to battle and hence every rising was bound to fail, this was the more senseless in that it disabled men for battle on the eve of decision, at a time when tremendous events could occur in a few days. When the ministry in Berlin hazarded a counterrevolution, that was the day for the people to hazard a revolution. The judicial investigation will confirm our assertion. The gentlemen of the *Kölnische Zeitung* would have done better if, instead of standing in front of the barricades "in the darkness of the night" with "folded arms and dark looks" and "reflecting on the future of the nation," they had stood on the barricades themselves and harangued the blinded masses with their words of wisdom. Of what use is wisdom *post festum?*

Worst was the treatment of the Civil Guard in the good Cologne press during the events in the city. Let us make a distinction. That the Civil Guard refused to sink to the level of a will-less servant of the police—that was its duty. That it voluntarily surrendered its arms—can be excused on one ground: the liberal portion of the guard knew that its illiberal portion joyfully seized the opportunity of ridding itself of its weapons. A partial resistance would have been useless.

The "Cologne Revolution" had *one* good result. It revealed the existence of a phalanx of more than 2,000 saints whose "satiated virtue and solvent morality"[5] demonstrate a "free life" only during a state of siege. Perhaps there will some day be an occasion for writing an *Acta Sanctorum*—the biographies of these saints. Our readers will then learn how the "treasures" that neither moth nor rust doth corrupt[6] are acquired, and in what way the economic background of "good intention" is conquered.

---

5. From Heinrich Heine, "Anno 1829."
6. Matthew VI: 19: "Lay not up for yourselves treasures upon earth, where moth and rust doth corrupt..."

Appeal of the Democratic Congress
to the German Nation*

Cologne, November 2

We reproduce below the Appeal of the "Democratic Congress":[1] "To the German Nation!

"For long disgraceful years the German nation sighed under the yoke of autocracy. The bloody deeds in Vienna and Berlin had given us reason to hope that the nation's freedom and unity would be realized in a single blow. The devilish artifices of a cursed reaction thwarted this development, cheating a heroic people of the fruits of its magnificent uprising. Vienna, a main bulwark of German freedom, stands momentarily in greatest peril. Sacrificed by the plots of a still powerful camarilla, it is to be delivered anew to the chains of despotism. But its noble population has risen as one man and confronts the armed hordes of its oppressors with deadly courage. The cause of Vienna is the cause of Germany, the cause of freedom. With the fall of Vienna, arbitrary government would raise its banner higher than ever; with Vienna's victory, it would be destroyed. It is up to us, German brothers, not to permit the destruction of Vienna's freedom or see it handed over to the armed barbaric hordes. It is the most sacred duty of all German governments to rush to the aid of the hard-pressed sister city with all their influence; but it is at the same time also the most sacred duty of the German people, in the interest of their own freedom, in the interest of self-preservation, to make every sacrifice to save Vienna. Never must they tolerate the disgrace of apathetic indifference

---

* *Neue Rheinische Zeitung*, November 3, 1848.
   1. The Second Democratic Congress met in Berlin from October 26 to 30, 1848, and passed a series of resolutions without preparing any means for their enforcement.

where the utmost is at stake. Therefore we appeal to you, brothers, that each of you, according to his means, contribute to save Vienna from destruction. What we do for Vienna, we do for Germany. Help yourselves! The men you sent to Frankfurt to establish freedom have rejected, with mocking laughter, the appeal to save Vienna. Now it is up to you to act! Demand, with strong and inflexible will, that your governments submit to your majority and save the cause of Germany and the cause of freedom in Vienna. Hurry! You are the power, your will is law! Arise! Ye men of freedom, arise in all the lands and wherever the idea of liberty and humanity glows in noble hearts! Arise, before it is too late! Save Vienna's freedom, save Germany's freedom. The present will admire you, the future will reward you with immortal glory!

    "October 29, 1848   "THE DEMOCRATIC CONGRESS
                                           IN BERLIN"

    This Appeal replaces the lack of revolutionary energy with preacher-like blubbering pathos, behind which is hidden the utmost poverty of ideas and passion.

    A few examples!

    The Appeal expected from the March revolutions in Vienna and Berlin the realization of the "freedom and unity" of the German nation *"in a single blow."* In other words: the Appeal dreamed of *"a single blow"* that would make the German people's "development" toward "freedom and unity" superfluous.

    Immediately after this, the fantastic "single blow," which replaces development becomes a "development" "thwarted" by the reactionaries. A phrase, a self-dissolving phrase!

    We overlook the monotonous repetition of the main theme: Vienna is in peril, and with Vienna, Germany's freedom; help Vienna and thereby you help yourselves! These ideas are not endowed with flesh and blood. The one phrase is wound around itself so often that it becomes a piece of rhetoric. We only remark that artificial, untrue pathos always degenerates into this kind of dull rhetoric.

    "It is up to us, German brothers, not to permit the destruction of Vienna's freedom or to see it handed over the armed barbaric hordes."

    And how do we begin to do this?

    Chiefly by an appeal to the sense of duty of the "German governments." *C'est incroyable!* [It is incredible!]

    "It is the most sacred duty of all German governments to rush to the aid of the hard-pressed sister city with all their influence."

    Is the Prussian Government to send Wrangel or Colomb or the Prince of Prussia against Auersperg, Jellachich, and Windischgrätz?

Did the "Democratic" Congress venture even for a moment, such a childish and conservative position toward the German governments? Did it, even for a moment, venture to separate the cause of the "most sacred interests" of the German governments from the cause and interests of "Croation order and freedom?" The governments will smile smugly at this maidenly reverie.

And the people?

The people in general are called upon "to make every sacrifice to save Vienna." Good! But the "people" expect specific demands from the Democratic Congress. He who demands everything demands nothing and receives nothing. The *specific* demand here is: "*Demand*, with strong and inflexible will, that *your governments* submit to your majority and save the cause of Germany and the cause of freedom in Vienna. Hurry! You are the power, your will is law! Arise!"

Assuming that magnificent people's demonstrations succeeded in moving the governments to take official steps to save Vienna, we would be blessed with a second edition of the Stein military order. To want to utilize the present "German governments" as "saviors of freedom"! As if in their "imperial buying and selling" they did not fulfill their true vocation, their "most sacred duties" as the Gabriels of "constitutional freedom"! The "Democratic Congress" should have kept silent about the German governments, or it should have unsparingly revealed their conspiracy with Olmütz and Petersburg.

Although the Appeal recommends "hurry"—and in truth there is no time to be lost—the humanistic phraseology pulls it beyond the frontiers of Germany, beyond all geographic frontiers, into the cosmopolitan never-never land of "noble hearts" in general!

"Hurry!" "Arise! Ye men of freedom, arise in all the lands and wherever the idea of liberty and humanity glows in noble hearts!"

We do not doubt that there are such "noble hearts" even in Lapland.

In Germany and *where else?* In wasting itself on this purely aimless phrase, the "Appeal" presented an authentic expression.

It is unforgivable that the "Democratic Congress" should have signed such a document. "The present" will not "admire" it for this, nor will "the future" reward it with "immortal glory."

Let us hope that despite the "Appeal of the Democratic Congress," the people will awake from their lethargy and bring to the Viennese the only kind of help that can still be brought at this moment—defeating the counterrevolution in its own house.

The Latest News from Vienna, Berlin, and Paris*

Cologne, November 4

There is light on the horizon.
There is still no direct news from Vienna. But from the reports of the official Prussian press itself, it appears that Vienna did not surrender, and that Windischgrätz has either deliberately or mistakenly sent out to the world a false telegram that found a ready, many-tongued, orthodox echo in the "good" press, no matter how much it tried to hide its malicious joy behind hypocritical and woeful, funereal words. Stripped of all the fictitious rubbish that dissolves into its own contradictions in the Silesian and Berlin reports, the following points appear: On October 29 the imperial bandits had only a few suburbs in their power. From the reports hitherto, it does *not* appear that they have as yet gained a foothold in the city of Vienna itself. The whole surrender of Vienna reduces itself to a few highly treasonable proclamations of the Vienna City Council. On October 30 the vanguard of the Hungarian army attacked Windischgrätz and was allegedly repulsed. On October 31 Windischgrätz again bombarded Vienna—in vain. He now finds himself between the Viennese and the Hungarian army of more than 80,000 men. Windischgrätz's infamous manifestoes gave the signal for revolt, or at least for very threatening motions, in all provinces. Even the Czech fanatics in Prague, the neophytes of the Slovanskà Lipa,[1] are awakening from their wild dreams and declare themselves in favor of Vienna against the Imperial *Schinderhannes*.[2] Never before had the

---

* *Neue Rheinische Zeitung*, November 5, 1848.
1. A Czech national society founded in 1848.
2. A nickname for Marshal Windischgrätz, deriving from the eighteenth-century German robber chieftain, Johann Bückler.

[450]

counterrevolution dared to trumpet so much its stupid and brazen plans. Even in Olmütz, the Austrian Coblenz, the ground is trembling under the feet of the crowned idiots. The leadership of the world-famous *Sipehsalar* [Supreme Commander] *Jellachich*, whose name is so great that "at the flash of his saber the frightened world hides in a cloud," a man to whom the "thunder of the cannon indicates the direction" he is to take every time he has to regroup, leaves no doubt that Hungarians and Viennese will:

> Whip the gang into the Danube,
> Scourge the insolent pack of scoundrels,
> The beggars, hungry, tired of life,
> A swarm of vagrants, rascals, vagabonds,
> Croatian scum, low peasant churls,
> Spewed by a sick and tired land
> Into frantic adventures and *sure destruction.*

Later reports will bring horrible details about the infamous actions of the Croats and other knights "of legal order and constitutional freedom." And from their seats on the stock exchanges and other comfortable viewers' loges, the European bourgeoisie applaud the unspeakable scenes of carnage—the same miserable characters who cried out in moral indignation at a few brusque acts of popular justice and whose thousands of lungs groaned a unanimous anathema against the "murderers" of the brave Latour and the noble Lichnowski.

In retaliation for the murders in Galicia, the Poles have again put themselves at the spearhead of the liberators of Vienna, as they are also at the spearhead of the Italian people, as they are everywhere the noble-minded generals of Revolution. Hurrah, three times hurrah, for the Poles!

The Berlin camarilla, intoxicated by the bloodshed in Vienna, blinded by the columns of smoke from the burning suburbs, deafened by the victorious shouts of the Croats and Haiducks, has dropped its veil. "Peace has been restored in Berlin." *Nous verrons.* [We shall see.]

From Paris, we hear at least the first subterranean rumblings that will bury the honest republic in its own ruins.

There is light on the horizon.

We Refuse to Pay Taxes*

THE CALM DEMEANOR of Berlin *delights* us; the ideals of the Prussian noncommissioned officer class are shattered on it.

But the National Assembly? Why does it not pass an act of outlawry, why does it not declare Wrangel an outlaw, why does not a single deputy walk up to Wrangel's bayonets and declare him in contempt and harangue the soldiery? . . .

And what do *we* do at this moment?

WE REFUSE TO PAY TAXES. A Wrangel, a Brandenburg understands —for these creatures learn Arabic from the Hyghlans[1]—that he carries a sword and that he draws a uniform and a salary. Whence come the sword and the uniform and the salary—that he does not understand.

There is only one way to defeat the monarchy. . . .

The monarchy not only defies the nation, it defies the citizens. Let us, therefore, defeat it in a citizen's way.

And how does one defeat the monarchy in a citizen's way?

By starving it out.

And how does one starve it out?

By refusing to pay taxes.

Consider it well! All the princes, all the Brandenburgs and the Wrangels, produce no—*army bread.* You yourselves produce the army bread.

---

* From an article in *Neue Rheinische Zeitung*, November 12, 1848.

1. On November 3, 1848, the *Kölnische Zeitung* carried a story, later ridiculed by the *Neue Rheinische Zeitung* (November 5), about the "Hyghlans," an African tribe that was supposedly a missing link between man and ape, many of whose members "learn the Arabic language."

The Ministry Under Indictment*

THE CITY OF BRANDENBURG [Berlin] WANTS TO HAVE NOTHING TO DO WITH THE MINISTRY OF BRANDENBURG AND IS SENDING AN ADDRESS OF THANKS TO THE NATIONAL ASSEMBLY.

THE WHOLE COUNTRY, IN ITS ADDRESSES, RECOGNIZES ONLY THE GOVERNMENT OF THE NATIONAL ASSEMBLY.

THE MINISTRY COMMITS HIGH TREASON ANEW WHEN, IN OPPOSITION TO THE HABEAS CORPUS ACT AND WITHOUT THE CONSENT OF THE NATIONAL ASSEMBLY, IT DECLARES A STATE OF SIEGE AND DRIVES THE NATIONAL ASSEMBLY ITSELF FROM THE SCHÜTZENHAUS WITH BAYONETS.

THE NATIONAL ASSEMBLY HAS ITS SEAT AMONG THE PEOPLE, AND NOT IN THIS OR THAT PILE OF STONES. DRIVEN FROM BERLIN, IT CAN SIT IN ANY OTHER PLACE, IN BRESLAU, COLOGNE, OR WHEREVER IT PLEASES. THIS IS THE DECISION IT MADE ON THE THIRTEENTH.

THE BERLINERS MOCK THE STATE OF SIEGE AND IN NO WAY LET THEMSELVES BE CURBED BY IT.

FROM MANY PARTS OF THE COUNTRY, ARMED MEN ARE RUSHING TO DEFEND THE NATIONAL ASSEMBLY.

THE GUARDS ARE REFUSING OBEDIENCE. THE SOLDIERS ARE FRATERNIZING WITH THE PEOPLE.

SILESIA AND THURINGIA ARE IN FULL REVOLT.

But, citizens, we appeal to you: Send money to the Democratic Central Committee in Berlin. And in return pay no taxes to the counterrevolutionary government. The National Assembly has stated that the refusal to pay taxes is legally sound. It has not yet decreed it out of consideration for officialdom. A *hunger cure* would teach

---

* Special edition of the *Neue Rheinische Zeitung*, November 15, 1848.

these officials the power of the citizens and make them good citizens themselves.

Starve the enemy and refuse to pay taxes! Nothing is more foolish than to provide a high-treason government with the means for a fight against the nation, and the means of all means is—money.

No More Taxes!*

Neue Rheinische Zeitung, November 17, 1848.

Cologne, November 16

ALL THE BERLIN newspapers, with the exception of the *Preussische Staats-Anzeiger,* the *Vossische Zeitung,* and the *Neue Preussische Zeitung,* have failed to appear. The city militia has been disarmed in the *Geheimratsviertel,*[1] but only in the *Geheimratsviertel.* It is the same battalion that assassinated the machine workers on October 31.[2] Its disarming is a gain for the cause of the people.

The National Assembly was once again driven out of the Köllnische City Hall by armed force.[3] It then moved to the Mielenz Hotel, where in the end, with 226 votes, it unanimously adopted the following resolution on *tax avoidance:*

"THE BRANDENBURG MINISTRY IS NOT AUTHORIZED TO DISPOSE OF GOVERNMENT MONEYS OR TO COLLECT TAXES, SO LONG AS THE NATIONAL ASSEMBLY IN BERLIN CANNOT CONTINUE ITS SESSIONS FREELY.

"THIS DECISION GOES INTO EFFECT ON NOVEMBER 17.

"THE NATIONAL ASSEMBLY OF NOVEMBER 15."

FROM THIS DAY ON, ALL TAXES ARE THEREFORE SUSPENDED! ! !

TAXPAYING IS HIGH TREASON, TAX AVOIDANCE IS THE FIRST DUTY OF THE CITIZEN!

---

1. The Privy Councilors District, in southwest Berlin, so called because it was inhabited primarily by Prussian officials.

2. On October 31, 1848, the Eighth Battalion of the Berlin Militia attacked an unarmed protest demonstration (against the cruel suppression of the revolt in Vienna) and killed several men.

3. On November 14, 1848, the National Assembly met in the Köllnische Rathaus, in the Kölln or Altkölln district of central Berlin.

The Bourgeoisie and the
Counterrevolution*

Cologne, December 9

WE NEVER concealed it. Our ground is not the *ground of legality;* it is the *ground of revolution.* The government, for its part, has now given up the hypocrisy about legal ground. It has placed itself on revolutionary ground, for counterrevolutionary ground is also revolutionary.

Article 6 of the Law of April 6, 1848, states: "The future representatives of the people shall in all cases have the right to approve all laws of governmental expenditure as well as of taxation."

Article 13 of the Law of April 8, 1848, states: "The Assembly, meeting pursuant to the present law, is convened to determine during this session, together with the crown, the future Constitution and the legal authorization of taxes."

The government tells the Assembly to go to the devil, dictates a *soi-disant* [so-called] constitution,[1] and of itself approves the taxes that the representatives of the people had denied it.

The Prussian Government has put a brilliant end to Camphausen-ism, a species of solemn *Law-Jobism.*[2] In revenge, the inventor of this epic, the great Camphausen, sits quietly in Frankfurt as the envoy of this selfsame Prussian Government and continues to intrigue with the Bassermanns in the service of this selfsame Prussian Government. This Camphausen, who invented the confederation theory to save the ground of legality—that is, in order to cheat the Revolution of the honors that belong to it—first invented the mines which were later

---

* Articles in the *Neue Rheinische Zeitung* during December, 1848.
1. On December 5, 1848, simultaneously with the dissolution of the National Assembly, the government proclaimed a "constitution for the Prussian State," which Marx and Engels called the "imposed constitution."
2. A play on *"Die Jobsiade,"* a mock-heroic poem by Karl Arnold Kortum.

[456]

to blow up the ground of legality and the confederation theory. This man contributed to the indirect election of an Assembly which yielded to the government and, in a moment of temporary uprising, could thunder: *Trop tard!* [Too late!] He recalled the Prince of Prussia, the chief of the counterrevolution, and did not disdain the official lie of calling his flight a study trip. He left in force the old Prussian laws on political offenses and the old courts. Under him the old bureaucracy and the old army again won time to recover from their scare and to reconstitute themselves completely. All the leaders of the old regime remained undisturbed in their positions. Under Camphausen the camarilla waged the war in Posen,[3] while he himself waged it in Denmark.[4] The Danish war was to be an outlet for the surplus patriotic energies of German youth, who after their return were duly put under police surveillance. He was expected to lend General Wrangel and his notorious Guards regiment a certain popularity and to rehabilitate the Prussian soldiery in general. As soon as the objective was attained, this sham war had to be strangled at all costs by an ignominious armistice, for Camphausen had to confederate again with the German National Assembly at Frankfurt am Main. The result of the Danish war was a commander in chief for both Margravates and the return of the Guards regiment to Berlin, whence it had been driven out in March.

And the war the camarilla at Potsdam waged under Camphausen's auspices in Posen! The war in Posen was more than a war against the Prussian revolution. It was the fall of Vienna, the fall of Italy, the defeat of the June heroes. It was the first decisive triumph achieved by the Russian Czar over the European revolution. And all this under the auspices of the great Camphausen, the thinking friend of history, the knight of the great debate, the hero of mediation.

Under and through Camphausen, the counterrevolution seized all critical positions and prepared an army ready for battle, while the Confederated Assembly debated. Under the Minister of Action, Hansemann-Pinto, the old police were put into new uniforms and a bitter and petty war was waged by the bourgeoisie against the people. Under Brandenburg final conclusions were drawn from these premises. All that was still required was—sideburns and a sword, instead of a brain.

When Camphausen resigned we commented: *"He sowed reaction in the bourgeois sense, he will reap it in the aristocratic and absolutist sense."*

We do not doubt that His Excellency the Prussian Envoy Camp-

---

3. In March, 1848, a Polish rebellion against Prussian domination broke out in Posen; it was crushed in May.
4. The Prusso-Danish war over Schleswig-Holstein in the spring of 1848.

hausen is now counted among the feudal gentlemen and has most peacefully accommodated himself to his "errors."

One should not, however, make a mistake; one should not ascribe to a Camphausen and a Hansemann, these men of the most subordinate greatness, any world-historical initiative. They were nothing but spokesmen of a class. Their language and their actions were merely the official echo of a class that had pushed them to the fore. They were the great bourgeois—only as front men.

The representatives of this class constitute the "liberal opposition" in the blissfully sleeping Assembly, which Camphausen awakened for a moment.

These gentlemen of the liberal opposition have been reproached for having become untrue to the principles of the March Revolution. This is an error.

The big landowners and capitalists, who were exclusively represented in the Assembly—in a word, the moneybags—augmented their wealth and education. On the one hand, with the development of bourgeois society in Prussia—that is, the development of industry, commerce, and agriculture—the old class differences lost their material foundations. The nobility itself became substantially bourgeoisified. Instead of Loyalty, Love, and Faith, it now, above all, produced beets, gin, and wool. The wool market became its main tournament. On the other hand, the old absolutist state, whose old social foundations were conjured away from under the nobles' feet by the course of development, became a restraining chain on the new bourgeois society with its changed means of production and changed needs. The bourgeoisie had to make a claim for its share in political rule, if only for its material interests. It was itself capable of legally vindicating its commercial and industrial needs. It had to take out of the hands of an obsolete, ignorant, and arrogant bureaucracy the administration of its "most sacred interests." It had to claim control of the national wealth, of which it believed itself to be the creator. It also had the ambition, after it had stolen the monopoly of so-called education from the bureaucracy and knew itself to surpass the latter by far in real knowledge of bourgeois social needs, to extort a political position corresponding to its social position. In order to achieve its purpose, it had to be able to debate freely its own interests, views, and the transactions of the government. This it called the "right to freedom of the press." It had to be able to associate without restraint. This it called the "right to free association." Religious freedom, etc., also had to be demanded as a necessary consequence of free competition. And before March, 1848, the Prussian bourgeoisie was well on its way to the realization of all its wishes.

The Prussian state found itself in financial difficulties. Its credit had run dry. That was the secret behind the convocation of the Assembly. The government, to be sure, resisted its fate, it ungraciously dissolved the "Confederate," but the irresistible need for money and lack of credit finally threw it into the arms of the bourgeoisie. Like the feudal barons, so also have the kings-by-the-grace-of-God always exchanged their privileges for cash. The emancipation of the serfs was the first, the constitutional monarchy the second, great act of this world-historical haggling in all the Christian-German states. *"L'argent n'a pas de maître"* ["Money has no master"], but the *maîtres* [masters] cease to be *maîtres* as soon as they are *démonétisés* [demonetized].

Thus the liberal opposition in the Confederated Assembly was nothing but the opposition of the bourgeoisie to a form of government which no longer corresponded to its interests and needs. In order to oppose the court, it had to court the people.

Perhaps the bourgeoisie really imagined that its opposition was made on *behalf* of the people.

The rights and freedoms which it won for itself, it naturally could claim only as the people's rights and the people's freedoms against the government.

This opposition, as we said, found itself well on the way, when the February storm erupted.

Cologne, December 11

As the March flood—a flood in miniature—subsided, it left on the Berlin surface no monster, no revolutionary colossus, but only effigies of the old style, thickset bourgeois figures—the liberals of the Confederate Diet, the representatives of the conscious Prussian bourgeoisie. The provinces—the Rhine Province and Silesia—which possess the most advanced bourgeoisie provided the main contingents of the new ministries. Behind them stood a whole array of Rhineland jurists. To the same degree that the bourgeoisie was pushed to the background by the feudalists, so also in the ministries of the Rhine Province and Silesia a place was made for the ancient Prussian provinces. The Brandenburg Ministry is connected with the Rhineland by only a single Tory from Elberfeld. Hansemann and von der Heydt! For the Prussian bourgeoisie, the entire difference between March and December, 1848, lies in these two names!

The Prussian bourgeoisie was exposed to public derision, not, as it hoped, because of a peaceful deal with the crown, but by revolution.

The bourgeoisie was to represent, not its own interests, but the people's interests against the crown, that is, against itself, for it was a people's movement that had prepared the way for it. But in bourgeois eyes the crown was still an umbrella-by-the-Grace-of-God, behind which it could hide its profane interests. The untouchability of *its* own interests and the political forms corresponding to them were to be translated into constitutional language, to read: Untouchability of the Crown. Hence the enthusiasm of the German, and especially the Prussian, bourgeoisie for the constitutional monarchy. But if the February Revolution, together with the afterpains in Germany, were welcome to the Prussian bourgeoisie, because it threw the control of the state into its hands, it reckoned without the host, for its rule was so tied up with stipulations that it neither would nor could comply with them.

The bourgeoisie did not lift a finger. It allowed the people to fight for it. Hence the authority it assumed was not the authority of a commander who has defeated his opponent, but the authority of a security committee to which the victorious people entrusted the care of their own interests.

Camphausen felt the embarrassment of his position, and the whole weakness of his ministry dated from this feeling and from the circumstances which conditioned it. Hence a kind of blush brightens the most shameless acts of his government. Frank shamelessness and brazenness were the prerogatives of Hansemann. The red complexion constituted the only difference between these two painters.

The Prussian March Revolution must not be confused with either the English Revolution of 1648 or that of the French in 1789.

In 1648 the bourgeoisie was allied with the modern aristocracy against the monarchy, the feudal nobility, and the dominant church.

In 1789 the bourgeoisie was allied with the people against the monarchy, the nobility, and the dominant church.

The Revolution of 1789 had for its model (at least in Europe) only the Revolution of 1648; the Revolution of 1648 had only the revolt of the Dutch against Spain. Both revolutions were a century apart not only in time but also in the content of their models.

In both revolutions the bourgeoisie was the class that really led the movement. The proletariat and segments of citizens not belonging to the bourgeoisie either had as yet no interests separate from those of the bourgeoisie or had not as yet developed independent classes or class divisions. Hence wherever it confronted the bourgeoisie, as, for example, in France from 1793 to 1794, it fought for the realization of bourgeois interests, if not quite in the same manner. The whole French Reign of Terror was nothing but a *plebeian way* of getting rid of the *enemies of the bourgeoisie,* of absolutism, of feudalism, of philistinism.

The revolutions of 1648 and 1789 were not English or French revolutions, but revolutions of a European type. They were not the triumph of a particular class of society over the old political order; they were the proclamation of the political order for a new European society. The bourgeoisie won that victory, but *the victory of the bourgeoisie* was then *the victory of a new order of society*—the victory of bourgeois over feudal property, of nationalism over provincialism, of competition over guilds, of equality of inheritance over primogeniture, of the domination of the owners of land over the rule through landowners, of enlightenment over superstition, of family over family name, of industriousness over gentlemanly slothfulness, of civic rights over medieval privileges. The Revolution of 1648 was the triumph of the seventeenth century over the sixteenth, the Revolution of 1789 was the victory of the eighteenth century over the seventeenth. These revolutions were more the expressions of the needs of the then existing world than of mere geographic sectors of that world—England and France—in which they occurred.

In the Prussian March Revolution there was nothing of all this.

The February Revolution abolished the constitutional monarchy in reality and the bourgeois rule in theory. The Prussian March Revolution was supposed to have established a constitutional monarchy in theory and a bourgeois rule in reality. Far from being a European revolution, it was merely the stunted aftereffect of a European revolution in a backward country. Instead of being in advance of its century, it was more than half a century behind its century. It was from the outset secondary, but it is known that secondary ailments are harder to cure, and at the same time waste the body more, than do primary ones. What was involved was not the establishment of a new society, but the rebirth in Berlin of a society that had died in Paris. The Prussian March Revolution was not even *national, German,* it was from the outset *provincial Prussian.* The Viennese, the Cassel, the Munich uprisings and all sorts of others paralleled and it challenged its supremacy.

While 1648 and 1789 had the inexhaustible self-reliance to be the spearhead of creativity, the ambition of the Berliners of 1848 was to create an anachronism. Its light was to be like the light of the stars, which reaches us earthlings only after the body that radiated it has been extinguished for a hundred thousand years. The Prussian March Revolution was in miniature, as everything Prussian is in miniature, such a star for Europe. Its light was the light of a long-gone social corpse.

The German bourgeoisie has developed in such a sluggish, cowardly, and crawling way that in the moment when it dangerously
confronted feudalism and absolutism, it saw itself endangered by the
proletariat and all the segments of the citizenry whose interests and
ideas were related to it. And the bourgeoisie not only had one class
behind it, but it viewed all of Europe *before* it as an enemy. The
Prussian bourgeoisie was not a class like the French one of 1789,
which, representing the *whole* modern society, confronted the representatives of the old society, the monarchy and the nobility. Rather,
it had sunk to a species of *class* that was in distinct opposition to the
crown as well as to the people, and was indecisive in the face of each
of its opponents, because it always saw both either in front of or
behind it. The Prussian bourgeoisie was inclined from the outset to a
betrayal of the people and to a compromise with the crowned representatives of the old society, since it belonged to the old order itself.
It represented, not the interests of a new society against the old, but
renewed interests within the aged society. It held the helm of the
revolution, not because the people were behind it, but because the
people pushed it forward. It was at the head, not because it represented the initiative of a new society, but merely the rancor of an
old social epoch. It came to the surface, but not for the new state
emerging from the earthquake that was breaking up the strata of the
old state. It was without faith in itself, without faith in the people,
snarling at those above it, trembling before those below it, egoistic in
the face of both, and conscious of its egoism. It was revolutionary
against conservatives, conservative against revolutionists. It mistrusted
its own slogans, using phrases instead of ideas. It was intimidated by
the world upheaval, it exploited the world upheaval. It had no energy
in any direction and plagiarized in all directions. Common, because
it had no originality, it was original in its commonness. Haggling over
its own wishes, it was without initiative, without faith in itself, without
faith in the people, without a sense of world history. It was an
execrated old man, condemned to direct and misdirect the youthful
energies of a robust people in its own age-enfeebled interests. It was
without eye, without ear, without tooth, without anything! Such was
the Prussian bourgeoisie at the helm of the Prussian state after the
March Revolution.

Cologne, December 15

The coalition theory, which the bourgeoisie that came to power
in the Camphausen Ministry immediately proclaimed as the "widest"

principle of the Prussian *contrat social*, was by no means a hollow theory. It had, rather, grown on the tree of the "golden" life.

The March Revolution did not subject the sovereign by the grace of God to the sovereignty of the people. It merely forced the crown, the absolutist state, to reconcile itself with the bourgeoisie, to come to an *understanding* with it.

The crown would sacrifice the nobility to the bourgeoisie; the bourgeoisie, the people to the crown. Under these conditions the monarchy would become bourgeois and the bourgeoisie monarchical.

After March, there were only these two forces. They served each other reciprocally as the lightning rods of the revolution. Everything, of course, on the "widest possible democratic foundation."

This was the secret of the coalition theory.

The oil and wool merchants,[5] who made up the first ministry after the March Revolution, were pleased with the role of covering the unmasked crown with their plebeian pinions. They reveled in the great delight of being accepted at court, and despite their rugged romanism —the romanism of the United Diet—out of pure magnanimity they covered the abyss that threatened to swallow the throne with the corpse of their erstwhile popularity. How he strutted as the midwife of the constitutional monarchy, this Minister Camphausen! The worthy man was obviously moved by himself, moved by his own magnanimity. The crown and its hangers-on reluctantly tolerated this humiliating protectorship, but made *bonne mine à mauvais jeu* [the best of a bad situation] and bided their time.

The partly dissolved army, with a few sweet words and curtsies, easily toppled the *bourgeois gentilhomme*,[6] the bureaucracy trembling for its positions and salaries, and the humiliated feudal class, whose leader was away on a constitutional study tour.

The Prussian bourgeoisie was in nominal possession of the government; it did not doubt for a moment that the forces of the old state had put themselves at its disposal and that its many loyal scions had given up their own power.

Not only in the ministry, but also throughout the kingdom was the bourgeoisie intoxicated with this delusion.

The only valorous deeds of the Prussian bourgeoisie after March, the often bloody chicaneries of the militia against the unarmed proletariat—did they not find submissive and willing helpers' helpers in the bureaucracy and even among the feudal gentlemen? The only exertions of the local representatives of the bourgeoisie, the communal

---

5. Ludolf Camphausen, head of the cabinet, had once been a dealer in fats and grain; David Justus Hansemann, the finance minister, had been a dealer in wool.
6. The vain and loutish "bourgeois gentleman" of Molière's play by that name.

464   GERMANY

councils—whose intrusive vileness was later appropriately booted by
a Windischgrätz, a Jellachich, and a Welden—the only valorous deeds
of these communal councils after the March Revolution, their pa-
triarchically earnest warnings to the people, were they not looked
upon with astonishment by the silenced prefects and the independent
generals of division? And the Prussian bourgeoisie still doubted
whether the old animosity of the army, of the bureaucracy, of the
feudalists, in worshipful submission to the generous victor, the bourgeoisie, out of fear of unbridled anarchy, was dead?

It was clear. The Prussian bourgeoisie had only one more task, the
task of making its rule comfortable by eliminating the troublesome
anarchists, restoring "peace and order," and collecting the taxes lost
during the March storms. It finally amounted only to reducing to a
minimum the production cost of its rule and the March Revolution
that conditioned it. The arms which the Prussian bourgeoisie in its
struggle with the feudal society and the crown was forced to claim
in the name of the people, the right of association, freedom of the
press, etc.—would not all these be broken at the hands of a deluded
people which no longer needed to use them on behalf of the bourgeoisie but gave notice of its desire to employ them against the
bourgeoisie?

The bourgeoisie was convinced that only one obstacle stood in
the way of its agreement with the crown, an agreement between the
markets of the bourgeoisie and the old state that had submitted to
its fate—a single obstacle, the people: *puer robustus sed malitiosus*,[7]
as Hobbes says. The *people* and the *revolution!*

The revolution was the people's legal title; on the revolution it
based its stormy claims. The revolution was the promissory note it
drew on the bourgeoisie. Through the revolution the bourgeoisie
came to power. The day of its accession to power was the due day
of this promissory note. The bourgeoisie had to lodge a protest against
the promissory note.

The revolution meant this to the people: You bourgeois are the
Comité du Salut Public,[8] the Welfare Committee, in whose hands we
put the power, not for you to concert with the crown on behalf of
your own interests, but for you to put through our interests, the
interests of the people, against the crown.

The revolution was the people's protest against an agreement
between the bourgeoisie and the crown. Hence the bourgeoisie, con-
certing with the crown, had to protest against—the *revolution.*

And this happened under the great Camphausen. The March

7. "A strong but malicious lad"; a paraphrase from Thomas Hobbes's *De Cive.*
8. Committee of Public Safety, which the French Revolution set up on April 6,
1793.

Revolution was not given recognition. The Berlin national representation constituted itself as a representation of the Prussian bourgeoisie, as a Coalition Assembly which repudiated any recognition of
the March Revolution.

The Camphausen Ministry undid what had been done. It proclaimed loudly to the Prussian people that it did not concert with the
bourgeoisie in order to make a revolution against the crown, but it
made a revolution in order that the crown and the bourgeoisie should
combine! The *title of legality* of the revolutionary people was destroyed and the *ground of legality* was won for the conservative
bourgeoisie.

The ground of legality!

Brüggemann, and through him the *Kölnische Zeitung*, have bab-
bled, fictionalized, and wailed about the "ground of legality" as much
and as often as the "ground of legality" was lost, won back, shot full
of holes, patched up, hurled from Berlin to Frankfurt, from Frankfurt
to Berlin, narrowed, widened, turned from a simple earth floor to an
inlaid floor, from an inlaid floor to a double floor—a well-known
trick of theatrical jugglers—from a double floor into a bottomless
trapdoor, so that, in the end, the ground of legality has rightly been
transformed for our readers into a floor of the *Kölnische Zeitung*, so
they could exchange the shibboleth of the Prussian bourgeoisie for
the private shibboleth of Herr Joseph Dumont, and a much-needed
idea of Prussian history for an arbitrary whim of the *Kölnische
Zeitung*, and see in the ground of legality only the ground on which
the *Kölnische Zeitung* grows.

The *ground of legality*, and particularly the *Prussian ground of
legality!*

The ground of legality—on which, after March, the knight of the
great debate, Camphausen, the resurrected ghost of the Confederated
Assembly, and the Assembly have moved—is the Constitutional Law
of 1815, or the Law of the Assembly of 1820, or the Patent of 1847,
or the Election and Unification Laws of April 8, 1848.

Nothing to all this.

The "legal ground" meant simply that the revolution did not win
and that the old society did not lose its ground, that the March
Revolution was only an "event" which provided an "impulse" for the
"understanding" between the old Prussian state and the bourgeoisie,
which had long been in preparation and the need for which had been
expressed in a most high proclamation but not considered "urgent"
before March. In a word, the "legal ground" meant that after March
the bourgeoisie wanted to negotiate with the crown on the same
footing as before March, as if no revolution had taken place and as
if the Coalition Assembly could have attained its objective without

the revolution. The "legal ground" meant that the people's legal title, the revolution, did not exist in the *contrat social* between the government and the bourgeoisie. *The bourgeoisie adduced its demands from the Old Prussian laws, so that the people would not adduce their demands from the new Prussian Revolution.*

It is known that the ideological cretins of the bourgeoisie, its newspaper scribblers, etc., claimed this extenuation of bourgeois interests to be the real interests of the bourgeoisie and had to imagine, to themselves and others, this to be the case. In the mind of a Brügge-mann the "legal ground" phrase became transformed into real substance.

The Camphausen Ministry discharged its task, the task of mediation and transition. Specifically, it carried out the mediation between the bourgeoisie raised on the shoulders of the people and the bourgeoisie which no longer needed the shoulders of the people; between the bourgeoisie which seemingly represented the people versus the crown and the bourgeoisie which really represented the crown versus the people; between the bourgeoisie which disengaged itself from the revolution and the bourgeoisie which was eliminated as the kernel of the revolution.

In keeping with its role, the Camphausen Ministry confined itself in virginal bashfulness to a passive resistance to the revolution.

It rejected the revolution in theory, to be sure, but in practice it strove only against its demands and tolerated only the reconstitution of the old political institutions.

In the meantime the bourgeoisie believed that it had reached the point where its passive resistance had to pass into active attack. The Camphausen Ministry resigned, not because it committed this or that blunder, but for the simple reason that it was the first ministry of the March Revolution, because it was *the* ministry of the March Revolution and, in keeping with its origins, still had to hide the bourgeoisie's representative behind the people's dictator. This ambiguous origin and its ambiguous character still imposed certain expediencies, reservations, and considerations for the sovereign people which had become burdensome to the bourgeoisie, but which a second ministry, emanating directly from the Confederated Assembly, need no longer observe.

The Camphausen Ministry's retirement was therefore a puzzle to the public-house politicians. The Ministry of Action, the Hansemann Ministry, succeeded it, because the bourgeoisie thought of passing from the period of passive betrayal of the people to the crown to a period of active subjection of the people to its rule in alliance with the crown. The Ministry of Action was the *second* ministry after the March Revolution. This was its whole secret.

Cologne, December 29

"*Gentlemen!* In money matters there is no friendship!"
In these words Hansemann summarized the entire United-Diet-Liberalism. This man was the head of the ministry that emerged by necessity from the United Assembly itself, a ministry which was to transform *passive resistance* to the people into *active attack* on the people, the Ministry of Action.

In no Prussian ministry had there been so many bourgeois names! Hansemann, Milde, Märker, Kühlwetter, Gierke! Even the one name in this ministry entitled to presentation at court, von Auerswald, belonged to the liberal, that is, the Königsberg nobility opposition that paid homage to the bourgeoisie. Only Roth von Schreckenstein represented the canaille of the old Prussian bureaucratic feudal nobility. Roth von Schreckenstein! Obsolete title of a robbers-and-knights novel of the past by the blessed Hildebrandt![9] But Roth von Schreckenstein was only the feudal setting in the bourgeois jewel. Roth von Schreckenstein, amidst the bourgeois ministry, proclaimed in big letters: the Prussian feudality, the army, the bureaucracy are following the rising star of the Prussian citizenry. These powers have put themselves at the disposal of the latter, which plants them before its throne the way the bear used to be planted as the heraldic symbol of the rulers over the people. Roth von Schreckenstein is to be the bear of the bourgeois ministry.

On June 26 the Hansemann Ministry presented itself to the National Assembly. It began to operate seriously only in July. The June Revolution was the background of the Ministry of Action, as the February Revolution had been the background of the Ministry of Mediation.

The Prussian bourgeoisie exploited against the people the bloody victory of the Paris bourgeoisie over the Paris proletariat, the way the Prussian crown exploited against the bourgeoisie the bloody victory of the Croats in Vienna. The woes of the Prussian bourgeoisie after the Austrian November are the settlement of accounts for the woes of the Prussian people after the French June. In their shortsighted narrow-mindedness these German philistines proved interchangeable with the French bourgeoisie. They overthrew no throne; they did not do away with the feudal society, let alone its last remnant; they did not have to defend any society created by themselves. After June as after February, as after the beginning of

---

9. In 1821 C. Hildebrandt published a knighthood romance called, *Kuno von Schreckenstein, oder die weissagende Traumgestalt* [*Kuno von Schreckenstein, or the Prophetic Vision*]. *Schreckenstein* means "terrifying rock."

the sixteenth century and in the eighteenth century, they thought they could, in their hereditary, cunning, profit-mad way, draw three-quarters' profit from foreign labor. They did not realize that behind the French June there lurked the Austrian November, and behind the Austrian November the Prussian December. They did not realize that while in France the bourgeoisie, which had smashed the throne, saw before it only one enemy, the proletariat—the Prussian bourgeoisie, grappling with the crown, had only one ally, the people. It was not that both did not possess opposing interests. It was, rather, that the same interest welded both together against a third, the power that oppressed them alike.

The Hansemann Ministry considered itself the Ministry of the June Revolution. And in every Prussian city the philistine citizens transformed themselves into "honest republicans" against the "red robbers"—and at the same time did not cease to be respectable royalists, and conveniently overlooked that their "reds" wore white-and-black[10] cockades.

In his speech from the throne on June 26, Hansemann made short shrift of Camphausen's mysteriously foggy "monarchy on the widest possible democratic foundation."

"A constitutional monarchy on the basis of a bicameral system and a combined exercise of legislative power by both chambers and the crown"—with this dry formula he turned back the portentous dictum of his enthusiastic predecessor.

"Changing the most necessary conditions that are not in accord with the new constitution; ridding property of the fetters which cripple its lucrative usefulness in most of the country; reorganization of the administration of justice; reformation of the tax laws, specifically, the elimination of tax privileges, etc.," and, above all, "strengthening the national power that is necessary for the protection" (from the citizens) "of the newly acquired freedom against reaction" (exploitation of freedom in the interest of the feudalists) "and anarchy" (exploitation of freedom in the interest of the people); "and the restoration of confidence that has been upset."[11]

Such was the ministerial program, the program of the Prussian bourgeoisie that had achieved ministerial status, whose classical representative was Hansemann.

---

10. The colors of the Prussian flag.
11. From Hansemann's speech in the National Assembly on June 26, 1848, in *Stenographische Berichte über die Verhandlungen der zur Vereinbarung der preussischen Staats-Verfassung berufenen Versammlung [Stenographic Reports on the Proceedings of the Assembly Convened for the Arrangement of a Prussian State Constitution]*, Vol. I.

In the Assembly, Hansemann was the most irate and cynical opponent of confidence, because—"Gentlemen! In money matters there is no friendship!" In the ministry Hansemann proclaimed the *"restoration of confidence that has been upset"* as the first priority, because—and this time he turned to the people, as he did formerly to the crown— *"Gentlemen! When it comes to money, good-fellowship is out!"*

What was involved at that time was the confidence that *provides* money; this time, the confidence that *produces* money. At that time feudal confidence, faithful and devoted trust in God, King, and Country; this time *bourgeois* confidence, confidence in commerce and trade, in interest on capital, in business friends' ability to pay, and commercial trust; not in Faith, Love, and Hope, but in *credit.*

"Restoration of confidence that has been upset!" In these words Hansemann expressed the *idée fixe* of the Prussian bourgeoisie.

Credit rests on the assurance that the exploitation of wage labor by capital, of the proletariat by the bourgeoisie, of the petty bourgeois by the big bourgeois, will continue in the traditional way. Every political agitation of the proletariat of whatever nature, be it even one directly commanded by the bourgeoisie, upsets confidence and credit. Hence in the mouth of Hansemann "restoration of confidence that has been upset" meant: *Suppression of every political movement among the proletariat* and among all strata of the population whose interests, in their view, do not coincide with those of the class at the helm.

Hence, next to "restoration of confidence that has been upset" Hansemann put "strengthening of the political power." He erred only in the nature of this "political power." He meant to strengthen the political power that would serve bourgeois confidence and credit, but he strengthened only the political power that demands confidence and which in an emergency resorts to grapeshot because it has no credit. He wanted to haggle with production costs of bourgeois rule and burden the bourgeoisie with the restoration of Prussian feudal rule, costing millions which it could ill afford.

To the workers Hansemann declared laconically that he had a great remedy for them in his pocket, but before he could take it out the "upset confidence" must first be restored. To restore confidence, the working class must put an end to its politicizing and meddling in political affairs and return to its old habits. If it follows his advice and confidence is restored, then the great mysterious remedy becomes effective because it is no longer necessary or applicable, since the illness—the upsetting of bourgeois order—has already been eliminated. And why remedies, when there is no illness? However, should the people persist in being headstrong, well and good, he would "strengthen the political power," the police, the army, the courts, the bureaucracy, he would turn the dogs on them, for "confidence" has become a "money question," and "Gentlemen! In money matters there is no friendship!"

No matter how Hansemann may smile over this, his program was an honest program, a well-intentioned program.

He wanted to strengthen the political power, not only against anarchy, that is, against the people; he wanted to strengthen it also against reaction, that is, the crown and the feudal interests, insofar as the latter sought to oppose the most modest ploitical claims of the bourgeoisie.

The Ministry of Action was in its entire composition already a protest against "reaction."

It distinguished itself from all previous Prussian ministries in that its real finance minister was the Prime Minister. For centuries the Prussian state had most carefully concealed the fact that the Ministries of War, Interior, and Foreign Affairs, Church and School Affairs, and even the Royal Court administration and Faith, Love, and Hope had been subordinated to profane *finances*. The Ministry of Action put this annoying bourgeois truth to the fore, in that it placed in the forefront Herr Hansemann, the man whose ministerial program, like his opposition program, was summed up in: "*Gentlemen! In money matters there is no friendship!*"

In Prussia, the monarchy became a "money question."

Let us now turn from the program of the Ministry of Action to its actions.

The threat of "strengthened political power" against "anarchy"— that is, against the working class and all segments of the citizenry which did not stay with Herr Hansemann's program—was made into a joke. One can say that, with the exception of the raising of taxes on beet sugar and brandy, this reaction against so-called anarchy— that is, against the revolutionary movement—was the only serious action of the Ministry of Action.

A large number of lawsuits against the press, based on provincial law or, where that was lacking, on the *Code Pénal;* numerous arrests based on the same "sufficient principles" (Auerswald's formula); the institution of a constabulary system in Berlin, whereby one constable was assigned for every two houses; police attacks on freedom of association; letting loose the soldiery on citizens who had become presumptuous; letting loose the militia on a proletariat that had become presumptuous; a state of siege by way of example—all this Hansemann Olympiad is still fresh in memory. It needs no further details.

Kühlwetter summed up this aspect of the efforts of the Ministry of Action in these words: "A state that wants to be truly free must have a truly large police personnel as its executive power."

To which Hansemann himself murmured what was to him a stabilizing comment: "This would also contribute essentially to the restoration of confidence, to the revival of business activity."

Hence under the Ministry of Action, the old Prussian police, the public procurators, the bureaucracy, the army were all "strengthened" because, Hansemann imagined, they were in the *pay* and hence in the *service* of the bourgeoisie. Enough: they were "*strengthened.*"

In contrast, the mood of the proletariat and the civil democracy can be described by one fact. While a few reactionaries manhandled a few democrats in Charlottenburg, the people stormed the hotel of the Prime Minister—so popular had the Ministry of Action become. On the following day Hansemann proposed a law against mob gatherings and public meetings. This is how slyly he intrigued against reaction.

Thus the real, palpable, popular activity of the Ministry of Action was a purely *police* one. In the eyes of the proletariat and the city democracy, the ministry and the Union Assembly, whose majority was represented in the ministry, and the Prussian bourgeoisie, whose majority formed the majority in the Union Assembly, represented nothing but the old, revived police and bureaucratic state. To this was added an embitterment against the bourgeoisie, because the bourgeoisie was in power and was working in the militia to become an integral part of the police.

This was the "March victory" in the eyes of the people; even the liberal gentlemen of the bourgeoisie took over *police* functions. Hence integral part of the police.

But only in the proposed organic laws, rather than from the actions of the Ministry of Action, does it become clear that the latter "strengthened" and spurred the "police," the ultimate expression of the old state, in favor of bourgeois interests.

In the laws that the Hansemann Ministry proposed for community regulation, jury courts, and militia it is *property*, in one form or another, that always forms the boundary between what is *legal* and *illegal*. In all these proposed laws, to be sure, the most servile concessions were made to the royal power, for here the bourgeois ministry believed itself to possess an ally that had become harmless, but in compensation the rule of capital became that much the more ruthless toward labor.

The militia law, which the Assembly sanctioned, was turned against the bourgeoisie itself and used to provide a legal excuse for its disarmament. Of course the bourgeoisie imagined that the law would become effective only after the community regulation decree and the promulgation of the constitution—after it has been fortified in its rule. The experiences which the Prussian bourgeoisie had with the militia law may contribute to its own enlightenment; it may learn from them that everything it once meant to do against the people was done against itself.

In *practice* therefore, the Hansemann Ministry summed itself up for the people in Old Prussian police jailing; and in theory, in the insulting Belgian differentiation between bourgeois and nonbourgeois.[12]

Let us now turn to the ministerial program, to the anarchy against reaction.

On this score the ministry has more pious wishes than actions to show.

To the pious bourgeois wishes belong the piecemeal sale of the demesnes to private owners, the surrender of banking institutions to free competition, the transformation of maritime commerce into a private institution.

The Ministry of Action was unfortunate in that all its economic attacks on the feudal party appeared under the aegis of a compulsory loan, and its reforming efforts in general appeared in the eyes of the people as mere financial expedients for filling the treasury of the strengthened "political power." In this way Hansemann reaped the hatred of one party without reaping approval from the other. And it cannot be denied that he ventured a serious attack on feudal privileges only where the immediate "money question"—the money question in the Finance Ministry's sense—forced itself upon him. It was in this narrow-minded sense that he cried out to the feudalists: "Gentlemen! In money matters there is no friendship!"

Thus even his positive bourgeois efforts against the feudalists contributed the same police coloring as his negative measures for the "revival of business activity." For in political economy *police* means *fisc*. The increase in the beet-sugar and brandy tax, which Hansemann put through the National Assembly and which became law, outraged the moneybags-for-King-and-Country in Silesia, in the Marches, in Saxony, in East and West Prussia, etc. But if these measures aroused the anger of the industrial landowners in the Old Prussian provinces, they stirred up no less discontent among the bourgeois distillers in the Rhineland Province, who saw themselves thereby placed in more unfavorable competitive conditions with the Old Prussian provinces. And to fill the measure to overflowing, the tax embittered the working

---

12. Under the Belgian Constitution of 1831 property qualifications for voting were so high that a large part of the population could not vote.

class in the old provinces for whom it meant nothing and could mean nothing but: *a rise in cost of indispensable provisions.* Nothing, therefore, was left of this measure but a filling up of the treasury of the "strengthened political power"! And this example suffices—for it is the only action of the Ministry of Action against the feudalists which *really* went into effect, the only proposed legislation in this direction that really became law.

Hansemann's "proposals" for the abolition of the class land-tax exemptions, like his project for an income tax, set off tarantellas among the landowning "for God, King, and Country" swarms. They denounced him as—a *communist;* and even now Prussian lady crusaders cross themselves three times when they mention the name Hansemann. It sounds to them like Fra Diavolo.[13] The abolition of the land-tax exemption, the only significant measure proposed by a Prussian minister during the rule of the Constituent Assembly, was defeated by the *narrow-minded principles of the left.* And Hansemann himself had justified this narrow-mindedness. He did not want to open up new financial resources for the ministry of "strengthened political power" before the constitution was fabricated and confirmed.

The bourgeois ministry par excellence was so unlucky that its most radical measure was paralyzed by the radical members of the Constituent Assembly. It was so paltry that its whole crusade against the feudality reduced itself to a tax increase, hateful to all classes alike, and its entire financial acumen aborted in a compulsory loan. Altogether, two measures which in the end merely provided *subsidies for the campaign of the counterrevolution against the bourgeoisie itself.* The feudalists, however, became convinced of the "malevolent" intentions of the bourgeois ministry. Thus even in its financial struggle with feudalism, the Prussian bourgeoisie, in its unpopular impotence, knew how to raise money only against itself, and—"Gentlemen! In money matters there is no friendship!"

Just as the bourgeois ministry succeeded in embittering the city proletariat, the bourgeois democracy, and the feudalists at the same time, so it also managed to alienate and to make an enemy of the peasant class enslaved by feudalism—all this with the eager support of the Constituent Assembly. In general, we should not forget that during half of its term, this Assembly found its appropriate representative in the Hansemann Ministry and that today's bourgeois martyrs were Hansemann's train bearers of yesterday.

---

13. *Brother Devil,* the name of an opera by the French composer Daniel François Auber (1782–1871), based on the exploits of a southern Italian bandit chieftain, Michele Pezza, who was hanged by the French conquerors in 1806.

The draft of the law for the exemption of feudal burdens, submitted by Patow under the Hansemann Ministry (see our previous criticism of it), was a wretched patchwork made up of the most impotent bougeois desires for the elimination of feudal privileges as "incompatible with the new constitutional relationships," and of the bourgeois fear of being revolutionary by touching any kind of property. A miserable, intimidated, narrow-minded egoism blinded the Prussian bourgeoisie to such an extent that it repulsed the allies it most needed—the peasant class.

On June 3, Deputy Hanow moved the motion "that all pending discussions regarding landowner-peasant relationships and the commutation of feudal services be postponed until the enactment of a law on this subject based on reasonable principles. . . ."

And it was not until the end of September, that is, four months later, under the Pfuel Ministry, that the Constituent Assembly resumed the suspended landowner-peasant deliberations, after it had rejected all liberal amendments and "reserved the determination of current contributions in the interim," depending "on the collection of the disputed contributions in arrears."

In August, if we are not mistaken, the Constituent Assembly accepted Nenstiel's motion that "an immediate abolition of compulsory peasant services to the manor" was "not urgent"—and still the peasants were expected to consider it urgent for them to fight for the Assembly which hurled them back into the material conditions that had existed before the March victory!

The French bourgeoisie began with the emancipation of the peasants. With the peasants, it conquered Europe. The Prussian bourgeoisie has been so possessed by its own narrow, selfish interests that it has forfeited even this ally and made it a tool in the hands of the counterrevolution.

The official history of the dissolution of the bourgeois ministry is known.

Under its wings the "political power" was so "strengthened" and the people's energy so depressed that as early as July 15 the *Dioscuri*, Kühlwetter-Hansemann, had to issue a warning to all the prefects of the country against the reactionary activities of the administrative officials, especially the subprefects; this resulted in an "Assembly of the nobility and the big landowners for the protection of their privileges" meeting alongside the Assembly in Berlin, and ending finally, in Oberlausitz, on September 4, in a convocation of the "Communal Diet for the maintenance of the threatened property rights of the big landowners," a Diet inherited from the Middle Ages, in opposition to the so-called Berlin National Assembly.

The energy which the government and the so-called National Assembly used against these constantly threatening counterrevolutionary symptoms was expressed in suitable paper admonitions. Bayonets, cannon balls, prisons, and jails the bourgeois ministry had only for the people, "for the restoration of the confidence that has been upset," and for the revival of business activity.

The incidents at Schweidnitz, where the soldiery directly assassinated the bourgeoisie in the militia, stirred the National Assembly out of its apathy. On August 9 it gathered up courage for a heroic deed, the Stein-Schultze Army Order, which means of coercion relied on the delicacy of feeling of the Prussian officers. What a means of coercion! And did not the royalist honor of the officers forbid them to pay attention to bourgeois honor?

One month after the Constituent Assembly prepared the Stein-Schultze Army Order, on September 7, it resolved again that its resolution was a real resolution and had to be carried out by the ministers. Hansemann refused, and resigned on September 11, after having appointed himself a bank director with an annual salary of six thousand taler, because—"Gentlemen! In money matters there is no friendship!"

Finally, on September 25, the Constituent Assembly gratefully accepted from Pfuel a completely eviscerated version of the Stein-Schultze Army Order, which in the meantime, because of the contradictory Army Order by Wrangel and the troop concentration in Berlin, had sunk to the level of a bad joke.

It needs only one look at the dates and the history of the Stein-Schultze Army Order to become convinced that the latter was not the real reason for Hansemann's resignation. Would Hansemann, who did not shrink from accepting the revolution, really have recoiled before that paper proclamation? Would Hansemann, who took any ministerial portfolio whenever it came his way, really have let one lie on the ministerial bench to be picked up by the first bidder, out of philistinish irritation? No! Our Hansemann is no visionary! Hansemann was simply duped, in much the same way he represented the duped bourgeoisie in general. They led him to believe that the crown would not let him fall under any circumstances. They let him lose the last pretense of popularity, in order finally to sacrifice him to the rancors of the bumpkin-Junkers and to get rid of bourgeois tutelage. Moreover, the campaign plan agreed upon between Russia and Austria called for a general from the camarilla, outside the Constituent Assembly, to be head of the cabinet. Under the bourgeois ministry the old "political power" was sufficiently "strengthened" to venture this coup.

They were disappointed in Pfuel. The victory of the Croats in Vienna made even a Brandenburg a useful instrument.

GERMANY

476

Under the Brandenburg Ministry the Assembly was ignominiously chased out, jeered, ridiculed, humiliated, and persecuted, and the *people were indifferent* in that critical moment. The people's defeat was the defeat of the Prussian bourgeoisie, the constitutionalists, hence a *victory of the democratic party*, no matter how dearly it had to pay for this victory.

But what about the imposed constitution?

At one time they said that a "piece of paper" would never interpose itself between the king and "his" people. Now they said: Only a piece of paper should interpose itself between the king and his people. The *real* constitution of Prussia is—*the state of siege*. The imposed French Constitution contained only one Article 14, which it abolished.[14] Every paragraph of the imposed Prussian Constitution is an Article 14.

By this constitution the crown decrees new privileges—namely, for itself.

It gives itself the liberty of dissolving the Chambers ad infinitum. It gives the ministers the liberty of issuing laws (including those about property) at will in the meantime. It gives the deputies the liberty of complaining against the ministers about the danger of being declared "internal enemies" in a period of siege. Finally, it gives itself the liberty, when the actions of the counterrevolution reach a peak in the spring, of replacing the "piece of paper" that floats in the air with a Magna Charta derived organically from the medieval Christian–Germanic Estates differentiation, or of giving up the constitution game altogether. Even in the latter case, the conservative portion of the bourgeoisie would fold its hands and intone: "The Lord hath given, the Lord hath taken away, praised be the name of the Lord!"

The history of the Prussian bourgeoisie, as well as the history from March to December of the German bourgeoisie in general, proves that in Germany a purely bourgeois revolution and the establishment of bourgeois rule in the form of a constitutional monarchy is impossible, and that the only possibilities are a feudal absolutist counterrevolution or a *social-republican revolution*.

But that the viable portion of the bourgeoisie must awake from its apathy again is guaranteed above all by the monster financial bill with which the counterrevolution will surprise it in the spring. As our Hansemann says so thoughtfully: "Gentlemen! In money matters there is no friendship!"

---

14. Article 14 of the *Charte constitutionelle,* issued by Louis XVII in 1814, read: "The King is the Chief of State . . . He decrees the stipulations and the ordinances necessary for the execution of the laws for the security of the state."

The House of Hohenzollern*

Cologne, May 9

IN THE LAST DAYS of its and the Prussian state's existence, the government of Herr von Hohenzollern seems again to verify fully the old reputation of the Prussian and Hohenzollern name.

Who does not know their character from Heine's poem:

> A child with a big pumpkin head,
> with long sideburns and gray pigtails,
> with spidery-long but strong little arms,
> with a gigantic gizzard but short entrails,
> A monster....[1]

Who does not know the breaches of faith, the perfidies, the legacy huntings by which this family of corporals bearing the name of Hohenzollern became great?

We know how the so-called Great Elector (as if an elector could be great!) committed his first treachery against Poland in that he, Poland's ally against Sweden, suddenly went over to the Swedes, the better to plunder Poland in the Peace of Oliva.[2]

We know the tasteless figure of Frederick I, the brutal coarseness of Frederick William I.

We know how Frederick II, the founder of patriarchal despotism,

---

* *Neue Rheinische Zeitung*, May 10, 1849.

1. Heinrich Heine, *"Der Wechselbalg"* ["The Monster"]: *"Ein Kind mit grossem Kürbiskopf,/Mit langem Schnurrbart, greisem Zopf,/Mit spinnig langen, doch starken Ärmchen,/Mit Riesenmagen, doch kurzen Gedärmchen,/Ein Wechselbalg...."*

2. At the Peace of Oliva, concluded between Sweden on the one side and Poland, Austria, and Brandenburg on the other, on May 3, 1660, Poland finally relinquished sovereignty over East Prussia.

[477]

the friend of the Enlightenment via flogging, auctioned off his country to the highest-bidding French entrepreneurs. We know how he allied with Russia and Austria to rape Poland,[3] an act which even now, after the Revolution of 1848, continues to be an unremoved stain on German history.

We know how Frederick William II helped to complete the rape of Poland, when he squandered the usurped Polish national and church estates on his courtiers.

We know how, in 1792, he formed a coalition with Austria and England to suppress the glorious French Revolution and to invade France; we also know how his "splendid army," covered with insult and shame, was driven out of France.

We know how he then left his allies in the lurch and hastened to make peace with the French Republic.[4]

We know how he, who used to pretend to enthusiasm for the King of France and Navarre, bought cheaply from the French Republic this same King's crown diamonds, and thus profited from the misfortune of his "Beloved Brother."

We know how he, whose whole life has been a real Hohenzollernish mixture of luxury and mysticism, of senile lasciviousness and childish superstition, trampled on freedom of speech in the Bischoffwerder Edicts.[5]

We know how his successor, Frederick William III, the "Just," betrayed his allies to Napoleon, having been tossed Hanover as bait.

We know how he thereupon immediately betrayed Napoleon to these quondam allies when he, in the pay of England and Russia, attacked the French Revolution embodied in the person of Napoleon.

We know what success that attack had: the unheard-of defeat of the "splendid army" at Jena; the sudden outbreak of a moral lice disease throughout the Prussian body politic; a series of betrayals, vilenesses, and cringings on the part of Prussian officials, from whom Napoleon and his generals turned away in disgust.

We know how, in 1813, Frederick William III, by means of fine words and splendid promises, brought the Prussian people to the point that they came to believe in a "war of liberty" against the French, although what was really involved was a suppression of the French Revolution and a restoration of the old order by the grace of God.

---

3. In 1772 Poland was first partitioned between Prussia, Austria, and Russia.
4. In 1795 Prussia and France concluded a separate peace at Basel.
5. In the edict on religion, of July 9, 1788, and on censorship, of December 19, 1788, issued at the suggestion of Frederick William II's favorite, Johann Rudolf von Bischoffwerder, religious and press freedom were restricted.

We know how the fine promises were forgotten as soon as the Holy Alliance marched into Paris on March 30, 1814.

We know how, by the time of Napoleon's return from Elba, the enthusiasm of the people was already so cooled that the Hohenzollern had to revive their extinguished zeal with the promise of a constitution (Edict of May 22, 1815) four weeks before the battle of Waterloo.

We recall the promises of the German Federal Acts and of the Vienna Curtain Acts:[6] freedom of the press, a constitution, etc.

We know how the "Just" Hohenzollern kept his word: the Holy Alliance and congresses for the suppression of nations, Carlsbad Decrees,[7] censorship, police despotism, rule by aristocracy, bureaucratic arbitrariness, justice by cabinets, demagogic persecutions, mass condemnations, financial waste—and no constitution.

We know how in 1820 the nation was assured of no increase in taxes and no rise in the national debt, and how the Hohenzollern kept his word: expansion of the Maritime Commerce Association into a secret state credit bank.

We know how the Hohenzollern replied to the appeal of the French people in the July Revolution: massing troops on the frontier, keeping down his own people, suppressing the movement in the smaller German states, and finally enslaving these states under the knout of the Holy Alliance.

We know how this same Hohenzollern violated neutrality in the Russo-Polish War,[8] letting the Russians pass through his territory and thereby get at the back of the Poles, putting the Prussian arsenals and magazines at the disposal of the Russians, offering a secure haven in Prussia to every defeated Russian army corps.

We know that the whole effort of the Hohenzollern Underlord, in accord with the objectives of the Holy Alliance, was directed at strengthening the aristocracy, the bureaucracy, and the military in their rule, and suppressing with brutal force all freedom of expression and all influence of the "limited intelligence of the subjects" on the government, not only in Prussia but also in the rest of Germany.

We know that there has rarely been a period when such laudable intentions have been carried out in a more brutal way than in the period of Frederick William III, especially between 1815 and 1840. Nowhere have so many people ever been condemned and sentenced,

---

6. The Acts passed by the Congress of Vienna, in June, 1815, confirming German federal constitutions.

7. The decrees passed by the ministers of the German federal states in August, 1819, establishing rigid censorship and surveillance of students and universities.

8. On January 31, 1831, Czar Nicholas I began a war against Poland, which ended on September 7, 1831, with the Russian occupation of Warsaw.

nowhere have the fortresses ever been so full of political prisoners, as under the "just" ruler. And having achieved this, one comes to realize what innocent blockheads these demagogues were.

Shall we revert also to the Hohenzollern who, according to the Monk of Lehnin,[9] "would be the last of his race"? Shall we speak of the rebirth of Christian-Germanic grandeur and the resurrection of pallid financial distress, of the Order of the Swan,[10] of the Chief Censorship Court, of the United Diet,[11] of the General Synod, of the "piece of paper,"[12] of the vain efforts to borrow money, and all the rest of the achievements of the glorious epoch of 1840–48? Shall we prove from Hegel that it takes a comedian to see the end of the Hohenzollern line?

It will not be necessary. The above-mentioned data fully suffices to characterize the Hohenzollern-Prussian name. It is true that the luster of this name was dimmed for a moment, but since the Pleiades of Manteuffel & Co. have surrounded the crown, the ancient grandeur has returned again. Once more, Prussia is, as of yore, a vice-kingdom under the Russian suzerainty; once more the Hohenzollern is the underlord of the Autocrat of all the Russians and the overlord of all the little boyars of Saxony, Bavaria, Hesse-Homburg, Waldeck, etc.; once more the limited understanding of the subjects is restored to its old right of obeying orders. "My splendid army," so long as the *Pravoslavny* [Orthodox] Czar does not use it himself, is to restore, in Saxony, Baden, Hesse, and the Palatinate, the kind of order that has prevailed in Warsaw for eighteen years, and to glue together, in its own country and in Austria, the cracked crown with the blood of the subjects. The word spoken in anxiety and in the distress of the heart concerns us as little as our forefathers resting with God; and as soon as we are finished at home we will move, with martial music and flying flags, against France, conquer the country which grows champagne, and destroy the great Babel, the mother of all sins!

These are the plans of our exalted rulers; this is the haven to which the noble Hohenzollern is steering us. Hence the piled-up edicts

---

9. In the so-called *Vaticinium Lehninense* [*Lehnin Prophecy*], a monk named Hermann, living in Lehnin, a cloister near Potsdam, prophesied in the year 1300 the decline of the House of Hohenzollern in the eleventh generation.

10. In 1843 Frederick William IV vainly tried to restore the knightly Order of the Swan, established in 1443.

11. The first United Diet sat from April 11 to June 26, 1847; it was dissolved after it would not vote a loan demanded by the King. The second United Diet, meeting on April 2, 1848, was dissolved on April 10, 1848, after it voted a loan of 25,000,000 taler.

12. In a speech at the opening of the Diet, on April 11, 1847, Frederick William IV referred to a constitution as a "piece of paper."

and strokes of violence; hence the repeated kicks at the cowardly Frankfurt Assembly; hence the states of siege, the arrests and the persecutions; hence the invasion of Dresden and South Germany by Prussian soldiery.

But there is still one power, which of course gets little attention from the gentlemen in Sans Souci, but which nevertheless will speak with the voice of thunder. The PEOPLE—the people who, in Paris as well as on the Rhine, in Silesia as well as in Austria, with teeth gnashing in anger, are awaiting the moment of revolt, and who knows how soon all the Hohenzollerns and all underlords and overlords will get what they deserve.

The Prussian Counterrevolution
and the Judiciary*

THE MAIN FRUIT of the revolutionary movement of 1848 is not what the nations have won, but what they have lost—*the loss of their illusions.*

June, November, December of the year 1848, these are the giant milestones, indicators of the disillusionment and the sobering of the European people's mind.

Among the last illusions which had held the German people in thrall was above all the superstition in regard to the judiciary.

The prosaic north wind of the Prussian counterrevolution has also blown the bloom off the people's chimera, whose true motherland is Italy—Eternal Rome.

The acts and declarations of the Rhenish Court of Cassation, the Supreme Tribunal of Berlin, the Supreme Courts of Münster, Bromberg, and Ratibor against Esser, Waldeck, Temme, Kirchmann, and Gierke prove once again that the French Convention [1792–95] is and remains the lighthouse of all revolutionary epochs. It inaugurated the Revolution in that it removed all officials by decree. Even judges are nothing but officials, as the above-named courts bear witness before all of Europe. Turkish cadis and Chinese Mandarin collegiums can comfortably endorse the latest judgments of those "high" courts against their colleagues.

Our readers are already familiar with the decrees of the Supreme Tribunal of Berlin and the Supreme Court of Ratibor. Today we will deal with the Supreme Court of Münster.

But first a few words about the Berlin-based Rhenish Court of Cassation, the *summus pontifex* [pope] of Rhenish jurisprudence.

* From article in *Neue Rheinische Zeitung*, December 24, 1848.

As is well known, the Rhenish jurists (with a few honorable exceptions) had nothing more precipitous to do in the Prussian Assembly than to cure the Prussian Government of its old prejudices and animosities. In reality they proved that their opposition to the government hardly amounted to even as much as that of the French *parlements* before 1789—a capricious and liberally self-aggrandizing validation of guild interests. The liberal Rhenish members of the Prussian Assembly were, like the liberals of the French National Assembly of 1789, the bravest of the brave in the army of servility. The Rhenish Prussian tribunals shamed the Old Prussian examining magistrates with their "political fanaticism." The Rhenish jurists had, of course, to maintain their reputation even after the dissolution of the Assembly. The laurels of the Old Prussian supreme tribunals caused the Rhenish Prussian Court of Cassation a loss of sleep. Its Chief President Sethe issued an order to Supreme Revision Councilor Esser (not to be confused with the "well-intentioned" Cologne Essers) similar to the one the President of the Supreme Tribunal Mühler issued to Privy Councilor Waldeck. But the Rhenish Prussian Court knew how to outbid the Old Prussian one. The President of the Rhenish Court of Cassation trumped his competitor by committing the perfidious incivility of informing the Berlin public by releasing the letter to *Die Deutsche Reform* before he sent it to Herr Esser himself. We are convinced that the *whole Rhine Province* will answer Herr Sethe's letter with a monster address to our gray and worthy countryman, Herr Esser.

It is not a little bit that is rotten in the "state of Denmark"; *everything* is.

Now to Münster!

Our readers have already heard about the Münster Supreme Court's protest against the reinstallation of its director, Temme.

The story hangs together as follows:

Directly or indirectly, the Ministry of the Counterrevolution had insinuated to the Privy Supreme Tribunal, the Rhenish Court of Cassation, and the Supreme Courts in Bromberg, Ratibor, and Münster that the King was reluctant to see Waldeck, Esser, Gierke, Kirchmann, and Temme return to their high judicial posts because of their participation in the Berlin National Assembly's decisions about withholding taxes. They were to protect against the withholding.

The high courts . . . all went along with this demand and sent protests from and to Berlin. The Supreme Court of Münster was dumb enough to turn directly to the King (the so-called Constitutional King) with a protest against Temme. . . .

The protest was signed by the whole Münster Collegium, with the exception of one Councilor, a brother-in-law of Minister of Justice Rintelen.

On December 18 Minister Rintelen sent a copy of this protest to Temme in Münster "for his decision," after the latter, without challenge by the cowards, had taken up his duties again.

On the morning of December 19, as the *Düsseldorfer Zeitung* reports, Temme "appeared for the first time at the plenary session of the Münster Supreme Court and took his place as Director alongside the Deputy Chief President von Olfers." . . .

The bravest of the brave were thunderstruck. They sat there silent, unmoving, stony, as if the head of Medusa had been hurled into this Mandarin collegium.

The brave Supreme Court of Münster! In its zealousness, it had ordered the examination and arrest of a number of people because they had tried to carry out the National Assembly's decision to withhold taxes. In its declaration of opinion against Temme, even directly at the steps of the throne, the brave Supreme Court had constituted itself a party—had passed a prejudiced judgment, and can therefore no longer play the judicial role vis-à-vis the other party. . . .

The Proletarian Revolution*

KARL MARX spoke on wages and capital and showed with great clarity how workers create capital, how they have been enslaved by the product of their own labor, and how capital is being constantly used to forge their chains ever more strongly. The so-called free worker has, to be sure, the consciousness of being a free worker, but he is the more in the power of capital as he is compelled to sell his labor for a miserable wage to maintain the barest existence. In most cases the free worker stands below the slaves and the serf. The working class does not have to abolish personal property—that has long been abolished and is being so daily—but what must be abolished is bourgeois property, which is founded on deceit.

In regard to social conditions in Germany, Marx remarked that the German proletariat is the first to be capable of carrying out successfully a radical cure. First, the Germans have largely emancipated themselves from all religious nonsense; second, they do not have to experience the protracted bourgeois movement as did the workers of other countries; third, their geographic situation will force them to declare war on the Eastern barbarism, for it was from there—from Asia—that all reaction against the West has come. Thereby the workers' party is forced into revolutionary ground, on which it must act in order to emancipate itself entirely.

---

* Report of a speech before the German Workers' Educational Society in London, February 28, 1867. Published in the magazine *Der Vorbote*, March 3, 1867.

Socialist Policy on the
Franco-Prussian War*

. . . THE MILITARY CAMARILLA, the academics, the bourgeoisie, and the pub politicians claim that [Prussia's proposed annexation of Alsace-Lorraine] is the means for protecting Germany from war with France forever. It is, on the contrary, the most proven way of transforming this war into a EUROPEAN INSTITUTION. To claim the necessity of a western Poland, which Alsace and Lorraine would be, is the surest means of perpetuating military despotism in a rejuvenated Germany. It is the infallible way of turning the coming peace into a mere armistice, once France has recovered sufficiently to reclaim the lost territory. It is the infallible way to ruin Germany and France through mutual laceration.

The scoundrels and fools who have found eternal peace in these guarantees should learn from Prussian history, from the example of Napoleon's *Pferdekur* [enough to kill a horse] in the Peace of Tilsit [July, 1807], how such forcible measures to subdue a vital people achieve a result opposite from that intended. And how can France, even after the loss of Alsace and Lorraine, be at all compared with Prussia after the Peace of Tilsit!

And if French chauvinism, so long as the status quo exists in international relations, has found a certain justification in the fact that since 1815 its capital and thereby all of France has had to surrender after a few lost battles—how much more will it be nurtured anew the moment its eastern border is on the Vosges and its northern one at Metz?

---

* From Marx and Engels, Letter to the Committee of the (German) Social-Democratic Labor Party, written between August 22 and 30, 1870; published as a brochure ("Manifesto of the Committee of the Social-Democratic Labor Party") September 5, 1870.

Even the most enraged Teuton would not dare claim that the Lorrainers and Alsatians desire the blessings of a German government. What is being proclaimed is Pan-Germanism and "secure" frontiers, and this is going to have fine consequences for Germany and Europe —from the East [Russia]!

Anyone who is not deafened by the cries of the moment, or who has no interest in deafening the German people, must see that the war of 1870 necessarily carries in its womb the seeds of a WAR BETWEEN GERMANY AND RUSSIA as much as the war of 1866 carried that of 1870.

I say NECESSARILY, UNAVOIDABLY, except only in the unlikely event of a previous outbreak of REVOLUTION IN RUSSIA.

If this unlikely event does not occur, then the war between Germany and Russia must even now be treated as a *fait accompli*.

Whether the present war is to be useful or harmful depends entirely on the present policy of the German victors. Should they take Alsace and Lorraine, France and Russia will war against Germany. It is superfluous to point out the disastrous consequences of this. Should they conclude an honorable peace with France, then Europe will be emancipated from a Muscovite dictatorship, Prussia will be elevated in Germany, the western part of the Continent will be allowed a peaceful development, and, finally, it will help the Russian social revolution, which needs such an external impetus for its development, and will also be of advantage to the Russian people.

BUT I FEAR THAT THE SCOUNDRELS AND FOOLS WILL PURSUE THEIR MAD COURSE UNLESS THE GERMAN WORKING CLASS RAISES ITS VOICE EN MASSE.

The present war opens a new world-historical epoch in that it has proved that even with the exclusion of German Austria, Germany is capable of going its own way, INDEPENDENTLY OF THE OUTSIDE. That it will now find its unity through the Prussian barracks is a punishment it richly deserves. But one advantage has been won directly. Petty rascalities, such as, for example, the conflict between North German national liberals and South German populists, will no longer stand uselessly in the way. Relations will develop and simplify on a large scale. If the German working class does not play its appropriate historic role, it will be its own fault. THIS WAR HAS MOVED THE CENTER OF GRAVITY OF THE CONTINENTAL LABOR MOVEMENT FROM FRANCE TO GERMANY. This places a greater responsibility on the German working class. . . .

Critique of the Gotha Program

Marginal Notes to the Program of the German Workers' Party, which follows this selection, is one of the major documents of Marxism. With the covering letter reproduced here (dated May 5, 1875), Marx sent it to Wilhelm Bracke, asking that it be submitted to the other leaders of the Social-Democratic Workers' party (the "Eisenachers"), which was meeting with the Lassalle-founded General Association of German Workers at Gotha, May 22–27, 1875. The Gotha Congress united both groups into the Socialist Labor party, which later became the powerful German Social-Democratic party.

Dear Bracke:

When you have read the following critical marginal notes on the Coalition Program,[1] please be so good as to send them on to Geib, Auer, Bebel, and Liebknecht for examination. The manuscript must be returned to you, so that it will be at my disposal in case of necessity. I am extremely busy and have to far exceed the amount of work the doctors allow me. Hence it was in no way a "pleasure" to write such a lengthy screed. It was, however, necessary, so that the steps I will take later will not be misinterpreted by the friends in the party for whom this communication is intended.

After the Coalition Congress has been held Engels and I will publish a short explanation to the effect that we will stay away from the said program of principles altogether, and that we have nothing to do with it.

This is indispensable because of the opinion—the entirely erroneous opinion—held abroad that we secretly guide the movement of the

---

1. *"Randglossen zum Programm der deutschen Arbeiterpartei."*

so-called Eisenach party from here. In a recently published Russian book,[2] for example, Bakunin not only holds me responsible for all the programs, etc., of that party but also for every step Liebknecht has taken from the day of his cooperation with the People's party.

Apart from this, it is my duty not to give recognition, even by diplomatic silence, to what in my opinion is a thoroughly objectionable program that demoralizes the party.

Every step of real movement is more important than a dozen programs. If therefore it was not possible—and the conditions of the time did not permit it—to go *beyond* the Eisenach program, one should simply have concluded an agreement for action against the common enemy. But if one constructs programs of principles (instead of postponing them until a prolonged period of common activity has prepared the ground), one sets up before the whole world landmarks which measure the level of party movement.

The Lassallean leaders are coming [to the Congress] because circumstances force them to do it. If it had been explained to them beforehand that there would be no haggling about principles, they would have had to be content with a program of action or a plan of organization for common action. Instead of this they are permitted to come armed with mandates, given recognition of them as binding, and thus one surrenders unconditionally to those who are in need of help. To crown the whole thing, they are holding a congress *before* the Congress of Compromise, while our own party is holding its congress *post festum*. Obviously they wanted to stifle all criticism and give our party no opportunity for reflection. We know that the mere fact of unification satisfies the workers, but it is a mistake to think this momentary success is not bought too dearly.

For the rest, the program is no good, even apart from its sanctification of the Lassallean articles of faith.

I shall be sending you in the near future the last parts of the French edition of *Capital*. The printing was held up for a considerable time by a French government ban. The thing will be ready this week or at the beginning of next week. Had you received the previous six sections? Please let me have the address of Bernhard Becker, to whom I must also send the final parts.

The bookshop of the *Volksstaat* has its peculiar ways. Up to this moment, for example, I have not received a single copy of my *Revelations About the Cologne Communist Trial*.

With best regards,

Your

KARL MARX

---

2. Mikhail Bakunin, *Gossudarstvennost i Anarchiya*, published anonymously in Switzerland in 1873.

Marginal Notes to the Program
of the German Workers' Party*

I

1. "Labor is the source of all wealth and all culture, and since useful labor is possible only in society and through society, the proceeds of labor belong undiminished with equal right to all members of society."

FIRST PART OF THE PARAGRAPH: "Labor is the source of all wealth and all culture."

Labor is *not the source* of all wealth. *Nature* is just as much the source of use values (and it is surely of such that material wealth consists!) as labor, which itself is only the manifestation of a force of nature, human labor power. The above phrase is to be found in all children's primers and is correct insofar as it is implied that labor is performed with the appurtenant subjects and instruments. But a socialist program cannot allow such bourgeois phrases to pass over in silence the *conditions* that alone give them meaning. And insofar as man from the beginning behaves toward nature, the primary source of all instruments and subjects of labor, as an owner, treats her as belonging to him, his labor becomes the source of use values, therefore also of wealth. The bourgeois have very good grounds for falsely ascribing *supernatural creative power* to labor; since precisely from the fact that labor depends on nature it follows that the man who possesses no other property than his labor power must, in all conditions of society and culture, be the slave of other men who have made themselves the owners of the

---

* Translation based on the edition of Progress Publishers, Moscow, 1968.

material conditions of labor. He can work only with their permission, hence live only with their permission.

Let us now leave the sentence as it stands, or rather limps. What could one have expected in conclusion? Obviously this:

"Since labor is the source of all wealth, no one in society can appropriate wealth except as the product of labor. Therefore, if he himself does not work, he lives by the labor of others and also acquires his culture at the expense of the labor of others."

Instead of this, by means of the verbal rivet "and since" a second proposition is added in order to draw a conclusion from this and not from the first one.

SECOND PART OF THE PARAGRAPH: "Useful labor is possible only in society and through society."

According to the first proposition, labor was the source of all wealth and all culture; therefore no society is possible without labor. Now we learn, conversely, that no "useful" labor is possible without society.

One could just as well have said that only in society can useless and even socially harmful labor become a branch of gainful occupation, that only in society can one live by being idle, etc., etc.—in short, one could just as well have copied the whole of Rousseau.

And what is "useful" labor? Surely only labor which produces the intended useful result. A savage—and man was a savage after he had ceased to be an ape—who kills an animal with a stone, who collects fruits, etc., performs "useful" labor.

THIRDLY, THE CONCLUSION: "And since useful labor is possible only in society and through society, the proceeds of labor belong undiminished with equal right to all members of society."

A fine conclusion! If useful labor is possible only in society and through society, the proceeds of labor belong to society—and only so much therefrom accrues to the individual worker as is not required to maintain the "condition" of labor, society.

In fact, this proposition has at all times been made use of by the champions of the *state of society prevailing at any given time*. First come the claims of the government and everything that sticks to it, since it is the social organ for the maintenance of the social order; then come the claims of the various kinds of private property, for the various kinds of private property are the foundations of society, etc. One sees that such hollow phrases can be twisted and turned as desired.

The first and second parts of the paragraph have some intelligible connection only in the following wording:

"Labor becomes the source of wealth and culture only as social labor," or, what is the same thing, "in and through society."

This proposition is incontestably correct, for although isolated labor (its material conditions presupposed) can create use values, it can create neither wealth nor culture.

But equally incontestable is this other proposition:

"In proportion as labor develops socially, and becomes thereby a source of wealth and culture, poverty and destitution develop among the workers, and wealth and culture among the nonworkers."

This is the law of all history hitherto. What, therefore, had to be done here, instead of setting down general phrases about "labor" and "society," was to prove concretely how in present capitalist society the material, etc., conditions have at last been created which enable and compel the workers to lift this social curse.

In fact, however, the whole paragraph, bungled in style and content, is only there in order to inscribe the Lassallean catchword of the "undiminished proceeds of labor" as a slogan at the top of the party banner. I shall return later to the "proceeds of labor," "equal right," etc., since the same thing recurs in a somewhat different form further on.

2. "In present-day society, the instruments of labor are the monopoly of the capitalist class; the resulting dependence of the working class is the cause of misery and servitude in all its forms."

This sentence, borrowed from the Rules of the International, is incorrect in this "improved" edition.

In present-day society the instruments of labor are the monopoly of the landowners (the monopoly of property in land is even the basis of the monopoly of capital) *and* the capitalists. In the passage in question, the Rules of the International do not mention either the one or the other class of monopolists. They speak of the *"monopolizer of the means of labor, that is, the sources of life."* The addition, *"sources of life,"* makes it sufficiently clear that land is included in the instruments of labor.

The correction was introduced because Lassalle, for reasons now generally known, attacked *only* the capitalist class and not the landowners. In England, the capitalist is usually not even the owner of the land on which his factory stands.

3. "The emancipation of labor demands the promotion of the instruments of labor to the common property of society and the cooperative regulation of the total labor, with a fair distribution of the proceeds of labor."

"Promotion of the instruments of labor to the common property" ought obviously to read their "conversion into the common property"; but this only in passing.

What are "proceeds of labor"? The product of labor or its value? And in the latter case, is it the total value of the product or only that part of the value which labor has newly added to the value of the means of production consumed?

"Proceeds of labor" is a loose notion which Lassalle has put in the place of definite economic conceptions.

What is "a fair distribution"?

Do not the bourgeois assert that the present-day distribution is "fair"? And is it not, in fact, the only "fair" distribution on the basis of the present-day mode of production? Are economic relations regulated by legal conceptions or do not, on the contrary, legal relations arise from economic ones? Have not also the socialist sectarians the most varied notions about "fair" distribution?

To understand what is implied in this connection by the phrase "fair distribution," we must take the first paragraph and this one together. The latter presupposes a society wherein the instruments of labor are common property and the total labor is cooperatively regulated, and from the first paragraph we learn that "the proceeds of labor belong undiminished with equal right to all members of society."

"To all members of society"? To those who do not work as well? What remains then of the "undiminished" proceeds of labor? Only to those members of society who work? What remains then of the "equal right" of all members of society?

But "all members of society" and "equal right" are obviously mere phrases. The kernel consists in this, that in this communist society every worker must receive the "undiminished" Lassallean "proceeds of labor."

Let us take first of all the words "proceeds of labor" in the sense of the product of labor; then the cooperative proceeds of labor are the *total social product*.

From this must now be deducted:

First, cover for replacement of the means of production used up.

Second, additional portion for expansion of production.

Third, reserve or insurance funds to provide against accidents, dislocations caused by natural calamities, etc.

These deductions from the "undiminished" proceeds of labor are an economic necessity and their magnitude is to be determined according to available means and forces, and partly by computation of probabilities, but they are in no way calculable by equity.

There remains the other part of the total product, intended to serve as means of consumption.

Before this is divided among the individuals, there has to be deducted again, from it:

First, the general costs of administration not belonging to production.

This part will from the outset be very considerably restricted in comparison with present-day society, and it diminishes in proportion as the new society develops.

Second, that which is intended for the common satisfaction of needs, such as schools, health services, etc.

From the outset this part grows considerably in comparison with present-day society and it grows in proportion as the new society develops.

Third, funds for those unable to work, etc., in short, for what is included under so-called official poor relief today.

Only now do we come to the "distribution" which the program, under Lassallean influence, alone has in view in its narrow fashion, namely, to that part of the means of consumption which is divided among the individual producers of the cooperative society.

The "undiminished" proceeds of labor have already unnoticeably become converted into the "diminished" proceeds, although what the producer is deprived of in his capacity as a private individual benefits him directly or indirectly in his capacity as a member of society.

Just as the phrase of the "undiminished" proceeds of labor has disappeared, so now does the phrase of the "proceeds of labor" disappear altogether.

Within the cooperative society based on common ownership of the means of production, the producers do not exchange their products; just as little does the labor employed on the products appear here as the *value* of these products, as a material quality possessed by them, since now, in contrast to capitalist society, individual labor no longer exists in an indirect fashion but directly as a component part of the total labor. The phrase "proceeds of labor," objectionable also today on account of its ambiguity, thus loses all meaning.

What we have to deal with here is a communist society, not as it has *developed* on its own foundations, but, on the contrary, just as it *emerges* from capitalist society; which is thus in every respect, economically, morally, and intellectually, still stamped with the birthmarks of the old society from whose womb it emerges. Accordingly, the individual producer receives back from society— after the deductions have been made—exactly what he gives to it.

What he has given to it is his individual quantum of labor. For example, the social working day consists of the sum of the individual hours of work; the individual labor time of the individual producer is the part of the social working day contributed by him, his share in it. He receives a certificate from society that he has furnished such and such an amount of labor (after deducting his labor for the common funds), and with this certificate he draws from the social stock of means of consumption as much as the same amount of labor costs. The same amount of labor which he has given to society in one form he receives back in another.

Here obviously the same principle prevails as that which regulates the exchange of commodities, as far as this is exchange of equal values. Content and form are changed, because under the altered circumstances no one can give anything except his labor, and because, on the other hand, nothing can pass to the ownership of individuals except individual means of consumption. But as far as the distribution of the latter among the individual producers is concerned, the same principle prevails as in the exchange of commodity equivalents: a given amount of labor in one form is exchanged for an equal amount of labor in another form.

Hence *equal right* here is still in principle—*bourgeois right*, although principle and practice are no longer at loggerheads, while the exchange of equivalents in commodity exchange exists only on the average and not in the individual case.

In spite of this advance, this equal right is still constantly stigmatized by a bourgeois limitation. The right of the producers is *proportional* to the labor they supply; the equality consists in the fact that measurement is made with an *equal standard*, labor.

But one man is superior to another physically or mentally and so supplies more labor in the same time, or can labor for a longer time; and labor, to serve as a measure, must be defined by its duration or intensity, otherwise it ceases to be a standard of measurement. This *equal* right is an unequal right for unequal labor. It recognizes no class differences, because everyone is only a worker like everyone else; but it tacitly recognizes unequal individual endowment, and thus productive capacity, as a natural privilege. *It is, therefore, a right of inequality, in its content, like every right.* Right by its very nature can consist only in the application of an equal standard; but unequal individuals (and they would not be different individuals if they were not unequal) are measurable only by an equal standard insofar as they are brought under an equal point of view, are taken from one definite side only, for instance, in the present case, are regarded *only as workers* and nothing more is seen in them, everything else being ignored. Further, one worker

is married, another not; one has more children than another, and so
on and so forth. Thus with an equal performance of labor, and
hence an equal share in the social consumption fund, one will in
fact receive more than another, one will be richer than another, and
so on. To avoid all these defects, right, instead of being equal, would
have to be unequal.

But these defects are inevitable in the first phase of communist
society as it is when it has just emerged after prolonged birth pangs
from capitalist society. Right can never be higher than the economic
structure of society and its cultural development conditioned thereby.

In a higher phase of communist society, after the enslaving subordination of the individual to the division of labor, and therewith
also the antithesis between mental and physical labor, has vanished;
after labor has become not only a means of life but life's prime
want; after the productive forces have also increased with the all-
round development of the individual, and all the springs of cooperative wealth flow more abundantly—only then can the narrow
horizon of bourgeois right be crossed in its entirety and society
inscribe on its banners: From each according to his ability, to each
according to his needs!

I have dealt more at length with the "undiminished" proceeds of
labor, on the one hand, and with "equal right" and "fair distribution," on the other, in order to show what a crime it is to attempt,
on the one hand, to force on our Party again, as dogmas, ideas
which in a certain period had some meaning but have now become
obsolete verbal rubbish, while again perverting, on the other, the
realistic outlook, which it cost so much effort to instill into the
Party but which has now taken root in it, by means of ideological
nonsense about right and other trash so common among the democrats and French socialists.

Quite apart from the analysis so far given, it was in general a
mistake to make a fuss about so-called distribution and put the
principal stress on it.

Any distribution whatever of the means of consumption is only
a consequence of the distribution of the conditions of production
themselves. The latter distribution, however, is a feature of the
mode of production itself. The capitalist mode of production, for
example, rests on the fact that the material conditions of production are in the hands of nonworkers in the form of property in
capital and land, while the masses are only owners of the personal
condition of production, of labor power. If the elements of production are so distributed, then the present-day distribution of the
means of consumption results automatically. If the material conditions of production are the cooperative property of the workers

themselves, then there likewise results a distribution of the means of consumption different from the present one. Vulgar socialism (and from it in turn a section of the democrats) has taken over from the bourgeois economists the consideration and treatment of distribution as independent of the mode of production and hence the presentation of socialism as turning principally on distribution. After the real relation has long been made clear, why retrogress again?

4. "The emancipation of labor must be the work of the working class, relative to which all other classes are only one reactionary mass."

The first strophe is taken from the introductory words of the Rules of the International, but "improved." There it is said: "The emancipation of the working class must be the act of the workers themselves"; here, on the contrary, the "working class" has to emancipate—what? "Labor." Let him understand who can.

In compensation, the antistrophe, on the other hand, is a Lassallean quotation of the first water: "relative to which" (the working class) "all other classes are only one reactionary mass."

In the *Communist Manifesto* it is said: "Of all the classes that stand face to face with the bourgeoisie today, the proletariat alone is a really revolutionary class. The other classes decay and finally disappear in the face of modern industry; the proletariat is its special and essential product."

The bourgeoisie is here conceived as a revolutionary class—as the bearer of large-scale industry—relative to the feudal lords and the lower middle class, who desire to maintain all social positions that are the creation of obsolete modes of production. Thus they do not form together with the bourgeoisie "only one reactionary mass."

On the other hand, the proletariat is revolutionary relative to the bourgeoisie because, having itself grown up on the basis of large-scale industry, it strives to strip off from production the capitalist character that the bourgeoisie seeks to perpetuate. But the *Manifesto* adds that the "lower middle class" is becoming revolutionary "in view of [its] impending transfer into the proletariat."

From this point of view, therefore, it is again nonsense to say that it, together with the bourgeoisie, and with the feudal lords into the bargain, "form only one reactionary mass" relative to the working class.

Has one proclaimed to the artisans, small manufacturers, etc., and peasants during the last elections: Relative to us, you, together with the bourgeoisie and feudal lords, form only one reactionary mass?

Lassalle knew the *Communist Manifesto* by heart, as his faithful followers know the gospels written by him. If, therefore, he has falsified it so grossly, this has occurred only to put a good color on his alliance with absolutist and feudal opponents against the bourgeoisie.

In the above paragraph, moreover, his oracular saying is dragged in by main force without any connection with the botched quotation from the Rules of the International. Thus it is here simply an impertinence, and indeed not at all displeasing to Herr Bismarck, one of those cheap pieces of insolence in which the Marat of Berlin deals.

> 5. "The working class strives for its emancipation first of all within the framework of the present-day national state, conscious that the necessary result of its efforts, which are common to the workers of all civilized countries, will be the international brotherhood of peoples."

Lassalle, in opposition to the *Communist Manifesto* and to all earlier socialism, conceived the workers' movement from the narrowest national standpoint. He is being followed in this—and that after the work of the International!

It is altogether self-evident that, to be able to fight at all, the working class must organize itself at home *as a class* and that its own country is the immediate arena of its struggle, insofar as its class struggle is national, not in substance, but, as the *Communist Manifesto* says, "in form." But the "framework of the present-day national state," for instance, the German Empire, is itself in its turn economically "within the framework" of the world market, politically "within the framework" of the system of states. Every businessman knows that German trade is at the same time foreign trade, and the greatness of Herr Bismarck consists, to be sure, precisely in his pursuing a kind of *international* policy.

And to what does the German Workers' party reduce its internationalism? To the consciousness that the result of its efforts will be "the international brotherhood of peoples"—a phrase borrowed from the bourgeois League of Peace and Freedom, which is intended to pass as equivalent to the international brotherhood of the working classes in the joint struggle against the ruling classes and their governments. Not a word, therefore, about the international functions of the German working class! And it is thus that it is to challenge its own bourgeoisie—which is already linked up in brotherhood against it with the bourgeois of all other countries—and Herr Bismarck's international policy of conspiracy.

In fact, the internationalism of the program stands *even infinitely below* that of the Free Trade party. The latter also asserts that the result of its efforts will be "the international brotherhood of peoples." But it also *does* something to make trade international and by no means contents itself with the consciousness that all peoples are carrying on trade at home.

The international activity of the working classes does not in any way depend on the existence of the International Working Men's Association. This was only the first attempt to create a central organ for the activity; an attempt which was a lasting success on account of the impulse which it gave but which was no longer realizable in its first historical form after the fall of the Paris Commune.

Bismarck's *Norddeutsche* was absolutely right when it announced, to the satisfaction of its master, that the German Workers' party had sworn off internationalism in the new program.

II

"Starting from these basic principles, the German workers' party strives by all legal means for the free state—and—socialist society: the abolition of the wage system together with the iron law of wages—and—exploitation in every form; the elimination of all social and political inequality."

I shall return to the "free" state later.

So, in future, the German Workers' party has got to believe in Lassalle's "iron law of wages"! That this may not be lost, the nonsense is perpetrated of speaking of the "abolition of the wage system" (it should read: system of wage labor), "together with the iron law of wages." If I abolish wage labor, then naturally I abolish its laws also, whether they are of "iron" or sponge. But Lassalle's attack on wage labor turns almost solely on this so-called law. In order, therefore, to prove that Lassalle's sect has conquered, the "wage system" must be abolished "together with the iron law of wages" and not without it.

It is well known that nothing of the "iron law of wages" is Lassalle's except the word "iron" borrowed from Goethe's "great, eternal iron laws." The word "iron" is a label by which the true believers recognize one another. But if I take the law with Lassalle's stamp on it, and consequently in his sense, then I must also take it with his substantiation for it. And what is that? As Lange already showed, shortly after Lassalle's death, it is the Malthusian theory of population (preached by Lange himself). But if this theory is correct, then again I cannot abolish the law even if I abolish wage labor a hundred times over, because the law then governs not only the system of wage labor but *every* social system. Basing themselves directly on this, the economists have been proving for fifty years and more that socialism cannot abolish poverty, which has its basis in nature, but can only make it *general,* distribute it simultaneously over the whole surface of society!

But all this is not the main thing. Quite apart from the false Lassallean formulation of the law, the truly outrageous retrogression consists in the following:

Since Lassalle's death there has asserted itself in our party the scientific understanding that wages are not what they appear to be—namely, the *value,* or *price, of labor*—but only a masked form for the *value,* or *price, of labor power.* Thereby the whole bourgeois conception of wages hitherto, as well as all the criticism hitherto directed against this conception, was thrown overboard once for all and it was made clear that the wage worker has permission to work for his own subsistence, that is, *to live,* only insofar as he works for a certain time gratis for the capitalist (and hence also for the latter's co-consumers of surplus value); that the whole capitalist system of production turns on the increase of this gratis labor by extending the working day or by developing the productivity, that is, increasing the intensity, of labor power, etc.; that, consequently, the system of wage labor is a system of slavery, and indeed of a slavery which becomes more severe in proportion as the social productive forces of labor develop, whether the worker receives better or worse payment. And after this understanding has gained more and more ground in our party, some return to Lassalle's dogmas although they must have known that Lassalle *did not know* what wages were, but, following in the wake of the bourgeois economists, took the appearance for the essence of the matter.

It is as if, among slaves who have at last got behind the secret of slavery and broken out in rebellion, a slave still in thrall to obsolete notions were to inscribe on the program of the rebellion: Slavery must be abolished because the feeding of slaves in the system of slavery cannot exceed a certain low maximum!

Does not the mere fact that the representatives of our party were capable of perpetrating such a monstrous attack on the understanding that has spread among the mass of our party prove by itself with what criminal levity and with what lack of conscience they set to work in drawing up this compromise program!

Instead of the indefinite concluding phrase of the paragraph, "the elimination of all social and political inequality," it ought to have been said that with the abolition of class distinctions all social and political inequality arising from them would disappear of itself.

III

"The German Workers' party, in order to pave the way to the solution of the social question, demands the establishment of producers' cooperative societies with state aid under the democratic control of the toiling people. The producers' cooperative societies are to be called into being for industry and agriculture on such a scale that the socialist organization of the total labor will arise from them."

After the Lassallean "iron law of wages," the physic of the prophet. The way to it is "paved" in worthy fashion. In place of the existing class struggle appears a newspaper scribbler's phrase: "the social *question*," to the "*solution*" of which one "paves the way." Instead of arising from the revolutionary process of transformation of society, the "socialist organization of the total labor" "arises" from the "state aid" that the state gives to the producers' cooperative societies and which the *state*, not the worker, "*calls into being*." It is worthy of Lassalle's imagination that with state loans one can build a new society just as well as a new railway!

From the remnants of a sense of shame, "state aid" has been put—under the democratic control of the "toiling people."

In the first place, the majority of the "toiling people" in Germany consists of peasants, and not of proletarians.

Second, "democratic" means in German "*volksherrschaftlich*" ["by the rule of the people"]. But what does "control by the rule of the people of the toiling people" mean? And particularly in the case of a toiling people which, through these demands that it puts to the state, expresses its full consciousness that it neither rules nor is ripe for ruling!

It would be superfluous to deal here with the criticism of the recipe prescribed by Buchez in the reign of Louis Philippe, in opposition to the French socialists and accepted by the reactionary workers, of the *atelier*. The chief offense does not lie in having inscribed this specific nostrum in the program, but in taking, in general, a retrograde step from the standpoint of a class movement to that of a sectarian movement.

That the workers desire to establish the conditions for cooperative production on a social scale, and first of all on a national scale, in their own country, only means that they are working to revolutionize the present conditions of production, and it has nothing in common with the foundation of cooperative societies with state aid. But as far as the present cooperative societies are concerned, they are of value *only* insofar as they are the independent creations of the workers and not protégés either of the governments or of the bourgeois.

IV

I come now to the democratic section.

A. "The free basis of the state."

First of all, according to II, the German Workers' party strives for "the free state."

Free state—what is this?

It is by no means the aim of the workers, who have got rid of the narrow mentality of humble subjects, to set the state free. In the German Empire the "state" is almost as "free" as in Russia. Freedom consists in converting the state from an organ superimposed upon society into one completely subordinate to it, and today, too, the forms of state are more free or less free to the extent that they restrict the "freedom of the state."

The German Workers' party—at least if it adopts the program —shows that its socialist ideas are not even skin-deep; in that, instead of treating existing society (and this holds good for any future one) as the *basis* of the existing state (or of the future state in the case of future society), it treats the state rather as an independent entity that possesses its own intellectual, ethical, and libertarian bases.

And what of the riotous misuse which the program makes of the words "present-day state," "present-day society," and of the still more riotous misconception it creates in regard to the state to which it addresses its demands?

"Present-day society" is capitalist society, which exists in all civilized countries, more or less free from medieval admixture, more or less modified by the particular historical development of each country, more or less developed. On the other hand, the "present-day state" changes with a country's frontier. It is different in the Prusso-German Empire from what it is in Switzerland, and different in England from what it is in the United States. The "present-day state" is therefore a fiction.

Nevertheless, the different states of the different civilized countries, in spite of their motley diversity of form, all have this in common, that they are based on modern bourgeois society, only one more or less capitalistically developed. They have, therefore, also certain essential characteristics in common. In this sense it is possible to speak of the "present-day state" in contrast with the future, in which its present root, bourgeois society, will have died off.

The question then arises: What transformation will the state undergo in communist society? In other words, what social functions will remain in existence there that are analogous to present state functions? This question can only be answered scientifically, and one does not get a flea-hop nearer to the problem by a thousand-fold combination of the word people with the word state.

Between capitalist and communist society lies the period of the revolutionary transformation of the one into the other. Corresponding to this is also a political transition period in which the state can be nothing but *the revolutionary dictatorship of the proletariat.*

Now the program does not deal with this nor with the future state of communist society.

Its political demands contain nothing beyond the old democratic litany familiar to all: universal suffrage, direct legislation, popular rights, a people's militia, etc. They are a mere echo of the bourgeois People's party, of the League of Peace and Freedom. They are all demands which, insofar as they are not exaggerated in fantastic presentation, have already been *realized.* Only the state to which they belong does not lie within the borders of the German Empire, but in Switzerland, the United States, etc. This sort of "state of the future" is a present-day state, although existing outside the "framework" of the German Empire.

But one thing has been forgotten. Since the German Workers' party expressly declares that it acts within "the present-day national state," hence within its own state, the Prusso-German Empire—its demands would indeed otherwise be largely meaningless, since one only demands what one has not got—it should not have forgotten the chief thing, namely, that all those pretty little gewgaws rest on the recognition of the so-called sovereignty of the people and hence are appropriate only in a *democratic republic.*

Since one has not the courage—and wisely so, for the circumstances demand caution—to demand the democratic republic, as the French workers' programs under Louis Philippe and under Louis Napoleon did, one should not have resorted, either, to the subterfuge, neither "honest" nor decent, of demanding things which have meaning only in a democratic republic from a state which is nothing but a police-guarded military despotism, embellished with parliamentary forms, alloyed with a feudal admixture, already influenced by the bourgeoisie and bureaucratically carpentered, and then to assure this state into the bargain that one imagines one will be able to force such things upon it "by legal means."

Even vulgar democracy, which sees the millennium in the democratic republic and has no suspicion that it is precisely in this last form of state of bourgeois society that the class struggle has to be fought out to a conclusion—even it towers mountains above this kind of democratism which keeps within the limits of what is permitted by the police and not permitted by logic.

That, in fact, by the word "state" is meant the government machine, or the state insofar as it forms a special organism separated from society through division of labor, is shown by the words "the German Workers' party demands as the economic basis of the state: a single progressive income tax," etc. Taxes are the economic basis of the government machinery and of nothing else. In the state of the future, existing in Switzerland, this demand has been pretty well fulfilled. Income tax presupposes various sources of income of the various social classes, and hence capitalist society. It is, therefore, nothing remarkable that the Liverpool financial reformers, bourgeois headed by Gladstone's brother, are putting forward the same demand as the program.

B. "The German Workers' party demands as the intellectual and ethical basis of the state:

"1. Universal and equal elementary education by the state. Universal compulsory school attendance. Free instruction."

"Equal elementary education"? What idea lies behind these words? Is it believed that in present-day society (and it is only with this one has to deal) education can be *equal* for all classes? Or is it demanded that the upper classes also shall be compulsorily reduced to the modicum of education—the elementary school—that alone is compatible with the economic conditions not only of the wage workers but of the peasants as well?

"Universal compulsory school attendance. Free instruction." The former exists even in Germany, the second in Switzerland and in the United States in the case of elementary schools. If in some states of the latter country higher educational institutions are also "free," that only means in fact defraying the cost of the education of the upper classes from the general tax receipts. Incidentally, the same holds good for "free administration of justice" demanded under A, 5. The administration of criminal justice is to be had free everywhere; that of civil justice is concerned almost exclusively with conflicts over property and hence affects almost exclusively the possessing classes. Are they to carry on their litigation at the expense of the national coffers?

The paragraph on the schools should at least have demanded technical schools (theoretical and practical) in combination with the elementary school.

"Elementary education by the state" is altogether objectionable. Defining by a general law the expenditures on the elementary schools, the qualifications of the teaching staff, the branches of instruction, etc., and, as is done in the United States, supervising the fulfilment of these legal specifications by state inspectors, is a very different thing from appointing the state as the educator of the people! Government and church should rather be equally excluded from any influence on the school. Particularly, indeed, in the Prusso-German Empire (and one should not take refuge in the rotten sub-terfuge that one is speaking of a "state of the future"; we have seen how matters stand in this respect) the state has need, on the contrary, of a very stern education by the people.

But the whole program, for all its democratic clang, is tainted through and through by the Lassallean sect's servile belief in the state, or, what is no better, by a democratic belief in miracles, or rather it is a compromise between these two kinds of belief in miracles, both equally remote from socialism.

"Freedom of science" says a paragraph of the Prussian Constitu-tion. Why, then, here?

"Freedom of conscience"! If one desired at this time of the *Kulturkampf*[1] to remind liberalism of its old catchwords, it surely could have been done only in the following form: Everyone should be able to attend to his religious as well as his bodily needs with-out the police sticking their noses in. But the Workers' party ought at any rate in this connection to have expressed its awareness of the fact that bourgeois "freedom of conscience" is nothing but the toleration of all possible kinds of religious freedom of conscience, and that for its part it endeavors rather to liberate the conscience from the witchery of religion. But one chooses not to transgress the "bourgeois" level.

I have now come to the end, for the appendix that now follows in the program does not constitute a characteristic component part of it. Hence I can be very brief here.

2. "Normal working day."

In no other country has the workers' party limited itself to such an indefinite demand, but has always fixed the length of the working day that it considers normal under the given circumstances.

3. "Restriction of female labor and prohibition of child labor."

The standardization of the working day must include the restric-tion of female labor, insofar as it relates to the duration, intermis-sions, etc., of the working day; otherwise it could only mean the exclusion of female labor from branches of industry that are

---

1. Cultural struggle; the reference is to Bismarck's struggle with the Catholic Church in Germany.

especially unhealthy for the female body or are objectionable morally for the female sex. If that is what was meant, it should have been said so.

"Prohibition of child labor." Here it was absolutely essential to state the age limit.

A general prohibition of child labor is incompatible with the existence of large-scale industry and hence an empty, pious wish. Its realization—if it were possible—would be reactionary, since, with a strict regulation of the working time according to the different age groups and other safety measures for the protection of children, an early combination of productive labor with education is one of the most potent means for the transformation of present-day society.

4. "State supervision of factory, workshop, and domestic industry."

In consideration of the Prusso-German state it should definitely have been demanded that the inspectors are to be removable only by a court of law; that any worker can have them prosecuted for neglect of duty; that they must belong to the medical profession.

5. "Regulation of prison labor."

A petty demand in a general workers' program. In any case, it should have been clearly stated that there is no intention from fear of competition to allow ordinary criminals to be treated like beasts, and especially that there is no desire to deprive them of their sole means of betterment, productive labor. This was surely the least one might have expected from socialists.

6. "An effective liability law."

It should have been stated what is meant by an "effective" liability law.

Be it noted, incidentally, that in speaking of the normal working day the part of factory legislation that deals with health regulations and safety measures, etc., has been overlooked. The liability law comes into operation only when these regulations are infringed.

In short, this appendix also is distinguished by slovenly editing. *Dixi et salvavi animam meam.* [I have spoken and saved my soul.]

Strategy and Tactics of the
Class Struggle*

It is an unavoidable phenomenon, well established in the course of development, that people from the ruling class also join the proletariat and supply it with educated elements. This we have already clearly stated in the *Manifesto*. Here, however, two remarks are to be made:

First, such people, in order to be useful to the proletarian movement, must bring with them really educated elements. This, however, is not the case with the great majority of German bourgeois converts. Neither the *Zukunft*[1] nor the *Neue Gesellschaft*[2] has provided anything to advance the movement one step. They are completely deficient in real, factual, or theoretical material. Instead, there are efforts to bring superficial socialist ideas into harmony with the various theoretical viewpoints which the gentlemen from the universities, or from wherever, bring with them, and among whom one is more confused than the other, thanks to the process of decomposition in which German philosophy finds itself today. Instead of first studying the new science [Marxist socialism] thoroughly, everyone relies rather on the viewpoint he brought with him, makes a short cut toward it with his own private science, and immediately steps forth with pretensions of wanting to teach it. Hence there are among those gentlemen as many viewpoints as there are heads; instead of

---

* From Marx and Engels, Circular Letter to August Bebel, Wilhelm Liebknecht, Frederick Wilhelm Fritzsche, Bruno Geiser, Wilhelm Hasenclever, and Wilhelm Bracke, September 17-18, 1879. First drafted by Engels, it was designed for "private circulation," as Marx wrote, among the social-democratic leadership in Germany.
1. A Berlin fortnightly magazine.
2. A Zurich monthly.

clarifying anything, they only produce arrant confusion—fortunately, almost always only among themselves. Such educated elements, whose guiding principle is to teach what they have not learned, the party can well dispense with.

Second, when such people from other classes join the proletarian movement, the first demand upon them must be that they do not bring with them any remnants of bourgeois, petty-bourgeois, etc., prejudices, but that they irreversibly assimilate the proletarian viewpoint. But those gentlemen, as has been shown, adhere overwhelmingly to petty-bourgeois conceptions. In so petty-bourgeois a country as Germany, such conceptions certainly have their justification, but only *outside* the Social-Democratic Labor party. If the gentlemen want to build a social-democratic petty-bourgeois party, they have a full right to do so; one could then negotiate with them, conclude agreements, etc., according to circumstances. But in a labor party they are a falsifying element. If there are grounds which necessitate tolerating them, it is a duty *only* to tolerate them, to allow them no influence in party leadership, and to keep in mind that a break with them is only a matter of time. In any case, the time seems to have come. It is inconceivable to us how the party can any longer tolerate in its midst the authors of that article.[3] If the party leadership more or less falls into the hands of such people, the party will simply be emasculated and, with it, an end to the proletarian order.

So far as we are concerned, after our whole past only one way is open to us. For nearly forty years we have raised to prominence the idea of the class struggle as the immediate driving force of history, and particularly the class struggle between the bourgeoisie and the proletariat as the great lever of the modern social revolution; hence we can hardly go along with people who want to strike this class struggle from the movement. At the founding of the International, we expressly formulated the battle cry: The emancipation of the working class must be the work of the working class itself. We cannot, therefore, go along with people who openly claim that the workers are too ignorant to emancipate themselves but must first be emancipated from the top down, by the philanthropic big and petty bourgeois. Should the new party [socialist] organ take a position that corresponds with the ideas of those gentlemen, become bourgeois and not proletarian, then there is nothing left for us,

---

3. "Retrospects on the Socialist Movement in Germany," in *Jahrbuch für Sozialwissenschaft und Sozialpolitik*, August, 1879, published in Zurich. The article, written by Karl Höchberg, Eduard Bernstein, and Carl August Schramm, advocated a transformation of the Social-Democratic party from a revolutionary to a reformist one.

sorry as we should be to do so, than to speak out against it publicly and dissolve the solidarity within which we have hitherto represented the German party abroad. But we hope it will not come to that.

This letter is to be communicated to all the five members of the Committee in Germany, as well as Bracke. . . .

On our part, we have no objection to this being communicated to the gentlemen in Zurich.

Personal Letters

From letter to Arnold Ruge
EN ROUTE, IN HOLLAND, MARCH, 1843

I am now traveling in Holland. As far as I can see from the local and French newspapers, Germany has plunged deep into muck and will go still deeper. I assure you that even if one feels little national pride, still one feels national shame, even in Holland. The smallest Dutchman is nevertheless a citizen compared to the biggest German. And the opinions foreigners have of the Prussian Government! In this there is a frightening unanimity; nobody has any illusions about that system and its simple nature . . . The pompous mantle of liberalism has fallen off, and the revolting despotism stands in all its nakedness before the eyes of the whole world.

This is also a manifestation, even if a reverse one. It is a truth that at least teaches us to recognize the hollowness of our patriotism and the unnaturalness of our political system. You look at me with a smile and ask: What is gained thereby? One does not make a revolution out of shame. I answer: Shame itself is a revolution; it is in reality the victory of the French Revolution over German patriotism, which defeated it in 1813. Shame is a sort of anger that turns on itself, and if a whole nation were really ashamed, it would be the lion that recoils in order to leap. I admit that shame is not yet to be found in Germany; on the contrary, those wretches are still patriots. But what system would drive out their patriotism if not this ridiculous one of the new knight [Frederick William IV]? The comedy of despotism being staged for us is as dangerous for him as the tragedy once was for the Stuarts and the Bourbons. And even if for a long time one does not see this comedy for what it is, it is still a revolution. The state is too serious a thing to be made into a buffoonery. One could perhaps for a time sail a ship full of fools before the wind, but it would meet its fate precisely because the fools would not believe the warnings. This fate is the revolution, which awaits us.

Letter to Arnold Ruge
COLOGNE, MAY, 1843

Your letter, my dear friend, is a good elegy, a breath-taking dirge; but politically it is altogether nothing. No nation despairs, and if it goes on hoping out of mere stupidity for a long time, nevertheless after many years it does realize its pious wishes out of sudden wisdom.

Still, you have infected me; your theme is not yet exhausted, I want to add the finale; and when everything is over, then give me your hand so that we can start again at the beginning. Let the dead bury and lament their dead. In contrast, it is enviable to be the first vigorously to enter a new life, this should be our destiny.

It is true, the old world belongs to the philistines. But we ought not to treat it like a scarecrow from which one turns away in alarm. We ought, rather, to look it straight in the eye. And it pays to study this master of the [philistine] world.

He is master of the world only, of course, insofar as he fills society with his own kind, as worms fill a corpse. The society of these gentlemen, therefore, needs nothing more than a number of slaves, and the owners of slaves need not be free. Even though as owners of landed property and people they are referred to as eminent masters, they are thereby no less philistinish than those they rule.

Men—means intellectual beings; free men—means republicans. The common philistines do not want to be either. Then what is left for them to be and want to be?

What they want—to live and to propagate their species (and further than that, as Goethe says, nobody can take it)—is also wanted by animals. The most a German politician might add to this is that the human being *knows* what he wants, and the German is so minded that he wants nothing more.

One will have to reawaken in the breast of these people the sense of the self-worth of men—freedom. Only such a sense, which vanished from the world with the Greeks and evaporated into the blue with Christianity, can transform society again into a community of people for their highest ends—a democratic state.

On the other hand, men who do not feel themselves to be men achieve the level of their masters, like a flock of slaves or horses. These hereditary masters are the goal of the whole society. That world belongs to them. They take it as it is and at face value. They take themselves as they find themselves, and stand where their feet grew, on the necks of these political animals who know no other destiny than to be "a vassal, propitiating and expectant."

The philistine world is the *political animal world*, and once we recognize its existence, we have no choice but simply to describe the status quo accurately. Centuries of barbarism have produced it and formed it, and here it stands now as a consistent system whose principle is a *dehumanized world*. The most fully realized philistine world, our Germany, must naturally remain far behind the French Revolution, which restored man again; and a German Aristotle who would derive his political ideas from our situation would have to write at the head of his chapter: "Man is a social, yet a thoroughly unpolitical animal," but he could not explain the German state more correctly than Mr. Zöpfl, author of *Constitutional Law in Germany*, has done already. According to him, Germany is a "union of families," which, to continue, belongs hereditarily and intrinsically to the most-high family, which is called Dynasty. The more fertile the families show themselves to be, the more happy the people; the greater the state, the mightier the dynasty; hence in normally despotic Prussia a premium of fifty Reichstaler is paid for every seventh son.

The Germans are such prudent realists that all their desires and high-flown thoughts do not reach beyond a bare existence. This realism, and no more, is accepted by those who rule them. These rulers are realists too; they are far removed from all thought and all human greatness, being mere officers and landowning Junkers; but they are not mistaken in that, being what they are, they are thoroughly efficient in using and dominating this animal kingdom, for domination and usufruct form a single concept, here as elsewhere. And when they permit themselves to receive homage and look over the heads of these teeming brainless creatures, what is closer to their minds than Napoleon on the Berezina River? It is recorded that when Napoleon looked at the swarm of drowning men in the river, he said to his companion: "*Voyez ces crapauds!*" ["Look at these toads!"] This remark is probably a lie, but it is nonetheless true. The only principle of despotism is contempt for man, dehumanized man, and this principle has the advantage over many others of being at the same time a fact. The despot always sees men as degraded. For him they are drowned before his eyes in the slime of abject existence, from which, like frogs, they too always reemerge. If men capable of great goals, as Napoleon was before his dynasty madness, can hold such a view, how can one expect an ordinary king to be an idealist under such conditions?

The general principle of monarchy is the despised, despicable, *dehumanized man;* and Montesquieu is very wrong in considering honor to be the principle of monarchy. He makes distinctions between monarchy, despotism, and tyranny. But all these are names for only one idea; at most it is a behavioral difference within the same principle. Where the monarchical principle is in the majority, human beings are in the minority; where there is no doubt, there are no people. Why should a man like the King of Prussia, who has no proof of being a problem, not simply follow his whim? And when he does it, what is the result? Contradictory purposes? Good, so nothing comes of it. Impotent tendencies? They are, nevertheless, the only political reality. Disgraces and embarrassments? There is only one disgrace and one embarrassment, that of abdication. So long as the whim stays in its place, it is right. Be it ever so unstable, brainless, and contemptible, it is always good enough to govern a nation that has never had any other law than the despotism of its kings. I do not say that a brainless system and the loss of respect internally and externally will never have consequences; I do not take this assurance of a ship of fools upon myself. I do maintain, however, that the King of Prussia will remain a man of his time so long as the topsy-turvy world continues to be a reality.

You know, I occupy myself a lot with this man. Even at the time when he still made the *Berlin Politische Wochenblatt* his organ, I recognized his worth and his destiny. When he took the oath at Königsberg he even then justified my conjecture that now the question would become purely a personal one. He declared himself heart and soul for the future basic laws of the Prussian domains, *his* state, and in reality in Prussia the King is the system. He is the only political person. His personality determines the system this way or that way. What he does or what one lets him do, what he thinks or what one puts in his mouth, in Prussia that is what the state thinks or does. Thus it is really a gain that the present King has declared all this plainly.

The only thing in which I erred for a time was the apparently exalted notion of what wishes and ideas the King needed for show. In fact, this did not matter, since the philistine is the material for the monarchy and the monarch is always only the king of the philistines; he cannot liberate either himself or his people, or make real men out of them, so long as both of them remain what they are.

The King of Prussia has tried to change the system with a theory his father [Frederick William III] did not have. The fate of this effort is known. It completely miscarried. Naturally. When one arrives at the political animal world there is no further place to go, and no way to advance except by abandoning its basis and crossing over to the human world of democracy.

The old King wanted nothing extravagant; he was a philistine and made no pretense to intellectualism. He knew that the servile state and his possession of it needed only a prosaic, quiet existence. The young King was more lively and alert, and thought much more about the monarch's absolutism, which is limited only by his heart and his understanding. The old vassal, servant-and-slave state revolted him. He wanted to bring it to life but permeated entirely with his desires, feelings, and ideas; and he could demand this, in *his* state, if it was to succeed. Hence his liberal speeches and heartfelt outpourings. Not dead law, but the full living heart of the King was to rule all his subjects. He wanted to set all hearts and spirits in motion toward his heart's desire, his long-nourished plans. A movement followed; but the other hearts did not beat in unison with his, and the subjugated people could not open their mouths without speaking of the abolition of the old government. The idealists, who had the temerity to want to make men out of the people, seized the word, and while the King fantasized in Old German, they thought it desirable to philosophize in New German. For a moment the old order of things seemed to have been turned on its head; indeed, things began to transform themselves into men; there were, in fact, well-known men, although naming names is not permitted in the Assembly; but the servants of the old despotism soon put an end to this un-German activity. It was not difficult to bring the wishes of the King, who had dreamed of a past full of priests, knights, and retainers, into palpable conflict with the aims of the idealists who wanted simply the consequences of the French Revolution—that is, in the last analysis, a republic and a free human order instead of a dead one. When this conflict became sharp and uncomfortable and the irascible King grew sufficiently enraged, the servants, who had hitherto conducted things so easily, came to him and said: the King was not well advised to encourage his subjects to make useless speeches, for it would be impossible to govern a race of talking men. The lord of all the rear-Russians also became disquieted over the movement in the heads of the fore-Russians[1] and demanded the restoration of the old, quiet conditions. And the consequence was a new edition of the old contempt for all wishes and ideas of the men who desired human rights and duties, that is, a restoration of the old vassal servile state, in which the slave serves silently and the owner of the land and people rules as silently as possible through his well-trained and obedient servants. Neither side can say what it wishes, neither the ones who want to be men nor the

---

1. Nicholas I, Czar of Russia, which Marx ironically referred to as "rear-Russia" in contrast to Prussia (Latin: *Borussia*), which he called "fore-Russia."

other, who has no use for men in his country. Silence is therefore the only recourse. *Muta pecora, prona et ventri oboedientia.* [The herd is mute, hangs its head, and obeys its stomach.]

Such has been the unfortunate attempt to elevate the philistine state on its own base; it resulted in making despotism's need for brutality and the impossibility of humanness evident before the whole world. A brutal situation can be maintained only with brutality. And at this point I finish with our common task—to look the philistine and his state firmly in the eye.

You cannot say that I hold the present too high; and if I do not altogether despair, it is only because its own desperate condition fills me with hope. I am not referring at all to the inability of the masters and the indolence of the servants and subjects who let everything go as God pleases; and yet both together already suffice to bring about a catastrophe. I am only calling your attention to the fact that the enemies of philistinism—in short, all thinking and suffering people— have arrived at an understanding, for which previously they lacked the means, and that even the passive continuation of the old vassals brings daily recruits in the service of the new humanity. The system of industry and commerce, of property and the exploitation of people, leads, even more quickly than does an increase in the population, to a breach inside the present society, which the old system will not be able to heal because none of it either heals or produces, but only exists and enjoys. The existence of suffering humanity, which thinks, and of thinking humanity, which is oppressed, must, however, necessarily become unusable and indigestible to the passive and brainlessly consuming animal world of philistinism.

From our side, the old world must be fully dragged into daylight and the new, positive one created. The longer the time that events allow for thinking humanity to ponder, and suffering humanity to assemble, the more completely will the product, which the present carries in its womb, enter the world.

Letter to Arnold Ruge
KREUZNACH, SEPTEMBER, 1843

I am pleased that you have decided to turn your thoughts from the past to undertake a new venture.[1] So be it in Paris, the ancient university of philosophy, *absit omen* [may there be no ill omen], and

---

1. The publication of *Deutsch-Französische Jahrbücher.*

the new capital of the new world. Necessity finds a way. Hence I do not doubt that all obstacles, whose gravity I do not ignore, will be overcome.

Whether the venture comes to fruition or not, I will be in Paris at the end of this month, since the atmosphere here enslaves and I see absolutely no room in Germany for any free activity.

In Germany everything is suppressed violently; a true anarchy of spirit, a regime of stupidity itself, has broken out, and Zurich obeys Berlin's orders. It is therefore increasingly evident that one has to look for a new rallying point for truly thoughtful and independent minds. I am convinced that our plan will correspond to the real needs, and the real needs must end in their fulfillment. Hence I have no doubt about the venture, if it is undertaken seriously.

The internal difficulties seem to be almost greater than the external obstacles. If there is no doubt about the "whence," there is the more confusion about the "whither." It is not only that a general anarchy has broken out among the reformers, but also that, as everybody would admit, none of them has an exact view of what the future should be. Still, this is the advantage of the new direction, that we do not anticipate the world dogmatically but we first try to discover the new world from a critique of the old one. Until now the philosophers have had the solution of all riddles lying on their lecterns, and the stupid exoteric world only had to open its mouth for the ready-roasted pigeons of absolute knowledge to fly in. Philosophy has become secularized, and the striking proof thereof is that the philosophical consciousness itself has been pulled into the torment of struggle not only externally but also internally. If the construction and preparation of the future is not our business, then it is the more certain what we do have to achieve—I mean the *ruthless criticism of all that exists*, ruthless also in the sense that criticism does not fear its results and even less so a struggle with the existing powers.

I am therefore not in favor of raising a dogmatic flag; quite the contrary. We should try to help the dogmatists clarify their ideas. Thus communism, in particular, is a dogmatic abstraction, and by this I do not mean some fanciful or possible communism, but the real, existing communism, as Cabet, Dézamy, Weitling, etc., teach and conceive it. This communism is itself separate from the humanist principle, merely a phenomenon affected by its opposite, private existence. Hence abolition of private property and communism are by no means identical, and communism has different doctrines from those of Fourier, Proudhon, etc., not accidentally, but necessarily in contradiction to them, because it is itself only a special, one-sided consummation of the socialist principle.

And the whole socialist principle is again only one aspect of *reality* as it affects the genuine human being. We must likewise concern ourselves with the other aspect, the theoretical existence of man—that is, religion, science, etc.—and make it the object of our criticism. In addition, we want to have an effect on our contemporaries, and especially our German contemporaries. One asks: How is one to achieve that? Two facts cannot be denied. First religion and then politics are the subjects that form the main interest of present-day Germany. We have to connect with these, but not to confront them with some ready-made system like the *Voyage en Icarie.*[2]

Reason has always existed, but not always in reasonable form. Hence the critic can choose any form of theoretical and practical consciousness and develop the true reality in its "ought" and final goal out of its own forms of existing reality. In regard to real life, the political state, even where it is not yet permeated with socialist demands, contains the demands of reason in all its *modern* forms. And it does not stop with that. Everywhere it subordinates reason to reality. But everywhere also it falls into the contradiction between its ideal destiny and its presuppositions.

Out of this conflict of the political state within itself, therefore, social truth can develop everywhere. Just as *religion* is the index to the theoretical struggles of mankind, so the *political state* is the index to its practical ones. Hence the political state expresses within its form *sub specie rei publicae* [as a special political form] all social conflicts, needs, truths, etc. It is therefore definitely not beneath the *hauteur des principes* [level of principles] to make the most specialized political questions—say, the difference between a *ständisch* [estate] system and a representative system—the object of criticism. For this question expresses only in a *political* way the difference between government by the people and the rule of private property. Hence the critic not only can but must enter into these political questions (which in the view of the crude socialists is beneath all dignity). In demonstrating the advantage of the representative system over the estate one, the critic interests a large part of the people in a *practical* subject. In raising the representative system out of its own political form to a general form and validating the true significance that lies at its foundation, he forces that part to rise above itself, for its victory is at the same time its loss.

Hence nothing prevents us from tying our criticism in with a criticism of and participation in politics, that is, in *real* conflicts, and in identifying with them. Thus we do not confront the world dog-

---

2. By Étienne Cabet, published in 1842.

matically with a new principle, proclaiming: Here is the truth, kneel before it! We develop for the world new principles out of the principles of the world. We do not say to the world: Give up your struggles, they are stupid stuff; we will provide you with the true watchword of the struggle. We merely demonstrate to the world why it really struggles, and consciousness is something that it *must* adopt, even if it does not want to do so.

The reform of the world's consciousness consists only in making it aware of its perception, in waking it up from its own dream, in explaining to it its own actions. Our whole purpose can consist of nothing else than in bringing out religious and political questions in self-aware human form, as Feuerbach did in his critique of religion.

Our slogan must therefore be: reform of consciousness, not through dogmas but through analysis of the mystic consciousness which is unclear to itself, regardless of whether it is religious or political. It will then be shown that the world has long possessed the dream of a thing, of which it only needs to have awareness in order to possess it in reality. It will be shown that what is involved is not a great stroke of thought between past and future, but a *consummation* of the ideas of the past. It will finally be shown that humanity begins no *new* task, but with consciousness consummates its old task.

Hence we can summarize the tendency of our paper in one word: Self-understanding (critical philosophy) of our epoch's struggles and desires. This is a task for the world and for us. It can only be the labor of combined forces. What is involved is a *confession*, and nothing else. In order to have its sins pardoned, mankind only needs to interpret them for what they are.

Letter to Frederick Engels (in Manchester)
LONDON, DECEMBER 2, 1856

What do you say about Neuchâtel and Valangin?[1] This case has induced me to supplement my highly defective knowledge of the history of Prussia. Indeed and indeed, the history of the world has never produced anything more lousy. The long history of how the nominal kings of France became real kings is also full of petty struggles, treacheries, and intrigues. But it is the history of the origins

---

1. In 1856 a conflict broke out between Prussia and Switzerland over the small principality of Neuchâtel, which Prussia claimed as its own dependency. Valangin was a part of Neuchâtel.

of a nation. Austrian history, showing how a vassal of the German Empire establishes power in its own house, becomes interesting due to the circumstance that, as a result of entanglements in the Orient, Bohemia, Italy, Hungary, etc., the vassal swindles himself into the position of emperor; and ultimately because the power of this house [Habsbourg] assumes such dimensions that Europe fears it may become a universal monarchy. Nothing of this sort in Prussia. It never subjugated a single Slavic nation, and in five hundred years it was not even able to get hold of Pomerania, until it finally got it by an "exchange."[2] Altogether, the Margravate of Brandenburg—since the Hohenzollerns acquired it—has never made any real conquests, except Silesia. As this is its only conquest, Frederick II is properly called the "Unique"! Petty thievery, bribery, direct corruption, underhand dealings to capture inheritances, etc.—all this shabbiness is what makes up Prussian history. And whatever else is interesting in feudal history— the struggle between overlord and vassal, trickery with the towns, etc.—is caricatured dwarfishly here, because the towns are petty and boring, the feudal lords insignificant louts, and the sovereign himself a cipher. In the Reformation, as in the French Revolution: vacillating perfidy, neutrality, separate peace treaties; the snapping up of a few morsels thrown to Prussia by Russia in the course of the various partitions arranged by the latter—as was the case with Sweden, Poland, Saxony. Added to this, in its list of rulers never any but three types—pietist, sergeant major, and clown—succeeding each other as night follows day, with irregularities which changed the sequence but never introduced a new type. What has kept the state on its legs through all this has been *mediocrity*—the *golden* mean—accurate bookkeeping, avoidance of extremes, precision in drill, a certain homebred coarseness, and "church regulations." *C'est dégoutant!* [It's disgusting!]

From letter to Johann Philipp Becker (in Geneva)
LONDON, FEBRUARY 26, 1862

... You must know that these Germans, young and old, are all oversmart, solid, practical men, who consider people like you and me immature fools not yet cured of their revolutionary fantasies. And that rabble is as bad here abroad as it is at home. During my stay in

---

2. In 1815 Prussia received Swedish Pomerania from Denmark in exchange for the Duchy of Lauenburg.

Berlin and elsewhere I convinced myself that any attempt to influence that canaille by literary means is completely futile. The self-complacent stupidity of those scamps for whom the press, that lamentable press, serves as an extraordinary elixir of life, is simply beyond belief. And then that lassitude of soul! Cudgeling is the only means of resurrection of the German Michael who, ever since he lost his philosophical illusions and took to money-making, to the idea of "Little Germany" and to "practical constitutionalism," has been nothing but a dull-witted, repulsive clown. Germany seemed to me to be entirely [word missing] a roomful of senile-smart, decrepit children.

Letter to Lion Philips (in Zaltbommel)
LONDON, MARCH 29, 1864

Dear Uncle:
    I assume that you are already, or are still, in Aachen and I therefore am writing this letter to you there. If you had waited for good weather you would have to be still in Bommel. Here at least, with the exception of one or two nice days, March was abominable, cold, wet, changeable from moment to moment. This is perhaps the reason why I have not yet got rid of the *verdummelinge* [accursed] furuncles. I curse them, but secretly.
    Little Eleanor has had a severe cough in the past two days and that prevents her from writing to you. She nevertheless commissions me to send you many greetings, and in regard to the Danish Question, begs me to tell you that "she don't care for such stuff," and that "she considers one of the parties to the quarrel as bad as the other, and perhaps worse."[1]
    The difficulty in understanding Prussian policy arises merely from the human predisposition to assume seriousness in far-reaching purposes and plans. In the same way, for example, the Mormon Bible is hard to understand, because there is not a spark of sense in it. In the first instance, Prussia, wishing to acquire popularity for its army, had already achieved its purpose in the Schleswig-Holstein campaigns of 1848. Second, it aimed at blocking off its own territory from German volunteers, democrats, and small states. Finally, Prussia and Austria aimed to make it possible for the Danish King [Christian IX], who played the same game as they, to force the Danes to certain conces-

---

1. The words in quotation marks were written in English.

sions through pressure from without. Of course Austria could not let Prussia play the main role, and so at the same time it used the opportunity to consummate a more precise alliance for other *peripeties* [solutions].

On April 12 the London Conference is to take place.[2] At the most, it will decide on a *personal union* between Schleswig and Holstein and Denmark; perhaps less, in no way more. Of what little seriousness the whole affair is, despite gunpowder, lead, and blood-spilling, you can see from the fact that up to this moment neither Prussia nor Austria has declared war on Denmark, nor has Denmark declared war on Prussia or Austria. There is no better way to throw sand in the eyes than letting armies march, horses trample, and cannons roar.

Despite all that, serious conflicts may be imminent. Bonaparte sees himself practically forced once again to make his *troupiers* [soldiers] an export business in "freedom" as a consequence of the great disaffection which exists not only in Paris but which has also shown itself provokingly in the last elections. And this time the dogs of Prussia have paved the way for him.

Garibaldi's trip to England, and the great ovations that he will receive here from all sides, are, or at least should be, a mere overture to a new rising against Austria. The latter, as an ally of the Prussians in Schleswig-Holstein and of Russia because of the siege conditions in Galicia,[3] has greatly eased the game for its enemies. A new Holy Alliance, with the present conditions of Poland, Hungary, Italy, the plebiscite in Germany, and the completely changed position of England, would enable even Napoleon the Little to play the Great Man. At the present moment a continuation of the peace would be best, for every war postpones the revolution in France.

God *verdumm* [damn] me! If there is anything more stupid than this political chessboard.[4]

I had really meant to write you about two more things, the Roman division and the astronomical darkness. But it is growing dark, the paper is coming to an end, and the post office will soon close, and so I must end now with the best regards of the whole family. Ditto to Karl [Philips] and wife Jean *enz* [not excluding].

Your devoted nephew,
K. MARX

---

2. The Conference on Schleswig-Holstein opened in London on April 25, 1864, and dragged on inconclusively until June.
3. On February 29, 1864, Austria declared a state of siege in insurrectionary Polish Galicia.
4. Sentence written in English.

Letter to Engels (in Manchester)
LONDON, FEBRUARY 11, 1865

Dear Fred:

Since this is Saturday, I assume you will not be sending off your piece[1] today, and hence there will still be time for these "supplementary" suggestions for alteration:

1. In the place where you ask, *What do the workers want?* I should not answer, as you do, that the workers in Germany, France, and England demand this and that. For the answer sounds as if we accepted ITZIG's ["Ikey": Lassalle] slogans (at least it would be so interpreted). I should rather say:

It would seem that the demands put forward by the most advanced workers in Germany at this time were directed toward, etc. This does not involve you at all, which is all the better in that later on you yourself criticize the demand for universal suffrage, if put forward without the necessary conditions. (The word "direct," moreover, would make no sense in England, for example, and is only the opposite of the "indirect" franchise invented by the Prussians.) The form in which the *Knoten* [philistines] in Germany conceive of state intervention à la Lassalle is of such a kind that one must anyhow be careful not to identify with "the same." It is much more distinguished (and safe) if you take the *Knoten* at their word and *let them say* what *they* want for themselves. (I say the *Knoten*, because they are the really argumentative, *Lassalle-ized* part).

2. I should not say that the movement of 1848-49 failed because the bourgeois resisted *direct universal suffrage*. On the contrary, the latter was declared as a German right by the Frankfurt parliament and proclaimed in every form by the Vice-Regent of the Reich [Archduke John of Austria]. (In my opinion, too, as soon as things can be discussed seriously in Germany, the franchise must be treated as part of rightfully *existing* law.) Since this is not the place for a longer exposition, I would use the phrase that the bourgeoisie at that time preferred peace with servitude to the mere *prospect* of fighting and freedom, or something like this.

On the whole, the article is very good and I am especially tickled

---

1. Engels' pamphlet, *The Prussian Military Question and the German Workers' Party* (Hamburg, 1865).

by the point made that the present *Knoten* movement only in fact exists *par la grâce de la police* [by the grace of the police].
In all haste.

> *Your*
> K.M.

I have crossed out the part where—I don't know why—you console the reactionary that by the third year of his service a soldier is no longer [radical], or at least not for long—although you later say the opposite.

From letter to Johann Baptist von Schweitzer (in Berlin)
LONDON, FEBRUARY 13, 1865

. . . Coalitions of the growing trade unions, as a means of the organized working-class struggle against the bourgeoisie, are not only of the highest importance—as is seen, among other things, in the United States, where the workers, despite the suffrage and republicanism, could not dispense with them—but also in Prussia and in Germany in general, where the right of coalition ruptures police rule and bureaucracy, tears up the regulation of servants [i.e., the semiserfs on the Junker estates] and the agricultural Junker economy; in short, it is a measure of maturation of the "subjects," which the Progesssive party[1]—that is, every bourgeois opposition party in Prussia—if not crazy, would a hundred times rather allow than the Prussian government, even the government of a Bismarck! In contrast, on the other side there is the royal Prussian government support of the cooperative societies—and anybody who knows Prussian conditions also knows beforehand their pygmy dimensions; as an economic measure they are nil, but at the same time they widen the guardianship system, bribe a portion of the working class, and emasculate its movement. Just as the bourgeois party in Prussia disgraced itself and brought on its present misery when it seriously believed that with the "New Era" [of King William I] the government would fall into its lap by the grace of the Prince Regent, so the labor party will disgrace itself even more if it imagines that through the Bismarck era, or some other Prussian era, golden apples will fall into its mouth by the grace of the king. That disappointment over Lassalle's unfortunate illusion of a socialist effort on the part of a Prussian government is bound to

---

1. The Progressive party, founded in June, 1861, had as its program a demand for the unification of Germany under Prussian leadership.

come, there can be no doubt. The logic of things will speak. But the *honor* of the labor party requires that it reject such phantom illusions even before their hollowness is exposed by experience. The working class is revolutionary or it is nothing.

From letter to Engels (in Manchester)
LONDON, SEPTEMBER 26, 1868

Dear Fred:

. . . For the German working class the most necessary thing is that it should cease conducting its agitation by kind permission of the higher authorities. A race so schooled in bureaucracy must go through a complete course of "self-help." On the other hand, they certainly have the advantage of beginning the movement at a period when conditions were much more advanced than they were for the English and, being Germans, of having heads on their shoulders capable of generalizing. . . .

Your
K.M.

From letter to Engels (in Manchester)
LONDON, AUGUST 10, 1869

Dear Freddy:

. . . It cannot be denied that the part of the speech (made by Wilhelm[1] in Berlin) reprinted in the supplement shows, underneath its stupidity, an undeniable cunning in arranging the affair to suit himself. For the rest, it is very nice! Because one should use the Reichstag only as instrument of agitation, one should never agitate there for anything reasonable directly affecting the interests of the workers! The worthy Wilhelm's illusion that because Bismarck is "fond of" using expressions friendly to the workers, he would therefore not oppose *genuine measures on behalf of the workers* is really charming. "As if"—as Bruno Bauer would say—Herr Wagener had not declared in the Reichstag that he was *for* the factory laws in

---

1. Wilhelm Liebknecht's speech, "On the Political Position of the Social-Democracy," delivered before the Berlin Democratic Labor Association May 31, 1869, and published in *Demokratisches Wochenblatt,* July 3 and August 7, 1869.

theory but against them in *practice*, "because they are useless under Prussian conditions"! "As if" Herr Bismarck, if he really wanted or was able to do anything for the workers, would not himself force the carrying out of the existing laws in Prussia itself! By the mere fact of its happening in Prussia, it would *have* to be followed by the liberal "Saxony," etc. What Wilhelm does not understand is that though the present governments flirt with the workers, they are well aware that their only support lies with the bourgeoisie; that therefore they scare the latter with phrases friendly to the workers but *cannot* ever really go against them.

The cow [Liebknecht] believes in the future "*Staat* DER *Demokratie*" [state OF democracy]! Privately, this means now constitutional England, now bourgeois United States, now the wretched Switzerland. "It" [the cow Liebknecht] has no idea of revolutionary politics. This is what he gives as proof—according to Schwabenmayer—of democratic energy: The railway to California was built by the bourgeoisie, the latter presenting to itself, through Congress, an enormous mass of "national land"; that is to say, they expropriated the workers from it by importing a rabble of Chinese to force down wages, and finally formed themselves into a new sprig of "financial aristocracy."

For the rest, I find it insolent on Wilhelm's part to introduce your and my names *ad vocem* [regarding] Brass.[2] I have warned him directly against selling himself to Brass and at the same time declared to him—viva voce—if this should lead to a scandal, we would publicly disavow him. . . .

Greetings.

IL MORO

Letter written in English to the Editor of the Daily News *(London)*
LONDON, JANUARY 16, 1871

Sir:

In accusing the French government of having "rendered impossible the free expression of opinion in France through the medium of the press and of national representatives," Bismarck did evidently but intend to crack a Berlin *Witz* [joke]. If you want to become acquainted with "true" French opinion please apply to Herr Stieber, editor of the Versailles *Moniteur* and notorious Prussian police spy!

2. In his speech of May 31, Liebknecht stated that August Brass, editor of *Norddeutsche Allgemeine Zeitung*, a Berlin daily, had put "at the disposal of Marx, Engels, and me two daily columns in his paper. . . ."

At Bismarck's command Messrs. Bebel and Liebknecht have been
arrested on the charge of high treason, simply because they dared to
fulfill their duties as German national representatives, viz., to protest
in the Reichstag against the annexation of Alsace and Lorraine, vote
against new war subsidies, express their sympathy with the French
Republic, and denounce the attempt at the conversion of Germany
into one Prussian barrack. For the utterance of the same opinions the
members of the Brunswick Social-Democratic Committee have, since
the beginning of last September, been treated like galley slaves, and
are still undergoing a mock prosecution for high treason. The same
lot has befallen numerous workmen who propagated the Brunswick
manifesto. On similar pretexts Mr. Hepner, subeditor of the Leipzig
Volksstaat, is prosecuted for high treason. The few independent
German journals existing outside Prussia are forbidden admission to
the Hohenzollern estates. German workmen's meetings in favor of a
peace honorable for France are daily dispersed by the police. According to the official Prussian doctrine, as naïvely laid down by General
Vogel von Falkenstein, every German "trying to counteract the
prospective aims of Prussian warfare in France" is guilty of high
treason. If M. Gambetta & Co. were, like the Hohenzollerns, forced
to violently put down popular opinion, they would only have to
apply the Prussian method and, on the plea of war, proclaim throughout France a state of siege. The only French soldiers on German soil
molder in Prussian jails. Still the Prussian Government feels itself
bound to rigorously maintain the state of siege, that is to say, the
crudest and most revolting form of military despotism, the suspension
of all law. French soil is infested by about a million German invaders.
Yet the French Government can safely dispense with that Prussian
method of "rendering possible the free expression of opinion." Look
at this picture and at that! Germany, however, has proved too petty a
field for Bismarck's all-absorbing love of independent opinion. When
the Luxemburgers gave vent to their sympathies with France, Bismarck made this expression of sentiment one of his pretexts for renouncing the London neutrality treaty. When the Belgian press committed a similar sin, the Prussian Ambassador at Brussels, Herr von
Balan, invited the Belgian ministry to put down not only all anti-
Prussian newspaper articles, but even the printing of mere news calculated to cheer the French on in their war of independence. A very
modest request this, indeed, to suspend the Belgian Constitution *"pour
le roi de Prusse"*! No sooner had some Stockholm papers indulged in
some mild jokes at the notorious "piety" of Wilhelm Annexander
than Bismarck came down on the Swedish cabinet with grim missives.
Even under the meridian of St. Petersburg he contrived to spy too

licentious a press. At his humble supplication the editors of the principal Petersburg papers were summoned before the censor in chief, who bade them beware of all strictures upon the real Borussian [Prussian] vassal of the Czar. One of those editors, M. Sagulyayev, was imprudent enough to emit the secret of his *avertissement* [warning] through the columns of the *Golos.* He was at once pounced upon by the Russian police and bundled off to some remote province.

It would be a mistake to believe that those gendarme proceedings are due only to the paroxysm of war fever. They are, on the contrary, the true methodical application of Prussian law principles. There exists in point of fact an odd proviso in the Prussian criminal code by dint of which every foreigner, on account of his doings or writings in his own or any other foreign country, may be prosecuted for "insult against the Prussian King" and "high treason against Prussia"! France—and her cause fortunately far from desperate— fights at this moment not only for her own national independence, but for the liberty of Germany and Europe.

I am, sir, yours respectfully,

KARL MARX

From letter to Friedrich Adolph Sorge (in Hoboken)
LONDON, OCTOBER 19, 1877

. . . The workers themselves, when like Herr Most & Co. they give up work and become "professional literary men," always breed "theoretical" mischief and are always ready to join muddleheads from the allegedly "learned" caste. Utopian socialism in particular, which for decades we have been sweeping out of German workers' heads with so much effort and labor—their freedom from it making them theoretically (and thereby also practically) superior to the French and English—this utopian socialism, playing with fantastic images of the future structure of society, is spreading again in a much more futile form; it is not to be compared with that of the great French and English utopians, but with—Weitling. It is natural that utopianism, which before the age of materialist-critical socialism concealed the latter within itself *in nuce* [in a nutshell], coming now *post festum* can only be silly—silly, stale, and basically reactionary.

From letter to Engels (in Littlehampton)
LONDON, SEPTEMBER 24, 1878

Dear Fred:
. . . After the opening of the Reichstag, I received a copy of the draft of the law prepared by the government and its rationale; yesterday I received from the same person (Bracke) the stenographic report of the Reichstag sessions of September 16 and 17.[1] I had no conception —even now—of the stupidity of the average German minister and the "genius" of his Master [Bismarck], as well as of the vileness of the representatives of the German bourgeoisie hanging on his coat-tails—until I saw this stereotyped report about the latest action. I am half-busy with extracts from the report for the English press, but I do not yet know if in the end it would be fitting for the *Daily News.* . . .

Yours,
MOHR

From letter to Friedrich Adolph Sorge (in Hoboken)
LONDON, SEPTEMBER 19, 1879

Dear Friend:
. . . In regard to Most & Co., we maintain a "passive" attitude toward them, that is, we have no relationship with them, although I see Most himself in my house now and then. Mr. Lübeck lies when he says that Engels and I have issued any "Statement" against Most or against the *Freiheit.* Jew-boy Bernstein[1] wrote to Engels from Zurich that Most wrote to Germany and Switzerland saying that we backed him. Whereupon Engels replied: If Bernstein submitted "proofs" of this, he would issue a public statement against these lies. But Bernstein (nephew of the Berlin Rabbi Rebenstein, of the Berlin *Volks-Zeitung*) did not, in fact, have an atom of proof to submit. Instead he whispered the false secret to the jackass Lübeck, who, with the customary discretion of these penny-a-liners, immediately sold it to the United States.

---

1. The days of the first debates preparing for the antisocialist laws.—Such anti-Semitic labels were fairly common in Marx's private correspondence.

Our points of dispute with Most are not in any way those of the trio of Zurich gentlemen—"Dr. Höchberg, Bernstein (Höchberg's secretary), and C. A. Schramm." We do not reproach Most for his *Freiheit*'s being *too revolutionary;* we reproach him for its having *no revolutionary content,* and for dealing merely in revolutionary phrases. We do not reproach him for not criticizing the party leaders in Germany, but, first, for making a public scandal instead of communicating his views to them in writing, that is, by letter, as we do; second, because he merely uses this as a pretext for making himself important and putting into circulation the idiotic secret conspiratorial plans of Messrs. Weber the Younger and Kaufmann. Long before his arrival here, these lads felt themselves called upon to take the "general labor movement" under their most-high direction, and they contrived multifarious attempts in every quarter to realize this "gracious" venture. The worthy Johann Most, a man of the most childish vanity, actually believes that world conditions have suffered a tremendous change because this same Most no longer lives in Germany but in London. The man is not without talent, but he kills it by too much writing. He is, in addition, without *espirit de suite* [consistency]. Every change of the wind blows him first in one direction and then in another, like a weathercock.

On the other hand, things may indeed reach a point where Engels and I might be compelled to issue a "public statement" against the Leipzigers[2] and their Zurich allies.

Here is the state of affairs. Bebel wrote us that they wanted to establish a party organ in Zurich and he requested our names as collaborators. Hirsch's name was given to us as the probable editor. Thereupon we accepted, and I wrote at once to Hirsch (then in Paris, whence he has since been expelled for the second time) to accept the editorship, since he alone affords us the certainty that such a pack of doctors and students, etc., and such a gang of professorial socialists, as now strut in the *Zukunft*, etc., and who have already begun to penetrate the *Vorwärts*, would be kept out and the party line would be strictly adhered to. But it turned out that Hirsch had uncovered a hornets' nest in Zurich. The five men—Dr. Höchberg (who has bought his way into the party with his money, an emotional driveler, the cousin of Sonnemann); Jew-boy Bernstein, his secretary; C. A. Schramm, a philistine, even though a well-meaning one; Viereck, sent from Leipzig (a philistine lout, the illegitimate son of the German Kaiser); and businessman Singer from Berlin (a petty bourgeois,

---

2. Members of the Executive Committee of the Social-Democratic party (August Bebel, Wilhelm Bracke, Wilhelm Liebknecht), which sat in Leipzig while Bismarck's antisocialist law was in effect.

paunchy; he visited me a few months ago)—these five men with the highest permission from Leipzig, made themselves the constituent committee and appointed the trio (Höchberg-Bernstein-Schramm) the *administrative and editorial supervisory committee* in Zurich, with the power of direct decision. Bebel, Liebknecht, and a few other German leaders were put above them as the final court of appeals. Hirsch demanded to know, first, from whom the money is to come; Liebknecht replied, from "the party plus Dr. Höchberg." Hirsch stripped off the rhetoric and reduced this quite correctly to "Höchberg." Second, Hirsch did not want to be subordinate to the trifolium Höchberg-Bernstein-C. A. Schramm, in which refusal he was the more justified as Bernstein, in answer to a letter in which Hirsch had asked for information, snapped at him with bureaucratic rudeness and condemned his *Laterne*[3]—*mirabile dictu*—as ultrarevolutionary, etc. After a prolonged correspondence, in which Liebknecht did not play a shining role, Hirsch withdrew. Engels informed Bebel that we were also withdrawing, as we had from the very beginning refused to write for the *Zukunft* (Höchberg) and the *Neue Gesellschaft* (Wiede). These fellows, theoretical ciphers and practical incompetents, want to take the teeth out of socialism (which they have trimmed according to university recipes) and out of the Social-Democratic party in particular, to enlighten the workers, or, as they say, to bring "elements of education" to their muddled superficiality, and above all, to make the party respectable in the eyes of the philistines. They are wretched counterrevolutionary windbags. Well, the weekly journal is now appearing (or is to appear) in Zurich, under the control and higher supervision of the Leipzigers (editor: Vollmar).

In the meantime, Höchberg came here to lure us. He found only Engels, who made clear to him the deep gulf between us and him by means of a critical review of the *Jahrbuch* published by Höchberg (under the pseudonym Dr. L. Richter). (Take a look at this *wretched* concoction: the article signed with the three *** is by the trio Höchberg-Bernstein-C. A. Schramm.) (But the worthy Johann Most also figures in it with the groveling article on the book scribbler Schäffle.) Nothing more reprehensible for the party has ever been printed. What a good turn Bismarck did, *not himself, but us*, when he made it possible for these fellows to make themselves clearly heard as a result of the enforced silence in Germany. Höchberg was stunned when Engels told him the plain truth; he is a "peaceable" evolutionary and really expects proletarian emancipation to come only from the "educated bourgeois," that is, people like himself. Liebknecht had told him that

---

3. A Social-Democratic weekly in Brussels which Hirsch edited.

au fond [at bottom] we all agreed. In Germany everybody—that is, all the leaders—shared his views, etc.

Indeed, Liebknecht, after making the great mistake of dealing with the Lassalleans, has opened the doors wide to all these half-humans, and thus paved the way *malgré lui* [despite himself] for a demoralization in the party which could be eliminated *only* by an [anti-] socialist law.

Now if the "weekly"—the party organ—should actually proceed along the lines initiated by Höchberg's *Jahrbuch,* we would be compelled to take a public stand against such dissipation of the party and its theory! Engels has drawn up a circular (letter) to Bebel, etc. (of course, for *private circulation* among the German party leaders), in which our standpoint is set forth without reserve. Thus the gentlemen have been forewarned and know us well enough to know that this means: Bend or break! If they want to compromise themselves, *tant pis* [so much the worse]! In no case will they be allowed to compromise us. You can see how low parliamentarism has already brought them from the fact that they are charging Hirsch with a great crime—of what? Because he has handled the scoundrel Kayser a bit roughly in the *Laterne* for the latter's disgraceful speech on Bismarck's tariff legislation. But now they say the party, that is, the handful of parliamentary representatives of the party, had authorized Kayser to speak like that! All the more shame for that handful! But even that is a wretched excuse. Actually, they were foolish enough to let Kayser speak for himself and in the name of his constituents; instead he spoke in the name of the party. However that may be, they are already so much affected by parliamentary idiocy that they believe they are above criticism, that they denounce criticism as a *crime de lèse majesté.*

In regard to the *Communist Manifesto,*[4] the matter has come to nought because first Engels, and then I, had no time. But one must get on with it in the end. . . .

Your loyally devoted

KARL MARX

Johann Most wrote me about Lübeck's babble in the Chicago paper.[5] I did not answer him; but now that I am back in London I will invite him personally and give him my opinion orally.

Hirsch is here since his expulsion from Paris. I have not seen him yet, as, of course, he could not find me at home while I was away.

I am mailing this in a "registered" envelope only because I have no other one at hand and did not want to postpone this any longer.

4. Preparation of an English edition for the American public.
5. *Chicagoer Arbeiter-Zeitung.*

From letter written in English to John Swinton (in New York)
LONDON, NOVEMBER 4, 1880

My Dear Sir:

. . . Liebknecht has to enter prison for six months. The antisocialist law having failed to overthrow or even to weaken the German Social-Democratic organization, Bismarck clings the more desperately to his panacea, and fancies that it *must* work, if only applied on a larger scale. Hence he has extended the state of siege to Hamburg, Altona, and three other northern towns. Under these circumstances our German friends have written me a letter of which one passage reads thus: "The socialist law, though it could not break and never will break our organization, does impose pecuniary sacrifices almost impossible to bear. To support the families ruined by the police, to keep alive the few papers left to us, to keep up the necessary communications by secret messengers, to fight the battle on the whole line—all this requires money. Our resources are nearly exhausted and we are forced to appeal to our friends and sympathizers in other countries." So much for the extract.

Now we here at London, Paris, etc., will do our best. At the same time I believe that a man of your influence might organize a subscription in the United States. Even if the monetary result were not important, denunciations of Bismarck's new *coup d'état* in public meetings held by you, reported in the American press, reproduced on the other side of the Atlantic, would sorely hit the Pomeranian *hobereau* [country squire] and be welcomed by all the socialists of Europe. More information you might get from Mr. Sorge (Hoboken). Any money forthcoming to be sent over to Mr. Otto Freytag, Landtagsabgeordneter [member of the Diet], Amtmannshof, Leipzig. His address ought, of course, not be made public; otherwise the German police would simply—*confiscate*.

Apropos. My youngest daughter [Eleanor]—who was not with us at Ramsgate —just tells me that she has cut my portrait from the copy of the *Capital* I sent you, on the pretext that it was a mere caricature. Well, I shall make up for it by a photogram to be taken on the first fine day.

Mrs. Marx and the whole family send you their best wishes.

Yours most sincerely,

KARL MARX

Letter to Friedrich Adolph Sorge (in Hoboken)
LONDON, NOVEMBER 5, 1880

Dear Sorge:

You must ascribe my long silence (1) to a very great pressure of work, and (2) to the dangerous illness of my wife, which has already lasted more than a year.

You have seen yourself to what heights Johann Most has developed, and on the other hand, how miserably the so-called party organ, the Zurich *Sozialdemokrat* (not to mention the *Jahrbuch* there), has been managed, *duce* [under the leadership of] Dr. Höchberg. Engels and I have therefore been in constant correspondence with the Leipzigers in this matter, often involving sharp clashes. But we have avoided intervening *publicly* in any way. For those who, *comparativement parlant* [comparatively speaking], sit quietly abroad, it is not fitting to undermine the position of those working within the country under the most difficult conditions and with the greatest personal sacrifices more difficult, to the delight of the bourgeois and the government. Liebknecht was here a few weeks ago, and "improvement" has been promised in every respect. The party organization is renewed, which could be done only in a secret way, that is, insofar as "secret" means a secret from the police.

It is only recently that I fully discovered Most's vileness—in a *Russian* socialist paper. He never dared print in German what can be read here in Russian vernacular. This is no more an attack on individuals, but the dragging of the *whole German labor movement through the dirt*. At the same time it shows grotesquely his absolute lack of understanding of the doctrine he had formerly peddled. It is a babbling so absurd, so illogical, so degenerate that it finally dissolves in *nothing*, that is to say, in Johann Most's boundless personal vanity. Since despite all his clamoring he could not accomplish anything in Germany—except a little among a certain Berlin crowd—he has allied himself with the younger generation of Bakuninists in Paris, the group which publishes the *Révolution Sociale* (whose circle of readers is exactly 210, but which has Pyat's *Commune* as its ally). The cowardly, melodramatic *farceur* Pyat—in whose *Commune* I figure as Bismarck's right hand—has a grudge against me because I have always treated him with absolute contempt and thwarted all his attempts to use the International for his stage effects. In any case, Most has performed a good service by having brought together all the ranters—Andreas Scheu, Hasselmann, etc., etc.—in one group.

As a result of Bismarck's new state-of-siege decrees and the persecution of our party organs, it is absolutely necessary to raise money for the party. I have, therefore, written yesterday to John Swinton (for a well-meaning bourgeois is best suited for this purpose), and told him to apply to you for detailed information on German conditions.

Apart from the trifles mentioned on the previous page—and how many of these have we seen evaporate and then vanish again without a trace during our long years of exile!—on the whole, things are going along splendidly (I mean by this the general developments in Europe), as well as within the circle of the really revolutionary party on the Continent.

You have probably noticed that, in particular, *Égalité* (thanks *en première instance* [primarily] to Guesde's coming over to us and to the work of my son-in-law Lafargue) has for the first time offered us a "French" *workers' paper* in the true sense of the word. Even Malon, in the *Revue Socialiste*—despite the inconsistencies inseparable from his eclectic nature—has had to espouse *socialisme moderne scientifique*, that is, *German* socialism (we were enemies, since he was originally a co-founder of the Alliance).[1] I wrote for him the *"Questionnaire,"* which was first printed in the *Revue Socialiste* and a large number of reprints were then distributed throughout France. Shortly thereafter Guesde came to London to draw up with us (myself, Engels, and Lafargue) a workers' election program for the coming general elections. With the exception of some trivialities, such as fixing the minimum wage by law, etc., which in spite of our protests Guesde found it necessary to throw to the French workers (I said to him: "If the French proletariat is still so childish as to require such bait, it is not worth while drawing up any program whatever"), the economic part of the very brief document consists solely of demands that have spontaneously arisen out of the labor movement itself, except for the introductory passages where the communist goal is defined in a few words. It was a tremendous step to pull the French workers down to earth from their fog of phraseology, and hence it was a shock to all the French giddy-heads, who live by "fog-making." After the most violent opposition by the anarchists, the program was first adopted in the *Région centrale*— that is, Paris and its environs—and later in many other workers' centers. The simultaneous formation of opposed groups of workers,

---

1. The *Alliance de la Democratie Socialiste* was founded by Mikhail Bakunin in October, 1868, with the aim of seizing control of the International for the anarchist movement.

which, however, accepted most of the "practical" demands of the program (except the anarchists, who do not consist of real workers but only of *déclassés* and a few duped workers as their rank-and-file soldiers), and the fact that very divergent standpoints were expressed in connection with other matters, prove to me that this is *the first real labor movement* in France. Until now, only sects existed there, and they naturally received their *mot d'ordre* [slogan] from the founder of the sect, whereas the mass of the proletariat followed the radical or pseudo-radical bourgeois and fought for them on the day of decision, only to be slaughtered, deported, etc., by the fellows they had put into power.

Émancipation, published a few days ago at Lyon, will be the organ of the *Parti Ouvrier* [Workers' party] that has arisen on the basis of German socialism.

In the meantime we also have had our champions in the camp of the enemy itself—that is, in the radical camp. Theisz has taken up the labor problem in *Intransigeant*, Rochefort's organ; after the defeat of the Commune he had come to London a Proudhonist, like all "thinking" French socialists, and there he changed completely— through personal contact with me and conscientious study of *Capital*. On the other hand, my son-in-law [Charles Longuet] gave up his professorship at King's College,[2] returned to Paris (his family, for-tunately, is still here), and became one of the most influential editors of *Justice*, which is owned by Clemenceau, head of the extreme left. He has done such good work that Clemenceau, who as late as last April came out publicly against socialism and as champion of American-democratic-republican views, in his latest speech against Gambetta in Marseilles, as well as in his general tendency and in essential points as contained in the minimum program, has swung over to us. Whether he will keep his promises is entirely immaterial. At any rate, he has introduced our element into the Radical party, whose organs, comically enough, consider something wonderful when it comes from the mouth of Clemenceau, while they had ig-nored or ridiculed it as long as it was merely issued as the slogan of the *Parti Ouvrier*.

I need hardly tell you—for you are familiar with French chauvin-ism—that the secret threads by which the leaders, from Guesde-Malon to Clemenceau, have been set in motion are *entre nous* [be-tween us]. *Il n'en faut pas parler. Quand on veut agir pour Messieurs les Français, il faut le faire anonymement, pour ne pas choquer le sentiment "national."* [One must not talk about this. When one

---

2. This part of the sentence was written in English.

wishes to influence Messrs. the French, one must do it anonymously, so as not to shock the "national" feeling.] As it is, the anarchists are already denouncing our cooperators as *Prussian* agents, under the dictatorship of the "notorious" Prussian agent—Karl Marx.[3]

In Russia—where *Capital* is more read and appreciated than anywhere else—our success is even greater. On the one hand we have the critics (mostly young university professors, some of them personal friends of mine, and also some writers for the reviews), and on the other hand the terrorist central committee,[4] whose program, secretly printed and issued in Petersburg recently, has provoked great rage among the Russian anarchists in Switzerland who are publishing in Geneva *The Black Redistribution* (this is the literal translation from the Russian: *Tshorny Peredel*). The people—most (not all) of whom left Russia *voluntarily*—constitute the so-called party of propaganda, in contrast to the terrorists, who risk their lives. (In order to carry on propaganda in Russia they move to Geneva! What a *quid pro quo!*) These gentlemen are against all political-revolutionary action. Russia is to leap in one breakneck jump into the anarchist-communist-atheist millennium! In the meantime they are preparing for this leap by a tiresome doctrinairism whose so-called *principes courent la rue depuis feu Bakounine* [principles have been commonplace since the late Bakunin].

And now enough for this time. Let me hear from you soon. Best regards from my wife.

Totus tuus [entirely yours],

KARL MARX

I should be very pleased if you could find me something good (substantial) on economic conditions in California, of course at my expense. California is very important to me, because nowhere else has the upheaval caused so shamelessly by capitalist centralization taken place—with such speed.

---

*From letter written in English to Henry Mayers Hyndman** (*in London*) LONDON, DECEMBER 8, 1880

Dear Sir:

. . . If you say that you do not share the views of my party for England I can only reply that that party considers an English revo-

---

3. Sentence written in English.
4. The Central Committee of the *Narodnaya Volya* [People's Will], founded in Petersburg in 1879.
* Reprinted from Hyndman, *The Record of an Adventurous Life* (London, 1911).

lution not necessary, but—according to historic precedents—*possible.* If the unavoidable evolution turns into a revolution, it would not only be the fault of the ruling classes, but also of the working class. Every pacific concession of the former has been wrung from them by "pressure from without." Their action kept pace with the pressure, and if the latter has more and more weakened, it is only because the English working class know now how to wield their power and use their liberties, both of which they possess legally.

In Germany the working class were fully aware from the beginning of their movement that you cannot get rid of a military despotism by a Revolution. At the same time they understood that such a Revolution, even if at first successful, would finally turn against them without previous organization, acquirement of knowledge, propaganda, and [illegible word]. Hence they moved within strictly *legal* bounds. The illegality was all on the side of the government, which declared them *en dehors la loi* [outside the law]. Their crimes were not *deeds,* but *opinions* unpleasant to their rulers. Fortunately, the same government—the working class having been pushed to the background with the help of the bourgeoisie—becomes now more and more unbearable to the latter, whom it hits on their most tender point—the pocket. This state of things cannot last.

Sincerely yours,

KARL MARX

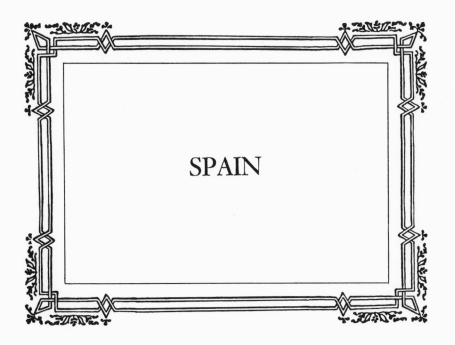

SPAIN

Chronology:
Spain, 1808-85

1808

MAY   *After the French occupation of Spain, a popular Spanish insurrection forces French General Joachim Murat to retire behind the Ebro River.*

JULY 20   *The French recapture Madrid; but on the same day another French force, marching on Cádiz, is defeated at Baylen.*

SEPTEMBER   *Napoleon I advances on Madrid, which the French have abandoned, with an army of 150,000 men.*

NOVEMBER 10–11   *The French defeat the Spaniards at Burgos and Espinosa.*

DECEMBER 13   *Madrid capitulates to Napoleon.*

1809

JANUARY 16   *In the Battle of Coruña a British invasion army under Sir John Moore is defeated and forced to evacuate Spain by French Marshal Nicolas Jean de Dieu Soult. But guerrilla warfare against the French continues.*

FEBRUARY 21   *Saragossa capitulates after a heroic defense. The French under Soult then invade Portugal and take Oporto, but are driven out by the British under Wellington.*

NOVEMBER 12   *In the Battle of Ocaña the Spaniards are defeated. The French then take Andalusia, except Cádiz.*

[541]

1810

JULY 10   The French take Ciudad Rodrigo in Portugal, forc-
             ing the British to fall back to the lines of Torres
             Vedras.

WINTER   After several engagements, the French under
             Marshal André Masséna withdraw to Spain and are
             besieged by the British in Almeida and Badajoz.

1811

MAY 5   Masséna is defeated in the Battle of Fuentes de
             Onoro.

MAY 16   The French under Soult are defeated by the British
             General William Beresford in the Battle of Albuera.

1812

JANUARY 19   The British take Ciudad Rodrigo.

APRIL 16   The British take Badajoz.

MAY 8   A Spanish National Assembly (Cortes), elected in
             1810 in Cádiz, the only uninvaded part of the coun-
             try, promulgates a democratic constitution providing
             for a one-chamber parliament, popular sovereignty,
             and universal suffrage.

JULY 22   In the battle of Salamanca, Wellington defeats the
             French under Marshal Auguste Frédéric Marmont.

AUGUST 12   Joseph Bonaparte, Napoleon's brother, whom he had
             made King of Spain, is forced to flee Madrid.

1813

JUNE 21   In the Battle of Vitoria, Wellington defeats French
             Marshal Jean Baptiste Jourdan, forces Joseph Bona-
             parte to escape to France.

AUGUST 21   The British capture San Sebastián.

OCTOBER 31   A force of British and Spaniards capture Pamplona.

NOVEMBER 10 Wellington crosses the French frontier and defeats
             Soult. The French invasion of Spain is over.

1814

MARCH   Ferdinand VII is restored to the Spanish throne,
             promising to maintain the democratic constitution of

1812; his failure to carry out his promise leads to a series of insurrections.

1820

JANUARY   *Spanish troops under Colonel Rafael Riego mutiny and march on Madrid. After other revolutionary movements break out, and the garrison in Madrid mutinies, Ferdinand VII restores the constitution. The King is a virtual prisoner until 1823.*

1823

SPRING   *Empowered by the Holy Alliance at the Congress of Verona (October, 1822), a French army invades Spain, marches on Madrid, and drives the revolutionaries south to Cádiz; the Spanish take Ferdinand VII with them.*

AUGUST 31   *In the Battle of the Trocadero the revolutionaries are defeated. The restored Ferdinand VII spends the next ten years of his life in what has been called an "orgy of repression."*

1833

JUNE 30   *Under the influence of his wife, Queen Christina (Cristina), Ferdinand VIII sets aside the Salic law, depriving his brother, Don Carlos, of succession to the throne in favor of his three-year-old daughter Isabella.*

SEPTEMBER 29   *Ferdinand VII dies; he is succeeded by his daughter, Isabella II, with the Queen ruling as regent.*

1834

Conservative elements, the Catholic Church, and much of the North (Navarre, Aragon, Catalonia) rebel against the government in support of Don Carlos, who claims the throne. The so-called Carlist War lasts until 1839.

1836

AUGUST 10   *Insurrections in Andalusia, Aragon, Catalonia, and Madrid, against the unpopular Queen Christina. She then restores the Constitution of 1812 and appoints a progressive ministry.*

1839

AUGUST 31   *The defeated Don Carlos leaves Spain for France.*

1840

OCTOBER   *Baldomero Espartero, a general who defeated the Carlists, revolts and forces Queen Christina to leave Spain. Espartero then becomes dictator-regent.*

1841

OCTOBER   *At Pamplona General Espartero defeats a pro-Christina insurrection.*

1842

NOVEMBER–   *Barcelona rises and declares a republic, but it is sup-*
DECEMBER   *pressed by Espartero.*

1843

JUNE   *An alliance of Moderates, Progressives, and Republicans moves against Espartero.*

JULY 15   *General Ramon Maria Narvaez, representing the new alliance, seizes Madrid and forces Espartero to flee the country.*

AUGUST   *Isabella II, thirteen years old, is declared of age; General Narvaez becomes Lieutenant General of the Kingdom.*

1844

MARCH   *Queen Christina returns, but Narvaez remains virtual dictator (until 1851).*

1845

A new constitution reestablishes the one of 1834 (Estatuto Real), providing for a bicameral legislature and giving the government power to control and dissolve the ministry.

1852

DECEMBER · *A camarilla eliminates the powers of the Cortes and establishes a dictatorship.*

1854

JULY · *A revolt led by General Leopoldo O'Donnell, a Moderate, and Espartero drives Queen Christina from the country. O'Donnell organizes a new party, the Liberal Union, with a moderate reform program; the Cortes confiscates Church lands.*

1856

JULY 15 · *Espartero resigns, and O'Donnell reestablishes the Constitution of 1845, with an amendment providing for an annual meeting of the Cortes.*

OCTOBER · *O'Donnell is dismissed; two years of reaction follow.*

1858–63

O'Donnell returns to power with the support of the Liberal Union party.

1864

SEPTEMBER · *General Narvaez becomes Premier, supported by reactionaries.*

1865

Censorship is restored and political clubs dissolved.

1866

JANUARY–JUNE · *General Juan Prim organizes an unsuccessful insurrection.*

1867

NOVEMBER 5 · *Death of General O'Donnell.*

1868

APRIL 23 · *Death of General Narvaez.*

SEPTEMBER 18 · *In Cádiz, Admiral Juan Baptista Topete proclaims a revolution which soon spreads throughout Spain.*

546   SPAIN

SEPTEMBER 28   *Marshal Francisco Serrano defeats royal forces at Alcolea.*

SEPTEMBER 29   *Queen Isabella flees to France and is declared deposed.*

OCTOBER 5   *Formation of a liberal provisional government under Serrano and Prim, abolishing the Jesuit order and providing for freedom of the press and universal suffrage.*

1869

MAY 21   *The Cortes votes for a monarchical government.*
JUNE 6   *A new constitution is proclaimed.*
JUNE 15   *Serrano becomes Regent and Prim head of the government.*

1873

FEBRUARY 12   *Proclamation of the first Spanish Republic.*

1874

NOVEMBER 24   *Alfonso, son of Isabella, comes of age and declares for a constitutional monarchy.*

DECEMBER 29–31 *With the help of antirepublican generals, Alfonso is declared King—Alfonso XII; the Carlist War continues (the Pope having recognized Don Carlos as Carlos VII, King of Spain).*

1876

JULY   *The Cortes accepts a new constitution, a compromise between those of 1845 and 1869.*

1885

Death of Alfonso XII. He is succeeded by his widow, Maria Christina, as Regent (until 1902).

Insurrection in Madrid*

MARX's intense interest in Spain began in the summer of 1854, when a revolution broke out in the Spanish army and spread across the land. Such an event in a country long considered backward and somnolent stirred Marx's curiosity. He undertook an investigation of Spanish history and political institutions.

"My principal study," he wrote to Engels on September 2, 1854, "is now Spain. Hitherto I have labored mostly through Spanish sources, covering the period from 1808 to 1814 and from 1820 to 1823. I now come to the period of 1824–33. The history is not without complications. It is even harder to trace the roots of the development. In any case, I began properly with Quixote. The whole thing, when very much condensed, will come to approximately six articles for the Tribune."

It came to much more. Altogether, Marx published in the New-York Daily Tribune in 1854 seventeen articles on Spain, eight of which —"Revolutionary Spain"—were a series. In 1856 he published two more pieces on the subject. The articles, which Marx wrote in English, are given here in full insofar as they deal with the subject of Spain. They not only show a detailed knowledge of Spanish political history but also contain flashes of acute insight into revolutionary activity (including guerrilla warfare) in general.

The news we receive of the military insurrection at Madrid continues to be of a very contradictory and fragmentary character. All the Madrid telegraphic dispatches are, of course, government statements, and of the same questionable faith as the bulletins published in the Gaceta. A review of the scanty materials at hand is consequently all I can give you. It will be recollected that O'Donnell was one of the

* New-York Daily Tribune, July 21, 1854. Written July 7, 1854.

generals banished by the Queen in February; that he refused to obey, secreted himself in Madrid, and from his hiding place kept up secret correspondence with the garrison of Madrid, and particularly with General Dulce, the Inspector General of the Cavalry. The government was aware of his sojourn at Madrid, and on June 27, at night, General Blaser, the Minister of War, and General Lara, the Captain General of New Castile, received warnings of an intended outbreak under the leadership of General Dulce. Nothing, however, was done to prevent or stifle the insurrection in its germ. On the twenty-eighth, therefore, General Dulce found no difficulty in assembling about 2,000 cavalry under pretext of a review, and marching with them out of the town, accompanied by O'Donnell, with the intention of kidnaping the Queen, then staying at the Escorial. The design failed, however, and the Queen arrived at Madrid on the twenty-ninth, attended by Count San Luis, the president of the Council, and held a review, while the insurgents took up quarters in the environs of the capital. They were joined by Colonel Echagüe and 400 men of the regiment "Prince," who brought along the regimental cash bag containing 1,000,000 francs. A column composed of seven battalions of infantry, one regiment of cavalry, one detachment of mounted gendarmerie, and two batteries of artillery left Madrid on the evening of the twenty-ninth inst., under command of General Lara, to meet the rebels quartered at the Venta del Espiritu Santo and the village of Vicalvaro. A battle took place on the thirtieth between the two armies, of which we have received three accounts—the official one addressed by General Lara to the Minister of War, published in the *Gaceta;* the second published by the *Messager de Bayonne,* and the third a report from the Madrid correspondent of the *Indépendance Belge,* an eyewitness of the affair. The first-named report, which may be found in all the London papers, is easily disposed of, General Lara stating at one time that he attacked the insurgents, and at another that they charged him, making prisoners in one place and losing them in another, claiming the victory and returning to Madrid—*enfin,* leaving the insurgents masters of the field, but covering it with the dead of the "enemy," while pretending himself to have only thirty wounded. . . . [Report of the *Messager de Bayonne* omitted.]

We come now to the report of the *Indépendance,* dated Madrid, July 1, which seems to be the most trustworthy. . . . [Report of the *Indépendance Belge* omitted.]

Up to the sixth inst. no papers or letters had arrived from Madrid. The *Moniteur* alone has the following laconic dispatch, dated Madrid, the fourth of July:

"Tranquillity continues to reign at Madrid and in the provinces."

A private dispatch states that the insurgents are at Aranjuez. If the battle anticipated for the first inst. by the correspondent of the *Indépendance* had resulted in a victory of the government, there would be wanting neither letters, nor papers, nor bulletins. Notwithstanding that the state of siege had been proclaimed at Madrid, the *Clamor Público*, the *Nación*, the *Diario*, the *España*, and the *Época* had reappeared without previous notice to the government, whose *fiscal* informed them of this dismal fact. Among the persons arrested at Madrid are named Messrs. Antonio Guillermo Moreno and José Manuel Collado, bankers. A warrant was issued against Sijora Sevillano, Marqués de Fuentes de Duero, a particular friend of Marshal Narvaez. Messrs. Mon and Pidal are placed under surveillance.

It would be premature to form an opinion on the general character of this insurrection. I may say, however, that it does not seem to proceed from the Progresista party, as General San Miguel, their soldier, remains quiet at Madrid. From all the reports it seems, on the contrary, that Narvaez is at the bottom of it, and that Queen Christina, whose influence had of late much decreased through the Queen's favorite Count San Luis, is not entirely a stranger to it.

There is perhaps no country, except Turkey, so little known to and so falsely judged by Europe as Spain. The numberless local pronunciamentos and military rebellions have accustomed Europe to view it on a level with Imperial Rome at the era of the praetorians. This is quite as superficial an error as was committed in the case of Turkey, by those who fancied the life of the nation extinct because its official history for the past century consisted only of palace revolutions and Janissary *émeutes* [mutinies]. The secret of this fallacy lies in the simple fact that historians, instead of viewing the resources and strength of these people in their provincial and local organizations, had drawn at the source of their court almanacs. The movements of what we are used to call the state have so little affected the Spanish people that they were quite content to leave that restricted domain to the alternative passions and petty intrigues of court minions, soldiers, adventurers, and a few so-called statesmen, and they have had little cause to repent themselves of their indifference. The character of modern Spanish history deserving to receive a very different appreciation than it has until now experienced, I will take an opportunity to treat this subject in one of my next letters. This much I may yet remark in this place, that little surprise ought to be felt if a general movement should now arise in the Peninsula from a mere military rebellion, since the late financial decrees of the government have converted the tax gatherer into a most efficient revolutionary propagandist. . . .

The Proclamations of Dulce and O'Donnell*

. . . THE SPANISH insurrection appears to assume a new aspect, as is evident from the proclamations of Dulce and O'Donnell, the former of whom is a partisan of Espartero, and the latter was a stout adherent of Narvaez and perhaps secretly of Queen Christina. O'Donnell, having convinced himself that the Spanish towns are not to be set in motion this time by a mere palace revolution, suddenly exhibits liberal principles. His proclamation is dated from Manzanares, a borough of the Mancha, not far from Ciudad Real. It says that his aim is to preserve the throne but to remove the camarilla; the rigorous observation of the fundamental laws; the amelioration of the election and press laws; the diminution of taxes; the advancement in the civil service according to merit; decentralization, and establishment of a national militia on a broad basis. It proposes provincial juntas and a general assembly of the Cortes at Madrid, to be changed with the revision of the laws.

The proclamation of General Dulce is even more energetic. He says: "There are no longer Progresistas and Moderados; all of us are Spaniards, and imitators of the men of July 7, 1822. Return to the Constitution of 1837; maintenance of Isabella II; perpetual exile of the Queen Mother; destitution of the present ministry; reestablishment of peace in our country; such is the end we pursue at every cost, as we shall show on the field of honor to the traitors whom we shall punish for their culpable folly."

According to the *Journal des Débats*, papers and correspondence have been seized at Madrid which are said to prove beyond doubt

---

* *New-York Daily Tribune*, August 3, 1854. Written July 18, 1854.

that it is the secret aim of the insurgents to declare the throne vacant, to reunite the Iberian Peninsula into one state, and to offer the crown to Don Pedro V, Prince of Saxe-Coburg-Gotha. The tender interest taken by the *Times* in the Spanish insurrection, and the simultaneous presence of the said Don Pedro in England, appear indeed to indicate that some new Coburg dodge is afloat. The court is evidently very uneasy, as all possible ministerial combinations have been tried. Isturiz and Martínez de la Rosa having been applied to in vain. The *Messager de Bayonne* asserts that the Count de Montemolín left Naples as soon as he received news of the insurrection.

O'Donnell has entered Andalusia, having crossed the Sierra Morena in three columns, one marching by Carolina, the other by Pozo Blanco, and the third by Despeñaperros. The *Gaceta* confesses that Colonel Buceta succeeded in surprising Cuenca, by the possession of which place the insurgents have secured their communications with Valencia. In the latter province the rising now comprises about four or five towns, besides Alora, where the government troops received a severe check.

It is stated also that a movement had broken out at Reus in Catalonia, and the *Messager de Bayonne* adds that disturbances had taken place in Aragon. . . .

The Spanish Revolution —
Greece and Turkey*

"*Ne touchez pas à la Reine*" (Touch not the Queen) is an old Castilian maxim, but the adventurous Mme. Muñoz and her daughter Isabella have too long overstepped the rights of even Castilian queens not to have outworn the loyal prejudices of the Spanish people.

The pronunciamentos of 1843[1] lasted three months; those of 1854 have scarcely lasted as many weeks. The ministry is dissolved, Count San Luis has fled, Queen Christina is trying to reach the French frontier, and at Madrid both troops and citizens have declared against the government.

The revolutionary movements of Spain since the commencement of the century offer a remarkably uniform aspect, with the exception of the movements in favor of provincial and local privileges which periodically agitate the northern provinces, every palace plot being attended by military insurrections, and these invariably dragging municipal pronunciamentos in their train. There are two causes for this phenomenon. In the first place, we find that what we call the state in a modern sense has, from the exclusively provincial life of the people, no national embodiment in opposition to the court except in the army. In the second place, the peculiar position of Spain and the Peninsular War created conditions under which it was only in the army that everything vital in the Spanish nationality was permitted to concentrate. Thus it happens that the only national demonstrations (those of 1812 and 1822) proceeded from the army; and thus the

---

* *New-York Daily Tribune*, August 4, 1854.
1. In May, 1843, a military revolt took place against the government of the Progresista party, forcing Espartero, the leader of the latter, to flee from Spain in July.

movable part of the nation has been accustomed to regard the army as the natural instrument of every national rising. During the troublesome epoch from 1830 to 1854, however, the cities of Spain came to know that the army, instead of continuing to uphold the cause of the nation, was changed into an instrument for the rivalries of the ambitious pretenders to the military guardianship of the court. Consequently we find the movement of 1854 very different even from that of 1843. The *émeute* of General O'Donnell was looked upon by the people as anything but a conspiracy against the leading influence at the court, especially as it was supported by the ex-favorite Serrano. The towns and country accordingly demurred to giving any response to the appeal made by the cavalry of Madrid. It was thus that General O'Donnell was forced to alter entirely the character of his operations in order not to remain isolated and exposed to failure. He was forced to assert in his proclamation three points equally opposed to the supremacy of the army: the convocation of the Cortes, an economical government, and the formation of a national militia—the last demand originating in the desire of the towns to recover their independence of the army. It is a fact, then, that the military insurrection has obtained the support of a popular insurrection only by submitting to the conditions of the latter. It remains to be seen whether it will be constrained to adhere to them and to execute these promises.

With the exception of the Carlists, all parties have raised their cry—Progresistas, partisans of the Constitution of 1837, partisans of the Constitution of 1812, Unionists (demanding the annexation of Portugal), and Republicans. The news concerning the latter party is to be received with caution, since it has to pass the censure of the Paris police. Beside these party struggles, the rival pretensions of the military leaders are in full development. Espartero had no sooner heard of the success of O'Donnell than he left his retreat at Leganes and declared himself the chief of the movement. But as soon as Caesar Narvaez learned [of] the appearance of his old Pompey in the field, he forthwith offered his services to the Queen, which were accepted, and he is to form a new ministry. From the details I am about to give you, it will be seen that the military has by no means taken the initiative in all places, but that in some they have had to yield to the overpowering pressure of the population.

Besides the pronunciamentos in Valencia, reported in my last, there has been one at Alicante. In Andalusia, pronunciamentos have taken place at Granada, Seville, and Jaén. In Old Castile, there has been a pronunciamento at Burgos; in León, at Valladolid; in Biscay, at San Sebastián and Vitoria; in Navarre, at Toledo, Pamplona, and Guipuzcoa; in Aragon, at Saragossa; in Catalonia, at Barcelona,

Tarragona, Lérida, and Gerona; there is said, also, to have been a pronunciamento in the Balearic Isles. In Murcia, pronunciamentos were expected to take place, according to a letter from Cartagena, dated July 12, which says: "In consequence of a *bando* [public notice] published by the military governor of the place, all the inhabitants of Cartagena possessed of muskets and other arms have been ordered to depose them with the civil authorities within twenty-four hours. On the demand of the Consul of France, the government has allowed the French residents to depose their arms, as in 1848, at the Consulate."

Of all these pronunciamentos, four only deserve particular mention, viz., those of San Sebastián in Biscay, Barcelona the capital of Catalonia, Saragossa the capital of Aragon, and Madrid.

In Biscay the pronunciamentos originated with the municipalities, in Aragon with the military. The municipality of San Sebastián was pronouncing in favor of the insurrection when the demand for the armament of the people was raised. The city was immediately covered with arms. Not till the seventeenth could the two battalions garrisoning the town be induced to join. The fusion between the citizens and military having been completed, 1,000 armed citizens accompanied by some troops set out for Pamplona, and organized the insurrection in Navarre. It was only the appearance of the armed citizens from San Sebastián which facilitated the rising of the Navarre capital. General Zabala joined the movement afterward and went to Bayonne, inviting the soldiers and officers of the Cordova regiment, who had fled there upon their late defeat at Saragossa, immediately to return to their country and to meet him at San Sebastián. According to some reports he subsequently marched upon Madrid to place himself under the orders of Espartero, while other reports state that he was on the march to Saragossa to join the Aragonese insurgents. General Mazzaredo, the commander of the Basque provinces, refusing to take part in the pronunciamento of Vitoria, was obliged to retire to France. The troops under orders of General Zabala are two battalions of the regiment of Bourbon, a battalion of carabiniers, and a detachment of cavalry. Before dismissing the subject of the Basque provinces, I may state as something characteristic that the Brigadier Barastequi, who has been named Governor of Guipuzcoa, is one of Espartero's former aides-de-camp.

At Barcelona the initiative was apparently taken by the military, but the spontaneity of their act becomes very doubtful from the additional information we have received. On the thirteenth of July, at seven o'clock P.M., the soldiers occupying the barracks of San Pueblo and of Bueno Suceso yielded to the demonstrations of the populace and declared their pronunciamento under the cry of *Vive la Reine, vive la Constitution;* death to the ministers, away with Christina! After having fraternized with the mass, and marched along with them over the Rambla, they halted at the Plaza of the Constitution. The cavalry, kept indoors at the Barcelonetta for the previous six days, because of the distrust it inspired in the Captain General, made a pronunciamento in its turn. From this moment the whole garrison passed over to the people, and all resistance on the part of the authorities became impossible. At ten o'clock General Marchesi, the military governor, yielded to the general pressure, and at midnight the Captain General of Catalonia announced his resolution to side with the movement. He went to the place of the Ayutamiento [local government], where he harangued the people, filling the place. On the eighteenth a junta was formed, composed of the Captain General and other eminent persons, with the cry of the Constitution, the Queen, and Morality. Further news from Barcelona states that some workmen had been shot on the order of the new authorities because they had destroyed machinery and violated property; also that a Republican Committee, convened in a neighboring town, had been arrested; but it should be recollected that this news passes through the hands of the Second of December,[2] whose special vocation it is to calumniate republicans and workmen.

At Saragossa it is said that the initiative proceeded from the military—a statement which becomes invalidated, however, by the additional remark that the formation of a militia corps was immediately resolved upon. So much is certain, and is confirmed by the Madrid *Gaceta* itself, that before the pronunciamento of Saragossa 150 soldiers of the Montesa regiment (cavalry) on the march to Madrid and quartered at Torrejón (five leagues from Madrid) revolted and abandoned their chiefs, who arrived at Madrid on the evening of the thirteenth with the regimental chest. The soldiers, under command of Captain Baraibán, mounted horse and took the road to Huete, being supposed to intend joining the force under Colonel Buceta at Cuenca. As for Madrid, against which Espartero is said to be marching with the "army of the center," and General Zabala with the army of the north, it was natural that a town which subsists upon the court should be the last to join in the insurrectionary movement. The *Gaceta* of the fifteenth inst. still published a bulletin from the Minister of War asserting the factions to be in flight and the enthusiastic loyalty of the troops increasing. Count San Luis, who seems to have very correctly judged the situation at Madrid, an-

---

2. December 2, 1851, was the date of Louis Napoleon's *coup d'état*, in which he made himself Napoleon III.

nounced to the workmen that General O'Donnell and the anarchists would deprive them of all employment, while if the government succeeded it would employ all workingmen on the public works for six reals (75 cents) a day. By this stratagem San Luis hoped to enroll the most excitable portion of the Madrileños under his banner. His success, however, was like that of the party of the *National* at Paris in 1848. The allies he had thus gained soon became his most dangerous enemies—the funds for their support being exhausted on the sixth day. How much the government dreaded a pronunciamento in the capital is evident from General Lara's (the Governor's) proclamation forbidding the circulation of any news respecting the progress of the insurrection. It appears, further, that the tactics of General Blaser were restricted to the care of avoiding any contact with the insurgents, lest his troops should catch the infection. It is said that the first plan of General O'Donnell was to meet the ministerial troops on the plains of La Mancha, so favorable to cavalry operations. This plan, however, was abandoned in consequence of the arrival of ex-favorite Serrano, who was in connection with several of the principal towns of Andalusia. The constitutional army thereupon determined, instead of remaining in the Mancha, to march upon Jaén and Seville.

It may be observed, *en passant*, that the *boletinos* of General Blaser bear a wonderful resemblance to the orders of the day of the Spanish generals of the sixteenth century, which gave such occasion for hilarity to Francis I, and of the eighteenth century, which Frederick the Great turned into ridicule.

It is plain that this Spanish insurrection must become a source of dissension between the governments of France and England, and the report given by a French paper that General O'Donnell was concealed, previous to the outbreak, in the palace of the British Ambassador is not likely to lessen the misgivings of Bonaparte on its account. There exists already some commencement of irritation between Bonaparte and Victoria; Bonaparte expected to meet the Queen at the embarkation of his troops from Calais, but Her Majesty answered his desire by a visit to the ex-Queen Amelia on the same day. Again, the English ministers when interpellated about nonblockade of the White Sea, the Black Sea, and the sea of Azov alleged as their excuse the alliance with France. Bonaparte retorted by an announcement of those very blockades in the *Moniteur*, without waiting for the formal consent of England. Lastly, a bad effect having been produced in France by the embarkation of French troops in British vessels only, Bonaparte published a list of French vessels destined for the same use and applied to it.

The Porte has communicated to the representatives of the four allied powers a note concerning the authority given to the Greek merchant ships again to enter Turkish ports. This authorization is to be valid for two months, on condition that the Greek Government does not render itself guilty of any act justifying its suspension. If at the expiration of this term the Greek Government shall have failed to give satisfactory reparation to the Porte, the latter reserves to itself the right of reestablishing the actual status quo. Greek ships in the Turkish ports will be subject to the local authorities, and deprived of any appeal to other protection. Within the two months the basis of an arrangement and of a commercial treaty will be negotiated. The indemnity claimed by the Porte for the immense damage done by the Greek insurrection is to be regulated by arbitration, on the report of a committee of inquiry, to be sent to the proper places, and composed of Frenchmen, Englishmen, Turks, and Greeks.

Shamyl has been officially invested by the Porte with the title of generalissimo of the army of Circassia and Georgia.

Three dragomans in the service of the French army have been shot at Varna, all of them having been found to correspond with the Russians. Two of them were Greeks and one Armenian. At the moment of his execution, one of them swallowed a paper of a compromising character.

We are informed from Hermannstadt, on the sixteenth inst., that no engagement has yet taken place in the vicinity of Frateshti.

The arrival of the allied forces at Rustshuk was, of course, a lie, and their whole aim, in the present instance, will be to keep under restraint—as the *Times* calls it—the barbarous fury of the victorious Turks.

Espartero*

IT IS ONE of the peculiarities of revolutions that just as the people seem about to take a great start and to open a new era, they suffer themselves to be ruled by the delusions of the past and surrender all the power and influence they have so dearly won into the hands of men who represent, or are supposed to represent, the popular movement of a by-gone epoch. Espartero is one of those traditional men whom the people are wont to take upon their backs at moments of social crises, and whom, like the ill-natured old fellow that obstinately clasped his legs about the neck of Sinbad the Sailor, they afterward find it difficult to get rid of. Ask a Spaniard of the so-called Progresista school what is the political value of Espartero, and he will promptly reply that "Espartero represents the unity of the great liberal party; Espartero is popular because he came from the people; his popularity works exclusively for the cause of the Progresistas." It is true that he is the son of an artisan, who has climbed up to be the Regent of Spain; and that, having entered the army as a common soldier, he left it as a field marshal. But if he be the symbol of the unity of the great liberal party, it can only be that indifferent point of unity in which all extremes are neutralized. And as to the popularity of the Progresistas, we do not exaggerate in saying that it was lost from the moment it became transferred from the bulk of that party to this single individual.

We need no other proof of the ambiguous and exceptional character of Espartero's greatness beyond the simple fact that, so far, nobody has been able to account for it. While his friends take refuge in allegoric generalities, his enemies, alluding to a strange feature of his private life, declare him but a lucky gambler. Both, then, friends and

---

* *New-York Daily Tribune,* August 19, 1854. Written August 4, 1854. (Lead article, unsigned.)

enemies, are at an equal loss to discover any logical connection between the man himself and the fame and the name of the man.

Espartero's military merits are as much contested as his political shortcomings are incontestable. In a voluminous biography published by Señor de Florez much fuss is made about his military prowess and generalship as shown in the provinces of Charcas, Paz, Arequipa, Potosí, and Cochabamba, where he fought under the orders of General Morillo, then charged with the reduction of the South American States under the authority of the Spanish crown. But the general impression produced by his South American feats of arms upon the excitable mind of his native country is sufficiently characterized by his being designated as the chief of the *Ayacuchismo*, and his partisans as *Ayacuchos*, in allusion to the unfortunate battle at Ayacucho, in which Peru and South America were definitely lost for Spain. He is, at all events, a very extraordinary hero whose historical baptism dates from a defeat instead of a success. In the seven years' war against the Carlists he never signalized himself by one of those daring strokes by which Narvaez, his rival, became early known as an iron-nerved soldier. He had certainly the gift of making the best of small successes, while it was mere luck that Maroto betrayed to him the last forces of the Pretender, Cabrera's rising in 1840 being only a posthumous attempt to galvanize the dry bones of Carlism. Señor de Marliani, himself one of Espartero's admirers, and the historian of modern Spain, cannot but own that the seven years' war is to be compared with nothing but the feuds waged in the tenth century between the petty lords of Gaul, when success was not the result of victory. It appears, by another mischance, that of all the Peninsular deeds of Espartero, that which made the liveliest impression upon the public memory was, if not exactly a defeat, at least a singularly strange performance in a hero of liberty. He became renowned as the bombarder of cities—of Barcelona and Seville. If the Spaniards, says a writer, should ever paint him as Mars, we should see the god figuring as a "wall batterer."

When Christina was forced, in 1840, to resign her regency and to fly from Spain, Espartero assumed, against the wishes of a very large section of the Progresistas, the supreme authority within the limits of parliamentary government. He surrounded himself with a sort of camarilla and affected the airs of a military dictator, without really elevating himself above the mediocrity of a constitutional king. His favor extended to Moderados rather than to old Progresistas, who, with a few exceptions, were excluded from office. Without conciliating his enemies, he gradually estranged his friends. Without the courage to break through the shackles of the parliamentary regime, he did not know how to accept it, how to manage it, or how to transform it

560SPAIN

into an instrument of action. During his three years' dictatorship the revolutionary spirit was broken step by step, through endless compromises, and the dissensions within the Progresista party were allowed to reach such a pitch as to enable the Moderados to regain exclusive power by a *coup de main*. Thus Espartero became so divested of authority that his own Ambassador at Paris conspired against him with Christina and Narvaez; and so poor in resources, that he found no means to ward off their miserable intrigues, or the petty tricks of Louis Philippe. So little did he understand his own position that he made an inconsiderate stand against public opinion when it simply wanted a pretext to break him to pieces.

In May, 1843, his popularity having long since faded away, he retained Seoane, Zurbano, and the other members of his military camarilla, whose dismissal was loudly called for; he dismissed the López Ministry, who commanded a large majority in the Chamber of Deputies, and he stubbornly refused an amnesty for the exiled Moderados, then claimed on all hands, by parliament, by the people, and by the army itself. This demand simply expressed the public disgust with his administration. Then, at once, a hurricane of pronunciamentos against the "tyrant Espartero" shook the Peninsula from one end to the other; a movement to be compared only, from the rapidity of its spreading, to the present one. Moderados and Progresistas combined for the one object of getting rid of the Regent. The crisis took him quite unawares—the fatal hour found him unprepared.

Narvaez, accompanied by O'Donnell, Concha, and Pezuela, landed with a handful of men at Valencia. On their side all was rapidity and action, considerate audacity, energetic decision. On the side of Espartero all was helpless hesitation, deadly delay, apathetic irresolution, indolent weakness. While Narvaez raised the siege of Teruel, and marched into Aragon, Espartero retired from Madrid, and consumed whole weeks in unaccountable inactivity at Albacete. When Narvaez had won over the corps of Seoane and Zurbano at Torrejón, and was marching on Madrid, Espartero at length effected a junction with Van Halen for the useless and odious bombardment of Seville. He then fled from station to station, at every step of his retreat deserted by his troops, till at last he reached the coast. When he embarked at Cádiz, that town, the last where he retained a party, bade its hero farewell by also pronouncing against him. An Englishman who resided in Spain during the catastrophe gives a graphic description of the sliding scale of Espartero's greatness: "It was not the tremendous crash of an instant, after a well-fought field, but a little and bit by bit descent, after no fighting at all, from Madrid to Ciudad Real, from Ciudad Real to Albacete, from Albacete to Cordova, from

Cordova to Seville, from Seville to Puerto Santa María, and thence to the wide ocean. He fell from idolatry to enthusiasm, from enthusiasm to attachment, from attachment to respect, from respect to indifference, from indifference to contempt, from contempt to hatred, and from hatred he fell into the sea."

How could Espartero have now again become the savior of the country, and "Sword of the Revolution," as he is called? This event would be quite incomprehensible were it not for the ten years of reaction Spain has suffered under the brutal dictatorship of Narvaez, and the brooding yoke of the Queen's minions, who supplanted him. Extensive and violent epochs of reaction are wonderfully fitted for reestablishing the fallen men of revolutionary miscarriages. The greater the imaginative powers of a people—and where is imagination greater than in the south of Europe?—the more irresistible their impulse to oppose to individual incarnations of despotism individual incarnations of the revolution. As they cannot improvise them at once, they excavate the dead men of their previous movements. Was not Narvaez himself on the point of growing popular at the expense of Sartorius? The Espartero who on the twenty-ninth of July held his triumphant entrance into Madrid was no real man; he was a ghost, a name, a reminiscence.

It is but due to justice to record that Espartero never professed to be anything but a constitutional monarchist; and if there had ever existed any doubt upon that point, it must have disappeared before the enthusiastic reception he met with during his exile at Windsor Castle and from the governing classes of England. When he arrived in London the whole aristocracy flocked to his abode, the Duke of Wellington and Palmerston at their head. Aberdeen, in his quality of Foreign Minister, sent him an invitation to be presented to the Queen; the Lord Mayor and the aldermen of the city entertained him with gastronomic homages at the Mansion House; and when it became known that the Spanish Cincinnatus passed his leisure hours in gardening, there was no botanical, or horticultural, or agricultural society which was not eager to present him with membership. He was quite the lion of that metropolis. At the end of 1847 an amnesty recalled the Spanish exiles, and the decree of Queen Isabella appointed him a senator. He was, however, not allowed to leave England before Queen Victoria had invited him and his Duchess to her table, adding the extraordinary honor of offering them a night's lodging at Windsor Castle. It is true, we believe, that this halo thrown around his person was somewhat connected with the supposition that Espartero had been and still was the representative of British interests in Spain. It is no less true that the Espartero demonstration looked something like a demonstration against Louis Philippe.

On his return to Spain he received deputation upon deputation, gratulations upon gratulations, and the city of Barcelona dispatched an express messenger to apologize for its bad behavior in 1843. But has anybody ever heard his name mentioned during the fatal period from January, 1846, till the late events? Has he ever raised his voice during that dead silence of degraded Spain? Is there recorded one single act of patriotic resistance on his part? He quietly retires to his estate at Logroño, cultivating his cabbages and flowers, waiting his time. He did not go even to the revolution till the revolution came for him. He did more than Mahomet. He expected the mountain to come to him, and the mountain came. Still, there is one exception to be mentioned. When the revolution of February burst out, followed by the general European earthquake, he caused to be published by Señor de Príncipe, and some other friends, a little pamphlet entitled *Espartero, His Past, His Present, His Future*, to remind Spain that it still harbored the man of the past, the present, and the future. The revolutionary movement soon subsiding in France, the man of the past, of the present, and of the future once more sank into oblivion.

Espartero was born at Granásula, in La Mancha, and like his famous fellow countryman, he also has his fixed idea—the Constitution; and his Dulcinea del Toboso—Queen Isabella. On January 8, 1848, when he returned from his English exile to Madrid, he was received by the Queen and took leave of her with the following words: "I pray your Majesty to call me whenever you want an arm to defend, or a heart to love you." Her Majesty has now called and her knight-errant appears, smoothing the revolutionary waves, enervating the masses by a delusive calm, allowing Christina, San Luis, and the rest to hide themselves in the palace, and loudly professing his unbroken faith in the words of the innocent Isabella.

It is known that this very trustworthy Queen, whose features are said to assume year after year a more striking resemblance to those of Ferdinand VII, of infamous memory, had her majority proclaimed on November 15, 1843. She was then only thirteen years old on November 21 of the same year. Olozaga, whom López had constituted her tutor for three months, formed a ministry obnoxious to the camarilla and the Cortes newly elected under the impression of the first success of Narvaez. He wanted to dissolve the Cortes, and obtained a royal decree signed by the Queen giving him power to do so, but leaving the date of its promulgation blank. On the evening of the twenty-eighth, Olozaga had the decree delivered to him from the hands of the Queen. On the evening of the twenty-ninth he had another interview with her; but he had hardly left her when an under-secretary of state came to his house and informed him that he was dismissed, and demanded back the decree which he had forced the Queen to sign. Olozaga, a lawyer by profession, was too sharp a man to be ensnared in this way. He did not return the document till the following day, after having shown it to at least one hundred deputies, in proof that the signature of the Queen was in her usual, regular handwriting. On December 13, Gonzalez Bravo, appointed as Premier, summoned the Presidents of the Chambers, the principal Madrid notables, Narvaez, the Marquis de la Santa Cruz, and others, to the Queen that she might make a declaration to them concerning what had passed between her and Olozaga on the evening of November 28. The innocent little Queen led them into the room where she had received Olozaga and enacted in a very lively, but rather overdone manner a little drama for their instruction. Thus had Olozaga bolted the door, thus seized her dress, thus obliged her to sit down, thus conducted her hand, thus forced her signature to the decree; in one word, thus had he violated her royal dignity. During this scene González Brabo took note of these declarations, while the persons present saw the alleged decree which appeared to be signed in a blotted and tremulous hand. Thus on the solemn declaration of the Queen, Olozaga was to be condemned for the crime of *laesa majestas*, to be torn in pieces by four horses, or at the best to be banished for life to the Philippines. But as we have seen, he had taken his measures of precaution. Then followed seventeen days' debate in the Cortes, creating a sensation greater even than that produced by the famous trial of Queen Caroline in England. Olozaga's defense in the Cortes contained among other things this passage: "If they tell us that the word of the Queen is to be believed without question, I answer, No! There is either a charge or there is none. If there be, that word is a testimony, like any other, and to that testimony I oppose mine." In the balance of the Cortes the word of Olozaga was found to be heavier than that of the Queen. Afterward he fled to Portugal to escape the assassins sent against him. This was Isabella's first *entrechat* on the political stage of Spain, and the first proof of her honesty. And this is the same little Queen whose words Espartero now exhorts the people to trust in, and to whom is offered, after eleven years' school for scandal, the "defending arm," and the "loving heart" of the "Sword of the Revolution."[1]

---

1. Marx to Engels, October 10, 1854: "In one of its recent numbers the *Tribune* permits itself to be congratulated by my competitor A.P.C. [London correspondent Ferenc Pulszky] for the 'splendid characterization' of my Espartero. Naturally, he does not realize that he 'complimented' me, but with a sure instinct he laid hold at the same time of a very silly concluding phrase, which properly belongs to the *Tribune*." The concluding phrase, which Marx did not write, read: "Our readers can judge whether the Spanish Revolution is likely to have any useful result or not."

Counterrevolution*

. . . THE BARRICADES were scarcely removed at Madrid, at the request of Espartero, before the counterrevolution was busy at work. The first counterrevolutionary step was the impunity allowed to Queen Christina, Sartorius, and their associates. Then followed the formation of the ministry, with the Moderado O'Donnell as Minister of War, and the whole army placed at the disposal of this old friend of Narvaez. There are in the list the names of Pacheco, Luján, Don Francisco Santa Cruz, all of them notorious partisans of Narvaez, and the first a member of the infamous Ministry of 1847. Another, Salazar, has been appointed on the sole merit of being a playfellow of Espartero. In remuneration for the bloody sacrifices of the people, on the barricades and in the public place, numberless decorations have been showered upon the Espartero generals on the one hand, and on the Moderado friends of O'Donnell on the other hand. In order to pave the way for an ultimate silencing of the press, the press law of 1837 has been reestablished. Instead of convoking a general Constituent Cortes, Espartero is said to intend convoking only the Chambers after the Constitution of 1837, and, as some say, even as modified by Narvaez. To secure as far as possible the success of all these measures and others that are to follow, large masses of troops are being concentrated near Madrid. If any consideration presses itself especially on our attention in this affair, it is the suddenness with which the reaction has set in.

On the first instant the chiefs of the barricades called upon Espartero, in order to make to him some observations on the choice

* New-York Daily Tribune, August 21, 1854. Written August 8, 1854.

of his ministry. He entered into a long explanation of the difficulties with which he was beset, and endeavored to defend his nominations. But the deputies of the people seem to have been little satisfied with his explanation. "Very alarming" news arrives at the same time, about the movements of the republicans in Valencia, Catalonia, and Andalusia. The embarrassment of Espartero is visible from his decree sanctioning the continued activity of the provincial juntas. Nor has he yet dared to dissolve the junta of Madrid, though his ministry is complete and installed in office.

The Demands of the Spanish People*

... SOME DAYS AGO the *Charivari*¹ published a caricature exhibiting the Spanish people engaged in battle and the two sabers—Espartero and O'Donnell—embracing each other over their heads. The *Charivari* mistook for the end of the revolution what is only its commencement. The struggle has already commenced between O'Donnell and Espartero, and not only between them, but also between the military chiefs and the people. It has been of little avail to the government to have appointed the toreador Pucheta as superintendent of the slaughter-houses, to have nominated a committee for the reward of the barricade combatants, and finally to have appointed two Frenchmen, Pujol and Delmas, as historiographers of the revolution. O'Donnell wants the Cortes to be elected according to the law of 1845, Espartero according to the Constitution of 1837, and the people by universal suffrage. The people refuse to lay down their arms before the publication of a government program, the program of Manzanares no longer satisfying their views. The people demand the annulment of the Concordat of 1852, confiscation of the estates of the counterrevolutionists, an *exposé* of the finances, canceling of all contracts for railways and other swindling contracts for public works, and lastly the judgment of Christina by a special court. Two attempts at flight on the part of the latter have been foiled by the armed resistance of the people. *El Tribuno* makes the following account of restitutions to be made by Christina to the National Exchequer: twenty-four millions illegally received as Regent from 1834 to 1840; twelve millions received on her return from France after an absence of three years; and thirty-five millions received of the Treasury of Cuba. This account even is a generous one. When Christina left Spain in 1840 she carried off large sums and nearly all the jewels of the Spanish crown.

---

* *New-York Daily Tribune*, August 25, 1854. Written August 11, 1854.
1. A French satiric daily published in Paris.

The Madrid Press*

. . . SOME MONTHS before the outbreak of the present Spanish revolution I told your readers that Russian influences were at work in bringing about a Peninsular commotion. For that Russia wanted no direct agents. There was the *Times*, the advocate and friend of King Bomba, of the "young hope" of Austria,[1] of Nicholas, of George IV, suddenly turned indignant at the gross immoralities of Queen Isabella and the Spanish court. There were, besides, the diplomatic agents of the English ministry, whom the Russian Minister Palmerston had no difficulty in bamboozling with visions of a Peninsular Coburg kingdom. It is now ascertained that it was the British Ambassador who concealed O'Donnell at his palace, and induced the banker Collado, the present Minister of Finance, to advance the money required by O'Donnell and Dulce, to start their pronunciamento. Should anybody doubt that Russia really had a hand in Peninsular affairs, let me remind him of the affair of the Isla de León. Considerable bodies of troops were assembled at Cádiz, in 1820, destined for the South American colonies. All at once the army stationed on the Isle declared for the Constitution of 1812, and its example was followed by troops elsewhere. Now we know from Chateaubriand, the French Ambassador at the Congress of Verona, that Russia stimulated Spain to undertake the expedition into South America, and forced France to undertake the expedition into Spain. We know, on the other hand, from the message of the United States President,[2] that Russia promised him to prevent the expedition against South America. It requires, then, but little judgment to infer as to the authorship of the insurrection of the Isla de León.

---

* *New-York Daily Tribune,* September 1, 1854. Written August 15, 1854.
1. Francis Joseph I, Emperor of Austria.
2. James Monroe's Message to Congress, December 2, 1823.

But I will give you another instance of the tender interest taken by Russia in the commotions of the Spanish Peninsula. In his *Historia política de la España moderna* (Barcelona, 1849) Señor de Marliani, in order to prove that Russia had no reason to oppose the constitutional movement of Spain, makes the following statement: "There were seen on the Neva Spanish soldiers swearing to the constitution" (of 1812) "and receiving their banners from imperial hands. In his extraordinary expedition against Russia Napoleon formed from the Spanish prisoners in France a special legion, who, after the defeat of the French forces, deserted to the Russian camp. Alexander received them with marked condescension, and quartered them at Peterhoff, where the Empress frequently went to visit them. On a given day Alexander ordered them to assemble on the frozen Neva, and made them take the oath for the Spanish constitution, presenting them at the same time with banners embroidered by the Empress herself. This corps, thenceforth named 'Imperial Alexander,' embarked at Kronstadt, and was landed at Cádiz. It proved true to the oath taken on the Neva, by rising, in 1821, at Ocaña for the reestablishment of the constitution."

While Russia is now intriguing in the Peninsula through the hands of England, it at the same time denounces England to France. Thus we read in the *New Prussian Gazette* that England has made the Spanish revolution behind the back of France.

What interest has Russia in fomenting commotions in Spain? To create a diversion in the West, to provoke dissensions between France and England, and lastly to seduce France into an intervention. Already we are told by the Anglo-Russian papers that French insurrectionists of June constructed the barricades at Madrid. The same was said to Charles X at the Congress of Verona. "The precedent set by the Spanish army had been followed by Portugal, spread to Naples, extended to Piedmont, and exhibited everywhere the dangerous example of armies meddling in measures of reform, and by force of arms dictating laws to their country. Immediately after the insurrection had taken place in Piedmont, movements had occurred in France, at Lyon, and in other places, directed to the same end. There was Berton's conspiracy at Rochelle in which twenty-five soldiers of the forty-fifth regiment had taken part. Revolutionary Spain retransfused its hideous elements of discord into France, and both leagued their democratic factions against the monarchical system."

Do we say that the Spanish revolution has been made by the Anglo-Russians? By no means. Russia only supports factious movements at moments when it knows revolutionary crises to be at hand. The real popular movement, however, which then begins, is always found to be as much opposed to the intrigues of Russia as to the oppressive agency of the government. Such was the fact in Wallachia in 1848—such is the fact in Spain in 1854.

The perfidious conduct of England is exhibited at full length by the conduct of its ambassador at Madrid, Lord Howden. Before setting out from England to return to his post, he assembled the Spanish bondholders, calling upon them to press the payment of their claims on the government, and in case of refusal to declare that they would refuse all credit to Spanish merchants. Thus he prepared difficulties for the new government. As soon as he arrived at Madrid, he subscribed for the victims fallen at the barricades. Thus he provokes ovations from the Spanish people.

The *Times* charges Mr. Soulé with having produced the Madrid insurrection in the interest of the present American administration. At all events, Mr. Soulé has not written the *Times*'s articles against Isabella II, nor has the party inclined to Cuban annexation gained any benefit from the revolution. With regard to this question, the nomination of General de la Concha as Captain General of the Island of Cuba is characteristic, he having been one of the seconds of the Duke of Alba in his duel with the son of Mr. Soulé. It would be a mistake to suppose that the Spanish liberals in any way partake in the views of the English liberal, Mr. Cobden, in reference to the abandonment of the colonies. One great object of the Constitution of 1812 was to retain the empire over the Spanish colonies by the introduction of a united system of representation into the new code. In 1811 the Spaniards even equipped a large armament, consisting of several regiments from Galicia, the only province in Spain then not occupied by the French, in order to combine coercion with their South American policy. It was almost the chief principle of that constitution not to abandon any of the colonies belonging to Spain, and the revolutionists of today share the same opinion.

No revolution has ever exhibited a more scandalous spectacle in the conduct of its public men than this undertaken in the interest of "morality." The coalition of the old parties forming the present government of Spain (the partisans of Espartero and the partisans of Narvaez) has been occupied with nothing so much as the division of the spoils of office, of place, of salaries, of titles, and of decorations. Dulce and Echagüe have arrived at Madrid, and Serrano has solicited permission to come, in order to secure their shares in the plunder. There is a great quarrel between Moderados and Progresistas, the former being charged with having named all the generals, the latter with having appointed all the political chiefs. To appease the jealousies of the "rabble," Buceta the toreador has been promoted from director of the slaughterhouses to director of police. Even the *Clamor Público*, a very moderate paper, gives vent to feelings of disappointment. "The conduct of the generals and chiefs would have been more dignified if they had resigned promotion, giving a noble example of disinterestedness, and conforming themselves to the principles of morality proclaimed by the revolution." The shamelessness of the distribution of the spoils is marked by the division of the ambassadors' places. I do not speak of the appointment of Señor Olozaga for Paris, although being the ambassador of Espartero at the same court in 1843, he conspired with Louis Philippe, Christina, and Narvaez; nor of the appointment for Vienna of Alejandro Mon, the Finance Minister of Narvaez in 1844; nor of that of Rios Rosas for Lisbon, and Pastor Díaz for Turin, both Moderados of very indifferent capacity. I speak of the nomination of González Bravo for the Embassy of Constantinople. He is the incarnation of Spanish corruption. In 1840 he published *El Guirigay* (*Gibberish*), a sort of Madrid *Punch*, in which he made the most furious attacks against Christina. Three years afterward his rage for office transformed him into a boisterous Moderado. Narvaez, who wanted a pliant tool, used him as Prime Minister of Spain, and then kicked him away as soon as he could dispense with him. Bravo, in the interval, appointed as his Minister of Finance one Carrasco, who plundered the Spanish treasury directly. He made his father Undersecretary of the Treasury, a man who had been expelled from his place as a subaltern in the Exchequer because of his malversation; and he transformed his brother-in-law, a hanger-on at the Principe Theater, into a state groom to the Queen. When reproached with his apostasy and corruption, he answered: "Is it not ridiculous to be always the same?" This man is the chosen ambassador of the revolution of morality.

It is somewhat refreshing to hear, in contrast with the official infamies branding the Spanish movement, that the people have forced these fellows at least to place Christina at the disposal of the Cortes, and to consent to the convocation of a National Constituent Assembly, without a Senate, and consequently neither on the election law of 1837 nor that of 1845. The government has not yet dared to prescribe an election law of its own, while the people are unanimously in favor of universal suffrage. At Madrid the elections for the National Guard have returned nothing but *Exaltados*.

In the provinces a wholesome anarchy prevails, juntas being constituted, and in action everywhere, and every junta issuing decrees in the interest of its locality—one abolishing the monopoly of tobacco, another the duty on salt. Contrabandists are operating on an enormous scale, and with the more efficiency as they are the only force never disorganized in Spain. At Barcelona the soldiers are in collision, now among each other, and now with the workmen. This anarchical state of the provinces is of great advantage to the cause of the revolution, as it prevents its being confiscated at the capital.

The Madrid press is at this moment composed of the following papers: *España, Novedadas, Nación, Época, Clamor Público, Diario Español, Tribuno, Esperanza, Iberia, Católico, Miliciano, Independencia, Guarda Nacional Esparterista, Unión, Europa, Espectador, Liberal, Eco de la Revolución.* The *Heraldo, Boletín del Pueblo,* and the *Mensajero* have ceased to exist.

The Course of the Revolution*

THE "LEADERS" [editorials] of the *Assemblée Nationale, Times,* and *Journal des Débats* prove that neither the pure Russian party, nor the Russo-Coburg party, nor the constitutional party is satisfied with the course of the Spanish revolution. From this it would appear that there is some chance for Spain, notwithstanding the contradiction of appearances.

On the eighth inst. a deputation from the Union Club waited on Espartero to present an address calling for the adoption of universal suffrage. Numerous petitions to the same effect were pouring in. Consequently a long and animated debate took place at the Council of Ministers. But the partisans of universal suffrage, as well as the partisans of the election law of 1846, have been beaten. The Madrid *Gaceta* publishes a decree for the convocation of the Cortes on the eighth of November, preceded by an *exposé* addressed to the Queen. At the elections the law of 1837 will be followed, with slight modifications. The Cortes is to be one Constituent Assembly, the legislative functions of the Senate being suppressed. Two paragraphs of the law of 1846 have been preserved, viz., the mode of forming the electoral *mesas* (boards receiving the votes and publishing the returns), and the number of deputies; one deputy to be elected for every 5,000 souls. The Assembly will thus be composed of from 420 to 430 members. According to a circular of Santa Cruz, the Minister of the Interior, the electors must be registered by the sixth of September. After the verification of the lists by the provincial deputations, the electoral lists will be closed on the twelfth of September. The elections will take place on the third of October, at the chief localities

* *New-York Daily Tribune,* September 4, 1854. Written August 18, 1854.

of the electoral districts. The scrutiny will be proceeded to on the sixteenth of October, in the capital of each province. In case of conflicting elections, the new proceedings which will thereby be necessitated must be terminated by the thirtieth of October. The *exposé* states expressly that "the Cortes of 1854, like that of 1837, will save the monarchy; it will be a new bond between the throne and the nation, objects which cannot be questioned or disputed." In other words, the government forbids the discussion of the dynastic question; hence the *Times* concludes the contrary, supposing that the question will now be between the present dynasty or no dynasty at all—an eventuality which, it is scarcely necessary to remark, infinitely displeases and disappoints the calculations of the *Times*.

The electoral law of 1837 limits the franchise by the conditions of having a household, the payment of the *mayores cuotas . . .* and the age of twenty-five years. There are further entitled to a vote the members of the Spanish academies of history and of the *artes nobles*, doctors, licentiates in the faculties of divinity, law, or medicine, members of ecclesiastical chapters, parochial curates and their assistant clergy, magistrates and advocates of two years' standing; officers of the army of a certain standing, whether on service or the retired list; physicians, surgeons, apothecaries of two years' standing; architects, painters, and sculptors honored with the membership of an academy; professors and masters in any educational establishment, supported by the public funds. Disqualified for the vote by the same law are defaulters to the common pueblo fund, or to local taxation, bankrupts, persons interdicted by the courts of law for moral or civil incapacity; lastly, all persons under sentence.

It is true that this decree does not proclaim universal suffrage, and that it removes the dynastic question from the forum of the Cortes. Still it is doubtful that even this Assembly will do. If the Spanish Cortes forbore from interfering with the crown in 1812, it was because the crown was only nominally represented—the King having been absent for years from Spanish soil. If they forbore in 1837, it was because they had to settle with absolute monarchy before they could think of settling with the constitutional monarchy. With regard to the general situation, the *Times* has truly good reasons to deplore the absence of French centralization in Spain, and that consequently even a victory over revolution in the capital decides nothing with respect to the provinces, so long as that state of "anarchy" survives there without which no revolution can succeed.

There are, of course, some incidents in the Spanish revolution peculiarly belonging to them. For instance, the combination of robbery with revolutionary transactions—a connection which sprang up in the guerrilla wars against the French invasions, and which was continued by the "royalists" in 1823, and the Carlists since 1835. No surprise will therefore be felt at the information that great disorders have occurred at Tortosa, in lower Catalonia. The *Junta Popular* of that city says, in its proclamation of July 31: "A band of miserable assassins, availing themselves of the pretext of the abolition of the indirect taxes, have seized the town and trampled upon all laws of society. Plunder, assassination, incendiarism have marked their steps." Order, however, was soon restored by the junta—the citizens arming themselves and coming to the rescue of the feeble garrison of the place. A military commission is sitting, charged with the pursuit and punishment of the authors of the catastrophe of July 30. This circumstance has, of course, given an occasion to the reactionary journals for virtuous declamation. How little they are warranted in this proceeding may be inferred from the remark of the *Messager de Bayonne*, that the Carlists have raised their banner in the provinces of Catalonia, Aragon, and Valencia, and precisely in the same contiguous mountains where they had their chief nest in the old Carlist Wars. It was the Carlists who gave origin to the *ladrones faceiosos*, that combination of robbery and pretended allegiance to an oppressed party in the state. The Spanish guerrillero of all times has had something of the robber since the time of Viriathus; but it is a novelty of Carlist invention that a pure robber should invest himself with the name of guerrillero. The men of the Tortosa affair certainly belong to this class.

At Lérida, Saragossa, and Barcelona matters are serious. The two former cities have refused to combine with Barcelona, because the military had the upper hand there. Still it appears that even there Concha is unable to master the storm, and General Dulce is to take his place, the recent popularity of that general being considered as offering more guarantees for a conciliation of the difficulties.

The secret societies have resumed their activity in Madrid, and govern the democratic party just as they did in 1823. The first demand which they have urged the people to make is that all ministers since 1843 shall present their accounts.

The ministry is purchasing back the arms which the people seized on the day of the barricades. In this way they have got possession of 2,500 muskets, formerly in the hands of insurgents. Don Manuel Zagasti, the Ayacucho *Jefe Político* of Madrid of 1843, has been reinstated in his functions. He has addressed to the inhabitants and the national militia two proclamations in which he announces his intention of energetically repressing all disorder. The removal of the creatures of Sartorius from the different offices proceeds rapidly.

It is, perhaps, the only thing rapidly done in Spain. All parties show themselves equally quick in that line.

Salamanca is not imprisoned, as was asserted. He had been arrested at Aranjuez, but was soon released, and is now in Málaga.

The control of the ministry by popular pressure is proved by the fact that the ministers of War, of the Interior, and of Public Works have effected large displacements and simplifications in their several departments, an event never known in Spanish history before.

The Unionist or Coburg-Braganza party is pitifully weak. For what other reason would they make such a noise about one single address sent from Portugal to the National Guard of Madrid? If we look nearer at it, it is even discovered that the address (originating with the Lisbon *Journal de Progrès*) is not of a dynastic nature at all, but simply of the fraternal kind so well known in the movements of 1848.

The chief cause of the Spanish revolution was the state of the finances, and particularly the decree of Sartorius, ordering the payment of six months' taxes in advance upon the year. All the public chests were empty when the revolution broke out, notwithstanding the circumstance that no branch of the public service had been paid; nor were the sums destined for any particular service applied to it during the whole of several months. Thus, for instance, the turnpike receipts were never appropriated to the use of keeping up the roads. The moneys set aside for public works shared the same destiny. When the chest of public works was subjected to revision, instead of receipts for executed works, receipts from court favorites were discovered. It is known that financiering has long been the most profitable business in Madrid. The Spanish budget for 1853 was as follows:

Civil List and Appanages	47,350,000 reals
Legislation	1,331,685 reals
Interest of Public Debt	213,271,423 reals
President of Council	1,687,860 reals
Foreign Office	3,919,083 reals
Justice	39,001,233 reals
War	273,646,284 reals
Marine	85,165,000 reals
Interior	43,957,940 reals
Police	72,000,000 reals
Finances	142,279,000 reals
Pensions	143,400,586 reals
Cultus	119,050,508 reals
Extras	18,387,788 reals
Total	1,204,448,390 reals

Notwithstanding this budget, Spain is the least taxed country of Europe, and the economic question is nowhere so simple as there. The reduction and simplification of the bureaucratic machinery in Spain are the less difficult as the municipalities traditionally administer their own affairs; so is reform of the tariff and conscientious application of the *bienes nacionales* not yet alienated. The social question in the modern sense of the word has no foundation in a country with its resources yet undeveloped, and with such a scanty population as Spain—15,000,000 only. . . .

The Reaction in Spain*

THE ENTRANCE into Madrid of the "Vicalvaro" regiments has encouraged the government to greater counterrevolutionary activity. The revival of the restrictive press law of 1837, adorned with all the rigors of the supplementary law of 1842, has killed all the "incendiary" portion of the press which was unable to offer the required *cautionnement* [security]. On the twenty-fourth the last number was given out of the *Clamor de las Barricadas* with the title of *Últimas Barricadas*, the two editors having been arrested. Its place was taken on the same day by a new reactionary paper called *Las Cortes*. "His Excellency, the Captain General, Don San Miguel," says the program of the last-mentioned paper, "who honors us with his friendship, has offered to this journal the favor of his collaboration. His articles will be signed with his initials. The men at the head of this enterprise will defend with energy that revolution which vanquished the abuses and excesses of a corrupt power, but it is in the *enceinte* of the Constituent Assembly that they will plant their banner. It is there that the great battle must be fought." The great battle is for Isabella II and Espartero. You will remember that this same San Miguel, at the banquet of the press, declared that the press had no other corrective but itself, common sense, and public education, that it was an institution which neither sword nor transportation, nor exile, nor any power in the world could crush. On the very day on which he offers himself as a contributor to the press, he has not a word against the decree confiscating his beloved liberty of the press.

The suppression of the liberty of the press has been closely followed by the suppression of the right of meeting, also by royal

* *New-York Daily Tribune*, September 16, 1854. Written September 1, 1854.

decree. The clubs have been dissolved at Madrid, and in the provinces the juntas and Committees of Public Safety, with the exception of those acknowledged by the ministry as "deputations." The Club of the Union was shut up in consequence of a decree of the whole ministry, notwithstanding that Espartero had only a few days previously accepted its honorary presidency, a fact which the London *Times* vainly labors to deny. This club had sent a deputation to the Minister of the Interior insisting on the dismissal of Señor Lagasti, the *Jefe Político* of Madrid, charging him with having violated the liberty of the press and the right of meeting. Señor Santa Cruz answered that he could not blame a public functionary for taking measures approved by the Council of Ministers. The consequence was that a serious trouble arose; but the Plaza de la Constitution was occupied by the National Guard, and nothing further occurred. The petty journals had scarcely been suppressed when the greater ones that had hitherto granted their protection to Lagasti found occasion to quarrel with him. In order to silence the *Clamor Público* its chief editor, Señor Corradi, was appointed minister. But this step will not be sufficient, as all editors cannot be attached to the ministry.

The boldest stroke of the counterrevolution, however, was the permission for Queen Christina's departure for Lisbon, after the Council of Ministers had engaged to keep her at the disposal of the Constituent Cortes—a breach of faith which they have tried to cover by an anticipated confiscation of Christina's estate in Spain, notoriously the least considerable portion of her wealth. Thus Christina had a cheap escape, and now we hear that San Luis, too, has safely arrived at Bayonne. The most serious part of the transaction is the manner in which the decree alluded to was obtained. On the twenty-sixth some patriots and National Guards assembled to consider the safety of the public cause, blaming the government on account of its vacillations and half-and-half measures, and agreeing to send a deputation to the ministry calling upon them to remove Christina from the palace, where she was plotting liberticide projects. There was a very suspicious circumstance in the adhesion of two aides-de-camp of Espartero, with Lagasti himself, to this proposition. The result was that the ministry met in council, and the upshot of their meeting was the elopement of Christina.

On the twenty-fifth the Queen appeared for the first time in public, on the promenade of the Prado, attended by what is called her husband, and by the Prince of Asturias. But her reception appears to have been extremely cold.

The committee appointed to report on the state of the finances at the epoch of the fall of the Sartorius Ministry has published its report in the *Gaceta,* where it is preceded by an *exposé* by Señor Collado, the Minister of Finance. According to this the floating debt of Spain now amounts to $33,000,000, and the total deficit to $50,000,- 000. It appears that even the extraordinary resources of the government were anticipated for years and squandered. The revenues of Havana and the Philippines were anticipated for two years and a half. The yield of the forced loan had disappeared without leaving a trace. The Almeda quicksilver mines were engaged for years. The balance in hand due to the *Caja* [strongbox] of deposits did not exist, nor did the fund for military substitution; 7,485,692 reals were due for the purchase of tobacco obtained, but not paid for. Ditto, 5,505,- 000 reals for bills on account of public works. According to the statement of Señor Collado the amount of obligations of the most pressing nature is 252,980,253 reals. The measures proposed by him for the covering of this deficit are those of a true banker, viz., to return to quiet and order, to continue to levy all the old taxes, and to contract new loans. In compliance with this advice Espartero has obtained from the principal Madrid bankers $2,500,000 on a promise of a pure Moderado policy. How willing he is to keep this promise is proved by his last measures.

It must not be imagined that these reactionary measures have remained altogether unresisted by the people. When the departure of Christina became known, on August 28, barricades were erected again; but if we are to believe a telegraphic dispatch from Bayonne, published by the French *Moniteur,* "the troops, united to the National Guard, carried the barricades and put down the movement."

This is the *cercle vicieux* in which abortive revolutionary governments are condemned to move. They recognize the debts contracted by their counterrevolutionary predecessors as national obligations. In order to be able to pay them they must continue their old taxes and contract new debts. To be able to contract new loans they must give guarantees of "order," that is, take counterrevolutionary measures themselves. Thus the new popular government is at once transformed into the handmaiden of the great capitalists, and an oppressor of the people. In exactly the same manner was the Provisional Government of France in 1848 driven to the notorious measure of the 45 centimes [tax] and the confiscation of the savings banks' funds in order to pay their interest to the capitalists. "The revolutionary governments of Spain," says the English author of the *Revelations on Spain,* "are at least not sunk so deep as to adopt the infamous doctrine of repudiation as practiced in the United States." The fact is that if any former Spanish revolution had once practiced repudiation, the infamous government of San Luis would not have found any banker willing to oblige it with advances. But perhaps our author holds the view that it is the privilege of the counterrevolution to contract, as it is the privilege of revolution to pay debts.

It appears that Saragossa, Valencia, and Algeciras do not concur in this view, as they have abrogated all taxes obnoxious to them.

Not content with sending Bravo Murillo as Ambassador to Constantinople, the government has dispatched Gonzales Bravo in the same capacity to Vienna.

On Sunday, August 27, the electoral reunions of the District of Madrid assembled in order to appoint, by general suffrage, the commissioners charged with the superintendence of the election at the capital. There exist two electoral committees in Madrid—the Liberal Union and the Union del Commercio.

The symptoms of reaction above collected appear less formidable to persons acquainted with the history of Spanish revolutions than they must to the superficial observer—since Spanish revolutions generally only date from the meeting of the Cortes, usually the signal for the dissolution of government. At Madrid, besides, there are only a few troops and at the highest 20,000 National Guards. But of the latter only about one-half are properly armed, while the people are known to have disobeyed the call to deliver up their arms.

Notwithstanding the tears of the Queen, O'Donnell has dissolved her bodyguard, the regular army being jealous of the privileges of this corps, from whose ranks a Godoy, noticed as a good player upon the guitar and a singer of *seguidillas graciosas y picantes* [gracious and piquant songs], could raise himself to become the husband of the King's niece, and a Muñoz, only known for his private advantages, become the husband of a Queen Mother.

In Madrid a portion of the republicans have circulated the following Constitution of a Federal Iberian Republic:

TÍTULO I. Organization of the Federal Iberian Republic

Art. 1. Spain and its isles and Portugal will be united and form the Federal Iberian Republic. The colors of the banner will be a union of the two actual banners of Spain and Portugal. Its device will be Liberty, Equality, Fraternity.

Art. 2. The sovereignty resides in the universality of the citizens. It is inalienable and imprescriptible. No individual, no fraction of the people can usurp its exercise.

Art. 3. The law is the expression of the national will. The judges are appointed by the people through universal suffrage.

Art. 4. All citizens of twenty-one years of age and enjoying their civil rights to be electors.

Art. 5. The punishment of death is abolished, for both political and common crimes. The jury is the judge in all cases.

Art. 6. Property is sacred. The estates taken from political emigrants are restored to them.

Art. 7. The contributions will be paid in proportion to incomes. There will be one tax only, direct and general. All indirect contributions, *octrois*, and on consumption are abolished. Likewise abolished are the government monopolies of salt and tobacco, the stamps, the patent dues, and the conscription.

Art. 8. The liberty of the press, of meeting, of association, of domicile, of education, of commerce, and of conscience, is granted. *Every religion will have to pay for its own ministers.*

Art. 13.[1] The administration of the republic is to be federal, provincial, and municipal.

TÍTULO II. Federal Administration

Art. 14. It will be entrusted to an Executive Council appointed and revocable by the Central Federal Congress.

Art. 15. The international and commercial relations, the uniformity of measures, weights and coins, the post office, and the armed forces are the domain of the Federal Administration.

Art. 16. The Central Federal Congress will be composed of nine deputies for every province, elected by universal suffrage and bound by their instructions.

Art. 17. The Central Federal Congress is in permanency.

Art. 20. Whenever a law is to be enacted, the administration thinking it necessary will bring the project under the cognizance of the confederation six months before it is before the Congress, and three months if it be for the Provincial Legislation.

Art. 21. Any deputy of the people failing to adhere to his instructions is handed over to justice.

TÍTULO III refers to the provincial and municipal administration and confirms similar principles. The last article of this chapter says: "*There are to be no longer any colonies;* they will be changed into provinces and administered on provincial principles. *Slavery shall be abolished.*"

TÍTULO IV. The Army

Art. 34. The whole people will be armed and organized in a national guard, one portion to be mobile and the other sedentary.

Art. 35. The mobile guard to consist of *celibaterios* [bachelors] between the ages of twenty-one and thirty-five; their officers to be chosen in the military schools by election.

Art. 36. The sedentary militia consists of all citizens between thirty-five and fifty-six years; officers to be appointed by election. Their service is the defense of the communities.

---

1. The missing articles here and subsequently were omitted by Marx.

Art. 38. The corps of artillery and engineers are recruited by voluntary enlistment, permanent, and garrisoning the fortresses on the coast of the frontiers. No fortresses shall be suffered in the interior.

Art. 39, alluding to the marines, contains similar provisions.

Art. 40. The staffs of the provinces and captain-generalcies are suppressed.

Art. 42. The Iberian Republic renounces all wars of conquest, and will submit its quarrels to the arbitration of governments disinterested in the question.

Art. 43. There shall be no standing armies.

The Press on Spain*

... THE REACTIONARY PRESS is not yet satisfied with the late measures of the Spanish Government; they grumble at the fact that a new compromise had been entered into with the revolution. Thus we read in the *Journal des Débats:* "It was only on August 7 when Espartero declared 'that in conformity with the wishes of the people of Madrid, the Duchess of Riansares should not leave the Capital, either by day or night, in any furtive manner.' It is only on August 28 that Queen Christina, after a detention of twenty-one days, is allowed to depart in broad day, with a sort of ostentation. But the government has been weak enough to order, simultaneously, the confiscation of her estates."

The *Débats* now hopes that this order will be canceled. But the hopes of the *Débats* are, perhaps, in this instance, even more doomed to disappointment than when it uttered faint hopes that the confiscation of the Orléans estates would not be carried out by Bonaparte. The *Jefe Político* of Oviedo has already proceeded to sequestrate the coal mines possessed by Christina in the province of Asturias. The directors of the mines of Siero, Langreo, and Piero Corril have received orders to make a statement and to place their administration under the government.

With regard to the "broad day" in which the *Débats* effects the departure of Christina, they are very wrongly informed. Queen Christina on leaving her apartments crossed the corridors in dead silence—everybody being studiously kept out of the way. The National Guard occupying the barracks in the court of the palace were not aware of her departure. So secretly was the whole plan arranged

---

* *New-York Daily Tribune,* September 30, 1854. Written September 12, 1854.

that even Garrigo, who was to have charge of her escort, only received his orders on the moment of starting. The escort only learned the mission with which they were entrusted at a distance of twelve miles from Madrid, when Garrigo had all sorts of difficulties in preventing his men from either insulting Christina or returning direct to Madrid. The chiefs of the National Guard did not learn anything of the affair until two hours after the departure of Mme. Muñoz. According to the statement of the *España* she reached the Portuguese frontier on the morning of September 3. She is said to have been in very good spirits on the journey, but her Duke was somewhat *triste*. The relations of Christina and this same Muñoz can only be understood from the answer given by Don Quixote to Sancho Panza's question why he was in love with such a low country wench as his Dulcinea, when he could have princesses at his feet: "A lady," answered the worthy knight, "surrounded by a host of high-bred, rich, and witty followers, was asked why she took for her lover a simple peasant. 'You must know,' said the lady, 'that for the office I use him he possesses more philosophy than Aristotle himself.' "

The view taken by the reactionary press in general on Spanish affairs may be judged of by some extracts from the *Kölnische Zeitung* and the *Indépendance Belge:* "According to a well-informed and trustworthy correspondent, himself an adherent of O'Donnell and the Moderado party," (says the former) "the position of affairs is grievous, a deep conflict continuing to exist among parties. The working classes are in a state of permanent excitement, being worked upon by the agitators."

"The future of the Spanish monarchy" (says the *Indépendance*) "is exposed to great dangers. All true Spanish patriots are unanimous on the necessity of putting down the revolutionary orgies. The rage of the libelers and of the constructors of barricades is let loose against Espartero and his government with the same vehemence as against San Luis and the banker Salamanca. But in truth this chivalrous nation cannot be held responsible for such excesses. The people of Madrid must not be confounded with the mob that vociferated 'Death to Christina,' nor for the infamous libels launched among the population, under the title of 'Robberies of San Luis, Christina, and the Acolytes.' The 1,800 barricades of Madrid and the ultracommunist manifestations of Barcelona bespeak the intermeddling of foreign democracy with the Spanish Saturnalia. So much is certain, that a great number of the refugees of France, Germany, and Italy have participated in the deplorable events now agitating the Peninsula. So much is certain, that Spain is on the brink of a social conflagration; the more immediate consequences will be the loss of the Pearl of the

Antilles, the rich Island of Cuba, because it places Spain in the impossibility to combat American ambition, or the patriotism of a Soulé or Sanders. It is time that Spain should open her eyes, and that all honest men of civilized Europe should combine in giving the alarm."

It certainly requires no intervention of foreign democracy to stir up the population of Madrid when they see their government break on the twenty-eighth the word given on the seventh; suspend the right of freely assembling, and restore the press law of 1837, requiring a *cautionnement* of 40,000 reals and 300 reals of direct taxes on the part of every editor. If the provinces remain agitated by uncertain and undecided movements, what other reason are we to find for this fact but the absence of a center for revolutionary action? Not a single decree beneficent to the provinces has appeared since the so-called revolutionary government fell into the hands of Espartero. The provinces behold it surrounded by the same sycophancy, intrigues, and place hunting that had subsisted under San Luis. The same swarm hangs about the government—the plague which has infested Spain since the age of the Philips.

Let us cast a glance at the last number of the Madrid *Gaceta* of September 6. There is a report of O'Donnell announcing a superabundance of military places and honors to such a degree that out of every three generals only one can be employed on active service. It is the very evil which has cursed Spain since 1823—this superencumbrance of generals. One would fancy that a decree was to follow abating the nuisance. Nothing of the sort. The decree following the report convokes a consultative junta of war, composed of a certain number of generals appointed by the government from among the generals holding at present no commission in the army. Besides their ordinary pay these men are to receive: each lieutenant general 5,000 reals, and each maréchal-de-camp 6,000 reals. General Manuel de la Concha has been named president of this military sinecurist junta. The same number of the *Gaceta* presents another harvest of decorations, appointments, etc., as if the first great distribution had failed to do its work. San Miguel and Dulce have received the grand cross of the order of Charles III; all the recompenses and provisional honors decreed by the junta of Saragossa are confirmed and enlarged. But the most remarkable portion of this number of the *Gaceta* is the announcement that the payment of the public creditors will be resumed on the eleventh inst. Incredible folly of the Spanish people not to be satisfied with these achievements of their revolutionary government!

Revolutionary Spain

I*

THE REVOLUTION in Spain has now so far taken on the appearance of a permanent condition that, as our correspondent in London has informed us, the wealthy and conservative classes have begun to emigrate and to seek security in France. This is not surprising; Spain has never adopted the modern French fashion, so generally in vogue in 1848, of beginning and accomplishing a revolution in three days. Her efforts in that line are complex and more prolonged. Three years seems to be the shortest limit to which she restricts herself, while her revolutionary cycle sometimes expands to nine. Thus her first revolution in the present century extended from 1808 to 1814; the second from 1820 to 1823; and the third from 1834 to 1843. How long the present one will continue, or in what it will result, it is impossible for the keenest politician to foretell; but it is not much to say that there is no other part of Europe, not even Turkey and the Russian war, which offers so profound an interest to the thoughtful observer as does Spain at this instant.

Insurrectionary risings are as old in Spain as that sway of court favorites against whom they are usually directed. Thus at the end of the fourteenth century the aristocracy revolted against King Juan II and his favorite, Don Álvaro de Luna. In the fifteenth century still more serious commotions took place against King Henry V and the head of his camarilla, Don Juan de Pacheco, Marquis de Villara. In the seventeenth century the people at Lisbon tore to pieces Vasconcellos, the Sartorius of the Spanish Viceroy in Portugal, as

---

* New-York Daily Tribune, September 9, 1854.

they did at Saragossa with San Colombo, the favorite of Philip V. At the end of the same century, under the reign of Carlos II, the people of Madrid rose against the Queen's camarilla, composed of the Countess of Berlias and the Counts Oropeza and Melgar, who had imposed on all provisions entering the capital an oppressive duty which they shared among themselves. The people marched to the royal palace, forced the King to appear on the balcony and himself denounce the Queen's camarilla. They then marched to the palaces of the Counts Oropeza and Melgar, plundered them, destroyed them by fire, and tried to lay hold of their owners, who, however, had the good luck to escape, at the cost of perpetual exile. The event which occasioned the insurrectionary rising in the fifteenth century was the treacherous treaty which the favorite of Henry IV, the Marquis de Villara, had concluded with the King of France, according to which Catalonia was to be surrendered to Louis XI. Three centuries later the Treaty of Fontainebleau, concluded on October 27, 1807—by which the favorite of Carlos IV and the minion of his Queen, Don Manuel Godoy, the Prince of Peace, contracted with Bonaparte for the partition of Portugal and the entrance of the French armies into Spain—caused a popular insurrection at Madrid against Godoy, the abdication of Carlos IV, the assumption of the throne by Ferdinand VII, his son, the entrance of the French army into Spain, and the following war of independence. Thus the Spanish War of Independence commenced with a popular insurrection against the camarilla, then personified in Don Manuel Godoy, just as the civil war of the fifteenth century commenced with the rising against the camarilla, then personified in the Marquis de Villara. So, too, the revolution of 1854 commenced with the rising against the camarilla, personified in the Count San Luis.

Notwithstanding these ever recurring insurrections, there has been in Spain, up to the present century, no serious revolution, except the war of the Holy League in the times of Carlos I, or Charles V, as the Germans call him. The immediate pretext, as usual, was then furnished by the clique who, under the auspices of Cardinal Adrian, the Viceroy, himself a Fleming, exasperated the Castilians by their rapacious insolence, by selling the public offices to the highest bidder, and by open traffic in lawsuits. The opposition against the Flemish camarilla was only at the surface of the movement. At its bottom was the defense of the liberties of medieval Spain against the encroachments of modern absolutism.

The material basis of the Spanish monarchy having been laid by the union of Aragon, Castile, and Granada, under Ferdinand the Catholic and Isabella I, Charles I attempted to transform that still feudal monarchy into an absolute one. Simultaneously he attacked the two pillars of Spanish liberty, the Cortes and the Ayuntamientos —the former a modification of the ancient Gothic *concilia*, and the latter transmitted almost without interruption from Roman times, the Ayuntamientos exhibiting the mixture of the hereditary and the elective character proper to the Roman municipalities. As to municipal self-government, the towns of Italy, of Provence, northern Gaul, Great Britain, and part of Germany offer a fair similitude to the then state of the Spanish towns; but neither the French Estates General nor the British Parliaments of the Middle Ages are to be compared with the Spanish Cortes. There were circumstances in the formation of the Spanish kingdom peculiarly favorable to the limitation of royal power. On the one side, small parts of the Peninsula were recovered at a time, and formed into separate kingdoms, during the long struggles with the Arabs. Popular laws and customs were engendered in these struggles. The successive conquests, being principally effected by the nobles, rendered their power excessive, while they diminished the royal power. On the other hand, the inland towns and cities rose to great consequence, from the necessity people found themselves under of residing together in places of strength, as a security against the continual irruptions of the Moors; while the peninsula formation of the country, and constant intercourse with Provence and Italy, created first-rate commercial maritime cities on the coast. As early as the fourteenth century, the cities formed the most powerful part in the Cortes, which were composed of their representatives, with those of the clergy and nobility. It is also worthy of remark that the slow recovery from Moorish dominion through an obstinate struggle of almost eight hundred years gave the Peninsula, when wholly emancipated, a character altogether different from that of contemporaneous Europe, Spain finding itself, at the epoch of European resurrection, with the manners of the Goths and the Vandals in the north, and with those of the Arabs in the south.

Charles I having returned from Germany, where the imperial dignity had been bestowed upon him, the Cortes assembled at Valladolid, in order to receive his oath to the ancient laws and to invest him with the crown. Charles, declining to appear, sent commissioners who, he pretended, were to receive the oath of allegiance on the part of the Cortes. The Cortes refused to admit these commissioners to their presence, notifying the monarch that if he did not appear and swear to the laws of the country he would never be acknowledged as King of Spain. Charles thereupon yielded; he appeared before the Cortes and took the oath—as historians say, with a very bad grace. The Cortes on this occasion told him: "You must

Revolutionary Spain   589

know, Señor, that the King is but the paid servant of the nation."
Such was the beginning of the hostilities between Charles I and the
towns. In consequence of his intrigues, numerous insurrections broke
out in Castile, the Holy League of Ávila was formed, and the united
towns convoked the assembly of the Cortes at Torteaillas, whence
on October 20, 1520, a "protest against the abuses" was addressed
to the King, in return for which he deprived all the deputies assembled
at Torteaillas of their personal rights. Thus civil war had become
inevitable; the commoners appealed to arms: their soldiers under
the command of Padilla seized the fortress of Torre Lobatón, but
were ultimately defeated by superior forces at the battle of Villalar
on April 23, 1521. The heads of the principal "conspiration" rolled
on the scaffold, and the ancient liberties of Spain disappeared.

Several circumstances conspired in favor of the rising power of
absolutism. The want of union between the different provinces deprived their efforts of the necessary strength; but it was above all
the bitter antagonism between the classes of the nobles and the citizens of the towns which Charles employed for the degradation of
both. We have already mentioned that since the fourteenth century
the influence of the towns was prominent in the Cortes, and since
Ferdinand the Catholic, the Holy Brotherhood (Santa Hermandad)
had proved a powerful instrument in the hands of the towns against
the Catholic nobles, who accused them of encroachments on their
ancient privileges and jurisdiction. The nobility, therefore, were
eager to assist Carlos I in his project of suppressing the Holy League.
Having crushed their armed resistance, Carlos occupied himself with
the reduction of the municipal privileges of the towns, which,
rapidly declining in population, wealth, and importance, soon lost
their influence in the Cortes. Carlos now turned round upon the
nobles, who had assisted him in putting down the liberties of the
towns, but who themselves retained a considerable political importance. Mutiny in his army for want of pay obliged him, in 1539, to
assemble the Cortes in order to obtain a grant of money. Indignant
at the misapplication of former subsidies to operations foreign to the
interests of Spain, the Cortes refused all supplies. Carlos dismissed
them in a rage: and, the nobles having insisted on a privilege of
exemption from taxes, he declared that those who claimed such a
right could have no claim to appear in the Cortes, and consequently
excluded them from that assembly. This was the death blow of the
Cortes, and their meetings were henceforth reduced to the performance of a mere court ceremony. The third element in the ancient
constitution of the Cortes, viz., the clergy, enlisted since Ferdinand
the Catholic under the banner of the Inquisition, had long ceased to

identify its interests with those of feudal Spain. On the contrary, by the Inquisition the Church was transformed into the most formidable tool of absolutism.

If after the reign of Carlos I the decline of Spain, in both a political and a social aspect, exhibited all those symptoms of inglorious and protracted putrefaction so repulsive in the worst times of the Turkish Empire, under the Emperor at least the ancient liberties were buried in a magnificent tomb. This was the time when Vasco Núñez Balboa planted the banner of Castile upon the shores of Darién, Cortez in Mexico, and Pizarro in Peru; when Spainsh influence reigned supreme in Europe, and the southern imagination of the Iberians was bewildered with visions of Eldorado, chivalrous adventures, and universal monarchy. Spanish liberty disappeared under the clash of arms, showers of gold, and the terrible illuminations of the auto-da-fé.

But how are we to account for the singular phenomenon that, after almost three centuries of a Habsburg dynasty, followed by a Bourbon dynasty—either of them quite sufficient to crush a people—the municipal liberties of Spain more or less survive? That in the very country where of all the feudal states absolute monarchy first arose in its most unmitigated form, centralization has never succeeded in taking root? The answer is not difficult. It was in the sixteenth century that were formed the great monarchies which established themselves everywhere on the downfall of the conflicting feudal classes—the aristocracy and the towns. But in the other great states of Europe absolute monarchy presents itself as a civilizing center, as the initiator of social unity. There it was the laboratory in which the various elements of society were so mixed and worked as to allow the towns to change the local independence and sovereignty of the Middle Ages for the general rule of the middle classes and the common sway of civil society. In Spain, on the contrary, while the aristocracy sank into degradation without losing their privilege, the towns lost their medieval power without gaining modern importance.

Since the establishment of absolute monarchy they have vegetated in a state of continuous decay. We have not here to state the circumstances, political or ecomonical, which destroyed Spanish commerce, industry, navigation, and agriculture. For the present purpose it is sufficient to simply recall the fact. As the commercial and industrial life of the towns declined, internal exchanges became rare, the mingling of the inhabitants of different provinces less frequent, the means of communication neglected, and the great roads gradually deserted. Thus the local life of Spain, the independence of its provinces and communes, the diversified state of society originally based on the physical configuration of the country, and historically developed by the detached manner in which the several provinces emancipated themselves from the Moorish rule and formed little independent commonwealths—was now finally strengthened and confirmed by the economic revolution which dried up the sources of national activity. And while the absolute monarchy found in Spain material in its very nature repulsive to centralization, it did all in its power to prevent the growth of common interests arising out of a national division of labor and the multiplicity of internal exchanges —the very basis on which alone a uniform system of administration and the rule of general laws can be created. Thus the absolute monarchy in Spain, bearing but a superficial resemblance to the absolute monarchies of Europe in general, is rather to be ranged in a class with Asiatic forms of government. Spain, like Turkey, remained an agglomeration of mismanaged republics with a nominal sovereign at their head. Despotism changed character in the different provinces with the arbitrary interpretation of the general laws by viceroys and governors; but despotic as was the government, it did not prevent the provinces from subsisting with different laws and customs, different coins, military banners of different colors, and with their respective systems of taxation. The oriental despotism attacks municipal self-government only when opposed to its direct interests but is very glad to allow those institutions to continue so long as they take off its shoulders the duty of doing something and spare it the trouble of regular administration.

Thus it happened that Napoleon, who like all his contemporaries considered Spain as an inanimate corpse, was fatally surprised at the discovery that while the Spanish state was dead, Spanish society was full of life, and every part of it overflowing with powers of resistance. By the Treaty of Fontainebleau he had got his troops to Madrid; by alluring the royal family into an interview at Bayonne he had forced Carlos IV to retract his abdication and then to make over to him his dominions; and he had intimidated Ferdinand VII into a similar declaration. Carlos IV, his Queen, and the Prince of Peace conveyed to Compiègne, Ferdinand VII and his brothers imprisoned in the castle of Valençay, Bonaparte conferred the throne of Spain on his brother Joseph, assembled a Spanish junta at Bayonne, and provided them with one of his ready-made constitutions. Seeing nothing alive in the Spanish monarchy except the miserable dynasty which he had safely locked up, he felt quite sure of this confiscation of Spain. But only a few days after his *coup de main* he received the news of an insurrection at Madrid. Murat, it is true, quelled that tumult by killing about 1,000 people; but when this massacre became known an insurrection broke out in Asturias, and soon afterward embraced the whole monarchy. It is to be remarked that this first spontaneous rising originated with the people, while the "better" classes had quietly submitted to the foreign yoke.

Thus it is that Spain was prepared for her more recent revolutionary career, and launched into the struggles which have marked her development in the present century. The facts and influences we have thus succinctly detailed still act in forming her destinies and directing the impulses of her people. We have presented them as necessary to an appreciation not only of the present crisis, but of all she has done and suffered since the Napoleonic usurpation—a period now of nearly fifty years—not without tragic episodes and heroic efforts—indeed, one of the most touching and instructive chapters in all modern history. [Let us hope that the additions now being made to their annals by the Spanish people may prove neither unworthy nor fruitless of good to themselves and to the world.][1]

II*

We have already laid before our readers a survey of the earlier revolutionary history of Spain, as a means of understanding and appreciating the developments which that nation is now offering to the observation of the world. Still more interesting, and perhaps equally valuable as a source of present instruction, is the great national movement that attended the expulsion of the Bonapartes and restored the Spanish crown to the family in whose possession it yet remains. But to rightly estimate that movement, with its heroic episodes and memorable exhibition of vitality in a people supposed to be moribund, we must go back to the beginning of the Napoleonic assault on the nation. The efficient cause of the whole was perhaps first stated in the Treaty of Tilsit, which was concluded on July 7, 1807, and is said to have received its complement through a secret convention, signed by Prince Kourakin and Talleyrand. It was published in the Madrid *Gaceta* on August 25, 1812, containing, among other things, the following stipulations:

"Art. I. Russia is to take possession of European Turkey, and to extend her possessions in Asia as far as she may think it convenient.

"Art. II. The Bourbon dynasty in Spain and the house of Braganza in Portugal will cease to reign. Princes of the Bonaparte family will succeed to both of those crowns."

---

1. This sentence was added by the editors.
* *New-York Daily Tribune*, September 25, 1854.

Supposing this treaty to be authentic, and its authenticity is scarcely disputed, even in the recently published memoirs of King Joseph Bonaparte, it formed the true reason for the French invasion of Spain in 1808, while the Spanish commotions of that time would seem to be linked by secret threads with the destinies of Turkey.

When, consequent upon the Madrid massacre and the transactions at Bayonne, simultaneous insurrections broke out in Asturias, Galicia, Andalusia, and Valencia, and a French army occupied Madrid, the four northern fortresses of Pamplona, San Sebastián, Figueras, and Barcelona had been seized by Bonaparte under false pretenses; part of the Spanish army had been removed to the island of Fünen, destined for an attack upon Sweden; lastly all the constituted authorities, military, ecclesiastic, judicial, and administrative, as well as the aristocracy, exhorted the people to submit to the foreign intruder. But there was one circumstance to compensate for all the difficulties of the situation. Thanks to Napoleon, the country was rid of its King, its royal family, and its government. Thus the shackles were broken which might else have prevented the Spanish people from displaying their native energies. How little they were able to resist the French, under the command of their kings and under ordinary circumstances, had been proved by the disgraceful campaigns of 1794 and 1796.

Napoleon had summoned the most distinguished persons in Spain to meet him at Bayonne, and to receive from his hands a king and a constitution. With very few exceptions, they appeared there. On June 7, 1808, King Joseph received at Bayonne a deputation of the grandees of Spain, in whose name the Duke of Infantado, Ferdinand VII's most intimate friend, addressed him as follows: "Sire, the grandees of Spain have at all times been celebrated for their loyalty to their Sovereign, and in them Your Majesty will now find the same fidelity and adhesion."

The Royal Council of Castile assured poor Joseph that he was "the principal branch of a family destined by heaven to reign." Not less abject was the congratulation of the Duke del Parque, at the head of a deputation representing the army. On the following day the same persons published a proclamation enjoining general submission to the Bonaparte dynasty. On July 7, 1808, the new constitution was signed by ninety-one Spaniards of the highest distinction: among them dukes, counts, and marquises, as well as several heads of the religious orders. During the discussions on that constitution all they found cause to remonstrate against was the repeal of their old privileges and exemptions. The first ministry and the first royal household of Joseph were the same persons who had formed the ministry and the royal household of Ferdinand VII. Some of the upper classes considered Napoleon as the providential regenerator of Spain; others as the only bulwark against revolution; none believing in the chance of national resistance.

Thus from the very beginning of the Spanish War of Independence the high nobility and the old administration lost all hold upon the middle classes and upon the people, because of their having deserted them at the commencement of the struggle. On the one side stood the *Afrancerados* [the Frenchified], and on the other the nation. At Valladolid, Cartagena, Granada, Jaén, San Lúcar, Carolina, Ciudad Rodrigo, Cádiz, and Valencia, the most prominent members of the old administration—governors, generals, and other marked personages presumed to be French agents and obstacles to the national movement—fell victims to the infuriated people. Everywhere the existing authorities were displaced. Some months previous to the rising, on March 19, 1808, the popular commotions that had taken place at Madrid, intended to remove from their posts *El Chorizero* (the sausage maker, a nickname of Godoy) and his obnoxious satellites. This object was now gained on a national scale, and with it the internal revolution was accomplished so far as contemplated by the masses, and as not connected with resistance to the foreign intruder. On the whole, the movement appeared to be directed rather *against* revolution than *for* it. National by proclaiming the independence of Spain from France, it was at the same time dynastic by opposing the "beloved" Ferdinand VII to Joseph Bonaparte; reactionary by opposing the old institutions, customs, and laws to the rational innovations of Napoleon; superstitious and fanatical by opposing "holy religion" against what was called French atheism, or the destruction of the special privileges of the Roman Church. The priests, terrified by the fate that had fallen upon their brethren in France, fostered the popular passions in the interest of self-preservation. "The patriotic fire," says Southey, "flamed higher for the holy oil of superstition."[2]

All the wars of independence waged against France bear in common the stamp of regeneration, mixed up with reaction; but nowhere to such a degree as in Spain. The King appeared in the imagination of the people in the light of a romantic prince, forcibly abused and locked up by a giant robber. The most fascinating and popular epochs of their past were encircled with the holy and miraculous traditions of the war of the cross against the crescent; and a great portion of the lower classes were accustomed to wear the livery of mendicants, and live upon the sanctified patrimony of the Church. A Spanish author, Don Joseph Clemente Carnicero, published in the

2. Robert Southey, *History of the Peninsular War* (3 vols.; London, 1823-32).

years 1814 and 1816 the following series of works: *Napoleon, the True Don Quixote of Europe; Principal Events of the Glorious Revolution of Spain; The Inquisition Rightly Reestablished.* It is sufficient to note the titles of these books to understand this one aspect of the Spanish revolution which we meet with in the several manifestoes of the provincial juntas, all of them proclaiming the King, their holy religion, and the country, and some even telling the people that "their hopes of a better world were at stake, and in very imminent danger."

However, if the peasantry, the inhabitants of small inland cities, and the numerous army of the mendicants, frocked and unfrocked, all of them deeply imbued with religious and political prejudices, formed the great majority of the National party, it contained on the other hand an active and influential minority which considered the popular rising against the French invasion as the signal given for the political and social regeneration of Spain. This minority was composed of the inhabitants of the seaports, commercial towns, and part of the provincial capitals, where, under the reign of Charles V, the material conditions of modern society had developed themselves to a certain degree. They were strengthened by the more cultivated portion of the upper and middle classes, authors, physicians, lawyers, and even priests, for whom the Pyrenees had formed no sufficient barrier against the invasion of the philosophy of the eighteenth century. As a true manifesto of this faction may be considered the famous memorandum of Jovellanos on the improvements of agriculture and the agrarian law, published in 1795, and drawn up by order of the Royal Council of Castile. There was, finally, the youth of the middle classes, such as the students of the university, who had eagerly adopted the aspirations and principles of the French Revolution and who, for a moment, even expected to see their country regenerated by the assistance of France.

So long as the common defense of the country alone was concerned, the two great elements composing the National party remained in perfect union. Their antagonism did not appear till they met together in the Cortes, on the battleground of a new constitution there to be drawn up. The revolutionary minority, in order to foment the patriotic spirit of the people, had not hesitated themselves to appeal to the national prejudices of the old popular faith. Favorable to the immediate objects of national resistance as these tactics might have appeared, they could not fail to prove fatal to this minority when the time had arrived for the conservative interests of the old society to entrench themselves behind these very prejudices and popular passions, with a view of defending themselves against the proper and ulterior plans of the revolutionists.

When Ferdinand left Madrid upon the summons of Bonaparte,

he had established a supreme junta of government under the presidency of the Infante Don Antonio. But in May this junta had already disappeared. There existed then no central government, and the insurgent towns formed juntas of their own, presided over by those of the provincial capitals. These provincial juntas constituted, as it were, so many independent governments, each of which set on foot an army of its own. The Junta of Representatives at Oviedo declared that the entire sovereignty had devolved into their hands, proclaimed war against Bonaparte, and sent deputies to England to conclude an armistice. The same was done afterward by the Junta of Seville. It is a curious fact that by the mere force of circumstances these exalted Catholics were driven to alliance with England, a power which the Spaniards were accustomed to look upon as the incarnation of the most damnable heresy, and little better than the Grand Turk himself. Attacked by French atheism, they were thrown into the arms of British Protestantism. No wonder that Ferdinand VII, on his return to Spain, declared, in a decree reestablishing the Holy Inquisition, that one of the causes "that had altered the purity of religion in Spain was the sojourn of foreign troops of different sects, all of them equally infected with hatred against the holy Roman Church."

The provincial juntas which had so suddenly sprung into life, altogether independent of each other, conceded a certain, but very slight and undefined, degree of ascendancy to the supreme Junta of Seville, that city being regarded as the capital of Spain while Madrid was in the hands of the foreigner. Thus a very anarchical kind of federal government was established, which the shock of opposite interests, local jealousies, and rival influences made a rather bad instrument for bringing unity into the military command, and to combine the operations of a campaign.

The addresses to the people issued by those several juntas, while displaying all the heroic vigor of a people suddenly awakened from a long lethargy and roused by an electric shock into a feverish state of activity, are not free from that pompous exaggeration, that style of mingled buffoonery and bombast, and that redundant grandiloquence which caused Sismondi to put upon Spanish literature the epithet of oriental. They exhibit no less the childish vanity of the Spanish character, the members of the juntas for instance assuming the title of highness and loading themselves with gaudy uniforms.

There are two circumstances connected with these juntas—the one showing the low standard of the people at the time of their rising, while the other was detrimental to the progress of the revolution. The juntas were named by general suffrage; but "the very zeal of the lower classes displayed itself in obedience." They generally elected

only their natural superiors, the provincial nobility and gentry backed
by clergymen and a very few notabilities of the middle class. So
conscious were the people of their own weakness that they limited
their initiative to forcing the higher classes into resistance against the
invader, without pretending to share in the direction of that resistance. At Seville, for instance, "the first thought of the people
was that the parochial clergy and the heads of the Convents should
assemble to choose the members of the junta." Thus the juntas were
filled with persons chosen on account of their previous station, and
very far from being revolutionary leaders. On the other hand, the
people when appointing these authorities did not think either of
limiting their power or of fixing a term to their duration. The juntas,
of course, thought only of extending the one and of perpetuating the
other. Thus these first creations of the popular impulse at the commencement of the revolution remained during its whole course as
so many dikes against the revolutionary current when threatening
to overflow.

On July 20, 1808, when Joseph Bonaparte entered Madrid, 14,000
French, under Generals Dupont and Vidal, were forced by Castanos
to lay down their arms at Baylen, and Joseph a few days afterward
had to retire from Madrid to Burgos. There were two events besides
which greatly encouraged the Spaniards; the one being the expulsion
of Lefebvre from Saragossa by General Palafox, and the other the
arrival of the army of the Marquis de la Romaña at Corsica, with
7,000 men who had embarked from the island of Fünen in spite of
the French, in order to come to the assistance of their country.

It was after the battle of Baylen that the revolution came to a
head, and that part of the high nobility who had accepted the Bonaparte dynasty or wisely kept back came forward to join the popular
cause—an advantage to that cause of a very doubtful character.

III*

The division of power among the provincial juntas had saved
Spain from the first shock of the French invasion under Napoleon,
not only by multiplying the resources of the country, but also by
putting the invader at a loss for a mark whereat to strike, the French
being quite amazed at the discovery that the center of Spanish resistance was nowhere and everywhere. Nevertheless, shortly after
the capitulation of Baylen and the evacuation of Madrid by Joseph,
the necessity of establishing some kind of central government be-

* *New-York Daily Tribune*, October 20, 1854.

came generally felt. After the first successes, the dissensions between the provincial juntas had grown so violent that Seville, for instance, was barely prevented by General Castanos from marching against Granada. The French army, which, with the exception of the forces under Marshal Bessières, had withdrawn to the line of the Ebro in the greatest confusion—so that if vigorously harassed it would then have easily been dispersed, or at least compelled to repass the frontier —was thus allowed to recover and to take up a strong position. But it was above all the bloody suppression of the Bilbao insurrection by General Merlin which evoked a national cry against the jealousies of the juntas and the easy laissez-faire of the commanders. The urgency of combining military movements; the certainty that Napoleon would soon reappear at the head of a victorious army collected from the banks of the Niemen, the Oder, and the shores of the Baltic; the want of a general authority for concluding treaties of alliance with Great Britain or other foreign powers, and for keeping up the connection with, and receiving tribute from Spanish America; the existence at Burgos of a French central power; and the necessity of setting up altar against altar—all these circumstances conspired to force the Seville Junta to resign, however reluctantly, its ill-defined and rather nominal supremacy, and to propose to the several provincial juntas to select each from its own body two deputies, the assembling of whom was to constitute a Central Junta, while the provincial juntas were to remain invested with the internal management of their respective districts, "but under due subordination to the general government." Thus the Central Junta, composed of thirty-five deputies from provincial juntas (thirty-four for the Spanish juntas, and one for the Canary Islands), met at Aranjuez on December 26, 1808, just one day before the potentates of Russia and Germany prostrated themselves before Napoleon at Erfurt.

Under revolutionary still more than under ordinary circumstances, the destinies of armies reflect the true nature of the civil government. The Central Junta, charged with the expulsion of the invaders from the Spanish soil, was driven by the success of the hostile arms from Madrid to Seville, and from Seville to Cádiz, there to expire ignominiously. Its reign was marked by a disgraceful succession of defeats, by the annihilation of the Spanish armies, and lastly by the dissolution of regular warfare into guerrilla exploits.

As said Urquizo, a Spanish nobleman, to Cuesta, the Captain General of Castile, on April 3, 1808: "Our Spain is a Gothic edifice, composed of heterogeneous morsels, with as many forces, privileges, legislations, and customs as there are provinces. There exists in her nothing of what they call public spirit in Europe. These reasons will prevent the establishment of any central power of so solid a structure as to be able to unite our national forces."

If, then, the actual state of Spain at the epoch of the French invasion threw the greatest possible difficulties in the way of creating a revolutionary center, the very composition of the Central Junta incapacitated it from proving a match for the terrible crisis in which the country found itself placed. Being too numerous and too fortuitously mixed for an executive government, they were too few to pretend to the authority of a national convention. The mere fact of their power having been delegated from the provincial juntas rendered them unfit for overcoming the ambitious propensities, the ill will, and the capricious egotism of those bodies. These juntas—the members of which, as we have shown in a former article, were elected on the whole in consideration of the situation they occupied in the old society, rather than of their capacity to inaugurate a new one—sent in their turn to the "Central" Spanish grandees, prelates, titularies of Castile, ancient ministers, high civil and military officials, instead of revolutionary upstarts. At the outset the Spanish revolution failed by its endeavor to remain legitimate and respectable.

The two most marked members of the Central Junta, under whose banners its two great parties ranged themselves, were Florida Blanca and Jovellanos, both of them martyrs of Godoy's persecution, former ministers, valetudinarians, and grown old in the regular and pedantic habits of the procrastinating Spanish regime, the solemn and circumstantial slowness of which had become proverbial even at the time of Bacon, who once exclaimed, "May death reach me from Spain: it will then arrive at a late hour."[3]

Florida Blanca and Jovellanos represented an antagonism, but an antagonism belonging to that part of the eighteenth century which preceded the era of the French Revolution; the former a plebeian bureaucrat, the latter an aristocratic philanthropist; Florida Blanca a partisan and a practicer of the enlightened despotism represented by Pombal, Frederick II, and Joseph II;[4] Jovellanos a "friend of the people," hoping to raise them to liberty by an anxiously wise succession of economical laws, and by the literary propaganda of generous doctrines; both opposed to the traditions of feudalism, the one by trying to disentangle the monarchical power, the other by seeking to rid civil society of its shackles. The part acted by either in the history of their country corresponded with the diversity of

---

3. The quotation from Francis Bacon is given by the Spanish historian José María Toreno in his *Historia des levantamiento, guerra y revolución de España* (vol. I, Paris, 1838).

4. See Saul K. Padover, *The Revolutionary Emperor: Joseph II* (1934, 1968).

their opinions. Florida Blanca ruled supreme as the Prime Minister of Charles III, and his rule grew despotic according to the measure in which he met with resistance. Jovellanos, whose ministerial career under Charles IV was but short-lived, gained his influence over the Spanish people, not as a minister, but as a scholar; not by decrees but by essays. Florida Blanca, when the storm of the times carried him to the head of a revolutionary government, was an octogenarian, unshaken only in his belief in despotism and his distrust of popular spontaneity. When delegated to Madrid he left with the municipality of Murcia a secret protest declaring that he had only ceded to force and to the fear of popular assassinations, and that he signed this protocol with the express view to prevent King Joseph from ever finding fault with his acceptance of the people's mandate. Not satisfied with returning to the traditions of his manhood, he retraced such steps of his ministerial past as he now judged to have been too rash. Thus he who had expelled the Jesuits from Spain was hardly installed in the Central Junta when he caused it to grant leave for their return "in a private capacity." If he acknowledged any change to have occurred since his time, it was simply this: that Godoy, who had banished him, and had dispossessed the great Count of Florida Blanca of his governmental omnipotence, was now again replaced by that same Count of Florida Blanca and driven out in his turn. This was the man whom the Central Junta chose as its President, and whom its majority recognized as an infallible leader.

Jovellanos, who commanded the influential minority of the Central Junta, had also grown old, and lost much of his energy in a long and painful imprisonment inflicted upon him by Godoy. But even in his best times he was not a man of revolutionary action, but rather a well-intentioned reformer, who, from overniceness as to the means, would never have dared to accomplish an end. In France he would perhaps have gone the length of Mounier or Lally-Tollendal, but not a step further. In England he would have figured as a popular member of the House of Lords. In insurrectionized Spain he was fit to supply the aspiring youth with ideas, but practically no match even for the servile tenacity of a Florida Blanca. Not altogether free from aristocratic prejudices, and therefore with a strong leaning toward the Anglomania of Montesquieu, this fair character seemed to prove that if Spain had exceptionally begot a generalizing mind, she was unable to do it except at the cost of individual energy, which she could only possess for local affairs.

It is true that the Central Junta included a few men—headed by Don Lorenzo Calvo de Rozas, the delegate of Saragossa—who, while adopting the reform views of Jovellanos, spurred on at the same time to revolutionary action. But their numbers were too few and their names too unknown to allow them to push the slow state coach of the Junta out of the beaten track of Spanish ceremonial.

This power, so clumsily composed, so nervelessly constituted, with such outlived reminiscences at its head, was called upon to accomplish a revolution and to beat Napoleon. If its proclamations were as vigorous as its deeds were weak, it was due to Don Manuel Quintana, a Spanish poet whom the Junta had the taste to appoint as their secretary and to intrust with the writing of their manifestoes.

Like Calderón's pompous heroes who, confounding conventional distinction with genuine greatness, used to announce themselves by a pompous enumeration of all their titles, the Junta has applied itself in the first place with decreeing the honors and decorations due to its exalted position. Their President received the predicate of "highness," the other members that of "excellency," while to the Junta in *corpore* was reserved the title of "majesty." They adopted a species of fancy uniform resembling that of a general, adorned their breasts with badges representing the two worlds, and voted themselves a yearly salary of 120,000 reals. It was a true idea of the old Spanish school that in order to make a great and dignified entrance upon the historical stage of Europe, the chiefs of insurgent Spain ought to wrap themselves in theatrical costumes.

We should transgress the limits of these sketches by entering into the internal history of the Junta and the details of its administration. For our end it will suffice to answer two questions. What was its influence on the development of the Spanish revolutionary movement? What on the defense of the country? These two questions answered, much that until now has appeared mysterious and unaccountable in the Spanish revolution of the nineteenth century will have found its explanation.

At the outset the majority of the Central Junta thought it their main duty to suppress the first revolutionary transports. Accordingly they tightened anew the old trammels of the press and appointed a new Grand Inquisitor, who was happily prevented by the French from resuming his functions. Although the greater part of the real property of Spain was then locked up in mortmain—in the entailed estates of the nobility and the unalienable estates of the Church —the Junta ordered the selling of the mortmains, which had already begun to be suspended, threatening even to amend the private contracts affecting the ecclesiastical estates that had already been sold. They acknowledged the national debt, but took no financial measure to free the civil list from a world of burdens with which a secular succession of corrupt governments had encumbered it, to reform their

proverbially unjust, absurd, and vexatious fiscal system, or to open
to the nation new productive resources by breaking through the
shackles of feudalism.

IV*

As early as the times of Philip V, Francisco Benito de la Soledad
had said: "All the evils of Spain are derived from the *legados*"
(lawyers). At the head of the mischievous magisterial hierarchy
of Spain was placed the *Consejo Real* [Royal Council] of Castile.
Sprung up in the turbulent times of the Don Juans and the En-
riques, strengthened by Philip II, who discovered in it a worthy
complement of the *Santo officio* [Holy Office], it had improved by
the calamities of the times and the weakness of the later kings to
usurp and accumulate in its hands the most heterogeneous attributes,
and to add to its functions of highest tribunal those of a legislator
and of an administrative superintendent of all the kingdoms of Spain.
Thus it surpassed in power even the French parliament which it
resembled in many points, except that it was never to be found on
the side of the people. Having been the most powerful authority in
ancient Spain, the *Consejo Real* was, of course, the most implacable
foe to a new Spain, and to all recent popular authorities threatening
to cripple its supreme influence. Being the great dignitary of the
order of the lawyers and the incarnate guarantee of all its abuses
and privileges, the *Consejo* naturally disposed of all the numerous
and influential interests vested in Spanish jurisprudence. It was therefore a power with which the revolution could enter into no compromise, but which had to be swept away unless it should be allowed
to sweep away the revolution in its turn. As we have seen in a former
article, the *Consejo* had prostituted itself before Napoleon, and by that
act of treason had lost all hold upon the people. But on the day of
their assumption of the office the Central Junta were foolish enough
to communicate to the *Consejo* their constitution, and to ask for its
oath of fidelity, after having received which they declared they would
dispatch the formula of the same oath to all the other authorities of
the kingdom. By this inconsiderate step, loudly disapproved by all the
revolutionary party, the *Consejo* became convinced that the Central
Junta wanted its support; it thus recovered from its despondency, and
after an affected hesitation of some days tendered a malevolent submission to the Junta, backing its oath by an expression of its own
reactionary scruples exhibited in its advice to the Junta to dissolve, by

* *New-York Daily Tribune*, October 27, 1854.

reducing its number to three or five members, according to Ley 3, Partita 2, Título 15; and to order the forcible extinction of the provincial juntas. After the French had returned to Madrid and dispersed the *Consejo Real*, the Central Junta, not contented with their first blunder, had the fatuity to resuscitate the *Consejo* by creating the *Consejo Reunido*—a reunion of the *Consejo Real* with all the other wrecks of the ancient royal councils. Thus the Junta spontaneously created for the counterrevolution a central power, which, rivaling their own power, never ceased to harass and counteract them with its intrigues and conspiracies, seeking to drive them to the most unpopular steps and then with a show of virtuous indignation to denounce them to the impassioned contempt of the people. It hardly need be mentioned that, having first acknowledged and then reestablished the *Consejo Real*, the Central Junta was unable to reform anything, either in the organization of Spanish tribunals or in their most vicious civil and criminal legislation.

That, notwithstanding the predominance in the Spanish rising of the national and religious elements, there existed in the two first years a most decided tendency to social and political reforms is proved by all the manifestations of the provincial juntas of that time, which, though composed as they mostly were of the privileged classes, never neglected to denounce the ancient regime and to hold out promises of radical reform. The fact is further proved by the manifestoes of the Central Junta. In their first address to the nation, dated November 10, 1808, they say: "A tyranny of twenty years, exercised by the most incapable hands, had brought them to the very brink of perdition; the nation was alienated from its government by hatred and contest. A little time only has passed since, oppressed and degraded, ignorant of their own strength, and finding no protection against the governmental evils, neither in the institutions nor in the laws, they had even regarded foreign dominion as less hateful than the wasting tyranny which consumed them. The dominion of a will always capricious, and most often unjust, had lasted too long; their patience, their love of order, their generous loyalty had too long been abused; it was time that law founded on general utility should commence its reign. Reform, therefore, was necessary throughout all branches. The Junta would form different committees, each entrusted with a particular department to whom all writings on matters of government and administration might be addressed."

In their address dated Seville, October 28, 1809, they say: "An imbecile despotism prepared the way for French tyranny. To leave the state sunk in old abuses would be a crime as enormous as to deliver you into the hands of Bonaparte."

There seems to have existed in the Central Junta a most original division of labor—the Jovellanos party being allowed to proclaim and to protocol the revolutionary aspirations of the nation, and the Florida Blanca party reserving to themselves the pleasure of giving them the lie direct, and of opposing to revolutionary fiction counter-revolutionary fact. For us, however, the important point is to prove from the very confessions of the provincial juntas deposited with the Central, the often-denied fact of the existence of revolutionary aspirations at the epoch of the first Spanish rising.

The manner in which the Central Junta made use of the opportunities for reforms afforded by the good will of the nation, the pressure of events, and the presence of immediate danger may be inferred from the influence exercised by their commissioners in the several provinces they were sent to. One Spanish author candidly tells us that the Central Junta, not overflowing with capacities, took good care to retain the eminent members at the center, and to dispatch those who were good for nothing to the circumference. These commissioners were invested with the power of presiding over the provincial juntas and of representing the Central in the plenitude of its attributes. To quote only some instances of their doings: General Romaña, whom the Spanish soldiers used to call Marquis de las Romerias, from his perpetual marches and countermarches—fighting never taking place except when he happened to be out of the way—this Romaña, when beaten by Soult out of Galicia, entered Asturias, and as a Commissioner of the Central. His first business was to pick a quarrel with the provincial junta of Oviedo, whose energetic and revolutionary measures had drawn down upon them the hatred of the privileged classes. He went the length of dissolving and replacing it by persons of his own invention. General Ney, informed of these discussions, in a province where the resistance against the French had been general and unanimous, instantly marched his forces into Asturias, expelled the Marquis de las Romerias, entered Oviedo, and sacked it during three days. The French having evacuated Galicia at the end of 1809, our Marquis and Commissioner of the Central Junta entered Coruña, united in his person all public authority, suppressed the district juntas, which had multiplied with the insurrection, and in their places appointing military governors, threatening the members of those juntas with persecution, actually persecuting the patriots, affecting a supreme benignity toward all who had embraced the cause of the invader, and proving in all other respects a mischievous, impotent, capricious blockhead. And what had been the shortcomings of the district and provincial juntas of Galicia? They had ordered a general recruitment without exemption of classes or persons; they had levied taxes upon the capitalists and proprietors; they had lowered the salaries of public functionaries; they had commanded the ecclesiastical corporations to keep at their disposition the revenues existing in their chests. In a word, they had taken revolutionary measures. From the time of the glorious Marquis de la Romerias, Asturias and Galicia, the two provinces most distinguished by their general resistance to the French, withheld from partaking in the war of independence whenever released from immediate danger of invasion.

In Valencia, where new prospects appeared to open as long as the people were left to themselves and to chiefs of their own choosing, the revolutionary spirit was broken down by the influence of the central government. Not content to place that province under the generalship of one Don José Caro, the Central Junta dispatched as "their own" commissioner the Baron Labazora. This Baron found fault with the provincial junta because it had resisted certain superior orders and canceled their decree by which the appointments to vacant canonship, ecclesiastical benefices, and commanderies had been judiciously suspended and the revenues destined for the benefit of the military hospitals. Hence bitter contests between the Central Junta and that of Valencia; hence, at a later epoch, the sleep of Valencia under the liberal administration of Marshal Suchet; hence its eagerness to proclaim Ferdinand VII on his return against the then revolutionary government.

At Cádiz, the most revolutionary place in Spain at the epoch, the presence of a Commissioner of the Central Junta, the stupid and conceited Marquis de Vittel, caused an insurrection to break out on February 22 and 23, 1809, which if not timely shifted to the War of Independence would have had the most disastrous consequences.

There exists no better example of the discretion established by the Central Junta in the appointment of their own commissioners than that of the delegate to Wellington, Señor Lozano de Torres, who, while humbling himself to servile adulation before the English General, secretly informed the Junta that the General's complaints on his want of provisions were altogether groundless. Wellington, having found out the double-tongued wretch, chased him ignominiously from his camp.

The Central Junta were placed in the most fortunate circumstances for realizing what they had proclaimed in one of the addresses to the Spanish nation. "It has seemed good to Providence that in this terrible crisis you should not be able to advance one step toward independence without advancing one likewise toward liberty." At the commencement of their reign the French had not yet obtained possession of one third of Spain. The ancient authorities they found either absent or prostrated by their connivance with the intruder, or dispersed at his bidding. There was no measure of social reform, transferring property and influence from the church and the aristocracy to the middle class and the peasants, which the cause of defending the common country could not have enabled them to carry. They had the same good luck as the French *Comité du salut public*—that the convulsion within was backed by the necessities of defense against aggressions from without; moreover they had before them the example of bold initiative which certain provinces had already been forced into by the pressure of circumstances. But not satisfied with hanging as dead weight on the Spanish revolution, they actually worked in the sense of the counterrevolution, by reestablishing the authorities, by forging anew the chains which had been broken, by stifling the revolutionary fire wherever it broke out, by themselves doing nothing and by preventing others from doing anything. During their stay at Seville, on July 20, 1809, even the English Tory government thought necessary to address them a note strongly protesting against their counterrevolutionary course, "apprehending that they were likely to suffocate the public enthusiasm." It has been remarked somewhere that Spain endured all the evils of revolution without acquiring revolutionary strength. If there be any truth in this remark, it is a sweeping condemnation passed upon the Central Junta.

We have thought it the more necessary to dwell upon this point as its decisive importance has never been understood by any European historian. Exclusively under the reign of the Central Junta, it was possible to blend with the actualities and exigencies of national defense the transformation of Spanish society, and the emancipation of the native spirit, without which any political constitution must dissolve like a phantom at the slightest combat with real life. The Cortes were placed in quite opposite circumstances—they themselves driven back to an insulated spot of the Peninsula, cut off from the main body of the monarchy during two years by a besieging French army, and representing ideal Spain, while real Spain was conquered or fighting. At the time of the Cortes, Spain was divided into two parts. At the Isla de León, ideas without action—in the rest of Spain, action wthout ideas. At the time of the Central Junta, on the contrary, particular weakness, incapacity, and ill will were required on the part of the supreme government to draw a line of distinction between the Spanish war and the Spanish revolution. The Cortes, therefore, failed, not, as French and English writers assert, because they were revolutionists, but because their predecessors had been reactionists and had missed the proper season of revolutionary action. Modern Spanish writers, offended by the Anglo-French critics, have nevertheless proved unable to refute them, and still wince under the *bon mot* of the Abbé de Pradt: "The Spanish people resemble the wife of Sganarelle, who wanted to be beaten."

V*

The Central Junta failed in the defense of their country because they failed in their revolutionary mission. Conscious of their own weakness, of the unstable tenor of their power, and of their extreme unpopularity, how could they have attempted to answer the rivalries, jealousies, and overbearing pretensions of their generals, common to all revolutionary epochs, but by unworthy tricks and petty intrigues? Kept as they were in constant fear and suspicion of their own military chiefs, we may give full credit to Wellington when writing to his brother, the Marquis of Wellesley, on September 1, 1809: "I am much afraid, from what I have seen of the proceedings of the Central Junta, that in the distribution of their forces they do not consider military defense and military operations so much as they do political intrigue and the attainment of trifling political objects."

In revolutionary times, when all ties of subordination are loosened, military discipline can be restored only by civil discipline sternly weighing upon the generals. As the Central Junta, from its incongruous complexion, never succeeded in controlling the generals, the generals always failed in controlling the soldiers, and to the end of the war the Spanish army never reached an average degree of discipline and subordination. This insubordination was kept up by the want of food, clothing, and all the other material requisites of an army—for the morale of an army, as Napoleon called it, depends altogether on its material condition. The Central Junta was unable regularly to provide for the army, because the poor poet Quintana's manifestoes would not do in this instance, and to add coercion to their decrees they must have recurred to the same revolutionary measures which they had condemned in the provinces. Even the general enlistment without respect to privilege and exemptions, and the facility granted to all Spaniards to obtain every grade in the army, was the work of the provincial juntas, and not of the Central Junta. If the defeats of the Spanish armies were thus produced by the counter-revolutionary incapacities of the Central Junta, these disasters in their turn still more depressed that government, and by making it the object of popular contempt and suspicion increased its dependence upon presumptuous but incapable military chiefs.

The Spanish standing army, if everywhere defeated, nevertheless

* *New-York Daily Tribune,* October 30, 1854.

presented itself at all points. More than twenty times dispersed, it was always ready again to show front to the enemy, and frequently reappeared with increased strength after a defeat. It was of no use to beat them, because, quick to flee, their loss in men was generally small, and as to the loss of the field they did not care about it. Retiring disorderly to the sierras, they were sure to reassemble and reappear when least expected, strengthened by new reinforcements, and able, if not to resist the French armies, at least to keep them in continual movement, and to oblige them to scatter their forces. More fortunate than the Russians, they did not even need to die in order to rise from the dead.

The disastrous battle of Ocaña, November 19, 1809, was the last great pitched battle which the Spaniards fought; from that time they confined themselves to guerrilla warfare. The mere fact of the abandonment of regular warfare proves the disappearance of the national before the local centers of government. When the disasters of the standing army became regular, the rising of the guerrillas became general, and the body of the people, hardly thinking of the national defeats, exulted in the local successes of their heroes. In this point at least the Central Junta shared the popular delusion. "Fuller accounts were given in the *Gaceta* of an affair of guerrillas than of the battle of Ocaña."

As Don Quixote had protested with his lance against gunpowder, so the guerrillas protested against Napoleon, only with different success. "These guerrillas," says the Austrian *Military Journal* (Vol. I, 1821), "carried their bases in themselves, as it were, and every operation against them terminated in the disappearance of its object."

There are three periods to be distinguished in the history of the guerrilla warfare. In the first period the population of whole provinces took up arms and made a partisan warfare, as in Galicia and Asturias. In the second period, guerrilla bands formed of the wrecks of the Spanish armies, of Spanish deserters from the French armies, of smugglers, etc., carried on the war in their own cause, independently of all foreign influence and agreeably to their immediate interest. Fortunate events and circumstances frequently brought whole districts under their colors. As long as the guerrillas were thus constituted, they made no formidable appearance as a body, but were nevertheless extremely dangerous to the French. They formed the basis of an actual armament of the people. As soon as an opportunity for a capture offered itself, or a combined enterprise was meditated, the most active and daring among the people came out and joined the guerrillas. They rushed with the utmost rapidity upon their booty, or placed themselves in order of battle, according to the object of their undertaking. It was not uncommon to see them standing out a whole day in sight of a vigilant enemy, in order to intercept a carrier or to capture supplies. It was in this way that the younger Mina captured the Viceroy of Navarre, appointed by Joseph Bonaparte, and that Julian made a prisoner of the Commandant of Ciudad Rodrigo. As soon as the enterprise was completed, everybody went his own way, and armed men were soon scattering in all directions; but the associated peasants quietly returned to their common occupation without "as much as their absence having been noticed." Thus the communication on all the roads was closed. Thousands of enemies were on the spot, though not one could be discovered. No courier could be dispatched without being taken; no supplies could set out without being intercepted; in short, no movement could be effected without being observed by a hundred eyes. At the same time there existed no means of striking at the root of a combination of this kind. The French were obliged to be constantly armed against an enemy who, continually flying, always reappeared, and was everywhere without being actually seen, the mountains serving as so many curtains. "It was," says the Abbé de Pradt, "neither battles nor engagements which exhausted the French forces, but the incessant molestations of an invisible enemy, who, if pursued, became lost among the people, out of which he reappeared immediately afterward with renewed strength. The lion in the fable tormented to death by a goat gives a true picture of the French army."[5] In their third period, the guerrillas aped the regularity of the standing army, swelled their corps to the number of from 3,000 to 6,000 men, ceased to be the concern of whole districts, and fell into the hands of a few leaders who made such use of them as best suited their own purposes. This change in the system of the guerrillas gave the French, in their contests with them, considerable advantage. Rendered incapable by their great numbers to conceal themselves, and to suddenly disappear without being forced into battle, as they had formerly done, the guerrillas were now frequently overtaken, defeated, dispersed, and disabled for a length of time from offering any further molestation.

By comparing the three periods of guerrilla warfare with the political history of Spain, it is found that they represent the respective degrees into which the counterrevolutionary spirit of the government had succeeded in cooling the spirit of the people. Beginning with the rise of whole populations, the partisan war was next carried on by guerrilla bands, of which whole districts formed the reserve, and

---

5. Dominique Georges Frédéric de Pradt, *Mémoires historiques sur la révolution d'Espagne* (Paris, 1816).

terminated in *corps francs* continually on the point of dwindling into banditti, or sinking down to the level of standing regiments.

Estrangement from the supreme government, relaxed discipline, continual disasters, constant formation, decomposition, and recomposition during six years of the *cadres* must have necessarily stamped upon the body of the Spanish army the character of praetorianism, making them equally ready to become the tools or the scourges of their chiefs. The generals themselves had necessarily participated in, quarreled with, or conspired against the central government, and always thrown the weight of their sword into the political balance. Thus Cuesta, who afterward seemed to win the confidence of the Central Junta at the same rate that he lost the battles of the country, had begun by conspiring with the *Consejo Real* and by arresting the Leónese deputies to the Central Junta. General Morla himself, a member of the Central Junta, went over into the Bonapartist camp after he had surrendered Madrid to the French. The coxcombical Marquis de la Romerias, also a member of the Junta, conspired with the vainglorious José Palafox, the wretched Montijo, and the turbulent Junta of Seville against it. The Generals Castaños, Blake, Abisbal (an O'Donnell) figured and intrigued successively at the times of the Cortes as regents, and the Captain General of Valencia, Don Xavier Elio, surrendered Spain finally to the mercies of Ferdinand VII. The praetorian elements was certainly more developed with the generals than with their troops.

On the other hand, the army and guerrilleros—which received during the war part of their chiefs, like Porlier, Lacy, Eroles, and Villacampa, from the ranks of distinguished officers of the line, while the line in its turn afterward received guerrilla chiefs, like Mina, Empecinado, etc.—were the most revolutionized portion of Spanish society, recruited as they were from all ranks, including the whole of the fiery, aspiring, and patriotic youth, inaccessible to the soporific influence of the central government; emancipated from the shackles of the ancient regime; part of them, like Riego, returning after some years' captivity in France. We are, then, not to be surprised at the influence exercised by the Spanish army in subsequent commotions, neither when taking the revolutionary initiative nor when spoiling the revolution by praetorianism.

As to the guerrillas, it is evident that, having for some years figured upon the theater of sanguinary contests, taken to roving habits, freely indulged all their passions of hatred, revenge, and love of plunder, they must in times of peace form a most dangerous mob, always ready at a nod in the name of any party or principle to step forward for him who is able to give them good pay or to afford them a pretext for plundering excursions.

VI*

On September 24, 1810, the Extraordinary Cortes assembled on the Isla de León; on February 20, 1811, they removed their sittings thence to Cádiz; on March 19, 1812, they promulgated the New Constitution; and on September 20, 1813, they closed their sittings, three years from the period of their opening.

The circumstances under which this Congress met are without parallel in history. While no legislative body had ever before gathered its members from such various parts of the globe, or pretended to control such immense territories in Europe, America, and Asia, such a diversity of races and such a complexity of interests— nearly the whole of Spain was occupied by the French, and the Congress itself, actually cut off from Spain by hostile armies, and relegated to a small neck of land, had to legislate in the sight of a surrounding and besieging army. From the remote angle of the Isla Gaditana they undertook to lay the foundation of a new Spain, as their forefathers had done from the mountains of Cavadonga and Sobrarve.⁶ How are we to account for the curious phenomenon of the Constitution of 1812, afterward branded by the crowned heads of Europe, assembled at Verona, as the most incendiary invention of Jacobinism, having sprung up from the head of old monastic and absolutist Spain at the very epoch when she seemed totally absorbed in waging a holy war against the Revolution? How, on the other hand, are we to account for the sudden disappearance of this same constitution, vanishing like a shadow—like the *"sueño de sombra,"* say the Spanish historians—when brought into contact with a living Bourbon? If the birth of that constitution is a riddle, its death is no less so. To solve the enigma, we propose to commence with a short review of this same Constitution of 1812, which the Spaniards tried again to realize at two subsequent epochs, first during the period from 1820 to 1823, and then in 1836.

The Constitution of 1812 consists of 334 articles and comprehends the following ten divisions: 1. On the Spanish nation and the Spaniards. 2. On the territory of Spain; its religion, government, and on Spanish citizens. 3. On the Cortes. 4. On the king. 5. On the tribunals and administration of justice in civil and criminal matters. 6. On the interior government of the provinces and communes. 7. On the taxes. 8. On the national military forces. 9. On public education. 10. On the observance of the constitution, and mode of proceeding to make alterations therein.

---

* *New-York Daily Tribune*, November 24, 1854.
6. In 718 the Spanish defeated the Arabs at Cavadonga; resistance against the Arabs continued in Sobrarve, in Aragon.

Proceeding from the principle that "the sovereignty resides essentially in the nation, to which, therefore, alone belongs exclusively the right of establishing fundamental laws," the constitution, nevertheless, proclaims a division of powers, according to which "the legislative power is placed in the Cortes jointly with the king"; "the execution of the laws is confided to the king"; "the application of the laws in civil and criminal affairs belongs exclusively to the tribunals, neither the Cortes nor the king being in any case empowered to exercise judicial authority, advocate pending cases, or command the revisal of concluded judgment."

The basis of the national representation is mere population, one deputy for every 70,000 souls. The Cortes consists of one house, viz., the commons, the election of the deputies being by universal suffrage. The elective franchise is enjoyed by all Spaniards, with the exception of menial servants, bankrupts, and criminals. After the year 1830, no citizen can enjoy this right who cannot read and write. The election is, however, indirect, having to pass through the three degrees of parochial, district, and provincial elections. There is no defined property qualification for a deputy. It is true that according to Article 92, "It is necessary, in order to be eligible as a deputy to the Cortes, to possess a proportionate annual income, proceeding from real personal property," but Article 93 suspends the preceding article until the Cortes in their future meetings declare the period to have arrived in which it shall take effect. The king has the right neither to dissolve nor to prorogue the Cortes, who annually meet at the capital on the first of March, without being convoked, and sit at least three months consecutively.

A new Cortes is elected every second year, and no deputy can sit in two Cortes consecutively; i.e., one can be reelected only after an intervening Cortes of two years. No deputy can ask or accept rewards, pensions, or honors from the king. The secretaries of state, the councilors of state, and those fulfilling offices of the royal household are ineligible as deputies to the Cortes. No public officer employed by government shall be elected deputy to the Cortes from the province in which he discharges his trust. To indemnify the deputies for their expenses, the respective provinces shall contribute such daily allowances as the Cortes, in the second year of every General Deputation, shall point out for the deputation that is to succeed it. The Cortes cannot deliberate in the presence of the king. In those cases where the ministers have any communication to make to the Cortes in the name of the king, they may attend the debates when, and in such manner, as the Cortes may think fit, and may speak therein, but they cannot be present at a vote. The king, the Prince of Asturias, and the regents have to swear to the constitution before the Cortes, who determine any question of fact or right that may occur in the order of the succession to the crown, and elect a regency if necessary. The Cortes are to approve, previous to ratification, all treaties of offensive alliance, or of subsidies and commerce, to permit or refuse the admission of foreign troops into the kingdom, to decree the creation and suppression of offices in the tribunals established by the constitution, and also the creation or abolition of public offices; to determine every year, at the recommendation of the king, the land and sea forces in peace and in war, to issue ordinances to the army, the fleet, and the national militia in all their branches; to fix the expenses of the public administration; to establish annually the taxes, to take property on loan, in cases of necessity, upon the credit of the public funds, to decide on all matters respecting money, weights and measures; to establish a general plan of public education, to protect the political liberty of the press, to render real and effective the responsibility of the ministers, etc. The king enjoys only a suspensive veto, which he may exercise during two consecutive sessions, but if the same project of new law should be proposed a third time, and approved by the Cortes of the following year, the king is understood to have given his assent, and has actually to give it. Before the Cortes terminate a session, they appoint a permanent committee, consisting of seven of their members, sitting in the capital until the meeting of the next Cortes, endowed with powers to watch over the strict observance of the constitution and administration of the laws; reporting to the next Cortes any infraction it may have observed, and empowered to convoke an extraordinary Cortes in critical times. The king cannot quit the kingdom without the consent of the Cortes. He requires the consent of the Cortes for contracting a marriage. The Cortes fix the annual revenue of the king's household.

The only privy council of the king is the Council of State, in which the ministers have no seat, and which consists of forty persons, four ecclesiastics, four grandees of Spain, and the rest formed by distinguished administrators, all of them chosen by the king from a list of one hundred and twenty persons nominated by the Cortes; but no actual deputy can be a councilor, and no councilor can accept offices, honors, or employment from the king. The Councilors of State cannot be removed without sufficient reasons, proved before the Supreme Court of Justice. The Cortes fix the salary of these councilors whose opinion the king will hear upon all important matters, and who nominate the candidates for ecclesiastical and judicial places. In the sections respecting the judicature, all the old *consejos* are abolished, a new organization of tribunals is introduced, a Supreme Court of Justice is established to try the ministers when impeached, to take cognizance of all cases of dismissal and suspension from office of Councilors of State and the officers of Courts of Justice, etc. Without proof that reconciliation has been attempted, no lawsuit can be commenced. Torture, compulsion, confiscation of property are suppressed. All exceptional tribunals are abolished but the military and ecclesiastic, against the decisions of which appeals to the Supreme Court are however permitted.

For the interior government of towns and communes (communes, where they do not exist, to be formed from districts with a population of 1,000 souls), Ayuntamientos shall be formed of one or more magistrates, aldermen, and public councilors, to be presided over by the chief of police (*corregidor*) and to be chosen by general election. No public officer actually employed and appointed by the king can be eligible as a magistrate, alderman, or public councilor. The municipal employments shall be public duty, from which no person can be exempt without lawful reason. The municipal corporations shall discharge all their duties under the inspection of the provincial deputation.

The political government of the provinces shall be placed in the governor (*jefe político*) appointed by the king. This governor is connected with a deputation over which he presides, and which is elected by the districts when assembled for the general election of the members for a new Cortes. These provincial deputations consist of seven members, assisted by a secretary paid by the Cortes. These deputations shall hold sessions for ninety days at most in every year. From the powers and duties assigned to them, they may be considered as permanent committees of the Cortes. All members of the Ayuntamientos and provincial deputations, in entering office, swear fidelity to the constitution. With regard to the taxes, all Spaniards are bound, without any distinction whatever, to contribute, in proportion to their means, to the expenses of the state. All customhouses shall be suppressed, except in the seaports and on the frontier. All Spaniards are likewise bound to military service, and, beside the standing army, there shall be formed corps of national militia in each province, consisting of the inhabitants of the same, in proportion to its population and circumstances. Lastly, the Constitution of 1812 cannot be altered, augmented, or corrected in any of its details until eight years have elapsed after its having been carried into practice.

When the Cortes drew up this new plan of the Spanish state, they were of course aware that such a modern political constitution would be altogether incompatible with the old social system, and consequently they promulgated a series of decrees with a view to organic changes in civil society. Thus they abolished the Inquisition. They suppressed the seignorial jurisdiction, with their exclusive, prohibitive, and privative feudal privileges, i.e., those of the chase, fishery, forests, mills, etc., excepting such as had been acquired on an onerous title, and which were to be reimbursed. They abolished the tithes throughout the monarchy, suspended the nominations of all ecclesiastic prebends not necessary for the performance of divine services, and took steps for the suppression of the monasteries and the sequestration of their property.

They intended to transform the immense wastelands, royal domains, and commons of Spain into private property, by selling one-half of them for the extinction of the public debt, distributing another part by lot as a patriotic remuneration for the disbanded soldiers of the War of Independence, and granting a third part, gratuitously, and also by lot, to the poor peasantry who should desire to possess but not be able to buy them. They allowed the enclosure of pastures and other real property, formerly forbidden. They repealed the absurd laws which prevented pasture from being converted into arable land or arable land converted into pasture, and generally freed agriculture from the old arbitrary and ridiculous rules. They revoked all feudal laws with respect to farming contracts, and the law according to which the successor of an entailed estate was not obliged to confirm the leases granted by his predecessor, the leases expiring with him who had granted them. They abolished the *Voto de Santiago,* under which name was understood an ancient tribute of a certain measure of the best bread and the best wine to be paid by the laborers of certain provinces principally for the maintenance of the Archbishop and Chapter of Santiago. They decreed the introduction of a large progressive tax, etc.

It being one of their principal aims to hold possession of the American colonies, which had already begun to revolt, they acknowledged the full political equality of the American and European Spaniards, proclaimed a general amnesty without any exception, issued decrees against the oppression weighing upon the original natives of America and Asia, canceled the *mitas,*[7] the *repartimientos,*[8] etc., abolished the monopoly of quicksilver, and took the lead of Europe in suppressing the slave trade.

The Constitution of 1812 has been accused on the one hand—for instance, by Ferdinand VII himself (see his decree of May 4, 1814)— of being a mere imitation of the French Constitution of 1791, trans-

---

7. Indians chosen by lottery for public works.
8. The right of employers to use as many aliens on their lands as they could support.

planted on the Spanish soil by visionaries, regardless of the historical traditions of Spain. On the other hand, it has been contended—for instance, by the Abbé de Pradt (*De la révolution actuelle de l'Espagne*)—that the Cortes unreasonably clung to antiquated formulas, borrowed from the ancient *Fueros* [statutes] and belonging to feudal times, when the royal authority was checked by the exorbitant privileges of the grandees.

The truth is that the Constitution of 1812 is a reproduction of the ancient *Fueros*, but read in the light of the French Revolution and adapted to the wants of modern society. The right of insurrection, for instance, is generally regarded as one of the boldest innovations of the Jacobin Constitution of 1793, but you meet this same right in the ancient *Fueros* of Sobrarve, where it is called the "*Privilegio de la Union.*" You find it also in the ancient Constitution of Castile. According to the *Fueros* of Sobrarve, the king cannot make peace nor declare war, nor conclude treaties, without the previous consent of the Cortes. The Permanent Committee, consisting of seven members of the Cortes, who are to watch over the strict observance of the constitution during the prorogation of the legislative body, was of old established in Aragon, and was introduced into Castile at the time when the principal Cortes of the monarchy were united in one single body. To the period of the French invasion a similar institution still existed in the kingdom of Navarre. Touching the formation of a State Council from a list of 120 persons presented to the king by the Cortes and paid by them—this singular creation of the Constitution of 1812 was suggested by the remembrance of the fatal influence exercised by the camarillas at all epochs of the Spanish monarchy. The State Council was intended to supersede the camarilla. Besides, there existed analogous institutions in the past. At the time of Ferdinand IV, for instance, the king was always surrounded by twelve commoners, designated by the cities of Castile, to serve as his privy councilors; and in 1419 the delegates of the cities complained that their commissioners were no longer admitted into the king's council. The exclusion of the highest functionaries and the members of the king's household from the Cortes, as well as the prohibition to the deputies to accept honors or office on the part of the king, seems, at first view, to be borrowed from the Constitution of 1812. But in fact we meet not only in the ancient Constitution of Castile with precedents, but we know that the people, at different times, rose and assassinated the deputies who had accepted honors or offices from the crown. As to the right of the Cortes to appoint regencies in case of minority, it had continually been exercised by the ancient Cortes of Castile during the long minorities of the fourteenth century.

It is true that the Cádiz Cortes deprived the king of the power he had always exercised of convoking, dismissing, or proroguing the Cortes, but as the Cortes had fallen into disuse by the very manner in which the kings improved their privileges, there was nothing more evident than the necessity of canceling it. The alleged facts may suffice to show that the anxious limitation of the royal power—the most striking feature of the Constitution of 1812—otherwise fully explained by the recent and revolting *souvenirs* of Godoy's contemptible despotism, derived its origin from the ancient *Fueros* of Spain. The Cádiz Cortes but transferred the control from the privileged estates to the national representation. How much the Spanish kings stood in awe of the ancient *Fueros* may be seen from the fact that when a new collection of the Spanish laws had become necessary, in 1805, a royal ordinance ordered the removal from it of all the remains of feudalism contained in the last collection of laws and belonging to a time when the weakness of the monarchy forced the kings to enter with their vassals into compromise derogatory to the sovereign power.

If the election of the deputies by general suffrage was an innovation, it must not be forgotten that the Cortes of 1812 were themselves elected by general suffrage, that all the juntas had been elected by it; that a limitation of it would therefore have been an infraction of a right already conquered by the people; and, lastly, that a property qualification, at a time when almost all the real property of Spain was locked up in mortmain, would have excluded the greater part of the population.

The meeting of the representatives in one single house was by no means copied from the French Constitution of 1791, as the morose English Tories will have it. Our readers know already that since Carlos I (the Emperor Charles V) the aristocracy and the clergy had lost their seats in the Cortes of Castile. But even at the time when the Cortes were divided into *brazas* (arms, branches) representing the different estates, they assembled in one single hall, separated only by their seats and voting in common. From the province in which alone the Cortes still possessed real power at the epoch of the French invasion, Navarre continued the old custom of convoking the Cortes by estates: but in the Vasongadas [Basque provinces] the altogether democratic assemblies admitted not even the clergy. Besides, if the clergy and aristocracy had saved their obnoxious privileges, they had long since ceased to form independent political bodies, the existence of which constituted the basis of the composition of the ancient Cortes.

The separation of the judiciary from the executive power, decreed by the Cádiz Cortes, was demanded as early as the eighteenth century by the most enlightened statesmen of Spain; and the general claim which the *Consejo Real* from the beginning of the revolution had concentrated upon itself made the necessity of reducing the tribunals to their proper sphere of action universally felt.

The section of the constitution which refers to the municipal government of the communes is a genuine Spanish offspring, as we have shown in a former article. The Cortes only reestablished the old municipal system while they stripped off its medieval character. As to the provincial deputations, invested with the same powers for the internal government of the provinces as the Ayuntamientos for the administration of the communes, the Cortes modeled them in imitation of similar institutions still existing at the time of the invasion in Navarre, Biscay, and Asturias. In abolishing the exemptions from the military service, the Cortes sanctioned only what had become the general practice during the War of Independence. The abolition of the Inquisition was also but the sanction of a fact, as the Holy Office, although reestablished by the Central Junta, had not dared to resume its functions, its holy members being content with pocketing their salaries and prudently waiting for better times. As to the suppression of feudal abuses, the Cortes went not even the length of the reforms insisted upon in the famous memorial of Jovellanos, presented in 1795 to the *Consejo Real* in the name of the economical society of Madrid.

The ministers of the enlightened despotism of the latter part of the eighteenth century, Florida Blanca and Campomanes, had already begun to take steps in this direction. Besides, it must not be forgotten that simultaneously with the Cortes there sat a French government at Madrid which, in all the provinces overrun by the armies of Napoleon, had swept away from the soil all monastic and feudal institutions and introduced the modern system of administration. The Bonapartist papers denounced the insurrection as entirely produced by the artifices and bribes of England, assisted by the monks and the Inquisition. How far the rivalry with the intruding government must have exercised a salutary influence upon the decisions of the Cortes may be inferred from the fact that the Central Junta itself, in its decree dated September, 1809, wherein the convocation of the Cortes is announced, addressed the Spaniards in the following terms: "Our detractors say that we are fighting to defend old abuses and the inveterate vices of our corrupted government. Let them know that your struggle is for the happiness as well as the independence of your country; that you will not depend henceforward on the uncertain will or the various temper of a single man," etc.

On the other hand, we may trace in the Constitution of 1812 symptoms not to be mistaken of a compromise entered into between the liberal ideas of the eighteenth century and the dark traditions of priestcraft. It suffices to quote Article 12, according to which "the religion of the Spanish nation is and shall be perpetually Catholic, Apostolic, and Roman, the only true religion. The nation protects it by wise and just laws, and prohibits the exercise of any other whatever"; or Article 173, ordering the king to take, on his accession to the throne, the following oath before the Cortes: "N., by the grace of God, and the Constitution of the Spanish Monarchy, the King of Spain, I swear by the Almighty and the Holy Evangelists that I will defend and preserve the Catholic, Roman, and Apostolic religion, without tolerating any other in the kingdom."

On a closer analysis, then, of the Constitution of 1812, we arrive at the conclusion that, so far from being a servile copy of the French Constitution of 1791, it was a genuine and original offspring of Spanish intellectual life, regenerating the ancient and national institutions, introducing the measures of reform loudly demanded by the most celebrated authors and statesmen of the eighteenth century, making inevitable concessions to popular prejudice.

VII*

There were some circumstances favorable to the assembling at Cádiz of the most progressive men of Spain. When the elections took place, the movement had not yet subsided, and the very disfavor which the Central Junta had incurred recommended its antagonists, who to a great extent belonged to the revolutionary minority of the nation. At the first meeting of the Cortes, the most democratic provinces, Catalonia and Galicia, were almost exclusively represented; the deputies from León, Valencia, Murcia, and the Balearic Isles not arriving till three months later. The most reactionary provinces, those of the interior, were not allowed, except in some few localities, to proceed with the elections for the Cortes. For the different kingdoms, cities and towns of old Spain, which the French armies prevented from choosing deputies, as well as for the ultramarine provinces of New Spain, whose deputies could not arrive in due time, supplementary representatives were elected from the many individuals whom the troubles of the war had driven from the provinces to Cádiz, and the numerous South Americans, merchants, natives, and others, whose curiosity or the state of affairs had likewise assembled at that place. Thus it happened that those provinces were represented by men more fond of innovation, and more impregnated with the ideas of the

---

eighteenth century, than would have been the case if they had been enabled to choose for themselves. Lastly, the circumstances of the Cortes meeting at Cádiz was of decisive influence, that city being then known as the most radical of the kingdom, more resembling an American than a Spanish town. Its population filled the galleries in the Hall of the Cortes and domineered the reactionists, when their opposition grew too obnoxious, by a system of intimidation and pressure from without.

It would, however, be a great mistake to suppose that the majority of the Cortes consisted of reformers. The Cortes was divided into three parties—the *Serviles*, the *Liberales* (these party denominations spread from Spain through the whole of Europe), and the *Americanos*, the latter voting alternately with the one or the other party, according to their particular interests. The Serviles, far superior in numbers, were carried away by the activity, zeal, and enthusiasm of the Liberal minority. The ecclesiastic deputies, who formed the majority of the Servile party, were always ready to sacrifice the royal prerogative, partly from the remembrance of the antagonism of the Church to the state, partly with a view to courting popularity, in order thus to save the privileges and abuses of their caste. During the debates on the general suffrage, the one-chamber system, the no-property qualification, and the suspensive veto the ecclesiastic party always combined with the more democratic part of the Liberals against the partisans of the English Constitution. One of them, the Canon Cañedo, afterward Archbishop of Burgos, and an implacable persecutor of the Liberals, addressed Señor Muñoz Torrero, also a canon, but belonging to the Liberal party, in these terms: "You suffer the king to remain excessively powerful, but as a priest you ought to plead the cause of the Church, rather than that of the king." Into these compromises with the Church party the Liberals were forced to enter, as we have already shown from some articles of the Constitution of 1812. When the liberty of the press was discussed, the parsons denounced it as "contrary to religion." After the most stormy debates, and after having declared that all persons were at liberty to publish their sentiments without special license, the Cortes unanimously admitted an amendment which, by inserting the word *political*, curtailed this liberty of half its extent, and left all writings upon religious matters subject to the censure of the ecclesiastic authorities, according to the decrees of the Council of Trent. On August 18, 1817, after a decree passed against all who should conspire against the constitution, another decree was passed, declaring that whoever should conspire to make the Spanish nation cease to profess the Catholic Roman religion should be prosecuted as a traitor, and suffer death. When the *Voto de Santiago* was abolished, a compensatory resolution was carried, declaring St. Teresa de Jesús the patroness of Spain. The Liberals also took care not to propose and carry the decrees about the abolition of the Inquisition, the tithes, the monasteries, etc., till after the constitution had been proclaimed. But from that very moment the opposition of the Serviles within the Cortes, and the clergy without, became inexorable.

Having now explained the circumstances which account for the origin and the characteristic features of the Constitution of 1812, there still remains the problem to be solved of its sudden and resistless disappearance at the return of Ferdinand VII. A more humiliating spectacle has seldom been witnessed by the world. When Ferdinand entered Valencia, on April 16, 1814, "the joyous people yoked themselves to his carriage, and testified by every possible expression of word and deed their desire of taking the old yoke upon themselves, shouting, 'Long live the absolute King!' 'Down with the constitution!' " In all the large towns the Plaza Mayor, or Great Square, had been named Plaza de la Constitucion, and a stone with these words engraved on it erected there. In Valencia this stone was removed and a "provisional" stone of wood set up in its place with the inscription: *Real Plaza de Fernando VII.* The populace of Seville deposed all the existing authorities, elected others in their stead to all the offices which had existed under the old regime, and then required those authorities to reestablish the Inquisition. From Aranjuez to Madrid Ferdinand's carriage was drawn by the people. When the King alighted the mob took him up in their arms, triumphantly showed him to the immense concourse assembled in front of the palace, and in their arms conveyed him to his apartments. The word "Liberty" appeared in large bronze letters over the entrance of the Hall of the Cortes in Madrid; the rabble hurried thither to remove it; they set up ladders, forced out letter by letter from the stone, and as each was thrown into the street the spectators renewed their shouts of exultation. They collected as many of the journals of the Cortes and of the papers and pamphlets of the Liberals as could be got together, formed a procession in which the religious fraternities and the clergy, regular and secular, took the lead, piled up these papers in one of the public squares, and sacrificed them there as a political auto-da-fé, after which high mass was performed and the Te Deum sung as a thanksgiving for their triumph. More important, perhaps—since these shameless demonstrations of the town mob partly paid for their performances, and like the *lazzaroni* of Naples preferring the wanton rule of kings and monks to the sober regime of the middle classes—is the fact that the second general elections resulted in a decisive victory of the Serviles; the Constituent Cortes being replaced by the ordinary Cortes on September 20, 1813, who transferred their sittings from Cádiz to Madrid on January 15, 1814.

We have shown in former articles how the revolutionary party itself had participated in rousing and strengthening the old popular prejudices, with a view to turn them into so many weapons against Napoleon. We have then seen how the Central Junta, at the only period when social changes were to be blended with measures of national defense, did all in their power to prevent them, and to suppress the revolutionary aspirations of the provinces. The Cádiz Cortes, on the contrary, cut off during the greater part of their existence from all connection with Spain, were not even enabled to make their constitution and their organic decrees known, except as the French armies retired. The Cortes arrived, as it were, *post factum*. They found society fatigued, exhausted, suffering, the necessary product of so protracted a war, entirely carried on upon the Spanish soil—a war in which, the armies being always on the move, the government of today was seldom that of tomorrow, while bloodshed did not cease one single day during almost six years throughout the whole surface of Spain, from Cádiz to Pamplona, and from Granada to Salamanca. It was not to be expected that such a society should be very sensible of the abstract beauties of any political constitution whatever. Nevertheless, when the constitution was first proclaimed at Madrid, and the other provinces evacuated by the French, it was received with "exultant delight," the masses being generally expecting a sudden disappearance of their social sufferings from mere change of government. When they discovered that the constitution was not possessed of such miraculous powers, the very overstrained expectations which had welcomed it turned into disappointment, and with these passionate southern peoples there is but one step from disappointment to hatred.

There were some particular circumstances which principally contributed to estrange the popular sympathies from the constitutional regime. The Cortes had published the severest decrees against the *Afrancesados* or Josephites. The Cortes were partly driven to these decrees by the vindictive clamor of the populace and the reactionists, who at once turned against the Cortes as soon as the decrees they had wrung from them were put to execution. Upwards of 10,000 families became thus exiled. A lot of petty tyrants let loose on the provinces evacuated by the French established their proconsular authority and began by inquiries, prosecution, prison, inquisitorial proceedings against those compromised through adherence to the French, by having accepted offices from them, bought national property from them, etc. The Regency, instead of trying to effect the transition from the French to the national regime in a conciliatory and discreet way, did all in their power to aggravate the evils and exasperate the passions inseparable from such changes of dominion. But why did they do so? In order to be able to ask from the Cortes a suspension of the Constitution of 1812, which, they told them, worked so very offensively. Be it remarked, *en passant*, that all the regencies, these supreme executive authorities appointed by the Cortes, were regularly composed of the most decided enemies of the Cortes and their constitution. This curious fact is simply explained by the Americans always combining with the Serviles in the appointment of the executive power, the weakening of which they considered necessary for the attainment of American independence from the mother country, since they were sure that an executive simply at variance with the sovereign Cortes would prove insufficient. The introduction by the Cortes of a single direct tax upon the rental of land, as well as upon industrial and commercial produce, excited also great discontent among the people, and still more so the absurd decrees forbidding the circulation of all Spanish specie coined by Joseph Bonaparte and ordering its possessors to exchange it for national coin, simultaneously interdicting the circulation of French money, and proclaiming a tariff at which it was to be exchanged at the national mint. As this tariff greatly differed from that proclaimed by the French in 1808 for the relative value of French and Spanish coins, many private individuals were involved in great losses. This absurd measure also contributed to raise the price of the first necessaries, already highly above the average rates.

The classes most interested in the overthrow of the Constitution of 1812 and the restoration of the old regime—the grandees, the clergy, the friars, and the lawyers—did not fail to excite to the highest pitch the popular discontent created by the unfortunate circumstances which had marked the introduction on the Spanish soil of the constitutional regime. Hence the victory of the Serviles in the general elections of 1813.

Only on the part of the army could the King apprehend any serious resistance, but General Elio and his officers, breaking the oath they had sworn to the constitution, proclaimed Ferdinand VII at Valencia without mentioning the constitution. Elio was soon followed by the other military chiefs.

In his decree, dated May 4, 1814, in which Ferdinand VII dissolved the Madrid Cortes and canceled the Constitution of 1812, he simultaneously proclaimed his hatred of despotism, promised to convene the Cortes under the old legal forms, to establish a rational liberty of the press, etc. He redeemed his pledge in the only manner which the reception he had met on the part of the Spanish people deserved—by rescinding all the acts emanating from the Cortes, by restoring everything to its ancient footing, by reestablishing the Holy Inquisition, by recalling the Jesuits banished by his grandsire, by consigning the most prominent members of the juntas, the Cortes, and their adherents to the galleys, African prisons, or to exile; and finally, by ordering the most illustrious guerrilla chiefs, Porlier and de Lacy, to be shot.

VIII*

During the year 1819 an expeditionary army was assembled in the environs of Cádiz for the purpose of reconquering the revolted American colonies. Henri O'Donnell, Count of Abisbal, the uncle of Leopold O'Donnell, the present Spanish Minister, was entrusted with the command. The former expeditions against Spanish America, having swallowed up 14,000 men since 1811 and being carried out in the most disgusting and reckless manner, had grown most odious to the army, and were generally considered a malicious means of getting rid of the dissatisfied regiments. Several officers, among them Quiroga, López Baños, San Miguel (the present Spanish Lafayette), O'Daly, and Arco Agüero, determined to improve the discontent of the soldiers, to shake off the yoke, and to proclaim the Constitution of 1812. Abisbal, when initiated into the plot, promised to put himself at the head of the movement. The chiefs of the conspiracy, in conjunction with him, fixed on July 9, 1819, as the day on which a general review of the expeditionary troops was to take place, in the midst of which act the grand blow was to be struck. At the hour of the review Abisbal appeared indeed, but instead of keeping his word ordered the conspiring regiments to be disarmed, sent Quiroga and the other chiefs to prison, and dispatched a courier to Madrid, boasting that he had prevented the most alarming of catastrophes. He was rewarded with promotion and decorations, but the court, having obtained more accurate information, afterward deprived him of his command and ordered him to withdraw to the capital. This is the same Abisbal who in 1814, at the time of the King's return to Spain, sent an officer of his staff with two letters to Ferdinand. Too great a distance from the spot rendering it impossible for him to observe the King's movements and to regulate his conduct according to that of the monarch, in one letter Abisbal made a pompous eulogy of the Constitution of 1812, on the supposition that the King would take the oath to support it, in the other, on the contrary, he represented the constitutional system as a scheme of anarchy and confusion, congratulated Ferdinand on

---

* New-York Daily Tribune, December 2, 1854.

his exterminating it, and offered himself and his army to oppose the rebels, demagogues, and enemies of the throne and altar. The officer delivered this second dispatch, which was cordially received by the Bourbon.

Notwithstanding the symptoms of rebellion which had shown themselves among the expeditionary army, the Madrid government, at the head of which was placed the Duke of San Fernando, then Foreign Minister and President of the Cabinet, persisted in a state of inexplicable apathy and inactivity, and did nothing to accelerate the expedition, or to scatter the army in different seaport towns. Meanwhile a simultaneous movement was agreed upon between Don Raphael del Riego, commanding the second battalion of Asturias, then stationed at Las Cabezas de San Juan, and Quiroga, San Miguel, and other military chiefs of the Isla de León, who had contrived to get out of prison. Riego's position was far the most difficult. The commune of Las Cabezas was in the center of three of the headquarters of the expeditionary army—that of the cavalry at Utrera, the second division of infantry at Lebrija, and a battalion of guides at Arcos, where the commander in chief and the staff were established. He nevertheless succeeded, on January 1, 1820, in surprising and capturing the commander and the staff, although the battalion centered at Arcos was double the strength of that of Asturias. On the same day he proclaimed in that very commune the Constitution of 1812, elected a provincial alcalde, and, not content with having executed the task devolved upon him, seduced the guides to his cause, surprised the battalion of Aragon lying at Bornos, marched from Bornos on Xeres, and from Xeres on Port St. Marie, everywhere proclaiming the constitution, till he reached the Isla de León, on the seventh of January, where he deposited the military prisoners he had made in the fort of St. Petri. Contrary to their previous agreement, Quiroga and his followers had not possessed themselves by a *coup de main* of the bridge of Suazo, and then of the Isla de León, but remained tranquil to the second of January, after Oltra, Riego's messenger, had conveyed to them official intelligence of the surprise of Arcos and the capture of the staff.

The whole forces of the revolutionary army, the supreme command of which was given to Quiroga, did not exceed 5,000 men, and their attacks upon the gates of Cádiz having been repulsed, they were themselves shut up in the Isla de León. "Our situation," says San Miguel, "was extraordinary, the revolution, stationary for twenty-five days without losing or gaining one inch of ground, presented one of the most singular phenomena in politics." The provinces seemed rocked into lethargic slumber. During the whole month of January, at the end of which Riego, apprehending the flame of revolution might be extinguished in the Isla de León, formed, against the councils of Quiroga and the other chiefs, a movable column of 1,500 men, and marched over a part of Andalusia, in presence of and pursued by a ten times stronger force than his own, proclaiming the constitution at Algeciras, Ronda, Málaga, Cordova, etc., everywhere received by the inhabitants in a friendly way, but nowhere provoking a serious pronunciamento. Meanwhile his pursuers, consuming a whole month in fruitless marches and countermarches, seemed to desire nothing but to avoid, as much as possible, coming to close quarters with his little army. The conduct of the government troops was altogether inexplicable. Riego's expedition, which began on January 27, 1820, terminated on March 11, he being then forced to disband the few men that still followed him. His small corps was not dispersed through a decisive battle, but disappeared from fatigue, from continual petty encounters with the enemy, from sickness and desertion. Meanwhile the situation of the insurrectionists in the Isla was by no means promising. They continued to be blocked up by sea and land, and within the town of Cádiz every declaration for their cause was suppressed by the garrison. How then did it happen that, Riego having disbanded in the Sierra Morena the constitutional troops on the eleventh of March, Ferdinand VII was forced to swear to the constitution, at Madrid, on the ninth of March, so that Riego really gained his end just two days before he finally despaired of his cause?

The march of Riego's column had riveted anew the general attention; the provinces were all expectation, and eagerly watched every movement. Men's minds, struck by the boldness of Riego's sally, the rapidity of his march, his vigorous repulses of the enemy, imagined triumphs never gained, and aggregations and reinforcement never obtained. When the tidings of Riego's enterprise reached the more distant provinces, they were magnified in no small degree, and those most remote from the spot were the first to declare themselves for the Constitution of 1812. So far was Spain matured for a revolution that even false news sufficed to produce it. So, too, it was false news that produced the hurricane of 1848.

In Galicia, Valencia, Saragossa, Barcelona, and Pamplona, successive insurrections broke out. Henri O'Donnell, alias the Count of Abisbal, being summoned by the King to oppose the expedition of Riego, not only offered to take arms against him but to annihilate his little army and seize on his person. He only demanded the command of the troops cantoned in the province of La Mancha, and money for his personal necessities. The King himself gave him a purse of gold and the requisite orders for the troops of La Mancha. But on his arrival at Ocaña, Abisbal put himself at the head of the troops and proclaimed the Constitution of 1812. The news of the defection roused the public spirit of Madrid, where the revolution burst forth immediately on the intelligence of this event. The government began then to negotiate with the revolution. In a decree dated March 6, the King offered to convoke the *ancient* Cortes, assembled in *Estamentos* (estates), a decree uniting no party, neither that of the old monarchy nor that of the revolution. On his return from France he had held out the same promise and failed to redeem his pledge. During the night of the seventh, revolutionary demonstrations having taken place in Madrid, the *Gaceta* of the eighth published a decree by which Ferdinand VII promised to swear to the Constitution of 1812. "Let all of us," he said in that decree, "and myself the first, fairly enter upon the path of the constitution." The people having got possession of the palace on the ninth, he saved himself only by reestablishing the Madrid Ayuntamiento of 1814, before which he swore to the constitution. He, for his part, did not care for false oaths, having always at hand a confessor ready to grant him full remission of all possible sins. Simultaneously a Consultative Junta was established, the first decree of which set free the political prisoners and recalled the political refugees. The prisons, now opened, sent the first constitutional ministry to the royal palace. Castro, Herreros, and A. Argüelles—who formed the first ministry—were martyrs of 1814 and deputies of 1812. The true source of the enthusiasm which had appeared on the accession of Ferdinand to the throne was joy at the removal of Charles IV, his father. And thus the source of general exultation at the proclamation of the Constitution of 1812 was joy at the removal of Ferdinand VII. As to the constitution itself, we know that, when finished, there were no territories in which to proclaim it. For the majority of the Spanish people it was like the unknown god worshiped by the ancient Athenians.

In our day it has been affirmed by English writers, with an express allusion to the present Spanish revolution, on the one hand that the movement of 1820 was but a military conspiracy, and on the other that it was but a Russian intrigue. Both assertions are equally ridiculous. As to the military insurrection, we have seen that, notwithstanding its failure, the revolution proved victorious; and besides, the riddle to be solved would not be the conspiracy of 5,000 soldiers, but the sanction of that conspiracy by an army of 35,000 men, and by a most loyal nation of twelve millions. That the revolution first acted through the ranks of the army is easily explained by the fact that, of all the bodies of the Spanish monarchy, the army was the only one thoroughly transformed and revolutionized during the War of Independence. As to Russian intrigue, it is not to be denied that Russia had her hands in the business of the Spanish revolution; that of all the European powers, Russia first acknowledged the Constitution of 1812, by the treaty concluded in Velike Luki, on July 20, 1812; that she first kindled the revolution of 1820, first denounced it to Ferdinand VII, first lighted the torch of counterrevolution on several points of the Peninsula, first solemnly protested against it before Europe, and finally forced France into an armed intervention against it. Monsieur de Tatishtshev, the Russian Ambassador, was certainly the most prominent character at the Court of Madrid—the invisible head of the camarilla. He had succeeded in introducing Antonio Ugarte, a wretch of low station, at court, and making him the head of the friars and footmen who, in their backstaircase council, swayed the nephew in the name of Ferdinand VII. By Tatishtshev, Ugarte was made director general of the expeditions against South America, and by Ugarte the Duke of San Fernando was appointed Foreign Minister and President of the Cabinet. Ugarte effected from Russia the purchase of rotten ships destined for the South American Expedition, for which the order of St. Ann was bestowed upon him. Ugarte prevented Ferdinand and his brother Don Carlos from presenting themselves to the army at the first moment of crisis. He was the mysterious author of the Duke of San Fernando's unaccountable apathy, and of the measures which led a Spanish Liberal to say at Paris in 1836: "One can hardly resist the conviction that the government was rendering itself the means for the overthrow of the existing order of things." If we add the curious fact that the President of the United States praised Russia in his message for her having promised not to suffer Spain to meddle with the South American colonies,[9] there can remain but little doubt as to the part acted by Russia in the Spanish Revolution. But what does all this prove? That Russia produced the revolution of 1820? By no means, but only that she prevented the Spanish Government from resisting it. That the revolution would have earlier or later overturned the absolute and monastic monarchy of Ferdinand VII is proved: (1) by the series of conspiracies which since 1814 had followed each other; (2) by the testimony of M. de Martignac, the French Commissary who accompanied the Duke of Angoulême at the time of the Legitimist invasion of Spain; (3) by testimony not to be rejected—that of Ferdinand himself.

In 1814 Mina intended a rising in Navarre, gave the first signal for resistance by an appeal to arms, entered the fortress of Pamplona,

---

9. James Monroe's Message to Congress, December 2, 1823, which enunciated the Monroe Doctrine.

but, distrusting his own followers, fled to France. In 1815 General Porlier, one of the most renowned guerrilleros of the War of Independence, proclaimed the constitution at Coruña. He was beheaded. In 1816 Richard intended capturing the King at Madrid. He was hanged. In 1817 Navarro, a lawyer, with four of his accomplices, expired on the scaffold at Valencia for having proclaimed the Constitution of 1812. In the same year the intrepid General Lacy was shot at Majorca for having committed the same crime. In 1818 Colonel Vidal, Captain Sola, and others, who had proclaimed the constitution at Valencia, were defeated and put to the sword. The Isla de León conspiracy then was but the last link in a chain formed by the bloody heads of so many valiant men from 1808 to 1814.

M. de Martignac who in 1833, shortly before his death, published his work *L'Espagne et ses Révolutions*,[10] makes the following statement: "Two years had passed away since Ferdinand VII had assumed his absolute power, and there continued still the proscriptions, proceeding from a camarilla recruited from the dregs of mankind. The whole state machinery was turned upside down; there reigned nothing but disorder, languor, and confusion—taxes most unequally distributed —the state of the finances was abominable—there were loans without credit, an impossibility of meeting the most urgent needs of the state, an army not paid, magistrates indemnifying themselves by bribery, a corrupt and do-nothing administration, unable to ameliorate anything, or even to preserve anything. Hence the general discontent of the people. The new constitutional system was received with enthusiasm by the great towns, the commercial and industrial classes, liberal professions, army, and proletariat. It was resisted by the monks, and it stupefied the country people."

Such are the confessions of a dying man who was mainly instrumental in subverting that new system. Ferdinand VII, in his decrees of June 1, 1817, March 1, 1817, April 11, 1817, November 24, 1819, etc., literally confirms the assertions of M. de Martignac, and resumes his lamentations in these words: "The miseries that resound in the ears of Our Majesty, on the part of the complaining people, overset one another." This shows that no Tatishtshev was needed to bring about a Spanish revolution.

---

10. The actual title of Martignac's work is *Essai historique sur la révolution d'Espagne et sur l'intervention de 1823* (Vol. I, Paris, 1832).

Coup d'État*

THE NEWS brought by the *Asia* yesterday, though later by three days than our previous advices, contains nothing to indicate a speedy conclusion of the civil war in Spain. O'Donnell's *coup d'état*, although victorious at Madrid, cannot yet be said to have finally succeeded. The French *Moniteur*, which at first put down the insurrection at Barcelona as a mere riot, is now obliged to confess that "the conflict there was very keen," but that "the success of the Queen's troops may be considered as secured." According to the version of that official journal, the combat at Barcelona lasted from five o'clock in the afternoon of July 18 till the same hour on the twenty-first—exactly three days—when the "insurgents" are said to have been dislodged from their quarters and fled into the country, pursued by cavalry. It is, however, averred that the insurgents still hold several towns in Catalonia, including Gerona, Junquera, and some smaller places. It also appears that Murcia, Valencia, and Seville have made their pronunciamentos against the *coup d'état;* that a battalion of the garrison of Pamplona, directed by the governor of that town on Soria, had pronounced against the government on the road, and marched to join the insurrection at Saragossa; and lastly that at Saragossa, from the beginning the acknowledged center of resistance, General Falcón had passed in review 16,000 soldiers of the line, reinforced by 15,000 militia and peasants from the environs.

At all events, the French Government considers the "insurrection" in Spain as not quelled, and Bonaparte, far from contenting himself with the sending of a batch of battalions to line the frontier, has

---

* *New-York Daily Tribune*, August 8, 1856. (Leading article, unsigned.)

[630]

ordered one brigade to advance to the Bidassoa, which brigade is being completed to a division by reinforcements from Montpellier and Toulouse. It seems also that a second division has been detached immediately from the army of Lyon, according to orders sent direct from Plombières on the 23d ult., and is now marching toward the Pyrenees, where by this time there is assembled a full *corps d'observation* of 25,000 men. Should the resistance to the O'Donnell government be able to hold its ground, should it prove formidable enough to inveigle Bonaparte into an armed invasion of the Peninsula, then the *coup d'état* of Madrid may have given the signal for the downfall of the *coup d'état* of Paris.

If we consider the general plot and the dramatis personae, this Spanish conspiracy of 1856 appears as the simple revival of the similar attempt of 1843, with some slight alterations, of course. Then, as now, Isabella at Madrid and Christina at Paris; Louis Philippe, instead of Louis Bonaparte, directing the movement from the Tuileries; on the one side, Espartero and his *Ayacuchos;* on the other, O'Donnell, Serrano, Concha, with Narvaez then in the proscenium, now in the background. In 1843, Louis Philippe sent two millions of gold by land and Narvaez and his friends by sea, the compact of the Spanish marriages being settled between himself and Mme. Muñoz. The complicity of Bonaparte in the Spanish *coup d'état*—who has, perhaps, settled the marriage of his cousin Prince Napoleon with a Mlle. Muñoz, or who at all events must continue his mission of mimicking his uncle—that complicity is not only indicated by the denunciations hurled by the *Moniteur* for the last two months at the communist conspiracies in Castile and Navarre, by the behavior before, during and after the *coup d'état* of M. de Turgot, the French Ambassador at Madrid, the same man who was the Foreign Minister of Bonaparte during his own *coup d'état;* by the Duke of Alba, Bonaparte's brother-in-law, turning up as the president of the new Ayuntamiento at Madrid immediately after the victory of O'Donnell; by Ros de Olano, an old member of the French party, being the first man offered a place in O'Donnell's ministry; and by Narvaez being dispatched to Bayonne by Bonaparte as soon as the first news of the affair reached Paris. That complicity was suggested beforehand by the forwarding of large quantities of ammunition from Bordeaux to Bayonne a fortnight in advance of the actual crisis at Madrid. Above all, it is suggested by the plan of operations followed by O'Donnell in his *razzia* against the people of that city. At the very outset he announced that he would not shrink from blowing up Madrid, and during the fighting he acted up to his word. Now, although a daring fellow, O'Donnell has never ventured upon a bold step without securing a safe retreat. Like his notorious uncle, the hero of treason, he never burned the bridge when he passed the Rubicon. The organ of combativeness is singularly checked in the O'Donnells by the organs of cautiousness and secretiveness. It is plain that any general who should hold forth the threat of laying the capital in ashes, and fail in his attempt, would forfeit his head. How then did O'Donnell venture upon such delicate ground? The secret is betrayed by the *Journal des Débats,* the special organ of Queen Christina. "O'Donnell expected a great battle, and at the most a victory hotly disputed. Into his previsions there entered the possibility of defeat. If such a misfortune had happened, the Marshal would have abandoned Madrid with the rest of his army, escorting the Queen, and turning toward the northern provinces, with a view to approach the French frontier." Does not all this look as if he had laid his plan with Bonaparte? Exactly the same plan had been settled between Louis Philippe and Narvaez in 1843, which, again, was copied from the secret convention between Louis XVIII and Ferdinand VII in 1823.

The plausible parallel between the Spanish conspiracies of 1843 and 1856 once admitted, there are still sufficiently distinct features in the movements to indicate the immense strides made by the Spanish people within so brief an epoch. These features are: the political character of the last struggle at Madrid; its military importance; and finally, the respective positions of Espartero and O'Donnell in 1856, compared with those of Espartero and Narvaez in 1843. In 1843 all parties had become tired of Espartero. To get rid of him, a powerful coalition was formed between the Moderados and Progresistas. Revolutionary juntas, springing up like mushrooms in all the towns, paved the way for Narvaez and his retainers. In 1856 we have not only the court and army on the one side against the people on the other, but within the ranks of the people we have the same divisions as in the rest of Western Europe. On the thirteenth of July the ministry of Espartero offered its forced resignation; in the night of the thirteenth and fourteenth the cabinet of O'Donnell was constituted; on the morning of the fourteenth the rumor spread that O'Donnell, charged with the formation of a cabinet, had invited Ríos Rosas, the ill-omened minister of the bloody days of July, 1854, to join him. At eleven A.M. the *Gaceta* confirmed the rumor. Then the Cortes assembled, ninety-three deputies being present. According to the rules of that body, twenty members suffice to call a meeting, and fifty to form a quorum. Besides, the Cortes had not been formally prorogued. General Infante, the President, could not but comply with the universal wish to hold a regular sitting. A proposition was submitted to the effect that the new cabinet did not enjoy the confidence of the Cortes, and that

Her Majesty should be informed of this resolution. At the same time the Cortes summoned the National Guard to be ready for action. Their committee, bearing the resolution of want of confidence, went to the Queen, escorted by a detachment of National Militia. While endeavoring to enter the palace they were driven back by the troops of the line, who fired upon them and their escort. This incident gave the signal for the insurrection. The order to commence the building of barricades was given at seven in the evening by the Cortes, whose meeting was dispersed immediately afterward by the troops of O'Donnell. The battle commenced the same night, only one battalion of the National Militia joining the royal troops. It should be noted that as early as the morning of the thirteenth, Señor Escosura, the Esparterist Minister of the Interior, had telegraphed to Barcelona and Saragossa that a *coup d'état* was at hand, and that they must prepare to resist it. At the head of the Madrid insurgents were Señor Madoz and General Valdez, the brother of Escosura. In short, there can be no doubt that the resistance to the *coup d'état* originated with the Esparterists, the citizens, and Liberals in general. While they, with the militia, engaged the line across Madrid from east to west, the workmen under Pucheta occupied the south and part of the north of the town.

On the morning of the fifteenth O'Donnell took the initiative. Even by the partial testimony of the *Débats*, O'Donnell obtained no marked advantage during the first half of the day. Suddenly, at about one o'clock, without any perceptible reason, the ranks of the National Militia were broken; at two o'clock they were still more thinned; and at six o'clock they had completely disappeared from the scene of action, leaving the whole brunt of the battle to be borne by the workmen, who fought it out till four in the afternoon of the sixteenth. Thus there were, in these days of carnage, two distinct battles—the one of the Liberal militia of the middle class, supported by the workmen against the army, and the other of the army against the workmen deserted by the militia. As Heine has it: "It is an old story, but is always new." Espartero deserts the Cortes; the Cortes desert the leaders of the National Guard; the leaders desert their men, and the men desert the people. On the fifteenth, however, the Cortes assembled again, when Espartero appeared for a moment. He was reminded by Señor Assensio and other members of his reiterated protestations to draw his grand sword of Luchana[1] on the first day when the liberty of the country should be endangered. Espartero called heaven to

1. Espartero was given the title of Count of Luchana for his victory over the Carlists in 1840.

witness his unswerving patriotism, and when he left, it was fully expected that he would soon be seen at the head of the insurrection. Instead of this, he went to the home of General Gurrea, where he buried himself in a bombproof cellar, à la Palafox, and was heard of no more. The commandants of the militia, who on the evening before had employed every means to excite the militiamen to take up arms, now proved as eager to retire to their private houses. At 2:00 P.M. General Valdez, who for some hours had usurped the command of the militia, convoked the soldiers under his direct command on the Plaza Mayor, and told them that the man who naturally ought to be at their head would not come forward, and that consequently everybody was at liberty to withdraw. Hereupon the National Guards rushed to their homes and hastened to get rid of their uniforms and hide their arms. Such is the substance of the account furnished by one well-informed authority. Another gives as the reason for this sudden act of submission to the conspiracy that it was considered that the triumph of the National Guard was likely to entail the ruin of the throne and the absolute preponderance of the republican democracy. The *Presse* of Paris also gives us to understand that Marshal Espartero, seeing the turn given to things in the congress by the democrats, did not wish to sacrifice the throne, or launch into the hazards of anarchy and civil war, and in consequence did all he could to produce submission to O'Donnell.

It is true that the details as to the time, circumstances, and breakdown of the resistance to the *coup d'état* are given differently by different writers; but all agree on the one principal point, that Espartero deserted the Cortes, the Cortes the leaders, the leaders the middle class, and that class the people. This furnishes a new illustration of the character of most of the European struggles of 1848–1849, and of those hereafter to take place in the western portion of that continent. On the one hand there are modern industry and trade, the natural chiefs of which, the middle classes, are averse to the military despotism; on the other hand, when they begin the battle against this same despotism, in step the workmen themselves, the product of the modern organization of labor, to claim their due share of the result of victory. Frightened by the consequences of an alliance thus imposed on their unwilling shoulders, the middle classes shrink back again under the protecting batteries of the hated despotism. This is the secret of the standing armies of Europe, which otherwise will be incomprehenseible to the future historian. The middle classes of Europe are thus made to understand that they must either surrender to a political power which they detest, and renounce the advantages of modern industry and trade, and the social relations based upon them, or forgo the privileges which the modern organization of the productive powers of society, in its primary phase, has vested in an exclusive class. That this lesson should be taught even from Spain is something equally striking and unexpected.

The End of the Revolution*

SARAGOSSA surrendered on August 1, at 1:30 P.M., and thus vanished the last center of resistance to the Spanish counterrevolution. There was, in a military point of view, little chance of success after the defeats at Madrid and Barcelona, the feebleness of the insurrectionary diversion in Andalusia, and the converging advance of overwhelming forces from the Basque provinces, Navarre, Catalonia, Valencia, and Castile. Whatever chance there might be was paralyzed by the circumstance that it was Espartero's old aide-de-camp, General Falcón, who directed the forces of resistance; that "Espartero and Liberty" was given as the battle cry; and that the population of Saragossa had become aware of Espartero's incommensurably ridiculous fiasco at Madrid. Besides, there were direct orders from Espartero's headquarters to his bottle holders at Saragossa that they were to put an end to all resistance, as will be seen from the following extract from the *Journal de Madrid* of July 29: "One of the Esparterist ex-ministers took part in the negotiations going on between General Dulce and the authorities of Saragossa, and the Esparterist member of the Cortes, Juan Alonso Martinez, accepted the mission of informing the insurgent leaders that the Queen, her ministers, and her generals were animated by a most conciliatory spirit."

The revolutionary movement was pretty generally spread over the whole of Spain. Madrid and La Mancha in Castile; Granada, Seville, Málaga, Cádiz, Jaén, etc., in Andalusia; Murcia and Cartagena in Murcia; Valencia, Alicante, Alcira, etc., in Valencia; Barcelona, Reus,

---

* *New-York Daily Tribune*, August 18, 1856. Written early August, 1856. (Lead article, unsigned.)

Figueras, Gerona, in Catalonia; Saragossa, Teruel, Huesca, Jaca, etc., in Aragon; Oviedo in Asturias; and Coruña in Galicia.

There were no moves in Estremadura, León, and Old Castile, where the revolutionary party had been put down two months ago, under the joint auspices of Espartero and O'Donnell—the Basque provinces and Navarre also remaining quiet. The sympathies of the latter provinces, however, were with the revolutionary cause, although they might not manifest themselves in sight of the French army of observation. This is the more remarkable if it be considered that twenty years ago these very provinces formed the stronghold of Carlism— then backed by the peasantry of Aragon and Catalonia, but who, this time, were most passionately siding with the revolution; and who would have proved a most formidable element of resistance, had not the imbecility of the leaders at Barcelona and Saragossa prevented their energies from being turned to account. Even the *London Morning Herald*, the orthodox champion of Protestantism, which broke lances for the Quixote of the auto-da-fé, Don Carlos, some twenty years ago, has stumbled over that fact, which it is fair enough to acknowledge. This is one of the many symptoms of progress revealed by the last revolution in Spain, a progress the slowness of which will astonish only those not acquainted with the peculiar customs and manners of a country, where "*a la mañana*" is the watchword of every day's life, and where everybody is ready to tell you that "our forefathers needed eight hundred years to drive out the Moors."

Notwithstanding the general spread of pronunciamentos, the revolution in Spain was limited only to Madrid and Barcelona. In the south it was broken by the cholera morbus, in the north by the Espartero murrain. From a military point of view, the insurrections at Madrid and Barcelona offer few interesting and scarcely any novel features. On the one side—the army—everything was prepared beforehand; on the other everything was extemporized; the offensive never for a moment changed sides. On the one hand, a well-equipped army, moving easily in the strings of its commanding generals; on the other, leaders reluctantly pushed forward by the impetus of an imperfectly armed people. At Madrid the revolutionists from the outset committed the mistake of blocking themselves up in the internal parts of the town, on the line connecting the eastern and western extremities —extremities commanded by O'Donnell and Concha, who communicated with each other and the cavalry of Dulce through the external boulevards. Thus the people were cutting off and exposing themselves to the concentric attack preconcerted by O'Donnell and his accomplices. O'Donnell and Concha had only to effect their junction and the revolutionary forces were dispersed into the north and south quarters of the town, and deprived of all further cohesion. It was a distinct feature of the Madrid insurrection that barricades were used sparingly and only at prominent street corners, while the houses were made the centers of resistance; and—what is unheard of in street warfare—bayonet attacks met the assailing columns of the army. But, if the insurgents profited by the experience of the Paris and Dresden insurrections, the soldiers had learned no less by them. The walls of the houses were broken through one by one, and the insurgents were taken in the flank and rear, while the exits into the streets were swept by cannon shot. Another distinguished feature in this battle of Madrid was that Pucheta, after the junction of Concha and O'Donnell, when he was pushed into the southern (Toledo) quarter of the town, transplanted the guerrilla warfare from the mountains of Spain into the streets of Madrid. The insurrection, dispersed, faced about under some arch of a church, in some narrow lane, on the staircase of a house, and there defended itself to the death.

At Barcelona the fighting was still more intense, there being no leadership at all. Militarily, this insurrection, like all previous risings in Barcelona, perished by the fact of the citadel, Fort Montjuich, remaining in the hands of the army. The violence of the struggle is characterized by the burning of 150 soldiers in their barracks at Gracia, a suburb which the insurgents hotly contested, after being already dislodged from Barcelona. It deserves mention that, while at Madrid, as we have shown in a previous article, the proletarians were betrayed and deserted by the bourgeoisie, the weavers of Barcelona declared at the very outset that they would have nothing to do with a movement set on foot by Esparterists, and insisted on the declaration of the republic. This being refused, they, with the exception of some who could not resist the smell of powder, remained passive spectators of the battle, which was thus lost—all insurrections at Barcelona being decided by its 20,000 weavers.

The Spanish revolution of 1856 is distinguished from all its predecessors by the loss of all dynastic character. It is known that the movement from 1804 to 1815 was national and dynastic. Although the Cortes in 1824 proclaimed an almost republican constitution, they did it in the name of Ferdinand VII. The movement of 1820–23, timidly republican, was altogether premature and had against it the masses to whose support it appealed, those masses being bound altogether to the Church and the crown. So deeply rooted was royalty in Spain that the struggle between old and modern society, to become serious, needed a testament of Ferdinand VII, and the incarnation of the antagonistic principles in two dynastic branches, the Carlist and

Christina ones. Even to combat for a new principle the Spaniard wanted a time-honored standard. Under these banners the struggle was fought out, from 1831 to 1843. Then there was an end of revolution, and the new dynasty was allowed its trial from 1843 to 1854. In the revolution of July, 1854, there was thus necessarily implied an attack on the new dynasty; but innocent Isabel was covered by the hatred concentrated on her mother, and the people reveled not only in their own emancipation but also in that of Isabel from her mother and the camarilla.

In 1856 the cloak had fallen and Isabel herself confronted the people by the *coup d'état* that fomented the revolution. She proved the worthy, coolly cruel, and cowardly hypocrite daughter of Ferdinand VII, who was so much given to lying that notwithstanding his bigotry he could never convince himself, even with the aid of the Holy Inquisition, that such exalted personages as Jesus Christ and his Apostles had spoken truth. Even Murat's massacre of the Madrileños in 1808 dwindles into an insignificant riot by the side of the butcheries of July 14–16, smiled upon by the innocent Isabel. Those days sounded the death knell of royalty in Spain. There are only the imbecile Legitimists of Europe imagining that, Isabel having fallen, Don Carlos may rise. They are forever thinking that when the last manifestation of a principle dies away, it is only to give its primitive manifestation another turn.

In 1856, the Spanish revolution has lost not only its dynastic, but also its military character. Why the army played such a prominent part in Spanish revolutions may be told in a very few words. The old institution of the captain generalships, which made the captains the pashas of their respective provinces; the war of independence against France, which not only made the army the principal instrument of national defense, but also the first revolutionary organization and the center of revolutionary action in Spain; the conspiracies of 1815–18, all emanating from the army; the dynastic war of 1831–1841, depending on the armies of both sides; the isolation of the liberal bourgeoisie forcing them to employ the bayonets of the army against clergy and peasantry in the country; the necessity for Christina and the camarilla to employ bayonets against the Liberals, as the Liberals had employed bayonets against the peasants; the tradition growing out of all these precedents; these were the causes which impressed on revolution in Spain a military, and on the army a praetorian character. Till 1854 revolution always originated with the army, and its different manifestations up to that time offered no external sign of difference beyond the grade in the army whence they originated.

Even in 1854 the first impulse still proceeded from the army, but there is the Manzanares manifesto of O'Donnell to attest how slender the base of the military preponderance in the Spanish revolution had become. Under what conditions was O'Donnell finally allowed to stay his scarcely equivocal promenade from Vicálvaro to the Portuguese frontiers, and to bring back the army to Madrid? Only on the promise to immediately reduce it, to replace it by the National Guard, and not to allow the fruits of the revolution to be shared by the generals. If the revolution of 1854 confined itself thus to the expression of its distrust, only two years later it finds itself openly and directly attacked by that army—an army that has now worthily entered the lists by the side of the Croats of Radetzky, the Africans of Bonaparte, and the Pomeranians of Wrangel. How far the glories of its new position are appreciated by the Spanish army is proved by the rebellion of a regiment at Madrid, on the twenty-ninth of July, which, not being satisfied with the mere *cigarros* of Isabel, struck for the five-franc pieces and sausages of Bonaparte, and got them, too.

This time, then, the army has been all against the people, or indeed, it has only fought against them, and the National Guards. In short, there is an end of the revolutionary mission of the Spanish army. The man in whom centered the military, the dynastic, and the bourgeois liberal character of the Spanish revolution—Espartero—has now sunk even lower than the common law of fate would have enabled his most intimate connoisseurs to anticipate. If, as is generally rumored, and is very probable, the Esparterists are about to rally under O'Donnell, they will have confirmed their suicide by an official act of their own. They will not save him.

The next European revolution will find Spain matured for cooperation with it. The years 1854 and 1856 were phases of transition she had to pass through to arrive at that maturity.

Bibliography

Collections

MARX'S WRITINGS, including his voluminous correspondence, are available primarily in German. The great collection is *Marx-Engels Werke* (39 vols., plus 2 vols. of Supplement and 1 vol. of Index), prepared by the Moscow Institute for Marxism-Leninism and published by Dietz Verlag, Berlin, 1964–68. There is also a Russian-language edition.

International Publishers in New York and Progress Publishers in Moscow have also brought out certain collections from time to time. One of the earliest is V. Adoratsky's *Karl Marx: Selected Works* (2 vols., 1933). There are also *Selected Correspondence,* and *Selected Works,* mostly in single volumes of varying dates. International Publishers has published a few specialized collections, among them Marx and Engels, *On Britain; Letters to Americans;* and *The Civil War in the United States.* The translation, especially in the latter two, is not infrequently garbled.

There are several relatively small collections of Marx's writings that are not connected with official Communist agencies. Most of them are in paperback. Among them:

Avineri, S. *Karl Marx on Colonialism and Modernization* (Doubleday, 1969); largely selections from Marx's articles in the *New-York Daily Tribune* and the Vienna *Presse.*

Blackstock, P. W., and Hoselitz, B. F., *The Russian Menace to Europe* (Free Press, 1952); a thoroughly garbled and distorted version of some of Marx's writings.

Bottomore, T. B., *Karl Marx: Selected Writings in Sociology and Social Philosophy* (McGraw-Hill, 1956); short but well-translated selections.

Bottomore, T. B., *Karl Marx: Early Writings* (McGraw-Hill, 1963); writings on "The Jewish Question" and some economic essays.

Christman, H. M., *The American Journalism of Marx and Engels* (The New American Library, 1966); a selection from the *New-York Daily Tribune.*

Easton, L. D., and Guddat, K. H., *Writings of the Young Marx on Philosophy and Society* (Doubleday, 1967); some well-translated selections from Marx's writings before 1847.

Feuer, L. S., *Basic Writings on Politics and Philosophy: Karl Marx and Friedrich Engels* (Doubleday, 1959); often inferior translations by others of excerpts.

Hook, S., *Marx and the Marxists* (D. Van Nostrand, 1955); a few short selections.

Marx's Books in English

In addition to *The Communist Manifesto*, which is universally available, individual books by Marx are to be found in English translation, most of them nowadays in paperback editions. Among them: *Capital* (3 vols., plus 2 parts of Vol. IV, entitled *Theories of Surplus Value*, published in Moscow in 1963 and 1968); *The Holy Family* (in collaboration with Engels); *The German Ideology* (in collaboration with Engels); *The Poverty of Philosophy; The Eighteenth Brumaire of Louis Napoleon; The Civil War in France; The Class Struggles in France, 1848 to 1850.*

Biographies

Most biographies of Marx tend to be both incomplete and strongly biased for or against him. The following are available in English, but should be read with caution:

Beer, M., *Life and Teaching of Karl Marx* (1925)
Berlin, I., *Karl Marx: His Life and Environment* (1939)
Carr, E. H., *Karl Marx: A Study in Fanaticism* (1934)
Korsch, K., *Karl Marx* (1936)
Lewis, J., *The Life and Teaching of Karl Marx* (1965)
Liebknecht, W., *Karl Marx: Biographical Memoirs* (1901)
Mehring, F., *Karl Marx: The Story of His Life* (1918)
Rühle, O., *Karl Marx: His Life and Work* (1928)
Payne, R., *Marx* (1968)
Schwartzschild, L., *The Red Prussian. The Life and Legend of Karl Marx* (1947)

Interpretations

Of books and articles interpreting Marxism there is no limit. The articles run into the tens of thousands, in every language in the world. Those who read German and French may consult E. Drahn's *Marx Bibliographie* (Berlin, 1923) and M. Rubel's *Bibliographie des Oeuvres de Karl Marx* (Paris, 1956) and his *Supplément à la Bibliographie des Oeuvres de Karl Marx* (Paris, 1960).

The following is a representative sample of books in English treating various aspects of Marxism:

Adoratsky, V., *Dialectical Materialism* (1934)
Bober, M. M., *Karl Marx's Interpretation of History* (1948)
D'Arcy, M., *Communism and Christianity* (n.d.)
Federn, K., *The Materialist Conception of History* (1939)
Fromm, E., *Marx's Conception of Man* (1961)
Garaudy, R., *Karl Marx: The Evolution of His Thought* (1964)
Gregor, A. J., *A Survey of Marxism: Problems in Philosophy and the Theory of History* (1965)
Hook, S., *Towards the Understanding of Karl Marx* (1933)
Lefebvre, H., *The Sociology of Marx* (1968)
Lichtheim, G., *Marxism in Modern France* (1966)
Livergood, N. D., *Activity in Marx's Philosophy* (1967)
Mayo, H. B., *Democracy and Marxism* (1955)
Meyer, A. G., *Marxism: The Unity of Theory and Practice* (1954)
Padover, Dr. S. K., *On the First International* (in preparation)
Schumpeter, J. A., *Capitalism, Socialism, and Democracy* (1942)
Somerville, J., *The Philosophy of Marxism: An Exposition* (1967)
Tucker, R. C., *Philosophy and Myth in Karl Marx* (1961)
Ulam, A. B., *The Unfinished Revolution: An Essay on the Sources of Influence of Marxism and Communism* (1960)
Venable, V., *Human Nature: The Marxian View* (1945)
Williams, W. A., *The Great Evasion: An Essay on the Contemporary Relevance of Karl Marx* (1964)
Wolfe, B. D., *Marxism: 100 Years in the Life of a Doctrine* (1965)

Biographical Index

Aberdeen, George Hamilton Gordon, earl of (1784–1860) British Tory statesman, 561

Abisbal (*see* O'Donnell, Henri)

Adrian (*see* Hadrian)

Aesop, sixth-century, B.C., Greek fabulist, 248n, 327n

Affre, Denis Auguste (1793–1848), Archbishop of Paris, 1840–1848, 367

Ailly, Pierre d' (1350–1420 or 1425), French Cardinal and theologian, 326

Allais, Louis Pierre Constant (b.*c.*-1821), French police agent, 287, 291

Alba (or Alva), Jacobo Luis, duke of (1821–1881), husband of Empress Eugénie's sister, 569, 631

Albert, Alexandre Martin (1815–1895), French Blanquist socialist, 53, 159, 161, 172

Alexander the Great (356–323 B.C.), King of Macedonia, 288, 383n

Alexander I (1777–1825), Czar of Russia, 1801–1825, 568

Alexander II (1818–1881), Czar of Russia, 1855–1881, 368, 398, 399

Alfonso XII (1857–1885), King of Spain, 1870–1885, 546

Angély, Saint Jean d', French General, 295

Anglès, François Ernest (1807–1861), French National Assembly deputy, 307

Angoulême, Louis Antoine, duke of (1775–1844), French General, son of King Charles X, 628

Anne (1665–1713), Queen of England and of Great Britain, 1707–1713, 46

Annenkov, Pavel V. (1812–1887), liberal Russian writer and landowner, xvii, xxi, 130n, 131

Annexander (*see* Wilhelm I)

Antonio, Pascual Bourbon, Don (1775–1817), Spanish Infante, son of King Charles III, 596

Arco, Augero Felipe (1790–1821), Spanish revolutionary leader, 624

Argüelles, Augustin (1776–1844), Spanish Liberal Party statesman, 627

Aristotle (384–322 B.C.), ancient Greek philosopher, 5, 512, 584

Arndt, Ernst Moritz (1769–1860), German patriotic writer, 383

Arsenius (*c.*354–*c.*450), Christian saint, 317

Assensio, Pedro Galvo, Spanish politician, active in the 1854–1856 revolution, 633

Athenaeus, third-century Greek writer, 300n

Auber, Daniel François (1782–1871), French composer of the opera, *Fra Diavolo*, 473n

Auer, Ignaz (1846–1907), German socialist, Reichstag deputy, 488

Auersperg, Karl von (1783–1859), Austrian General, 40, 448

Auerswald, Rudolf von (1795–1866), Prussian Foreign Minister in 1848, 413, 467

Aurelle de Paladines, Louis Jean Baptiste d' (1804–1877), French General, Paris National Guard commander in March, 1871, 340, 341, 342, 390n

Azy, Benoit d', 299, 303

* International Working Men's Association (First International)

† International Working Men's Association

father of Frederick Engels, xvii

Epicurus (341–270 B.C.), Greek philosopher, one of the subjects of Marx's Ph.D. dissertation, xiv, xxxii

Erolés, Joaquin de (1785–1825), Spanish General, 610

Escosura, Patricio de la (1807–1878), Spanish writer and politician, 633

Espartero, Baldomero (1793–1879), Spanish General, Regent, 1841–1843; Premier, 1854–1856, 336, 544, 550, 552n, 553–555, 558–566, 569–570, 572, 577–579, 583–585, 632–634, 640

Esser, J. P. III, Cologne Privy Councillor, Prussian National Assembly deputy, 1848–1849, 482–483

Falcon, Antonio, Spanish General, active in the 1854–56 revolution, 630, 636

Falloux, Frédéric de (1811–1886), French politician and historian, 186, 195, 204, 213, 264–265, 276–277, 304, 306, 394

Faucher, Léon (1803–1854), French journalist and politician, 155, 186, 191, 193, 223, 282–283, 299, 304

Favre, Claude Gabriel Jules (1809–1880), French politician, member of the Provisional governments of 1848 and 1871, 330, 333–335, 338, 340, 343, 357, 362–363, 371–372, 375, 379–380, 387–388 & n, 391–393, 394, 396–397, 404

Favre, Mme, wife of above, 345

Ferdinand II (1830–1859), King of Sicily and Naples, 1830–1859, 336, 567

Ferdinand IV (1285–1312), King of Spain, 1295–1312, 616

Ferdinand V, the Catholic (1452–1516), King of Castile, 1474–1506; King of Aragon (Ferdinand II), 1479–1516, 589

Ferdinand VII (1784–1833), King of Spain, 1808–1833, 542–543, 587, 591, 593–595, 605, 610, 615, 621–625, 626–629, 632, 638–639

Ferry, Jules (1832–1893), French politician and member of Parliament, 335

Feuerbach, Ludwig (1804–1872), German materialist philosopher, 518, xi, xiv, xxxv

Fleury, Charles (real name: Krause, Carl Friedrich August) (b.1824), Prussian police agent in London, 127

Flocon, Ferdinand (1800–1866), French politician, editor of *La Réforme*,

member of the 1848 Provisional government, 159

Florez, José Segundo (b.1789), Spanish historian, 559

Florida Blanca, José Monini, Count de (1728–1808), Spanish statesman, representative of Enlightened Despotism, 599, 600, 618

Flourens, Gustave (1838–1871), French scientist, friend of Marx, killed as a Communard, 340, 343, 346, 373, 401–402

Fould, Achille (1800–1867), French banker, Minister under Napoleon III, 167, 179, 189, 214, 216–217, 278, 295, 299, 306

Fouquier-Tinville, Antoine Quentin (1746–1795), French Revolutionist, Public Procurator, 196

Fourier, François Marie Charles (1772–1837), French utopian socialist theorist, xvi, xxxiii, 6, 104, 106, 516

Francis I (1494–1547), King of France, 1515–1547, 556

Francis Joseph I (1830–1916), Emperor of Austria, 1848–1916, 412, 567

Frankel, Leo (1844–1896), Hungarian revolutionist, Communard, 356, 402 & n

Frederick I (Barbarossa) (c.1122–1190), Emperor of Germany, 1155–1190, 136–137

Frederick I (1657–1713), Elector of Brandenburg, first King of Prussia, 1701–1713, 477

Frederick II (1194–1250), Grandson of Emperor Frederick I, Emperor of Germany, 1220–50, 136, 477–478

Frederick II (the Great) (1712–1786), King of Prussia, 1740–1786, 46, 372, 478 & n, 519, 556, 599

Frederick William (1831–1888), Crown Prince of Prussia, 329, 448, 457

Frederick William I (1688–1740), King of Prussia, 1713–1740, 477

Frederick William III (1770–1840), King of Prussia, 1797–1840, 390, 478, 479–80, 513–514

Frederick William IV (1795–1861), King of Prussia, 1840–1861, 7–22, 412, 413, 423, 480 & n, 483, 510, 513–514

Freiligrath, Ferdinand (1810–1876), German poet, refugee in London, friend of Marx, xx, 123n, 124, 127

Freytag, Otto, German lawyer, defender of Liebknecht and other socialists in 1872, 532

652

Fritzsche, Friedrich Wilhelm (1825–1905), German labor leader and editor, emigrated to U.S. in 1881, 507n

Galileo, Galilei (1564–1642), Italian physicist and astronomer, 128 & n

Gallifet, Gaston Alexandre Auguste, Marquis de (1830–1909), French General, fought against the Paris Commune, 345, 346, 370

Gambetta, Léon (1838–1882), French statesman, Premier, 1881–1882, 330, 334, 392 & n, 393, 397, 398, 526, 535

Ganesco, Grégori (c.1830–1877), Roumanian-born French Bonapartist journalist, 356

Gans, Eduard (1797–1839), German jurist, Marx's professor at the University of Berlin, xii

Garcia de la Cuesta, Gregorio (1741–1811), Spanish General, 598–599, 610

Garibaldi, Giuseppe (1807–1882), Italian patriot and soldier, 521

Garnier-Pagès, Louis Antoine (1803–1887), French politician, member of the government of National Defense, 1870–1871, 236, 388

Geib, August (1842–1879), Hamburg bookdealer, a founder of the German Social Democratic Party, 488

Geiser, Bruno (1846–1898), German Social Democratic journalist and Reichstag deputy, 507n

George I (1660–1727), King of England, 1714–1727, 46

George II (1683–1760), King of England, 1727–1760, 46

George IV (1762–1830), King of England, 1820–1830, 567

Gessner, Salomon (1730–1788), Swiss painter and poet, 29

Gierke, Stettin Syndicus, Prussian Minister of Agriculture, 1848, 467, 482–483

Gigot, Philippe Charles (1819–1860), Belgian communist, friend of Marx, 130–131 & n, 132, 133

Girardin, Delphine de (1804–1855), French author, wife of Émile de Girardin, 328n

Girardin, Émile (1806–1881), French journalist, 235, 293

Giraud, Charles Joseph Barthélemy (1802–1881), French jurist, monarchist, 312

Gladstone, Robert (1811–1872), Eng-

lish merchant and philanthropist, 504

Gladstone, William Ewart (1809–1898), British Liberal Party leader, four times Prime Minister, 62, 391, 398

Gneisenau, August Wilhelm Anton von (1760–1831), German Field Marshal, 390

Godoy, Manuel (1767–1851), Spanish statesman, known as "Prince of Peace," chief Minister of Charles IV after 1793, 580, 587, 591, 594, 599, 600, 617

Goethe, Johann Wolfgang von (1749–1832), German poet, dramatist, and novelist, 128n, 249n, 499, 511

Goetz, Ferdinand (1826–1915), German physician, and Liberal Reichstag deputy, 417

Gonzalez Bravo, Luis (1811–1871), Spanish statesman, Moderate, Prime Minister in 1843 and 1868, 563, 570, 580

Goudchaux, Michel (1797–1862), French banker, 177

Gracchus, Gaius Sempronius (153–121 B.C.), Roman Tribune, 246

Gracchus, Tiberius Sempronius (163–133 B.C.), Roman Tribune, brother of Gaius, 246

Granier de Cassagnac, Bernard Adolphe (1806–1880), French journalist and politician, 236, 328

Greif(f), Prussian police agent in London, 127

Grousset, Pascal (1844–1909), Blanquist member of the Paris Commune, 404

Guesde, Jules (1845–1922), French Marxist socialist, 534, 535

Guiod, Alphonse Simon (b.1805), French General, commander of artillery during siege of Paris, 1870–71, 334

Guise, Duc de (1614–1664), French leader of the uprising known as the Fronde, 327

Guizot, François Pierre Guillaume (1787–1874), French historian and statesman, head of the government, 1840–1848, 38, 45–50, 80, 134, 145, 148, 155, 158, 159, 186, 192, 209, 213, 246, 256, 303, 304, 318, 328, 336–337

Gumpert, Eduard (d.1893), German physician in Manchester, whom Marx often consulted, li

Gurrea, Ignacio, Spanish Progressist General, 634

* International Working Men's Association

* International Working Men's Association

* International Working Men's Association

* International Working Men's Association

Tridon, Edmé Marie Gustave (*cont.*) member of the Paris Commune, 395, 405

Trochu, Louis Jules (1815–1896), French General and politician, commander of the army in Paris, September, 1870 to January, 1871, 330, 332, 333–334, 342–344, 366, 392, 396

Turgot, Louis Félix Étienne, marquis de (1796–1866), French diplomat, Foreign Minister, 1851–1852, 631

Ugarte y Larrizabal, Antonio (1780–*c*.1833), Spanish politician, favorite of Ferdinand VII, 628

Urquhart, David (1805–1877), British diplomat and editor, xli

Urquijo (or Urquizo), Mariano Luis de (1708–1817), Spanish writer and politician, 598–99

Vaïsse, Claude Marius (1799–1864), French Bonapartist politician, 298

Valentin, Louis Ernest, French General, Paris Police Prefect in 1871, 340–341, 360

Varlin, Louis Eugène (1839–1871), French Proudhonist, shot as a Communard on May 28, 402, 405

Vasconcellos, Miguel de (d.1640), Spanish statesman, 586

Vatimesnil, Antoine François Henri de (1789–1860), French politician, 299

Vauban, Sébastien le Prêtre, marquis de (1633–1707), French Marshal and military engineer, 218

Vermorel, Auguste (1841–1871), French Proudhonist, Communard, editor of *Courrier Français*, 395

Vésinier, Pierre (1826–1902), IWA* member, Communard, anti-Marx refugee in London, 404

Victoria (1819–1901), Queen of England, 1837–1901, 391, 556

Vidal, Joaquin (d.1819), liberal Spanish officer, executed for rebellion, 227, 228, 233, 282, 597, 629

Viereck, Louis (1851–1921), German editor, Social Democratic Reichstag deputy, emigrated to U.S. in 1890, 529

Vieyra, French officer, active in Bonapartist coup of December 2, 1851, 273

Villèle, Jean Baptiste (1773–1854),

French statesman, Prime Minister, 1822–27, 304

Vinoy, Joseph (1800–1880), French General, appointed governor of Paris, January, 1871, 340, 341, 342, 344, 345, 400

Virgil (or Vergil) (70 B.C.–19 B.C.), Roman poet, 211n

Viriathus, Lusitanian rebel against the Romans, murdered in 139 A.D., 574

Vittel, member of the Spanish Junta in 1808, 605

Vivien, Alexandre François Auguste (1799–1854), French lawyer and Orleanist politician, 182

Vogel von Falkenstein, Eduard (1797–1885), Prussian General and politician, 526

Vogt, Karl (1817–1895), German émigré in Switzerland, in pay of Napoleon III, attacked by Marx in his pamphlet, *Herr Vogt* (1860), xliii, 401

Vollmar, Georg Heinrich von (1850–1922), German socialist and editor, 530

Voltaire, François Marie Arouet de (1694–1778), French man of letters, leading figure in the Enlightenment, 38, 211, 223, 224, 278, 346 & n

Wade, John (1788–1875), British economist and historian, 134

Wagener, Hermann (1815–1889), German conservative official and newspaper publisher, 524–525

Wakefield, Edward Gibbon (1796–1862), British statesman and economist, 134

Walpole, Sir Robert (1676–1745), British Whig statesman, Prime Minister, 1721–1742, 47

Weber, Louis, German communist, watchmaker, refugee in London, 529

Weerth, Georg (1822–1856), German poet and journalist, friend of Marx, xvii, xx

Weitling, Christian Wilhelm (1808–1871), German tailor, member of the League of the Just, propagator of utopian communism, xvi, xxi–xii, xxxv, 3, 18, 130–132, 516, 527

Welden, Franz Ludwig von (1782–1853), Austrian General, commanding against Austrian and Hungarian revolutionists, 464

---

* International Working Men's Association

Subject Index